The Master Reader/Writer

D. J. Henry

Daytona State College

Boston Columbus Indianapolis New York San Francisco
Amsterdam Cape Town Dubai London Madrid Milan Munich Paris Montreal Toronto
Delhi Mexico City São Paulo Sydney Hong Kong Seoul Singapore Taipei Tokyo

Executive Editor: Matt Wright
Editorial Assistant: Laura Marenghi
Program Manager: Lauren Finn
Development Editor: Erin Dye
Product Marketing Manager: Jennifer Edwards
Production Manager: Ellen MacElree
Digital Editor: Kara Noonan
Digital Content Specialist: Anne Leung
Project Coordination: Cenveo® Publisher Services
Cover Design Lead: Heather Scott
Cover Photos: (Ferris Wheel): Lookpol/Shutterstock
(Hand with Phone): Piotr Pabijan/Shutterstock
Senior Manufacturing Buyer: Roy L. Pickering, Jr.
Printer/Binder: LSC Communications
Cover Printer: LSC Communications

Acknowledgments of third party content appear on pages 638–640, which constitute an extension of this copyright page.

Library of Congress Cataloging-in-Publication Data

Henry, D. J. (Dorothy Jean)
The master reader/writer / D.J. Henry, Daytona State College.
pages cm
Includes index.
ISBN 978-0-321-92739-2
1. English language—Rhetoric—Study and teaching. 2. College readers. 3. Report writing—Study and teaching. I. Title.
PE1417.H39 2016
808'.0427—dc23
2015014345

Student ISBN-13: 978-0-321-92739-2
Student ISBN-10: 0-321-92739-7

ALC ISBN-13: 978-0-321-92742-2
ALC ISBN-10: 0-321-92742-7

www.pearsonhighered.com

Brief Contents

Detailed Contents iv

Preface xv

Unit 1 The Reading and Writing Processes

MODULE 1 An Introduction to Reading and Writing 2

MODULE 2 Develop a Reading/Writing Strategy 54

Unit 2 Develop Vocabulary and Analyze Language

MODULE 3 Learn and Use New Words 94

MODULE 4 Word Choice, Tone, and Purpose 138

MODULE 5 Distinguish Between Fact and Opinion 178

Unit 3 Reading and Writing Essays

MODULE 6 Understanding the Essay 218

MODULE 7 A Reading/Writing Strategy for Research 258

Unit 4 Rhetorical Modes and Methods of Development

MODULE 8 Time and Space Order Patterns: *Narration*, *Process*, and *Description* 300

MODULE 9 The Cause and Effect Pattern 344

MODULE 10 The Example Patterns 384

MODULE 11 The Classification, Comparison, and Contrast Patterns 426

MODULE 12 Argument 464

Unit 5 10 Essential Grammar Skills with MySkillsLab

MODULE 13 The Comma 508

MODULE 14 Comma Splices and Fused Sentences 511

MODULE 15 Fragments and Consistent Use of Point of View, Number, and Tense 513

MODULE 16 Subject-Verb Agreement: Present Tense 518

MODULE 17 Adjectives and Adverbs 521

MODULE 18 Parallelism 524

MODULE 19 Misplaced and Dangling Modifiers 527

MODULE 20 Quotation Marks 530

MODULE 21 The Apostrophe 533

MODULE 22 Improving Your Spelling 536

Unit 6 Reading Selections 550

Photo Credits 638

Text Credits 639

Index 641

Detailed Contents

Preface **xv**

UNIT 1 The Reading and Writing Processes

MODULE 1
An Introduction to Reading and Writing 2

LEARNING AND USING LANGUAGE

LO1 Answer the Question: "What the Point of Reading and Writing?" 3

PHOTOGRAPHIC ORGANIZER: Reasons to Read and Write 3

LO2 Connect Reading and Writing 4

READING: "Intrinsic Versus Extrinsic Motivation," Aronson, Wilson, and Akert 5

READING: "Definition of Learning," Ciccarelli and White 7

LO3 Assess the Reading/Writing Situation 10

READING: Excerpt from *An American Slave: Written by Himself*, 1849, Frederick Douglass 13

LO4 Recognize the Elements of Text 16

READING: Excerpt from *Huckleberry Finn*, Mark Twain 17

READING: Excerpt from *Pygmalion*, George Bernard Shaw 18

READING: "A View from Within," D.J. Henry 19

READING: "The Well-Adjusted Individual," Hunt and Colander 20

READING: "Symbols and Language," Macionis 21

LO5 Develop Tools to Create Meaning through Reading/Writing 25

Activate Prior Knowledge 25

READING: "The Indian Who Developed an Alphabet" 26

Make Inferences and Implications 28

Create Concept Maps and Outlines 30

READING: "Sigmund Freud's Elements of Personality," Macionis 32

Write a Summary 34

READING: "Jean Piaget's Theory of Cognitive Development," Macionis 35

READING: "The Story of My Life: Chapter IV," Helen Keller 37

Workshop: Introduction to Reading and Writing 40

READING: "I Won't Learn from You," Herbert Kohl 40

Reading and Writing Assignments MySkillsLab™ 45

Review Test 1 MySkillsLab™ 49

READING: "Learning Preferences," Woolfolk 49

Review Test 2 MySkillsLab™

Academic Learning Log: Module Review MySkillsLab™ 52

MODULE 2
Develop a Reading/Writing Strategy 54

HARDSHIP AND LOSS

LO1 Answer the Question, "What's the Point of Developing a Reading/Writing Strategy?" 55

PHOTOGRAPHIC ORGANIZER: Develop a Reading/Writing Strategy 55

LO2 Recognize the Phases of a Reading/Writing Strategy 56

LO3 Apply the Reading/Writing Strategy: Before, During, and After Reading 58

Preread to Survey 58

Question 58

READING: "Stress and Human Resilience," Aronson, Elliot, Wilson, and Akert 59

READING: "Reframing: Finding Meaning in Traumatic Events," Aronson, Wilson, and Akert 61

Read and Question 64

Annotate 64

Recite and Review 66

Brainstorm 66

READING: "At What a Cost!," Samuel Bates, 1875 70

READING: "The Gettysburg Address," Abraham Lincoln, 1863 71

LO4 Apply the Reading/Writing Strategy: After Prewriting, Write a Draft 72

LO5 Apply the Reading/Writing Strategy: After Writing, Review, Revise, and Proofread Your Draft 74

Review 74

Revise 74

Proofread 75

Workshop: Develop a Reading/Writing Strategy 79

READING: "Bereavement," Macionis 79

READING: Excerpt from *The Year of Magical Thinking*, Joan Didion 79

Reading and Writing Assignments MySkillsLab™ 85

Review Test 1 MySkillsLab™ 89

READING: "Small Group Roles," DeVito 90

Review Test 2 MySkillsLab™

Academic Learning Log: Module Review MySkillsLab™ 92

UNIT 2 Develop Vocabulary and Analyze Language

MODULE 3
Learning and Using New Words 94

PERCEPTION AND REALITY

L❶ Answer the Question: "What's the Point of Learning and Using New Words?" 95

PHOTOGRAPHIC ORGANIZER: Learning and Using New Words 95

L❷ Employ Context Clues to Comprehend and Make a Point 96

Synonyms 96

READING: "Interpreting Dreams," Wood, Wood, and Boyd 97

Antonyms 100

READING: "An Introduction to Metaphysics," Steward, Blocker, and Petrik 100

General Context 103

READING: "Vagabonds," Arthur Rimbaud 104

Examples 106

READING: "Why Zombies, Robots, and Clowns Freak Us Out," Landau 106

READING: "Sensation and Perception," Gerrig 109

L❸ Use Vocabulary Resources in Textbooks to Comprehend and Make a Point 112

Identify Content (Subject Area) Words 112

Look for Textbook Definitions 112

Use a Glossary 112

READING: "The Dreamwork of Surrealist Painting," Sayre 113

READING: "In the Beginning: Psychoanalysis," Ciccarelli and White 116

Workshop: Using and Learning New Words 119

READING: *Hamlet*, Act I, Scenes iv-v, Shakespeare 119

Reading and Writing Assignments MySkillsLab™ 129

Review Test 1 MySkillsLab™ 133

READING: "The Process of Urbanization," Henslin 133

Review Test 2 MySkillsLab™

Academic Learning Log: Module Review MySkillsLab™ 136

MODULE 4

Word Choice, Tone, and Purpose 138

IDENTITY AND CHANGE

L❶ Answer the Question: "What's the Point of Word Choice, Tone, and Purpose?" 139

PHOTOGRAPHIC ORGANIZER: Word Choice, Tone, and Purpose 139

L❷ Connect Topic, Audience, Word Choice, Tone, and Purpose 140

READING: "The Role of Myth in Cultural Life," Sayre 141

READING: "Aristotle," Sayre 146

L❸ Question and Annotate to Identify Tone and Purpose 148

READING: "The Story of Narcissus," Ovid 149

READING: Excerpt from *The Origin of Species*, Charles Darwin 155

L❹ Brainstorm and Draft to Establish Tone and Purpose 158

L❺ Review and Revise for Word Choice, Tone, and Purpose 161

Workshop: Word Choice, Tone, and Purpose 162

READING: Excerpt from "Rappaccini's Daughter," Nathaniel Hawthorne 162

Reading and Writing Assignments MySkillsLab™ 170

Review Test 1 MySkillsLab™ 174

READING: "The Death Camps: Murder by Assembly Line," Leva, Muir, Veldman, and Maas 174

Review Test 2 MySkillsLab™

Academic Learning Log: Module Review MySkillsLab™ 176

MODULE 5

Distinguish Between Fact and Opinion 178

RIGHT TO LIFE, LIBERTY, AND THE PURSUIT OF HAPPINESS

LO1 Answer the Question, "What's the Point of Fact and Opinion?" 179

PHOTOGRAPHIC ORGANIZER: Fact and Opinion 179

LO2 Distinguish Between Fact and Opinion 180

READING: "Report of the 1848 Women's Rights Convention," Elizabeth Cady Stanton 183

LO3 Survey, Question, and Annotate to Analyze Facts and Opinions 187

READING: "A San Francisco Merchant Protests Discrimination Against the Chinese," 1852, Norman Asing 188

READING: Transcript of President Andrew Jackson's Message to Congress "On Indian Removal" (1830) 194

LO4 Brainstorm and Draft Using Facts and Opinions 198

LO5 Review, Revise, and Proofread for Effective Use of Facts and Opinions 201

Basic Language Rules for Quotes 201

Basic Language Rules for Reported Speech 202

Workshop: Distinguish Between Fact and Opinion 203

READING: The Declaration of Independence 203

Reading and Writing Assignments MySkillsLab™ 209

Review Test 1 MySkillsLab™ 213

READING: "The Politics of Immigrants: Power, Ethnicity, and Social Class," Henslin 213

Review Test 2 MySkillsLab™

Academic Learning Log: Module Review MySkillsLab™ 216

UNIT 3 Reading and Writing Essays

MODULE 6

Understanding the Essay 218

PROTECTING THE ENVIRONMENT

LO1 Answer the Question, "What's the Point of the Essay?" 219

PHOTOGRAPHIC ORGANIZER: The Essay 219

The Levels of Information in an Essay 220

The Levels of Information in a Paragraph 221

LO2 Question, Read, Annotate, and Review an Essay 221

READING: "Climate Change: Reducing the Climate Footprint," U.S. Environmental Protection Agency 222

READING: "The Dangers of Climate Change," Withgott and Laposata 227

READING: From *Silent Spring*, "A Fable for Tomorrow," Rachel Carson 230

LO3 Prewrite a Draft of a Central Idea: Thesis Statement 232

LO4 Prewrite to Generate and Organize Relevant Details 235

LO5 Compose a Draft Using Logical Order 237

LO6 Revise and Proofread for Effective Language: Word Choice 240

Workshop: Understanding the Essay 243

READING: "Marine Debris and the Environment," National Oceanic and Atmospheric Administration 244

Reading and Writing Assignments MySkillsLab™ 249

Review Test 1 MySkillsLab™ 253

READING: "Conflict Defined," Folger, Poole, and Stutman 253

Review Test 2 MySkillsLab™

Academic Learning Log: Module Review MySkillsLab™ 256

MODULE 7

A Reading/Writing Strategy for Research 258

LO1 Answer the Question, "What's the Point of Developing a Reading/Writing Strategy for Research?" 259

PHOTOGRAPHIC ORGANIZER: What Is the Point of Developing a Reading/Writing Strategy for Research? 259

LO2 Develop Your Reading/Writing Strategy for Research 260

LO3 Choose a Topic to Research 262

STEP BY STEP: Discover a Research Topic 262

LO4 Find and Evaluate Sources of Research Information 264

What Kind of Information Do I Need? 264

Where Can I Find the Information I Need? 264

Library Resources and Sources 264

Internet Resources and Sources 267

How Can I Know the Information I Find Is Reliable or Trustworthy? 269

LO5 Avoid Plagiarism Throughout the Research Process 271

LO6 Master the Basics of Documentation Styles: MLA and APA 274

The Basics of MLA 274

Key Differences between MLA and APA 282

Sample Student Research Essay: MLA 283

Sample Student Research Essay: APA 287

Workshop: Applying the Reading/Writing Strategy to Research 292

Reading and Writing Assignments MySkillsLab™ 294

Review Test 1 MySkillsLab™ 295

READING: "Dating in Cyberspace," Schwartz and Scott 295
Review Test 2 MySkillsLab™
Academic Learning Log: Module Review MySkillsLab™ 298

UNIT 4 Rhetorical Modes and Methods of Development

MODULE 8
Time and Space Order Patterns: *Narration, Process,* and *Description* 300

BREAKING DOWN BARRIERS TO COMMUNICATION

LO1 Answer the Question, "What's the Point of Time and Space Order?" 301

PHOTOGRAPHIC ORGANIZER: How Do We Learn to Communicate? 301

LO2 Question, Read, Annotate, and Review Passages Using Time and Space Order 302

READING: "Language," Ciccarelli and White 303

READING: "Mother Tongue," Amy Tan 307

READING: "Annie Sullivan's Letters about Educating Helen Keller" 312

LO3 Prewrite a Draft of a Thesis Statement Using Time and Space Order 316

LO4 Prewrite to Generate Relevant Details Using Time and Space Order 318

LO5 Compose a Draft Using Logical Order: Time and Space Order 320

STUDENT ESSAY: "Overcoming Communication Barriers," Reagan Earnest 321

LO6 Revise and Proofread for Effective Language with Time and Space Order 323

Workshop: Comprehend and Create Time and Space Order 326

READING: "Do Women and Men Speak Different Languages?", Renzetti 326

READING: "Sex, Lies, and Conversation: Why Is It So Hard for Men and Women to Talk to Each Other?", Deborah Tannen 328

READING: Excerpt from *My English*, Julia Alvarez 329

Reading and Writing Assignments MySkillsLab™ 334

Review Test 1 MySkillsLab™ 338

READING: "Listening in Public Speaking," DeVito 338

Review Test 2 MySkillsLab™

Academic Learning Log: Module Review MySkillsLab™ 342

MODULE 9
The Cause and Effect Pattern 344

MOTIVATION AND ACHIEVEMENT

LO1 Answer the Question, "What's the Point of Cause and Effect?" 345

PHOTOGRAPHIC ORGANIZER: What Are the Causes and Effects of Human Motivation and Achievement? 345

LO2 Question, Read, and Annotate Passages Using Cause and Effect 346

READING: "Understanding Motivation," Ciccarelli and White 347

READING: Excerpt from *The Space Economy*, Michael Griffin (NASA) 352

READING: Excerpt from *Around the World in 72 Days*, 1890, Nellie Bly 356

L3 Prewrite a Draft of a Thesis Statement Using Cause and Effect 358

L4 Prewrite to Generate Relevant Details Using Cause and Effect 360

L5 Compose a Draft Using Logical Order: Cause and Effect 362

STUDENT ESSAY:"Let Your Life Speak," Alex Obed 362

L6 Revise and Proofread for Effective Language with Cause and Effect 366

Workshop: Comprehend and Create a Cause and Effect Essay 368

READING: Remarks by President Obama on the BRAIN Initiative and American Innovation 368

READING: "Explosion of the Space Shuttle *Challenger* Address to the Nation, January 28, 1986," Ronald Reagan 370

READING: "New America," Robert D. Ballard 371

Reading and Writing Assignments MySkillsLab™ 375

Review Test 1 MySkillsLab™ 379

READING: "What Risks Are Involved in Tattooing?," USFDA 379

Review Test 2 MySkillsLab™

Academic Learning Log: Module Review MySkillsLab™ 382

MODULE 10

The Example Patterns 384

LIVING IN THE DIGITAL AGE

L1 Answer the Question, "What's the Point of the Example Patterns?" 385

PHOTOGRAPHIC ORGANIZER: What Are Examples of the Pros and Cons of Living in the Digital Age? 385

L2 Question, Read, Annotate, and Review Passages Using Examples 386

READING: "Ethics in Computing," Evans, Martin, and Poatsy 388

READING: "What Is Cyberbullying?" Stopbullying.gov 396

READING: "E-Readers Mark a New Chapter in the Developing World," Lynn Neary 397

L3 Prewrite a Draft of a Thesis Statement Using Examples 399

L4 Prewrite to Generate Relevant Details Using Examples 401

L5 Compose a Draft Using Logical Order: Examples 404

READING: Student Essay: "The Pros and Cons of Living in the Digital Age," Madelyn Miller 405

L6 Revise and Proofread for Effective Language with Examples 408

Workshop: Comprehend and Create an Essay Using Examples 409

READING: "The HIVE," D.J. Henry 409

READING: "What Is GPS?" gps.gov 411

READING: "Who Is Watching?" Evans, Martin, and Poatsy 413

Reading and Writing Assignments MySkillsLab™ 418

Review Test 1 MySkillsLab™ 421

READING: "Gossip," DeVito 421

Review Test 2 MySkillsLab™

Academic Learning Log: Module Review MySkillsLab™ 424

MODULE 11
The Classification, Comparison, and Contrast Patterns 426

CONFLICT AND RESOLUTION

LO1 Answer the Question, "What's the Point of the Classification, Comparison, and Contrast Patterns?" 427

PHOTOGRAPHIC ORGANIZER: What Is Conflict, and How Do We Resolve It? 427

LO2 Question, Read, Annotate, and Review Passages Using Classification, Comparison, and Contrast 428

READING: "Elements of War and Peace," Macionis 430

READING: Excerpt from Aung San Suu Kyi's Nobel Peace Prize Lecture, 2012 434

READING: Excerpt from President John F. Kennedy's Commencement Address at the American University, 10 June 1963 438

LO3 Prewrite a Draft of a Thesis Statement Using Classification, Comparison, and Contrast 441

LO4 Prewrite to Generate Relevant Details Using Classification, Comparison, and Contrast 443

LO5 Compose a Draft Using Logical Order: Classification, Comparison, and Contrast 445

STUDENT ESSAY: "The War Machine," Bethany Cobb 446

LO6 Revise and Proofread for Effective Language with Classification, Comparison, and Contrast 448

Workshop: Comprehend and Create an Essay Using Classification, Comparison, and Contrast 450

READING: Broadcast, Outbreak of War with Germany, September 3, 1939, King George VI of England 450

READING: "I Will Fight No More Forever," Chief Joseph of the Nez Perce 451

READING: "United States-Soviet Space Cooperation During the Cold War," NASA 451

Reading and Writing Assignments MySkillsLab™ 455

Review Test 1 MySkillsLab™ 459

READING: "Categorizing Personality by Types," Gerrig and Zimbardo 459

Review Test 2 MySkillsLab™

Academic Learning Log: Module Review MySkillsLab™ 462

MODULE 12
Argument 464

CIVIC DUTY

LO1 Answer the Question "What's the Point of Argument?" 465

PHOTOGRAPHIC ORGANIZER: Argument 465

LO2 Question, Read, and Annotate Passages Using Argument 466

READING: "The Price of Greatness," Winston Churchill 469

READING: United Nations Charter 475

READING: Excerpt from "The Truman Library Speech," Kofi Annan 477

LO3 Prewrite a Draft of a Thesis Statement Using Argument 480

LO4 Prewrite to Generate Relevant Details Using Argument 481

LO5 Compose a Draft Using Logical Order: Argument 483

STUDENT ESSAY: "The Recipe for Good Citizenship," Colleen Fahrenbach 484

LO6 Revise and Proofread for Effective Language with Argument 487

Workshop: Comprehend and Create an Essay Using Argument 489

READING: Excerpt from *On the Duty of Civil Disobedience*, Henry David Thoreau 489

READING: "Is it a Crime for a U.S. Citizen to Vote?" Susan B. Anthony 491

READING: Speech on the Eve of Historic Dandi March, Mahatma Gandhi 494

Reading and Writing Assignments MySkillsLab™ 499

Review Test 1 MySkillsLab™ 503

READING: "Do Lie Detectors Really Detect Lies?," Zimbardo, Johnson, and Hamilton 503

Review Test 2 MySkillsLab™

Academic Learning Log: Module Review MySkillsLab™ 506

UNIT 5 10 Essential Grammar Skills with MySkillsLab™

MODULE 13
The Comma 508

LO1 Use Commas with Items in a Series 508

LO2 Use Commas with Introductory Elements 509

LO3 Use Commas to Join Independent Clauses 509

LO4 Use Commas with Parenthetical Ideas 501

LO5 Use Commas with Quotations 510

MODULE 14
Comma Splices and Fused Sentences 511

LO1 Identify Comma Splices 511

LO2 Identify Fused Sentences 511

LO3 Correct Comma Splices and Fused Sentences Using Four Strategies 512

MODULE 15
Fragments and Consistent Use of Point of View, Number, and Tense 513

LO1 Recognize the Difference Between Sentences and Fragments 513

LO2 Edit to Correct Types of Fragments 513

LO3 Use Consistent Person and Point of View 515

LO4 Use Consistent Number 516

LO5 Use Consistent Tense 517

MODULE 16
Subject-Verb Agreement: Present Tense 518

LO1 Recognize Subject-Verb Agreement 518

LO2 Create Agreement Using Key Verbs in the Present Tense: *To Have, To Do, To Be* 518

LO3 Create Subject-Verb Agreement 520

MODULE 17
Adjectives and Adverbs 521
LO1 Recognize Types and Uses of Adjectives 521
LO2 Recognize Types and Uses of Adverbs 522

MODULE 18
Parallelism 524
LO1 Use Parallel Words 524
LO2 Use Parallel Phrases 525
LO3 Use Parallel Clauses 525
LO4 Punctuate for Parallelism 526

MODULE 19
Misplaced and Dangling Modifiers 527
LO1 Edit Misplaced Modifiers 527
LO2 Edit Dangling Modifiers 528

MODULE 20
Quotation Marks 530
LO1 Format and Punctuate Direct Quotations 530
LO2 Use Speech Tags with Direct Quotations 531
LO3 Use Quotation Marks Correctly with Titles 532

MODULE 21
The Apostrophe 533
LO1 Use the Apostrophe to Show Ownership 533
LO2 Use the Apostrophe for Contractions 534
LO3 Avoid Common Misuses of the Apostrophe 535

MODULE 22
Improving Your Spelling 536
LO1 Rules for Improving Your Spelling 536
Rule 1: Understand How Suffixes Are Used 536
Rule 2: Add -*s* or -*es* to Nouns and Verbs to Form the Plural 537
Rule 3: Double the Final Consonant in Words with One Syllable 537
Rule 4: Double the Final Consonant in Words with More Than One Syllable 537
Rule 5: Drop or Keep the Final *E* 538
Rule 6: Change or Keep the Final *Y* 538
Rule 7: Choose *ie* or *ei* 538
LO2 Identify Three Reasons for Word Confusion 539
LO3 Correctly Use 30 Commonly Confused Words 540

UNIT 6 Reading Selections 550

1. **An Account of Alfred C. Cooley's Plight in the Face of Hurricane Katrina**
   Sandra Offiah-Hawkins (NARRATION) 552
2. **Seven Ages of Man from *As You Like It***
   William Shakespeare (PROCESS) 560
3. **Niagara Falls**
   Rupert Brooke (DESCRIPTION) 565
4. **Beauty from Ashes**
   Anne Smith (CAUSE AND EFFECT) 573
5. ***A Doll's House*, Act III, Final Scene**
   Henrik Ibsen (CAUSE AND EFFECT) 584
6. **Fannie Lou Hamer**
   Maya Angelou (GENERALIZATION AND EXAMPLE) 594
7. **I Hear America Singing**
   Walt Whitman (DEFINITION AND EXAMPLE) 600
8. **Shaking Hands**
   Edward Everett (CLASSIFICATION) 605
9. **On the Difference Between Wit and Humor**
   Charles S. Brooks (COMPARISON AND CONTRAST) 612
10. **The Morality of Birth Control**
    Margaret Sanger (ARGUMENT) 620
11. **Nobel Lecture: The Nobel Peace Prize 2014**
    Malala Yousafzai (ARGUMENT) 628

Photo Credits 638
Text Credits 639
Index 641

Preface

The Master Reader/Writer offers a balanced approach to literacy by bringing instruction for reading and writing together in one textbook. Research indicates that when reading and writing are taught together, students achieve better in both areas (Tierney & Shanahan, 1991). Reading and writing are similar and complementary communication processes. They both have recursive before, during, and after phases, and the outcome of both is that the individual constructs his or her own meaning. *The Master Reader/Writer* builds on these similarities.

How Does *The Master Reader/ Writer* Emphasize Process?

Emphasis on reading and writing as processes is embedded in instruction throughout the textbook. The reading/writing process is introduced and illustrated in Unit 1 with two-page four-color graphics that explain this process as a strategy that students apply to reading and writing in everyday life, college life, and working life to comprehend and compose text.

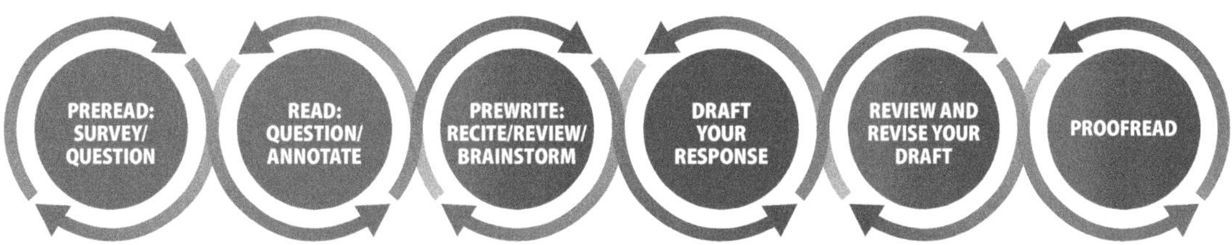

Appropriate process icons appear throughout the textbook as signals to guide students through the reading and writing process of particular assignments.

How Does *The Master Reader/Writer* Help Students Think Critically?

One of the most significant benefits of teaching reading and writing together is that students become better critical thinkers (Langer & Applebee, 1987). A critical thinker raises questions; considers multiple perspectives; gathers, analyzes, and assesses information; synthesizes ideas; applies new knowledge; and reflects to self-improve. *The Master Reader/Writer* recognizes the important role of critical thinking in the process of making meaning by teaching high-level skills in Unit 1. To lay an early and firm foundation, students learn to think critically by determining and establishing purpose and tone, inferring and implying ideas, and distinguishing between fact and opinion. Then, each subsequent module calls for students to apply these critical thinking steps to comprehend and compose text. In addition, *The Master Reader/Writer* deepens critical thinking by asking students to assume the role of both readers and writers within each and every module. Furthermore, *The Master Reader/Writer* engages critical thinking skills by using a thematic approach with an overall guiding question for readings in each module. To answer the guiding question about the modules' themes, students employ critical thinking skills. For example,

- Students learn to clarify an author's purpose when they read and to clarify their own purposes when they write.
- Students learn to ask and answer questions to comprehend and compose texts.
- Students learn to assess supporting details in what they read and in preparation for what they write.
- Students learn to evaluate the impact of word choices made by authors in what they read and as they prepare to write for a specific audience.
- Students learn to develop logical inferences and conclusions based on what they read and in preparation for what they write.
- Students learn to distinguish between fact and opinion as they read and to effectively use fact and opinion in their writing.
- Students learn to identify and analyze sources in what they read and in preparation for what they write.
- Students learn to synthesize ideas from multiple sources.
- Students learn to analyze and provide text evidence as supporting details.
- Students learn to read closely and write meaningfully.

Critical thinkers are engaged learners who think about their thinking (metacognition). *The Master Reader/Writer* fosters and encourages engaged learning and metacognition. Mirroring the before, during, and after phases of reading/writing, each module fosters students' critical thinking skills before, during, and after learning.

Before Learning:

In each module opener, the photographic organizer introduces the concept or main topic of the module and guides students to think critically about the concept. To prepare to learn, students . . .

- **Call up prior knowledge:** Students analyze the engaging set of photographs to compose captions that state how each photograph represents or relates to the topic of the module.
- **Make predictions:** By answering the question "What's the point of . . .?," students make written predictions about the significance of the topic and how it applies to everyday, college, and working life.
- **Engage visual and tactile learning modes:** Students consider photographs to call up their prior knowledge, analyze what the images represent, and respond with written predictions about the importance of the concept.

During Learning:

Throughout each module, examples and explanations engage students as active learners; then practices offer opportunities for students to apply what they learn and test their understanding. To learn, students . . .

- **Engage with examples:** Examples are designed as directed thinking activities that reinforce instruction by guiding students to complete an exercise that applies the instruction to a specific situation. Explanations follow immediately. Modules 8–12 also include authentic student model essays so students can learn from peer analysis and writing.
- **Model think-alouds:** Each think-aloud records one student's answer to the example and explains the thought process or decisions he or she made as he or she completed the example. Students are encouraged to use writing-to-learn to record their own think-alouds about what and how they are learning.
- **Apply core concepts to specific situations:** Practices guide students to apply what they are learning to situations or content encountered in everyday, college, or working life.

After Learning:

Each module ends with a series of after learning activities, such as Workshops; Reading/Writing Assignments for Everyday, College, and Working Life; Review Tests; and an Academic Learning Log. These varied activities reinforce learning and offer students the opportunity to track and reflect upon their mastery of the concepts studied in the module. To think critically after learning, students . . .

- **Apply concepts:** The module Workshop guides students to apply the concepts they have learned in the module as a strategy throughout the reading/writing process. In each workshop, students write a formal response or essay in which they synthesize readings from the Workshop and the rest of the module. The Reading/Writing Assignments are designed as choices students can select to apply what they have learned in the Workshop.
- **Review concepts and test ongoing mastery:** Each module offers two Review Tests (one in print and one in MySkillsLab). Students read a passage and answer objective reading comprehension questions. These questions also cover concepts taught in previous modules.
- **Respond to reading passages:** Most Review Tests ask students to think critically to summarize the passage. All Review Tests conclude with two writing prompts, one in which students summarize the passage, and another in which they respond critically to the passage. Students think critically to use information from the reading passage to address a specific writing situation.
- **Reflect upon learning:** In the Academic Learning Logs students recall key vocabulary and concepts for each learning outcome. Students use their own words or create concept maps to call up what they have learned. Students also analyze their level of mastery, identify what they still need to study, and explain how they plan to continue their studies.

The Workshop:

Each module features a Workshop as a capstone academic reading and writing assignment. This capstone assignment offers one to three readings related to the module's overall theme. The Workshop guides students through each phase of the reading/writing strategy, affording students the opportunity to independently apply what they have learned throughout the module. The Workshop reminds students of the module's guiding question and provides a relevant cluster of questions that can be used for prereading, discussion, and writing-to-sources prompts. To accomplish this capstone reading/writing assignment, students engage in the following critical thinking activities before, during, and after reading and writing:

- Questioning and surveying the text.
- Annotating the text to comprehend the author's central idea and key supports and to generate details to include in their own writing.
- Synthesizing ideas from a variety of sources.
- Composing original text in response to sources.
- Revising and proofreading to produce a quality final draft.

How Does *The Master Reader/ Writer* Provide Students with Purpose and Self-Assessment Tools?

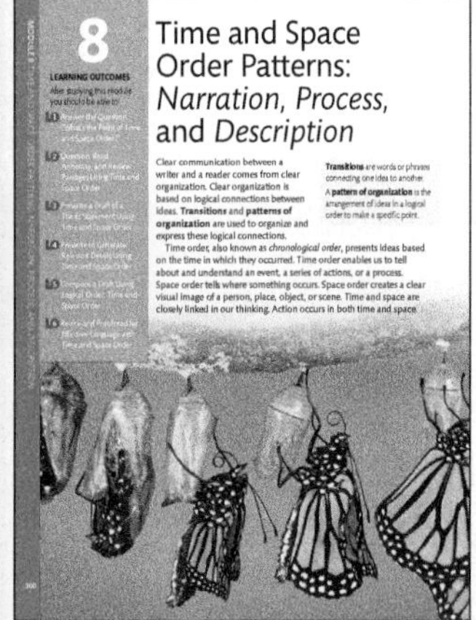

Learning Outcomes

Each module in Units 1–4 begins by stating student learning outcomes and offering pre-learning activities called "What's the Point?" that guide students in the use of predicting, questioning, and setting a purpose for learning. Throughout the modules, students learn by applying core concepts to meaningful reading and writing situations, thereby developing and internalizing reading and writing processes. Modules end with after learning summaries and applications tied to the module's student learning outcomes so students may self-assess, monitor progress, and address individual needs. Each module is also aligned to an additional Review Test in MySkillsLab.

Levels of Learning

The best way *to learn* is *to do*. Thus, one of the primary aims of this text is to give students plentiful opportunities to apply what they are learning. Every concept introduced in the book is accompanied by an explanation of the concept, an example with explanation of the example, and one or more practice examples.

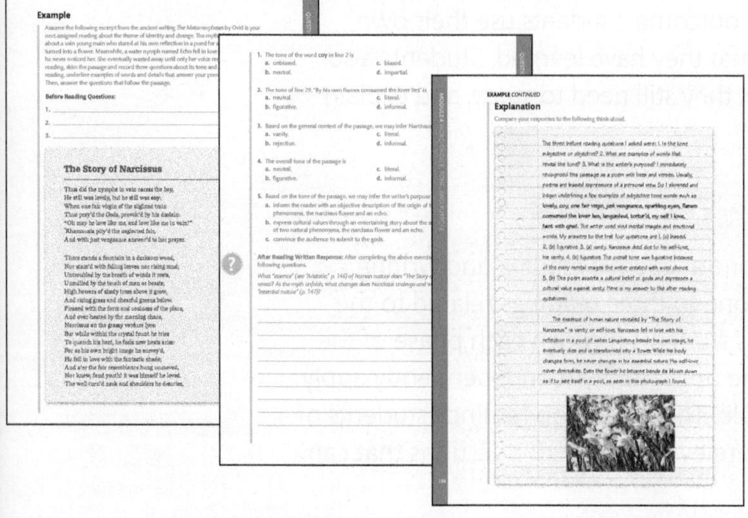

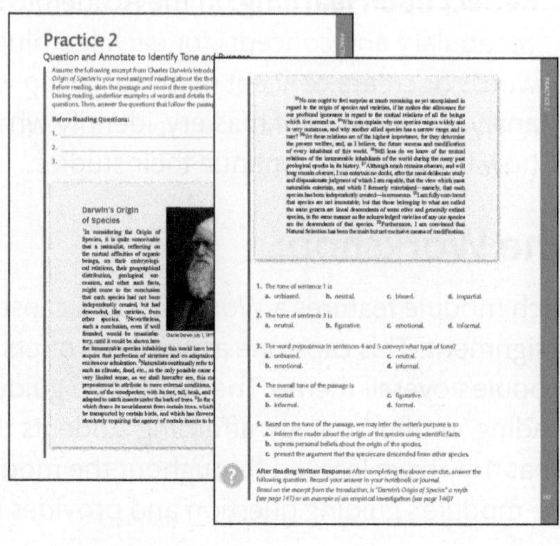

Each module also contains **two review tests**, one in the printed textbook and one in MySkillsLab, in which students read passages to practice their reading skills and then respond to the passage in writing based on a *Reader Response* writing prompt.

Review Test

Conflict Defined

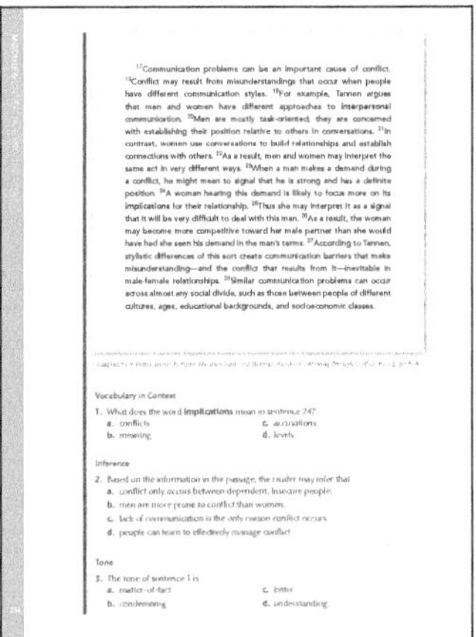

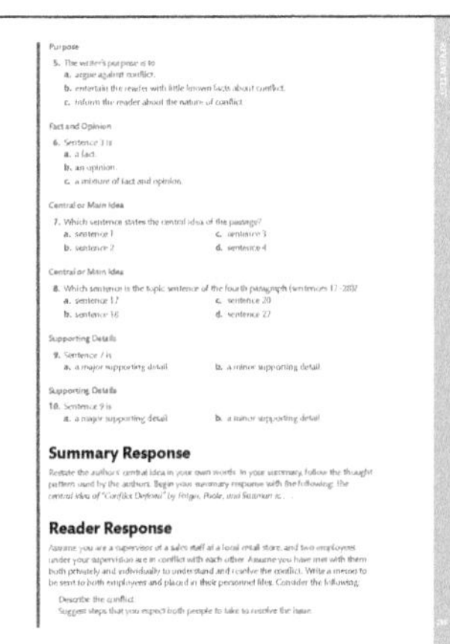
Summary Response

Reader Response

Finally, each module closes with an **Academic Learning Log**. Each module also features a section of **reading and writing assignments**. These assignments create realistic writing situations that direct students to consider audience and purpose as they respond to topics and situations relevant to "Everyday Life," "College Life," and "Working Life." Thus, the text offers several levels of learning. Not only are students given an abundance of practice so that they focus on individual skills, but they are also provided with challenging writing situations in which to employ their reading/writing process.

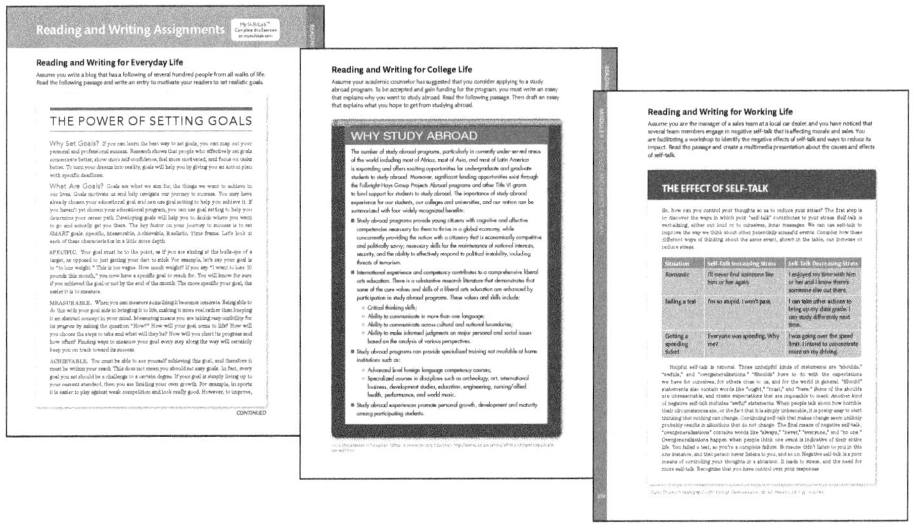
Reading and Writing Assignments

Reading and Writing for Everyday Life

THE POWER OF SETTING GOALS

Reading and Writing for College Life

WHY STUDY ABROAD

Reading and Writing for Working Life

THE EFFECT OF SELF-TALK

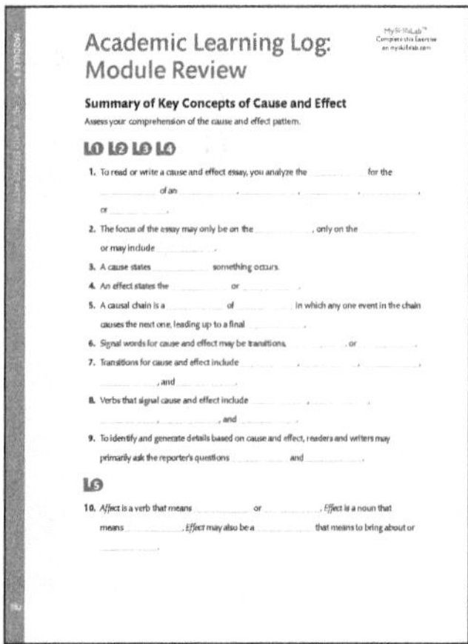
Academic Learning Log: Module Review

Summary of Key Concepts of Cause and Effect

High-Interest Thematic Approach with Guiding Questions

The Master Reader/Writer follows a thematic approach to the readings for each module. The themes are common high-interest, real-world, or academic concepts that students will encounter in their daily lives, such as "Identify and Change," and "Motivation and Achievement."

Each module provides students with a "Guiding Question" that they work toward answering through each Example, Practice, and ultimately, the Workshop. In every module, the first reading is given as an Example that is annotated with interactive prereading questions about the reading's text structure. Students are directed to annotate the text to answer these prereading questions. In addition, after reading questions ask students to summarize the reading and/or complete a concept map with details from the reading. The Example is followed by a Practice made up of two additional readings on the module's theme. Each of these readings also has prereading and after reading questions. However, the after reading questions guide students to begin the process of synthesizing ideas from the passages they have read. The Workshop is the capstone activity of each module. During the Workshop, students answer a cluster of thematic questions to guide them to synthesize the passages they've read and apply the module's instruction into their reading/writing processes. In both the Practices and the Workshop, students apply the reading/writing strategy to compose their own essays.

The authentic readings in this text come from well-known authors and sources including primary documents in the forms of essays and speeches, providing students with real-world and academic practice in decoding and understanding complex texts. *The Master Reader/Writer* provides students with tools and strategies they need in order to understand these passages.

Text Structure

The Master Reader/Writer offers students access to and experience with materials that present both professional and student writing that span various patterns of organization and genres (such as essays, textbook excerpts, articles from books, articles, online sources, and speeches). Through immersion in text structure, students develop a sense of why an author chooses a particular organizational pattern or genre for a specific purpose. Students experience the power of well-organized text to convey a message.

Visual Instruction and Learning Activities

The Master Reader/Writer uses photographs, graphics, and annotation of instructional examples to reach visual learners and drive concepts home. For example, each module opens with a photographic organizer that activates the thinking process by introducing and illustrating the skill in question, and stimulating prewriting activities. As another example, visual learning activities introduce and facilitate writing assignments; concept maps, charts, graphs, and annotated examples enable students to "see" the concept clearly.

WHAT'S THE POINT of Argument? LO

Argument is often a call to action or a challenge to a change of mind. The following photos represent a call to good citizenship. Study the photographs. In the space provided, identify the claim, reasons, and an opposing point of view about what it means to be a good citizen. Then answer the question "What's the point of argument?"

Photographic Organizer: Argument

ISSUE: WHAT MAKES A GOOD CITIZEN?

SUPPORTING POINTS

What is this reason? What is this reason? What is this reason?

COUNTERCLAIM (Opposing Point)

What is this opposing view?

What is the claim?

Refute the counterclaim.

What's the point of argument?

EXAMPLE CONTINUED

Term	Definition	Trait	What It Is Not	Examples
Relativism			Judeo-Christian ethics	None given
Situational ethics		None given	Judeo-Christian ethics	None given
Societal ethics		None given		None given
Rule utilitarianism			Situational ethics	
Unethical behavior		None given	Amoral behavior—no sense of right or wrong	

Explanation

Compare your answers to the following think-aloud, completed by Madelyn, another student in your class.

The writers of this passage used both the generalization-example and the definition-example patterns. Almost every paragraph begins with a general statement followed by examples as supporting details. For example, sentence 61 makes a general statement, and sentences 62–65 give examples to support it. The writer also

How Is *The Master Reader/Writer* Organized?

The Master Reader/Writer's structure taps into the similarities between reading and writing by systematically integrating reading and writing skills and concepts into units/modules of instruction. The sequence of units is designed to offer comprehensive coverage of the reading/writing processes and skills while at the same time providing distinct modules that allow for individualization of instruction based on the needs of specific teaching-learning situations.

Unit 1 teaches comprehension tools for reader/writers to make or construct meaning. These tools are reinforced throughout the book as they recur in each subsequent module. Examples of tools for constructing meaning include the following:

- Making Inferences and Implications
- Summarizing
- Questioning and Annotating Techniques

Unit 2 teaches vocabulary acquisition and language choice, as well as skills to analyze subjective and objective language to distinguish fact from opinion. Instruction also offers guidelines for using direct speech with quotation marks and indirect or reported speech.

Unit 3 teaches essay writing and research as a foundational strategy. Thus, research becomes a recurring strategy and skill incorporated throughout subsequent modules. Students apply appropriate research and documentation strategies and skills throughout the rest of the textbook as they read and respond to text.

Unit 4 offers instruction for using rhetorical modes to comprehend passages, synthesize details from several readings, and compose a response to what has been read.

- The traditional patterns of organization are taught as foundational concepts upon which students construct higher levels of meaning.
- Instruction is scaffolded from guided activities to independent application of key strategies in the use of rhetorical devices throughout the reading/writing process.
- Examples and practices guide students through the reading/writing process to comprehend and compose text.

Research indicates that teaching reading and writing together reduces the need for direct instruction in grammar and increases a student's mastery of organization, argument, and various other writing skills. Combined reading/writing instruction develops a "sentence sense" that serves as the foundation of grammatical awareness (Haussamen, NCTE, 2004).

Thus, Unit 5, "10 Essential Grammar Skills with MySkillsLab," supports individualized grammar instruction. As student and teacher partner together to identify specific patterns of a student's needs, Unit 5 serves as a quick hard-copy reference handbook that defines and illustrates the rules for the 10 most common grammatical errors committed by students. In addition, each grammar lesson is amplified by and supplemented with access to MySkillsLab for in-depth practice and assessment of specific skills. Furthermore, as students discover additional needs, individualized study plans can be created in MySkillsLab.

Unit 6, "Reading Selections," offers students rich opportunities to interact with text as both readers and writers—applying the literacy skills attained as they progress through instruction. Selections are authentic, published pieces that reflect diverse voices addressing high-interest cultural topics. Each selection features a vocabulary prompt and after reading activities that include objective reading comprehension items, after reading discussion questions, and reader response prompts.

How Does *The Master Reader/Writer* Prepare Students for Success?

Perhaps one of the greatest motivations and underlying goals of *The Master Reader/Writer* is to offer an opportunity to develop the literacy skills of our students as quickly as possible. To do so, *The Master Reader/Writer* taps into brain-based learning, fosters metacognition, places instruction in meaningful contexts, and engages students with high-interest content and visual presentation. Your work as a classroom instructor is of the utmost value; the opportunity to partner with you to nurture student success is a great honor. My hope is that *The Master Reader/Writer* complements your aspirations as a teacher and inspires your students to realize their full potential.

Instructor Support and Professional Development

Pearson is pleased to offer a variety of support materials to help make teaching reading and writing easier for teachers and to help students excel in their coursework. Many of our student supplements are available free or at a greatly reduced price when packaged with *The Master Reader/Writer.* Visit www.pearsonhighered.com, contact your local Pearson sales representative, or review a detailed listing of the full supplements package in the *Instructor's Resource Manual* for more information.

Book-Specific Ancillary Material

Annotated Instructor's Edition for The Master Reader/Writer
ISBN 0-321-92740-0 / 978-0-321-92740-8
The AIE offers in-text answers to all exercises, practice sets, and reading/writing assignments. It also indicates which activities are offered simultaneously in MySkillsLab. It is a valuable resource for experienced and first-time instructors alike.

Instructor's Resource Manual for The Master Reader/Writer
ISBN 0-321-92741-9 / 978-0-321-92741-5
The material in the *IRM*, written by Loretta Rodgers of Eastfield College, is designed to save instructors time and provide them with effective options for teaching the integrated reading/writing course. It offers suggestions for setting up their course; provides sample syllabus models, provides lots of extra practice for students who need it; and offers quizzes and grammar tests, including unit tests. This valuable resource is exceptionally useful for adjuncts who might need advice in setting up their initial classes or who might be teaching a variety of courses with too many students and not enough time.

Test Bank for The Master Reader/Writer
ISBN 0-13-392908-6 / 978-0-13-392908-9
An abundance of extra practice exercises are included in the Test Bank for *The Master Reader/Writer.* The *Test Bank*, created by Loretta Rodgers—Eastfield College, can also be used to create tests in Pearson's MyTest test creation tool.

PowerPoint Presentation for The Master Reader/Writer
ISBN 0-321-92744-3 / 978-0-321-92744-6
PowerPoint presentations have been created to accompany each module of *The Master Reader/Writer*; these consist of classroom-ready lecture outline slides, lecture tips and classroom activities, and module review questions. It is available for download from the Instructor Resource Center.

Answer Key for The Master Reader/Writer
ISBN 0-321-96370-9 / 978-0-321-96370-3
The Answer Key contains the solutions to the exercises in the student edition of the text. It is available for download from the Instructor Resource Center.

Professional Development
Pearson offers a variety of professional development programs and resources to support full- and part-time instructors. These include Pedagogy & Practice, an open-access digital resource gallery [http://pedagogyandpractice.pearsonhighered.com/], and our Speaking About English online conference series, featuring scholar/educators addressing pedagogical topics via web-based presentations. These conferences are held twice a year and are free of cost to attend. Information about future conferences, as well as archives of past sessions, can be found on the conference website [http://www.pearsonhighered.com/speakingabout/english/]. Updated information about any and all of these Partnership Programs can always be found on our catalog page [http://www.pearsonhighered.com/english/].

Looking for more Grammar coverage? Here are some options that are FREE when bundled with *The Master Reader/Writer!*
The Prentice Hall Grammar Workbook 3e by Jeanette Adkins, Tarrant County CC
ISBN: 0-205-73907-5
This workbook is a comprehensive source of instruction for students who need additional grammar, punctuation, and mechanics assistance. Covering such topics as subject-verb agreement, conjunctions, modifiers, capital letters, and vocabulary, each chapter provides helpful explanations, examples, and exercises. It is available to bundle for FREE!

The Pearson Lab Manual for Developing Writers by Linda Copeland, St. Louis CC-Merramac
This three-volume workbook is an ideal supplement for any developmental writing sequence. All three are available to bundle individually for FREE!

1. **Volume A: Sentences (0-205-63409-5)**
At this level, exercises and applications of grammar, punctuation, and mechanics stress rules rather than simply skill and drill. There are many composing exercises that apply sentence skills explained in the students' primary textbook.

2. **Volume B: Paragraphs (0-205-69341-5) & Volume C: Essays (0-205-69340-7)**
The exercises encourage students to apply key concepts covered in most writing classes—that is, topic sentences, thesis statements, coherence, unity, and levels

of development. *Analysis* exercises give further illustration of concepts explained in class and in the primary textbook; *Building* exercises give students the "raw materials" to develop paragraphs and/or essays along the various modes. Revision prompts encourage students to look at specific key elements of their own writing and assess whether they have met the needs of their reading audience.

MySkillsLab™ **www.myskillslab.com**

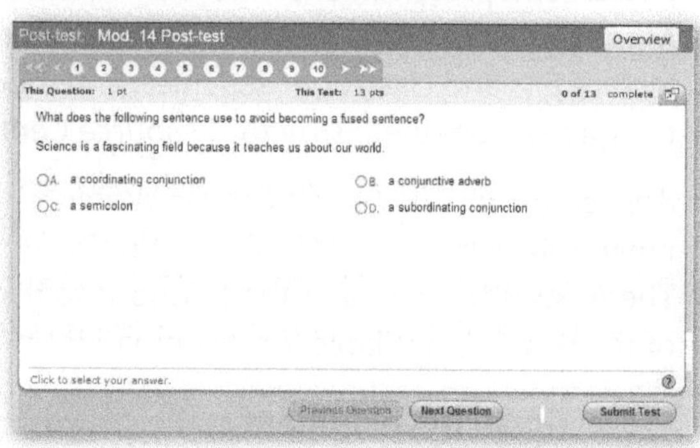

Efficiently blending the market-leading and proven practice from MyWritingLab and MyReadingLab into a single application and learning path, MySkillsLab offers a wealth of practice opportunity, additional instruction/content support, and extensive progress tracking for integrated reading/writing courses. For more than half a decade, MySkillsLab has been the most widely used online learning application for the integrated reading/writing course across two- and four-year institutions. We have published case studies demonstrating how MySkillsLab (or, individually, MyReadingLab and MyWritingLab) consistently benefits students' mastery of key reading skills, reading comprehension, writing skills, and critical thinking.

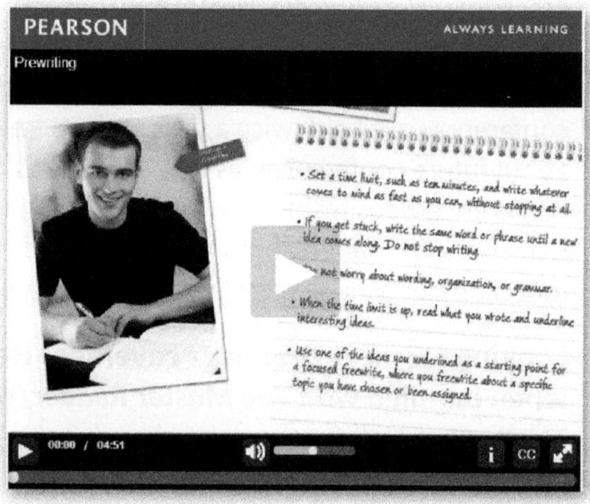

Reading MySkillsLab improves students' mastery of 26 reading skills across four levels of difficulty via mastery-based skill practice, and improves students' reading levels with the Lexile® framework (www.Lexile.com) to measure both reader ability and text difficulty on the same scale and pair students with readings within their Lexile range.

Writing MySkillsLab offers skill remediation in grammar and punctuation, paragraph development, essay development, and research, and improves students' overall writing through automatic scoring by Pearson's proven Intelligent Essay Assessor (IEA).

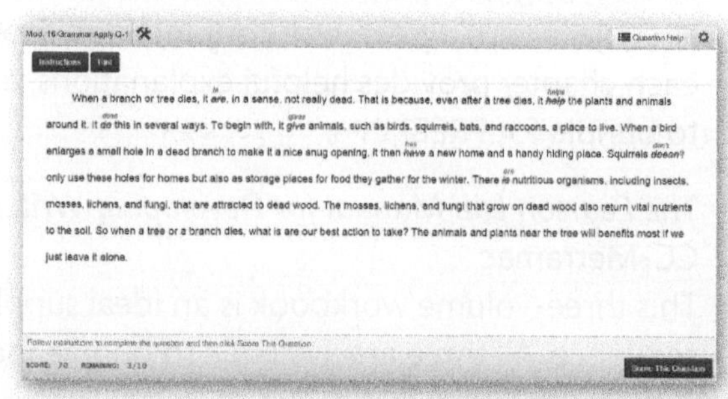

A Deeper Connection Between Print and Media
Pearson's MySkillsLab (www.myskillslab.com) is deeply integrated into the assignments and activities in *The Master Reader/Writer*. Students can complete and submit various exercises and activities within the eText/MySkillsLab course and some of the results flow right to the Instructor Gradebook. Additionally, all professional readings are also available in MySkillsLab with the corresponding apparatus associated with them along with book-specific videos that expand upon the reading, writing, and thinking processes.

Acknowledgments

Composing *The Master Reader/Writer* has been a joyous process: The opportunity to serve the learning community as a textbook author continues to fill me with a wondrous sense of gratitude and humility. I owe much to the entire Pearson team, including Eric Stano, Editor-in-Chief, Developmental Reading and Writing; Matthew Wright, Executive Editor, Developmental English; Erin Dye, Project Manager at Nieman Inc., for her wisdom and creativity that always inspires and improves my writing; Kathy Smith with Cenveo Publisher Services, for her tireless devotion to excellence; Ellen MacElree and the entire production team for their work ethic and gracious attitudes. The entire Pearson team, from the editorial team, to production, to representatives in the field, each one passionately strives to provide teachers and students with the best possible resources to foster literacy. In addition, I would like to thank Loretta Rodgers—Eastfield College for authoring the various supplements that accompany *The Master Reader/Writer.* I owe a special debt of gratitude to my own assistant, Heather Brady, without whom I could not have accomplished the monumental task of composing this series. Her ability to locate engaging passages from appropriate sources, write content for examples, practices, and reading/writing assignments, as well as edit all the various stages of the manuscript make her contribution invaluable.

For nearly twenty-five years, I worked with an amazing group of faculty from across the State of Florida as an item-writer, reviewer, or scorer of statewide assessment exams for student learning and professional certification. The work we accomplished together continues to inform me as a teacher, writer, and consultant. I count myself greatly blessed to have worked with these who sacrificed much for the good of our students.

Finally, I would like to gratefully recognize the outstanding insights provided by the following colleagues and reviewers. I deeply appreciate their investment of time and energy:

Janice Brantley, University of Arkansas at Pine Bluff
Leslie Brian, Houston Community College and Lonestar College System
Christopher Brockman, Vance-Granville Community College
Nelda Contreras, Brookhaven College
Deborah Davis, Richland College
Barbara S. Doyle, Arkansas State University
Christine Fisher, Trinity Valley Community College
Patricia Kilbourn Haller, Saginaw Valley State University
Janis Innis, Houston Community College
Julie Kelly, St. Johns River State College
Vickie Kelly, Hinds Community College
Kimberly Koledoye, Houston Community College
Patty Kunkel, Santa Fe College
Dawn Reno Langley, Piedmont Community College
Alice Leonhardt, Blue Ridge Community College
Alexandria Leyton, City College of San Francisco and University of San Francisco
Leslie Lovenstein, Pulaski Technical College
Irma Luna, San Antonio College
Gladys Montalvo, Palm Beach State College
Donna Nalley, South University Online
Jen Osborne, St. Philip's College
Nancy M. Risch, Caldwell Community College and Technical Institute
Dixie Shaw-Tillmon, The University of Texas at San Antonio
Susan Silva, El Paso Community College
Angel T. Solomon, Piedmont Community College
Alexandr Tolj, John Tyler Community College
Alexandra Wagman, Holyoke Community College
Shari Waldrop, Navarro College

1 An Introduction to Reading and Writing

LEARNING OUTCOMES

After studying this module you should be able to:

- LO 1 Answer the Question "What's the Point of Reading and Writing?"
- LO 2 Connect Reading and Writing
- LO 3 Assess the Reading/Writing Situation
- LO 4 Recognize the Elements of Text
- LO 5 Develop Tools to Create Meaning through Reading/Writing

Reading and writing are thinking processes in which we make and express meaning through our interactions with text. During the reading process, we draw information from a text to create meaning. **Reading** is an active process during which we get information from and make meaning of text. When what you've read makes sense, you've achieved **comprehension**, an understanding of the material. Master readers rely on the reading process to ask questions, find answers, and react to a writer's ideas. **Writing** is an active process during which we express information in text form to create meaning. Writers create meaning by developing and organizing ideas and communicating them to other people. Master writers rely on the writing process to discover, organize, and express information as clearly as possible. Master writers seek to build comprehension in readers.

Reading is the act of comprehending text.

Comprehension is the act of making meaning or gaining knowledge.

Writing is the act of composing text.

WHAT'S THE POINT of Reading and Writing? LO 1

A mastery of reading and writing helps you build a foundation for success in everyday life, college life, and working life. Before you study this module, predict the importance of reading and writing. Study the following photographs. State a reason for or benefit of reading and writing situations in our everyday, college, and working lives. Then state the point of becoming a master reader/writer.

Photographic Organizer: Reasons to Read and Write

EVERYDAY LIFE	READING	WRITING

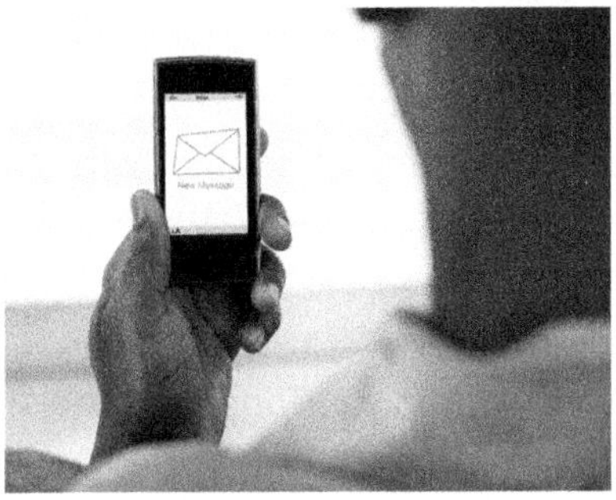

COLLEGE LIFE	READING	WRITING

WORKING LIFE	READING	WRITING

What's the point of reading and writing?

LO2 Connect Reading and Writing

Reading and writing are closely related thinking processes. A writer (author) sends a message, and a reader (audience) receives a message. A master writer thinks about what the reader needs to know. A master reader thinks about the writer's purpose. Thus, writing and reading rely on and strengthen each other.

Think of writing and reading as a conversation between the writer and the reader. One writes; the other reads. But the conversation often doesn't end there. A reader's response to a piece of writing keeps the dialogue going. When you write a summary, your response is to restate the author's ideas. It's like saying to the author, "If I understood you correctly, you said. . . ." When you write to analyze the text for deeper meaning, you are answering questions a writer may **imply**, such as, "What is the significance of this idea?" A master reader draws conclusions about or **infers** the writer's meaning. Connecting reading and writing benefits both reader and writer.

To **imply** is to suggest meaning rather than directly state an idea.
To **infer** is to determine meaning based on reasoning, evidence, or details.

By reading, a writer gains . . .

- New vocabulary
- Additional facts about a topic
- Different opinions on a topic
- Details that support an opinion
- Connections between prior knowledge and new ideas
- Varying ways to apply writing techniques:
  - Ways to use punctuation
  - Ways to write sentences
  - Ways to organize ideas
  - Ways to open and close an essay

Writing helps a reader to learn. **Writing-to-learn** is a powerful way to connect reading and writing. Writing-to-learn activities use questions and written responses to focus attention on an important concept, idea, or task. At times, you may write to learn about a specific concept or idea. At other times, you may write to learn more about how you think or approach a reading or writing task. One writing-to-learn activity is to state what you already know, what you need to learn, and what you discovered about a topic from reading the text.

Writing-to-learn is the use of focused, informal writings to deepen understanding of a concept, idea, or skill.

By writing, a reader gains . . .

- Ways to engage with text
- Ways to connect text to the world
- Ways to use text structure to write
- Ways to respond to ideas
- Improved skills in areas such as spelling
- Deeper understanding of ideas

For Module 1, assume you are taking a college course in psychology and your class is beginning to study the theme of learning and using language. Each reading in this module follows this theme. The question you will seek to answer as you read is "What is the importance of learning and using language?" After completing all readings, you will write about what you have learned.

Example

Read the following passage. Answer the questions that come before and after the passage.

1. What is the passage about?

2. What do I already know about this idea?

Intrinsic Versus Extrinsic Motivation

[1]Imagine that you are an elementary school teacher who wants your students to develop a love of reading. [2]Not only do you want your students to read more, but you also want them to develop a love of books. [3]How might you go about accomplishing this?

[4]If you are like many educators, you might decide that a good approach would be to reward the children for reading. [5]Teachers have always rewarded kids with a smile or a gold star on an assignment, of course, but recently they have turned to more powerful incentives. [6]A chain of pizza restaurants offers elementary school students in some school districts a certificate for a free pizza when they have read a certain number of books (see "Book It!" at www.bookitprogram.com). [7]One school district has taken this a step further by rewarding high school students with cash prizes if they do well on Advanced Placement exams.

[8]There is no doubt that rewards are powerful motivators and that pizzas and money will get kids to read more. [9]One of the oldest and most fundamental psychological principles says that giving a reward each time a behavior occurs will increase the frequency of that behavior. [10]Whether it be a food pellet delivered to a rat pressing a bar or a free pizza given to a child for reading, rewards can change behavior.

[11]But people are not rats, and we have to consider the effects of rewards on what's inside—people's thoughts about themselves, their self-concept, and their motivation to read in the future. [12]Does being paid to read, for example, change people's ideas about *why* they are reading? [13]The danger of reward programs such as Book It! is that kids will begin to think they are reading to earn something, not because they find reading to be an enjoyable activity in its own right. [14]When the reward programs end and pizzas are no longer forthcoming, children may actually read less than they did before.

CONTINUED

EXAMPLE *CONTINUED*

[15]This is especially likely to happen to children who already liked to read. [16]Such children have high **intrinsic motivation**: the desire to engage in an activity because they enjoy it or find it interesting, not because of external rewards or pressure. [17]Their reasons for engaging in the activity have to do with themselves—the enjoyment and pleasure they feel when reading a book. [18]In other words, reading is play, not work.

[19]What happens when the children start getting rewards for reading? [20]Their reading, originally stemming from intrinsic motivation, is now also spurred by **extrinsic motivation**, which is people's desire to engage in an activity because of external rewards or pressures, not because they enjoy the task or find it interesting. [21]According to self-perception theory, rewards can hurt intrinsic motivation. [22]Whereas before many children read because they enjoyed it, now they are reading so that they will get the reward. [23]The unfortunate outcome is that replacing intrinsic motivation with extrinsic motivation makes people lose interest in the activity they initially enjoyed. [24]This result is called the **overjustification effect**, which results when people view their behavior as caused by compelling extrinsic reasons (e.g., a reward), making them underestimate the extent to which their behavior was caused by intrinsic reasons.

—Adapted from Aronson, Wilson, and Akert, *Social Psychology*, 8th ed., Pearson, 2013, pp. 10–11.

3. What do I still need or want to learn or clarify about specific ideas in the passage?

____

____

4. What did I learn from reading this passage?

____

____

Explanation

Compare your answers to the following think-aloud.

The title states the topic as intrinsic and extrinsic motivation. I already knew about "Book It!" because my school used that program. The writer is right. Once the program was over, many of my friends stopped reading. I want to learn more about self-perception theory. I was surprised to learn that rewards can harm motivation.

Practice 1

Connect Reading and Writing: Writing-to-Learn

Read the following passage from a college psychology textbook. Use writing-to-learn to connect your reading and writing about the text by answering the questions that come before and after the passage.

1. What is the passage about?

2. What do I already know about this idea?

Definition of Learning

[1]**Learning** is any relatively permanent change in behavior brought about by experience or practice. [2]The "relatively permanent" part of the definition refers to the process of memory, for without the ability to remember what happens, people cannot learn anything.

[3]As for the inclusion of experience or practice, think about the last time you did something that caused you a lot of pain. [4]Did you do it again? [5]Probably not. [6]You didn't want to experience that pain again, so you changed your behavior to avoid the painful consequences. [7]This is how children learn not to touch hot stoves. [8]In contrast, if a person does something resulting in a very pleasurable experience, that person is more likely to do that same thing again. [9]This change in behavior is known as the *law of effect.*

[10]In the early 1900s, the Russian scientist Ivan Pavlov (1849–1936) pioneered the empirical study of the basic principles of a particular kind of learning.

[11]Studying the digestive system in his dogs, Pavlov had built a device that would accurately measure the amount of saliva produced by the dogs when they were fed a measured amount of food. [12]Normally, when food is placed in the mouth of any animal, the salivary glands automatically start releasing saliva to help with chewing and digestion. [13]This is a normal *reflex*—an unlearned, involuntary response that is not under personal control or choice—one of many that occur in both animals and humans. [14]The food causes a particular reaction, the salivation. [15]A *stimulus* can

CONTINUED

be defined as any object, event, or experience that causes a *response,* the reaction of an organism. [16]In the case of Pavlov's dogs, food is the stimulus and salivation is the response.

Pavlov and the Salivating Dogs

[17]Pavlov soon discovered that his dogs began salivating when they weren't supposed to be salivating. [18]Some dogs would start salivating when they saw the lab assistant bringing food, others when they heard the clatter of the food bowl from the kitchen, and still others when it was the time of day they were usually fed. [19]Pavlov spent the rest of his career studying what eventually he termed **classical conditioning**, learning to elicit an involuntary, reflex-like response to a stimulus other than the original, natural stimulus that normally produces the response.

Elements of Classical Conditioning

[20]Pavlov eventually identified several key elements that must be present and experienced in a particular way for conditioning to take place.

Unconditioned Stimulus

[21]The original, naturally occurring stimulus is called the **unconditioned stimulus (UCS)**. [22]The term *unconditioned* means "unlearned." [23]This is the stimulus that ordinarily leads to the involuntary response. [24]In the case of Pavlov's dogs, food is the unconditioned stimulus.

Unconditioned Response

[25]The automatic and involuntary response to the unconditioned stimulus is called the **unconditioned response (UCR)** for much the same reason. [26]It is unlearned and occurs because of genetic "wiring" in the nervous system. [27]For example, in Pavlov's experiment, the salivation to the food is the UCR (unconditioned response).

Conditioned Stimulus

[28]Pavlov determined that almost any kind of stimulus could become associated with the unconditioned stimulus (UCS) if it is paired with the UCS often enough. [29]In his original study, the sight of the food dish itself became a stimulus for salivation *before* the food was given to the dogs. [30]Every time they got food (to which they automatically salivated), they saw the dish. [31]At this point, the dish was a **neutral stimulus (NS)** because it had no effect on salivation. [32]After being paired with the food so many times, the dish came to produce a salivation response, although a somewhat weaker one, as did the food itself. [33]When a previously neutral stimulus, through repeated pairing with the unconditioned stimulus, begins to cause the same kind of involuntary response, learning has occurred. [34]The previously neutral stimulus can now be called a **conditioned stimulus (CS)**. [35](*Conditioned*

means "learned," and, as mentioned earlier, *unconditioned* means "unlearned.")

Conditioned Response [36]The response that is given to the CS (conditioned stimulus) is not usually quite as strong as the original unconditioned response (UCR), but it is essentially the same response. [37]However, because it comes as a learned response to the conditioned stimulus (CS), it is called the **conditioned response (CR)**.

[38]Classical conditioning is actually one of the simplest forms of learning. [39]It happens to people all the time without them even being aware of it. [40]Does your mouth water when you merely see an advertisement for your favorite food on television? [41]Do you feel anxious every time you hear the high-pitched whine of the dentist drill? [42]These are both examples of classical conditioning.

[43]Another type of learning is observational learning. [44]**Observational learning** is the learning of new behavior through watching the actions of a model (someone else who is doing that behavior). [45]Sometimes that behavior is desirable, and sometimes it is not. [46]Albert Bandura (1986) concluded from his studies and others that observational learning required the presence of four elements.

Attention [47]To learn anything through observation, the learner must first pay attention to the model. [48]For example, a person at a fancy dinner party who wants to know which utensil to use has to watch the person who seems to know what is correct. [49]Certain characteristics of the model can make attention more likely. [50]For example, people pay more attention to those they perceive as similar to them, and to those they perceive as attractive.

Memory [51]The learner must also be able to retain the memory of what was done, such as remembering the steps in preparing a dish that was first seen on a cooking show.

Imitation [52]The learner must be capable of reproducing, or imitating, the actions of the model. [53]A 2-year-old might be able to watch someone tie shoelaces and might even remember most of the steps, but the child's chubby little fingers will not have the skill necessary for actually tying the laces.

Desire [54]Finally, the learner must have the desire or motivation to perform the action. [55]That person at the fancy dinner, for example, might not care which fork is the "proper" one.

—Adapted from Ciccarelli and White, *Psychology*, 4th ed., Pearson, 2015, pp. 176–179, 187, 209–211.

CONTINUED

PRACTICE 1 *CONTINUED*

3. What do I still need or want to learn or clarify about specific ideas in the passage?

4. What did I learn about the importance of learning and using language from reading this passage?

LO3 Assess the Reading/Writing Situation

Although reading and writing are closely related and interactive, usually you are mainly doing one or the other. In a specific **reading situation** there is a **purpose** or goal for reading, a **topic** or subject about which you are reading, and you, the **audience**. Likewise, a specific **writing situation** has a purpose for writing, addresses a particular topic, and is directed toward the audience or reader. A **reading/writing situation** occurs when both reading and writing are required to understand and share information or respond to it for a particular purpose. The graphic to the right illustrates the reading/writing situation.

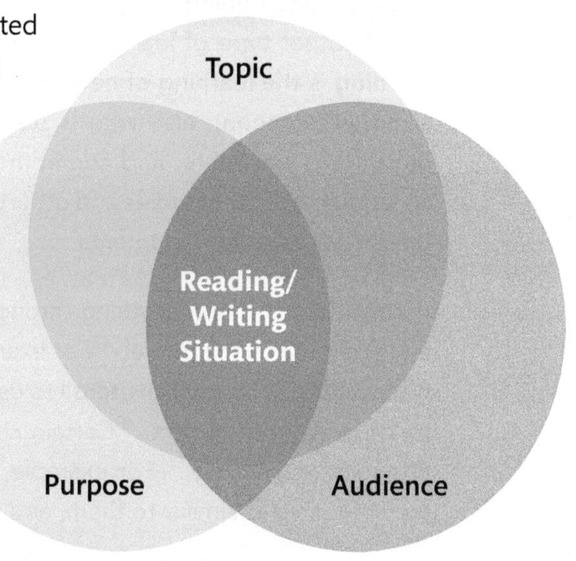

A **reading situation** is a circumstance in which a reader (or audience) has a purpose or goal for reading about a specific topic.

The **purpose** is the reason for reading or writing.

A **topic** is the subject matter developed in a piece of text.

The **audience** is a person or group of people who read a piece of text.

A **writing situation** is a circumstance in which a writer has a purpose for writing about a specific topic for a specific audience.

A **reading/writing situation** is a circumstance in which a person purposefully reads about a specific topic and responds in writing with a specific purpose for a specific audience.

Most often, purpose is the element that links the topic and the audience. The following chart presents three basic purposes for reading/writing situations. As you look at this chart, think about the relationships among topic, audience, and purpose.

Three Purposes for Reading/Writing

To Inform

READING
The purpose is to learn, gather, and grasp information.

WRITING
The purpose is to share, explain, or demonstrate information.

Example:
An informative text explains the cycle of metamorphosis, describes the steps to change a tire, or details the causes of addiction.

To Entertain or Be Expressive

READING
The purpose is to gain pleasure or to broaden experiences or imagination.

WRITING
The purpose is to share personal views or amuse the reader.

Example:
An expressive text explores topics of personal and universal significance (such as poverty, faith, or loss) in poems, short stories, or essays.

To Argue

READING
The purpose is to critically evaluate ideas as logical and reliable.

WRITING
The purpose is to change the reader's opinions or actions.

Example:
An argumentative text states a claim and provides logical supports to convince the reader to agree or disagree with an idea, such as a brochure listing reasons to recycle or vote for someone.

Example

Read the following statements. Identify the topic, audience, and purpose of each one. Next, compose a sentence of your own for a specific audience and with a specific purpose. Share your responses with a peer.

1. Learning Resources is pleased to offer you the position of Assistant Manager, Community Education; your skills and experience make you an ideal fit.

   TOPIC: ______________________________

   AUDIENCE: ______________________________

   PURPOSE: ______________________________

2. As the principal, you must put a stop to bullying at Norton Middle School.

   TOPIC: ______________________________

   AUDIENCE: ______________________________

   PURPOSE: ______________________________

3. Oh, fair youth, to love learning is to love your life!

   TOPIC: ______________________________

   AUDIENCE: ______________________________

   PURPOSE: ______________________________

MY SENTENCE: ______________________________

____

Explanation

Compare your responses to the following think-aloud.

The topic of statement 1 is a job offer based on the words "pleased to offer you the position" written to inform a job applicant that he or she has the job. The topic of statement 2 is "bullying" addressed to the principal of Norton Middle School. The purpose is to persuade the principal to "put a stop to bullying." The topic of statement 3 is "learning" addressed to "fair youth" or young people in general to express the value of learning. My sentence persuades young people to choose their friends carefully: Peer pressure leads to imitation of certain behaviors to fit in, so carefully choose your friends.

Practice 2

Assess the Reading/Writing Situation

Assume the following passage is the next assigned reading on the theme "the importance of learning and using language." Read the following excerpt from Fredrick Douglass's autobiography about his journey from slavery to freedom in the nineteenth century. Use writing-to-learn to connect reading and writing and to assess the reading/writing situation. Before reading, look at the questions that follow the passage. Answer as many as you can before reading. Answer the remaining questions after you read. Use information from the text to support your responses.

An American Slave: Written by Himself Chapter VII

[1]Very soon after I went to live with Mr. and Mrs. Auld, she very kindly commenced to teach me the A, B, C. [2]After I had learned this, she assisted me in learning to spell words of three or four letters. [3]Just at this point of my progress, Mr. Auld found out what was going on, and at once forbade Mrs. Auld to instruct me further, telling her, among other things, that it was unlawful, as well as unsafe, to teach a slave to read.

[4]"It would forever unfit him to be a slave. [5]He would at once become unmanageable, and of no value to his master. [6]As to himself, it could do him no good, but a great deal of harm. [7]It would make him discontented and unhappy." [8]These words sank deep into my heart, stirred up sentiments within that lay slumbering, and called into existence an entirely new train of thought. [9]It was a new and special revelation, explaining dark and mysterious things, with which my youthful understanding had struggled, but struggled in vain. [10]I now understood what had been to me a most perplexing difficulty—to wit, the white man's power to enslave the black man. [11]It was a grand achievement, and I prized it highly. [12]From that moment, I understood the pathway from slavery to freedom. [13]It was just what I wanted, and I got it at a time when I the least expected it. [14]Whilst I was saddened by the thought of losing the aid of my kind mistress, I was gladdened by the invaluable instruction which, by the merest accident, I had gained from my master.

***

CONTINUED

PRACTICE 2 *CONTINUED*

[15]Though conscious of the difficulty of learning without a teacher, I set out with high hope, and a fixed purpose, at whatever cost of trouble, to learn how to read.

***

[16]The first step had been taken. [17]Mistress, in teaching me the alphabet, had given me the *inch*, and no precaution could prevent me from taking the *ell*.

[18]The plan which I adopted, and the one by which I was most successful, was that of making friends of all the little white boys whom I met in the street. [19]As many of these as I could, I converted into teachers. [20]With their kindly aid, obtained at different times and in different places, I finally succeeded in learning to read. [21]When I was sent of errands, I always took my book with me, and by going one part of my errand quickly, I found time to get a lesson before my return. [22]I used also to carry bread with me, enough of which was always in the house, and to which I was always welcome; for I was much better off in this regard than many of the poor white children in our neighborhood. [23]This bread I used to bestow upon the hungry little urchins, who, in return, would give me that more valuable bread of knowledge. [24]I am strongly tempted to give the names of two or three of those little boys, as a testimonial of the gratitude and affection I bear them; but prudence forbids;—not that it would injure me, but it might embarrass them; for it is almost an unpardonable offence to teach slaves to read in this Christian country.

***

[25]The idea as to how I might learn to write was suggested to me by being in Durgin and Bailey's ship yard, and frequently seeing the ship carpenters, after hewing, and getting a piece of timber ready for use, write on the timber the name of that part of the ship for which it was intended. [26]When a piece of timber was intended for the larboard side, it would be marked thus—"L." [27]When a piece was for the starboard side, it would be marked thus—"S." [28]A piece for the larboard side forward, would be marked thus—"L. F." [29]When a piece was for starboard side forward, it would be marked thus—"S. F." [30]For larboard aft, it would be marked thus—"L. A." [31]For starboard aft, it would be marked thus—"S. A." [32]I soon learned the names of these letters, and for what they were intended when placed upon a piece of timber in the ship-yard. [33]I immediately commenced copying them, and in a short time was able to make the four letters named. [34]After that, when I met with any boy who I knew could write, I would tell him I could write as well as he. [35]The next word would be, "I don't believe you. [36]Let me see you try it." [37]I would then make the letters which I had been so fortunate as to learn, and ask him to beat that. [38]In this way I got a good many lessons in writing, which it is quite possible I should never have gotten in any other way. [39]During this time, my copy-book was the board fence, brick wall, and pavement; my pen and ink was a lump of chalk. [40]With these, I learned mainly how to write. [41]I then commenced and continued copying the Italics in Webster's

Spelling Book, until I could make them all without looking on the book. [42]By this time, my little Master Thomas had gone to school, and learned how to write, and had written over a number of copy-books. [43]These had been brought home, and shown to some of our near neighbors, and then laid aside. [44]My mistress used to go to class meeting at the Wilk Street meeting house every Monday afternoon, and leave me to take care of the house. [45]When left thus, I used to spend the time in writing in the spaces left in Master Thomas's copy-book, copying what he had written. [46]I continued to do this until I could write a hand very similar to that of Master Thomas. [47]Thus, after a long, tedious effort for years, I finally succeeded in learning how to write.

—Douglass, Frederick, *An American Slave: Written by Himself*. The Anti-Slavery Office, Boston, 1849. pp. 32–34, 38.

1. What is the topic of this passage?

2. What do I already know that is related to this topic?

3. Who is the intended audience?

4. What is the writer's purpose?

5. What more do I need or want to learn about this topic?

6. According to Douglass, what is the importance of learning and using language?

LO4 Recognize the Elements of Text

Master readers and writers use the elements of text structure to comprehend and compose ideas. **Text structure** refers to the way a writer organizes **supporting details** to convey a **central idea** or a **theme**. Master readers tap into text structure to connect ideas, make predictions, and monitor their comprehension. Master writers choose a particular type or **genre** of text structure to create meaning for their readers. While distinct differences exist based on the genre of text, some similarities exist as well. The following chart gives a brief overview of some of the elements of text based on genre.

Text structure refers to the ways in which information is organized and presented in print.

Supporting details are the specific ideas that develop, define, explain, or illustrate a central idea or theme.

A **central idea** is the main point of a nonfiction passage.

A **theme** is the focus, lesson, or moral presented in a piece of fiction.

Genre is a form of expression marked by common traits or qualities.

Elements of Text by Genre

	Fiction			**Nonfiction**
Genre	Poetry	Drama	Short Story/Novel	Essays/Articles/Books
General Form	Verse Rhymed Free (unrhymed) Lines/Stanzas	Script	Narration	Logical Order Narration/Process Description Cause/Effect Comparison/ Contrast Problem/Solution
Elements	Title Meter Descriptions Imagery Rhythm Theme	Title Setting Characters Stage directions Dialogue Plot Theme	Title Setting Characters Descriptions Dialogue Plot Theme	Title Introduction Central Idea Supporting Details Effective Expression Conclusion

Example

Assume the following passage is the next assigned reading on the theme "the importance of learning and using language." Read the following four pieces of text, several of which are excerpts from longer works. Identify the genre of each one. Then, pair with a peer and share your responses to the questions "What specific text features helped you identify each one?" "How do these passages differ in text structure?" "In what ways are they similar?" Give examples to support your answer. Then, share your paired responses with your class.

1. Genre: ____________________

Excerpt from *Huckleberry Finn*: Chapter V, "Pap Starts in on a New Life"

[1]He kept a-looking me all over. [2]By and by he says:

[3]"Starchy clothes—very. [4]You think you're a good deal of a big-bug, don't you?"

[5]"Maybe I am, maybe I ain't," I says.

[6]"Don't you give me none o' your lip," says he. [7]"You've put on considerable many frills since I been away. [8]I'll take you down a peg before I get done with you. [9]You're educated, too, they say—can read and write. [10]You think you're better'n your father, now, don't you, because he can't? [11]I'll take it out of you. [12]Who told you you might meddle with such hifalut'n foolishness, hey?—who told you you could?"

[13]"The widow. [14]She told me."

[15]"The widow, hey?—and who told the widow she could put in her shovel about a thing that ain't none of her business?"

[16]"Nobody never told her."

[17]"Well, I'll learn her how to meddle. [18]And looky here—you drop that school, you hear? [19]I'll learn people to bring up a boy to put on airs over his own father and let on to be better'n what he is. [20]You lemme catch you fooling around that school again, you hear? [21]Your mother couldn't read, and she couldn't write, nuther, before she died. [22]None of the family could before they died. [23]I can't; and here you're a-swelling yourself up like this. [24]I ain't the man to stand it—you hear? [25]Say, lemme hear you read."

[26]I took up a book and begun something about General Washington and the wars. [27]When I'd read about a half a minute, he fetched the book a whack with his hand and knocked it across the house, He says:

[28]"It's so. [29]You can do it. [30]I had my doubts when you told me. [31]Now looky here; you stop that putting on frills. [32]I won't have it. [33]I'll lay for you, my smarty; and if I catch you about that school I'll tan you good. [34]First you know you'll get religion, too. [35]I never see such a son."

–Twain, Mark, *The Adventures of Huckleberry Finn*. Harper & Brothers NY, 1884, pp. 26–29.

CONTINUED

EXAMPLE *CONTINUED*

2. Genre: ____________________

Excerpt from *Pygmalion*, Act I

All the rest have gone except the note taker, the gentleman, and the flower girl, who sits arranging her basket, and still pitying herself in murmurs.

THE FLOWER GIRL. Let him mind his own business and leave a poor girl—

THE NOTE TAKER [*explosively*] Woman: cease this detestable boohooing instantly; or else seek the shelter of some other place of worship.

THE FLOWER GIRL [*with feeble defiance*] I've a right to be here if I like, same as you.

THE NOTE TAKER. A woman who utters such depressing and disgusting sounds has no right to be anywhere—no right to live. Remember that you are a human being with a soul and the divine gift of articulate speech: that your native language is the language of Shakespeare and Milton and The Bible; and don't sit there crooning like a bilious pigeon.

THE FLOWER GIRL [*quite overwhelmed, and looking up at him in mingled wonder and deprecation without daring to raise her head*] Ah-ah-ah-ow-ow-ow-oo!

THE NOTE TAKER [*whipping out his book*] Heavens! what a sound! [He writes; then holds out the book and reads, reproducing her vowels exactly] Ah-ah-ah-ow-ow-ow-oo!

THE FLOWER GIRL [*tickled by the performance, and laughing in spite of herself*] Garn!

THE NOTE TAKER. You see this creature with her kerbstone English: the English that will keep her in the gutter to the end of her days. Well, sir, in three months I could pass that girl off as a duchess at an ambassador's garden party. I could even get her a place as lady's maid or shop assistant, which requires better English. That's the sort of thing I do for commercial millionaires. And on the profits of it I do genuine scientific work in phonetics, and a little as a poet on Miltonic lines.

THE GENTLEMAN. I am myself a student of Indian dialects; and—

THE NOTE TAKER [*eagerly*] Are you? Do you know Colonel Pickering, the author of Spoken Sanscrit?

THE GENTLEMAN. I am Colonel Pickering. Who are you?

THE NOTE TAKER. Henry Higgins, author of Higgins's Universal Alphabet.

—Shaw, Bernard. Act 1, *Pygmalion.*

3. **Genre:** ______________________________

A View from Within

Stupid me
full of stops and nos, and don'ts and can'ts
stalked by failure
running from rejection trippin' over needs
stubbing against most everything.
Sometimes the striving goes hard:
I hope against hope
(or maybe it's my mama's hope)
and enroll in my future and find myself
here today,
in your class
beneath your scrutiny,
hoping the glint in your Teacher eyes
comes from a good light,
while that bear fierce fear breathes hot down my neck.
and my brain freezes to stupor.
I don't think
my slowness to rise comes from any dullness in my head.
After all, I can be sly survivor
but then again stupid me
got this far knowing nothing, so most think.
So, show me, I dare you, Go on!
Show me
My Worth!

—Henry, D. J.

CONTINUED

EXAMPLE *CONTINUED*

4. Genre: ______________________________

The Well-Adjusted Individual

[1]Probably the most famous theory of the development of a healthy personality is that of Abraham Maslow, known as Maslow's hierarchy. [2]**Maslow's hierarchy** states that there are five levels of human achievement, each of which must be satisfied before the next is attempted. [3]They are shown in the figure "Abraham Maslow's Hierarchy."

[4]**Self-actualization,** the level of human achievement in which one is well adjusted to one's reality, is the highest level, according to Maslow. [5]A person need not be famous, or the best in the field, in order to be self-actualized. [6]Rather, we are self-actualized when content with life and capable of handling the problems that all of us must face. [7]Because each level of the hierarchy must be satisfied before the next can be attempted, few of us reach self-actualization; even for those few who attain that highest level, it is a constant effort to stay there and not slide back down.

Figure: Abraham Maslow's Hierarchy

—Hunt and Colander, *Social Science: An Introduction to the Study of Society*, 14th ed., Pearson, 2014, p. 127.

Explanation

Compare your answers to the following think-aloud.

I already knew Huckleberry Finn was a novel, and novels usually tell the story with dialogue between characters. The second example is a play because the title said, "Act I," and plays are divided up into acts. Also, there were stage directions in brackets and italics telling actors how to speak and move. The third example is a poem set up in short lines that don't rhyme. The last is an essay with paragraphs. These features are the ways that each one is different from the others. The play, the novel, and the poem all use the speech of people or a person and tell a story. In contrast, this essay explains the words in bold print and uses a figure to illustrate them.

Practice 3

Recognize the Elements of Text

Assume the following passage is another reading on the theme "the importance of learning and using language." You are expected to answer the question "What is the importance of language?" As you read, underline the elements of the text structure that you will use in your written and oral response to the question. After reading, answer the writing-to-learn questions that follow the passage.

Symbols and Language

SYMBOLS

[1]Like all creatures, humans use their senses to experience the surrounding world, but unlike others, we also try to give the world meaning. [2]Humans transform elements of the world in symbols. [3]A **symbol** *is anything that carries a particular meaning recognized by people who share a culture, a shared*

CONTINUED

PRACTICE 3 *CONTINUED*

إقرأوا Arabic	**Read** English	독서 Korean
կարդա Armenian	διαβαζω Greek	بخوانيد. Farsi
អាន Cambodian	קְרָא Hebrew	**читать** Russian
閱讀 Chinese	पढ़ना Hindi	**¡Ven a leer!** Spanish

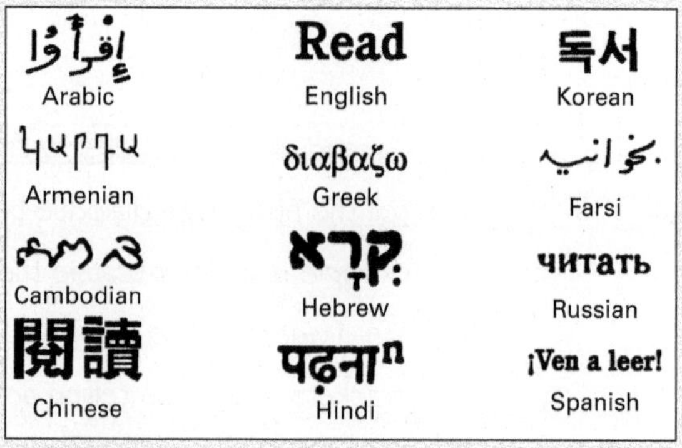

Figure: Human Languages, A Variety of Symbols. Here the English word "read" is written in twelve languages.

way of life. [4]A word, a whistle, a wall covered with graffiti, a flashing red light, a raised fist—all serve as symbols. [5]We can see the human capacity to create and manipulate symbols reflected in the very different meanings associated with the simple act of winking an eye, which can convey interest, understanding, or an insult.

[6]Societies create new symbols all the time. [7]We are so dependent on our culture's symbols that we take them for granted. [8]However, we become keenly aware of the importance of a symbol when someone uses it in an unconventional way, as when a person burns a U.S. flag during a political demonstration. [9]Entering an unfamiliar culture also reminds us of the power of symbols. [10]Culture shock is really the inability to "read" meaning into strange surroundings. [11]Not understanding symbols of a culture leaves a person feeling lost and isolated, unsure of how to act, and sometimes frightened.

[12]Culture shock is a two-way process. [13]On the one hand, travelers experience culture shock when encountering people whose way of life is different. [14]For example, North Americans who consider dogs beloved household pets might be put off by the Masai of eastern Africa, who ignore dogs and never feed them. [15]The same travelers might be horrified to find that in parts of Indonesia and the People's Republic of China, people roast dogs for dinner.

[16]On the other hand, travelers might inflict culture shock on local people by acting in ways that offend them. [17]A North American who asks for a steak in an Indian restaurant may unknowingly offend Hindus, who consider cows sacred and never to be eaten. [18]Global travel provides almost endless opportunities for this kind of misunderstanding.

[19]Symbolic meanings also vary within a single society. [20]To some people in the United States, a fur coat represents a prized symbol of success, but to others it represents the inhumane treatment of animals.

LANGUAGE

[21]An illness in infancy left Helen Keller (1880–1968) blind and deaf. [22]Without these two senses, she was cut off from the symbolic world, and her social development was greatly limited. [23]Only when her teacher, Anne

Mansfield Sullivan, broke through Keller's isolation using sign language did Helen Keller begin to realize her human potential.

[24]**Language** is *a system of symbols that allows people to communicate with one another.* [25]Humans have created many alphabets to express the hundreds of languages we speak. [26]Several examples are shown in the Figure: Human Languages, A Variety of Symbols. [27]Most people in Western societies write from left to right, but people in Africa and western Asia write from right to left. [28]Three of the most widely spoken languages are English, Chinese, and Spanish.

[29]Language not only allows communication but is also the key to cultural transmission, the process by which one generation passes culture to the next. [30]Just as our bodies contain the genes of our ancestors, our culture contains countless symbols of those who came before us. [31]Language is the key that unlocks centuries of accumulated wisdom.

[32]Throughout human history, every society has transmitted culture by using speech, a process sociologists call the "oral cultural tradition." [33]Some 5,000 years ago, humans invented writing, although at that time only a privileged few learned to read and write. [34]Not until the twentieth century did high-income nations boast of nearly universal literacy. [35]Still, about 14 percent of U.S. adults (more than 30 million people) are functionally illiterate, unable to read or write in a society that increasingly demands such skills. [36]In low-income countries of the world, at least one-third of adults are illiterate (U.S. Department of Education, 2008, World Bank, 2012).

[37]Language skills may link us to the past, but they also spark the human imagination to connect symbols in new ways, creating an almost limitless range of future possibilities. [38]Language sets humans apart as the only creatures who are self-conscious, aware of our limitations and ultimate mortality, yet able to dream and to hope for a future better than the present.

Does Language Shape Reality? [39]Does someone who thinks and speaks using Cherokee, an American Indian language, experience the world differently from other North Americans who think in, say, English or Spanish? [40]Edward Sapir and Benjamin Whorf claimed that the answer is yes since each language has its own distinctive symbols that serve as the building blocks of reality. [41]Further, they noted that each language has words or expressions not found in any other symbolic system [42]Finally, all languages fuse symbols with distinctive emotions so that, as multilingual people know, a single idea may "feel" different when spoken in Spanish rather than in English or Chinese.

[43]Formally the **Sapir-Whorf thesis** holds that *people see and understand the world through the cultural lens of language.* [44]In the decades since Sapir

CONTINUED

and Whorf published their work, however, scholars have taken issue with this proposition. [45]The widespread belief that, for example, Eskimos experience "snow" differently because they have many more words for it is not true. [46]Inuit speakers have about the same number of words for snow as English speakers do.

[47]So how does language affect our reality? [48]Current thinking is that although we do fashion reality out of our symbols, evidence supports the claim that language does not determine reality in the way Sapir and Whorf claimed. [49]For example, we know that children understand the idea of "family" long before they learn the word. [50]Similarly, adults can imagine new ideas or things before devising a name for them.

—Macionis, *Society: The Basics*, 13th ed., Pearson, 2015, pp. 52–56.

1. What is the topic of this passage? ______________________________

2. What do I already know that is related to this topic? ______________________________

____

3. Who is the writer's intended audience? ______________________________

4. What is the writer's purpose? ______________________________

5. What is my purpose for reading? ______________________________

6. What is my purpose for writing? ______________________________

7. Who is my audience? ______________________________

8. What more do I need or want to learn about this topic? ______________________________

____

9. What have I learned from reading this passage that I will use in my response?

____

____

10. How does text structure help me read and write? ______________________________

____

Develop Tools to Construct Meaning through Reading/Writing

LO5

To comprehend or make a point, master readers and writers use a variety of tools or strategies to create meaning. Some of the most common include activating prior knowledge, making inferences and implications, creating concept maps and outlines, and writing summaries.

Activate Prior Knowledge

We all have learned and stored in our memory a large body of information gained from our life experiences; this information is called **prior knowledge**. For example, "Trekkers" are avid fans of the *Star Trek* movies and television series. They pride themselves on knowing all there is to know about *Star Trek*. They spend much time and effort building up their prior knowledge about the characters, the story lines, and production details. Then, they compare new story lines to what they already know. Likewise, writers of new *Star Trek* stories study past versions and take into consideration the audience's prior knowledge and their expectations based on that prior knowledge. Both writer and reader build on their prior knowledge.

Prior knowledge is the large body of information that is learned throughout a lifetime of experience.

Activate Prior Knowledge

The Body of Knowledge Learned Throughout a Lifetime of Experience

	Call up prior knowledge	Check new information against prior knowledge	Expect growth or change of knowledge
	BEFORE READING	DURING READING	AFTER READING
	What do I already know? What do I need to know?	Does this idea/detail make sense based on what I already know?	What did I learn?
	BEFORE WRITING	DURING WRITING	AFTER WRITING
	What does my reader already know? What does my reader need to know?	Does this idea/detail make sense based on what my reader already knows?	What did my reader learn?

Example

A key assignment in your study of the theme of learning language is to read, write, and present to the class a report about a significant historical figure of your choice. You have located the following historical article about Sequoyah, the inventor of the Cherokee alphabet. Before you read, answer the questions to determine your prior knowledge about the topic. After reading, answer the questions to consider the prior knowledge of your audience.

1. What do I know about Sequoyah, the Cherokee nation, or Native Americans?

____

____

2. What do I know about an alphabet and its function?

____

____

The Indian Who Invented an Alphabet

[1]It goes without saying that inventors of alphabets are few and far between in this day and age of the world. [2]The A B C of civilization is centuries past. [3]For this reason great interest attaches to Sequoyah, the Cherokee, who, having seen the whites communicate with one another by writing, composed an alphabet to represent the sounds of his own language.

[4]The story of his invention of the alphabet and its final adoption by the Cherokee government is one that all the old-time Cherokees still remember and talk of with pride. [5]At first the Indians did not have much faith in Sequoyah's alphabet. [6]Up to that time his standing among his people had not been the highest, and they did not consider him one of their wise men. [7]They said he was a dreamer and that he was lazy. [8]Some even hinted that he was crazy, and at best he was considered harmless. [9]From boyhood he had been scratching his hieroglyphics on rocks and chips and trees, or made them with strands of pebbles in the sand. [10]The older heads of the tribe paid little attention to him, as they thought his pastime of making letters was merely something to keep him busy and amuse his clouded intellect. [11]But as time passed Sequoyah's alphabet began to assume a definite form, and he finally announced that he could teach it to others so that they could send messages. [12]When completed it consisted of eighty-five characters, which represented syllables and sounds and was phonetic in kind. [13]In its conception it is the very foundation of the method by which children are taught to read today, and he asked to be allowed to teach it by establishing schools in the tribe.

[14]But the wise men of the tribe were incredulous, and said it would only be fooling away time to teach it to the children.

[15]At that time Sequoyah was married and had a family. [16]He taught his alphabet to his own little girl, at that time a child of about eight, and also to several

other children of the tribe. [17]He was then living in Alabama, but contemplated emigrating to the Indian Territory, and he said his object in teaching it to the children was that it might be preserved in case he was lost, as the Cherokees had no material upon which his alphabet could be written and kept with certainty.

[18]He first made the trip to the Cherokee Nation alone in order to look up a location. [19]After his arrival he wrote a letter to his little daughter, and sent it back by some Cherokees who were returning to Alabama. [20]When the little girl read the letter, and told of the things that had happened and where her father was, the other members of the tribe were surprised and the wise men were impressed. [21]There began to dawn upon them the usefulness of all of Sequoyah's dreaming, and shortly they began to teach it to their children.

[22]Not long after this Sequoyah emigrated to the Cherokee Nation, where his alphabet was soon adopted by the Cherokee government, who established it in a system of public schools. [24]An official paper of the nation was also established and printed in those characters, and that paper lasted and was printed in Cherokee up to the final dissolution of the tribe, in 1906. [24]The Cherokee government voted Sequoyah an annuity in recognition of his Work, and at his death it went to his wife.

[25]The primal object of Sequoyah in the use of his alphabet was to find a means by which he might unify and hold together the various bands and tribes of his nation. [26]From time to time bodies of Cherokees would become dissatisfied with acts of the tribe, and go off to live by themselves. [27]There was no medium of intercourse among them by which they might understand one another. [28]Sequoyah saw in that the final disintegration of his nation, and all the powers of his great mind were bent to stop the clannish discontent and weld all of the parties and sub-tribes into one uniform nation.

[29]Of all the brilliant Cherokees, Sequoyah was the greatest, and his name is still held by the Cherokees in profound reverence. [30]He was unlettered and knew no English, but that did not affect the powers of his active mind. [31]Not only his own people, but also the whites recognized his genius and strove to do him honors. [32]It is after him that scientists have named the big trees of California *Sequoyah Gigantus*. [33]He is said to have been the only person in the Western Hemisphere to have invented an alphabet, and historians call him the American Cadmus.

—*Harpers Weekly*, 8 May 1909 ,Vol. LIII No. 2733, p. 29.

3. What did I learn (how have my views changed based on reading this information)?

____

____

4. What does my audience know about Sequoyah, the Cherokee Nation, or Native Americans?

____

____

5. What do I want my audience to learn? ______________________

____

Explanation

Compare your answers to the following student's think-aloud.

I never heard of Sequoyah before. I have heard about Cherokees; I know very little about them. We all know that Native Americans were forced off their lands and suffered greatly. An **alphabet** is "a system of symbols that allow people to communicate." When asked, my classmates' prior knowledge seemed the same as mine. Learning about Sequoyah deepened my respect for Native Americans and our own alphabet. I want my audience to know who he is and what he did, and to come to respect him like I have.

Make Inferences and Implications

A master writer carefully chooses words, examples, illustrations, or other types of details to imply or suggest a point. A master reader thoughtfully analyzes the writer's choices to infer or determine the appropriate meaning suggested by the writer. The following graphic illustrates this exchange of information.

Inferring and Implying Meaning as Readers and Writers

Writer Chooses Words to Imply Ideas

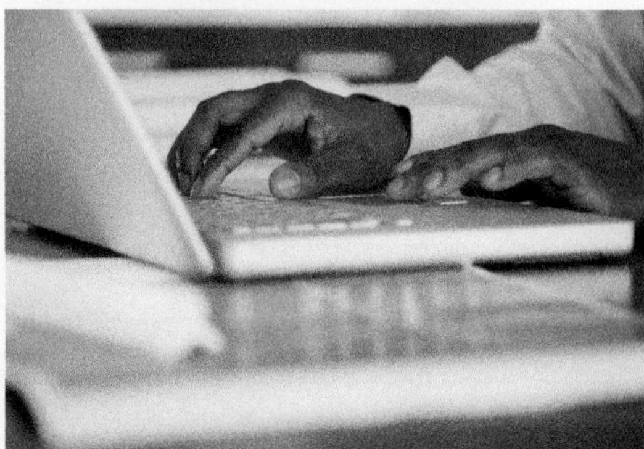

Writer Sends Message

Reader Analyzes Words to Infer Ideas

Reader Receives Message

To imply a point, a writer chooses words to suggest a strong attitude or emotion. To comprehend the writer's point, a reader analyzes the words chosen by the writer. This exchange relies on both the reader's and the writer's prior knowledge of the literal definition and emotional meaning of words. Consider the following piece of dialogue from *Pygmalion*, Act I, that you read in the Example on page 18.

Message Implied by Writer's Word Choice

Dictionary definition: nauseated **Attitude:** disagreeable

Implication: annoying

don't sit there crooning like a bilious pigeon

Inference drawn: The Note Taker is annoyed by the sound of the Flower Girl's voice.

Message Inferred by Reader's Analysis of Writer's Word Choice

Example

Reconsider the following lines from the poem "A View from Within" that you read in the Example on page 19. In the given spaces, write your inferences based on your understanding of what the writer is implying. Then, compose a sentence about your learning experience or the learning experience of someone you know. Word your sentence to imply a positive or negative emotion about the learning experience.

1. ". . . I hope against hope
(or maybe it's my mama's hope)
and enroll in my future and find myself
here today, in your class. . . ."

Inference: ______________________________

____

2. ". . . while that bear fierce fear breathes hot down my
neck and my brain freezes to stupor."

Inference: ______________________________

____

My sentence: ______________________________

____

Explanation

Compare your answers to the following think-aloud.

1. I infer that the writer is implying hopelessness. First, the phrase "hope against hope" expresses a desperate feeling that suggests a lack of faith. When she said, "or maybe it's my mama's hope," I inferred that the mother has more hope or faith in the writer's ability to learn than the writer has. 2. The word **bear** suggests danger. Then, the writer implies the physical effect of fear being "hot down my neck." I have felt this same heat from stress. Then, her brain freezes or becomes numb. The dictionary says the word **stupor** means weary or dull. So I infer that the writer's fear of learning causes an inability to learn. I wrote, "Learning is a lamp of hope."

Create Concept Maps and Outlines

Master readers and writers rely on concept maps and outlines to comprehend and compose text. Both a **concept map** and an **outline** show the writer's plan or flow of information from topic to central idea to specific details. A master writer often uses a concept map or outline to generate and organize ideas before writing. Frequently, after reading, a master reader creates a concept map or outline based on the ideas in the passage to check comprehension. The following thinking guides can help you use concept maps and outlines as you read and write.

A **concept map**, cluster, or web creates a visual picture of the logical flow and relationships among ideas in a piece of text.

An **outline** is a list of ideas in blocks of thoughts using headings and subheadings to indicate the relationships among general ideas and supporting details in a piece of text.

Concept Mapping

- ❑ Draw a circle in the middle of your page and write your topic in the circle.
- ❑ Write a word that relates to the topic, circle the word, and connect it to the topic circle with a line.
- ❑ Repeat this process so that a set of major supports radiates out from the topic circle.
- ❑ Write a word that relates to one of the major supports, circle it, and connect it to that major support circle.
- ❑ Repeat this process for each of the major supports to create clusters of minor supports.

Outlining

- ❑ Create an outline from other prewriting activities such as freewrites, lists, and concept maps.
- ❑ List and identify each item using the following order: Roman numerals, capital letters, Arabic numerals, and lowercase letters, in that order, to show the flow of ideas, as illustrated below:

  I. Main Idea

    A. Major supporting detail

      1. Minor supporting detail

        a. Minor supporting detail

- ❑ Place a period after each numeral or letter.
- ❑ Capitalize each item.
- ❑ For topic outlines, state each item with a word or phrase.
- ❑ For sentence outlines, state each item as a complete thought.

The following examples illustrate the use of a concept map and a topic outline based on the passage "Symbols and Language" on page 21.

Concept Map

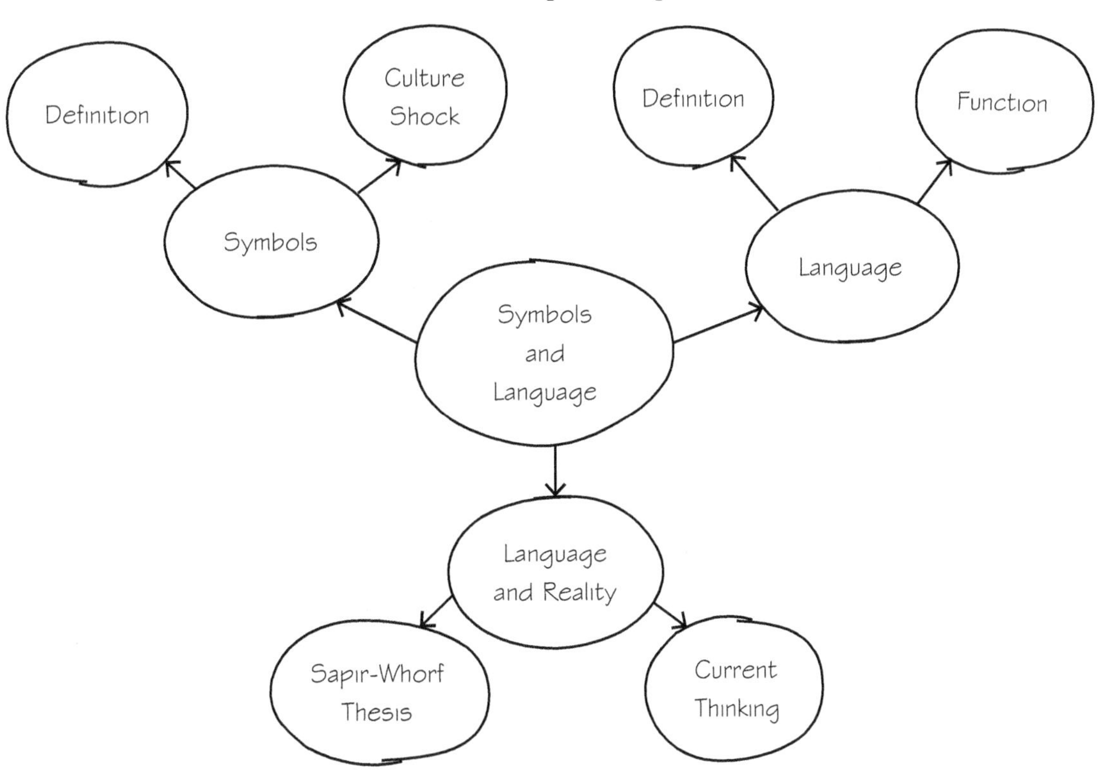

Outline

Topic: Symbols and Language

I. A Symbol
   A. Definition
   B. Culture Shock

II. Language
   A. Definition
   B. Function

III. Language and Reality
   A. Sapir-Whorf thesis
   B. Current Thinking

Example

Assume your psychology professor has stated that the following information will be on the next written exam based on the following question: "How do Freud's elements of personality relate to learning language as in the experience of Frederick Douglass?" To comprehend the text and prepare your written response, complete the outline or concept map with ideas from the text.

Sigmund Freud's Elements of Personality

[1]Sigmund Freud (1856–1939), trained as a physician, studied personality and mental disorders and eventually developed the celebrated theory of psychoanalysis. [2]Freud combined basic needs and the influence of society into a model of personality with three parts: id, ego, and superego. [3]The **id** (Latin for "it") represents the *human being's basic drives, which are unconscious and demand immediate satisfaction.* [4]Rooted in biology, the id is present at birth, making a newborn a bundle of demands for attention, touching, and food. [5]But society opposes the self-centered id, which is why one of the first words a child typically learns is "no."

[6]To avoid frustration, a child must learn to approach the world realistically. [7]This is done through the **ego** (Latin for "I"), which is *a person's conscious efforts to balance innate pleasure-seeking drives with the demands of society.* [8]The ego arises as we become aware of our distinct existence and face the fact that we cannot have everything we want.

[9]In the human personality, the **superego** (Latin for "above or beyond the ego") is *the cultural values and norms internalized by an individual.* [10]The superego operates as our conscience, telling us why we cannot have everything we want. [11]The superego begins to form as a child becomes aware of parental demands and matures as the child comes to understand that everyones' behavior should take account of cultural norms.

—Macionis, *Sociology*, 15th Ed., Pearson, 2014, pp. 129–130.

Topic: Sigmund Freud's Elements of Personality

I. ______________________________

A. ______________________________

B. ______________________________

II. ______________________________

A. ______________________________

B. ______________________________

III. ______________________________

A. ______________________________

B. ______________________________

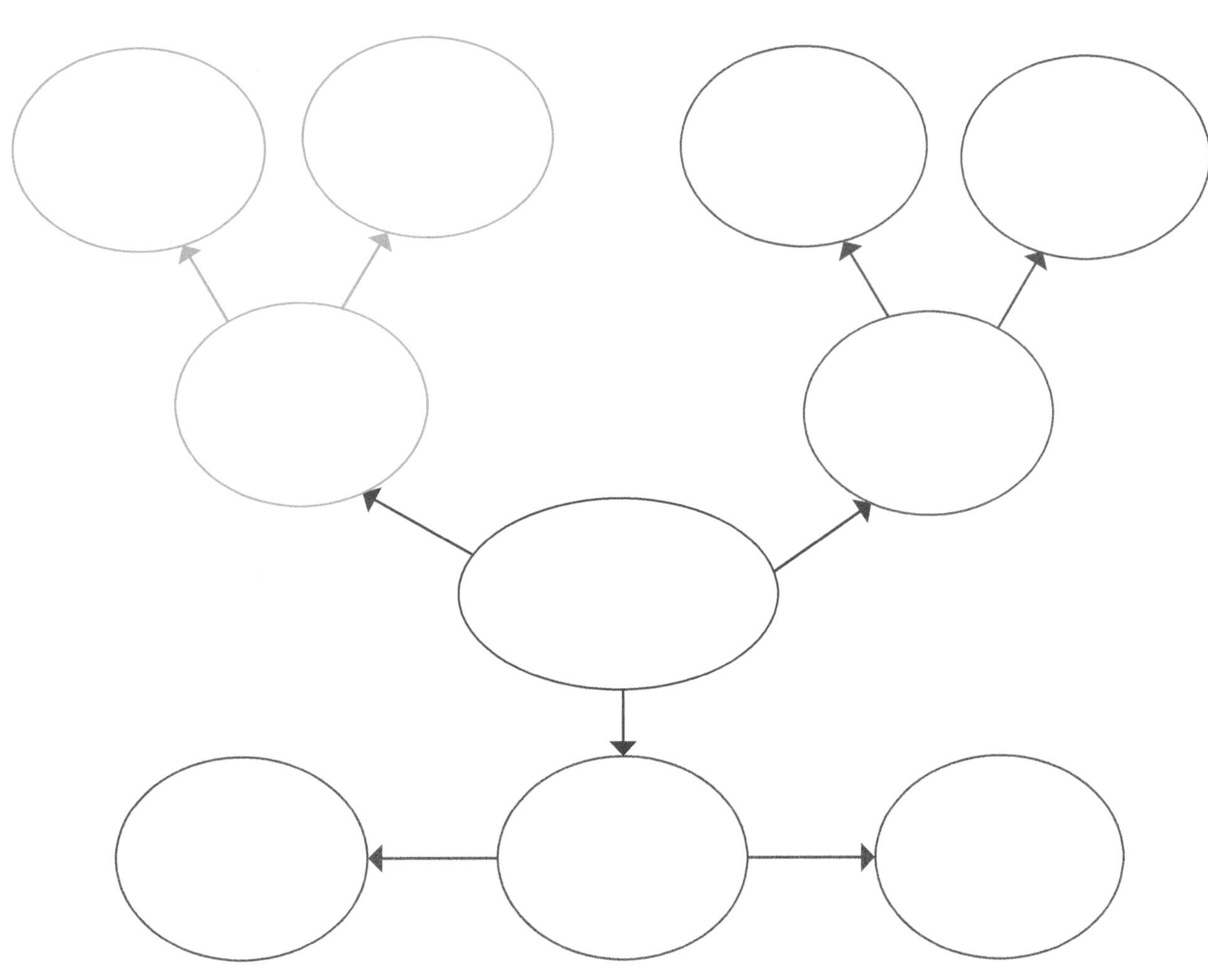

Explanation

Compare your answers to the following think-aloud.

The elements of the text were very helpful guides to the key details I needed to learn and use in the outline and concept map. The topic, which appears in the center of the concept map, is "Freud's Elements of Personality." There are three elements, the id, the ego, and the superego, which are identified by Roman numerals I., II., and III. in the outline and are in the circles that radiate from the center circle or topic circle in the concept map. The writer provided a definition for each element and explained when or why each element developed. These are identified as A. and B. in the outline. In the concept map, arrows from the three elements point to the circles with this information.

Write a Summary

The fundamental connection between reading and writing is *thinking*: thinking about the meaning of what you read and the connection between what you read and what you write. Two active thinking-reading-writing tasks are **annotating** a text and writing a **summary**. Often you will want to **paraphrase**, that is, repeat the ideas using your own words. The length of a summary varies based on the length of the original text.

To **annotate** is to take notes on the page of the text by marking the text or writing brief responses in the margins.

A **summary** is a brief, clear restatement of the most important points of a piece of text.

To **paraphrase** is to restate an idea in your own words.

To create a summary, you annotate, or mark your text during reading. As you read, you highlight the central idea and key details and cross out unnecessary or repetitive information. Then, after reading, you refer to your annotations to condense the material into its most important points. The following guideline offers one strategy for writing a summary.

A STRATEGY FOR WRITING A SUMMARY

1. **Delete**

   unnecessary material (such as detailed examples).

   repetitive material.

2. **Condense**

   by inserting a word to replace a list.

   by inserting a word to replace individual parts of an action.

3. **Restate**

   the central idea.

OR

4. **Compose**

   a sentence that states the implied central idea or theme.

Example

Apply the strategy for summarization to the following selection.

JEAN PIAGET'S THEORY OF COGNITIVE DEVELOPMENT

[1]The Swiss psychologist Jean Piaget (1896–1980) studied human *cognition,* how people think and understand; he developed four stages of cognitive development.

[2]Stage one is the **sensorimotor stage**, *the level of human development at which individual experience the world only through their senses.* [3]For about the first two years of life, the infant knows the world only through the five senses: touching, tasting, smelling, looking, and listening. [4]"Knowing" to young children amounts to what their senses tell them.

[5]About age two, children enter the **preoperational stage**, *the level of human development at which individuals first use language and other symbols.* [6]Now children begin to think about the world mentally and use imagination. [7]But "pre-op" children between about two and six still attach meaning only to specific experiences and objects. [8]They can identify a toy as their "favorite" but cannot explain what types of toys they like.

[9]Lacking abstract concepts, a child also cannot judge size, weight, or volume. [10]In one of his best-known experiments, Piaget placed two identical glasses containing equal amounts of water on a table. [11]He asked several children aged five and six if the amount in each glass was the same. [12]They nodded that it was. [13]The children then watched Piaget take one of the glasses and pour its contents into a taller, narrower glass so that the level of the water in the glass was higher. [14]He asked again if each glass held the same amount. [15]The typical five- or six-year-old now insisted that the taller glass held more water. [16]By about age seven, children are able to think abstractly and realize that the amount of water stays the same.

[17]Next comes the **concrete operational stage**, *the level of human development at which individuals first see causal connections in their surroundings.* [18]Between the ages of seven and eleven, children focus on how and why things happen. [19]In addition, children now attach more than one symbol to a particular event or object. [20]If, for example, you say to a child of five, "Today is Wednesday," she might respond, "No, it's my birthday!" –indicating that she can use just one symbol at a time. [21]But a ten-year-old at the concrete operational stage would be able to respond, "Yes, and it's also my birthday."

[22]The last stage in Piaget's model is the **formal operational stage**, *the level of human development at which individuals think abstractly and critically.* [23]At about age twelve, young people begin to reason abstractly rather than thinking only of concrete situations. [24]If, for example, you were to ask a seven-year-old, "What would you like to be when you grow up?" you might receive a concrete response such as "a teacher." [25]But most teenagers can think more abstractly and might reply, "I would like a job that helps others." [26]As they gain the capacity for abstract thought, young people also learn to understand metaphors. [27]Hearing the phrase "A penny for your thoughts" might lead a child to ask for a coin, but a teenager will recognize a gentle invitation to intimacy.

—Macionis, *Sociology*, 15th ed., Pearson, 2014, pp. 130–131.

Explanation

Compare your answers to the following think-aloud.

I mostly used steps 1 and 3 to annotate the text and write my summary; once in a while I used step 2. I condensed and restated the central idea in sentence 1. To condense information, I underlined the definitions and facts about each stage. Next, I crossed out most of the examples and explanations in all the paragraphs. For example, I crossed out the entire third paragraph, sentences 9–16. Then, I restated the definitions for each stage by combining the facts I underlined into my restatement of the definitions. Here is my summary:

Psychologist Jean Piaget (1896–1980) identified four stages of cognitive or mental development. During the sensorimotor stage, from birth to two, knowing comes through the experience of the five senses. During the preoperational stage, ages two to six, the use of language and symbols develops. During the concrete operational stage, between ages 7 and 11, comes awareness of cause-effect relationships. Finally, in the formal operational stage, at age 12, abstract and critical thinking occurs.

Practice 4

Develop Tools to Create Meaning through Reading and Writing

Assume that your next assignment on the theme of learning language will be a written response to the following reading. Helen Keller (1880–1968) became deaf and blind at the age of 19 months, yet went on to become a famous author, political activist, and lecturer. Apply the tools you have learned about in this module to create meaning. Answer question 1 before you read. Answer questions 2 through 7 after reading the passage.

1. What prior knowledge do I have about overcoming significant barriers?

THE STORY OF MY LIFE: CHAPTER IV

by Helen Keller

[1]The most important day I remember in all my life is the one on which my teacher, Anne Mansfield Sullivan, came to me. [2]I am filled with wonder when I consider the immeasurable contrast between the two lives which it connects. [3]It was the third of March, 1887, three months before I was seven years old.

[4]On the afternoon of that eventful day, I stood on the porch, dumb, expectant. [5]I guessed vaguely from my mother's signs and from the hurrying to and fro in the house that something unusual was about to happen, so I went to the door and waited on the steps. [6]The afternoon sun penetrated the mass of honeysuckle that covered the porch, and fell on my upturned face. [7]My fingers lingered almost unconsciously on the familiar leaves and blossoms which had just come forth to greet the sweet southern spring. [8]I did not know what the future held of marvel or surprise for me. [9]Anger and bitterness had preyed upon me continually for weeks and a deep languor had succeeded this passionate struggle.

[10]Have you ever been at sea in a dense fog, when it seemed as if a tangible white darkness shut you in, and the great ship, tense and anxious, groped her way toward the shore with plummet and sounding-line, and you waited with beating heart for something to happen? [11]I was like that ship before my education began, only I was without compass or sounding-line, and had no way of knowing how near the harbour was. [12]"Light! give me light!" was the wordless cry of my soul, and the light of love shone on me in that very hour.

[13]I felt approaching footsteps. I stretched out my hand as I supposed to my mother. [14]Some one took it, and I was caught up and held close in the arms of her who had come to reveal all things to me, and, more than all things else, to love me.

[15]The morning after my teacher came she led me into her room and gave me a doll. [16]The little blind children at the Perkins Institution had sent it and Laura Bridgman had dressed it; but I did not know this until afterward. [17]When I had played with it a little while, Miss Sullivan slowly spelled into my hand the word "d-o-l-l." [18]I was at once interested in this finger play and tried to imitate it. [19]When I finally succeeded in making the letters correctly I was flushed with childish pleasure and pride. [20]Running downstairs to my mother I held up my hand and made the letters for doll. [21]I did not know that I was spelling a word or even that words existed; I was simply making my

CONTINUED

PRACTICE 4 *CONTINUED*

fingers go in monkey-like imitation. [22]In the days that followed I learned to spell in this uncomprehending way a great many words, among them *pin, hat, cup* and a few verbs like *sit, stand* and *walk.* [23]But my teacher had been with me several weeks before I understood that everything has a name.

[24]One day, while I was playing with my new doll, Miss Sullivan put my big rag doll into my lap also, spelled "d-o-l-l" and tried to make me understand that "d-o-l-l" applied to both. [25]Earlier in the day we had had a tussle over the words "m-u-g" and "w-a-t-e-r." [26]Miss Sullivan had tried to impress it upon me that "m-u-g" is mug and that "w-a-t-e-r" is water, but I persisted in confounding the two. [27]In despair she had dropped the subject for the time, only to renew it at the first opportunity. [28]I became impatient at her repeated attempts and, seizing the new doll, I dashed it upon the floor. [29]I was keenly delighted when I felt the fragments of the broken doll at my feet. [30]Neither sorrow nor regret followed my passionate outburst. [31]I had not loved the doll. [32]In the still, dark world in which I lived there was no strong sentiment or tenderness. [33]I felt my teacher sweep the fragments to one side of the hearth, and I had a sense of satisfaction that the cause of my discomfort was removed. [34]She brought me my hat, and I knew I was going out into the warm sunshine. [35]This thought, if a wordless sensation may be called a thought, made me hop and skip with pleasure.

[36]We walked down the path to the well-house, attracted by the fragrance of the honeysuckle with which it was covered. [37]Someone was drawing water and my teacher placed my hand under the spout. [38]As the cool stream gushed over one hand she spelled into the other the word water, first slowly, then rapidly. [39]I stood still, my whole attention fixed upon the motions of her fingers. [40]Suddenly I felt a misty consciousness as of something forgotten—a thrill of returning thought; and somehow the mystery of language was revealed to me. [41]I knew then that "w-a-t-e-r" meant the wonderful cool something that was flowing over my hand. [42]That living word awakened my soul, gave it light, hope, joy, set it free! [43]There were barriers still, it is true, but barriers that could in time be swept away.

[44]I left the well-house eager to learn. [45]Everything had a name, and each name gave birth to a new thought. [46]As we returned to the house every object which I touched seemed to quiver with life. [47]That was because I saw everything with the strange, new sight that had come to me. [48]On entering the door I remembered the doll I had broken. [49]I felt my way to the hearth and picked up the pieces. [50]I tried vainly to put them together. [51]Then my eyes filled with tears; for I realized what I had done, and for the first time I felt repentance and sorrow.

[52]I learned a great many new words that day. [53]I do not remember what they all were; but I do know that *mother, father, sister, teacher* were among them—words that were to make the world blossom for me, "like Aaron's rod, with flowers." [53]It would have been difficult to find a happier child than I was as I lay in my crib at the close of that eventful day and lived over the joys it had brought me, and for the first time longed for a new day to come.

—Keller, Helen. *The Story of My Life.* Grosset & Dunlap: NY, 1905, pp. 19–22.

2. What is the most important (or central) idea Helen Keller wants her readers to remember? ______

3. How is Helen Keller's learning experience similar to or different from Frederick Douglass's? ______

4. According to Piaget's stages of cognitive development, at what stage is Keller at the beginning of the passage? Based on sentence 51, what stage of cognitive development, according to Piaget, has Keller now reached? ______

5. Complete the following outline with details from the passage:

   Topic: The Story of My Life: Chapter IV

   I. On the afternoon of that eventful day, ______

   II. The morning after my teacher came, ______

   III. One day, I became impatient ______

   IV. Suddenly, the mystery of ______

   V. I left the well-house ______

6. Write a summary of the passage. Use your own paper. In the first sentence of your summary, state the title of the passage and the author's name: *In Chapter IV of* The Story of My Life, *Helen Keller. . . .*

7. Write a response to the following question: "How does Helen Keller's story illustrate the importance of language?" Use your own paper.

Master readers and writers often use a **reading/writing journal** to record the information generated throughout the reading/writing process. For example, look back over the seven questions you answered in Practice 4. These questions and answers would be excellent entries in a reading/writing journal. By recording your prereading questions, notes of answers taken during reading, outlines, and summaries composed after reading, you are better able to track your comprehension and prepare your written response to what you have read.

A **reading/writing journal** is a notebook in which a reader/writer records information and tracks the reading/writing strategies used to comprehend and compose text.

Workshop: Introduction to Reading and Writing

Assume you are continuing your study of the theme of learning and using language in your college psychology course. The following excerpt from the autobiography of Herbert Kohl is your capstone reading assignment on this theme. The capstone writing assignment will be a formal written response to the Guiding Question "What is the importance of learning and using language?" Read the passage and complete the activities that follow.

I Won't Learn from You

By Herbert Kohl

[1]I want to share one of my own early ventures into not-learning and self-definition. I cannot speak Yiddish, though I have had opportunities to learn from the time I was born. My father's parents spoke Yiddish most of the time and since my family lived downstairs from them in a two-family house for fourteen of my first seventeen years, my failure to learn wasn't from lack of exposure. My father speaks both Yiddish and English and never indicated that he wouldn't teach me Yiddish. Nor did he ever try to coerce me to learn the language, so I never had educational traumas associated with learning Yiddish. My mother and her family had everything to do with it. They didn't speak Yiddish at all. Learning Yiddish meant being party to conversations that excluded my mother. I didn't reject my grandparents and their language. It's just that I didn't want to be included in conversations unless my mother was also included. In solidarity with her, I learned how to not-learn Yiddish.

[2]There was Yiddish to be heard everywhere in my environment, except at public school: on the streets, at home, in every store. Learning to not-learn Yiddish meant that I had to forget Yiddish words as soon as I heard them. When words stuck in my head I had to refuse to associate the sounds with any meaning. If someone told a story in Yiddish, I had to talk to myself quietly in English or hum to myself. If a relative greeted me in Yiddish I responded with the uncomprehending look I had rehearsed for those occasions. I also remember learning to concentrate on the component sounds of words and thus shut out the speaker's meaning or intent. In doing so, I allowed myself to be satisfied with understanding the emotional flow of a conversation without knowing what people were saying. I was doing just the reverse of what beginning readers are expected to do—read words and understand meanings instead of getting stuck on particular letters and the sounds they make. In effect I used phonics to obliterate meaning.

[3]In not-learning Yiddish, I had to ignore phrases and gestures, even whole conversations, as well as words. And there were many lively, interesting

conversations upstairs at my grandparents'. They had meetings about union activities, talked about family matters and events in Europe and later in Israel. They discussed articles in the *Daily Forward,* the Yiddish newspaper, and plays downtown in the Yiddish theatre. Everyone was a poet, and everybody had an opinion. I let myself read hands and faces, and I imagined ideas and opinions bouncing around the room. I experienced their conversations much in the way I learned to experience Italian opera when I was fourteen. I had a sense of plot and character and could follow the flow and drama of personal interaction, yet I had no idea of the specifics of what was being said. To use another image: it was as if I were at a foreign-language movie with my father, my uncles, and my grandmother providing English subtitles whenever I asked for help understanding what was going on. I allowed myself to be content with this partial knowledge, but now I mourn the loss of the language and culture of my father's family that it entailed.

[4]Deciding to actively not-learn something involves closing off part of oneself and limiting one's experience. It can require actively refusing to pay attention, acting dumb, scrambling one's thought and overriding curiosity. The balance of gains and losses resulting from such a turning away from experience is difficult to assess. I still can't tell how much I gained or lost by not-learning Yiddish. I know that I lost a language that would have enriched my life, but I gained an understanding of the psychology of active not-learning that has been very useful to me as a teacher.

[5]Because not-learning involves willing rejection of some aspect of experience, it can often lead to what appears to be failure. For example, in the case of some youngsters, not-learning to read can be confused with failing to learn to read if the rejection of learning is overlooked as a significant factor. I had that happen to me when I was eleven and expanded not-learning Yiddish to not-learning Hebrew. I was sent to *chedah,* Hebrew school, to learn that part of the Torah that I would have to read aloud in front of the whole congregation during my bar mitzvah. My family was not at all religious, and though we belonged to a temple, we attended services only on Yom Kippur. From my perspective, the point of going to Hebrew school was not to learn Hebrew but to ensure that I didn't embarrass my parents when I had to recite part of the Torah on my bar mitzvah. As I figured it, if I not-learned Hebrew it would save me a lot of effort and time I could use for science projects and my rather tentative experiments with writing. And so for two years I applied what I had learned about not-learning Yiddish and I not-learned Hebrew. I could read the sounds and recite my way through the *Mahzor,* the daily prayer book, and the Torah. I listened to our teacher/rabbi drone on about the righteousness of the Jews and our special role in history, and I was silent though cynical.

[6]I did, however, get in trouble for my arrogant not-learning. One day the rabbi gave us a test with questions written in Hebrew. Since I couldn't

CONTINUED

translate a word from Hebrew to English, much less an entire question, my prospects for passing the test were not good. I was too proud to show the rabbi that I couldn't do the test, so I set it up with my friend Ronnie that I would copy his test. Cheating in Hebrew school was not a moral issue to me but a matter of saving face. Ronnie understood my dilemma perfectly and told me he would have loved to not-learn Hebrew too, only his father insisted on testing him every night on his Hebrew school lessons.

7During the test I succeeded in copying Ronnie's whole paper which I knew was a sure "A," only I failed worse than if I had written letters at random in mock Hebrew on the test sheet. The rabbi returned all of the papers except Ronnie's and mine. Then he called the class to attention and said he felt a need to give special appreciation to Ronnie, for not only had Ronnie gotten one "A," he also received a second "A" which, the rabbi said, was the first time in his career that any student had done that well. And, he added, Herbert didn't hand in any paper at all, which he told the class was worse than trying and failing. It seems that I had copied Ronnie's paper so accurately that I had answered the Hebrew question "What is your name?" with Ronnie's Hebrew name. I was thoroughly humiliated in front of all of my friends and, for all my arrogance about getting away with not-learning Hebrew, felt very stupid.

8I never forgot this humiliation, and when I became a teacher I resolved never to humiliate any of my students. I also decided to assume that there were complex factors behind any apparent failure, which, if understood, could be used to transform it into positive learning. Not-learning Yiddish and Hebrew has made me very sensitive to the difference between not-learning and failing to learn. Failure is characterized by the frustrated will to know, whereas not-learning involves the will to refuse knowledge. Failure results from a mismatch between what the learner wants to do and is able to do. The reasons for failure may be personal, social, or cultural, but whatever they are, the results of failure are most often a loss of self-confidence accompanied by a sense of inferiority and inadequacy. Not-learning produces thoroughly different effects. It tends to strengthen the will, clarify one's definition of self, reinforce self-discipline, and provide inner satisfaction. Not learning can also get one in trouble if it results in defiance or a refusal to become socialized in ways that are sanctioned by dominant authority.

9Not-learning tends to take place when someone has to deal with unavoidable challenges to her or his personal and family loyalties, integrity, and identity. In such situations there are forced choices and no apparent middle ground. To agree to learn from a stranger who does not respect your integrity causes a major loss of self. The only alternative is to not-learn and reject the stranger's world.

—Kohl, Herbert. "I Won't Learn from You." *Milkweed Editions: Thistle Series,* 1991, pp. 11–16.

Activate Prior Knowledge, Read, and Annotate

As you read, annotate key ideas.

A. Questions to Activate Prior Knowledge

1. What prior knowledge do I have about "the importance of learning language"?

2. What other texts have I read that remind me of Kohl's essay?

B. Questions to Make Connections within the Text

3. What is the most important (or central) idea Herbert Kohl wants his readers to remember?

4. How did Kohl's experience with his own learning influence his role as a teacher?

C. Questions to Make Connections with Other Texts

5. How is Kohl's experience with learning language similar to or different from the experiences of Helen Keller and Frederick Douglass?

6. How does the use of language and symbols relate to Maslow's hierarchy of human achievement? Support your point with examples from the lives of Frederick Douglass, Helen Keller, Sequoyah, and/or Herbert Kohl.

Summarize the Passage

Refer to your answers to the questions. **Map** the relationship among ideas you have annotated in the text. **Outline** or list key ideas and details in blocks of thought. **Summarize** the central point and key supporting details. Paraphrase ideas.

Write a Response

Discuss changes in your understanding about learning and using language based on the new information you have read. In the space below, create a concept map or outline of ideas for your written response to the guiding question "What is the importance of learning and using language?" On your own paper, use the ideas you generated to compose a draft of your response.

Pair and Share

Once you have composed your response to the text, pair with a peer and share your written responses with each other. Discuss the ways in which you connected reading and writing to comprehend and compose your responses. Discuss the specific tools you developed, such as activating prior knowledge, making inferences and implications, concept mapping, outlining, and summarizing.

Reading and Writing Assignments

MySkillsLab™
Complete this Exercise
on myskillslab.com

Reading and Writing for Everyday Life

Assume your mother has just been diagnosed with pre-diabetes; her blood sugar levels are higher than normal and this can lead to serious health problems. She does not exercise; she eats fried foods, chips, sodas, and desserts, and very few fruits or vegetables. You have found the following information in your college health textbook. Read the passage and write her an e-mail that summarizes the key information and makes helpful recommendations.

NUTRITION FOR LIFE

What Is Nutrition, and Why Is It Important?

Nutrition is *the scientific study of food and how food nourishes our body and influences our health.* It encompasses how we consume, digest, metabolize, and store nutrients and how these nutrients affect our body. Nutrition science also studies the factors that influence our eating patterns, makes recommendations about the amount we should eat of each type of food, and addresses issues related to food safety and the global food supply. You can think of nutrition, then, as the discipline that encompasses everything about food.

Proper nutrition can help us improve our health, prevent certain diseases, achieve and maintain a healthy weight, and maintain our energy and vitality. Think about it: if you eat three meals a day, then by this time next year, you'll have had more than a thousand chances to influence your body's functioning! Let's take a closer look at how nutrition supports health and wellness.

Wellness can be defined in many ways. Traditionally considered simply the absence of disease, **wellness** is now described as *a multidimensional state of being that includes physical, emotional, and spiritual health.* Wellness is not an end point in our lives but is an active process we work on every day.

A critical aspect of wellness is physical health, which is influenced by both our nutrition and our level of physical activity. The two are so closely related that you can think of them as two sides of the same coin: our overall state of nutrition is influenced by how much energy we expend doing daily activities, and our level of physical activity has a major impact on how we use the nutrients in our food. Several studies have even suggested that healthful nutrition and regular physical activity can increase feelings of well-being and reduce feelings of anxiety and depression. In other words, wholesome food and physical activity just plain feel good!

—Adapted from Thompson and Moore. *Nutrition for Life*, 3rd ed., Pearson, 2013, p. 2.

Reading and Writing for College Life

Assume you are a Student Government Ambassador. You are scheduled to talk at the upcoming Freshman Orientation session for new students. You have chosen to speak about how to handle stress in college life. Read the following passage. Write a draft of your speech that gives examples from college life for each type of stress. Offer advice about how to handle each type.

Types of Stress: Eustress, Hypostress, Hyperstress, and Distress

Stress is experienced as a biochemical reaction within the body due to the way in which we interpret and respond to external pressures, which may be positive or negative. Contrary to popular belief, stress does not cause this reaction; it *is* the reaction. Interestingly, while some stresses upset us, not all stress is bad for us. Selye has identified four kinds of stress.

1. A good kind of stress, **eustress** is a short-term stress that encourages us to take more seriously and expend more energy on important activities. For example, hitters stepping up to the plate in a baseball game may experience eustress, if they are psyched up to perform.

2. **Hypostress** is underload. This happens when we start feeling anxious because we're bored or unchallenged by our situation. This problem is easily resolved when you switch to "being productive and doing something worthwhile."

3. **Hyperstress** occurs when too many tasks and responsibilities pile up on us and we are unable to adapt to the changes or cope with all that is happening at once. This is the kind of stress frequently experienced by students and teachers.

4. **Distress** arises when we lose control over a situation and the source of stress is unclear to the individual. It is related to anxiety, which may cause us to suppress the real issues. There are those who may tell you that everything is OK but they aren't happy and find that they are having trouble getting along with other people. It may take the help of others to determine exactly what the problem is.

Distress is more encompassing than the other forms of stress. It relates more to our world view, personality (Type A, too controlling, workaholic, etc.), and self-fulfilling prophecy (or expectations). Because distress can make us appear difficult or act in ways that appear unpleasant to others, it can contribute to conflict proneness.

–Adapted from Cahn and Ruth, *Managing Conflict through Communication*, 5th ed., Pearson, 2014. pp 178–179.

Reading and Writing for Working Life

Assume you are on staff at a human resource department for a national retail chain store or restaurant such as the GAP or Cracker Barrel. Your supervisor wants to update the employee training program and has asked you to read the following article and make your recommendations. Read the article and compose a memo making three suggestions for employee training.

TRAINING METHODS AND REQUIREMENTS

Orientation can be as simple as an overview of an organization and the distribution of basic information, such as company procedures and expectations. Today, however, many companies are going beyond the traditional orientation program of explaining rules and regulations, as reflected in the orientation checklist that follows.

New Employee Orientation Checklist

Your First Day

- ☑ You will be introduced to the current staff and your appointed mentor.
- ☑ You will see your new workspace and have a tour of the facilities.
- ☑ You will review the job description, including the job's responsibilities and expectations.
- ☑ You will receive a copy of the company handbook.
- ☑ You will review any health or financial benefits that are available.
- ☑ You will be introduced to general administrative practices used by the department.
- ☑ You will have an opportunity to ask questions.

Your First Week

- ☑ You can expect to have brief, daily meetings with your direct manager so that you understand your responsibilities for the day.
- ☑ You will meet with your appointed mentor to discuss issues or problems.
- ☑ At the end of the week, you will have a meeting with your employer to discuss any professional questions or personal concerns you may have.

Training begins where orientation ends. Training should teach skills or ways to improve on existing skills. For example, a salesperson might know how to sell a product but may not know all the intricacies of selling a new product. Often, other employees in the department or the recent hire's mentor can conduct on-the-job training. With on-the-job training, employees learn skills by performing them. An **apprentice training program** trains individuals through classroom or formal instruction and on-the-job training. Once the employee has proven sufficient skills, he or she can advance in status.

Some jobs are more readily learned through a programmed learning approach in which an employee is asked to perform step-by-step instructions or respond to questions. These often come in the form of computerized multiple-choice tests that provide immediate feedback The benefit of programmed learning is that an employee can progress at his or her own pace, picking up information piece by piece. For some settings, though, this kind of training may not match the type of complex decision making needed to teach employees. It also requires a commitment in providing computer access to employees and in acquiring and maintaining the automated training software.

Improvements in technology provide companies with other training options, such as simulated training and interactive multimedia training. *Gamification*, the application of game design concepts to nongame settings, has led to some training tools that are very engaging. Cold Stone Creamery, the U.S. Army, and Hilton are all turning once-dull training into an interactive video experience by taking advantage of "serious games" to train their employees. One study by the Entertainment Software Association showed that 70 percent of major U.S. employers have used interactive software and games for training.

Other companies are offering simulation training that allows their employees to really get a taste for their jobs. **Simulation training** provides realistic job-task training in a manner that is challenging but does not create the threat of failure. It is suitable for airline pilots, astronauts, and medical professionals for whom making mistakes during training is not an option or is too costly. However, other organizations take advantage of simulation training as well. For example, at the Institute for Simulation & Training at the University of Central Florida, students interact with virtual students in a classroom simulation program.

Online training allows employees to take college classes on the Internet at their convenience, enabling them to obtain specific job-related education or pursue a degree. Other forms of Internet-based distance learning training involve instructors in a centralized location teaching groups of employees at remote locations via television hookups (*teletraining*) or through a combination of audiovisual equipment (*videoconferencing*). Modern webconferencing allows users to share documents, share application software, and swap control of an attendee's desktop. Attendees can ask questions in real time, comment to the group as videos are being shown, and archive the session for later viewing.

Electronic Performance Support Systems (EPSSs) are another form of training technology. These systems provide employees with information and training when they need it, automatically, instead of sending employees to long, formal trainings, disconnected from their daily work. EPSSs can act as an in-house automated training alternative. With the quality of training interaction that users have with modern technologies, this is an increasingly attractive option. One case study reported that a client implemented EPSS and saw the system answer over 300,000 requests for support the first year, generating savings of $2.6 million.

—Adapted from Solomon, *Better Business*, 3rd ed., Pearson, 2014, pp. 264–265.

Review Test

MySkillsLab™
Complete this Exercise
on myskillslab.com

Score (number correct) ______ × 25 = ______%

An Introduction to Reading and Writing

Read the following passage from a college textbook for an education course. Answer the questions that follow the passage.

Glossary

preferences (sentence 9): favored choices
solitary (sentence 11): private, alone, independent
distinction (sentence 19): difference, trait
dimension (see chart): aspect, feature, trait
facets (sentence 21): aspect, feature, trait
cognitive (sentence 21): mental
spatial (sentence 21): physical space

LEARNING PREFERENCES

[1]Since the late 1970s, a great deal has been written about differences in students' learning preferences. [2]Learning preferences are often called *learning styles* in these writings, but I believe preferences is a more accurate label because the "styles" are determined by your preferences for particular learning environments—for example, where, when, with whom, or with what lighting, food, or music you like to study. [3]I like to study and write during large blocks of time—all day, if I don't have classes. [4]I usually make some kind of commitment or deadline every week so that I have to work in long stretches to finish the work before that deadline. [5]Then I take a day off. [6]When I plan or think, I have to see my thinking in writing. [7]I have a colleague who draws diagrams of relationships when she listens to a speaker or plans a paper. [8]You may be similar or very different, but we all may work effectively. [9]But are these **preferences** important for learning?

[10]Some proponents of learning styles believe that students learn more when they study in their preferred setting and manner. [11]And there is evidence that very bright students need less structure and prefer quiet, **solitary** learning. [12]But most educational psychologists are skeptical about the value of learning preferences. [13]"The reason researchers roll their eyes at learning styles research is the utter failure to find that assessing children's learning styles and matching to instructional methods has any effect on their learning" (Stahl, 2002, p. 99).

[14]Students, especially younger ones, may not be the best judges of how they should learn. [15]Sometimes, students, particularly those who have difficulty, prefer what is easy and comfortable; real learning can be hard and uncomfortable. [16]Sometimes, students

CONTINUED

prefer to learn in a certain way because they have no alternatives; it is the only way they know how to approach the task. [17]These students may benefit from developing new—and perhaps more effective—ways to learn. [18]One final consideration: Many of the learning styles advocates imply that the differences in the learner are what matter.

VISUAL/VERBAL DISTINCTIONS

[19]There is one learning styles **distinction** that has research support. [20]Richard Mayer has been studying the distinction between visual and verbal learners, with a focus on learning from computer-based multimedia. [21]He is finding that there is a visualizer-verbalizer dimension and that it has three **facets:** ***cognitive spatial*** *ability* (low or high), *cognitive style* (visualizer vs. verbalizer), and *learning preference* (verbal learner vs. visual learner), as shown in the following table.

Three Facets of the Visualizer-Verbalizer Dimension

[22]There are three **dimensions** to visual versus verbal learning: ability, style, and preference. [23]Individuals can be high or low on any or all of these dimensions.

Facet	Types of Learners	Definition
Cognitive Ability	High spatial ability	Good abilities to create, remember, and manipulate images and spatial information
	Low spatial ability	Poor abilities to create, remember, and manipulate images and spatial information
Cognitive Style	Visualizer	Thinks using images and visual information
	Verbalizer	Thinks using words and verbal information
Learning Preference	Visual learner	Prefers instruction using pictures
	Verbal learner	Prefers instruction using words

—Mayer, Richard E., *Journal of Educational Psychology*, American Psychological Association, © 2003. Reproduced with the permission of American Psychological Association.

[24]The picture is more complex than simply categorizing a student as either a visual or a verbal learner. [25]Students might have preferences for learning with pictures, but their low spatial ability could make using pictures to learn less effective. [26]These differences can be reliably measured, but research has not identified the effects of teaching to these styles.

—Woolfolk, *Educational Psychology*, 10th ed., pp. 124–127.

1. What do I already know about learning styles? ______________________________

____

____

____

2. What do I need to learn? ______________________________

____

____

____

3. According to the chart, the three dimensions to visual versus verbal learning are

______________, ______________, and ______________.

4. Based on the passage, the best definition for the word **distinction** is

a. similarity. **b.** contrast. **c.** effect.

5. Based on the information in the passage, we may infer that

a. most students know their individual learning styles or preferences.

b. visual learners perform better academically than verbal learners.

c. students are always the best judges of how they should learn.

d. no specific learning style or preference is better than another.

Summary Response

Restate the writer's ideas in your own words. Begin your summary response with the following: *The most important idea of "Learning Preferences" by Woolfolk is. . . .*

Reader Response

Assume you have been asked to become a peer counselor in the learning center of your college or university. You have been asked to prepare a report about learning preferences. Refer to the chart in the passage, and consider the following:

- Identify and describe the ways in which you or someone you know is a visualizer-verbalizer.
- Give examples based on experiences and/or observations.

Academic Learning Log: Module Review

Summary of Key Concepts of the Introduction to Reading and Writing

Assess your comprehension of the Introduction to Reading and Writing.

LO1 LO2

1. Reading is the ______________; writing is the ______________.
2. To imply is to ______________________________;

   to infer is to ______________________________.

LO1 LO2 LO3

3. ______________ is the use of focused, informal writings to deepen understanding.
4. A ______________ is a circumstance in which a person purposefully reads about a specific topic and responds in writing with a specific purpose for a specific audience.
5. A __________ is the subject matter developed in a piece of text; the __________ is the person or group who reads a piece of text; the __________ is the reason for reading or writing. Three purposes for reading and writing are __________, __________, and __________.

LO1 LO2 LO3 LO4

6. Elements of ______________ are the ways in which information is organized and presented in text. Elements include a ______________, a ______________, and ______________.
7. Genres of text include __________, __________, __________, __________, __________, __________, and __________.

Test Your Comprehension of Reading and Writing

Respond in your own words to the following questions and prompts.

LO1 LO2 LO3 LO4

Define prior knowledge.

How do readers and writers use outlines and concept maps to comprehend and compose text?

Explain the steps in the strategy for writing a summary.

LO1 LO2 LO3 LO4

1. **How will I use what I have learned?** In your reading/writing journal, discuss how you will apply to your own reading/writing strategy what you have learned about reading and writing. When will you apply this knowledge as you read and write?
2. **What do I still need to study about reading and writing?** In your journal, discuss your ongoing study needs. Describe what, when, and how you will continue studying and using reading and writing.

MySkillsLab™

Complete the Post-test for Module 1 in MySkillsLab.

2

Develop a Reading/ Writing Strategy

LEARNING OUTCOMES

After studying this module you should be able to:

1. Answer the Question "What's the Point of Developing a Reading/ Writing Strategy?
2. Recognize the Phases of a Reading/Writing Strategy
3. Apply the Reading/ Writing Strategy: Before, During, and After Reading
4. Apply the Reading/ Writing Strategy: After Reading, Write a Draft
5. Apply the Reading/ Writing Strategy: After Writing, Review, Revise, and Proofread Your Draft

When we tap into the power of the reading/writing cycle as an exchange of information, we build both our knowledge and our communication skills. Written language allows an exchange of ideas between a writer and a reader. A master writer makes every effort to present ideas clearly so the reader can understand and respond to them. Likewise, a master reader makes every effort to understand and respond to the ideas of the writer.

WHAT'S THE POINT of Developing a Reading/Writing Strategy?

LO1

As two equal parts of the communication process, writing and reading are essential to your success in your everyday life, your college life, and your work life. Before you study this module, predict the importance of developing a reading/writing strategy. For each of the photographs below, write a caption that identifies the reading/writing situation as everyday life, college life, and working life. Also, predict the type of reading and writing required for each situation. Finally, state the point of developing a reading/writing strategy.

Photographic Organizer: Develop a Reading/Writing Strategy

What's the point of developing a reading/writing strategy?

L2 Recognize the Phases of a Reading/Writing Strategy

Often, we find it necessary to read something and then respond to it in writing. This creates a reading/writing situation. For example, in everyday life, we read and respond to e-mails, letters to the editor in publications, or postings on blogs or social networks. In college life, we read textbooks and articles, along with a wide variety of other material across the curriculum. Then, we respond to what we have read by composing essays and reports. In working life, we read and respond in writing to e-mails, memos, reports, training materials, company policies, and other material.

As we know, reading and writing are closely related and use similar thinking processes. By coordinating these two types of processes, you can improve both your reading and your

A Reading/Writing Strategy

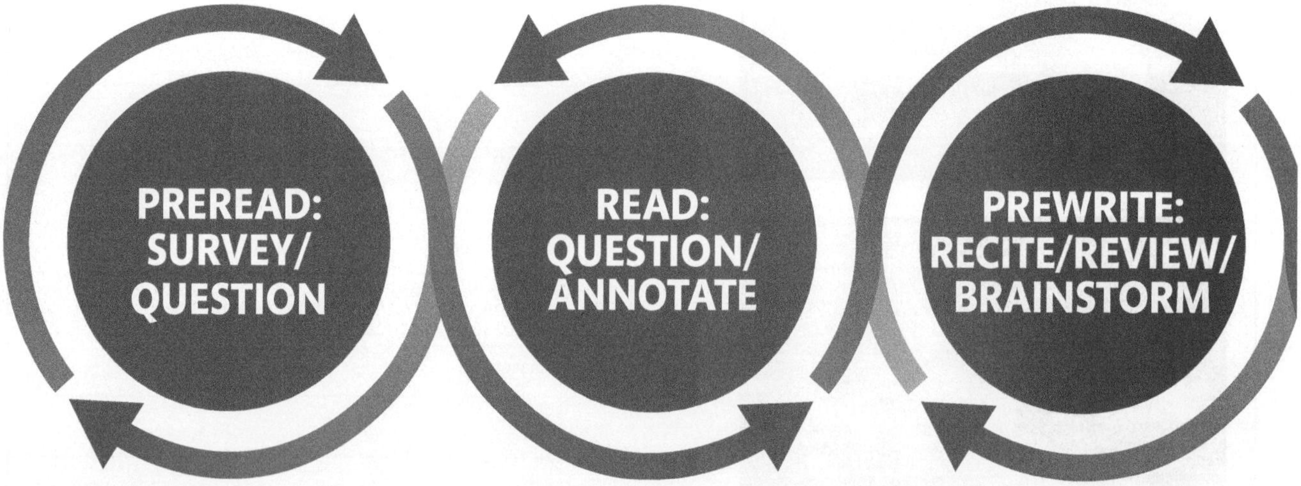

PREREAD: SURVEY/ QUESTION

READ: QUESTION/ ANNOTATE

PREWRITE: RECITE/REVIEW/ BRAINSTORM

Preread: Survey/Question

- Create questions based on a survey of titles, headings, bold/italic terms, and visuals.

Ask:

- What is my prior knowledge of this topic?
- What is my purpose for reading?
- Who is the intended audience?

Read: Question/Annotate

- Continue to ask/record questions.
- Underline main ideas.
- Circle new or key words.
- Highlight key supporting details.
- Restate ideas out loud.

Ask:

- What prior knowledge can I use to make Inferences about the text's meaning?
- What evidence allows me to make those Inferences?

Prewrite: Recite/Review/ Brainstorm

List, cluster, or outline topics based on your survey; leave room to fill in details during reading. Record predicted answers.

- Freewrite to analyze prior knowledge, purpose for reading, and audience.
- Freewrite a first response to the text.
- Take notes/Recite ideas: Record main ideas in your own words.
- Add supporting details from the reading to the list, cluster, or outline of key topics.
- Brainstorm/list topics from the reading to respond to in writing.
- Identify the intended audience of your writing.
- Compose an outline of ideas for your written response.

writing. A **reading/writing strategy** is a series of steps that coordinates the reading and writing processes. The graphic below offers a reading/writing strategy.

A **reading/writing strategy** is a series of steps that coordinates the reading process with the writing process to comprehend and respond in writing to text.

Your purpose in any reading/writing situation is to respond to what you are reading. Your response may vary. At times, you may only restate or summarize the writer's main point. At other times, you may analyze the writer's logic or expressions, agree or disagree with particular points, or explore your own treatment of the particular topic. As you develop your reading/writing strategy, apply the tools you learned in Module 1 to comprehend and create meaning, including activating prior knowledge, asking questions, making inferences and implications, and creating outlines and concept maps. The close relationship and similarities between reading and writing can be developed into a reading/writing strategy that you can use in your everyday life, college life, and working life.

DRAFT YOUR RESPONSE

REVIEW AND REVISE YOUR DRAFT

PROOFREAD

Draft

- Read your annotated text.
- Freewrite a response based on the completed list, cluster, or outline of key topics and details.
- Compose a thesis statement for your response.
- Compose an introduction, body, and conclusion of your response to the reading.

Review and Revise your Drafted Response

- Review your draft for clear use of wording, details, and organization.
- Annotate your draft with needed revisions.
- Rewrite your draft based on your review and annotations.

Proofread

- Reread your draft to identify/correct errors.
- Annotate your draft with needed corrections.
- Create and publish a polished draft.

L3 Apply the Reading/Writing Strategy: Before, During, and After Reading

Before Reading/Writing: Survey and Ask Questions

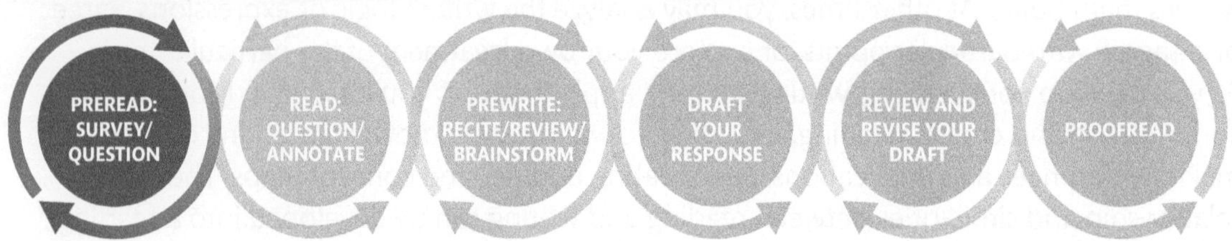

The process of creating *before reading strategies* is a vital step to take as your prewriting process in any reading/writing situation.

PREREAD TO SURVEY

Quickly look over, or skim, the reading to activate prior knowledge and clarify your purpose for reading and writing. As you skim, note the genre and structure of the text.

QUESTION

To aid in comprehension and to prewrite your response, ask questions before you read. Use the reporter's questions—*who, what, when, where, why,* and *how*—to turn key terms and headings into questions. Use **question-answer relationships (QAR)** to activate prior knowledge, locate answers to your questions, and track any changes in your own views as you read. The following thinking guide can help you preread, survey, and question as a reading/writing strategy.

Question-Answer Relationships (QAR) are questions and answers that connect a piece of text to itself, to the reader, to the world, and to other texts.

Step by Step: Survey and Question

- ☐ **Survey** a reading passage to discover the topic and text structure. Create questions based on text features: italics, bold type, titles, introductions, headings, pictures, captions, and graphics. Read the first paragraph, summaries, and questions.
- ☐ **Ask QAR questions** before you read as a prewriting step for your written response.

Right There:	What is the passage about? How is the material organized?
On My Own:	What do I already know about this idea? (What is my prior knowledge?)
	How is this text similar to or different from other texts I've read?
	What is my purpose for reading/writing?
Writer and Me:	What points may I want to address or include in my written response?
	How does this text relate to current events or to my own life?

For Module 2, assume you are taking a college course in sociology, and your class is beginning a study on the theme of loss and hardship. The Guiding Question that you will seek to answer during your study is "In what ways do humans experience and respond to hardship and loss?" Each reading in this module follows this theme. After completing all assigned readings, you will write about what you have learned.

Example

The following section from a textbook is the first assigned reading on the theme of loss and hardship. Begin the process of understanding and responding to ideas. Preview the passage. Then create questions that you will answer in the next phase. Use the "Step by Step: Survey and Question" thinking guide.

Stress and Human Resilience

[1]Joanne Hill suffered an unimaginable amount of loss over a 4-year period. [2]It began when her husband, Ken, died of heart failure at the age of 55, followed shortly by the deaths of her brother, stepfather, mother, aunt, two uncles, two cousins, her cousin's partner, her stepmother, and, finally, her son, who died suddenly of a heart attack at the age of 38. [3]Joanne helped care for several of these loved ones before they died, including her mother, who suffered from Alzheimer's and breast cancer, her brother, who died of lung cancer, and her aunt who died of liver cancer. [4]"Everyone I loved seemed to need help." [5]How could anyone endure so much loss? [6]Maybe Joanne is one of those rare people born with a huge reservoir of inner strength. [7]However, Hill attributes her survival to a series of "rainbow remedies" that she learned, through hard experience, to apply to her life.

[8]There is more to our physical health than germs and disease—we also need to consider the amount of stress in our lives and how we deal with that stress. [9]Early research in this area documented some extreme cases in which people's health was influenced by stress. [10]Consider these examples, reported by psychologist W. B. Cannon (1942):

- [11]A New Zealand woman eats a piece of fruit and then learns that it came from a forbidden supply reserved for the chief. [12]Horrified, her health deteriorates, and the next day she dies—even though it was a perfectly fine piece of fruit.
- [13]A man in Africa has breakfast with a friend, eats heartily, and goes on his way. [14]A year later, he learns that his friend had made the breakfast from a wild hen, a food strictly forbidden in his culture. [15]The man immediately begins to tremble and is dead within 24 hours.
- [16]An Australian man's health deteriorates after a witch doctor casts a spell on him. [17]He recovers only when the witch doctor removes the spell.

[18]These examples probably sound bizarre, like something you would read in *Ripley's Believe It or Not.* [19]But let's shift to the present in the United States, where many similar cases of sudden death occur following a psychological trauma. [21]When people undergo a major upheaval in their lives, such as losing a spouse, declaring bankruptcy, or being forced to resettle in a new culture, their chance of dying increases. [22]Soon after a major earthquake in the Los Angeles area on

CONTINUED

EXAMPLE *CONTINUED*

January 17, 1994, there was an increase in the number of people who died suddenly of heart attacks. [23]And many people experienced psychological and physical problems after the terrorist attacks on September 11, 2001. [24]One study measured the heart rates of a sample of adults in New Haven, Connecticut, the week after the attacks. [25]Compared to a control group of people studied before the attacks, the post–September 11 sample showed lower heart rate variability, which is a risk factor for sudden death. [26]On the other hand, as we will see in a moment, studies of the long-term effects of the 9/11 attacks have found relatively little evidence of prolonged negative reactions. [27]What exactly are the effects of stress on our psychologies and physical health, and how can we learn to cope most effectively?

Resilience

[28]The first thing to note is that humans are remarkably resilient. [29]To be sure, we all must contend with the blows life deals us, including day-to-day hassles and major, life altering events. [30]And although it is true that such events can have negative effects on psychological and physical health, many people, such as Joanne Hill, cope with them extremely well. [31]Researchers have examined people's reactions over time to major life events, including the death of loved ones and the 9/11 terrorist attacks. [32]The most common response to such traumas is **resilience**, which can be defined as mild, transient reactions to stressful events, followed by a quick return to normal, healthy functioning.

[33]Take life's most difficult challenge—dealing with the loss of a loved one. [34]For years, mental health professionals assumed that the "right" way to grieve was to go through an intense period of sadness and distress, in which people confronted and worked through their feelings, eventually leading to acceptance of the loss. [35]People who did not show symptoms of extreme distress were said to be in a state of denial that would lead to greater problems down the road. [36]When researchers looked systematically at how people respond to the death of loved ones, however, an interesting fact emerged: Many people never experienced significant distress and recovered quickly. [37]Studies of bereaved spouses, for example, typically find that fewer than half show signs of significant, long-term distress. [38]The remainder, like Joanne Hill, show no signs of depression and are able to experience positive emotions.

[39]Although one might think that such people are in a state of denial, or that they were never very attached to their spouses, there is little evidence to support these possibilities. [40]Rather, there is increasing evidence that although life's traumas can be quite painful, many people have the resources to recover from them quickly. [41]The same pattern has been found in people's responses to other highly stressful events, such as emergency workers' reactions to the bombing of the federal building in Oklahoma City in 1995 and New Yorkers' reactions to the 9/11 terrorist attacks. [42]Surprisingly few people show prolonged, negative reactions to these tragedies. [43]Nonetheless, some people do have severe negative reactions to stressful events.

[44]Hans Selye (1956, 1976) defines *stress* as the body's physiological response to threatening events. [45]Holmes and Rahe (1967) suggested that stress is the degree to which people have to change and readjust their lives in response to an external event. [46]The more change, the greater the stress.

—Adapted from Aronson, Wilson, and Akert, *Social Psychology*, 8th ed. Pearson, 2013, pp. 416–418.

1. ______________________________

____

2. ______________________________

____

3. ______________________________

____

4. ______________________________

____

Explanation

Compare your responses to the following student's think-aloud.

I referred to the thinking guide to form my questions. I used the title, headings, and words in bold and italic print to make up my questions. Just asking these questions has already helped me. My purpose for reading will now be to find the answers. I asked the following questions: "What is the topic, and how is the information organized?" "How is this text related to what I already know or have read?" "How is this passage related to loss and hardship?" "What is the meaning of **resilience** and **stress**?"

Practice 1

Before Reading/Writing: Survey and Ask Questions

Assume the following textbook passage is the second assigned reading about hardship and loss in your sociology class. Survey the passage and form prereading questions using the "Step by Step: Survey and Question" thinking guide. Record your questions in the spaces provided after the passage.

Reframing: Finding Meaning in Traumatic Events

[1]When something traumatic happens to you, is it best to try to bury it as deep as you can and never talk about it, or to spend time thinking about the event and discuss it with others? [2]Although folk wisdom has long held that it is best to open up, only recently has this assumption been put to the

CONTINUED

test. [3]James Pennebaker and his colleagues (Pennebaker, 1990, 1997, 2004; Sloan et al., 2008; Smyth & Pennebaker, 2008) have conducted a number of interesting experiments on the value of writing about traumatic events. [4]Pennebaker and Beale (1986), for example, asked college students to write, for 15 minutes on each of 4 consecutive nights, about a traumatic event that had happened to them. [5]Students in a control condition wrote for the same amount of time about a trivial event. [6]The traumas that people chose to write about included tragedies such as rape and the death of a sibling.

[7]Writing about these events was certainly upsetting in the short run. [8]Students who wrote about traumas reported more negative moods and showed greater increases in blood pressure. [9]But there were also dramatic long-term benefits. [10]The same students were less likely to visit the student health center during the next 6 months, and they reported having fewer illnesses. [11]Similarly, first-year college students who wrote about the problems of entering college, survivors of the Holocaust who wrote about their World War II experiences, and patients who had had a heart attack and wrote about it improved their health over the several months after putting their experiences in writing (Pennebaker, Barger, & Tiebout, 1989; Pennebaker, Colder, & Sharp, 1990; Willmott et al., 2011).

[12]What is it about opening up that leads to better health? [13]People who write about negative events construct a more meaningful narrative or story that reframes the event. [14]Pennebaker (1997) has analyzed the hundreds of pages of writing his participants provided and found that the people who improved the most were those who began with rather incoherent, disorganized descriptions of their problem and ended with coherent, organized stories that explained the event and gave it meaning. [15]Subsequent research has shown that reframing is especially likely to occur when people take a step back and write about a negative life event like an observer would, rather than immersing themselves in the event and trying to relive it (Kross & Ayduk, 2011). [16]The result? [17]Once people have reframed a traumatic event in this way, they think about it less and are less likely to try to suppress thoughts about it when it does come to mind. [18]Trying to suppress negative thoughts can lead to a preoccupation with those very thoughts, because the act of trying not to think about them can actually make us think about them more, leading to intrusive memories (Wegner, 1994).

[19]You may recall that in an earlier chapter we discussed an intervention called Critical Incident Stress Debriefing (CISD), in which people who have witnessed a horrific event are asked to relive the event as soon as possible in a 3- to 4-hour session, describing their experiences in detail and discussing their emotional reactions to the event. [20]As we saw, CISD has been shown, in well-controlled studies, *not* to be beneficial. [21]But why does writing about an

event help people recover when reliving it in a CISD session does not? [22]One reason appears to be the timing. [23]The writing exercise works best if enough time has passed to allow people to gain a new perspective on the incident. [24]In contrast, right after the event occurs is not a good time to try to relive it, reframe it, or understand it in a different way. [25]In fact, one problem with CISD is that it can solidify memories of the bad things that occurred, rather than helping people to reframe them.

[26]In sum, research shows that humans are often remarkably resilient in the face of adversity, particularly if they can maintain a sense of control. [27]Seeking social support can help. [28]If people continue to be troubled by the memories of stressful events, it may help to use Pennebaker's writing technique to help make sense of what happened and what it means.

—Adapted from Aronson, Wilson, and Akert, *Social Psychology*, 8th ed. Pearson, 2013, pp. 427–428.

1. ____

2. ____

3. ____

4. ____

During Reading: Read, Question, Annotate

The process of identifying *during reading strategies* is also a vital step to take as part of your prewriting process in any reading/writing situation. As you read, annotate the text with ideas that answer the questions you formed before reading.

READ AND QUESTION

As you read, *continue to ask questions* about what you are reading. Compare new ideas to your prior knowledge. Repair confusion. Stay focused and alert.

ANNOTATE

Annotation is marking the text to highlight key ideas or adding your own margin notes. Annotations draw information from the text for use in your written response. The following thinking guide can help you read, question, and annotate as a reading/writing strategy.

Step by Step: Read, Question, and Annotate

- ❑ **Read** and think about the information by continuing to ask questions:
  - Reread the parts you don't understand.
  - Reread when your mind drifts during reading.
  - Read ahead to see if the idea becomes clearer.
  - Determine the meaning of words from the context. Look up new or different words.
- ❑ **Question**, acknowledge, and resolve any confusion as it occurs.
  - Use QAR questions based on the headings, subheadings, and words in **bold type** and *italics.*
  - Does this new information agree or disagree with what I already know?
  - What is the significance of this information?
  - What inferences or conclusions can I make based on the text?
- ❑ **Annotate** to make the material your own by marking the text or adding notes in the margins.
  - Create a picture, chart, or concept map in the margin.
  - Mark your text by underlining, circling, or otherwise highlighting topics, key terms, and main ideas.
  - Rephrase an idea in the margin.
  - Answer questions that were created based on the headings and subheadings.
  - Write a brief summary of the section or passage.

Example

Assume you are continuing to study hardship and loss in your sociology class. You are now ready to reread and annotate the passage "Stress and Human Resilience" on p. 59. As you read, annotate the text for answers to the questions you created before reading. Also, ask new questions to resolve confusion. Use the thinking guide "Step by Step: Read, Question, and Annotate."

Explanation

Compare your answers to the following student's think-aloud.

It was helpful to have the before reading questions, and I found the answers pretty easily. However, I had to reread a few paragraphs and ask new questions when I got confused. For example, I had to ask about the meaning of several words. I looked up and wrote the following definitions in the margins. **Transient** means short-term, **subjective** means personal, and **objective** means factual. I was surprised to read that 9/11 survivors did not have long-term negative effects. I underlined the following details to answer my questions. What is the topic, and how is the information organized? I underlined the title "Stress and Human Resilience." How is this text related to what I already know or have read? I underlined the details about 9/11; I will never forget watching those planes on TV. I also underlined details about change and death. I have had to move and I have lost loved ones. How is this passage related to loss and hardship? This passage talks about the connections among loss, hardship, stress, and resilience. What is the meaning of resilience and stress? I underlined sentences 44 and 45 for the definitions of stress. And I underlined the definition for **resilience** given in sentence 32.

Practice 2

During Reading/Writing: Read, Question, Annotate

Using the thinking guide "Step by Step: Read, Question, and Annotate," annotate the answers to your prereading questions to the passage about "Reframing" in Practice 1.

After Reading–Prewriting: Recite, Review, Brainstorm

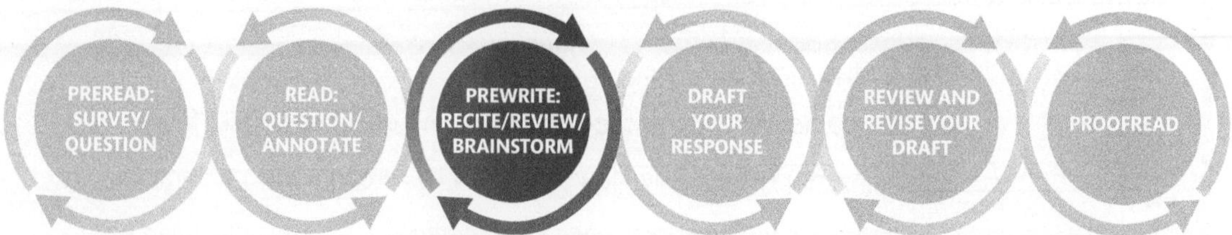

Master readers/writers use the *after reading strategies* of reciting and reviewing as prewriting steps to brainstorm their written responses to the text. Basically, there are two general types of responses. The first is a summary that only restates the writer's ideas. The second type is an analytical response in which you agree or disagree with the writer's ideas, explain the significance of the ideas, or connect the information to other texts, the world, or yourself.

RECITE AND REVIEW

Use the annotations, summaries, notes, and questions/answers you created earlier to recount what you have read. When you recite, you review by rereading and recalling ideas. However, a review also connects new information to your prior knowledge, the world, and other texts.

BRAINSTORM

Use your questions and annotations to focus your brainstorming. Include logical inferences based on the connections you have made. The following thinking guide can help you recite, review, and brainstorm ideas as a reading/writing strategy.

Step by Step: Recite, Review, Brainstorm

- ☐ **Recite** the information in your notebook.
  - **Record** answers to QAR questions.
  - **Paraphrase** ideas using your own words.
  - **Summarize** the passage.
- ☐ **Review** the information.
  - **Review** new or specialized words based on the context of the passage.
  - **Connect** information to prior knowledge, the world, and other texts.
- ☐ **Brainstorm** ideas for your written response to the passage.
  - **Freewrite** ideas. Consider the following questions:
    - How do ideas connect to my prior knowledge, the world, or other texts?
    - Which ideas do I agree or disagree with, and why?
    - Who needs to know certain information, and why?
  - **Map** the relationships among concepts you have annotated in the text.
  - **Outline** or list key ideas in blocks of thought.

Example

Assume you are continuing to study hardship and loss in your sociology class. Your professor has required you to write a response to the following question: "What is the relationship among the ideas in the passages 'Stress and Human Resilience' and 'Reframing: Finding Meaning in Traumatic Events'?" To brainstorm ideas for your response, use the annotations you made about both passages. Focus on the connections among key terms and their definitions. Follow the thinking guide "Step by Step: Recite, Review, Brainstorm." Complete the following concept map with the ideas you brainstorm.

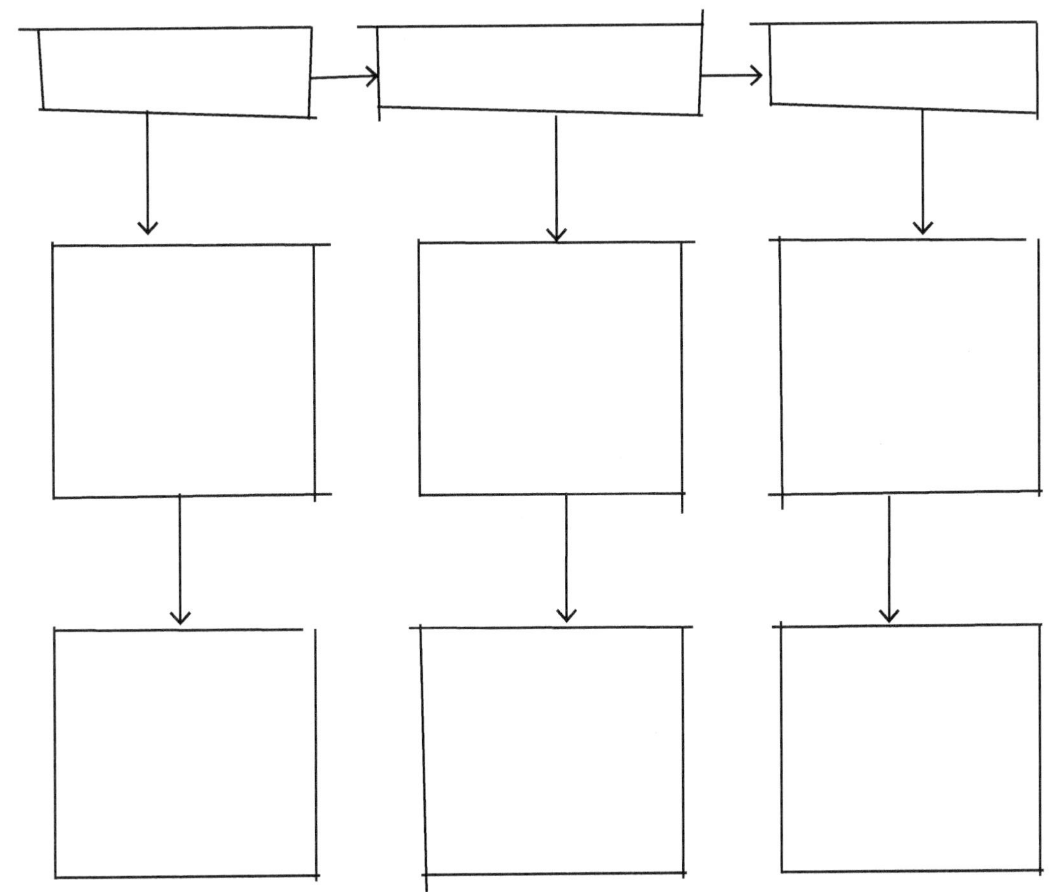
How Do Stress, Human Resilience,
and Reframing Connect?

EXAMPLE *CONTINUED*

Explanation

Compare your answers to the following think-aloud.

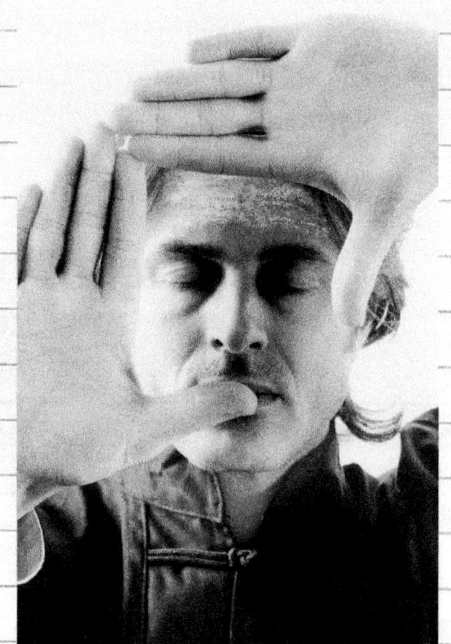

To understand the connection among stress, human resilience, and reframing, I defined each term. The definitions of **reframing** and **resilience** included the word **stress**. As I thought about it, I saw that reframing reduces stress by giving it meaning; and by reducing stress, people become more resilient. It's like a process of cause and effect. A threatening event or change of life causes stress to occur. Reframing gives the stress meaning. Once the meaning of the stress is understood, resilience—or a quick recovery of well-being—occurs.

So I filled in the three top boxes in the concept map to show this flow from stress to reframing to resilience.

Then, I filled in the two boxes below stress with the two definitions given by experts in the passage "Stress and Human Resilience."

In the two boxes below reframing in the middle column, I gave the definition of **reframing** from the passage "Reframing: Finding Meaning in Traumatic Events."

Finally, in the two boxes below resilience in the third column, I gave the definition of **resilience** and stated that reframing is a way to achieve resilience.

Practice 3

Apply the Reading/Writing Strategy: Before, During, and After Reading

Assume the following passages are assigned readings about hardship and loss for your sociology class. Both passages are about the U.S. Civil War battle at Gettysburg. Your writing assignment is to connect these passages to what you have learned about *stress, human resilience*, and *reframing* from prior readings. First, preread each passage by surveying the QAR questions given below. Then, read and annotate key ideas and answers to the questions. Finally, on your own paper, brainstorm details for your written response. Use the thinking guides on pages 58, 64, and 66.

QAR Questions:

1. How are these passages related to loss and hardship?

2. How does Samuel Bates' description of the Gettysburg battle reveal the two types of stress defined in the passage "Stress and Human Resilience" (page 59)?

3. How does Lincoln's Gettysburg Address illustrate the act of "reframing" as defined in the passage "Reframing: Finding Meaning in Traumatic Events" (page 61)?

4. What meaning did Lincoln give to the battlefield?

5. How does Lincoln's Gettysburg Address illustrate human resilience?

CONTINUED

PRACTICE 3 *CONTINUED*

At What a Cost!

[1]A great triumph had been achieved by the Union arms. [2]But at what a cost! [3]And what a spectacle did that field present! [4]Amidst "the thunder of the captains, and the shouting," thousands of the gallant and brave, who three days before had marched as joyfully as the boldest, had been stricken down, and had poured out their life-blood like water; and thousands, cold in death, were scattered on every conceivable part of that gory field.

The Battlefield of Gettysburg, Little Round Top and Round Top

[5]Professor Jacobs, in his "Later Rambles," says: "For several days after the battle, the field everywhere bore the fresh marks of the terrible struggle. [6]The soil was yet red with the blood of the wounded and slain, and large numbers of the dead of both armies were to be seen lying in the place where the fatal missiles struck them. . . . [7]The work of interring 9000 dead, and removing about 20,000 wounded to comfortable quarters, was a herculean task. [8]The rebel army had left the most of their dead lying unburied on the field, as also large numbers of their badly wounded, and had fled for safety. . . . [9]There was considerable delay in properly interring the corpses that lay on the field of battle. [10]It was only after rebel prisoners, who had been taken in the vicinity after the battle, were impressed into this service, especially into that of covering up the bodies of their fallen comrades, that the work was finally completed. [11]Whilst some of these prisoners went into this work with reluctance and murmuring, others did it cheerfully, saying, 'It is just what we have compelled the Yankees to do for us!' [12]Although the field was thoroughly searched, the dead were not all discovered until it was impossible to perform for them what humanity, under other circumstances, would have demanded. [13]In front of Little Round Top, amongst huge rocks, lay all summer long the decaying bodies of half a dozen or more of rebels, who had probably belonged to Hood's division, and, having been wounded on July 2d, in their desperate effort to take Little Round Top, may have crept into the open spaces between these rocks for shelter or for water. [14]There they died undiscovered, and when found they were so far gone in decomposition that they could not be removed. [15]And such also was the position in which they lay that it was impossible to cover them with earth.

[16]Great surprise is sometimes expressed by visitors because they do not find so many graves as they had expected to see. [17]"You tell us," say they, "that there were about 3500 Union, and about 5500 rebel soldiers killed in this battle; but we do not see so many graves. [18]Where were they buried?" [19]The answer has uniformly been, "The whole ground around Gettysburg is one vast cemetery." [20]The men are buried everywhere. [21]When they could conveniently be brought together, they were buried in clusters of ten, twenty, fifty, or more; but so great was their number, and such the advanced stage of decomposition of those that had lain on the field for several days

during the hot weather of July, together with the unavoidable delay, that indicating by the freshly turned up earth, and perhaps by a board, a shingle, a stick, or stone, that the mortal remains of a human being lie there. . . . [22]Rose's farm, especially a wheat field, and Sherfy's peach orchard, were points of desperate and bloody contest. [23]The wheat field was strewn with rebel dead, and one grave near Rose's garden alone contains 400 of them. . . . [24]Their remains will probably never be removed from the spot they now occupy, and doubtless in future time the plough will turn up their crumbling bones, together with the remnants of the weapons they used in the atrocious warfare. [25]The vicinity of Gettysburg will thus remain a vast charnel-house, and for years to come will be visited by mourning friends.

—Bates, Samuel, P. *The Battle of Gettysburg*. Philadelphia: T.H. Davis & Co., 1875, pp. 256–258.

The Gettysburg Address (1863)

by Abraham Lincoln

[1]Four score and seven years ago our fathers brought forth on this continent, a new nation, conceived in liberty, and dedicated to the proposition that all men are created equal.

Abraham Lincoln Delivering His Gettysburg Address, 1863

[2]Now we are engaged in a great civil war, testing whether that nation, or any nation so conceived, and so dedicated, can long endure. [3]We are met on a great battlefield of that war. [4]We have come to dedicate a portion that field, as a final resting place for those who here gave their lives that that nation might live. [5]It is altogether fitting and proper that we should do this.

[6]But, in a larger sense, we can not dedicate—we can not consecrate—we can not hallow—this ground. [7]The brave men, living and dead, who struggled here, have consecrated it, far above our poor power to add or detract. [8]The world will little note, nor long remember what we say here; while it can never forget what they *did* here. [9]It is for us the living, rather, to be dedicated here to the unfinished work which they who fought here have thus far so nobly advanced. [10]It is rather for us to be here dedicated to the great task remaining before us—that, from these honored dead we take increased devotion to that cause for which they gave the last full measure of devotion—that we here highly resolve these dead shall not have died in vain—that this nation, under God, shall have a new birth of freedom—and that government of the people, by the people, for the people, shall not perish from the earth.

—Abraham Lincoln, *The Gettysburg Address.*

L4 Apply the Reading/Writing Strategy: After Prewriting, Write a Draft

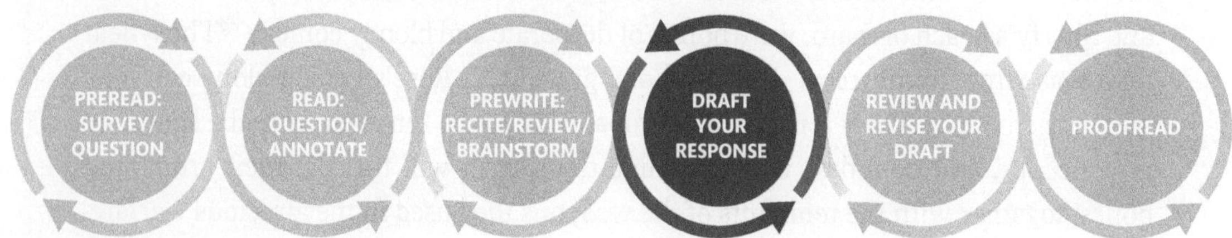

The drafting stage of the reading/writing process takes the ideas generated during prewriting and develops them into an initial version of your written response to what you have read. This first draft may be revised several times during the next phases of the reading/writing process. This phase may also include several tasks, depending on the reading/writing situation. An essay or letter may require the drafting of an introduction, a main idea (such as a topic sentence or thesis statement), supporting details, and a conclusion. A stand-alone paragraph, such as a summary, may require only the main idea and major supporting details. The following thinking guide can help you draft your written response as a reading/writing strategy.

Step by Step: Drafting

- ☐ Write your main idea in a complete sentence.
- ☐ As you write a thesis statement or topic sentence, assert an idea instead of announcing your topic. Avoid the following announcements:
  - "I am going to write about . . ."
  - "My paragraph (or essay) is about . . ."
  - "My topic is . . ."
- ☐ As you write your first draft, do not worry about issues such as spelling and grammar.
- ☐ Generate major and minor details to support your main idea.
- ☐ As you write, include new ideas as they occur to you without self-criticism or editing before you have a complete draft; this first draft does not need to be perfect. You will use the revision process to evaluate details for logic and relevance once your draft is complete.
- ☐ Use the first draft to discover how your ideas flow and fit together.
- ☐ Resolve to write multiple drafts to produce your best work.

Example

Assume you are continuing your work to write a response to the question "What is the relationship among the ideas in the passages 'Stress and Human Resilience' and 'Reframing: Finding Meaning in Traumatic Events'?" Based on your prewrite (see page 68), write a draft of your response. Use the thinking guide "Step by Step: Drafting."

Explanation

Compare your use of the reading/writing strategy and your draft to the following think-aloud and draft.

I closely followed the concept map I had created. In this first draft, I did not check for any errors in grammar or word choices. I just wanted to get the general ideas stated.

Stress, Reframing, and Human Resiliance

Reframing is one way for you to reduce the negative effects of stress and foster resilience in the face of traumatic events.

To understand the relationship among stress, reframing, and resiliance, you must first define **stress** or **traumatic events.** Sociologist Hans Selye defines stress as a physical reaction to a threatening event. Sociologists Holmes and Rahe define **stress** as the degree to which an event changes people's lives.

According to the passage Reframing: Finding Meaning in Traumatic Events, writing about a trauma reduces its long-term negative effects. They believe writing about a stressful event allows the person to "reframe" the trauma into a meaningful experience. Writing enables the person to express and let go of the pain rather than ignore it or hold on to it.

In the passage Stress and Human Resilience, **resilience** is defined as a short-term response to a traumatic or stressful experience, soon after which recovery of well-being occurs. Reframing offers a healthy, positive way to quickly recover from a stressful threat or life change.

Practice 4

Apply the Reading/Writing Strategy: After Reading, Write a Draft

Assume you are continuing your work on the response you brainstormed in Practice 3 (page 68). Based on your prewrite, draft your written response on your own paper. Use the thinking guide "Step by Step: Drafting."

L5 Apply the Reading/Writing Strategy: After Writing, Review, Revise, and Proofread Your Draft

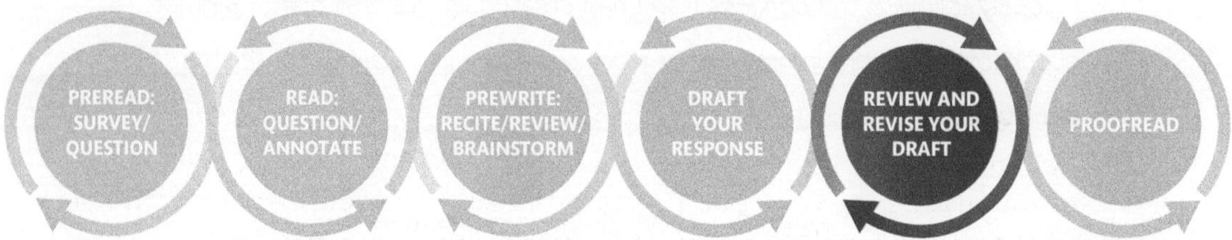

Now that you have gotten your ideas on paper, you can review your work to make sure your paragraph offers a focused, unified, well-supported, and coherent chunk of information. As you revise your draft, review and apply what you have learned.

REVIEW

Take another look at what you have written. Ask questions that your reader would ask. Think about the flow of your ideas and how easily a reader can follow your thoughts. Annotate your own writing with the revisions you think will improve the writing.

REVISE

Revising is re-seeing your work through the eyes of your reader. Revising is reworking your draft for clarity, logic, interest, and believability.

Step by Step: Review and Revise

- ❑ Read your draft out loud to identify parts that may be unclear or awkward.
- ❑ Annotate your draft, as needed, with the revisions you will make.
- ❑ Refer to the author and title of the passage to which you are responding as needed.
- ❑ Clearly state or imply your central idea.
- ❑ Move information as needed into the most logical order.
- ❑ Add transitions as needed to clarify the relationship between ideas.
- ❑ Add details and examples as needed to strengthen or clarify specific points.
- ❑ Delete irrelevant details.
- ❑ Replace vague words and details with vivid and precise expressions.

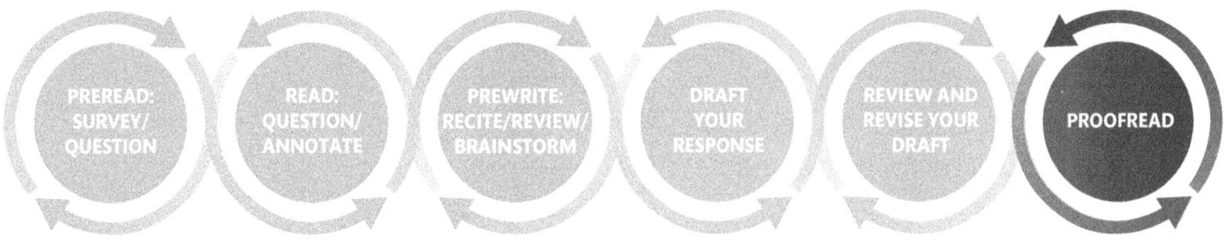

PROOFREAD

Once you have revised your paragraph, take time to carefully proofread your work. Proofreading is correcting errors in punctuation, capitalization, mechanics, grammar, and spelling. When you proofread, you are both a reader looking for errors that need correction and a writer creating a clean, polished copy. Publishing a clean, error-free draft proves you are committed to excellence and that you take pride in your work. Many student writers struggle with common errors, and every writer has her or his own pattern or habit of careless errors. To create a polished draft, a master writer masters the rules of writing and edits to eliminate careless errors. The following thinking guide can help you review, revise, and proofread your written response as a reading/writing strategy.

Step by Step: Proofread

Allow some time to pass between revising and proofreading.

- ☐ Read your work one sentence at a time from the end to the beginning. Reading your work from the end to the beginning allows you to focus on each sentence.
- ☐ Read again from the beginning with a cover sheet of paper that you slide down the page as you read so that you focus on one sentence at a time.
- ☐ Use a highlighter to mark mistakes.
- ☐ Proofread more than once; focus on one type of error at a time.
- ☐ Proofread for the types of errors you commonly make.
- ☐ Use word processing spell checkers carefully (they don't know the difference between words such as *there, their,* or *they're*).
- ☐ Use a dictionary to double check your spelling.

Example

Assume you are continuing to work on your written response to the passages about stress, human resilience, and reframing. Review and revise your draft, and then proofread it. Use the thinking guides "Step by Step: Review and Revise" and "Step by Step: Proofread."

Explanation

Compare your use of the reading/writing strategy and your revised and proofread drafts to the following think-aloud and revised and proofread drafts.

Upon review of my first draft, I saw the need to add details to make my general points more clear. So I used my own understanding about stress and fight or flight, and I returned to the passages for additional details. I did not address errors in grammar or word choice.

Stress, Reframing, and Human Resiliance

Reframing is one way for you to reduce the negative effects of stress and foster resiliance in the face of traumatic events.

To understand the relationship among stress, reframing, and resiliance, you must first define **stress** or **traumatic** events. Sociologist Hans Selye defines **stress** as a physical reaction to a threatening event. Sociologists Holmes and Rahe defined **stress** as the degree to which an event changes people's lives.

According to the passage Reframing: Finding Meaning in Traumatic Events writing about a trauma reduces its long-term negative effects. They believe writing about a stressful event allows the person to "reframe" the trauma into a meaningful experience. Writing enables the person to express and let go of the pain rather hold on to it. Reframing offers a healthy,

Insert: In the passage Stress and Human Resiliance

Explain flight or flight and give examples from passage

Give examples from passage.

Give examples from passage to support the underlined idea.

Move underlined sentence to be last, concluding sentence.

positive way to quickly recover from a stressful threat or life change. In the passage Stress and Human Resiliance **resiliance** is defined as a short-term response to a stressful experience soon after which recovery of well-being occurs. Reframing offers a healthy, positive way to quickly recover from a stressful threat or life change.

As I proofread, I inserted quotation marks around the titles and commas after phrases that introduced a sentence. I also fixed misspellings.

Resilience
Stress, Reframing, and Human ^ ~~Resiliance~~

Reframing is one way ~~for you~~ to reduce the negative effects of stress and foster ^resilience ~~resiliance~~ in the face of traumatic events.

To understand the relationship among stress, reframing, and ^resilience ~~resiliance~~, ~~you must~~ first define **stress** or traumatic events. In the passage ^" Stress and Human ~~Resiliance~~ ^Resilience," sociologist Hans Selye defines **stress** as a physical reaction to a threatening event. The body faces a threat by increasing the heart's rate and releasing extra energy in order to stand and fight or to take flight. This effect can be dangerous. For example, according to the passage ^" Stress and Human ~~Resiliance~~ ^Resilience," there was an increase of fatal heart attacks immediately following the 1994 earthquake in Los Angeles. Sociologists Holmes and Rahe defined **stress** as the degree to which an event changes people's lives. For example ^, the death of a spouse may cause great change in your family. The more the family has to readjust daily routines, the greater their stress.

CONTINUED

EXPLANATION *CONTINUED*

According to the passage "Reframing: Finding Meaning in Traumatic Events," writing about a trauma reduces its long-term negative effects. Research showed improved health for those who had written about surviving the holocaust, surviving a heart attack, or their World War II experiences. ~~They~~ Experts believe writing about a stressful event allows the person to "reframe" the trauma into a meaningful experience. Writing enables the person to express and let go of the pain rather than ignore it or hold on to it. In the passage "Stress and Human ~~Resiliance~~ Resilience," ~~resiliance~~ resilience is defined as a short-term response to a traumatic or stressful experience soon after which recovery of well-being occurs. Reframing offers a healthy, positive way to quickly recover from a stressful threat or life change.

Practice 5

Apply the Reading/Writing Strategy: After Writing, Review and Revise Your Draft

Review and revise the draft you composed about stress, resilience, reframing, and the passages about the Civil War in Practice 4 (page 73). Use the thinking guide "Step by Step: Review and Revise."

Practice 6

Apply the Reading/Writing Strategy: Proofread

Proofread the draft you composed about stress, resilience, reframing, and the passages about the Civil War in Practice 5. Use the thinking guide "Step by Step: Proofread."

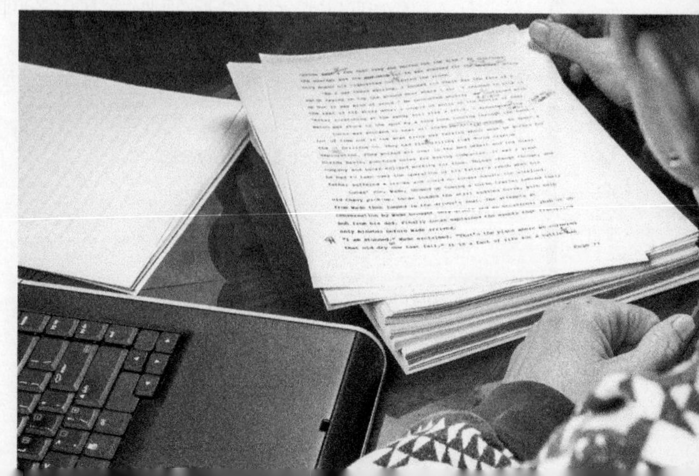

Workshop: Develop a Reading/ Writing Strategy

Assume you are continuing your study of the theme of hardship and loss in your college sociology course. All of the passages you have read throughout this module have been part of your ongoing reading assignments. Your capstone writing assignment will be a formal response to the Guiding Question "In what ways do humans experience and respond to hardship and loss?" The following excerpts are your capstone reading assignments on this theme. The first passage is from a sociology textbook and briefly defines one theory about grief. The second passage is an excerpt from Joan Didion's memoir *The Year of Magical Thinking*. Didion chronicles the year after her husband died from a heart attack, while their daughter, Quintana, was in a coma. Skim the prereading questions to guide your reading, read the passages, and complete the activities that follow.

Bereavement

1Elisabeth Kubler-Ross (1969) found that most people confront their own death in stages. Initially, individuals react with *denial*, followed by *anger*, then they try *negotiation*, hoping for divine intervention. Gradually, they fall into *resignation* or *depression* and finally reach *acceptance*. According to some researchers, bereavement follows the same pattern of stages. The people closest to a dying person may initially deny the reality of impending death and then gradually reach a point of acceptance.

2Reaching closure is not possible when a death is unexpected, and survivors' social disorientation may last for years. One study of middle-aged women who had recently experienced the death of their husbands found that many felt they had *lost* not only a spouse but also their reason for living. Therefore, dealing successfully with bereavement requires the time and social support necessary to form a new sense of self and recognize new options.

—Macionis, *Sociology*, 15th ed., Pearson, pp. 444–446.

THE YEAR OF MAGICAL THINKING

by Joan Didion

1*Life changes fast.*

2*Life changes in the instant.*

3*You sit down to dinner and life as you know it ends.*

4*The question of self-pity.*

CONTINUED

[5]Those were the first words I wrote after it happened. The computer dating on the Microsoft Word file ("Notes on change.doc") reads "May 20, 2004, 11:11p.m.," but that would have been a case of my opening the file and reflexively pressing save when I closed it. I had made no changes to that file in May. I had made no changes to that file since I wrote the words, in January 2004, a day or two or three after the fact. For a long time I wrote nothing else.

[6] *Life changes in the instant.*

[7] *The ordinary instant.*

[8]At some point, in the interest of remembering what seemed most striking about what had happened, I considered adding those words, "the ordinary instant." I saw immediately that there would be no need to add the word "ordinary," because there would be no forgetting it: the word never left my mind. It was in fact the ordinary nature of everything preceding the event that prevented me from truly believing it had happened, absorbing it, incorporating it, getting past it. I recognize now that there was nothing unusual in this: confronted with sudden disaster we all focus on how unremarkable the circumstances were in which the unthinkable occurred, the clear blue sky from which the plane fell, the routine errand that ended on the shoulder with the car in flames, the swings where the children were playing as usual when the rattlesnake struck from the ivy. "He was on his way home from work—happy, successful, healthy—and then, gone," I read in the account of a psychiatric nurse whose husband was killed in a highway accident. In 1966 I happened to interview many people who had been living in Honolulu on the morning of December 7, 1941; without exception, these people began their accounts of Pearl Harbor by telling me what an "ordinary Sunday morning" it had been. "It was just an ordinary beautiful September day," people still say when asked to describe the morning in New York when American Airlines 11 and United Airlines 175 got flown into the World Trade towers. Even the report of the 9/11 Commission opened on this insistently premonitory and yet still dumbstruck narrative note: "Tuesday, September 11, 2001, dawned temperate and nearly cloudless in the eastern United States."

[9]"And then—gone." In the midst of life we are in death, Episcopalians say at the graveside. Later I realized that I must have repeated the details of what happened to everyone who came to the house in those first weeks, all those friends and relatives who brought food and made drinks and laid out plates on the dining room table for however many people were around at lunch or dinner time, all those who picked up the plates and froze the leftovers and ran the dishwasher and filled our (I could not yet think my) otherwise empty house even after I had gone into the bedroom (our bedroom, the one in which there still lay on a sofa a faded terrycloth XL robe bought in the 1970s at Richard Carroll in Beverly Hills) and shut the door. Those moments when I was abruptly overtaken by exhaustion are what I remember most clearly about the first days and weeks. I have no memory of telling anyone the details, but I must have done so, because everyone seemed to know them. At one point I considered the possibility that they had picked up the details of the story from

one another, but immediately rejected it: the story they had was in each instance too accurate to have been passed from hand to hand. It had come from me.

10Another reason I knew that the story had come from me was that no version I heard included the details I could not yet face, for example the blood on the living room floor that stayed there until José came in the next morning and cleaned it up. José. Who was part of our household. Who was supposed to be flying to Las Vegas later that day, December 31, but never went. José was crying that morning as he cleaned up the blood. When I first told him what had happened he had not understood. Clearly I was not the ideal teller of this story, something about my version had been at once too offhand and too elliptical, something in my tone had failed to convey the central fact in the situation (I would encounter the same failure later when I had to tell Quintana), but by the time José saw the blood he understood. I had picked up the abandoned syringes and ECG electrodes before he came in that morning but I could not face the blood.

11In outline.

12It is now, as I begin to write this, the afternoon of October 4, 2004.

13Nine months and five days ago, at approximately nine o'clock on the evening of December 30, 2003, my husband, John Gregory Dunne, appeared to (or did) experience, at the table where he and I had just sat down to dinner in the living room of our apartment in New York, a sudden massive coronary event that caused his death. Our only child, Quintana, had been for the previous five nights unconscious in an intensive care unit at Beth Israel Medical Center's Singer Division, at that time a hospital on East End Avenue (it closed in August 2004) more commonly known as "Beth Israel North" or "the old Doctors' Hospital," where what had seemed a case of December flu sufficiently severe to take her to an emergency room on Christmas morning had exploded into pneumonia and septic shock. This is my attempt to make sense of the period that followed, weeks and then months that cut loose any fixed idea I had ever had about death, about illness, about probability and luck, about good fortune and bad, about marriage and children and memory, about grief, about the ways in which people do and do not deal with the fact that life ends, about the shallowness of sanity, about life itself. I have been a writer my entire life. As a writer, even as a child, long before what I wrote began to be published, I developed a sense that meaning itself was resident in the rhythms of words and sentences and paragraphs, a technique for withholding whatever it was I thought or believed behind an increasingly impenetrable polish. The way I write is who I am, or have become, yet this is a case in which I wish I had instead of words and their rhythms a cutting room, equipped with an Avid, a digital editing system on which I could touch a key and collapse the sequence of time, show you simultaneously all the frames of memory that come to me now, let you pick the takes, the marginally different expressions, the variant readings of the same lines. This is a case in which I need more than words to find the meaning. This is a case in which I need whatever it is I think or believe to be penetrable, if only for myself.

—Didion, Joan. *The Year of Magical Thinking.* Knopf: NY, 2005, pp. 3–8.

Preread: Survey and Question

Survey the following questions. Answer the questions about your prior knowledge. Then, skim the passages to locate key details to annotate during reading.

1. What prior knowledge do I have about "the ways humans experience and respond to hardship and loss"?

____

____

2. What prior knowledge do I have about bereavement or the stages of grief?

____

____

3. What other texts have I read related to hardship, loss, and bereavement?

____

____

4. What is the most important (or central) idea in the textbook passage "Bereavement"?

____

____

5. What is the most important (or central idea) in the excerpt from *The Year of Magical Thinking*?

____

____

6. How do the stages of grief as described in the passage "Bereavement" relate to the ideas in the passage "Stress and Human Resilience" (page 59)?

____

____

7. How do the stages of grief as described in the passage "Bereavement" relate to the ideas in the passage "Reframing: Finding Meaning in Traumatic Events" (page 61)?

____

____

8. How do the stages of grief as described in the passage "Bereavement" relate to the ideas in the passage "At What a Cost!" (page 70)?

9. How do the stages of grief as described in the passage "Bereavement" relate to the ideas in the passage "The Gettysburg Address" (page 71)?

10. How do the stages of grief as described in the passage "Bereavement" relate to Didion's description of her loss in the excerpt from *The Year of Magical Thinking*?

11. How do the ideas in the passage "Stress and Human Resilience" relate to Didion's description of her loss in the excerpt from *The Year of Magical Thinking*?

12. How do the experiences of hardship and loss described in the passage "At What a Cost!" relate to Didion's experience of her loss in the excerpt from *The Year of Magical Thinking*?

13. How does Abraham Lincoln's response to hardship and loss in his Gettysburg Address differ from and/or compare to Didion's response to her loss?

14. How does the concept of reframing relate to the passage from Module 1 "Symbols and Language" (page 21)?

15. Which ideas or details will I use from other texts to make my point about hardship and loss?

Read and Annotate

As you read, annotate key ideas, particularly those details that answer your prereading questions.

Recite, Review, and Brainstorm

Recite and **Review** the information. Paraphrase ideas. Summarize the most important parts. **Brainstorm** ideas for your written response to the passage. Answer your prereading questions. *Freewrite* or *map* the relationship among answers to questions or ideas you have annotated in the text. *Outline* or *list* key ideas and details in blocks of thought. Use your own paper.

Write a Draft of Your Response

Using the ideas you generated by brainstorming, compose a draft of your response. Use your own paper.

Revise Your Draft

Once you have created a draft, read it to answer the questions in the "Questions for Revising" box that follows. Indicate your answers by annotating your paper. If you answer "yes" to a question, underline, check, or circle examples. If you answer "no" to a question, write needed information in the margins and draw lines to indicate the placement of additional details. Revise your essay based on your reflection. (*Hint:* Experienced writers create several drafts as they focus on one or two questions per draft.)

Step by Step: Questions for Revising

- ☐ Have I stated or implied a focused central idea?
- ☐ Is the logical order of ideas clear? Have I used strong transitions to guide my reader, such as *first, second, next,* etc.?
- ☐ Have I made my point with adequate details?
- ☐ Have I included only the details that are relevant to my point?
- ☐ What impact will my essay have on my reader?

Proofread Your Draft

Once you have made any revisions to your essay that may be needed, proofread your essay to eliminate careless errors.

Reading and Writing Assignments

MySkillsLab™
Complete this Exercise on myskillslab.com

Reading and Writing for Everyday Life

Assume the FDA is planning to revise current regulations so that food labels provide information that is clearer to consumers and more consistent with recent updates in the Dietary Guidelines. The FDA is asking for consumers' feedback about what information should be included on food labels. Read the following lists about the changes and write a letter of response to the FDA. In your letter, include at least three types of information you would like to see on a food label, and why.

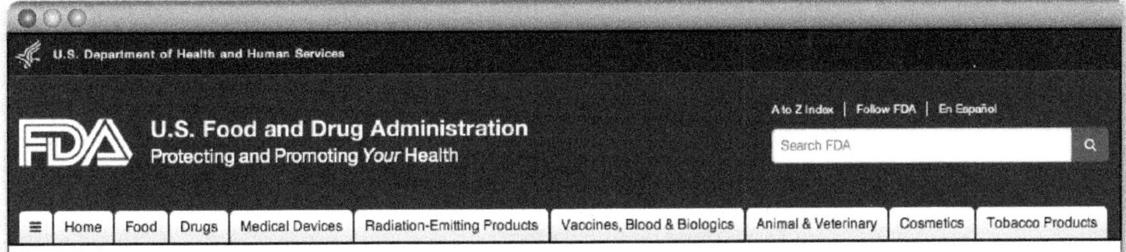

Proposed Changes to Nutrition Facts Label

Possible Changes Under Consideration:

- More concise and consistent front-of-package information.
- More appropriate information on number of servings contained within the entire package of food.
- Less complex ingredient information.
- Stricter regulation of health claims made by manufacturers.

The following sections describe what is currently required on food labels.

Label Formats

Original vs. Proposed

Nutrition Facts (Original)

Serving Size 2/3 cup (55g)
Servings Per Container About 8

Amount Per Serving	
Calories 230	Calories from Fat 72
	% Daily Value*
Total Fat 8g	12%
Saturated Fat 1g	5%
Trans Fat 0g	
Cholesterol 0mg	0%
Sodium 160mg	7%
Total Carbohydrate 37g	12%
Dietary Fiber 4g	16%
Sugars 1g	
Protein 3g	
Vitamin A	10%
Vitamin C	8%
Calcium	20%
Iron	45%

* Percent Daily Values are based on a 2,000 calorie diet. Your daily value may be higher or lower depending on your calorie needs.

	Calories:	2,000	2,500
Total Fat	Less than	65g	80g
Sat Fat	Less than	20g	25g
Cholesterol	Less than	300mg	300mg
Sodium	Less than	2,400mg	2,400mg
Total Carbohydrate		300g	375g
Dietary Fiber		25g	30g

Nutrition Facts (Proposed)

8 servings per container
Serving size 2/3 cup (55g)

Amount per 2/3 cup
Calories 230

% DV*	
12%	**Total Fat** 8g
5%	Saturated Fat 1g
	Trans Fat 0g
0%	**Cholesterol** 0mg
7%	**Sodium** 160mg
12%	**Total Carbs** 37g
14%	Dietary Fiber 4g
	Sugars 1g
	Added Sugars 0g
	Protein 3g
10%	Vitamin D 2mcg
20%	Calcium 260mg
45%	Iron 8mg
5%	Potassium 235mg

* Footnote on Daily Values (DV) and calories reference to be inserted here.

Five Components Must Be Included on Food Labels:

1. *A statement of identity:* The common name of the product or an appropriate identification must be prominently displayed on the label.
2. *The net contents of the package:* This information accurately describes the quantity of the food product in the entire package and is listed as weight (e.g., grams), volume (e.g., fluid ounces), or numerical count (e.g., four bars).
3. *Ingredient list:* The ingredients must be listed by their common name, in descending order by weight. This means that the first product listed in the ingredient list is the predominant ingredient in that food.
4. *The name and address of the food manufacturer, packer, or distributor:* This information can be used to contact the company.
5. *Nutrition Facts Panel:* This panel is the primary tool to assist you in choosing more healthful foods.

—Adapted from Thompson and Moore. *Nutrition for Life*, 3rd ed., Pearson, 2013, p. 22.

Reading and Writing for College Life

Assume you are taking a student success course. Your teacher has assigned your class to read the following passage and to write a response to the prompt under the heading "Determining Your Good Stress Zone." In your response discuss some of the skills you will focus on to ensure your success as a student.

7 NAVIGATING YOUR FUTURE SUCCESS

GOOD STRESS: STAY IN YOUR ZONE

Develop a system to keep you in your "good stress zone," so you can perform at your best and seize personal, academic, and professional opportunities. The first step is assessment and awareness. Recognizing your own stressors and the symptoms they cause can help you determine when your stress is out of balance and you have entered your bad stress zone. Notice we are not focusing as much on the triggers, for you will always have triggers that come and go, but more so on the physical and mental symptoms caused by a trigger. These symptoms represent a wake-up call to cope with what's going on in your life before it overtakes you.

Not all stress is bad for you. Survival stress is an important and necessary stress. If confronted by a life-threatening event, part of your nervous system called the sympathetic nervous system—the fight-or-flight system—will kick in. The impact on the sympathetic system causes certain responses to maximize your chance for survival. In other words, your body gets ready to either fight or flee the dangerous situation. Responses may include:

- Increased adrenaline levels for more energy
- Faster heart rate to supply more oxygen to muscles
- Increased blood pressure to get more blood flow to the brain
- Pupil dilation to bring in more light to see better

Good Stress

The fight-or-flight response shows a good stress response in life-threatening situations. But what about everyday events such as a big exam, a job interview, or giving a speech in front of the class? Studies show that you actually perform better if you have moderate stress and are not totally "cool as a cucumber." Without enough stress, your performance may suffer because you are bored or unmotivated. However, if you let stress get out of hand and you panic, you have entered into bad stress, where you perform poorly or even not at all.

Determining Your Good Stress Zone

Write at least three adjectives or phrases that describe you when you are in "your good stress zone." The better you describe your good stress zone, the more likely you are to spend time there. Thus, select words that describe you when you are functioning well, running on all cylinders, and so on. Some adjectives may include *happy, focused,* and a *sense of humor*. Phrases may include "I'm more productive" or "I feel lighter." Choose words that best describe you when you are doing well. Write a passage that describes your good stress zone and at least two steps you can take to stay in your good zone.

—Adapted from Colbert, *Navigating Your Future Success.* 2nd ed., Pearson, 2015, p. 7.

Reading and Writing for Working Life

Assume you are applying for a management position at a national corporation such as FedEx, UPS, Google, Disney, Starbucks, or Wal-Mart. You have received from the company an article to read about corporate social responsibility, a topic of great concern to the company. You are expected to review the article before your interview. Read the information and prepare a response. In your response, indicate which three of "The Five Pillars of Corporate Social Responsibility" you think the company to which you are applying should be concerned with and why.

THE FIVE PILLARS OF CORPORATE SOCIAL RESPONSIBILITY

Corporate social responsibility (CSR) is defined as a company's obligation to conduct its activities with the aim of achieving social, environmental, and economic development. All business organizations, regardless of their size, have a corporate responsibility. By being socially responsible, a company makes decisions in five major areas:

1. Human rights and employment standards in the workplace
2. Ethical sourcing and procurement
3. Marketing and consumer issues
4. Environmental, health, and safety concerns
5. Community and good neighbor policies

Human Rights and Employment Standards in the Workplace

CSR concerns affect the world outside the office in both local and global communities. For example, employment standards—how a company respects and cares for its employees—are reflected locally in the policies a company sets and the impact a company has on the community. As a business interacts more with the global marketplace, a company will have to make decisions about ethical standards on tough issues such as child labor, pollution, fair wages, and human rights. For example, when Vedanta Resources, a United Kingdom mining and aluminum refining company, came into the Indian community of Orissa, it promised great gains in the quality of life for its employees and the entire region. However, due to the company's practices, no gains have occurred, the air is hard to breathe, and the main source of drinking water is polluted.

Ethical Sourcing and Procurement

Finding a source for raw materials and making agreements with suppliers is an aspect of many businesses. In today's global marketplace, many companies find themselves working with international suppliers. Once a business considers purchasing materials from a supplier in a different country or even a deferent region of their home country, the company is tied to environmental and social concerns in that area. Consider a company that has an assembly plant in a different country. That company is now tied to the social conditions there. To keep its supplier operating or keep an assembly plant running smoothly, the company has a vested interest in the quality of the schools in that area so that the local workforce is educated.

Many people have purchased the Apple iPhone but few were aware of the working conditions of Apple suppliers. An audit of Apple's supplier factories in China revealed the use of underage workers, environmental violations, and unsafe worker conditions sometimes so severe that there were suicide attempts by workers.

Marketing and Consumer Issues

Marketing can often present ethical challenges. In addition to issues regarding truth in advertising, marketers must consider messages that may be manipulative even if they are not outright lies. For example, several major fashion labels like Prada, Versace, and Armani have agreed to ban size-zero models from their fashion shows. As more medical authorities have linked the viewing of these images with an increase in eating disorders, the fashion industry is faced with a decision. There are many marketing and consumer issues that companies must consider if they are to behave in a socially responsible way. What do you think? Is the use of size-zero professional models socially irresponsible? How do we judge when responsible behavior turns into irresponsible behavior?

Environmental, Health, and Safety Concerns

Many industries, even small companies, make decisions every day that affect the environment and the safety of their workers or neighbors. From multinational manufacturing giants to the local auto body shop, any industry involved with processes that produce toxic waste must make decisions that directly affect the environment. Meanwhile, the production of toxic materials is moving at a far faster pace than the growth of proper storage and disposal facilities and techniques, so disposal becomes more and more expensive. One of the most infamous cases was documented in the award-winning book *A Civil Action* (Vintage, 1996). A high incidence of childhood leukemia appeared in a small Massachusetts town. A civil action lawsuit filed by one boy's mother ultimately found that the town water supply had been poisoned by trichloroethylene dumped by two local businesses. What are the short- and long-term costs of ignoring these concerns? Companies that have a CSR focus concentrate on ways to make such decisions in a socially sound way.

Community and "Good Neighbor" Policies

Finally, CSR is concerned with how a company affects the community, particularly the surrounding neighborhood. This issue has been a challenge for Wal-Mart for years. In the documentary *Wal-Mart: The High Cost of Low Price*, film director Robert Greenwald argues that Wal-Mart pays its associates so little that the arrival of a Wal-Mart outlet in a community actually costs the community. Because workers are paid poorly and are not offered medical benefits to cover their children, Medicaid expenditures increase. In addition, Greenwald argues that many local and smaller businesses cannot compete with the giant and are forced to close. Adding insult to injury, often a community has given Wal-Mart subsidies to attract them to the area. Finding a way to be a good corporate neighbor is important to avoid the tensions and bad publicity that Wal-Mart has struggled against.

—Adapted from Solomon, *Better Business*, 3rd ed., Pearson, 2014, pp. 64–66.

Review Test

MySkillsLab™
Complete this Exercise
on myskillslab.com

Score (number correct) ______× 10 =______%

Develop a Reading/Writing Strategy

Apply the reading/writing strategy to comprehend and respond to the following passage from a college communication textbook.

Glossary

elaborator (sentence 12): one who carefully or thoughtfully explains complicated details
procedural (sentence 17): related to the steps or process of a task
harmonizer (sentence 24): one who brings different views into agreement
expediter (sentence 28): one who ensures progress is made to complete a task

SMALL GROUP ROLES

[1]Group member roles fall into three general classes: group task roles, group building and maintenance roles, and individual roles—a classification introduced in early research (Benne & Sheats, 1948) and still widely used today (Beebe & Masterson, 2012). [2]These roles are frequently served by leaders as well.

Group Task Roles

[3]Group task roles help the group focus on achieving its goals. [4]Effective group members serve several roles. [5]Some people lock into a few specific roles, but this single focus is usually counterproductive—it's better for the roles to be spread more evenly among the members and for the roles to be alternated frequently. [6]Here are some examples of group task roles.

- [7]*The information seeker or giver or the opinion seeker or giver* asks for or gives facts or opinions, seeks clarification of issues being discussed, and presents facts or opinions to group members. [8]"Sales for May were up 10 percent. [9]Do we have the sales figures for June?"
- [10]*The initiator-contributor* presents new ideas or new perspectives on old ideas, suggests new goals, or proposes new procedures or organizational strategies. [11]"We need to also look at the amount of time visitors spend on our new site."
- [12]*The **elaborator*** gives examples and tries to work out possible solutions, trying to build on what others have said. [13]"That three-part division worked at ABC and should work here as well."
- [14]*The evaluator-critic* evaluates the group's decisions, questions the logic or practicality of the suggestions, and provides the group with both positive and negative feedback. [16]"That's a great idea, but it sounds expensive."
- [17]*The **procedural** technician or recorder* takes care of various mechanical duties, such as distributing group materials and arranging the seating; writing down the group's activities, suggestions, and decisions; and/or serving as the group's memory. [18]"We have another meeting scheduled to discuss just this issue, so perhaps we can skip it for today."

CONTINUED

Group Building and Maintenance Roles

[19]No group can be task oriented at all times. [20]Group members have varied interpersonal relationships, and these need to be nourished if the group is to function effectively. [21]Group members need to be satisfied if they are to be productive. [22]Group building and maintenance roles serve these relationship needs. [23]Here are some examples of these roles.

- [24]*The encourager or* ***harmonizer*** provides members with positive reinforcement through social approval or praise for their ideas and mediates the various differences between group members. [25]"Pat, another great idea."
- [26]*The compromiser* tries to resolve conflict between his or her ideas and those of others and offers compromises. [27]"This looks like it could work if each department cut back at least 10 percent."
- [28]*The gatekeeper-**expediter*** keeps the channels of communication open by reinforcing the efforts of others. [29]"Those were really good ideas; we're on a roll."
- [30]*The standard setter* proposes standards for the functions of the group or for its solutions. [31]"We need to be able to increase the number of visits by several thousand a day."
- [32]*The follower* goes along with members, passively accepts the ideas of others, and functions more as an audience than as an active member. [33]"If you all agree, that's fine with me."

Individual Roles

[34]Whereas group task and group building and maintenance roles are productive and help the group achieve its goal, individual roles are counterproductive. [35]They hinder the group from achieving its goal and are individual rather than group oriented. [36]Such roles, often termed dysfunctional, hinder the group's effectiveness in terms of both productivity and personal satisfaction. [37]Here are some examples of individual roles.

- [38]*The aggressor* expresses negative evaluation of members and attacks the group. [39]"That's a terrible idea. [40]It doesn't make any sense."
- [41]*The recognition seekers and self-confessors* try to focus attention on themselves, boast about their accomplishments rather than the task at hand, and express their own feelings rather than focus on the group. [42]"The system I devised at B&B was a great success; everyone loved it. [43]We should just go with that."
- [44]*The blocker* provides negative feedback, is disagreeable, and opposes other members or suggestions regardless of their merit. [45]"You're dreaming if you think that will work."
- [46]*The special interest pleader* disregards the goals of the group and pleads the case of some special group. [47]"This solution isn't adequate; it doesn't address the needs of XYZ."
- [48]*The dominator* tries to run the group or members by pulling rank, flattering members, or acting the role of boss. [49]"I've been here the longest; I know what works and what doesn't work."

—DeVito, *The Essential Elements of Public Speaking*, 5th ed., Pearson, 2015, pp. 276–277.

Mapping: Complete the following concept map with information from the passage.

Central Idea: Group member roles fall into three general classes.		
1.	**4.**	**7.**
The information seeker/giver The opinion seeker/giver	The encourager or harmonizer	**8.**
2.	**5.**	The recognition seekers and self-confessors
The elaborator	The gatekeeper-expediter	**9.**
3.	The standard setter	The special interest pleader
The procedural technician	**6.**	The dominator

10. Based on the information in the passage, we may infer that a group member who says "What a dumb idea" is acting as
a. a dominator. **b.** an aggressor. **c.** a standard setter. **d.** a gatekeeper.

Summary Response

Restate the writer's ideas in your own words. Begin your summary response with the following: *The most important idea of "Small Group Roles" by DeVito is. . . .*

Reader Response

Assume you are a team leader of a group of workers in a local recycling business. You are meeting to discuss ways to promote your business to the community. To ensure that everyone profits from the insights of others, compose a response or two that you as a leader could make in order to deal with the five individual roles that might get in the way.

Academic Learning Log: Module Review

Summary of Key Concepts of Developing a Reading/Writing Strategy

Assess your comprehension of the reading/writing strategy.

LO1 LO2 LO3 LO4 LO5

1. The six basic phases of the reading/writing strategy are ________, ________, ________, ________, ________, and ________.

LO1 LO2 LO3

2. Before reading/writing, preread, ________, and ________.
3. A survey is a ____.
4. During reading, read, ________, and ________.
5. After reading–before writing, recite, ________, and ________.
6. Prewriting is ____.
7. Three ways to brainstorm are to ________, ________, and ________.

LO1 LO2 LO4

8. After reading, ____

LO1 LO2 LO5

9. After writing, ________, ________, and ________ your draft.
10. Proofreading is ____.

Test Your Comprehension of the Reading/Writing Strategy

Respond in your own words to the following questions and prompts.

LO1 LO2 LO3 LO4 LO5

In your own words, explain the point of developing a reading/writing strategy.

Create a concept map to illustrate the reading/writing strategy.

1. **How will I use what I have learned?** In your notebook, discuss how you will apply what you have learned about the reading/writing strategy. When will you apply this knowledge to your reading/writing strategy?
2. **What do I still need to study about the reading/writing strategy?** In your notebook, discuss your ongoing study needs. Describe what, when, and how you will continue studying and using the reading/writing strategy.

MySkillsLab™

Complete the Post-test for Module 2 in MySkillsLab.

3

LEARNING OUTCOMES

After studying this module you should be able to:

LO 1 Answer the Question "What's the Point of Learning and Using New Words?"

LO 2 Employ Context Clues to Comprehend and Make a Point

LO 3 Use Vocabulary Resources in Textbooks to Comprehend and Make a Point

Learning and Using New Words

Words are the building blocks of meaning. Have you ever watched a child with a set of building blocks such as Legos®? Hundreds of separate pieces can be joined together to create buildings, planes, cars, or even spaceships. Words are like that, too. A word is a small block of thought. Words properly joined create meaning. The more words you know, the better you can understand a writer's point. Likewise, words are the writer's most important tool. A rich **vocabulary**, the words you know, enables you to write exactly what you mean. How many words do you have in your vocabulary? If you are like most people, you know about 60,000 words by the time you are 18 years old. During your college studies, you will most likely learn an additional 20,000 words. Each subject you study will have its own set of words that you will be expected to read, comprehend, and use in writing. In everyday life, you are exposed to new words as you engage in hobbies, read and negotiate legal contracts, and purchase products and services. In working life, each job or career brings with it a specialized set of words that you will be expected to use in your communications with supervisors, coworkers, and the public. Master readers and writers constantly learn and use new words to understand and make a point.

Vocabulary is all the words a person uses or understands.

WHAT'S THE POINT of Learning and Using New Words?

Before you study this module, predict the importance of vocabulary. Consider the following images and captions. Next to each photograph, predict how learning new words relates to reading and writing in academic life, everyday life, and working life. Finally, answer the question "What's the point of learning and using new words?"

Photographic Organizer: Learning and Using New Words

What's the point of learning and using new words?

L2 Employ Context Clues to Comprehend and Make a Point

Master readers and writers interact with new words in a number of ways. One way is to use **context clues**. The word *context* means "surroundings." The meaning of a word is shaped by the words surrounding it—by its context. Master readers use context clues to learn new words or different uses for known words. Master writers employ context clues to communicate clearly and effectively to their readers.

A **context clue** is the information surrounding a new or specialized word that is provided to clarify its meaning.

There are four types of context clues:

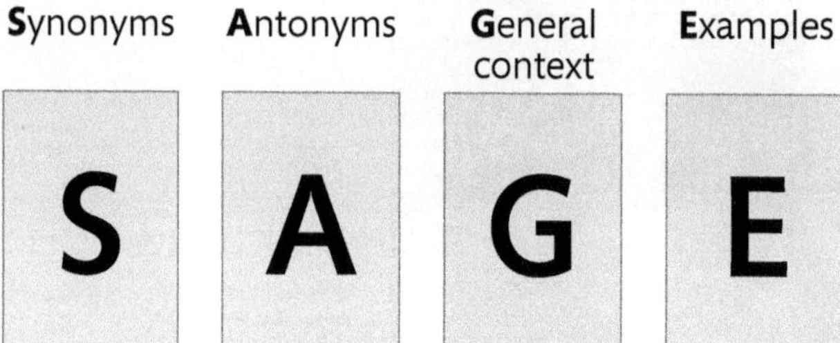

Notice that when the first letters of each type of context clue are put together, they spell the word **SAGE**. The word *sage* means "wise." Using context clues throughout the reading/writing process is a wise—SAGE—strategy.

Synonyms

A **synonym** is a word that has a meaning similar to that of another word. Many times, a writer will place a synonym near a new or difficult word or term as a context clue to the word's meaning. Usually, a synonym is set off with a signal word and a pair of commas, a pair of dashes, or a pair of parentheses before or after it.

A **synonym** is a word that has the same or nearly the same meaning as another word.

Synonym Signal Words		
or	*that*	*is*

For Module 3, assume you are taking a college philosophy course and are studying the theme of perception and reality. The Guiding Question that you will seek to answer during the module is "How do we know what is real and what is not?" After completing all assigned readings, you will write about what you have learned about perception and reality.

Example

The following passage explores the connections between our dreams and the reality of our everyday life. Before reading, skim the passage and underline the terms in **bold** and *italic* print. During reading, circle the signal words for each synonym and underline the synonym for the word in bold or italics. After reading, complete the "Write to Learn: Synonyms as Context Clues" chart with the key terms, their synonyms from the passage, and an example that you have observed or experienced. Finally, write a response to the after reading question that follows the passage.

INTERPRETING DREAMS

[1]You may have wondered whether dreams, especially those that frighten us or that recur, have hidden meanings. [2]Sigmund Freud believed that dreams function to satisfy unconscious sexual and aggressive desires. [3]Because such wishes are unacceptable to the dreamer, they have to be disguised and therefore appear in dreams in *symbolic* or representative forms. [5]Freud differentiated between the **manifest content** of a dream —the straightforward material of the dream as recalled by the dreamer—and the **latent content**—or the underlying, hidden meaning of the dream—which he considered more significant.

[6]Beginning in the 1950s, psychologists began to move away from the Freudian interpretation of dreams. [7]For example, Hall (1953) proposed a **cognitive theory** of dreaming—that is dreaming is simply thinking while asleep. [11]Hobson and McCarley (1977) advanced the **activation-synthesis hypothesis** of dreaming. [12]This *hypothesis* or explanation suggests that dreams are simply the brain's attempt to make sense of the random firing of brain cells during REM-sleep. [13]Just as people try to make sense of input from the environment during their waking hours, they try to find meaning in the *synthesis* (combination) of sensations and memories that are *activated*, or triggered, internally by this random firing of brain cells. [14]Hobson (1989) believes that dreams also have psychological significance, because the meaning a person imposes on the random mental activity reflects that person's experiences, remote memories, associations, drives, and fears.

[15]Some dream experts suggest that dreams may have more meaning than Hobson and McCarley originally theorized. [16]A survey questioning subjects about their dream content, for example, concluded that much of the content of dreams is meaningful, consistent over time, and fits in with past or present emotional concerns rather than being bizarre, meaningless and random (Damhoff, 1996, 2005). [17]Hobson and colleagues have reworked the activation-synthesis hypothesis to reflect concerns about dream meaning, calling it the **activation-information mode model**, or AIM (Hobson, et al., 2000). [18]In this newer version, information that is accessed during waking hours can have an influence on the synthesis of dreams. [19]In other words, when the brain is "making up" a dream to explain its own activation, it uses meaningful bits and pieces of the person's experiences from the previous day or last few days rather than just random items from memory.

—Adapted from Wood, Wood, and Boyd, *Mastering the World of Psychology*, 3rd ed., p. 127. and Ciccarelli and White. *Psychology*, 4th ed., Pearson, 2015, p. 152.

CONTINUED

EXAMPLE *CONTINUED*

Write to Learn: Synonyms as Context Clues		
Key Term	**Synonym**	**Example**
1. symbolic		
2. manifest content		
3. latent content		
4. hypothesis		
5. synthesis		

After Reading Written Response: After completing the chart "Write to Learn: Synonyms as Context Clues," answer the following question in the given space. Use information from your completed chart.

What is the connection between our dreams and our waking life?

Explanation

Compare your answers to the following think-aloud.

Completing the vocabulary chart deepened my understanding and helped me make connections between my prior knowledge and the new information. The chart also helped me answer the after reading question. Here are the key words, their synonyms in parentheses, and my examples. 1. Symbolic (representative); a wedding ring is symbolic of commitment. 2. Manifest content (straightforward material); I dreamed I was a child climbing a ladder I own that disappeared into the sky. 3. Latent content (underlying, hidden meaning); the disappearing ladder may symbolize life after death, success, or overcoming a problem. Latent content means both the details in a dream and the meaning of those details. 4. Synthesis (combination); my dream combined or synthesized details such as how I looked as a child and a ladder I now own. 5. Hypothesis (explanation, theory); I have studied other scientific hypotheses or theories about evolution and relativity. I noticed that the words **theory** and **hypothesis** are synonyms in this passage. Here is my written response to the question "What is the connection between our dreams and our waking life?"

Experts offer several theories about the connection between our dreams and our waking life. Freud believed that our dreams are ways we work out unconscious sexual desires and aggression. He believed our emotions greatly influence our dreams. Other experts believe that our physical brains create our dreams. When we sleep, brain cells activate physical feelings and memories and create dreams that make sense of that information. The activation-information mode model explains that our recent experiences become meaningful details in our dreams.
A recent dream of mine is an example. The manifest content was that I was a child climbing a ladder that disappeared into the sky. The dream synthesized details of my appearance as a child with a ladder I now own. I think anxiety about my new job triggered the dream.
The child may represent my new life with a new job. The ladder may symbolize my hope for success. The latent content could be that I want to be successful in my new job.

Antonyms

An **antonym** has the opposite meaning of another word. Antonyms help you understand a word's meaning by showing you what the original word is *not*. Writers use antonyms to make a point more vivid or powerful and to guide the reader to understand a deeper meaning. The following contrast words often act as signals that an antonym is being used.

An **antonym** is a word that has the opposite meaning of another word.

Antonym Signal Words			
but	*however*	*in contrast*	*instead*
not	*on the other hand*	*unlike*	*yet*

Sometimes antonyms appear next to the contrasting word. In those cases, commas, dashes, or parentheses set them off. At other times, writers place antonyms in other parts of the sentence to emphasize the difference between the ideas.

When writers use an antonym to clarify the meaning of a word, they assume that the reader knows the meaning of the antonym. However, if you are not sure of the meaning of the antonym, you can use two steps to understand the key term based on its antonym. First, identify the antonym given for the key term. Second, supply a word that means the opposite of the antonym used in the sentence.

Example

Assume you are continuing your study of the theme of perception and reality. Skim the following passage from a philosophy textbook to preview the terms in **bold** print. During reading, circle the signal words for antonyms and underline the key terms and their antonyms. After reading, complete the vocabulary chart. Finally, write a response to the after reading question that follows the passage.

An Introduction to Metaphysics

1Metaphysics is an area of philosophy that tries to answer this question: what is reality? 2Metaphysics seeks to discover general standardized criteria for what is real and how that differs from what may seem to be real but actually is not.

3The distinction between appearance and **reality** is already familiar to us, of course, through common sense and ordinary language. 4That is, we know what someone means who says that the building *appeared* to be structurally sound, but *really* was severely damaged by termites. 5What philosophers try to do is explain this difference, that is, to say why something is said to be real, or what counts as reality; in short, to state clearly the standards or criteria for what is real.

[6]Metaphysics is by far the most ancient branch of philosophy, beginning with the pre Socratic Milesian philosopher-scientists (sixth century B.C.E.), who proposed a system of methods to study **observable** rather than unseen entities. [7]They speculated on the "ageless, deathless" substance underlying the changing **temporal** world. [8]Some thought this was water, others air, and still others felt there had to be more than one basic ingredient in order to account for the enormous variety of things in the world. [9]For many centuries this occupied the central place in philosophy. [10]Originally called First Philosophy, metaphysics was thought to be the necessary starting point, or foundation, for all the other areas of philosophy. [11]Before one could reasonably decide in moral philosophy, one must consider the nature of values. [12]For example, if values are relative opposed to **absolute**, one must first decide whether values are the kind of thing that can exist independently of human perception. [13]If so, then values could indeed be absolute, but if not, then all values would be relative to an individual's or a society's point of view. [14]Similarly, before one could reasonably speculate on the fate of the soul after death, one would first have to determine if there *is* a soul. [15]In this sense metaphysics was seen as the most fundamental part of philosophy, presupposed by all the rest.

[16]Metaphysics, then, attempts to determine the difference between appearance and reality. [17]However, one may ask, "Is it not obvious what is real and what is not?" [18]Reality is what one can touch, see, feel, smell, taste, and hear. [19]This definition of reality establishes what can be discovered by the five senses as the basis for what is real. [20]This theory of knowledge is called **empiricism.** [21]Empirical knowledge is the kind of knowledge that comes from the senses. [22]But since there are other plausible criteria for reality that may conflict with the empiricist criterion, it is clearly not obvious that reality is limited to what we can see and touch. [23]In opposition to empiricism is a view of reality known as rationalism. [24]Rationalism relies on intellect or **reason**, not the senses, as the source of knowledge. [25]What is most real is what we know through the intellect. [26]In this sense one might conclude that the chemical elements that make up the physical world are more real than the objects that they comprise. [27]The wood is converted into paper and the paper finally burned, but the particles of carbon, which existed all along, linger on in the air. [28]One could then go a step further and reason that since the chemical elements are made out of still simpler elements (atoms and molecules), these entities are more real than the chemical elements of which they are a part.

—Adapted from Steward, Blocker, and Petrik. *Fundamentals of Philosophy*, 7th ed., Pearson, 2010, pp. 85–86.

CONTINUED

EXAMPLE *CONTINUED*

Write to Learn: Antonyms as Context Clues		
Key Term	**Antonym**	**Meanings**
1. reality		**Key term:** **Antonym:**
2. observable		**Key term:** **Antonym:**
3. absolute		**Key term:** **Antonym:**
4. empiricism		**Key term:** **Antonym:**
5. reason		**Key term:** **Antonym:**

After Reading Written Response: Answer the following question in the given space. Use information from the chart you completed.

How may metaphysics help us explain our dreams?

Explanation

Compare your answers to the following think-aloud.

Key words are followed by their definitions. Their antonyms and definitions are in parentheses. 1. Reality: things as they exist (appearance: things as they seem). 2. Observable: seen (unseen: unnoticed, invisible, hidden). 3. Absolute: independent (relative: dependent). At first, I thought **absolute** meant "unchanging." But the writer used the synonym **independently**. Thus, **relative** means that a view is dependent on something else. Like my taste in food is relative to how I feel at the time. 4. Empirical: knowledge based on the senses (rationalism: knowledge based on reason). 5. Reason: intellect (senses: feelings). The writer used the word **intellect** as a synonym for **reason**. Here is my written response:

Metaphysics seeks to explain the difference between reality and appearance. And dreams may appear as a link to reality in two ways. First, Freud stated that dreams have a manifest content that can be recalled or observed by the dreamer. The manifest content of a dream taps into the things we experience or feel during our waking life. Other experts state that dreams are the result of the physical brain activating feelings and memories to make sense of waking life. Thus, we could use empiricism to explain the feelings or sensations in our dreams. Freud also stated that dreams have latent content or hidden, symbolic meaning. To explain the symbolic meaning of our dreams we could use reason or rationalism. For example, in my dream with the ladder, I reasoned that the ladder represented success.

G

General Context

Often you will find that the writer has chosen not to provide either a synonym clue or an antonym clue. In that case, the writer expects the reader to rely on the **general context** of the passage to understand the meaning of the unfamiliar word. This involves either reading the entire sentence or looking ahead in the text for information that will help clarify the meaning of the new word.

General context is the information (words and sentences) that surrounds a word and influences or clarifies its meaning.

Information about the word can be included in the passage in several ways. Sometimes, a writer gives a definition. Other times, a writer uses vivid descriptions of a situation to convey the word's meaning. A reader has to use logic to figure out the meaning of the word.

Example

Read the following poem that, according to some critics, depicts a nightmare. Before you read, skim the poem and predict the meaning of the word *vagabonds.* During reading, underline clues to the meaning of the title. After reading, complete the vocabulary graphic organizer and write a response to the after reading question.

"Vagabonds" by Arthur Rimbaud

Pitiful brother—the dreadful nights I owed him! "I've got no real involvement in the business. I toyed with his weakness, so—it was my fault—we wound up back in exile and enslavement."

He saw me as a loser, a weird child; he added his own prods.

I answered my satanic doctor, jeering, and made it out the window. All down a landscape crossed by unheard-of music, I spun my dreams of a nighttime wealth to come.

After that more or less healthy pastime, I'd stretch out on a pallet. And almost every night, soon as I slept, my poor brother would rise—dry mouth and bulging eyes (the way he'd dreamt himself!)—and haul me into the room, howling his stupid dream.

Truly convinced, I'd vowed to take him back to his primal state—child of the sun—and so we wandered, fed on wine from the caves and gypsy bread, me bound to find the place itself and the code.

After Reading Written Response: Answer the following question in the given space. Use information from the chart you completed. *Based on details given in this poem—the manifest content of the nightmare—how does Rimbaud define the word* vagabonds?

Write to Learn: General Sense of the Passage as a Context Clue

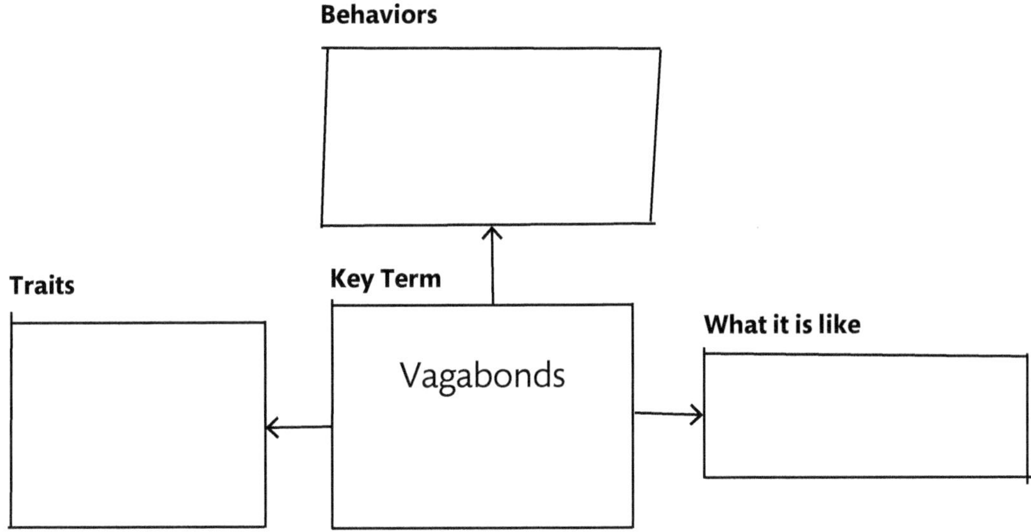

Explanation

Compare your answers to the following student's think-aloud.

I underlined these clues: Traits—pitiful, no involvement, loser, and weird. Behaviors—made it out the window, stretch out on a pallet, wandered, to find. What it is like—exile and enslavement, a gypsy. Here is my response to the after reading question:

The manifest content of vagabonds are images of them as "pitiful . . . loser . . . weird," with "no involvement," gypsies in "exile and enslavement." They "wander . . . to find" a place, crawl out windows, and "stretch out on pallets." Vagabonds are drifters outside of society.

Examples

Many times a writer will state the meaning of a new or difficult word and then provide **examples** of it. To further clarify, a writer may also include examples of what the word is *not*. The following signal words often introduce an example.

An **example** is a person, place, or thing that represents, illustrates, or models a meaning of a word.

Example Signal Words				
consists of	*for example*	*for instance*	*including*	*such as*

Colons and dashes can also indicate examples.

Example

Assume you are continuing your studies on the theme of perception and reality. Read the following article. Before reading, skim the passage and underline the key terms each time they are repeated. During reading, circle examples of the terms. After reading, complete the vocabulary graphic organizer. Then write a response to the after reading question.

Why Zombies, Robots, and Clowns Freak Us Out

1What do zombies and androids have in common? 2They're almost human, but not quite. 3That disconnect is creepy, in a way that scientists are searching to understand.

4The *uncanny valley* is the idea that as a robot's appearance becomes more and more humanlike, we don't always respond to it more positively. 5Rather, there's a point on the scale between robot and human where we are repulsed. 6If it's mechanical but not entirely human, a robot seems disturbing.

7Why would that be? 8It would make sense that as human likeness increases in a robot, so would our comfort with it. 9But on a graph showing that relationship, there's a "valley" where this familiarity dips down into creepiness, and then comes back up again with more human characteristics.

[10]You may have experienced feeling this while watching animated movies that incorporate humanlike forms. [11]It's also the reason that you might get freaked out by clowns or by photos of people with extreme plastic surgeries who don't look quite real anymore. [12]Our brains come to an impasse when we see something that resembles a member of our species but just doesn't make the cut.

[13]Some animators sidestep the issue: in the movie "WALL-E," for example, the main character has eyes but is not very humanlike otherwise; he is clearly a robot. [14]His friend, EVE, looks like a white shape with eyes. [15]Both express emotions clearly but don't try to mimic the human shape or form [16]And HAL 9000 from "2001: A Space Odyssey" is just a red camera eye, but it too conveys feelings.

[17]But when you get more humanlike, things get weird. [18]Some reviewers were put off by the characters in the film "Polar Express," for instance.

[19]Then there are the Na'vi in "Avatar," who have many physical human characteristics in addition to morphed features and tails. [20]But they are also blue, creating a sense of "otherness" that may have made them less distasteful to viewers—in other words, they were sufficiently un-human.

—From "Why Zombies, Robots, and Clowns Freak Us Out," by Elizabeth Landau, CNN.com, 27 Sept 2012. <http://www.cnn.com/2012/07/11/health/uncanny-valley-robots/> Reprinted with permission.

Write to Learn: Examples as Context Clues

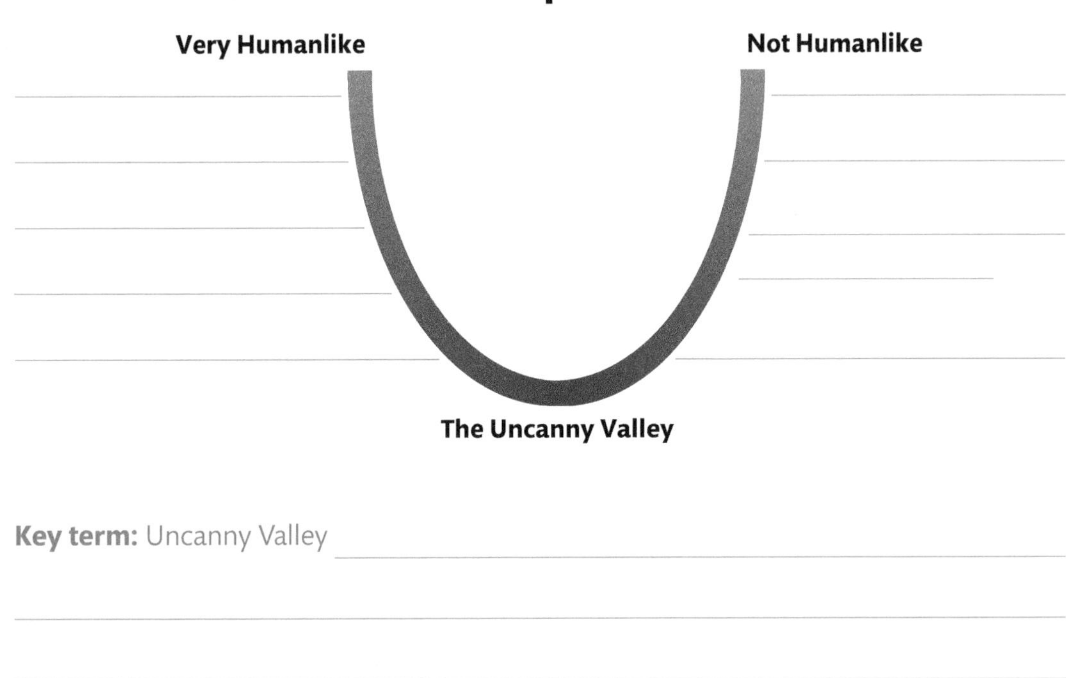

Key term: Uncanny Valley

CONTINUED

EXAMPLE *CONTINUED*

After Reading Written Response: Answer the following question in the given space. Use information from the chart you completed. *How does the "uncanny valley" engage empirical knowledge (see page 101) in our attempt to make the distinction between appearance and reality?*

Explanation

Compare your answers to the following think-aloud.

I combined and condensed the details from sentences 4 and 5 to summarize a definition for **uncanny valley** in one sentence. Examples of creatures on the too-humanlike side of the uncanny valley include zombies, androids (humanlike robots), clowns, extreme plastic surgeries, and the characters from **Polar Express.** To clarify the meaning of this "valley," the writer also gave examples of what are on the opposite side of the valley or how some animators avoid the "creepiness" issue. These examples include WALL-E, his friend EVE, Hal 9000, from **2001: A Space Odyssey,** and the Na'vi in **Avatar**. All of these examples have traits that make it clear they are not human. Here is my response to the after reading question:

Empirical knowledge is based on the information we gain from our five senses. The uncanny valley comes into play through our sense of sight. When we see an image of something like a zombie or an android that looks almost human, but isn't, we are uncomfortable with the visual distortion; it creeps us out.

So far, you have used context clues and vocabulary graphic organizers to comprehend a passage. Often, writers also use vocabulary graphic organizers or outlines to brainstorm ideas. By identifying key terms and generating context clues using **SAGE**, a master writer creates details to summarize or support a central point about an idea or topic.

Practice 1

Employ Context Clues to Understand and Make a Point

Assume you are continuing to read and learn about the theme "perception and reality" and have been assigned the following reading from a college psychology textbook. Before reading, skim the passage to underline the key terms highlighted in bold and italic print. During reading, annotate the passage by underlining the context clues given for key terms. After reading, complete the outline of the key concepts and answer the questions that follow the passage.

Sensation and Perception

[1]Have you ever wondered how your brain—locked in the dark, silent chamber of the skull—experiences the blaze of color in a van Gogh painting, the driving melodies and rhythms of rock 'n' roll, the refreshing taste of watermelon on a hot day, the soft touch of a child's kiss, or the fragrance of wildflowers in the springtime?

[2]Your experience of the world relies on processes of *perception.* [3]The term **perception**, in its broad usage, refers to the overall process of apprehending objects and events in the environment—to sense them, understand them, recognize and label them, and prepare to react to them. [4]A *percept* is what is perceived—the ***phenomenological***, or experienced, outcome of the process of perception. [5]Your perceptual processes serve the dual functions of *survival* and *sensuality.* [6]These processes help you survive by sounding alarms of danger, priming you to take swift action to ward off hazards, and directing you toward agreeable experiences. [7]These processes also provide you with sensuality. [8]Sensuality is the quality of being devoted to the gratification of the senses; it entails enjoying the experiences that appeal to your various senses of sight, sound, touch, taste, and smell.

[9]The process of perception is best understood divided into three stages: sensation, perceptual organization, and identification (or recognition) of objects. [10]**Sensation** is the process by which stimulation of ***sensory receptors***—the structures in your eyes: ears, and so on—produces neural impulses that represent experiences inside or outside the body. [11]For example, sensation provides the basic facts of the visual field. [12]Nerve cells in your eyes pass information along to cells in your brain.

[13] **Perceptual organization** refers to the stage in which your brain integrates evidence from your senses with prior knowledge of the world to form an ***internal*** representation of an external stimulus. [14]With respect to vision, organizational processes provide estimates of an object's likely size, shape, movement, distance, and orientation. [15]These mental activities most often occur swiftly and efficiently, without conscious awareness.

[16]The processes of **identification and recognition** assign meaning to percepts. [17]With respect to vision, earlier stages of perception answer the question "What does the object look like?" [18]At this stage, the questions become those of identification—"What is this object?"—and recognition "What is the object's function?" [20]You identify circular objects as baseballs, coins, clocks, oranges, and moons; you identify people as male or female, friend or foe, relative or rock star.

[21]In everyday life, perception seems to be entirely effortless. [22]You have very little awareness that you require these different stages of processing to arrive at a meaningful understanding of the world.

—Gerrig, *Psychology and Life*, 20th ed., Pearson, 2013, p. 80.

CONTINUED

PRACTICE 1 *CONTINUED*

1. The best meaning of the word **perception** as used in sentence 3 is
   - **a.** emotion.
   - **b.** intellect.
   - **c.** comprehension.
   - **d.** distortion.

2. The context clue given for *perception* is ________________________.

3. The best meaning of the word **phenomenological** as used in sentence 4 is
   - **a.** events one lives through.
   - **b.** natural.
   - **c.** unrealistic.
   - **d.** imagined.

4. The context clue given for *phenomenological* is ____________.

5. The best meaning of **sensory receptors** as used in sentence 10 is
   - **a.** organs with nerve endings.
   - **b.** the ears.
   - **c.** visual receivers.
   - **d.** deliberate responses.

Vocabulary Graphic Organizer: The Process of __________

Stage 1:	→ **Stage 2:**	→ **Stage 3:**
Definition:	**Definition:**	**Definition:**
Example:	**Example:**	**Example:**

6. The context clue given for *sensory receptors* is ____________.

7. The best meaning of the word **internal** as used in sentence 13 is
   a. inward. **b.** outside. **c.** unknown. **d.** understood.

8. The context clue given for *internal* is ____________.

After Reading Written Response: Answer the following question in the given space. Use information from the chart you completed. *How is the* uncanny valley *an example of the process of perception?* To brainstorm ideas for your response, complete the vocabulary graphic organizer with information from the passages "Sensation and Perception" and "Why Zombies, Robots, and Clowns Freak Us Out" (see pages 106–107 and 109).

Vocabulary Graphic Organizer: The Process of Perception of the Uncanny Valley

Stage 1:	Stage 2:	Stage 3:
Explanation:	Explanation:	Explanation:
Example:	Example:	Example:

L3 Use Vocabulary Resources in Textbooks to Comprehend and Make a Point

Writers and publishers offer a wide range of vocabulary resources in textbooks to support learning and deepen understanding. The following three suggestions offer ways to tap into a textbook's vocabulary resources.

Identify Content (Subject Area) Words

Many students think they should be able to pick up a textbook and simply read it. However, a textbook is written for a content or subject area, such as math, history, or English. Each content area has its own vocabulary. For example, a history textbook takes a different approach than a literature textbook. Various courses may use the same words, but these words often take on a new or different meaning in the context of the content area. Usually, new or specialized content words are highlighted in **bold** or *italic* print. Before reading or writing, skim a passage for content words.

Look for Textbook Definitions

In addition to highlighting new or specialized content words, textbooks usually also provide a definition for the word. Many times an example is given to illustrate the word's meaning. Context clues are helpful. As you read, annotate key terms, definitions, and examples.

Use a Glossary

Since each subject or content area has its own specific vocabulary, many textbooks provide an extra section at the back of the book called a **glossary** that alphabetically lists all the specialized terms, along with their definitions. Other textbooks may provide short glossaries within each chapter; in these cases, the glossaries may appear in the margins or in highlighted boxes where the words first appear, or they may appear at the end of each chapter. The meanings given in a glossary are limited to the way in which the word is used in that content area.

A **glossary** is a list of selected words and their definitions as used in a specific area of study.

There are many opportunities to use content words, textbook definitions, and glossaries in your reading/writing strategy. Before reading, skim the section for specialized terms (these words may be in **bold** or *italic* print). Call up prior knowledge—what you already know—about the terms. During reading, annotate the glossary words where they appear in the text. After reading, write vocabulary review lists using glossary terms by paraphrasing or restating the definitions in your own words. Before writing, use content words, textbook definitions, or the glossary to brainstorm ideas for a draft. During revision and proofreading, check your usage and spelling against the textbook's vocabulary resources.

Example

The following selection is from a college humanities textbook. Before reading, use the textbook resources to survey the text and call up your prior knowledge. As you read the passage, annotate the terms where they appear in the text. After reading, complete the vocabulary review list and answer the after reading question that follows the passage.

The Dreamwork of Surrealist Painting

Andre Breton

[1]In his 1924 *Surrealist Manifesto,* the French writer, poet, and theorist Andre Breton [bruh-TOHN] (1896–1966) credited Freud with encouraging his own creative endeavors: [2]"It would appear that it is by sheer chance that an aspect of intellectual life—and by far the most important in my opinion—about which no one was supposed to be concerned any longer has, recently, been brought back to light. [3]Credit for this must go to Freud. [4]On the evidence of his discoveries a current of opinion is at last developing which will enable the explorer of the human mind to extend his investigations, since he will be empowered to deal with more than merely summary realities." [5]Breton had trained as a doctor and had used Freud's technique of free association when treating shell-shock victims in World War I. [6]As his definition indicates, he had initially conceived of **Surrealism** as a literary movement, with Breton himself at its center. [7]All of the Surrealists had been active Dadaists, but as opposed to **Dada's** "anti-art" spirit, their new "surrealist" movement believed in the possibility of a "new art." [8]Nevertheless, Surrealism retained much of Dada's spirit of revolt.

Picasso's Surrealism

[9]Breton argued that Picasso led the way to Surrealist art in his *Les Demoiselles d'Avignon,* which jettisoned art's dependence on external reality. [10]The great founder of **Cubism**, Breton said, possessed "the facility to give materiality to what had hitherto remained in the domain of pure fantasy." [11]Picasso was attracted to the Surrealist point of view because it offered him new directions and possibilities. [12]He was obsessed with the duality of experience, the same opposition between Thanatos (the death drive) and Eros (the sex drive) that Freud had outlined in *Beyond the* ***Pleasure Principle****.* [13]Picasso's work addresses Surrealism's most basic theme—the self in all its complexity. [14]And he adds one more important theme—the self in relation to the **Other**—the dynamic interplay between the conscious and the unconscious selves.

Surrealism A 20th-century movement in art and literature that sought to release the creative potential of the unconscious mind.

Dada A 20th-century movement that developed among European artists and writers as a result of disillusionment with World War I; its founders claimed that it meant nothing, just as in the face of war, life itself had come to seem meaningless.

Cubism An art style developed by Pablo Picasso and Georges Braque, noted for the geometry of its forms, its fragmentation of the object, and its abstraction.

Pleasure Principle The instinctual seeking of pleasure and avoiding of pain in order to satisfy biological and psychological needs.

Other A general term in philosophy that opposes the given norm, identity, or self.

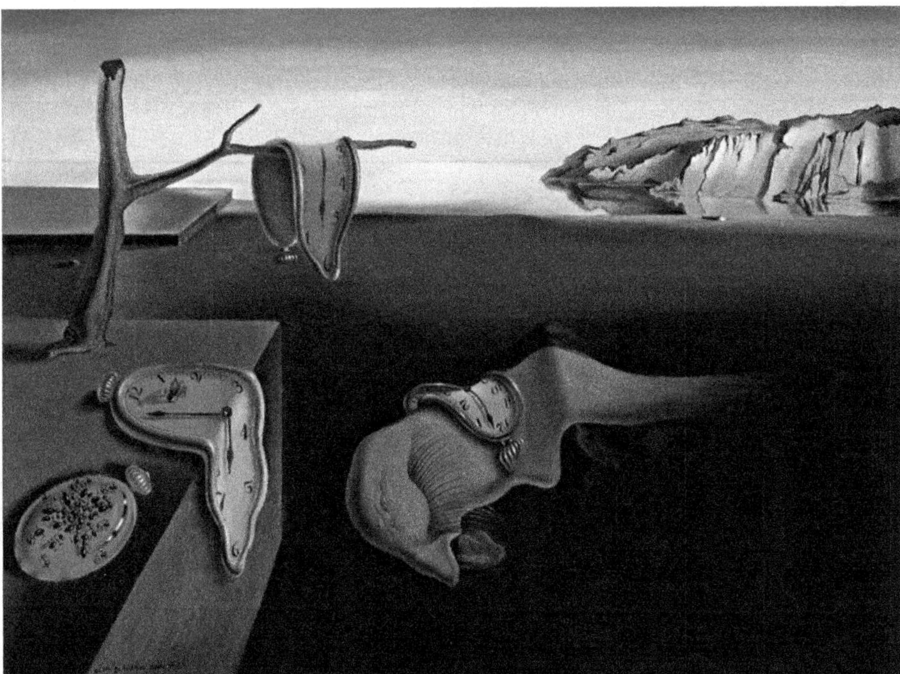

Figure 24-42; *The Persistence of Memory,* Salvador Dalí, 1931

CONTINUED

EXAMPLE *CONTINUED*

Paranoiac Description of a mental state of distrust, involving distorted views, delusions, or hallucinations.

Automatism A technique involving a trancelike state to express the creative force of the unconscious mind in art.

Salvador Dalí's Surrealism

[15]This sense of self-alienation is central to work of Spanish artist Salvador Dalí [dah-LEE] (1904–1989), who in 1928, at age 24, was introduced to the Surrealists by Joan Miró. [16]Already eccentric and flamboyant, Dalí had been expelled from the San Fernando Academy of Fine Arts two years earlier for refusing to take his final examination, claiming that he knew more than the professor who was to examine him. [17]He brought this same daring self-confidence to the Surrealist movement. [18]Among the first paintings he executed under the influence of the Surrealists is *The Lugubrious Game*, in which he confronts the "lugubrious"—or mournful and gloomy—side of sexuality. [19]He followed, he said a "**paranoiac** critical method," a brand of self hypnosis that he claimed allowed him to hallucinate freely. [20]"I believe the moment is at hand," he wrote in a description of his method, "when, by a paranoiac and active advance of the mind, it will be possible (simultaneously with **automatism**...) to systematize confusion and thus to help to discredit the world of reality." [21]He called his images "new and menacing," and works such as the famous 1931 *The Persistence of Memory* (fig. 24-42) are precisely that. [22]This work is a self-portrait of the sleeping Dalí, who lies slug like in the middle of the painting draped beneath the coverlet of time. [23]Ants, which are the symbol of death, crawl over a watchcase. [24]A fly alights on the watch dripping over the ledge, and another limp watch hangs from a dead tree that gestures towards the sleeping Dalí.

—Sayre, *Discovering the Humanities*. Pearson, 2010, pp. 446–447.

Vocabulary Review List		
Key Terms	**Definition**	**Example**
Cubism		
Dada		
Paranoiac		
Surrealism		

After Reading Written Response: Answer the following questions in the given space. Use information from the chart you completed. *What is the relationship among surrealism, reality, sensation, and perception (page 109)? How does the poem "Vagabonds" by Arthur Rimbaud (page 104) illustrate this relationship?*

Explanation

Compare your responses to the following think-aloud.

Before I read the passage, I looked over all the terms in the glossary and read their definitions. Then, as I read, I underlined the following key details: Surrealism retained much of Dada's spirit of revolt; Picasso, founder of Cubism, gives materiality to pure fantasy; Picasso addresses Surrealism's most basic theme—the self in all its complexity; the conscious and the unconscious selves; artist Salvador Dalí followed "paranoiac critical method," a brand of self hypnosis that he claimed allowed him to hallucinate freely, "to systematize confusion and thus to help to discredit the world of reality."

My annotations have created a summary of the key points in the passage. Here is my response to the after reading question:

Surrealism is an artistic revolt against the world of reality. Surrealism, like Dada, sees the real world as meaningless and distrustful. Thus, the artist seeks to express the creativity of the unconscious mind as seen in distortions, delusions, or hallucinations. Picasso created Cubism, which uses geometric forms to create artistic images. And Dalí used his "paranoiac critical method" of self hypnosis to hallucinate and create "new and menacing" images. In "Vagabonds," Rimbaud depicts his relationship with his "brother" in a nightmarish scene. In each, surrealism plays with the process of perception. Surrealist art draws a distorted view of sensations to startle us out of perceptual organization based on prior knowledge. The distorted or dreamlike images foster deeper thought about how we identify, recognize, and assign meaning to what we experience.

Practice 2

Use Vocabulary Resources in Textbooks to Comprehend and Make a Point

The following selection is from a college psychology textbook. Before reading, use the textbook resources to survey the text and call up your prior knowledge. As you read the passage, annotate the terms where they appear in the text. After reading, complete the vocabulary review list and answer the after reading question that follows the passage.

In the Beginning: Psychoanalysis

[1]So what exactly happens in psychoanalysis? [2]I've heard lots of stories about it, but what's it really like? [3]In a sense, Freud took the old method of physical cleansing to a different level. [4]Instead of a physical purge, cleansing for Freud meant removing all the "impurities" of the unconscious mind that he believed were responsible for his patients' psychological and nervous disorders. [5](Freud was a medical doctor and referred to the people who came to him for help as "patients.") [6]The impurities of the unconscious mind were considered to be disturbing thoughts, socially unacceptable desires, and immoral urges that originated in the id, the part of the personality that is itself unconscious and driven by basic needs for survival and pleasure.

[7]Because these unconscious thoughts were used by the person to prevent anxiety and would not be easily brought into conscious awareness, Freud designed a technique to help his patients feel more relaxed, open, and able to explore their innermost feelings without fear of embarrassment or rejection. [8]This method was called **psychoanalysis**, an insight therapy that emphasizes revealing the unconscious conflicts, urges, and desires that are assumed to cause disordered emotions and behavior (Freud, 1904; Mitchell & Black, 1996). [9]This is the original reason for the couch in Freud's version of psychoanalysis; people lying on the couch were more relaxed and would, Freud thought, feel more dependent and childlike, making it easier for them to get at those early childhood memories. [10]An additional plus was that he could sit behind the patients at the end of the couch and take notes. [11]Without the patients being able to see his reactions to what they said, they remained unaffected by his reactions.

psychoanalysis an insight therapy based on the theory of Freud, emphasizing the revealing of unconscious conflicts.

[12]Freud also made use of two techniques to try to get at the repressed information in his patients' unconscious minds. [13]These techniques were the interpretation of dreams and allowing patients to talk freely about anything that came to mind.

Dream Interpretation

[14]Dream interpretation, or the analysis of the elements within a patient's reported dream, formed a large part of Freud's psychoanalytic method. [15]Freud believed that repressed material often surfaced in dreams, although in symbolic form. [16]The **manifest content** of the dream was the actual dream and its events, but the **latent content** was the hidden, symbolic meaning of those events that would, if correctly interpreted, reveal the unconscious conflicts that were creating the nervous disorder (Freud, 1900).

manifest content the actual content of one's dream.

latent content the symbolic or hidden meaning of dreams.

Free Association

[17]The other technique for revealing the unconscious mind was a method originally devised by Freud's coworker, Josef Breuer (Breuer & Freud, 1895). [18]Breuer encouraged his patients to freely say whatever came into their minds without fear of being negatively evaluated or condemned. [19]As the patients talked, they began to reveal things that were loosely associated with their flow of ideas, often revealing what Breuer felt were hidden, unconscious concerns. [20]Freud adopted this method, believing that repressed impulses and other material were trying to "break free" into consciousness and would eventually surface in his patients' **free associations**.

free association psychoanalytic technique in which a patient was encouraged to talk about anything that came to mind without fear of negative evaluations.

Resistance

[21]A key element in psychoanalysis was the analysis of **resistance**, the point at which the patient becomes unwilling to talk about certain topics. [22]Freud believed that resistance from the patient meant that the conversation was coming uncomfortably close to repressed material.

resistance occurring when a patient becomes reluctant to talk about a certain topic, either changing the subject or becoming silent.

Transference

[23]In revealing more and more of their innermost feelings to the doctor, patients would begin to trust the therapist who accepted anything they said and did not criticize or punish them for saying it, as they once trusted their parents. [24]Freud believed that the therapist would then become a symbol of a parental authority figure from the past in a process he called **transference**. [25]In transference, the patient would at first transfer positive feelings for some authority figure from the past such as a mother or father. [26]"When the therapist remained neutral and seemingly unresponsive, the patient would transfer negative feelings."

transference In psychoanalysis, the tendency for a patient or client to project positive or negative feelings for important people from the past onto the therapist.

– Ciccarelli and White, *Psychology*, 2nd ed. Prentice Hall, 2009, pp. 600–601.

CONTINUED

PRACTICE 2 *CONTINUED*

After Reading Written Response: To brainstorm ideas for your response, complete the chart with definitions from this passage and give possible connections to each concept from the passage "The Dreamwork of Surrealist Painting" (page 113). Then, write your response on your own paper.

What could be possible connections between Surrealism and psychoanalysis?

Vocabulary Review List		
Key Terms	**Definition**	**Connection to "Surrealism"**
Psychoanalysis		
Manifest content		
Latent content		
Free association		
Resistance		
Transference		

Workshop: Using and Learning New Words

Assume you are continuing your study about the theme of perception and reality. All of the passages you have read throughout this module have been part of your ongoing reading assignments. Your capstone writing assignment will be a formal response to the question "How do we know what is real and what is not?" The following excerpt from Shakespeare's play *Hamlet* is your capstone reading assignment for this theme. In this scene, the ghost of the murdered King appears to his son Hamlet and Hamlet's companions. Skim through the prereading questions and then read the following passage. Then complete the activities that follow. As you read, use the footnotes as a glossary of terms to identify what the words and phrases mean as they are used in the context of the passage.

Hamlet

Act I, Scenes iv-v

SCENE IV.
The platform.

...

Enter Ghost.

HORATIO Look, my lord, it comes!

HAMLET Angels and ministers of grace defend us!
Be thou a spirit of health or goblin damned,
Bring with thee airs from heaven or blasts from hell,
Be thy intents wicked or charitable,
Thou com'st in such a questionable shape
That I will speak to thee. I'll call thee Hamlet,
King, father, royal Dane. O, answer me!
Let me not burst in ignorance, but tell
Why thy canonized bones, hearsèd in death,
Have burst their cerements; why the sepulcher,
Wherein we saw thee quietly inurned,

---

39 **ministers of grace** messengers of God
40 **Be thou** whether you are. **spirit of health** good angel
41 **Bring** whether you bring
42 **Be thy intents** whether your intentions are
43 **questionable** inviting question
47 **canonized** buried according to the canons of the church. **Hearsèd** coffined
48 **cerements** grave clothes
49 **inurned** entombed

CONTINUED

Hath oped his ponderous and marble jaws
To cast thee up again. What may this mean,
That thou, dead corpse, again in complete steel
Revisits thus the glimpses of the moon,
Making night hideous, and we fools of nature
So horridly to shake our disposition
With thoughts beyond the reaches of our souls?
Say, why is this? Wherefore? What should we do?

[*The Ghost*] *beckons* [*Hamlet*].

HORATIO It beckons you to go away with it,
As if it some impartment did desire
To you alone,

MARCELLUS Look, with what courteous action
It wafts you to a more removéd ground.
But do not go with it.

HORATIO No, by no means.

HAMLET It will not speak. Then I will follow it.

HORATIO Do not, my lord!

HAMLET Why, what should be the fear?
I do not set my life at a pin's fee,
And for my soul, what can it do to that,
Being a thing immortal as itself?
It waves me forth again: I'll follow it.

HORATIO What if it tempt you toward the flood,
my lord,
Or to the dreadful summit of the cliff

---

52 **complete steel** full armor
53 **glimpses of the moon** pale and uncertain moonlight
54 **fools of nature** mere men, limited to natural knowledge and subject to nature
55 **So . . . disposition** to distress our mental composure so violently
59 **impartment** communication
65 **fee** value
69 **flood** sea

That beetles o'er his base into the sea,
And there assume some other horrible form
Which might deprive your sovereignty of reason
And draw you into madness? Think of it.
The very place puts toys of desperation,
Without more motive, into every brain
That looks so many fathoms to the sea
And bears it roar beneath.

HAMLET It wafts me still.—Go on, I'll follow thee.

MARCELLUS You shall not go, my lord.

[They try to stop him].

HAMLET Hold off your hands!

HORATIO Be ruled. You shall not go.

HAMLET My fate cries out,
And makes each petty artery in this body
As hardy as the Nemean lion's nerve.
Still am I called. Unhand me, gentlemen.
By heaven, I'll make a ghost of him that lets me!
I say, away! Go on, I'll follow thee.

Exeunt Ghost and Hamlet.

HORATIO He waxes desperate with imagination.

MARCELLUS Let's follow. 'Tis not fit thus to obey him.

HORATIO Have after. To what issue will this come?

MARCELLUS Something is rotten in the state of Denmark.

HORATIO Heaven will direct it.

MARCELLUS Nay, let's follow him.

Exeunt.

---

71 **beetles o'er** overhangs threateningly (like bushy eyebrows) **his** its

73 **deprive . . . reason** take away the rule of reason over your mind

75 **toys of desperation** fancies of desperate acts, i.e., suicide

81 **My fate cries out** my destiny summons me

82 **petty** weak. **Artery** (through which the vital spirits were thought to have been conveyed)

83 **Nemean lion** one of the monsters slain by Herclues in his twelve labors. **Nerve** sinew

85 **lets** hinder

89 **Have after** let's go after him. **Issue** outcome

91 **it** i.e., this outcome

CONTINUED

SCENE V.

The Battlements of the castle.

Enter Ghost and Hamlet.

HAMLET Where wilt thou lead me? Speak. I'll go no further.
GHOST Mark me.
HAMLET I will
GHOST My hour is almost come,
When I to sulfurous and tormenting flames
Must render up myself.
HAMLET Alas, poor ghost!
GHOST Pity me not, but lend thy serious hearing
To what I shall unfold.
HAMLET Speak. I am bound to hear.
GHOST So art thou to revenge, when thou shalt hear.
HAMLET What?
GHOST I am thy father's spirit,
Doomed for a certain term to walk the night,
And for the day confined to fast in fires,
Till the foul crimes done in my days of nature
Are burnt and purged away. But that I am forbid
To tell the secrets of my prison house,
I could a tale unfold whose lightest word
Would harrow up thy soul, freeze thy young blood,
Make thy two eyes like stars start from their spheres,
Thy knotted and combinéd locks to part,
And each particular hair to stand an end
Like quills upon the fretful porcupine.

---

7 **bound** (1) ready (2) obligated by duty and fate. (The Ghost, in line 8, answers in the second sense.)

12 **fast** do penance by fasting

13 **crimes** sins. **Of nature** as a mortal

14 **But that** were it not that

17 **harrow up** lacerate, tear

18 **spheres** i.e., eye sockets, were compared to the orbits or transparent revolving spheres in which, according to Ptolemaic astronomy, the heavenly bodies were fixed

19 **knotted . . . locks** hair neatly arranged and confined

	But this eternal blazon must not be
	To ears of flesh and blood. List, list, O, list!
	If thou didst ever thy dear father love—
HAMLET	O God!
GHOST	Revenge his foul and most unnatural murder.
HAMLET	Murder!
GHOST	Murder most foul, as in the best it is,
	But this most foul, strange and unnatural.
HAMLET	Haste me to know 't, that I, with wings as swift
	As meditation or the thoughts of love,
	May sweep to my revenge.
GHOST	I find thee apt;
	And duller shouldst thou be than the fat weed
	That roots itself in ease on Lethe wharf,
	Wouldst thou not stir in this. Now, Hamlet, hear.
	'Tis given out that, sleeping in my orchard,
	A serpent stung me. So the whole ear of Denmark
	Is by a forgéd process of my death
	Rankly abused. But know, thou noble youth,
	The serpent that did sting thy father's life
	Now wears his crown.
HAMLET	O my prophetic soul! My uncle!
GHOST	Ay, that incestuous, that adulterate beast,
	With witchcraft of his wit, with traitorous gifts,—
	O wicked wit and gifts, that have the power
	So to seduce!—won to his shameful lust

22 **eternal blazon** revelation of the secrets of eternity
28 **in the best** even at best
33 **shouldst thou be** you were have to be. **fat** torpid, lethargic
34 **Lethe** the river of forgetfulness in Hades
36 **orchard** garden
38 **forgéd process** falsified account
39 **abused** deceived
43 **adulterate** adulterous
44 **gifts** (1) talents (2) presents

CONTINUED

The will of my most seeming-virtuous queen:
O Hamlet, what a falling off was there!
From me, whose love was of that dignity
That it went hand in hand even with the vow
I made to her in marriage, and to decline
Upon a wretch whose natural gifts were poor
To those of mine!
But virtue, as it never will be moved,
Though lewdness court it in a shape of heaven,
So lust, though to a radiant angel linked,
Will sate itself in a celestial bed
And prey on garbage.
But, soft! methinks I scent the morning air.
Brief let me be. Sleeping within my orchard,
My custom always of the afternoon,
Upon my secure hour thy uncle stole,
With juice of curséd hebona in a vial,
And in the porches of my ears did pour
The leprous distilment, whose effect
Holds such an enmity with blood of man
That swift as quicksilver it courses through
The natural gates and alleys of the body,

---

50 **even with the vow** with the very vow

53 **To** compared to

54 **virtue, as it** as virtue

55 **shape of heaven** heavenly form

57 **sate . . . bed** cease to find sexual pleasure in a virtuously lawful marriage

62 **secure** confident, unsuspicious

63 **hebona** a poison (The word seems to be a form of *ebony*, though it is thought perhaps to be related to *henbane*, a poison, or to *ebenus*, "yew.")

64 **porches of my ears** ears as a porch or entrance of the body

65 **leprous distilment** distillation causing leprosylike disfigurement

And with a sudden vigor it doth posset
And curd, like eager droppings into milk,
The thin and wholesome blood. So did it mine,
And a most instant tetter barked about,
Most lazar-like, with vile and loathsome crust,
All my smooth body.
Thus was I, sleeping, by a brother's hand
Of life, of crown, of queen at once dispatched,
Cut off even in the blossoms of my sin,
Unhouseled, disappointed, unaneled,
No reckoning made, but sent to my account
With all my imperfections on my head.
O, horrible! O, horrible, most horrible!
If thou hast nature in thee, bear it not.
Let not the royal bed of Denmark be
A couch for luxury and damnéd incest.
But, howsoever thou pursues this act,
Taint not thy mind nor let thy soul contrive
Against thy mother aught. Leave her to heaven
And to those thorns that in her bosom lodge,
To prick and sting her. Fare thee well at once.
The glowworm shows the matin to be near,
And 'gins to pale his uneffectual fire.
Adieu, adieu, adieu! Remember me.

Exit.

---

69 **posset** coagulate, curdle

70 **eager** sour, acid

72 **tetter** eruption of scabs. **Barked** covered with a rough covering, like bark on a tree

73 **lazar-like** leperlike

76 **dispatched** suddenly deprived

78 **Unhouseled** without having received the Sacrament. **Disappointed** unread (spiritually) for the last journey. **Unaneled** without having received extreme unction

79 **reckoning** settling of accounts

82 **nature** i.e., the promptings of a son

84 **luxury** lechery

90 **matin** morning

91 **his** its

CONTINUED

WORKSHOP *CONTINUED*

HAMLET

O all you host of heaven! O earth! What else?
And shall I couple hell? O, fie! Hold, hold, my heart,
And you, my sinews, grow not instant old,
But bear me stiffly up. Remember thee!
Ay, thou poor ghost, while memory holds a seat
In this distracted globe. Remember thee?
Yea, from the table of my memory
I'll wipe away all trivial fond records,
All saws of books, all forms, all pressures past
That youth and observation copied there,
And thy commandment all alone shall live
Within the book and volume of my brain,
Unmixed with baser matter. Yes, by heaven!
O most pernicious woman!
O villain, villain, smiling, damnéd villain!
My tables—meet it is I set it down
That one may smile, and smile, and be a villain.
At least I'm sure it may be so in Denmark.

[*Writing*.]

So, uncle, there you are. Now to my word:
It is "Adieu, adieu! I remember me."
I have sworn't.

---

94 **couple** add. **Hold** hold together
95 **instant** instantly
98 **globe** (1) head (2) world
99 **table** tablet, slate
100 **fond** foolish
101 **saws** wise sayings. **Forms** shapes or images copied onto the slate; general ideas. **Pressures** impressions stamped
108 **tables** writing tablets. **Meet it is** it is fitting
111 **there you are** i.e., there, I've written that down against you

–Shakespeare, William. *Hamlet, Prince of Denmark.* in The Complete Works of Shakespeare, 4th Ed. David Bevington. New York: Longman, 1997.

Preread: Survey and Question

Survey the following lists of questions that you will answer during and after reading. After surveying the questions, skim the passage to note the location of possible answers.

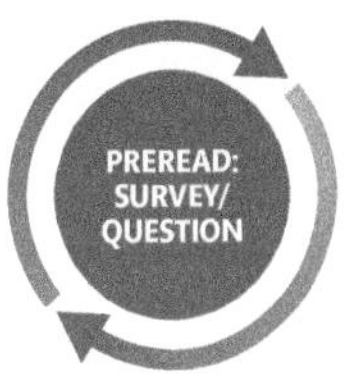

1. Is this scene a presentation of the manifest content (page 97) of a dream or does Hamlet really see his father's ghost? Explain.

2. What empirical proof (pages 101, 117) is given to support the belief that Hamlet is talking with his father's ghost? What rational explanation could be offered to support or refute that he is talking to the ghost?

3. How does your understanding of the "uncanny valley" help you identify with Hamlet in this passage? Explain. (See pages 106–107.)

4. How could the ghost of the King be a "percept" based on the three stages of perception? (See page 109.)

5. How does this scene from Hamlet answer the question "How do we know what is real and what is not?"

Read and Annotate

As you **read**, **annotate** key ideas, particularly those details that answer your prereading questions.

Recite, Review, and Brainstorm

Recite and **Review** the information: Paraphrase ideas. Summarize the most important parts. **Brainstorm** ideas for your written response to the passage: Answer your prereading questions. *Freewrite* or *map* the relationship among answers to questions or ideas you have annotated in the text. *Outline* or *list* key ideas and details in blocks of thought. Use your own paper.

Write a Draft of Your Response

Using the ideas you generated by brainstorming, compose a draft of your response. Use your own paper.

Revise Your Draft

Once you have created a draft, read it over to answer the questions in the "Questions for Revising" box that follows. Indicate your answers by annotating your paper. If you answer "yes" to a question, underline, check, or circle examples. If you answer "no" to a question, write needed information in the margins and draw lines to indicate the placement of additional details. Revise your essay based on your reflection. (*Hint:* Experienced writers create several drafts as they focus on one or two questions per draft.)

Step by Step: Questions for Revising

- ☐ Have I stated or implied a focused central idea?
- ☐ Is the logical order of ideas clear? Have I used strong transitions to guide my reader, such as *first, second, next,* etc.?
- ☐ Have I made my point with adequate details?
- ☐ Have I included only the details that are relevant to my central point?
- ☐ Have I offered context clues to clarify the meaning of key words?

Proofread Your Draft

Once you have made any revisions to your essay that may be needed, proofread your essay to eliminate careless errors.

MySkillsLab™
Complete this Exercise on myskillslab.com

Reading and Writing for Everyday Life

Assume you or someone you know is a caregiver to an elderly person who has been diagnosed with low bone density. The doctor has given you the following information to review. Read the information and write a plan of action that will help combat the loss of bone density for the person you care about. Use your own paper.

HOW DO BONES STAY HEALTHY?

Although the shape and size of bones do not significantly change after puberty, bone density—the compactness and strength of bones—continues to develop into early adulthood. *Peak bone density* is the point at which bones are strongest because they are at their highest density. About 90% of a woman's bone density is built by 17 years of age. For men, peak bone density occurs during their twenties. However, male or female, before we reach the age of 30 years, our bones have reached peak density, and by age 40, our bone density has begun its irreversible decline.

Just as other body cells die off and are continually replaced, bone mass is regularly recycled. This process, called remodeling, involves two steps: the breakdown of existing bone and the formation of new bone. Bone is broken down by cells called osteoclasts, which erode the bone surface by secreting enzymes and acid that dig grooves into the bone matrix. New bone is formed through the action of cells called osteoblasts, or "bone builders." These cells work to synthesize new bone matrix in the eroded areas. Around 40 years of age, bone breakdown begins to outpace bone formation, and this imbalance results in a gradual loss in bone density.

Achieving a high peak bone density requires adequate intake of the four minerals: calcium, phosphorus, magnesium, and fluoride. Adequate protein and vitamins D and K are also essential. In addition to nutrients, healthy bone density requires regular weight bearing exercises, such as weight lifting, strength training, rope jumping, tennis, jogging and walking, even jumping jacks, all of which appropriately stress bones and stimulate their growth.

—Adapted from Thompson and Moore. *Nutrition for Life*, 3rd ed., Pearson, 2013, pp. 211–213.

Reading and Writing for College Life

Assume you volunteer as a student counselor at your college or university, and you have been asked to lead a training session for the other counselors on positive thinking for success. In your research to prepare for your training seminar, you found the following information in your student success textbook. Read the passage and write a multimedia presentation using key words from the passage that identify the need for reframing one's thinking and illustrate ways to do so. Use your own paper.

REFRAME YOUR THINKING: WHAT ATTITUDE DO YOU PRESENT? 20

REFRAME YOUR THINKING: What Attitude Do You Present?

Your attitude will influence not only what you think about yourself but also what others think about you. You really have two choices: You can assume a positive or a negative attitude in any situation; in the same way you can choose to have good or bad stress dominate your life.

Did you ever hear a weather forecaster describe the conditions as partly sunny or partly cloudy? Aren't these the same conditions stated from a different perspective? Is this going to be a good day or a bad day for you? Which would you pick? Your answer depends on your attitude: You decide whether the glass is half empty or half full. People with *positive attitudes* would say the glass is half full: It's a partly sunny day and it is going to be a good one. However, people with *negative attitudes* see a half-empty glass and complain about the partly cloudy weather and the lousy day they are sure they will have. In addition, they might try to blame it all on someone else. Which person is more enjoyable to work with? The two following images shows how just a look can convey an attitude.

Reframing your attitude simply means looking at things in a more positive way. It's best to start off believing you are going to have a good day but, in reality, things may happen to make your day go differently than planned. That's life. Positive thinkers will make the best of it and *reframe* their thinking. Let's say you were in a doctor's waiting room for over an hour, waiting for your appointment. Look at how people with two different attitudes would approach the situation:

The Negative Attitude. As you might expect, the people with negative attitudes would become very upset. Their blood pressure would rise, and the interaction with their doctor would not be pleasant. In their anger, they may not thoroughly communicate information that could *affect* their treatment. After they leave, things could *snowball*: The rest of their *interactions* that day might be somewhat *hostile*; they might have a bad day at work or school, develop a tension headache, and have a difficult time sleeping at night. Because of a lack of restful sleep, the next day will already start off on a bad note.

The Positive Attitude. People with positive attitudes may initially feel upset, but they will regain their composure and reframe their thinking from anger to *acceptance*. They realize they have *no control* over the situation and must simply wait to see their doctor. There is no sense ruining the rest of their day. Positive people may sit back and take a few deep breaths and then do something *constructive*. They may have taken some work with them to the doctor's office just in case this happens. By getting their work done while waiting, they have turned a *potentially negative experience* into a positive one and can later go out to that movie they wanted to see.

Though written over 100 years ago, this poetic quote continues to ring true:

PIECE OF WISDOM

"Mind is the Master power that moulds and makes,
And Man is Mind, and evermore he takes
The tool of Thought, and, shaping what he wills,
Brings forth a thousand joys, a thousand ills: -
He thinks ill secret, and it comes to pass:
Environment is but his looking-glass."

—James Allen, Author of As a Man Thinketh

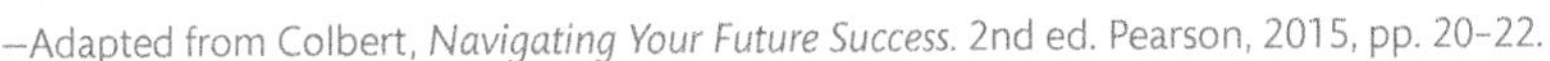

–Adapted from Colbert, *Navigating Your Future Success*. 2nd ed. Pearson, 2015, pp. 20–22.

Reading and Writing for Working Life

Assume you work at a small business that is under new management. The new leadership is offering employees an opportunity to voice their preferences for the type of retirement plan the company would like to offer. Read the following memo from the Human Resources Department. Compose an e-mail in response as requested. Use your own paper.

To: All employees
From: Human Resources
RE: Retirement Plans

Our company is in the process of researching various retirement plans to implement in the near future. As part of our research, we are asking for your input. Please read over the attachment about three types of retirement plans. Please indicate which one you prefer and why.

A **401(k) plan** is a defined contribution plan in which pretax dollars are invested in a bundle of investments that are generally managed by an outside investment company, such as the Vanguard Group or Fidelity Investments. The amount of the annual contribution is determined by the employee as a percentage of salary up to a specified legal limit. In some cases, a company will match a portion of the employee's contribution to the account.

Pension plans are another kind of retirement benefit that some companies offer their full-time employees. There are two types of pension plans:

- With *defined benefit plans,* employees know ahead of time how much pension they will receive when they retire. Defined benefit plans are not popular with employers, as a company takes on the financial risk if the fund's investments do not perform as expected.
- *Defined contribution plans* specify the annual amount employees will contribute to their pension plan through payroll deductions. With defined contribution plans, the actual amount received at retirement depends on the amount contributed and the fund's investment earnings. The burden of risk falls on employees with defined contribution plans, and there is no way they can determine how much will ultimately be available until they actually retire.

Profit-sharing plan is a term used for a range of different types of compensation options. At many businesses, profit sharing means that if the company hits certain profit targets, then there is a bonus structure for employees. Sometimes the term *profit sharing* is used for company contributions to an employee retirement plan. Profit sharing plans are often offered as a part of executive compensation in larger companies, but in many small companies, they are a way to motivate employees, especially during the start-up phase when cash is tight and salaries may be low.

—Solomon, *Better Business*, 3rd ed., Pearson, 2014, p. 268.

Review Test

MySkillsLab™
Complete this Exercise
on myskillslab.com

Score (number correct) _____ × 10 = _____%

Study the glossary and survey the passage from a college sociology textbook. Locate the terms from the glossary in the passage; circle the terms and underline the definitions as they are worded in context. Then read the passage and respond to the questions and activities.

Glossary

megacity (sentence 29): a city of 10 million or more residents
megalopolis (sentence 24): an urban area consisting of at least two metropolises and their many suburbs
metropolis (sentence 14): a central city surrounded by smaller cities and their suburbs
urbanization (sentence 2): the process by which an increasing proportion of the population live in cities and have growing influence on the culture

The Process of Urbanization

[1]Although cities are not new to the world scene, urbanization is. [2] **Urbanization** refers to masses of people moving to cities, and these cities having a growing influence on society. [3]Urbanization is taking place all over the world. [4]In 1800, only 3 percent of the world's population lived in cities (Hauser and Schnore 1965). [5]Then in 2007, for the first time in history, more people lived in cities than in rural areas. [6]Urbanization is uneven across the globe. [7]For the industrialized world, it is 77 percent, and for the Least Industrialized Nations, it is 41 percent (Haub 2006; Robb 2007). [8]Without the Industrial Revolution, this remarkable growth could not have taken place, for an extensive infrastructure is needed to support hundreds of thousands and even millions of people in a relatively small area.

[9]To understand the city's attraction, we need to consider the "pulls" of urban life. [10]Because of its exquisite division of labor, the city offers incredible variety—music ranging from rap and salsa to country and classical, shops that feature imported delicacies from around the world and those that sell special foods for vegetarians and diabetics. [11]Cities also offer anonymity, which so many find refreshing in light of the tighter controls of village and small-town life. [12]And, of course, the city offers work.

[13]Some cities have grown so large and have so much influence over a region that the term *city* is no longer adequate to describe them. [14]The term **metropolis** is used instead. [15]This term refers to a central city surrounded by smaller cities and their suburbs. [16]They are linked by transportation and communication and connected economically, and sometimes politically, through county boards and regional governing bodies. [17]St. Louis is an example.

[18]Although this name, St. Louis, properly refers to a city of 340,000 people in Missouri, it also refers to another 2 million people who live in more than a hundred separate towns in both Missouri and Illinois. [19]Altogether, the

CONTINUED

region is known as the "St. Louis or Bi-State Area." [20]Although these towns are independent politically, they form an economic unit. [21]They are linked by work (many people in the smaller towns work in St. Louis or are served by industries from St. Louis), by communications (they share the same area newspaper and radio and television stations), and by transportation (they use the same interstate highways, the Bi-State Bus system, and international airport). [22]As symbolic interactionists would note, shared symbols (the Arch, the Mississippi River, Busch Brewery, the Cardinals, the Rams, the Blues—both the hockey team and the music) provide the residents a common identity.

[23]Most of the towns run into one another, and if you were to drive through this metropolis, you would not know that you were leaving one town and entering another—unless you had lived there for some time and were aware of the fierce small town identifications and rivalries that coexist within this overarching identity.

[24]Some metropolises have grown so large and influential that the term **megalopolis** is used to describe them. [25]This term refers to an overlapping area consisting of at least two metropolises and their many suburbs. [26]Of the twenty or so megalopolises in the United States, the three largest are the Eastern seaboard running from Maine to Virginia, the area in Florida between Miami, Orlando, and Tampa, and California's coastal area between San Francisco and San Diego. [27]The California megalopolis extends into Mexico and includes Tijuana and its suburbs.

[28]This process of urban areas turning into a metropolis, and a metropolis developing into a megalopolis, occurs worldwide. [29]When a city's population hits 10 million, it is called a **megacity**. [30]In 1950, New York City was the only megacity in the world. [31]Today there are 19. [32]The largest of these are shown in the figure "The 20 Largest Cities in the World." [33]Megacities are growing so rapidly that by the year 2025 there are expected to be twenty-seven. [34]As you can see, most megacities are located in the Least Industrialized Nations.

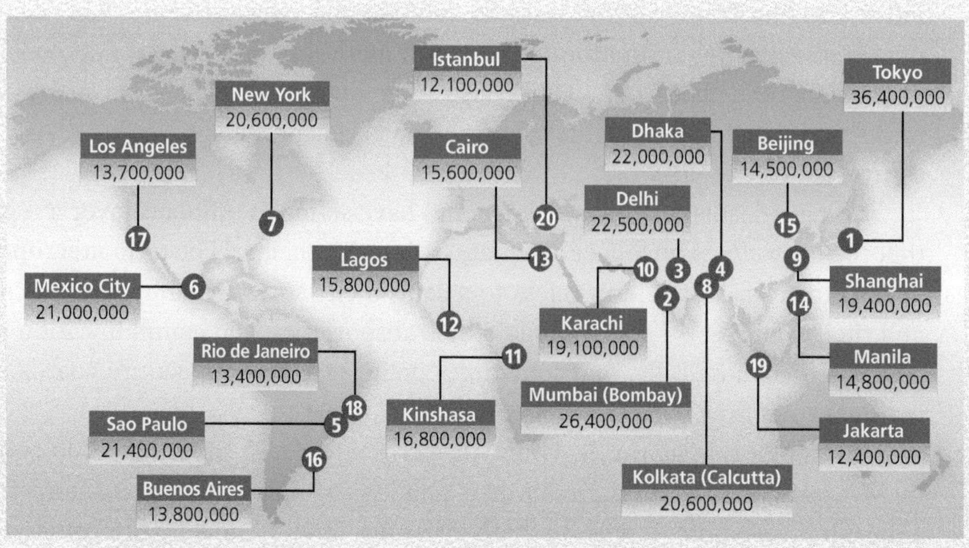

—Henslin, *Sociology: A Down-to-Earth Approach*, 10th ed., pp. 608–609. Figure source: By the author. Based on United Nations 2008: Table 3.

1. According to the passage, St. Louis is an example of a
   a. megalopolis. **c.** metropolis.
   b. megacity. **d.** city.

2. According to the passage, the area of California that extends into Mexico and includes Tijuana and its suburbs is an example of a
   a. megalopolis. **c.** metropolis.
   b. megacity. **d.** city.

3. According to the passage, New York City is an example of a
   a. megalopolis. **c.** metropolis.
   b. megacity. **d.** city.

4. Based on information in the passage, we may infer that urbanization focuses on
   a. the process and influence of expanding populations in cities.
   b. the problems of overpopulation of cities.
   c. the attractions of large cities.
   d. the flight of people from large cities.

Complete the following flow chart with key words from the passage.

Urbanization: **(5)** ______

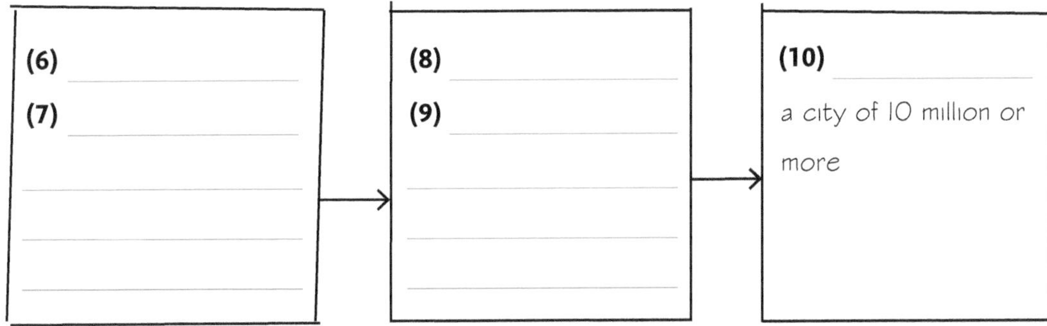

Summary Response

Restate the author's most important idea in your own words using some of the words in **bold** print. Begin your summary response with the following: *The most important idea of "The Process of Urbanization" by Henslin is. . . .*

Reader Response

What type of community do you live in? How has urbanization affected your area? Write an article for a local publication that describes your vision for how the city should grow or control growth. Consider the following:

Describe your community.
Identify strengths in your community.
Identify problems in your community.

MySkillsLab™
Complete this Exercise
on myskillslab.com

Academic Learning Log: Module Review

Summary of Key Concepts of Learning and Using New Words

Assess your comprehension of learning and using new words.

LO1 LO2

1. Vocabulary is ____.
2. **SAGE** stands for the four context clues: ____.
3. A synonym is ____.
4. An antonym is a ____.
5. General context is ____.
6. A reader ____________ and a writer ____________ the meaning of a word based on the general context of a passage.
7. An example is ____.

LO1 LO3

8. Textbook vocabulary resources include ____________, ____________, and a ____________.
9. Content words are often indicated by ____________ or ____________ print.
10. A glossary is a ____.

Test Your Comprehension of Learning and Using New Words

Respond in your own words to the following questions and prompts.

LO1 LO2 LO3

In your own words, what is vocabulary? Identify the most helpful skill you have learned.

Create a glossary of four terms that you have learned about the reading/writing strategy in Modules 1, 2, and 3. Quickly skim each module for words in bold print or that have textbook definitions provided. (For example, you may choose to include the words *audience*, *purpose*, *inference*, *context clues*, and so on.) Provide context clues in your definitions. Use the following chart to create a draft of your glossary:

A Glossary of Terms for a Reading/Writing Strategy	
Term	**Definition**

1. **How will I use what I have learned?** In your notebook, discuss how you will apply learning and using new words to your own reading/writing strategy. When will you apply this knowledge to your reading/writing strategy?
2. **What do I still need to study about learning and using new words?** In your notebook, discuss your ongoing study needs. Describe what, when, and how you will continue learning and using new words.

MySkillsLab™

Complete the Post-test for Module 3 in MySkillsLab.

4 Word Choice, Tone, and Purpose

LEARNING OUTCOMES

After studying this module you should be able to:

- **LO 1** Answer the question "What's the Point of Word Choice, Tone, and Purpose?"
- **LO 2** Connect Topic, Audience, Word Choice, Tone, and Purpose
- **LO 3** Question and Annotate to Identify Tone and Purpose
- **LO 4** Brainstorm and Draft to Establish Tone and Purpose
- **LO 5** Review and Revise for Word Choice, Tone, and Purpose

Every piece of text reveals the writer's personal attitude or opinion about the chosen topic and his or her specific reason or purpose for sharing the information with a particular audience. Think about when you are really angry and you want to express how you feel. Which words pop into your mind first? Would you say those words to anyone at any time, or would you choose different words depending on who is with you or where you are? Do you choose the same words or details to share with children that you would choose to communicate with your teacher or best friend? The words we choose reveal our emotions, attitudes, and reasons for thinking the way we do. Thus, master writers carefully choose their words to make a specific point. Likewise, to comprehend the point, master readers thoughtfully consider the words a writer uses.

WHAT'S THE POINT of Word Choice, Tone, and Purpose?

Before you study this module, predict the relationship between purpose and tone. Consider the following images and captions. Each person represents a role or a job. Next to each photograph, predict the following based on each person's role: the purpose for communicating and the emotion or tone likely used to communicate. Finally, answer the question "What's the point of word choice, tone, and purpose?"

Photographic Organizer: Word Choice, Tone, and Purpose

A telemarketer in a call center

Purpose (reason to communicate): ____________________

____

Tone (emotion): ____________________

____

A valedictorian giving a graduation speech

Purpose (reason to communicate): ____________________

____

Tone (emotion): ____________________

____

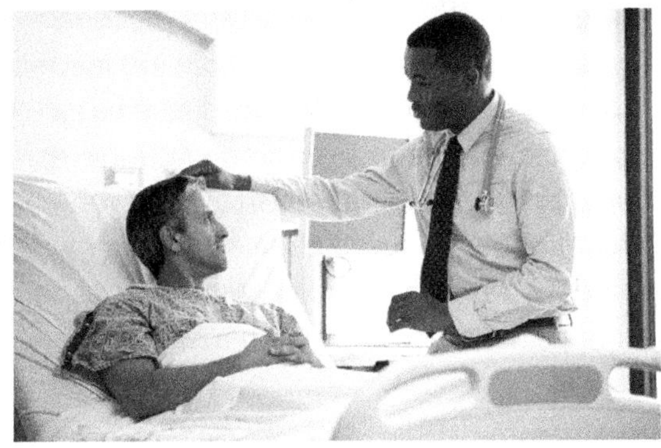

A doctor speaking with a patient

Purpose (reason to communicate): ____________________

____

Tone (emotion): ____________________

____

What's the point of word choice, tone, and purpose?

____

____

L2 Connect Topic, Audience, Word Choice, Tone, and Purpose

Words are power tools with which readers and writers create meaning. Words are the means for both *what* we say and *how* we say it. Think about the different shades of meaning of the following three words: *crib*, *house*, and *home*. All three words share a literal or basic **denotative** meaning—a dwelling, a building in which people live. However, the words *crib* and *home* imply different **connotative** meanings, emotions, or attitudes. Why use the word *crib* instead of *house* or *home*? Who is the most likely audience for the word *crib*—a friend or an employer? A master writer not only chooses words to imply or suggest a **tone**, emotion, or attitude, but also carefully selects words to fulfill his or her purpose for writing. **Word choice** reveals both your attitude and your purpose for communicating, whether in conversation or in writing. As you may recall from Module 1 (see page 11), the three basic purposes for reading and writing are to inform, to entertain or be expressive, and to argue. The following chart illustrates a small sample of possible relationships among word choice, tone, and purpose.

Denotation is the direct, literal, or dictionary meaning of a word.

Connotation is the cultural or emotional meaning associated with or implied by a word.

Tone is a manner of expression that communicates an attitude, emotion, or lack of emotion.

Word Choice is the writer's careful selection of words.

Word Choice: Tone and Purpose		
Word	**Denotative Meaning: To Inform**	**Connotative Meaning: To Entertain or Express; To Argue**
antibiotic	countermeasure, medicine	cure, potion
genetic	biological, heredity	natural, inbred
metamorphosis	change, modification	transformation, mutation
naturalist	scientist, biologist	environmentalist, tree-hugger

Often, when the purpose is to inform, the writer chooses words that state denotative meanings that are straightforward and free of emotion or attitude. To express a personal view, entertain an audience, or argue a point, a writer often chooses words that are loaded with either positive or negative connotative meanings. For example, the word *cure* has a positive connotation. *Cure* implies that an *antibiotic* heals through a method or course of medical treatment. In contrast, the word *potion* suggests a drink that has magical, even dangerous powers. The writer's purpose has a direct impact on word choice. A master writer carefully chooses words to imply or suggest a point or to support a point. A master reader thoughtfully analyzes the writer's word choice to infer the writer's intended meaning.

? For Module 4, assume you are taking a college course in humanities, and your class is beginning a study on the theme of identity and change. Each reading in this module follows this theme. As you read, you will seek to answer the guiding question "How do our experiences change our identity?" After completing all assigned readings, you will write about what you have learned about identity and change.

Example

The following section from a college humanities textbook is the first assigned reading on the theme of identity and change. Survey the passage for the writer's use of words with denotative and connotative meanings. During reading, underline key terms. After reading, answer the questions based on the writer's choice of words.

The Role of Myth in Cultural Life

[1]A myth is a story that a culture assumes is true. [2]It also embodies the culture's views and beliefs about its world, often serving to explain otherwise mysterious natural phenomena. [3]Myths stand apart from scientific explanations of the nature of reality. [4]However, as a mode of understanding and explanation, myth has been one of the most important forces driving the development of culture. [5]Although myths are speculative they are not pure fantasy, like fairytales. [6]They are grounded in observed experience. [7]They serve to rationalize the unknown and to explain to people the nature of the universe and their place in it.

—Sayre, *The Humanities: Culture, Continuity & Change*, Vol. I, 3rd ed., Pearson, 2015, p. 18.

1. Overall, which type of meaning does the writer use to define *myth*?
   a. denotative
   b. connotative

2. The writer's purpose is to
   a. inform the reader about the role of myth in cultural life.
   b. entertain the reader with myths.
   c. argue for or against the role of myth in cultural life.

Explanation

Compare your answers to the following think-aloud.

The writer mainly uses (a) denotative meaning of words to define **myth**, including **explain**, **natural phenomena**, **scientific explanations**, **observed experience**, and **rationalize**. The writer uses a few words with connotative meanings such as **mysterious**, **fantasy**, and **fairytales**. The main use of denotative meanings suggests that the writer's purpose is (a) to inform the reader about the role of myth in cultural life.

Reading/Writing: Connect Topic, Audience, Word Choice, Tone, and Purpose

Word choice is a key tool for comprehending and making a point. A master reader analyzes the writer's chosen words to identify the intended audience and to understand the writer's tone and purpose. A master writer thoughtfully chooses words to establish a clear tone to reach a specific audience of readers for a particular purpose.

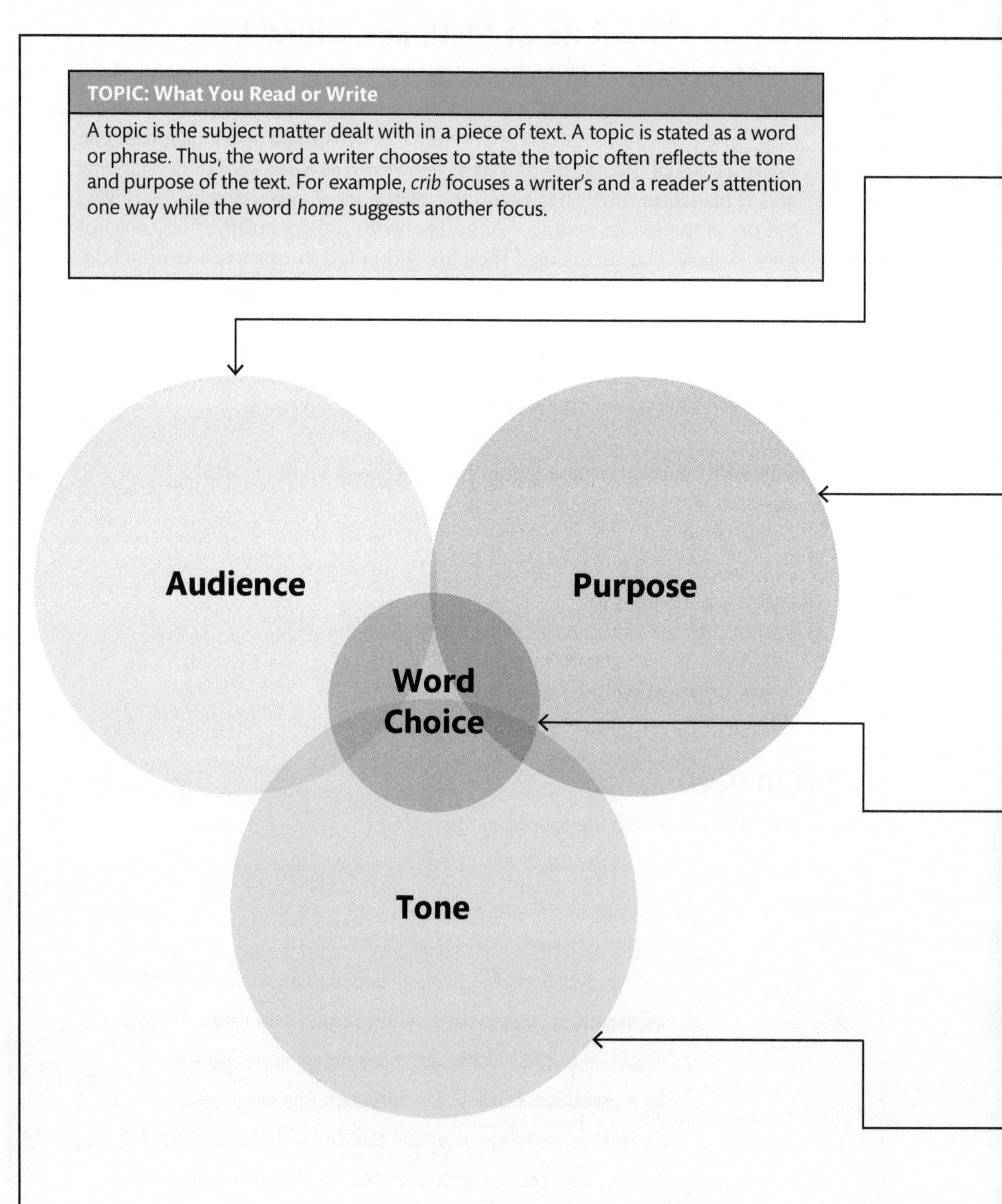

TOPIC: What You Read or Write
A topic is the subject matter dealt with in a piece of text. A topic is stated as a word or phrase. Thus, the word a writer chooses to state the topic often reflects the tone and purpose of the text. For example, *crib* focuses a writer's and a reader's attention one way while the word *home* suggests another focus.
Audience
Purpose
Word Choice
Tone

THE AUDIENCE: Who Reads the Text

The audience is the individual or group of people for whom the text is written. A writer chooses words appropriate for the age and education of the audience. The writer who chooses to use the word *crib* for *house* is most likely writing to an audience of peers.

THE PURPOSE: Why You Read or Write

Purpose is the reason a writer writes about a topic. A reader seeks to understand and respond to a writer's purpose. Three general purposes are to inform, to entertain or be expressive, and to argue. Word choice establishes purpose. The applicant writing a cover letter to apply for a job describes work experiences as having "worked from my *house*" rather than "worked from my *crib*." A neighbor inviting friends over for a visit may say, "Drop by my *crib* around 6 p.m."

WORD CHOICE: What Words a Writer Uses to Make a Point

A writer chooses words based on the writing situation. An e-mail to a friend uses a different set of words than a writer would use in a cover letter to a prospective employer.

THE TONE: How You Write—How You Are Influenced by What You Read

Tone is the writer's attitude toward a topic. The word *crib* suggests a casual, informal attitude. In contrast, *house* suggests a professional, formal attitude. The writer who chooses the word *crib* also taps into positive or negative emotions based on the experience of the reader. Writers choose words that will have the greatest impact on the audience. Word choice establishes tone.

Example

Read the following paragraphs to deepen your understanding of the term *myth*. Each entry appeals to one of the audiences depicted in the following photos. First, write the letter of the paragraph next to the picture that shows its intended audience. Then, answer the after reading question. Share your responses with a peer or small group. Discuss how word choice, tone, and purpose helped you identify the audience for each piece.

A. "Once upon a time there lived a sweet little girl in a cottage with her mother. Not far away lived her old grandmother, who loved her dearly and often brought her toys and gifts. One day she went to the market and came home with a red cap and cloak for her little granddaughter. The child liked them so much that she wore them everywhere she went. So she came to be called little Red Riding Hood."
–"Little Red Riding Hood." *Grimm's Fairy Tales. Google books.*

B. ***Fact or Myth?*** It's cool to drink. Alcohol isn't as harmful as other drugs.

Answer: Myth. There is nothing cool about stumbling around, passing out, and puking on yourself. Drinking alcohol also can cause bad breath and weight gain. Alcohol increases your risk for many deadly diseases, such as cancer. Drinking too much alcohol too quickly can lead to alcohol poisoning, which can kill you.
–"Underage Drinking: Myths vs. Facts." SAMHSA. "http://www.stopalcoholabuse.gov/media/pdf/MythsFactsBrochure_508compliant.pdf

C. Publis Ovidius Naso (20 March 43 BC–AD 17/18), known as Ovid, possessed a talent for love songs designed to satisfy the notoriously loose sexual mores of the Roman aristocrats. His work, *The Metamorphoses* is a collection of poetic stories describing or revolving around one sort of supernatural change in shape or another, from the divine to the human, the animate to the inanimate, the human to the vegetal. Few poems have contributed so importantly to later literature. It is so complete in its survey of the best-known Classical myths, plus stories from Egypt, Persia, and Italy, that it remains a standard work today.
–Sayre, *The Humanities: Culture, Continuity & Change*, Vol. I, 3rd ed., Pearson, 2015, p. 191.

1. ______

2. ______

3. ______

After Reading Writing Response: After completing the above exercise, answer the following question in the given space. *How do each of these entries serve as an example for the definition of* myth *given in the paragraph "The Role of Myth in Cultural Life" (page 141)?*

Explanation

Compare your answers to the following think-aloud.

Photograph 1 matches passage B; Photograph 2, passage C; Photograph 3, passage A. My answer to the after reading question explains my reasoning:

The audience, tone, and purpose of each passage helped me see "the role of myth in culture." For example, passage A is amusing make-believe and an example of what a myth is not. "Myth vs. Fact" (passage B) warns teens to beware of false beliefs based on "observed experiences." Passage C discusses a scholarly ancient source for Classical myths.

Practice 1

Connect Topic, Audience, Word Choice, Tone, and Purpose

Assume the following passage from a college humanities textbook is your second assigned reading on the theme of identity and change. Read the passage and answer the questions that follow.

Aristotle

[1]Greek philosopher and scientist, Aristotle (384–322 BCE) was a student of Plato's. [2]Recall that, for Plato, all reality is a mere reflection of a higher, spiritual truth, a higher dimension of Ideal Forms that we glimpse only through philosophical contemplation.

[3]Aristotle disagreed. [4]Reality was not a reflection of an ideal form, but existed in the material world itself, and by observing the material world, one could come to know universal truths. [5]So Aristotle observed and described all aspects of the world in order to arrive at the essence of things. [6]His methods of observation came to be known as ***empirical** investigation.* [7]And though he did not create a formal **scientific method**, he and other early empiricists did create procedures for testing their theories about the nature of the world that, over time, would lead to the great scientific discoveries of Bacon, Galileo, and Newton. [8]Aristotle studied biology, zoology, physics, astronomy, politics, logic, ethics, and the various genres of literary expression. [9]Based on his observations of lunar eclipses, he concluded as early as 350 BCE that the Earth was spherical, an observation that may have motivated Alexander to cross India in order to sail back to Greece. [10]He described over 500 animals in his *Historia Animalium,* including many that he dissected himself. [11]In fact, Aristotle's observations of marine life were unequaled until the seventeenth century and were still much admired by Charles Darwin in the nineteenth.

Greek philosopher and scientist Aristotle

[12]He also understood the importance of formulating a reasonable *hypothesis* to explain phenomena. [13]His *Physics* is an attempt to define the first principles governing the behavior of matter—the nature of weight, motion, physical existence, and variety in nature. [14]At the heart of Aristotle's philosophy is a question about the relation of *identity* and *change* (not far removed, incidentally, from one of the governing principles of this text, the idea of continuity and change in the humanities). [15]To discuss the world

coherently, we must be able to say what it is about a thing that makes it the thing it is, that separates it from all the other things in the world. [16]In other words, what is the attribute that we would call its material identity or **essence**? [17]What it means to be human, for instance, does not depend on whether one's hair turns gray. [18]Such "accidental" changes matter not at all. [19]At the same time, our experience of the natural world suggests that any coherent account requires us to acknowledge process and change—the change of seasons, the changes in our understanding associated with gaining knowledge in the process of aging, and so on. [20]For Aristotle, any account of a thing must accommodate both aspects: We must be able to say what changes a thing undergoes while still retaining its essential nature, and Aristotle thus approached all manner of things—from politics to the human condition—with an **eye** toward determining what constituted its essence.

—Sayre, *The Humanities: Culture, Continuity & Change*, 3rd ed., Pearson, 2015, pp. 159–160.

1. Based on context clues, the best meaning of the word **empirical** in sentence 6 is

a. assumed.
b. observed.
c. imagined.
d. important.

2. Based on context clues, the best meaning of the word **essence** in sentence 16 is

a. image.
b. outside.
c. spirit.
d. identity.

3. Based on context clues, the best meaning of the word **eye** in sentence 20 is

a. physical sight.
b. light.
c. feel.
d. understanding.

4. Overall the writer uses the meanings of words that are

a. connotative.
b. denotative.

5. The writer's purpose is to

a. inform the reader about a key historical figure.
b. entertain the reader with personal views about a key historical figure.
c. argue about the contributions of a key historical figure.

After Reading Written Response: After completing the above exercise, answer the following questions. Record your answers in your notebook or journal.

What are the meanings of the following terms: myth, empirical evidence, the scientific method, *and* essence? *How do these terms suggest the different ways we identify and understand natural phenomena?*

L3 Question and Annotate to Identify Tone and Purpose

To comprehend a passage and prepare to prewrite a response, survey the passage and ask questions about word choice, tone, and purpose. Many master readers/writers record prereading questions in their notebook or journal before they read. Then, during reading, they annotate or underline tone words that suggest the writer's attitude and purpose. The following charts offer a few examples of questions you may ask to infer tone and purpose from the writer's choice of words.

Word Choice: Tone Questions to Ask Before and During Reading	
Is the tone **OBJECTIVE?**	Is the tone **SUBJECTIVE?**
Is the tone **impartial**? Which words establish a fair-minded and balanced view of the topic?	Is the tone **personal**? Which words express an individual's views about the topic?
Is the tone **unbiased**? Which words establish an unemotional and accurate view of the topic?	Is the tone **biased**? Which words suggest a narrow-minded or slanted view of the topic?
Is the tone **neutral**? Which words offer an impersonal or unaffected view of the topic?	Is the tone **emotional**? Which words suggest a mood or connotation, or stir feelings?
Is the tone **formal**? Does the wording offer a third-person academic or professional view of the topic?	Is the tone **informal**? Which words express a first person or conversational view of the topic?
Is the tone **literal**? Which words state denotative or exact meanings?	Is the tone **figurative**? Which words suggest vivid, fresh, or imaginative mental images or symbols?

Word Choice: Purpose Questions to Ask Before and During Reading		
Is the purpose to **INFORM?**	Is the purpose to **ENTERTAIN** or be **EXPRESSIVE**?	Is the purpose to **ARGUE**?
Does the passage: Give instruction? Discuss concepts? Clarify ideas? Describe events? Analyze views or events? Use an informative tone?	Does the passage: Evoke emotion? Create vivid, fresh, or imaginative mental pictures? Express personal, cultural, or universal values? Use an entertaining or expressive tone?	Does the passage: Call for a change in attitude or action? Assert a claim and discuss supporting and opposing views? Use an argumentative or convincing tone?

Example

Assume the following excerpt from the ancient writing *The Metamorphoses* by Ovid is your next assigned reading about the theme of identity and change. The myth of Narcissus is about a vain young main who stared at his own reflection in a pond for so long that he turned into a flower. Meanwhile, a water nymph named Echo fell in love with him, but he never noticed her. She eventually wasted away until only her voice remained. Before reading, skim the passage and record three questions about its tone and purpose. During reading, underline examples of words and details that answer your prereading questions. Then, answer the questions that follow the passage.

Before Reading Questions:

1. ______________________________

2. ______________________________

3. ______________________________

The Story of Narcissus

Thus did the nymphs in vain caress the boy,
He still was lovely, but he still was **coy**;
When one fair virgin of the slighted train
Thus pray'd the Gods, provok'd by his disdain:
"Oh may he love like me, and love like me in vain!"
*Rhamnusia pity'd the neglected fair,
And with just vengeance answer'd to her prayer.

There stands a fountain in a darksom wood,
Nor stain'd with falling leaves nor rising mud;
Untroubled by the breath of winds it rests,
Unsullied by the touch of men or beasts;
High bowers of shady trees above it grow,
And rising grass and chearful greens below.
Pleased with the form and coolness of the place,
And over-heated by the morning chace,
Narcissus on the grassy verdure lyes:
But while within the crystal fount he tries
To quench his heat, he feels new heats arise:
For as his own bright image he survey'd,
He fell in love with the fantastic shade;
And o'er the fair resemblance hung unmoved,
Nor knew, fond youth! it was himself he loved.
The well-turn'd neck and shoulders he descries,

***Rhamnusia,** also known as Nemesis, the Greek goddess of revenge.

CONTINUED

EXAMPLE *CONTINUED*

*__Bacchus__, also known as Dionysus, the roman god of wine and intoxication.

*__Apollo__, the Greek and Roman god of light and music, represented the ideal youth.

The spacious forehead, and the sparkling eyes;
The hands that *Bacchus might not scorn to show,
And hair that round *Apollo's head might flow;
With all the purple youthfulness of face,
That gently blushes in the wat'ry glass.
By his own flames consumed the lover lies,
And gives himself the wound by which he dies.
To the cold water oft he joins his lips,
Oft catching at the beauteous shade he dips
His arms, as often from himself he slips.
Nor knows he who it is his arms pursue
With eager clasps, but loves he knows not who.

What could, fond youth, this helpless passion move?
What kindled in thee this unpity'd love?
Thy own warm blush within the water glows,
With thee the colour'd shadow comes and goes,
Its empty being on thy self relies;
Step thou aside, and the frail charmer dies.

Still o'er the fountain's wat'ry gleam he stood,
Mindless of sleep, and negligent of food;
Still view'd his face, and languish'd as he view'd.
At length he rais'd his head, and thus began
To vent his griefs, and tell the woods his pain.
"You trees," says he, "and thou surrounding grove,
Who oft have been the kindly scenes of love,
Tell me, if e'er within your shades did lye
A youth so tortur'd, so perplex'd as I?
I, who before me see the charming fair,
Whilst there he stands, and yet he stands not there:
In such a maze of love my thoughts are lost:
And yet no bulwark'd town, nor distant coast,
Preserves the beauteous youth from being seen,
No mountains rise, nor oceans flow between.
A shallow water hinders my embrace;
And yet the lovely mimick wears a face
That kindly smiles, and when I bend to join
My lips to his, he fondly bends to mine.
Hear, gentle youth, and pity my complaint,
Come from thy well, thou fair inhabitant.
My charms an easy conquest have obtain'd
O'er other hearts, by thee alone disdain'd.

But why should I despair? I'm sure he burns
With equal flames, and languishes by turns.
When-e'er I stoop, he offers at a kiss,
And when my arms I stretch, he stretches his.
His eye with pleasure on my face he keeps,
He smiles my smiles, and when I weep he weeps.
When e'er I speak, his moving lips appear
To utter something, which I cannot hear.

"Ah wretched me! I now begin too late
To find out all the long-perplex'd deceit;
It is my self I love, my self I see;
The gay delusion is a part of me.
I kindle up the fires by which I burn,
And my own beauties from the well return.
Whom should I court? how utter my complaint?
Enjoyment but produces my restraint,
And too much plenty makes me die for want.
How gladly would I from my self remove!
And at a distance set the thing I love.
My breast is warm'd with such unusual fire,
I wish him absent whom I most desire.
And now I faint with grief; my fate draws nigh;
In all the pride of blooming youth I die.
Death will the sorrows of my heart relieve.
Oh might the visionary youth survive,
I should with joy my latest breath resign!
But oh! I see his fate involv'd in mine."

This said, the weeping youth again return'd
To the clear fountain, where again he burn'd;
His tears defac'd the surface of the well,
With circle after circle, as they fell:
And now the lovely face but half appears,
O'er-run with wrinkles, and deform'd with tears.
"Ah whither," cries Narcissus, "dost thou fly?
Let me still feed the flame by which I die;
Let me still see, tho' I'm no further blest."
Then rends his garment off, and beats his breast:
His naked bosom redden'd with the blow,
In such a blush as purple clusters show,
Ere yet the sun's autumnal heats refine

CONTINUED

EXAMPLE *CONTINUED*

Their sprightly juice, and mellow it to wine.
The glowing beauties of his breast he spies,
And with a new redoubled passion dies.
As wax dissolves, as ice begins to run,
And trickle into drops before the sun;
So melts the youth, and languishes away,
His beauty withers, and his limbs decay;
And none of those attractive charms remain,
To which the slighted Echo su'd in vain.

She saw him in his present misery,
Whom, spight of all her wrongs, she griev'd to see.
She answer'd sadly to the lover's moan,
Sigh'd back his sighs, and groan'd to ev'ry groan:
"Ah youth! belov'd in vain," Narcissus cries;
"Ah youth! belov'd in vain," the nymph replies.
"Farewel," says he; the parting sound scarce fell
From his faint lips, but she reply'd, "farewel."
Then on th' wholsome earth he gasping lyes,
'Till death shuts up those self-admiring eyes.
To the cold shades his flitting ghost retires,
And in the Stygian waves it self admires.
For him the Naiads and the Dryads mourn,
Whom the sad Echo answers in her turn;
And now the sister-nymphs prepare his urn:
When, looking for his corps, they only found
A rising stalk, with yellow blossoms crown'd.

Metamorphosis of Narcissus (1937) by Salvador Dalí

—*Story of Narcissus*, Ovid, trans. Dryden, Pope, Congreve, Addison, and others, vol. 1, Harper, NY, 1872.

1. The tone of the word **coy** in line 2 is
   a. unbiased.
   b. neutral.
   c. biased.
   d. impartial.

2. The tone of line 29, "By his own flames consumed the lover lies" is
   a. neutral.
   b. figurative.
   c. literal.
   d. informal.

3. Based on the general context of the passage, we may infer Narcissus represents
   a. vanity.
   b. rejection.
   c. literal.
   d. informal.

4. The overall tone of the passage is
   a. neutral.
   b. figurative.
   c. literal.
   d. informal.

5. Based on the tone of the passage, we may infer the writer's purpose is to
   a. inform the reader with an objective description of the origin of two natural phenomena, the narcissus flower and an echo.
   b. express cultural values through an entertaining story about the supernatural origin of two natural phenomena, the narcissus flower and an echo.
   c. convince the audience to submit to the gods.

?

After Reading Written Response: After completing the above exercise, answer the following questions.

What "essence" (see "Aristotle," p. 146) of human nature does "The Story of Narcissus" reveal? As the myth unfolds, what changes does Narcissus undergo and what remains of his "essential nature" (p. 147)?

CONTINUED

EXAMPLE *CONTINUED*

Explanation

Compare your responses to the following think-aloud.

The three before reading questions I asked were: 1. Is the tone subjective or objective? 2. What are examples of words that reveal the tone? 3. What is the writer's purpose? I immediately recognized this passage as a poem with lines and verses. Usually, poems are biased expressions of a personal view. So I skimmed and began underlining a few examples of subjective tone words such as **lovely, coy, one fair virgin, just vengeance, sparkling eyes, flames consumed the lover lies, languished, tortur'd, my self I love, faint with grief.** The writer used vivid mental images and emotional words. My answers to the first four questions are 1. (c) biased. 2. (b) figurative. 3. (a) vanity. Narcissus died due to his self-love, his vanity. 4. (b) figurative. The overall tone was figurative because of the many mental images the writer created with word choice. 5. (b) This poem asserts a cultural belief in gods and expresses a cultural value against vanity. Here is my answer to the after reading questions:

The essence of human nature revealed by "The Story of Narcissus" is vanity or self-love. Narcissus fell in love with his reflection in a pool of water. Languishing beside his own image, he eventually dies and is transformed into a flower. While his body changes form, he never changes in his essential nature. His self-love never diminishes. Even the flower he became bends its bloom down as if to see itself in a pool, as seen in this photograph I found.

Practice 2

Question and Annotate to Identify Tone and Purpose

Assume the following excerpt from Charles Darwin's Introduction to his publication *The Origin of Species* is your next assigned reading about the theme of identity and change. Before reading, skim the passage and record three questions about its tone and purpose. During reading, underline examples of words and details that answer your prereading questions. Then, answer the questions that follow the passage.

Before Reading Questions:

1. ______________________________

2. ______________________________

3. ______________________________

Darwin's Origin of Species

Charles Darwin July 1, 1877

[1]In considering the Origin of Species, it is quite conceivable that a naturalist, reflecting on the mutual affinities of organic beings, on their embryological relations, their geographical distribution, geological succession, and other such facts, might come to the conclusion that each species had not been independently created, but had descended, like varieties, from other species. [2]Nevertheless, such a conclusion, even if well founded, would be unsatisfactory, until it could be shown how the innumerable species inhabiting this world have been modified so as to acquire that perfection of structure and co-adaptation, which most justly excites our admiration. [3]Naturalists continually refer to external conditions, such as climate, food, etc., as the only possible cause of variation. [4]In one very limited sense, as we shall hereafter see, this may be true; but it is preposterous to attribute to mere external conditions, the structure, for instance, of the woodpecker, with its feet, tail, beak, and tongue, so admirably adapted to catch insects under the bark of trees. [5]In the case of the mistletoe, which draws its nourishment from certain trees, which has seeds that must be transported by certain birds, and which has flowers with separate sexes absolutely requiring the agency of certain insects to bring pollen from one

CONTINUED

flower to the other, it is equally preposterous to account for the structure of this parasite, with its relations to several distinct organic beings, by the effects of external conditions, or of habit, or of the volition of the plant itself.

[6]It is, therefore, of the highest importance to gain a clear insight into the means of modification and coadaptation. [7]At the commencement of my observations it seemed to me probable that a careful study of domesticated animals and of cultivated plants would offer the best chance of making out this obscure problem. [8]Nor have I been disappointed; in this and in all other perplexing cases I have invariably found that our knowledge, imperfect though it be, of variation under domestication, afforded the best and safest clue. [9]I may venture to express my conviction of the high value of such studies, although they have been very commonly neglected by naturalists.

[10]From these considerations, I shall devote the first chapter of this Abstract to Variation under Domestication. [11]We shall thus see that a large amount of hereditary modification is at least possible, and, what is equally or more important, we shall see how great is the power of man in accumulating by his Selection successive slight variations. [12]I will then pass on to the variability of species in a state of nature; but I shall, unfortunately, be compelled to treat this subject far too briefly, as it can be treated properly only by giving long catalogues of facts. [13]We shall, however, be enabled to discuss what circumstances are most favourable to variation. [14]In the next chapter the Struggle for Existence amongst all organic beings throughout the world, which inevitably follows from their high geometrical powers of increase, will be treated of. [15]This is the doctrine of Malthus, applied to the whole animal and vegetable kingdoms. [16]As many more individuals of each species are born than can possibly survive; and as, consequently, there is a frequently recurring struggle for existence, it follows that any being, if it vary however slightly in any manner profitable to itself, under the complex and sometimes varying conditions of life, will have a better chance of surviving, and thus be naturally selected. [17]From the strong principle of inheritance, any selected variety will tend to propagate its new and modified form.

[18]This fundamental subject of Natural Selection will be treated at some length in the fourth chapter; and we shall then see how Natural Selection almost inevitably causes much Extinction of the less improved forms of life and induces what I have called Divergence of Character. [19]In the next chapter I shall discuss the complex and little known laws of variation and of correlation of growth. [20]In the four succeeding chapters, the most apparent and gravest difficulties on the theory will be given: namely, first, the difficulties of transitions, or understanding how a simple being or a simple organ can be changed and perfected into a highly developed being or elaborately constructed organ; secondly the subject of Instinct, or the mental powers of animals, thirdly, Hybridism, or the infertility of species and the fertility of varieties when intercrossed; and fourthly, the imperfection of the Geological Record. [21]In the next chapter I shall consider the geological succession of organic beings throughout time; in the eleventh and twelfth, their geographical distribution throughout space; in the thirteenth, their classification or mutual affinities, both when mature and in an embryonic condition. [22]In the last chapter I shall give a brief recapitulation of the whole work, and a few concluding remarks.

[23]No one ought to feel surprise at much remaining as yet unexplained in regard to the origin of species and varieties, if he makes due allowance for our profound ignorance in regard to the mutual relations of all the beings which live around us. [24]Who can explain why one species ranges widely and is very numerous, and why another allied species has a narrow range and is rare? [25]Yet these relations are of the highest importance, for they determine the present welfare, and, as I believe, the future success and modification of every inhabitant of this world. [26]Still less do we know of the mutual relations of the innumerable inhabitants of the world during the many past geological epochs in its history. [27]Although much remains obscure, and will long remain obscure, I can entertain no doubt, after the most deliberate study and dispassionate judgment of which I am capable, that the view which most naturalists entertain, and which I formerly entertained—namely, that each species has been independently created—is erroneous. [28]I am fully convinced that species are not immutable; but that those belonging to what are called the same genera are lineal descendants of some other and generally extinct species, in the same manner as the acknowledged varieties of any one species are the descendants of that species. [29]Furthermore, I am convinced that Natural Selection has been the main but not exclusive means of modification.

–Darwin, *The Origin of Species by Means of Natural Selection*, D. Appleton and Co, NY, 1883.

1. The tone of sentence 1 is

a. unbiased. **b.** neutral. **c.** biased. **d.** impartial.

2. The tone of sentence 3 is

a. neutral. **b.** figurative. **c.** emotional. **d.** informal.

3. The word *preposterous* in sentences 4 and 5 conveys what type of tone?

a. unbiased.
b. emotional.
c. neutral.
d. informal.

4. The overall tone of the passage is

a. neutral.
b. informal.
c. figurative.
d. formal.

5. Based on the tone of the passage, we may infer the writer's purpose is to

a. inform the reader about the origin of the species using scientific facts.
b. express personal beliefs about the origin of the species.
c. present the argument that the species are descended from other species.

?

After Reading Written Response: After completing the above exercise, answer the following question. Record your answer in your notebook or journal.

Based on the excerpt from the Introduction, is "Darwin's Origin of Species" a myth *(see page 141) or an example of an* empirical investigation *(see page 146)?*

L4 Brainstorm and Draft to Establish Tone and Purpose

Use your questions and annotations to brainstorm a response to what you have read. Include logical inferences based on the connections you have made. Use an outline or concept map to organize connections among the key terms you want to include in your writing.

Example

Assume your humanities teacher provided the following study question to prepare for an in-class essay exam:

How does "The Story of Narcissus" illustrate the theme of identity and change?

To brainstorm and draft your response:

- Refer to your answers to the After Reading Questions in the Example (page 153):
  - What essence of human nature does "The Story of Narcissus" reveal?
  - As the myth unfolds, what changes does Narcissus undergo and what remains of his "essential nature"?
- Complete the following concept map with the appropriate details from "The Story of Narcissus" and your earlier answers.
- Use the completed concept map and your own paper to draft your response to the exam's study question.

I. Narcissus' Youthful Essence or Identity	II. Narcissus' Aging Essence or Identity	III. Narcissus' Transformation Essence or Identity
Handsome- ______________ ______________ (2) **Desirable-** "of the slighted train" (3) **Unloving-** ______________ ______________ (2) **Self absorbed-** "It is my self I love" (75)	**Miserable-** ______________ ______________ (73) **Suicidal-** "Death will the sorrows of my heart relieve" (88) **Dying-** ______________ ______________ (107)	**Dead-** ______________ ______________ (124) **Reborn-** "a rising stalk, with yellow blossoms crowned" (130)

What's the central point?

____

____

Explanation

Compare your answers to the following think-aloud.

I found my answers to the after reading questions from earlier readings summed up a response to the exam study question. I had written that the essence of Narcissus is vanity or self-love. His essence didn't change, just his physical form. This thought helped me complete the concept map with details from the story. I completed the map with details from the story's line numbers as indicated in parentheses. Handsome— "lovely"; Unloving—"coy"; Miserable— "Ah, wretched me"; Dying "as wax dissolves"; Dead— "his flitting ghost retires." The first sentence of my draft states the central point:

I think the identity or essence of Narcissus doesn't change even though his physical body transforms into another life form. Narcissus' identity or essential self is vanity, and he never wavers in his self-devotion.

In his youth, Narcissus' identity is tied to his physical looks. He is handsome, even "lovely" (2) and desired by many. For example, Echo, one of the "slighted train" of rejected lovers, prays for him to suffer the pain of unreturned love. Although he was physically beautiful, his essence was unloving or "coy" (3). He has one love, "It is my self I love" (75).

As he ages, Narcissus' essence doesn't change. His emotional and physical state change, but his self-absorption doesn't. Miserable, he complains "Ah, wretched me!" (73). He sounds suicidal when he says, "Death will the sorrows of my heart relieve" (88). However, he doesn't express any remorse or concern for hurting

CONTINUED

EXAMPLE *CONTINUED*

others. Instead, he talks only of his own suffering. He doesn't acknowledge Echo who remains by his side as he dies. She doesn't leave him even though he hurt her greatly. He doesn't gain any understanding of the misery he caused others. He loves only himself even as he watches himself "as wax dissolves" (line 107).

Narcissus eventually dies and "his flitting ghost retires" (124). It is fitting that his essence is reborn as a beautiful flower, "a rising stalk, with yellow blossoms crowned" (130). The physical nature of Narcissus was as beautiful as a flower. Perhaps, the gods chose to honor and preserve his physical essence, by turning him into the beautiful flower that is named for him. Yet his name, his identity, has become the word **narcissism**, a widely used label for the essence of human self-centeredness and arrogance.

Practice 3

Brainstorm and Draft to Establish Tone and Purpose

Assume your humanities teacher provided additional study questions to prepare for an in-class essay exam:

> *How do the terms* myth, empirical evidence, the scientific method, *and* essence *relate to the theme of identity and change?*

To brainstorm and draft your response:

- Refer to your answers to the After Reading Questions in Practice 1 (page 147) or Practice 2 (page 153):
  - How do these terms suggest the different ways we identify and understand natural phenomena?
  - Based on the excerpt from the Introduction, is "Darwin's Origin of Species" a *myth* or an example of an *empirical investigation*?
- Create a concept map with the appropriate details from "Aristotle" (page 146) and "Darwin's Origin of Species" (page 155).
- Refer to your earlier answers for useful details and insights.
- Use the completed concept map to draft your response to the exam's study question.

Review and Revise for Word Choice, Tone, and Purpose

LO 5

Master writers review and revise for word choice, tone, and purpose. First, a master writer reads the draft silently or out loud. During this review, he or she underlines specific words or phrases that should be revised to establish a consistent tone in keeping with the audience and purpose. Once this initial review is completed, master writers make revisions to rework the draft.

Example

Assume that you are a peer editor for the writer who composed the following draft in response to the study question, *"How does 'The Story of Narcissus' illustrate the theme of identity and change?"* (Example, page 158.) Review the draft. Underline the wording that you think should be revised based on tone, audience, and purpose. Offer suggestions for revising at least three words or phrases.

Explanation

Compare your answers to the following think-aloud.

The audience, tone, and purpose of this written response are academic. I underlined and revised the following words to create a formal and objective tone. In the first paragraph, I suggest deleting the informal personal pronoun I think. The sentence should begin with "The identity…" In the second paragraph, revise looks to "appeal." The contraction doesn't appears six times and should be revised to "does not" or replaced. For example, in the third paragraph, revise doesn't express to "never expresses," doesn't acknowledge to "never acknowledges," and doesn't leave to "never leaves."

Practice 4

Review and Revise for Word Choice, Tone, and Purpose

Review and revise the draft you composed in Practice 3 (page 160). On a print copy of your draft, underline the wording that you should revise based on tone, audience, and purpose. Provide revised wording on the draft near the underlined idea. Create a new draft with your revisions completed.

Workshop: Word Choice, Tone, and Purpose

The following selection offers two excerpts from the short story "Rappaccini's Daughter" by Nathaniel Hawthorne and is your capstone reading assignment on the theme of identity and change. This short story, published in 1846, recounts the tale of a young student, Giovanni, who falls in love with Beatrice, the beautiful daughter of a brilliant scientist. The scientist is conducting a long-term experiment that involves the young couple. Your capstone writing assignment will be a formal response that addresses the Guiding Question "How do our experiences change our identity?" To complete your writing assignment, skim the prereading questions to guide your reading, read the selection, and complete the activities that follow.

RAPPACCINI'S DAUGHTER

1A young man, named Giovanni Guasconti, came, very long ago, from the more southern region of Italy, to pursue his studies at the University of Padua. Giovanni, who had but a scanty supply of gold ducats in his pocket, took lodgings in a high and gloomy chamber of an old edifice, which looked not unworthy to have been the palace of a Paduan noble, and which, in fact, exhibited over its entrance the armorial bearings of a family long since extinct. The young stranger, who was not unstudied in the great poem of his country, recollected that one of the ancestors of this family, and perhaps an occupant of this very mansion, had been pictured by Dante as a partaker of the immortal agonies of his Inferno. These reminiscences and associations, together with the tendency to heart-break natural to a young man for the first time out of his native sphere, caused Giovanni to sigh heavily, as he looked around the desolate and ill-furnished apartment.

2"Holy Virgin, signor," cried old dame Lisabetta, who, won by the youth's remarkable beauty of person, was kindly endeavoring to give the chamber a habitable air, "what a sigh was that to come out of a young man's heart! Do you find this old mansion gloomy? For the love of heaven, then, put your head out of the window, and you will see as bright sunshine as you have left in Naples."

3Guasconti mechanically did as the old woman advised, but could not quite agree with her that the Lombard sunshine was as cheerful as that of southern Italy. Such as it was, however, it fell upon a garden beneath the window, and expended its fostering influences on a variety of plants, which seemed to have been cultivated with exceeding care.

4"Does this garden belong to the house?" asked Giovanni.

5Heaven forbid, signor! —unless it were fruitful of better pot-herbs than any that grow there now," answered old Lisabetta. "No; that garden is cultivated by the own hands of Signor Giacomo Rappaccini, the famous Doctor, who, I warrant him, has been heard of as far as Naples. It is said he distils these plants into medicines that are as potent as a charm. Oftentimes you may see the Signor Doctor at work, and perchance the Signora his daughter, too, gathering the strange flowers that grow in the garden."

6The old woman had now done what she could for the aspect of the chamber, and, commending the young man to the protection of the saints, took her departure.

7Giovanni still found no better occupation than to look down into the garden beneath his window. From its appearance, he judged it to be one of those botanic gardens, which were of earlier date in Padua than elsewhere in Italy, or in the world. Or, not improbably, it might once have been the pleasure-place of an opulent family; for there was the ruin of a marble fountain in the center, sculptured with rare art, but so woefully shattered that it was impossible to trace the original design from the chaos of remaining fragments. The water, however, continued to gush and sparkle into the sunbeams as cheerfully as ever. A little gurgling sound ascended to the young man's window, and made him feel as if a fountain were an immortal spirit, that sung its song unceasingly, and without heeding the vicissitudes around it; while one century embodied it in marble, and another scattered the perishable garniture on the soil. All about the pool into which the water subsided, grew various plants, that seemed to require a plentiful supply of moisture for the nourishment of gigantic leaves, and, in some instances, flowers gorgeously magnificent. There was one shrub in particular, set in a marble vase in the midst of the pool, that bore a profusion of purple blossoms, each of which had the lustre and richness of a gem; and the whole together made a show so resplendent that it seemed enough to illuminate the garden, even had there been no sunshine. Every portion of the soil was peopled with plants and herbs, which, if less beautiful, still bore tokens of assiduous care; as if all had their individual virtues, known to the scientific mind that fostered them. Some were placed in urns, rich with old carving, and others in common garden-pots; some crept serpent-like along the ground, or climbed on high, using whatever means of ascent was offered them. One plant had wreathed itself round a statue of Vertumnus, which was thus quite veiled and shrouded in a drapery of hanging foliage, so happily arranged that it might have served a sculptor for a study.

8While Giovanni stood at the window, he heard a rustling behind a screen of leaves, and became aware that a person was at work in the garden. His figure soon emerged into view, and showed itself to be that of no common laborer, but a tall, emaciated, sallow, and sickly looking man, dressed in a scholar's garb of black. He was beyond the middle term of life, with gray hair, a thin gray beard, and a face singularly marked with intellect and cultivation, but which could never, even in his more youthful days, have expressed much warmth of heart.

9Nothing could exceed the intentness with which this scientific gardener examined every shrub which grew in his path; it seemed as if he was looking into their inmost nature, making observations in regard to their creative essence, and discovering why one leaf grew in this shape, and another in that, and wherefore such and such flowers differed among themselves in hue and perfume. Nevertheless, in spite of the deep intelligence on his part, there was no approach to intimacy between himself and these vegetable existences. On the contrary, he avoided their actual

CONTINUED

touch, or the direct inhaling of their odors, with a caution that impressed Giovanni most disagreeably; for the man's demeanor was that of one walking among malignant influences, such as savage beasts, or deadly snakes, or evil spirits, which, should he allow them one moment of license, would wreak upon him some terrible fatality. It was strangely frightful to the young man's imagination, to see this air of insecurity in a person cultivating a garden, that most simple and innocent of human toils, and which had been alike the joy and labor of the unfallen parents of the race. Was this garden, then, the Eden of the present world? —and this man, with such a perception of harm in what his own hands caused to grow, was he the Adam?

10The distrustful gardener, while plucking away the dead leaves or pruning the too luxuriant growth of the shrubs, defended his hands with a pair of thick gloves. Nor were these his only armor. When, in his walk through the garden, he came to the magnificent plant that hung its purple gems beside the marble fountain, he placed a kind of mask over his mouth and nostrils, as if all this beauty did but conceal a deadlier malice. But finding his task still too dangerous, he drew back, removed the mask, and called loudly, but in the infirm voice of a person affected with inward disease:

11"Beatrice! —Beatrice!"

12"Here am I, my father! What would you?" cried a rich and youthful voice from the window of the opposite house; a voice as rich as a tropical sunset, and which made Giovanni, though he knew not why, think of deep hues of purple or crimson, and of perfumes heavily delectable. —"Are you in the garden?"

13"Yes, Beatrice," answered the gardener, "and I need your help."

14Soon there emerged from under a sculptured portal the figure of a young girl, arrayed with as much richness of taste as the most splendid of the flowers, beautiful as the day, and with a bloom so deep and vivid that one shade more would have been too much. She looked redundant with life, health, and energy; all of which attributes were bound down and compressed, as it were, and girdled tensely, in their luxuriance, by her virgin zone. Yet Giovanni's fancy must have grown morbid, while he looked down into the garden; for the impression which the fair stranger made upon him was as if here were another flower, the human sister of those vegetable ones, as beautiful as they—more beautiful than the richest of them—but still to be touched only with a glove, nor to be approached without a mask. As Beatrice came down the garden-path, it was observable that she handled and inhaled the odor of several of the plants, which her father had most sedulously avoided.

15"Here, Beatrice," said the latter, —"see how many needful offices require to be done to our chief treasure. Yet, shattered as I am, my life might pay the penalty of approaching it so closely as circumstances demand. Henceforth, I fear, this plant must be consigned to your sole charge."

16"And gladly will I undertake it," cried again the rich tones of the young lady, as she bent towards the magnificent plant, and opened her arms as if to embrace it. "Yes, my sister, my splendor, it shall be Beatrice's task to nurse and serve thee; and thou shalt reward her with thy kisses and perfume breath, which to her is as the breath of life!"

17 Then, with all the tenderness in her manner that was so strikingly expressed in her words, she busied herself with such attentions as the plant seemed to require; and Giovanni, at his lofty window, rubbed his eyes, and almost doubted whether it were a girl tending her favorite flower, or one sister performing the duties of affection to another. The scene soon terminated. Whether Doctor Rappaccini had finished his labors in the garden, or that his watchful eye had caught the stranger's face, he now took his daughter's arm and retired. Night was already closing in; oppressive exhalations seemed to proceed from the plants, and steal upward past the open window; and Giovanni, closing the lattice, went to his couch, and dreamed of a rich flower and beautiful girl. Flower and maiden were different and yet the same, and fraught with some strange peril in either shape.

* * *

18 "Beatrice," asked he abruptly, "whence came this shrub!"

19 "My father created it," answered she, with simplicity.

20 "Created it! created it!" repeated Giovanni. "What mean you, Beatrice?"

21 "He is a man fearfully acquainted with the secrets of nature," replied Beatrice; "and, at the hour when I first drew breath, this plant sprang from the soil, the offspring of his science, of his intellect, while I was but his earthly child. Approach it not!" continued she, observing with terror that Giovanni was drawing nearer to the shrub. "It has qualities that you little dream of. But I, dearest Giovanni—I grew up and blossomed with the plant, and was nourished with its breath. It was my sister, and I loved it with a human affection: for—alas! hast thou not suspected it? there was an awful doom."

22 Here Giovanni frowned so darkly upon her that Beatrice paused and trembled. But her faith in his tenderness reassured her, and made her blush that she had doubted for an instant.

23 "There was an awful doom," she continued, —"the effect of my father's fatal love of science—which estranged me from all society of my kind. Until Heaven sent thee, dearest Giovanni, Oh! how lonely was thy poor Beatrice!"

24 "Was it a hard doom?" asked Giovanni, fixing his eyes upon her.

25 "Only of late have I known how hard it was," answered she tenderly. "Oh, yes; but my heart was torpid, and therefore quiet."

26 Giovanni's rage broke forth from his sullen gloom like a lightning-flash out of a dark cloud.

27 "Accursed one!" cried he, with venomous scorn and anger. "And finding thy solitude wearisome, thou hast severed me, likewise, from all the warmth of life, and enticed me into thy region of unspeakable horror!"

28 "Giovanni!" exclaimed Beatrice, turning her large bright eyes upon his face. The force of his words had not found its way into her mind; she was merely thunder-struck.

29 "Yes, poisonous thing!" repeated Giovanni, beside himself with passion. "Thou hast done it! Thou hast blasted me! Thou hast filled my veins with poison! Thou hast made me as hateful, as ugly, as loathsome and deadly a creature as thyself—a world's wonder of hideous monstrosity! Now—if our breath be happily as fatal to ourselves as to all others—let us join our lips in one kiss of unutterable hatred, and so die!"

CONTINUED

30"What has befallen me?" murmured Beatrice, with a low moan out of her heart. "Holy Virgin pity me, a poor heartbroken child!"

31"Thou! Dost thou pray?" cried Giovanni, still with the same fiendish scorn. "Thy very prayers, as they come from thy lips, taint the atmosphere with death. Yes, yes; let us pray! Let us to church, and dip our fingers in the holy water at the portal! They that come after us will perish as by a pestilence. Let us sign crosses in the air! It will be scattering curses abroad in the likeness of holy symbols!"

32"Giovanni," said Beatrice calmly, for her grief was beyond passion, "Why dost thou join thyself with me thus in those terrible words? I, it is true, am the horrible thing thou namest me. But thou! —what hast thou to do, save with one other shudder at my hideous misery, to go forth out of the garden and mingle with thy race, and forget that there ever crawled on earth such a monster as poor Beatrice?"

33"Dost thou pretend ignorance?" asked Giovanni, scowling upon her. "Behold! This power have I gained from the pure daughter of Rappaccini!"

34There was a swarm of summer-insects flitting through the air, in search of the food promised by the flower-odors of the fatal garden. They circled round Giovanni's head, and were evidently attracted towards him by the same influence which had drawn them, for an instant, within the sphere of several of the shrubs. He sent forth a breath among them, and smiled bitterly at Beatrice, as at least a score of the insects fell dead upon the ground.

35"I see it! I see it!" shrieked Beatrice. "It is my father's fatal science? No, no, Giovanni; it was not I! Never, never! I dreamed only to love thee, and be with thee a little time, and so to let thee pass away, leaving but thine image in mine heart. For, Giovanni—believe it–though my body be nourished with poison, my spirit is God's creature, and craves love as its daily food. But my father! —he has united us in this fearful sympathy. Yes; spurn me! —tread upon me! —kill me! Oh, what is death, after such words as thine? But it was not I! Not for a world of bliss would I have done it!"

36Giovanni's passion had exhausted itself in its outburst from his lips. There now came across him a sense, mournful, and not without tenderness, of the intimate and peculiar relationship between Beatrice and himself. They stood, as it were, in an utter solitude, which would be made none the less solitary by the densest throng of human life. Ought not, then, the desert of humanity around them to press this insulated pair closer together? If they should be cruel to one another, who was there to be kind to them? Besides, thought Giovanni, might there not still be a hope of his returning within the limits of ordinary nature, and leading Beatrice—the redeemed Beatrice—by the hand? Oh, weak, and selfish, and unworthy spirit, that could dream of an earthly union and earthly happiness as possible, after such deep love had been so bitterly wronged as was Beatrice's love by Giovanni's blighting words! No, no; there could be no such hope. She must pass heavily, with that broken heart, across the borders of Time—she must bathe her hurts in some fount of Paradise, and forget her grief in the light of immortality—and there be well!

37But Giovanni did not know it.

38"Dear Beatrice," said he, approaching her, while she shrank away, as always at his approach, but now with a different impulse—"dearest Beatrice, our fate is not yet so desperate. Behold! There is a medicine, potent, as a wise physician has assured me, and almost divine in its efficacy. It is composed of ingredients the most opposite to those by which thy awful father has brought this calamity upon thee and me. It is distilled of blessed herbs. Shall we not quaff it together, and thus be purified from evil?"

39"Give it me!" said Beatrice, extending her hand to receive the little silver phial which Giovanni took from his bosom. She added, with a peculiar emphasis: "I will drink—but do thou await the result."

40She put Baglioni's antidote to her lips; and, at the same moment, the figure of Rappaccini emerged from the portal, and came slowly towards the marble fountain. As he drew near, the pale man of science seemed to gaze with a triumphant expression at the beautiful youth and maiden, as might an artist who should spend his life in achieving a picture or a group of statuary, and finally be satisfied with his success. He paused—his bent form grew erect with conscious power, he spread out his hand over them, in the attitude of a father imploring a blessing upon his children. But those were the same hands that had thrown poison into the stream of their lives! Giovanni trembled. Beatrice shuddered very nervously, and pressed her hand upon her heart.

41"My daughter," said Rappaccini, "thou art no longer lonely in the world! Pluck one of those precious gems from thy sister shrub, and bid thy bridegroom wear it in his bosom. It will not harm him now! My science, and the sympathy between thee and him, have so wrought within his system, that he now stands apart from common men, as thou dost, daughter of my pride and triumph, from ordinary women. Pass on, then, through the world, most dear to one another, and dreadful to all besides!"

42"My father," said Beatrice, feebly—and still, as she spoke, she kept her hand upon her heart—"wherefore didst thou inflict this miserable doom upon thy child?"

43"Miserable!" exclaimed Rappaccini. "What mean you, foolish girl? Dost thou deem it misery to be endowed with marvelous gifts, against which no power nor strength could avail an enemy? Misery, to be able to quell the mightiest with a breath? Misery, to be as terrible as thou art beautiful? Wouldst thou, then, have preferred the condition of a weak woman, exposed to all evil, and capable of none?"

44"I would fain have been loved, not feared," murmured Beatrice, sinking down upon the ground. —"But now it matters not; I am going, father, where the evil, which thou hast striven to mingle with my being, will pass away like a dream—like the fragrance of these poisonous flowers, which will no longer taint my breath among the flowers of Eden. Farewell, Giovanni! Thy words of hatred are like lead within my heart—but they, too, will fall away as I ascend. Oh, was there not, from the first, more poison in thy nature than in mine?"

45To Beatrice—so radically had her earthly part been wrought upon by Rappaccini's skill—as poison had been life, so the powerful antidote was death. And thus the poor victim of man's ingenuity and of thwarted nature, and of the fatality that attends all such efforts of perverted wisdom, perished there, at the feet of her father and Giovanni. Just at that moment, Professor Pietro Baglioni looked forth from the window, and called loudly, in a tone of triumph mixed with horror, to the thunder-stricken man of science:

46"Rappaccini! Rappaccini! And is *this* the upshot of your experiment?"

—Nathanial Hawthorne, "Rappaccini's Daughter" from *Mosses from on Old Manse*, MacMillan & Co, NY, 1908.

Preread: Survey and Question

Survey the following questions. Answer the questions about your prior knowledge. Then, skim the passages to locate key details to annotate during reading.

1. Describe the essence or essential identity of Dr. Rappaccini, Beatrice Rappaccini, and Giovanni.

2. How does Dr. Rappaccini use empirical investigation to conduct his scientific experiment?

3. How has Rappaccini's experiment changed the essence, or nature, of Beatrice? In what ways has she remained, in essence, unchanged?

4. How has Rappaccini's experiment changed the essence, or nature, of Giovanni? In what ways has he remained, in essence, unchanged?

5. In "The Origin of Species," Darwin states, "how great is the power of man in accumulating by his Selection successive slight variations" in a species. How does "Rappaccini's Daughter" illustrate this power?

6. How does the story illustrate the dangers of man's scientific power?

7. In what ways are Dr. Rappaccini and Giovanni narcissistic?

Read and Annotate

As you read, annotate key ideas, particularly those details that answer your prereading questions.

Recite, Review, and Brainstorm

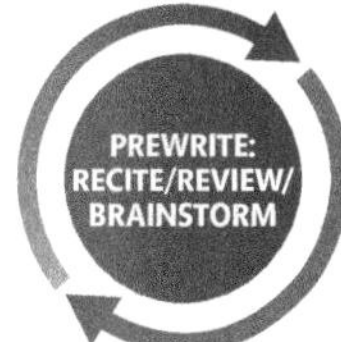

Recite and **Review** the information. Paraphrase ideas. Summarize the most important parts. **Brainstorm** ideas for your written response to the passage. Answer your prereading questions. *Freewrite* or *map* the relationship among answers to questions or ideas you have annotated in the text. *Outline* or *list* key ideas and details in blocks of thought. Identify the central point you want to make. Use your own paper.

Write a Draft of Your Response

Using the ideas you generated by brainstorming, compose a draft of your response. Use your own paper.

Revise Your Draft

Once you have created a draft of your response, read it over to answer the questions in the "Questions for Revising" box that follows. Indicate your answers by annotating your paper. If you answer, "yes" to a question, underline, check, or circle examples. If you answer "no" to a question, write needed information in the margins and draw lines to indicate the placement of additional details. Revise your essay based on your reflection. (*Hint:* Experienced writers create several drafts as they focus on one or two questions per draft.)

Step by Step: Questions for Revising

- ☐ Have I stated or implied a focused main idea?
- ☐ Have made my purpose clear?
- ☐ Is my tone appropriate for my audience and purpose?
- ☐ Is the logical order of ideas clear? Have I used words to clearly guide my reader, such as *first*, *second*, *next*, etc.?
- ☐ Have I used concrete details to make my point?
- ☐ Have I made my point with adequate details?
- ☐ Do all the details support my point?

Proofread Your Draft

Once you have made any revisions to your essay that may be needed, proofread your essay to eliminate careless errors.

Reading and Writing Assignments

MySkillsLab™
Complete this Exercise
on myskillslab.com

Reading and Writing for Everyday Life

Assume you volunteer as a youth outreach assistant at a Child and Family Services non-profit organization in your community. You have been asked to lead a discussion about eating disorders at the next student workshop your organization will host. Your organization has given you the following information to use in your discussion. Read the information and write a draft of your multimedia presentation.

DISORDERED EATING: ARE YOU AT RISK?

disordered eating A general term used to describe a variety of abnormal or atypical eating behaviors that are used to keep or maintain a lower body weight.

eating disorder A clinically diagnosed psychiatric disorder characterized by severe disturbances in body image and eating behaviors.

anorexia nervosa A serious, potentially life-threatening eating disorder that is characterized by self-starvation, which eventually leads to a deficiency in the energy and essential nutrients the body requires to function normally.

bulimia nervosa A serious eating disorder characterized by recurrent episodes of binge eating and recurrent inappropriate compensatory behaviors in order to prevent weight gain, such as self-induced vomiting, fasting, excessive exercise, or misuse of laxatives, diuretics, enemas, or other medications.

body image A person's perception of his or her body's appearance and functioning.

Disordered eating is a general term used to describe a variety of atypical eating behaviors that people use to achieve or maintain a lower body weight. These behaviors may be as simple as going on and off diets or as extreme as refusing to eat any fat. Such behaviors don't usually continue for long enough to make the person seriously ill, nor do they significantly disrupt the person's normal routine. In contrast, some people restrict their eating so much or for so long that they become dangerously underweight. These people have an **eating disorder**. The two more commonly diagnosed eating disorders are *anorexia nervosa* and *bulimia nervosa*. Anorexia nervosa is characterized by self-starvation, leading to a severe nutrient deficiency. In contrast, bulimia nervosa is characterized by extreme overeating and followed by self-induced vomiting, misuse of laxatives, fasting, or excessive exercise.

EATING BEHAVIORS OCCUR ON A CONTINUUM

When does normal dieting cross the line into disordered eating? Eating behaviors occur on a continuum, a spectrum that can't be divided neatly into parts. An example is a rainbow—where exactly does the red end and the orange begin? Thinking about eating behaviors as a continuum makes it easier to understand how a person can progress from normal eating behaviors to a pattern that is disordered. For instance, let's say that for several years you've skipped breakfast in favor of a midmorning snack, but now you find yourself avoiding the cafeteria until early afternoon. Is this normal? To answer that question, you'd need to consider your feelings about food and your *body image*.

MANY FACTORS CONTRIBUTE TO DISORDERED EATING BEHAVIORS

Research indicates that a number of psychological, interpersonal, social, and biological factors may contribute in any particular individual.

Influence of Family Research suggests that family conditioning, structure, and patterns of interaction can influence the development of an eating disorder. Based on observational studies, families with an anorexic member show more rigidity in their family structure, have less clear interpersonal boundaries, and tend to avoid open discussions on topics of disagreement. Conversely, families with a member diagnosed with bulimia nervosa tend to have a less stable family organization and to be less nurturing, more angry, and more disruptive. Childhood physical or sexual abuse also increases the risk for an eating disorder.

Influence of Media As media saturation has increased, so has the incidence of eating disorders among white women. Every day, we are confronted with advertisements in which images of lean, beautiful women promote everything from beer to cars. Most adults understand that these images are unrealistic, but adolescents, still developing a sense of identity and body image, lack the ability to distance themselves from what they see. It is likely that the barrage of media models is contributing to the increase in eating disorders. However, scientific evidence that the media are *causing* this increase is difficult to obtain.

Influence of Social and Cultural Values Eating disorders are significantly more common in white females in Western societies than in other women worldwide. This may be due in part to the white Western culture's association of slenderness with health, wealth, and high fashion. In contrast, until recently, the prevailing view in developing societies has been that excess body fat is desirable as a sign of health and wealth. The members of society with whom we most often interact—our family members, friends, classmates, and co-workers—also influence the way we see ourselves.

Influence of Personality A number of studies suggest that people with anorexia nervosa exhibit increased rates of obsessive-compulsive behaviors and perfectionism. They also tend to be socially inhibited, compliant, and emotionally restrained. Unfortunately, many studies observe these behaviors only in individuals who are very ill and in a state of starvation, which may affect personality. Thus, it is difficult to determine if personality is the cause or the effect of the disorder. In contrast, people with bulimia tend to be more impulsive, have low self-esteem, and demonstrate an extroverted, erratic personality style that seeks attention and admiration.

Influence of Genetic Factors Overall, the diagnosis of anorexia nervosa or bulimia nervosa is several times more common in siblings and other blood relatives who also have the diagnosis than in the general population. This observation might imply the existence of an "eating disorder gene"; however, it is difficult to separate the genetic factors from the environmental factors within families.

—Adapted from Thompson and Moore. *Nutrition for Life*, 3rd ed., Pearson, 2013, pp. 284–286.

Reading and Writing for College Life

Assume you are taking a student success course. You are to read the following passage and write a short essay that identifies and explains which intelligences are your strengths and which intelligences you need to develop.

78 Navigating Your Future Success?

Howard Gardner's Multiple Intelligences

Howard Gardner, a university professor, developed a theory of multiple intelligences. He argued that we have different types of intelligences. Within each person, some intelligences are better developed than others. For example, if you prefer math and science classes over English, you have a well-developed logic/math intelligence. Please do not take any of this to mean that if you struggle in an area you cannot do it because of your innate intelligence. Instead, take steps to develop these skills, perhaps by drawing on strengths in other areas of Gardner's framework.

Linguistic Intelligence. Someone with strong linguistic intelligence has an aptitude for using and understanding language. Writers, speakers, and lawyers typically have great linguistic intelligence.

Logical/Mathematical Intelligence. Someone with logical/mathematical intelligence can understand how systems work and can work well with numbers. Scientists, accountants, computer programmers, and mathematicians rely on this type of intelligence.

Musical/Rhythmic Intelligence. Someone with musical/rhythmic intelligence can recognize patterns and rhythms with relative ease. Musical performers/composers are the most obvious example of people who embody this type of intelligence.

Bodily/Kinesthetic Intelligence. Someone with bodily kinesthetic intelligence often does something physical to solve a problem or to learn. Examples include athletes, firefighters, and performing artists.

Spatial Intelligence. Someone with spatial intelligence can imagine and understand the three-dimensional world in their own minds. Airplane pilots and engineers rely on spatial intelligence in their work.

Naturalist Intelligence. Someone with naturalist intelligence understands the features of and differences among living things and the natural world. Farmers, foresters, and others who work on the land and with animals demonstrate naturalist intelligence.

Intrapersonal Intelligence. Someone with intrapersonal intelligence has strong self-awareness. Those with intrapersonal intelligence are very aware of their strengths as well as any limitations and often work at self-improvement. Researchers and philosophers demonstrate this intelligence.

Interpersonal Intelligence. Someone with interpersonal intelligence is able to understand and relate to other people. Educators, politicians, counselors, health care professionals, and salespeople demonstrate interpersonal intelligence.

–Adapted from Colbert, *Navigating Your Future Success*, 2nd ed., Pearson, 2015, pp. 78–79.

Reading and Writing for Working Life

Assume you are applying for a job in middle management for a national retail store chain such as Apple or Old Navy. Assume you found the following article in a workforce magazine. In your letter of application, describe the skills you possess that will make you a successful manager.

The Skills of Successful Managers

Because they are responsible for a variety of jobs and because these jobs can change quite rapidly, managers need to possess 5 basic skills.

A manager must have **conceptual skills**—the ability to think abstractly and to picture an organization as a whole and understand its relationship to the remainder of the business community. Such skills also include understanding the relationships between the parts of an organization itself. Whenever new market opportunities or potential threats arise, managers rely on their conceptual skills to predict outcomes of their decisions. Conceptual skills are often developed with time and experience.

Technical skills include the abilities and knowledge that enable employees to carry out the specific tasks required of a discipline or a department, such as drafting skills for an architect, programming skills for a software developer, or market analysis skills for a marketing manager. Technical skills may also include how to operate certain machinery. Managers must be comfortable with technology and possess good analytical skills to interpret a variety of data Managers must also know how to perform or at least have a good understanding of the skills required of the employees they supervise.

Managers who possess **time management skills** are effective and productive with their time. Effective managers eliminate time wasters, such as constant interruptions, set aside time each day to return phone calls and e-mail, ensure that meetings have a clear agenda, and successfully delegate work to others to increase the productive use of available time. Analyzing your day to track carefully how your time is spent can also be an important key to improving time management.

Managers achieve their goals by working with people both inside and outside an organization, so it is critical that they have strong **interpersonal skills**. Interpersonal skills enable managers to interact with other people to motivate them and to develop trust and loyalty. It is becoming increasingly important for managers to take into consideration the needs, backgrounds, and experiences of many different people when communicating with individuals and groups in an organization

It is critical that managers have good **decision-making skills**—the ability to identify and analyze a challenge, identify and examine the alternatives, choose and implement the best plan of action, and evaluate the results. Successful managers work with their teams during the decision making process, and if changes need to be made, the entire process begins again

—Adapted from Solomon, *Better Business*, 3rd ed., Pearson, 2014, pp. 205–207.

Review Test

MySkillsLab™
Complete this Exercise on myskillslab.com

Score (number correct) ______ × 10 = ______%

Word Choice, Tone, and Purpose

Read the following passage from a college history textbook. Answer the questions that follow.

The Death Camps: Murder by Assembly Line

[1]On January 20, 1942, senior German officials met in a villa in Wannsee, outside Berlin, to finalize plans for killing every Jew in Europe. [2]**SS** lieutenant colonel Adolf Eichmann (1906–1962) listed the number of Jews in every country. [3]To accomplish mass murder, the **Einsatzgruppen** had become killing machines. [4]By trial and error, they discovered the most efficient ways of rounding up Jews, shooting them quickly, and burying the bodies. [5]However, shooting took time, used up valuable ammunition, and required large numbers of men.

[6]Moreover, even the best-trained and carefully **indoctrinated** soldiers eventually cracked under the strain of shooting unarmed women and children at close range. [7]A systematic approach was needed. [8]This perceived need resulted in a key Nazi innovation: the death camp.

[9]The death camp was a specialized form of a concentration camp. [10]From 1933 on, Hitler's government had sentenced communists, Jehovah's Witnesses, the **Roma**, and anyone else defined as an enemy of the regime to forced labor in concentration camps. [11]After the war began, the concentration camp system expanded dramatically. [12]Scattered throughout Europe, concentration camps became an essential part of the Nazi war economy. [13]Some firms, such as the huge chemical **conglomerate** I. G. Farben, established factories inside or right next to camps, which provided vital supplies of forced labor. [14]All across Europe during the war, concentration camp inmates died in huge numbers from the brutal conditions. [15]But only in Poland did the Nazis construct death camps, specialized concentration camps with only one purpose—murder, primarily the murder of Jews.

[16]The death camps marked the final stage in a vast assembly line of murder. [17]In early 1942 the trains conveying victims to the death camps began to rumble across Europe. [18]Individuals selected for **extermination** followed orders to gather at the railway station for deportation to "work camps." [19]They were then packed into cattle cars, more than 100 people per car, all standing up for the entire journey. [20]Many Jews died en route. [21]The survivors stumbled off the trains into a nightmare world. [22]At some camps, SS guards **culled** stronger Jews from each transport to be worked to death as slaves. [23]Most, however, walked straight from the trains into a room, where they were told to undress, and then herded into a "shower room"—actually a gas chamber. [24]Carbon monoxide gas or a pesticide called Zyklon-B killed the victims. [25]Jewish slaves burned the bodies in vast crematoria, modeled after industrial bake ovens. [26]The Nazis thus constructed a vast machine of death.

SS (2): abbreviation for the German word *Schutzstaffel*, which translates as Protective Squadron, a personal guard unit for Hitler, responsible for the mass murder of Jews and others deemed undesirable

Einsatzgruppen (3): strike or task force, SS units given the task of murdering Jews and Communist Party members in the areas of the Soviet Union occupied by Germany during World War II

indoctrinated (6): instructed, taught

Roma (10): gypsies

conglomerate (13): corporation, business

extermination (18): execution, death

—Levack, Muir, Veldman, and Maas, *The West: Encounters & Transformations*, Atlas Edition, Combined Edition, 2nd ed., pp. 870–871.

Vocabulary in Context

1. What does the word **culled** mean in sentence 22?
   - **a.** rejected
   - **b.** inserted
   - **c.** picked
   - **d.** beat

Inference

2. Based on information from the passage, we may infer that
   - **a.** only Jews died in concentration camps.
   - **b.** only the Nazi government was financially involved with the concentration camps.
   - **c.** all concentration camps across Europe specialized in killing prisoners.
   - **d.** racism was a driving force behind the death camps.

Tone

3. The tone of sentence 1 is
   - **a.** matter-of-fact.
   - **b.** condemning.
   - **c.** bitter.
   - **d.** understanding.

Tone

4. The overall tone of the passage is
   - **a.** horrified.
   - **b.** neutral.
   - **c.** condemning.
   - **d.** sorrowful.

Purpose

5. The writer's purpose is to
   - **a.** argue about the brutality of the Nazi death camps.
   - **b.** shock the reader with graphic details about Nazi death camps.
   - **c.** inform the reader about the development of Nazi death camps.

Summary Response

Restate the authors' central idea in your own words. In your summary, state the authors' tone and purpose. Begin your summary response with the following: *The central idea of "Death Camps: Murder by Assembly Line" by Levack, Muir, Veldman, and Maas is. . . .*

Reader Response

Assume a local chapter of the American Jewish League is sponsoring an essay contest to honor those who suffered under the Nazi regime and to educate youth about the effects of prejudice. Write a 500-word essay to submit to the contest.

MySkillsLab™
Complete this Exercise
on myskillslab.com

Academic Learning Log: Module Review

Summary of Key Concepts of Word Choice, Tone, and Purpose

Assess your comprehension of word choice, tone, and purpose.

LO1 LO2

1. Tone is ____
____.
2. Word choice is ____
____.
3. Connotation is ____
____.
4. Denotation is ____
____.
5. An ______________ tone is impartial, unbiased, neutral, formal, or literal.
6. A ______________ tone is personal, biased, emotional, informal, or figurative.
7. To inform, the writer chooses words that state ______________ meanings. To express a personal view, entertain an audience, or argue a point, a writer often chooses words with ______________ meanings.

LO3 LO4 LO5

8. Question and annotate to ______________ tone before and during reading.
9. Brainstorm and ______________ to ______________ tone and purpose.
10. ______________, ______________, and proofread to verify appropriate tone and purpose.

Test Your Comprehension of Word Choice, Tone, and Purpose

Respond in your own words to the following questions and prompts.

LO1 LO2

What is the relationship among word choice, tone, and purpose?

LO3 LO4 LO5

Describe how the reading/writing strategy enables a reader/writer to comprehend and establish tone in a passage.

LO1 LO2 LO3 LO4 LO5

1. **How will I use what I have learned?** In your notebook, discuss how you will apply to your own reading/writing strategy what you have learned about word choice, tone, and purpose. When will you apply this knowledge to your reading/writing strategy?
2. **What do I still need to study about word choice, tone, and purpose?** In your notebook, discuss your ongoing study needs. Describe what, when, and how you will continue studying and using word choice, tone, and purpose.

MySkillsLab™

Complete the Post-test for Module 4 in MySkillsLab.

5 Distinguish Between Fact and Opinion

LEARNING OUTCOMES

After studying this module you should be able to:

- **LO 1** Answer the Question "What's the Point of Fact and Opinion?"
- **LO 2** Distinguish Between Fact and Opinion
- **LO 3** Survey, Question, and Annotate to Analyze Facts and Opinions
- **LO 4** Brainstorm and Draft Using Facts and Opinions
- **LO 5** Review, Revise, and Proofread for Effective Use of Facts and Opinions

Carlos and Nashawn were driving in opposite directions when their cars collided. Carlos accused Nashawn, saying her distracted driving caused the accident since she was putting on her makeup and talking on her cellphone. Nashawn blamed Carlos for the accident, saying that he was speeding and weaving in and out of lanes. The fact is that a car accident occurred. The drivers involved gave two different opinions about the cause of the accident. The traffic officer who responds to the accident will gather evidence or **objective proof** to separate fact from opinion and determine the true cause of the accident. The evidence may come from eyewitnesses who observed the accident as it occurred. Or the evidence may be physical evidence such as skid marks on the road or the specific damage to the cars. **Facts** can be proven by evidence; **opinions** cannot be proven. The ability to distinguish between fact and opinion affects how you react to what you see or read and how you pass the information on as a writer. Master readers and writers are able to accurately recognize and clearly communicate facts and opinions.

Objective proof can be physical evidence, an eyewitness account, or the result of an accepted scientific method.

A **fact** is a specific detail that is true based on objective proof.

An **opinion** is an interpretation, value judgment, or belief that cannot be proved or disproved.

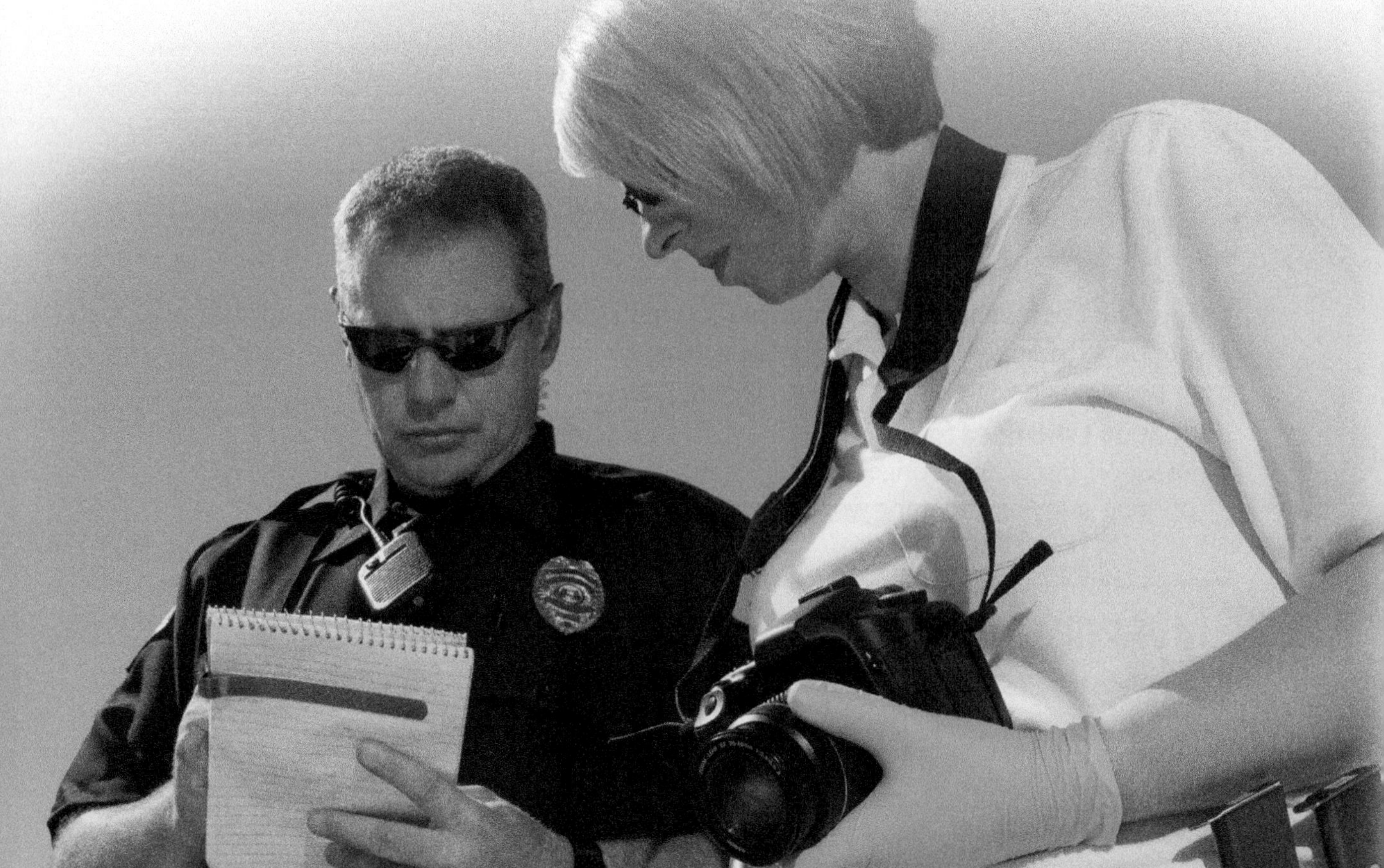

WHAT'S THE POINT of Fact and Opinion? 

You probably are familiar with the terms *fact* and *opinion*, and you may already have an idea about what each one means. Test what you know about the difference between fact and opinion. Study the following photographs that illustrate the nature of facts and opinions. In the blanks below each photograph, state the purpose of the opinion or fact as illustrated. Then predict how fact and opinion differ by answering the question "What's the point of fact and opinion?"

Photographic Organizer: Fact and Opinion

Study each photograph and predict the purpose of using facts and opinions.

FACT

Purpose: ______________________

____

Purpose: ______________________

____

OPINION

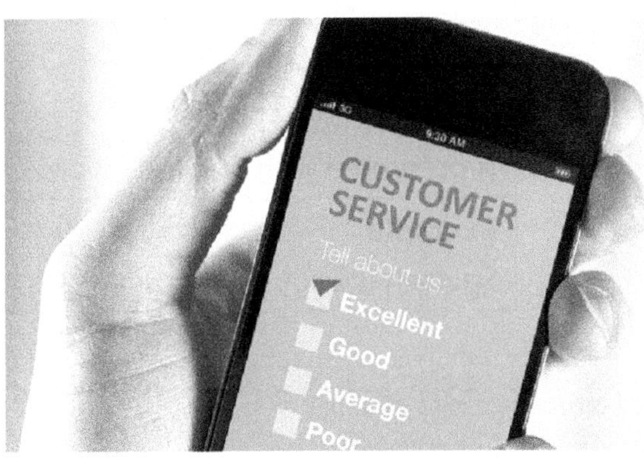

Purpose: ______________________

____

Purpose: ______________________

____

What's the point of fact and opinion? ______________________

____

L2 Distinguish Between Fact and Opinion

Both readers and writers must distinguish between fact and opinion to effectively comprehend and make a point. Consider the following two statements.

> Andrew Jackson served as the seventh President of the United States.
> Andrew Jackson was a cruel and violent leader.

The first sentence states a detail that can be proven as true or false. The second sentence relays a personal view with which others may agree or disagree. Separating fact from opinion requires you to think critically because opinion is often presented as fact. The following clues will help you separate fact from opinion.

A Fact . . .	**An Opinion . . .**
is objective is discovered states reality can be verified is presented with unbiased words	is subjective is created interprets reality cannot be verified is presented with biased words
Example Spinach is a source of iron.	**Example** Spinach tastes awful.

Biased words express opinions, value judgments, and interpretations.

Qualifiers are words that limit or enhance of the meaning of another word.

Word choice reveals the use of facts and opinions. **Biased words** often imply an emotion. A **qualifier** may express an absolute, unwavering opinion using words such as *always* or *never*. Qualifiers may also express an opinion in the form of a command as in *must*, or the desirability of an action with a word such as *should*. Qualifiers may indicate different degrees of doubt with words such as *seems* or *might*. The box below contains a few examples of these types of words.

Biased Words					
amazing	best	favorite	great	magnificent	stupid
awful	better	frightful	greatest	miserable	ugly
bad	disgusting	fun	handsome	poor	unbelievable
beautiful	exciting	good	key	smart	value
Qualifiers					
all	could	likely	never	possibly, possible	sometimes
always	every	may	often	probably, probable	think
appear	has/have to	might	only	seem	though
believe	it is believed	must	ought to	should	usually

Often, we base our ideas and beliefs on a blend of fact and opinion. Three questions help master readers and writers to distinguish between facts and opinions.

Questions to Distinguish Between Fact and Opinion

- Can the statement be proved or demonstrated to be true?
- Can the statement be observed in practice or operation?
- Can the statement be verified by witnesses, manuscripts, or documents?

If the answer to any of these questions is "no," the statement is an opinion—not a fact. Often, you will find the answer is both "yes" and "no," as many statements include both fact and opinion.

? For Module 5, assume you are taking a college course in American History, and your class is beginning a study on the theme of the Right to Life, Liberty, and the Pursuit of Happiness. Each reading in this module follows this theme. After completing all assigned readings, you will be asked to answer the guiding question "What is the importance and effect of the phrase 'the Right to Life, Liberty, and the Pursuit of Happiness' in the Declaration of Independence?"

Example

Read the following sentences taken from a passage in a college history textbook. Mark each as **F** if it states a fact, **O** if it expresses an opinion, or **F/O** if it combines fact and opinion. Underline biased words and qualifiers as needed.

Clearing the Land of Indians

_____ 1. The first major political controversy of Jackson's presidency involved Indian Policy.

_____ 2. At the time Jackson took office, 125,000 Native Americans still lived east of the Mississippi River.

_____ 3. Cherokee, Choctaw, Chickasaw, and Creek Indians held millions of acres in what would become the southern cotton kingdom stretching across Georgia, Alabama, and Mississippi.

_____ 4. Since Jefferson's presidency, two differing policies, assimilation and removal, had governed the treatment of Native Americans.

_____ 5. The goal of assimilation was for Indians to adopt the customs and economic practices of white Americans.

_____ 6. Removal was believed to be the only way to ensure the survival of the Native American culture.

_____ 7. The goal of the removal policy was the voluntary migration of Indians westward to tracts of land where they could live free from white harassment; however, Jackson stated that if the Indians refused to move west, he would destroy their nation.

CONTINUED

EXAMPLE *CONTINUED*

____ 8. During the winter of 1831, the Choctaw became the first tribe to walk the "Trail of Tears" westward.

____ 9. Malnutrition, exposure, and a cholera epidemic killed many members of the Choctaw nation; in 1836, about 35,000 of the Creek tribes' 15,000 members died along the westward removal trek.

____ 10. Jackson's Indian policy was both callous and inhumane.

—Adapted from Martin, Roberts, Mintz, McMurry, and Jones. *America and Its Peoples*, 5th ed., Pearson, 2004, pp. 258–259.

Explanation

Compare your answers to the following think-aloud.

I was surprised to see how often biased words and qualifiers appeared in these sentences from a textbook. I usually think of textbooks as offering only facts. However, these sentences are about an emotional time during which one group of people suffered defeat and removal from their ancestral lands. Sentences 2, 4, and 5 state facts (F) without use of biased words or qualifiers. Sentence 1 (F/O) uses the qualifier **major.** And the word **controversy** states an opinion by suggesting a negative meaning about the facts of Jackson's Indian Policy. In sentence 3 (F/O), the amount of land owned by Native Americans at this time can be verified by research. However, the biased word **kingdom** describes the future use of that land. Sentence 6 (O) uses the qualifiers **believed to be** and **only** to reflect an opinion about the removal policy. Sentence 7 (F/O) offers details that can be verified. However, the sentence also uses the biased word **harassment** and reports Jackson's threatening stance. Sentence 8 (F/O) states facts that are documented. However, the vivid picture created by the figurative words **Trail of Tears** gives an emotional name to the removal policy. Sentence 9 (F/O) mostly states facts that are documented. However, the word **trek** does have a negative connotation that suggests the difficulty of the trip. Choosing **trek** instead of **journey** or **walk** offers an opinion. Sentence 10 states a strong negative opinion about Jackson's policy. The reader may likely agree with this opinion based on the facts.

Practice 1

Distinguish Between Fact and Opinion

Assume the following primary document is your second assigned reading on the theme of the Right to Life, Liberty, and the Pursuit of Happiness. Read the passage and answer the questions that follow.

Report of the 1848 Women's Rights Convention

[1]The text of this report is from the original tract produced after the Convention in the North Star Printing Office owned by Frederick Douglass, Rochester, New York. [2]It was reprinted several times and circulated as a sales item at local and national women's rights conventions.

[3]Held at Seneca Falls, N.Y., July 19th and 20th, 1848. Rochester:

[4]Printed by John Dick at the North Star Office Thursday Morning

[5]The Convention assembled at the hour appointed, James Mott, of Philadelphia, in the Chair. [6]The minutes of the previous day having been read, E. C. Stanton again read the Declaration of Sentiments, which was freely discussed by Lucretia Mott, Ansel Bascom, S. E. Woodworth, Thomas and Mary Ann M'clintock, Frederick Douglass, Amy Post, Catharine Stebbins, and Elizabeth C. Stanton, and was unanimously adopted, as follows:

Declaration of Sentiments

[7]When, in the course of human events, it becomes necessary for one portion of the family of man to assume among the people of the earth a position different from that which they have hitherto occupied, but one to which the laws of nature and of nature's God entitle them, a decent respect to the opinions of mankind requires that they should declare the causes that impel them to such a course. [8]We hold these truths to be self-evident; that all men and women are created equal; that they are endowed by their Creator with certain inalienable rights; that among these are life, liberty, and the pursuit of happiness; that to secure these rights governments are

Elizabeth Cady Stanton and her daughter, Harriet, 1856

CONTINUED

instituted, deriving their just powers from the consent of the governed. [9]Whenever any form of Government becomes destructive of these ends, it is the right of those who suffer from it to refuse allegiance to it, and to insist upon the institution of a new government, laying its foundation on such principles, and organizing its powers in such form as to them shall seem most likely to effect their safety and happiness. [10]Prudence, indeed, will dictate that governments long established should not be changed for light and transient causes; and accordingly, all experience hath shown that mankind are more disposed to suffer, while evils are sufferable, than to right themselves, by abolishing the forms to which they are accustomed. [11]But when a long train of abuses and usurpations, pursuing invariably the same object, evinces a design to reduce them under absolute despotism, it is their duty to throw off such government, and to provide new guards for their future security. [12]Such has been the patient sufferance of the women under this government, and such is now the necessity which constrains them to demand the equal station to which they are entitled.

[13]The history of mankind is a history of repeated injuries and usurpations on the part of man toward woman, having in direct object the establishment of an absolute tyranny over her. [14]To prove this, let facts be submitted to a candid world.

[15]He has never permitted her to exercise her inalienable right to the elective franchise.

[16]He has compelled her to submit to laws, in the formation of which she had no voice.

[17]He has withheld from her rights which are given to the most ignorant and degraded men—both natives and foreigners.

[18]Having deprived her of this first right of a citizen, the elective franchise, thereby leaving her without representation in the halls of legislation, he has oppressed her on all sides.

[19]He has made her, if married, in the eye of the law, civilly dead.

[20]He has taken from her all right in property, even to the wages she earns.

[21]He has made her, morally, an irresponsible being, as she can commit many crimes, with impunity, provided they be done in the presence of her husband. [22]In the covenant of marriage, she is compelled to promise obedience to her husband, he becoming, to all intents and purposes, her master—the law giving him power to deprive her of her liberty, and to administer chastisement.

[23]He has so framed the laws of divorce, as to what shall be the proper causes of divorce; in case of separation, to whom the guardianship of

the children shall be given, as to be wholly regardless of the happiness of women—the law, in all cases, going upon the false supposition of the supremacy of man, and giving all power into his hands.

[24]After depriving her of all rights as a married woman, if single and the owner of property, he has taxed her to support a government which recognizes her only when her property can be made profitable to it.

[25]He has monopolized nearly all the profitable employments, and from those she is permitted to follow, she receives but a scanty remuneration.

[26]He closes against her all the avenues to wealth and distinction, which he considers most honorable to himself. [27]As a teacher of theology, medicine, or law, she is not known.

[28]He has denied her the facilities for obtaining a thorough education—all colleges being closed against her.

[29]He allows her in Church as well as State, but a subordinate position, claiming Apostolic authority for her exclusion from the ministry, and with some exceptions, from any public participation in the affairs of the Church.

[30]He has created a false public sentiment, by giving to the world a different code of morals for men and women, by which moral delinquencies which exclude women from society, are not only tolerated but deemed of little account in man.

[31]He has usurped the prerogative of Jehovah himself, claiming it as his right to assign for her a sphere of action, when that belongs to her conscience and her God.

[32]He has endeavored, in every way that he could to destroy her confidence in her own powers, to lessen her self-respect, and to make her willing to lead a dependent and abject life.

[33]Now, in view of this entire disfranchisement of one-half the people of this country, their social and religious degradation,—in view of the unjust laws above mentioned, and because women do feel themselves aggrieved, oppressed, and fraudulently deprived of their most sacred rights, we insist that they have immediate admission to all the rights and privileges which belong to them as citizens of these United States.

[34]In entering upon the great work before us, we anticipate no small amount of misconception, misrepresentation, and ridicule; but we shall use every instrumentality within our power to effect our object. [35]We shall employ agents, circulate tracts, petition the State and national Legislatures, and endeavor to enlist the pulpit and the press in our behalf. [36]We hope this Convention will be followed by a series of Conventions, embracing every part of the country.

[37]Firmly relying upon the final triumph of the Right and the True, we do this day affix our signatures to this declaration.

—National Park Service. *Women's Rights*. 7 July 2014.

CONTINUED

PRACTICE 1 *CONTINUED*

1. Sentence 1 is a statement of
   a. fact. **b.** opinion. **c.** fact and opinion.

2. Sentence 5 is a statement of
   a. fact. **b.** opinion. **c.** fact and opinion.

3. Sentence 6 is a statement of
   a. fact. **b.** opinion. **c.** fact and opinion.

4. Sentence 13 is a statement of
   a. fact. **b.** opinion. **c.** fact and opinion.

5. Sentence 15 is a statement of
   a. fact. **b.** opinion. **c.** fact and opinion.

6. Sentence 20 is a statement of
   a. fact. **b.** opinion. **c.** fact and opinion.

7. Sentence 32 is a statement of
   a. fact. **b.** opinion. **c.** fact and opinion.

8. Sentence 37 is a statement of
   a. fact. **b.** opinion. **c.** fact and opinion.

9. The purpose of the text is to
   a. inform. **b.** entertain. **c.** argue.

10. The overall tone of the text is
    a. neutral. **b.** condemning. **c.** approving.

After Reading Question: *How were Native Americans (page 181) and women in the 1800s (page 183) denied the right to life, liberty, and the pursuit of happiness?* Record your answers in your notebook or journal.

Survey, Question, and Annotate to Analyze Facts and Opinions

LO3

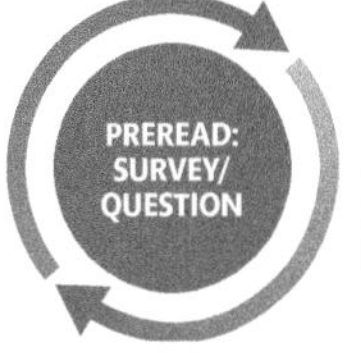

Distinguishing between fact and opinion is a key strategy throughout the reading/writing process. Even though opinions can't be proved true in the same way that facts can, many opinions are sound and valuable. To infer the reliability of an opinion you may consider the source or the author of the opinion. Writers offer two types of valid opinions: **informed opinions** and **expert opinions**. For example, you may develop an informed opinion about a physical illness through your own research. In contrast, a doctor offers an expert opinion based on years of education, training, and experience.

An **informed opinion** expresses a view based on the gathering and analyzing of information about a given topic.

An **expert opinion** expresses a view based on training and extensive knowledge in a given field.

A **fallacy** is an error in logical thought, a mistaken belief, or a deceptive opinion.

Some writers may use an emotional appeal or **fallacy** instead of valid opinions or facts to convince the reader to support a particular point or view. The word *fallacy* comes from a Latin word that means "to deceive or trick." Fallacies mislead readers by powerfully stating or implying irrelevant and inadequate details. The following chart offers a few examples of fallacies.

Examples of Fallacies

Fallacy	Definition	Example
Bandwagon	Suggests that "everyone is doing it" so it must be valid	The fact that the majority of our citizens support gun control proves that gun control is morally right.
Begging the Question	Assumes that an unproven or unsupported point is true; restates the point as a supporting detail	If such actions were not illegal, then they would not be prohibited by the law.
Glittering Generality	Offers general positive statements that cannot be verified	America is the land of the free and the home of the brave.
Personal Attack/ Name Calling	Uses abusive remarks to discredit a person in place of evidence	Andrew Jackson, murderer and adulterer, is unfit to be President of the United States.
Plain Folks	Appeals to the simple, practical, no nonsense, everyday experience or commonly shared values	"Don't Swap Horses in the Middle of the Stream," Abraham Lincoln campaign slogan, 1864.
Transfer	Associates a product or idea with a symbol that has positive or negative values	The Republican Party is the party of Abraham Lincoln.

To analyze the writer's use of facts and opinions to determine if the writer has provided relevant or adequate support, ask questions and annotate the text.

Example

Assume this primary document is your next assigned reading on the theme of the Right to Life, Liberty, and the Pursuit of Happiness. In addition to the passage, your professor provided you an introductory paragraph to the reading as part of your assignment. Before reading, skim the passages and record three questions about the use of fact and opinion. Also note new or difficult words to define before reading. For example, survey one reader's Before Reading Glossary defining difficult words; then identify words you need to define before reading. During reading, annotate examples of words and details that answer your prereading questions. Then, answer the questions that follow the passage.

Before Reading Questions:

1. ______________________________

____

____

2. ______________________________

____

____

3. ______________________________

____

____

Before Reading Glossary

retrograde (sentence 14): moving or bending backwards; moving toward an earlier worse condition

naturalized (sentence 33): granted citizenship in the United States after fulfilling certain requirements

infringement (sentence 34): violation or abuse of a law or a right

talismanic (sentence 38): an object or idea that has a powerful, supernatural influence

cupidity (sentence 41): greed

A SAN FRANCISCO MERCHANT PROTESTS DISCRIMINATION AGAINST THE CHINESE

[1]The Gold Rush brought tens of thousands of people from around the world, including China, to California. [2]In 1849, there were only 54 Chinese immigrants in California, but by 1877, the number had increased to 116,000. [3]Although emigrants from China made up only a small proportion of California's immigrants, they faced intense prejudice and discrimination. [4]In 1852, California Governor John Bigler proposed restricting immigration from China. [5]In the following public letter, published in a newspaper, Norman Asing, a prominent San Francisco merchant, restaurant owner, and community leader, responds to the governor's proposal.

–Martin, et. al. *America and Its Peoples*, 5th ed., Pearson, p. 356.

[6]To His Excellence Gov. Bigler

[7]Sir.—I am a Chinaman, a republican, and a lover of free institutions, am much attached to the principles of the Government of the United States, and therefore take the liberty of addressing you the chief of the Government of this State.

[8]Your official position gives you a great opportunity to good or evil. [9]Your opinions through a message to a legislative body have weight, and perhaps none more so with the people, for the effects of your late message has been thus far to prejudice the public mind against my people, to enable those who wait the opportunity to hunt them down, and rob them of the rewards of their toil. [10]You may not have meant that this should be the case, but you can see what will be the result of your propositions.

[11]I am not much acquainted with your logic, that by excluding population from this State you enhance its wealth. [12]I always have considered that population was wealth: particularly a population of producers, of men who by the labor of their hands or intellect, enrich the warehouses or the granaries of the country with the products of nature and art.

[13]You are deeply convinced you say "that to enhance the prosperity and to preserve the tranquility of this State, Asiatic immigration must he checked." [14]This, your Excellency, is but one step towards a retrograde movement of the Government, which, on reflection, you will discover; and which the citizens of this country ought never to tolerate. [15]It was one of the principal causes of quarrel between you (when colonies) and England; when the latter pressed laws against emigration you looked for immigration; it came, and immigration made you what you are—your nation what it is. [16]It transferred you at once from childhood to manhood and made you great and respectable throughout the nations of the earth.

[17]I am sure your Excellency cannot, if you would, prevent your being called the descendant of an immigrant, for I am sure you do not boast of being a descendant of the red men. [18]But your further logic is more reprehensible. [19]You argue that this is a republic of a particular race—that the constitution of the United States admits of no asylum to any other than the pale face. [20]This proposition is false in the extreme—, and you know it. [21]The declaration of your independence, and all the acts of your government, your people, and your history, are against you.

[22]It is true, you have degraded the negro because of you holding him in involuntary servitude, and because for the sake of union in some of your States such was tolerated and amongst this class you would endeavor to place us and no doubt it would be pleasing to some would-be freemen to mark the brand of servitude upon us. [23]But we would beg to remind you that when your nation was

CONTINUED

EXAMPLE *CONTINUED*

a wilderness, and the nation from whom you sprung barbarous, we exercised most of the arts and virtues of civilized life; that we are possessed of a language and literature, and that men skilled in science and the arts numerous amongst us; that the productions of our manufactories, our sail and work-shops, form no small share of the commerce of the world; and that for centuries our schools, charitable institutions, asylums and hospitals been as common as in your own land.

[24]That our people cannot be reproved for their idleness, and that your historians have given them due credit for the variety and richness of their works of art, and for their simplicity of manners, and particularly their industry. [25]And we beg to remark, that so far as the history of our race in California goes, it stamps with the test of truth the fact that we are not the degraded race you would make us. [26]We came amongst you as mechanics or traders, and following every honorable business of life. [27]You do not find us pursuing occupations of a degrading character, except you consider labor degrading, which I am sure you do not; and if our countrymen save the proceeds of their industry from the tavern and the gambling house, to spend it on the purchase of farms or town lots or on their families, surely you will admit that even these are virtues.

[28]You say "you desire to see no change in the generous policy of this Government as far as regards to Europeans." [29]It is out of your power to say, however, in what way or to whom the doctrines of the constitution shall apply. [30]You have no more right to propose a measure for checking immigration, than you have to assume the right of sending a message to the Legislature on the subject. [31]As for the color and complexion of our race, we are perfectly aware that our population have been a little more tanned than yours.

[32]Your Excellency will discover, however, that we are as much allied to the African race and the red man as you are yourself, and that as far as the aristocracy of skin is concerned, ours might compare with many of the European races; nor do we consider that your Excellency, as a Democrat, will make us believe that the framers of your declaration of rights ever suggested the propriety of establishing an aristocracy of skin.

[33]I am a naturalized citizen, your Excellency, of Charleston, South Carolina, and a Christian too: and so hope you will stand corrected in your assertion that "none of the Asiatic class," as you are pleased to term them, "have applied for benefits under our naturalization act." [34]I could point out to you numbers of citizens, all over the whole continent, who have taken advantage of your hospitality and citizenship, and I defy you to say that our race have ever abused that hospitality or forfeited their claim on this or any of the governments of South America, by an infringement on the laws of the countries into which

they pass. [35]You find us peculiarly peaceable and orderly. [36]It does not cost your State much for our criminal prosecution. [37]We apply less to your courts for redress, and so far as I know, there are none that are a charge upon the State, as paupers. [38]You say that "gold, with its talismanic power, has overcome those natural habits of non-intercourse we have exhibited." [39]I ask you, has not gold had the same effect upon your people, and the people of other countries, who have migrated hither? [40]Why, it was gold that filled your country, (formerly a desert) with people; filled the harbor with ships, and opened our much-coveted trade to the enterprise of your merchants.

[41]You cannot, in the face of facts that stare you in the face, assert that the cupidity of which you speak is ours alone: so that your Excellency will perceive that in this age a change of cupidity would not tell. [42]Thousands of citizens come here to dig gold, with the idea of returning as speedily as they can. [43]We think you are in error, however, in this respect, as many of us, and many more, will acquire a domicile amongst you. [44]But, for the present, I shall take leave of your Excellency, and shall resume this question upon another occasion; which I hope you will take into consideration in a spirit of candor. [45]Your predecessor pursued a different line of conduct towards us, as will appear by reference to this message.

[46]I have the honor to be your Excellency's very obedient servant. Norman Asing.

"The Chinese Question." Harper's Magazine, 1871

—*Daily Alta California* (May 5, 1852)

CONTINUED

EXAMPLE *CONTINUED*

1. Overall, sentences 1 through 5 present
a. facts.
b. informed opinions.
c. expert opinions.
d. fallacies.

2. The use of the word *republican* in sentence 7 is an example of
a. personal attack.
b. plain folks.
c. glittering generality.
d. transfer.

3. The use of the words *lover of free institutions* and *liberty* in sentence 7 are examples of
a. personal attack.
b. plain folks.
c. glittering generality.
d. begging the question.

4. The phrase "to enhance the prosperity and to preserve the tranquility of this State" in sentence 13 is an example of
a. bandwagon.
b. plain folks.
c. glittering generality.
d. transfer.

5. The use of the term *red men* in sentence 17 is an example of
a. personal attack.
b. plain folks.
c. glittering generality.
d. transfer.

6. Sentence 26, "We came amongst you as mechanics or traders, and following every honorable business of life," is an example of
a. plain folks.
b. bandwagon.
c. glittering generality.
d. transfer.

7. The use of the phrase "generous policy of this Government" in sentence 28 is an example of
a. personal attack.
b. bandwagon.
c. glittering generality.
d. transfer.

8. The use of the phrases *naturalized citizen* and *Christian, too* in sentence 33 are examples of
a. personal attack.
b. plain folks.
c. glittering generality.
d. transfer.

9. The overall tone of Norman Asing's letter is
a. neutral.
b. angry.
c. bitter.
d. respectful.

10. Based on the tone of the passage, we may infer the writer's purpose is to
a. inform the public about Governor Bigler's proposal to limit "Asiatic immigration."
b. entertain the public with positive details about Chinese workers.
c. present a public stand against Governor Bigler's proposal to limit "Asiatic immigration."

After Reading Question: *How are the experiences of the Chinese in California, as described by Asing in 1852, similar to or different from the experiences of U.S. women in 1848 (page 183)?* Record your response in your notebook or journal.

Explanation

Compare your responses to the following think-aloud.

Based on my survey of the introductory paragraph and Asing's letter, I recorded the following before-reading questions. Here are my questions and answers, as well as the details I underlined to answer each one:

1. What are the key facts? In 1849, only 54 Chinese immigrants in California. By 1877, numbers had increased to 116,000. In 1852, Governor Bigler proposed restricting immigration from China. Asing, San Francisco merchant, restaurant owner, community leader, responds to governor's proposal. 2. Does the writer offer informed or expert opinions? Norman Asing offers an informed opinion about discrimination against the Chinese. He begins his letter with a personal introduction: I am a Chinaman, a republican, and a lover of free institutions. His success in business makes him an expert in that subject. However, he has no formal education in immigration issues and offers no sources outside of his own experience and observations. His life experiences have greatly informed his opinion about this situation and make his informed opinion credible. 3. Which fallacies does the writer employ? Asing's letter contains many emotional appeals or fallacies. For example, the opening sentence uses glittering generalities with the phrase "lover of free institutions" and transfer with the word **republican.** Many of the fallacies I underlined are contained in the following questions and answers: 1. (a); 2. (d); 3. (c); 4. (c); 5. (a); 6. (a); 7. (c); 8. (d); 9. (d); 10. (c).

After Reading Question: In the mid 1800s, the experiences of the Chinese in California as described by Asing are similar to the experiences of U.S. women. Both the Chinese and U.S. women faced discrimination that was supported by the government. Both groups had strong leaders. Both groups publically declared their right to life, liberty, and the pursuit of happiness.

Practice 2

Survey, Question, and Annotate to Analyze Facts and Opinions

Assume the following speech to Congress by President Andrew Jackson, a primary document, is your next assigned reading on the theme of the Right to Life, Liberty, and the Pursuit of Happiness. Before reading, skim the passage. In your journal or notebook, record three questions about the use of fact and opinion. Also note new or difficult words to define before reading. For example, survey one reader's Before Reading Glossary defining difficult words; then identify words you need to define before reading. During reading, annotate examples of words and details that answer your prereading questions. After reading, answer the questions that follow the passage.

Before Reading Glossary

consummation (sentence 1): realization, completion, fulfillment, perfection

pecuniary (sentence 4): related to money, financial, economics

annihilation (sentence 12): total destruction

Transcript of President Andrew Jackson's Message to Congress "On Indian Removal" (1830)

[1]It gives me pleasure to announce to Congress that the benevolent policy of the Government, steadily pursued for nearly thirty years, in relation to the removal of the Indians beyond the white settlements is approaching to a happy consummation. [2]Two important tribes have accepted the provision made for their removal at the last session of Congress, and it is believed that their example will induce the remaining tribes also to seek the same obvious advantages.

[3]The consequences of a speedy removal will be important to the United States, to individual States, and to the Indians themselves. [4]The pecuniary advantages which it promises to the Government are the least of its recommendations. [5]It puts an end to all possible danger of collision between the authorities of the General and State Governments on account of the Indians. [6]It will place a dense and civilized population in large tracts of country now occupied by a few savage hunters. [7]By opening the whole territory between Tennessee on the north and Louisiana on the south to the settlement of the whites it will incalculably strengthen the southwestern frontier and render the adjacent States strong enough to repel future invasions without remote aid. [8]It will relieve the whole State of Mississippi and the western part of Alabama of Indian occupancy, and enable those States to advance rapidly in population, wealth, and power. [9]It will separate the Indians from immediate contact with settlements of whites; free them from the power of the States; enable them to pursue happiness in their own way and under their own rude institutions; will retard the progress of decay, which is lessening their numbers, and perhaps cause them gradually, under the protection of the Government and through the influence of good counsels, to

Trail of Tears by Robert Lindneux on canvas

cast off their savage habits and become an interesting, civilized, and Christian community.

[10]What good man would prefer a country covered with forests and ranged by a few thousand savages to our extensive Republic, studded with cities, towns, and prosperous farms embellished with all the improvements which art can devise or industry execute, occupied by more than 12,000,000 happy people, and filled with all the blessings of liberty, civilization and religion?

[11]The present policy of the Government is but a continuation of the same progressive change by a milder process. [12]The tribes which occupied the countries now constituting the Eastern States were annihilated or have melted away to make room for the whites. [13]The waves of population and civilization are rolling to the westward, and we now propose to acquire the countries occupied by the red men of the South and West by a fair exchange, and, at the expense of the United States, to send them to land where their existence may be prolonged and perhaps made perpetual. [14]Doubtless it will be painful to leave the graves of their fathers; but what do they more than our ancestors did or than our children are now doing? [15]To better their condition in an unknown land our forefathers left all that was dear in earthly objects. [16]Our children by thousands yearly leave the land of their birth to seek new homes in distant regions. [17]Does Humanity weep at these painful separations from everything, animate and inanimate, with which the young heart has become entwined? [18]Far from it. [19]It is rather a source of joy that our country affords scope where our young population may range unconstrained in body or in mind, developing the power and facilities of man in their highest

CONTINUED

PRACTICE 2 *CONTINUED*

perfection. [20]These remove hundreds and almost thousands of miles at their own expense, purchase the lands they occupy, and support themselves at their new homes from the moment of their arrival. [21]Can it be cruel in this Government when, by events which it can not control, the Indian is made discontented in his ancient home to purchase his lands, to give him a new and extensive territory, to pay the expense of his removal, and support him a year in his new abode? [22]How many thousands of our own people would gladly embrace the opportunity of removing to the West on such conditions! [23]If the offers made to the Indians were extended to them, they would be hailed with gratitude and joy.

[24]And is it supposed that the wandering savage has a stronger attachment to his home than the settled, civilized Christian? [25]Is it more afflicting to him to leave the graves of his fathers than it is to our brothers and children? [26]Rightly considered, the policy of the General Government toward the red man is not only liberal, but generous. [27]He is unwilling to submit to the laws of the States and mingle with their population. [28]To save him from this alternative, or perhaps utter annihilation, the General Government kindly offers him a new home, and proposes to pay the whole expense of his removal and settlement.

1. Overall, the passage relies mostly on
a. facts.
b. informed opinions.
c. expert opinions.
d. fallacies.

2. The use of the phrase *benevolent policy* in sentence 1 is an example of
a. personal attack.
b. plain folks.
c. glittering generality.
d. transfer.

3. The use of the statement *happy consummation* in sentence 1 is an example of
a. personal attack.
b. plain folks.
c. glittering generality.
d. begging the question.

4. The statement "their example will induce the remaining tribes also to seek the same . . ." in sentence 2 is an example of
a. bandwagon.
b. transfer.
c. glittering generality.
d. begging the question.

5. The use of the phrase *obvious advantages* in sentence 2 is an example of
   a. personal attack.
   b. plain folks.
   c. glittering generality.
   d. transfer.

6. The expression *savage hunters* in sentence 6 is an example of
   a. personal attack.
   b. bandwagon.
   c. glittering generality.
   d. transfer.

7. The use of the phrase *to pursue happiness* in sentence 9 is an example of
   a. personal attack.
   b. bandwagon.
   c. glittering generality.
   d. transfer.

8. The use of the words *rude institutions* in sentence 9 is an example of
   a. personal attack.
   b. bandwagon.
   c. glittering generality.
   d. transfer.

9. The use of the word *Republic* in sentence 10 is an example of
   a. personal attack.
   b. bandwagon.
   c. glittering generality.
   d. transfer.

10. The use of the words *studded, happy, blessings,* and *liberty* in sentence 10 are examples of
   a. personal attack.
   b. bandwagon.
   c. glittering generality.
   d. transfer.

11. The use of the words *Republic, civilization,* and *religion* in sentence 10 are examples of
   a. personal attack.
   b. bandwagon.
   c. glittering generality.
   d. transfer.

12. Sentences 21 through 23 are examples of
   a. personal attack.
   b. plain folks.
   c. glittering generality.
   d. begging the question.

13. The overall tone of President Jackson's address to Congress is
   a. neutral.
   b. arrogant.
   c. resentful.
   d. humble.

14. Based on the tone of the passage, we may infer the writer's purpose is to
   a. inform.
   b. entertain.
   c. argue.

After Reading Question: *How do the experiences of the Native Americans during the Indian Removal in 1830 compare those of the Chinese in California, in 1852 (page 188), and U.S. women in 1848 (page 183)?* Record your response in your notebook or journal.

LO4 Brainstorm and Draft Using Facts and Opinions

After reading and before writing, refer to your questions and annotations to brainstorm your response to what you have read. Include logical inferences based on the connections you have made. Brainstorm by using an outline or concept map to organize connections among the key terms you want to include in your writing. Then, use your completed outline or concept map to compose a rough or first draft of your response.

Example

Assume your history course requires a formal written response to the three passages you have read related to the theme of the Right to Life, Liberty, and the Pursuit of Happiness. To direct your thinking, your professor has provided the following prompt:

> ***In the mid 1800s in the United States, in what ways were women, Chinese immigrants, and Native Americans denied the right to life, liberty, and the pursuit of happiness?***

To brainstorm and draft your response:

- Use details from your answers to the following after reading questions:
  - "Report of the 1848 Women's Rights Convention," Practice 1 (page 183).
  - "To His Excellency," by Norman Asing, Example (page 188).
  - "On Indian Removal," by Andrew Jackson, Practice 2 (page 194).
- Complete the following concept map to brainstorm the details of your writing.
- Refer to the completed concept map to write a rough draft.

	Women	**Chinese Immigrants**	**Native Americans**
Right to Life			
Liberty			
Pursuit of Happiness			

Explanation

Compare your answers to the following think-aloud.

The concept map showed me that I could organize my thoughts by discussing each group separately, or I could combine them into a point-by-point discussion. I chose to go point-by-point. In my draft, I underlined the details from the chart:

In the 1800s in the United States, women, Chinese immigrants, and Native Americans were denied the right to life, liberty, and the pursuit of happiness. Each group was denied the right to life. According to the Record of the Report of the 1848 Women's Rights Convention, ruthless men made women, if married, in the eye of the law, civilly dead. According to Norman Asing's letter, Governor Bigler, obviously a racist, proposed immigration laws that prejudiced the public against the Chinese immigrants and put them in danger of those who would hunt them down and rob them. President Jackson's address to Congress stated, Native American tribes were annihilated or melted away to make room for whites.

These three groups were also denied liberty. Men had never permitted a woman to exercise her inalienable right to vote. Governor Bigler declared, Asiatic immigration must be checked. And President Jackson called for Indian removal from their ancient lands.

These peoples were also denied the pursuit of happiness. White men had monopolized nearly all the profitable employments, and women earned a scanty wage for the jobs they did hold. Asing pointed out that Bigler would deny the Chinese immigrant from following every honorable business of life. Native Americans unwillingly left the graves of their fathers.

Practice 3

Brainstorm and Draft Using Facts and Opinions

Assume your history professor has provided an alternate writing prompt for the required formal written response to the three passages you have read related to the theme of the Right to Life, Liberty, and the Pursuit of Happiness:

> ***Based on the three passages you have read, how would women, Chinese immigrants, and Native Americans define the terms "right to life," "liberty," and the "pursuit of happiness"?***

To brainstorm and draft your response:

- Use details from your answers to the following after reading questions:
  - "Report of the 1848 Women's Rights Convention," Practice 1 (page 183).
  - "To His Excellency," by Norman Asing, Example (page 188).
  - "On Indian Removal," by Andrew Jackson, Practice 2 (page 194).
- Complete the following concept map to brainstorm the details of your writing.
- Refer to the completed concept map to write a rough draft.

Term	**Definition**	**Examples**
Right to Life		
Liberty		
Pursuit of Happiness		

Review, Revise, and Proofread for Effective Use of Facts and Opinions

L5

Master writers review and revise for accurate use of facts and opinions. First, a master writer reads the draft silently or out loud. During this review, he or she underlines specific words or phrases that should be revised to eliminate irrelevant details or fallacies. Once this initial review is completed, master writers make revisions to rework the draft.

Attribution is the means of giving credit to the source of a fact or opinion.

A **quote,** or direct speech, states the exact words of a person or passage.

In **reported speech,** or indirect speech, the words of a speaker or passage are recounted with a reporting verb (such as *said*), along with the necessary changes in person and tense.

Once a draft has been revised, master writers proofread for accurate attribution of facts and opinions. **Attribution** is an effective way to distinguish between fact and opinion. It is also an effective tool to evaluate the reliability of a source. Two types of attribution are **quotes** and **reported speech**. Consider the following statements. What is similar and different between the two?

Quote: Dr. Martin Luther King, Jr., states, "I have a dream."
Reported speech: Dr. Martin Luther King, Jr., stated that he had a dream.

The quote identified the speaker and placed quotation marks before and after the speaker's exact words. The reported speech also identified the speaker, but did not use the speaker's exact words. In the reported speech, the word *that* linked the speaker's name to his ideas and the writer changed the verb tense and pronouns. A quote captures a statement made in the time it was spoken and a speaker often uses present tense. Thus, this quote used the present tense verbs *states* and *have.* However, reported speech retells what was said in the past, so *states* was revised to *stated* and *have* was changed to *had.* Likewise, the first-person pronoun *I* in the quote changed to *he* in the reported speech.

Effective use of attribution is based on several rules of language. Use the following guidelines as you proofread your writing for effective use of facts and opinions.

Basic Language Rules for Quotes

- Quotation marks appear before and after the exact words of the speaker.

  Patrick Henry stated, "Give me liberty or give me death."

- Set off the attribution phrase that gives credit to the speaker or source with a comma.

  Patrick Henry stated, "Give me liberty or give me death."

- Place a comma or period at the end of the quote inside the closing quotation mark.

  Patrick Henry stated, "Give me liberty or give me death."
  "Give me liberty or give me death," stated Patrick Henry.

- Begin the first sentence of quoted material with a capital letter.

  Patrick Henry stated, "Give me liberty or give me death."

- When a quote is interrupted by an attribution phrase, the quoted material after the attribution is not capitalized.

  "Give me liberty," Patrick Henry stated, "or give me death."

Basic Language Rules for Reported Speech

- Reword the original idea of the speaker or the passage.

  Patrick Henry demanded that he be **given liberty or death**.
- Use *that* to link the speaker to the reported speech, the reworded original idea.

  Patrick Henry demanded **that** he be given liberty or death.
- Change the pronouns and tense of verbs as appropriate for sense.

  Patrick Henry demanded that **he be given** liberty or death.

Example

Assume that you are a peer editor for the writer of the draft composed in response to the writing prompt in the Example on page 198:

> ***In the mid 1800s in the United States, in what ways were women, Chinese immigrants, and Native Americans denied the right to life, liberty, and the pursuit of happiness?***

To review, revise, and proofread the draft, complete the following steps:

1. Review the draft. Underline at least three words or phrases that state irrelevant facts or opinions, such as fallacies.
2. Suggest revisions in the margin near the underlined details.
3. Proofread: Circle errors in attribution such as lack of attribution, improper use of pronouns, verb tense, or punctuation.

Explanation

Compare your answers to the following think-aloud.

I underlined and suggested deleting the following words in paragraph 1 to avoid use of fallacies: The phrase obviously a racist and the word ruthless are personal attacks. I also suggested the use of quotation marks around the following exact words quoted from the original passages. In paragraph 1: "if married, in the eye of the law, civilly dead." and "who would hunt them down and rob them." and "were annihilated" and "melted away to make room for whites." In paragraph 2: "Asiatic immigration must be checked." In paragraph 3: "monopolized nearly all the profitable employments," and "a scanty" and "following every honorable business of life" and "the graves of their fathers."

There were many uses of reported speech that did not need quotation marks.

Practice 4

Review, Revise, and Proofread for Effective Use of Facts and Opinions

Use a print copy of the draft you composed in Practice 3 (page 200). To review, revise, and proofread the draft, complete the following steps:

1. Review the draft. Underline at least three words or phrases that state irrelevant facts or opinions, such as fallacies.
2. Suggest revisions in the margin near the underlined details.
3. Proofread: Circle errors in attribution such as lack of attribution, improper use of pronouns, verb tense, or punctuation.
4. Create a new, corrected, draft.

Workshop: Distinguish Between Fact and Opinion

Assume you are continuing your study of the theme of the Right to Life, Liberty, and the Pursuit of Happiness in your college history class. The following passage, the text of the United States Declaration of Independence, is your capstone reading assignment. Your capstone writing assignment is to write a formal response to the question "What is the importance and effect of the phrase 'the Right to Life, Liberty, and the Pursuit of Happiness' in the Declaration of Independence?" To complete your writing assignment, skim the prereading questions to guide your reading, read the passage, and then complete the activities that follow.

The Declaration of Independence

In Congress, July 4, 1776.

The unanimous Declaration of the thirteen united States of America,

[1]When in the Course of human events, it becomes necessary for one people to dissolve the political bands which have connected them with another, and to assume among the powers of the earth, the separate and equal station to which the Laws of Nature and of Nature's God entitle them, a decent respect to the opinions of mankind requires that they should declare the causes which impel them to the separation.

[2]We hold these truths to be self-evident, that all men are created equal, that they are endowed by their Creator with certain unalienable Rights, that among these are Life, Liberty and the pursuit of Happiness.—That to secure these rights, Governments are instituted among Men, deriving their just powers from the consent of the governed,—

CONTINUED

That whenever any Form of Government becomes destructive of these ends, it is the Right of the People to alter or to abolish it, and to institute new Government, laying its foundation on such principles and organizing its powers in such form, as to them shall seem most likely to effect their Safety and Happiness. Prudence, indeed, will dictate that Governments long established should not be changed for light and transient causes; and accordingly all experience hath shewn, that mankind are more disposed to suffer, while evils are sufferable, than to right themselves by abolishing the forms to which they are accustomed. But when a long train of abuses and usurpations, pursuing invariably the same Object evinces a design to reduce them under absolute Despotism, it is their right, it is their duty, to throw off such Government, and to provide new Guards for their future security.—Such has been the patient sufferance of these Colonies; and such is now the necessity which constrains them to alter their former Systems of Government. The history of the present King of Great Britain is a history of repeated injuries and usurpations, all having in direct object the establishment of an absolute Tyranny over these States. To prove this, let Facts be submitted to a candid world.

3He has refused his Assent to Laws, the most wholesome and necessary for the public good.

4He has forbidden his Governors to pass Laws of immediate and pressing importance, unless suspended in their operation till his Assent should be obtained; and when so suspended, he has utterly neglected to attend to them.

5He has refused to pass other Laws for the accommodation of large districts of people, unless those people would relinquish the right of Representation in the Legislature, a right inestimable to them and formidable to tyrants only.

6He has called together legislative bodies at places unusual, uncomfortable, and distant from the depository of their public Records, for the sole purpose of fatiguing them into compliance with his measures.

7He has dissolved Representative Houses repeatedly, for opposing with manly firmness his invasions on the rights of the people.

8He has refused for a long time, after such dissolutions, to cause others to be elected; whereby the Legislative powers, incapable of Annihilation, have returned to the People at large for their exercise; the State remaining in the mean time exposed to all the dangers of invasion from without, and convulsions within.

9He has endeavoured to prevent the population of these States; for that purpose obstructing the Laws for Naturalization of Foreigners; refusing to pass others to encourage their migrations hither, and raising the conditions of new Appropriations of Lands.

10He has obstructed the Administration of Justice, by refusing his Assent to Laws for establishing Judiciary powers.

11He has made Judges dependent on his Will alone, for the tenure of their offices, and the amount and payment of their salaries.

12He has erected a multitude of New Offices, and sent hither swarms of Officers to harrass our people, and eat out their substance. He has kept among us, in times of peace, Standing Armies without the Consent of our legislatures.

13He has affected to render the Military independent of and superior to the Civil power.

14He has combined with others to subject us to a jurisdiction foreign to our constitution, and unacknowledged by our laws; giving his Assent to their Acts of pretended Legislation:

15For Quartering large bodies of armed troops among us:

[16]For protecting them, by a mock Trial, from punishment for any Murders which they should commit on the Inhabitants of these States: For cutting off our Trade with all parts of the world:

[17]For imposing Taxes on us without our Consent:

[18]For depriving us in many cases, of the benefits of Trial by Jury: For transporting us beyond Seas to be tried for pretended offences

[19]For abolishing the free System of English Laws in a neighbouring Province, establishing therein an Arbitrary government, and enlarging its Boundaries so as to render it at once an example and fit instrument for introducing the same absolute rule into these Colonies:

[20]For taking away our Charters, abolishing our most valuable Laws, and altering fundamentally the Forms of our Governments:

[21]For suspending our own Legislatures, and declaring themselves invested with power to legislate for us in all cases whatsoever.

[22]He has abdicated Government here, by declaring us out of his Protection and waging War against us.

[23]He has plundered our seas, ravaged our Coasts, burnt our towns, and destroyed the lives of our people.

[24]He is at this time transporting large Armies of foreign Mercenaries to compleat the works of death, desolation and tyranny, already begun with circumstances of Cruelty & perfidy scarcely paralleled in the most barbarous ages, and totally unworthy the Head of a civilized nation.

[25]He has constrained our fellow Citizens taken Captive on the high Seas to bear Arms against their Country, to become the executioners of their friends and Brethren, or to fall themselves by their Hands.

[26]He has excited domestic insurrections amongst us, and has endeavoured to bring on the inhabitants of our frontiers, the merciless Indian Savages, whose known rule of warfare, is an undistinguished destruction of all ages, sexes and conditions.

[27]In every stage of these Oppressions We have Petitioned for Redress in the most humble terms: Our repeated Petitions have been answered only by repeated injury. A Prince whose character is thus marked by every act which may define a Tyrant, is unfit to be the ruler of a free people.

[28]Nor have We been wanting in attentions to our British brethren. We have warned them from time to time of attempts by their legislature to extend an unwarrantable jurisdiction over us. We have reminded them of the circumstances of our emigration and settlement here. We have appealed to their native justice and magnanimity, and we have conjured them by the ties of our common kindred to disavow these usurpations, which, would inevitably interrupt our connections and correspondence. They too have been deaf to the voice of justice and of consanguinity. We must, therefore, acquiesce in the necessity, which denounces our Separation, and hold them, as we hold the rest of mankind, Enemies in War, in Peace Friends.

[29]We, therefore, the Representatives of the united States of America, in General Congress, Assembled, appealing to the Supreme Judge of the world for the rectitude of our intentions, do, in the Name, and by Authority of the good People of these Colonies, solemnly publish and declare, That these United Colonies are, and of Right ought to be Free and Independent States; that they are Absolved from all Allegiance to the British Crown, and that all political connection between them and the State of Great Britain, is and ought to be totally dissolved; and that as Free and Independent States, they have full Power to levy War, conclude Peace, contract Alliances, establish Commerce, and to do all other Acts and Things which Independent States may of right do. And for the support of this Declaration, with a firm reliance on the protection of divine Providence, we mutually pledge to each other our Lives, our Fortunes and our sacred Honor.

Preread: Survey and Question

Survey the following questions. Answer the questions about your prior knowledge. Then, skim the passages to locate key details to annotate during reading.

1. What is your prior knowledge about the Declaration of Independence?

____

____

2. What did the statement "All men are created equal" (paragraph 2) mean at the time the Declaration of Independence was written?

____

____

3. Explain and illustrate the grievances/abuses discussed within the Declaration of Independence.

____

____

4. How do the grievances/abuses discussed within the Declaration of Independence compare to the grievances/abuses asserted by women (page 183), Chinese immigrants (page 188), and Native Americans (page 194) of the 1800s?

____

____

5. What does the statement "All men are created equal" (paragraph 2) mean for us today?

____

____

6. Discuss the meaning of the three natural rights that Jefferson identified in the Declaration of Independence: "Life, Liberty, and the Pursuit of Happiness."

____

____

7. How is the Report of the Women's Conference in 1848 similar to and different from the Declaration of Independence? Explain the reasons for the similarities and differences.

8. How does the Declaration of Independence support Norman Asing's protest about discrimination against the Chinese immigrants?

9. How did Andrew Jackson use the values of the Declaration of Independence to support his call for Indian Removal?

10. What does the Right to Life specifically refer to in our lives today?

11. What does the Right to Liberty specifically refer to in our lives today?

12. What does the Right to the Pursuit of Happiness specifically refer to in our lives today?

13. Has the United States lived up to the ideals set forth in the Declaration of Independence?

Read and Annotate

As you read, annotate key ideas, particularly those details that answer your prereading questions.

Recite, Review, and Brainstorm

Recite and **Review** the information. Paraphrase ideas. Summarize the most important parts. **Brainstorm** ideas for your written response to the passage. Answer your prereading questions. *Freewrite* or *map* the relationship among answers to questions or ideas you have annotated in the text. *Outline* or *list* key ideas and details in blocks of thought. Identify the central point you want to make. Use your own paper.

Write a Draft of Your Response

Using the ideas you generated by brainstorming, compose a draft of your response. Use your own paper.

Revise Your Draft

Once you have created a draft of your response, read it over to answer the questions in the "Questions for Revising" box that follows. Indicate your answers by annotating your paper. If you answer "yes" to a question, underline, check, or circle examples. If you answer "no" to a question, write needed information in the margins and draw lines to indicate the placement of additional details. Revise your essay based on your reflection. (*Hint:* Experienced writers create several drafts as they focus on one or two questions per draft.)

Step by Step: Questions for Revising

- ☐ Have I stated or implied a focused main idea?
- ☐ Have made my purpose clear?
- ☐ Is my tone appropriate for my audience and purpose?
- ☐ Is the logical order of ideas clear? Have I used words to clearly guide my reader, such as *first, second, next*, etc.?
- ☐ Have I used concrete details to make my point?
- ☐ Have I made my point with adequate details?
- ☐ Do all the details support my point?
- ☐ Have I used proper attribution styles for quotes and reported speech?

Proofread Your Draft

Once you have made any revisions to your essay that may be needed, proofread your essay to eliminate careless errors.

Reading and Writing Assignments

MySkillsLab™
Complete this Exercise
on myskillslab.com

Reading and Writing for Everyday Life

Assume a friend or family member recently learned she has developed symptoms of cardiovascular disease. You found the following article about a popular diet that you think she should follow. Read the article. Compose a letter to your friend or relative recommending the diet.

The Mediterranean Diet: Myth or Fact?

A Mediterranean-style diet has received significant attention in recent years, as the rates of cardiovascular disease in many Mediterranean countries are substantially lower than the rates in the United States. These countries include Portugal, Italy, France, Greece, Turkey, and Israel. Each country has unique dietary patterns; however, they share the following traits: Meat is eaten monthly, and eggs, poultry, fish, and sweets are eaten weekly, making the diet low in saturated fats and refined sugars. The fat used predominantly for cooking and flavor is olive oil, making the diet high in monounsaturated fats. Foods eaten daily include grains, such as bread, pasta, couscous, and bulgur; fruits; beans and other legumes; nuts; vegetables; and cheese and yogurt. These choices make this diet high in fiber and rich in vitamins and minerals.

The Mediterranean Diet Pyramid, like the USDA Food Patterns, suggests daily physical activity and a daily intake of whole grain breads, cereals, other grains, fruits, and vegetables. Unlike the USDA Food Patterns, this diet includes the daily consumption of beans, other legumes, and nuts and less frequent consumption of meat, fish, poultry, and eggs. Cheese and yogurt, not milk, are the primary dairy sources. A unique feature of the Mediterranean diet is the consumption of wine and olive oil daily.

The Mediterranean diet is not lower in fat; in fact, about 40% of the total energy in this diet is derived from fat, which is much higher than the U.S. dietary fat recommendations. However, the majority of fat in the Mediterranean diet is from plant oils, which are more healthful sources than the animal fats found in the U.S. diet, making the Mediterranean diet more protective against cardiovascular disease. Thus, far from being a fad diet, the Mediterranean Diet is an excellent example of a healthy eating pattern that you can follow.

—Adapted from Thompson and Manore, *Nutrition for Life*, 3rd ed., Pearson, 2013, p. 21.

Reading and Writing for College Life

Assume you are taking a student success class. Your professor has assigned the following sections from your textbook for you to teach to the class. Read the material and create a PowerPoint presentation of key points. In your presentation demonstrate a memory aid. Create a list of key ideas to remember. Create mnemonics to remember the items. Use at least two of the strategies discussed in the mnemonics section.

AIDING YOUR MEMORY

Although the purpose of education is to encourage thinking skills rather than memorization, you will recognize that memory is vital. Memory is used as an index of success because most techniques used to measure learning rely on it. Therefore, a good memory is a definite asset. Researchers have theorized we all have several types of memory usually based on time of storage. Sensory memory is a very brief recall of what we just saw or heard and is stored for only seconds or minutes. If we act on, or focus on this experience, it can be stored in short-term memory where it can stay for a few days. Long-term memory stores experience and knowledge for days or even decades. Ideally, your studying is placing your knowledge in long-term memory, and one of the keys to facilitate long-term memory storage is the amount of focus you place on the material and the *number of senses* you engage while learning the material. This is why discussion and effective study groups help long-term memory and test performance.

Test your memory in the following exercise:

Testing Your Memory

Time yourself for 1 minute and memorize the following food items. Then, try to recite them from memory.

Meat loaf	Frankfurters	Iced tea
Grapefruit	Jam	Hummus
Burrito	Lemonade	Cherries
Kiwi	Diet soda	

Were you able to finish and recite them all? ______

If not do not worry. This seemingly random list of food items would be hard to memorize, in large part because of its length. Another difficulty would be your familiarity with each item. Depending on the foods that were available in your home, you would be more familiar with some items than with others. You lack of context, or connection, would make these items harder to remember.

At times, we do have to memorize information. The key is to have a system for memorizing and, even more importantly, to make your learning meaningful. This time, take the food items in the previous exercise and place them in alphabetical order and in groups of three:

burritos, cherries, diet soda
frankfurters, grapefruit, hummus
iced tea, jam, kiwi
lemonade, meat loaf

This memorization technique is called clustering, or grouping.

Grouping

There's a reason that our phone numbers are interrupted with a hyphen between the third and fourth number in the sequence. This technique makes it easier for us to remember the sequence. Rather than remembering a long sequence, we can more easily remember two shorter groups of numbers. In the case of our food list, we first grouped the items in alphabetical order and in clusters of three. We can also group the items by type of food:

Entrees: burrito, frankfurters, meat loaf
Fruits: cherries, grapefruit, kiwi
Drinks: diet soda, iced tea, lemonade
Spreads: hummus, jam

Mnemonics

Another effective memorization technique is the use of mnemonics, which are words, rhymes, or formulas that aid your memory. For example, did you have to memorize the names of the eight planets in order (Mercury, Venus, Earth, Mars, Jupiter, Saturn, Uranus, and Neptune)? Perhaps, then, you heard this mnemonic (or a similar one):

My **v**ery **e**ducated **m**other **j**ust **s**erved **us** **n**achos

This mnemonic is known as an acrostic: You take the first letter of every item to be memorized and form a sentence that will help you to remember vocabulary, terms, or concepts.

Another mnemonic device is an acronym, which is similar to an acrostic. Acronyms are words formed from the first letters of the terms you need to memorize. For example, the ABCs of CPR remind you that A = establish Airway, B = rescue Breathing, and C = establish Circulation. This mnemonic helps you to remember the steps and their proper order in a critical situation. Another classic mnemonic is the word HOMES to memorize the names of the Great Lakes (Huron, Ontario, Michigan, Erie, and Superior).

Rhymes or formulas are also helpful mnemonic devices. "In 1492, Columbus sailed the ocean blue." Many students in the United States are familiar with this age-old mnemonic. Formulas that appeal to your sense of logic can also help memory. For example, "Spring forward, Fall back" helps us adjust our clocks accordingly for daylight saving time. You can also make up silly stories to help remember facts. In fact, often the sillier the story, the easier it is to remember.

—Colbert, *Navigating Your Future Success*, 2nd ed., Pearson, 2015, pp. 80–82.

Reading and Writing for Working Life

Assume you are training as an intern in a human resources department at a local bottling company. Most of the employees are older, white males. Your supervisor has asked you to assist in putting together information to educate management about diversity in the workforce. Read the article. Write a memo to your supervisor that summarizes the key points. Suggest possible actions the company might implement to improve the diversity of its workforce.

How Is A Diverse Workforce Beneficial

Diversity is an important component of the modern workplace. A diverse workforce helps companies offer a broad range of viewpoints that are necessary to compete in a world that is more globalized. Such variety in viewpoints promotes creativity in problem solving with improved results.

In addition, products and services need to cater to customers and clients with diverse backgrounds, so it's vital to have a workforce that understands the nuances of different cultural needs. Additionally, a diverse staff helps strategize ways to handle markets that have become segmented, both culturally and demographically. For example, PepsiCo's Frito-Lay division launched a Doritos guacamole-flavored tortilla chip to appeal especially to Latino consumers. The Latino Employee Network provided valuable feedback on taste and packaging to ensure that the Latino community would consider these chips as authentic. The product generated more than $100 million in sales in its first year, making it the most successful product launch in the company's history.

Because promoting diversity is a priority for most companies in today's global marketplace, so too is the implementation of diversity training programs. These often-costly programs typically involve workshops and seminars that teach managers about the benefits of a diverse workforce. And yet, according to a recent study, most of them simply don't work. After analyzing years of national employment statistics, the study concluded that standard diversity training rarely had an effect on the number of women or minority managers employed at companies where it was used. Why not? Some theorize that mandatory training inevitably leads to backlash; others say altering people's inner biases is a nearly impossible task. However; the study also found that two techniques had significant, beneficial effects on workplace diversity: (1) the appointment of a specific person or committee who is specifically accountable for addressing diversity issues within the company led to 10 percent increases in the number of women and minorities in management positions; (2) mentorships increased the number of African American women in leadership positions by 23.5 percent.

—Adapted from Solomon, Poatsy, and Martin. *Better Business*, 3rd ed., Pearson, 2014, pp. 275–276.

Review Test

MySkillsLab™
Complete this Exercise
on myskillslab.com

Score (number correct) ______ x 10 = ______%

Distinguishing Between Fact and Opinion

Read the following passage from a college sociology textbook. Answer the questions that follow.

Glossary
truism (sentence 1): a statement whose truth is well known
sojourners (sentence 7) a temporary resident, one who stays for a while
primacy (sentence 16): the state of being first in rank or importance

The Politics of Immigrants: Power, Ethnicity, and Social Class

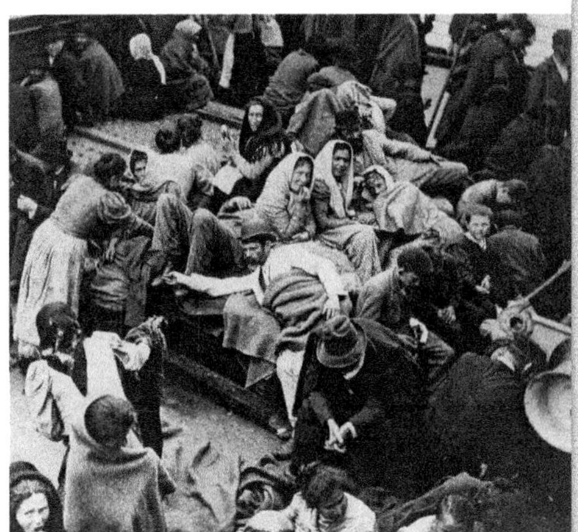

Over 12 million immigrants arrived in the U. S. between 1870 and 1900 through the portal of Ellis Island in New York Harbor.

[1]That the United States is the land of immigrants is a **truism**. [2]Every schoolchild knows that since the English Pilgrims landed on Plymouth Rock, group after group has sought relief from hardship by reaching U.S. shores. [3]Some, such as the Irish immigrants in the late 1800s and early 1900s, left to escape brutal poverty and famine. [4]Others, such as the Jews of czarist Russia, fled religious persecution. [5]Some sought refuge from lands ravaged by war. [6]Others, called **entrepreneurial** immigrants, came primarily for better economic opportunities. [7]Still others were **sojourners** who planned to return home after a temporary stay. [8]Some, not usually called immigrants, came in chains, held in bondage by earlier immigrants.

[9]Today, the United States is in the midst of its second largest wave of immigration. [10]In the largest wave, immigrants accounted for 15 percent of the U.S. population. [11]Almost all of those immigrants in the late 1800s and early 1900s came from Europe. [12]In our current wave, immigrants make up 13 percent of the U.S. population, with a mix that is far more diverse. [13]Immigration from Europe has slowed to a trickle, with twice as many of our recent immigrants coming from Asia as from Europe (Statistical Abstract 2011: Tables 38, 42). [14]In the past 20 years, about 20 million immigrants have settled legally in the United States, and another 11 million are here illegally (Statistical Abstract 2011: Tables 43, 45).

[15]In the last century, U.S.-born Americans feared that immigrants would bring socialism or communism with them. [16]Today's fear is that the millions of immigrants from Spanish-speaking countries threaten the **primacy** of the English language. [17]Last century brought a fear that immigrants would take jobs away from U.S.-born citizens. [18]This fear has returned. [19]In addition, African Americans fear a loss of political power as immigrants from Mexico and Central and South America swell the Latino population.

CONTINUED

[20]What path do immigrants take to political activity? [21]In general, immigrants first organize as a group on the basis of ethnicity rather than class. [22]They respond to common problems, such as discrimination and issues associated with adapting to a new way of life. [23]This first step in political activity is their cultural identity. [24]As sociologists Alejandro Portes and Rubén Rumbaut (1990) note, "By mobilizing the collective vote and by electing their own to office, immigrant minorities have learned the rules of the democratic game and absorbed its values in the process."

[25]Immigrants, then, don't become "American" overnight. [26]Instead, they begin by fighting for their own interests as an ethnic group—as Irish, Italians, and so on. [27]However, according to Portes and Rumbaut, once a group gains representation somewhat proportionate to its numbers, a major change occurs. [28]At this point, social class becomes more significant than race–ethnicity. [29]Note that the significance of race–ethnicity in politics does not disappear, but that it recedes in importance.

[30]Irish immigrants to Boston illustrate this pattern. [31]Banding together on the basis of ethnicity, they built a power base that put the Irish in political control of Boston. [32]As the significance of ethnicity faded, social class became prominent. [33]Ultimately, they saw John F. Kennedy, one of their own, from the upper class, sworn in as president of the United States. [34]Even today, being "Irish" continues to be a significant factor in Boston politics.

—Henslin, *Sociology: A Down-to-Earth Approach*, 11th ed., p. 423.

Vocabulary in Context

1. What does the word **entrepreneurial** mean in sentence 6?

a. business
b. poor
c. leisure
d. wealthy

Inference

2. Based on the information in the passage, we may infer that immigrants

a. never gain political power.
b. easily overcome challenges.
c. want to return to their homelands.
d. founded the United States.

Tone

3. The tone of sentence 1 is

a. matter-of-fact.
b. condemning.
c. bitter.
d. understanding.

Tone

4. The overall tone of the passage is

a. admiring.
b. neutral.
c. condemning.
d. resentful.

Purpose

5. The writer's purpose is to
   a. argue against immigration.
   b. entertain the reader with little known facts about immigration.
   c. inform the reader about the historical and current issues related to immigration.

Fact and Opinion

6. Sentence 3 is
   a. a fact.
   b. an opinion.
   c. a mixture of fact and opinion.

7. Sentence 10 is
   a. a fact.
   b. an opinion.
   c. a mixture of fact and opinion.

8. The statement "once a group gains representation somewhat proportionate to its numbers, a major change occurs" is
   a. a fact.
   b. an opinion.
   c. a mixture of fact and opinion.

9. Alejandro Portes and Ruben Rumbaut offer
   a. facts.
   b. expert opinions.
   c. informed opinions.
   d. fallacies.

10. The term *American* (sentence 25) taps into the fallacy of
    a. bandwagon.
    b. name calling.
    c. glittering generality.
    d. transfer.

Summary Response

Restate the author's central idea in your own words. In your summary, follow the thought pattern used by the author. Begin your summary response with the following: *The central idea of "The Politics of Immigrants: Power, Ethnicity, and Social Class" by Henslin is. . . .*

Reader Response

Think about the changing population demographics in the United States. Assume you work for the local newspaper in your area, and write an editorial that addresses this topic. In your article, respond to the following two excerpts from the passage.

> "Today's fear is that the millions of immigrants from Spanish-speaking countries threaten the primacy of the English language." (sentence 16)
>
> "However, according to Portes and Rumbaut, once a group gains representation somewhat proportionate to its numbers, a major change occurs. At this point, social class becomes more significant than race-ethnicity." (sentences 27–28)

Academic Learning Log: Module Review

Summary of Key Concepts of Distinguishing Between Fact and Opinion

Assess your comprehension of fact and opinion.

LO1 LO2

1. A fact is ______________________________.
2. An opinion is ______________________________.
3. Objective proof can be ______________________________ ______________________________.
4. An informed opinion is developed by ______________________________.
5. An expert opinion is developed through ______________________________ ______________________________.
6. A fact ______________ reality and uses ______________ words; an opinion ______________ reality and uses ______________ words.
7. A qualifier may express an ______________________ using words like ______________ or ______________ .

LO3 LO4 LO5

8. A fallacy is an error in ______________, a ______________, or a ______________; examples of fallacies include ______________, ______________, ______________, ______________, ______________, and ______________.
9. ______________ is the act of giving credit to the source of a piece of information.
10. A ______________, or direct speech, states the ______________ words of a person or passage. ______________, or indirect speech, recounts the words of a speaker or passage with a reporting verb (such as ______________) with the necessary changes in ______________ and ______________.

Test Your Comprehension of Distinguishing Between Fact and Opinion

Respond in your own words to the following questions and prompts.

L1 L2 L3 L4 L5

Describe how to distinguish between a fact and an opinion.

Why is it important to distinguish between fact and opinion?

L1 L2 L3 L4 L5

1. **How will I use what I have learned?** In your notebook, discuss how you will apply to your own reading/writing strategy what you have learned about distinguishing between fact and opinion. When will you apply this knowledge to your reading/writing strategy?
2. **What do I still need to study about distinguishing between fact and opinion?** In your notebook, discuss your ongoing study needs. Describe what, when, and how you will continue studying and using fact and opinion.

MySkillsLab™

Complete the Post-test for Module 5 in MySkillsLab.

6

LEARNING OUTCOMES

After studying this module you should be able to:

- L1 Answer the Question "What's the Point of an Essay?"
- L2 Question, Read, Annotate, and Review an Essay
- L3 Prewrite a Draft of a Central Idea: Thesis Statement
- L4 Prewrite to Generate and Organize Relevant Details
- L5 Compose a Draft Using Logical Order
- L6 Revise and Proofread for Effective Language: Word Choice

Understanding the Essay

All of us of have had some experience studying, writing, or reading essays. Perhaps the most common and flexible form of writing, the essay allows powerful personal expression. The **essay** is used for academic papers, business reports, newspaper and magazine articles, Web articles, and letters to the editor of a newspaper or journal. By mastering the tasks of reading and writing an essay, you will enhance your ability to think, to reason, and to communicate.

An **essay** expresses a writer's point about a topic in a series of closely connected paragraphs.

An essay is a series of closely related blocks of ideas that develops and supports the writer's point about a topic. Paragraphs serve as these building blocks since an essay is composed of several paragraphs.

WHAT'S THE POINT of the Essay?

Before you study this module, predict the significance of the essay. The following set of pictures depicts several situations in which people are reading different types of essays written for specific audiences. Examine each photograph. Then predict the topic or purpose for the types of essays written for each audience (write your predictions in the given spaces). Finally, answer the question "What's the point of an essay?"

Photographic Organizer: The Essay

What's the point of the essay?

The Levels of Information in an Essay

Title
Introduction
Explains the importance of topic and the writer's point.
Offers background information about the topic.
Hooks the reader's interest.
Thesis Statement
States the central idea in a complete sentence.
Uses specific, effective wording.
Relates to all the details in the essay.
Paragraph's Topic Sentence
States the main idea of the paragraph.
Offers one primary support for the thesis statement.
Relates to all the details in the paragraph.
Links the details in the paragraph to the thesis statement.
Major Detail
Supports the topic sentence.
Is a secondary support for the thesis statement.
Is more general than a minor detail.
Minor Detail
Supports a major detail.
Is a secondary support for the thesis statement.
Offers the most specific details in the essay.
Conclusion
Reinforces the importance of the writer's overall point.
A Body Paragraph: Use as many body paragraphs as needed to fully develop the thesis statement.

The word *essay* means "attempt," to make an effort to accomplish an end. An essay has a specific audience for a particular purpose. An effective essay supports a *central idea* or *thesis statement* with relevant and adequate **supporting details** in **logical order**, using **effective expression**. An effective essay also often begins with an introduction and ends with a conclusion. The graphic above illustrates four levels of information in an essay: title, introduction, body, and conclusion.

Note that each level of information serves a specific function in the essay.

A **paragraph** is an essential component of an essay. A paragraph is a smaller block of ideas that joins with other blocks of ideas to develop the writer's central idea. Paragraphs vary in purpose, such as the introductory paragraph, the body paragraph, and the concluding paragraph. A writer may use several body paragraphs to fully develop a point. The main idea of a paragraph, often

Supporting details are the specific ideas that develop, explain, or support a central or main idea.

Logical order is the pattern of organization that controls the flow of ideas within a paragraph or essay; examples include narration, description, and classification.

Effective expression is the writer's use of words and structure to impact the reader.

A **paragraph** is a series of closely related sentences that develop and support one point or subtopic within a piece of writing.

stated in a **topic sentence**, focuses on a subtopic or specific point that supports the writer's central point. A paragraph begins on a new line and is indented. The following chart shows the levels of information in a paragraph. Notice the flow of ideas from general to specific, from **major details** to **minor details**.

A **topic sentence** is a sentence that states the main idea of a paragraph.

A **major detail** directly explains, develops, or illustrates a main idea in a paragraph or the central point in an essay.

A **minor detail** directly explains, develops, or illustrates a major detail.

The Levels of Information in a Paragraph

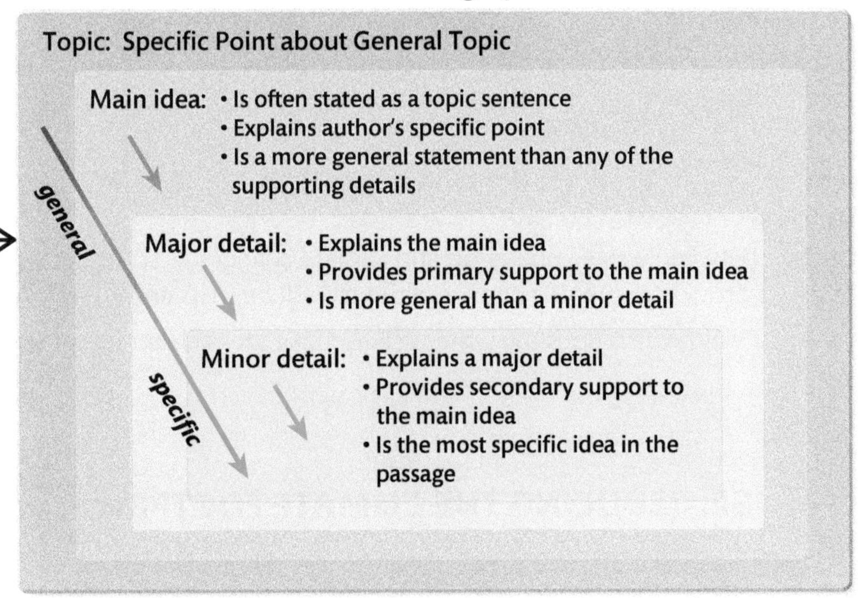

Question, Read, Annotate, and Review an Essay

Before reading, master readers ask questions and skim an essay to identify the topic, the writer's central point, and the key supporting details. During reading, they annotate key details. After reading, they often make an outline or map that illustrates the flow of the writer's ideas. The master reader's goal is to determine the writer's point of the essay.

For Module 6, assume you are taking a college course in earth science and your class is beginning a study on the theme of "protecting the environment." Each reading in this module follows this theme. After completing all assigned readings, you will write in response to the following guiding question "What are the dangers to the environment, and what should we do to protect it?"

Example

Assume the following passage from the U.S. Environmental Protection Agency's (EPA) Website is your first assigned reading on the theme "protecting the environment." Your professor has provided before and during reading questions and guided annotations to prepare you to read about and respond to the theme. Before reading, survey the questions and skim the passage for possible answers. Next, read the passage and the annotations. As you read, add your own annotations by completing the prompts in **bold** print in the annotations. After reading, use your own words to answer the questions. Record your answers in your reading/writing journal. Finally, complete the outline with information from the passage.

Before and During Reading Questions:

Logical Order: Did the writer provide an introduction, body, and conclusion?
Central Idea: What is the writer's central point?
Relevant Details: What are greenhouse gases?

What is the greenhouse effect?
What are the basic causes of climate change?
What is the connection between waste generation and climate change?
How do life cycle stages provide numerous opportunities to reduce GHG emissions?

Effective Language: What vivid words does the writer use to make ideas clear or easy to remember?

CLIMATE CHANGE: REDUCING THE CLIMATE FOOTPRINT

Greenhouse Gases and the Greenhouse Effect

Effective Language: Vivid words such as *Greenhouse* create a mental picture in the reader's mind to make the point clear and easy to remember. **Circle one more vivid word or phrase.**

Relevant Details: The details highlighted in sentences 2 and 7 make up a list of greenhouse gases. This list of details answers the question "What are greenhouse gases?" **Underline details that answer the other Before and During Reading Questions.**

[1]Understanding the greenhouse effect is critical to understanding global climate change. [2]The Earth's atmosphere includes various gases—water vapor, carbon dioxide (CO_2), methane (CH_4), and nitrous oxide (N_2O). [3]Together these gases act as a greenhouse. [4]They prevent too much heat from escaping from the Earth's atmosphere. [5]They are, therefore, classified as greenhouse gases (GHGs). [6]Other powerful GHGs result from industrial processes and are not naturally occurring. [7]These include hydrofluorocarbons (HFCs), perfluorocarbons (PFCs), and sulfur hexafluoride (SF_6).

[8]GHGs are essential for regulating our climate because they absorb and hold heat from the sun in the atmosphere around the Earth; the greenhouse effect is the warming of the Earth's surface and lower atmosphere by these gases. [9]The climate control process begins with a wave of solar radiation passing through the atmosphere. [10]Most of this radiation is absorbed by the Earth's surface. [11]But some of the energy is reflected off the Earth's surface back into space as infrared radiation. [12]Infrared waves can be trapped by GHGs. [13]This process helps keep the planet at a temperature suitable for life. [14]Each GHG differs in its ability to absorb this heat. [15]HFCs and PFCs are the most heat-absorbent. [16]CH_4 traps around 23 times more heat per molecule than CO_2. [17]And N_2O absorbs 270 times more heat per molecule than CO_2.

[18]Without the GHGs' effect on the atmosphere, the average temperature on Earth would be minus 2 degrees Fahrenheit. [19]Currently, the average temperature is 60 degrees Fahrenheit. [20]The average temperature, however, has increased by 1 degree Fahrenheit during the last century. [21]This change is a result of the recent increase in GHG concentrations in our atmosphere.

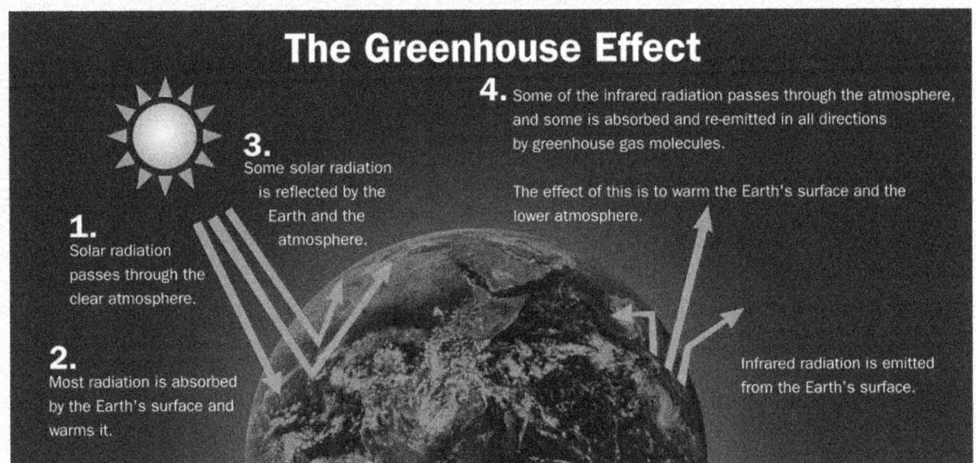

Climate Change–The Basics

[22]At one time, all climate changes occurred naturally. [23]During the Industrial Revolution, however, humans began altering the climate and environment through changing agricultural and industrial practices. [24]These activities have changed the makeup of the Earth's atmosphere by increasing the levels of GHGs, primarily CO_2, CH_4, and N_2O. [25]CO_2 is released to the atmosphere by the burning of fossil fuels, wood and wood products, and solid waste. [26]CH_4 is released from the decomposition of organic wastes in landfills, the raising of livestock, and the production and transport of coal, natural gas, and oil. [27]N_2O is released during agricultural and industrial activities as well as during the burning of solid waste and fossil fuels.

[28]The increased levels of GHGs in the Earth's atmosphere have the potential to cause global climate change. [29]According to the National Academy of Sciences (NAS), GHGs are accumulating in the Earth's atmosphere as a result of human activities. [30]This development is likely contributing to an increase in the global mean surface air temperature and ocean temperature below the surface. [31]These temperature increases are threats. [32]Human health, agriculture, water resources, forests, wildlife, and coastal areas are vulnerable to the changes that global warming may bring. [33]Waste prevention and recycling can play a significant role in reducing greenhouse gas emissions.

Central Idea: The central idea is the point the writer makes about the topic of the passage. The topic is "reducing greenhouse emissions." **Double underline the writer's point about the topic.**

Waste Generation and Climate Change

[34]Every stage of a product's life cycle impacts climate change. [35]In addition, each stage requires the use of natural resources and the consumption of energy—human activities that result in the release of GHGs and impact the Earth's environment.

CONTINUED

EXAMPLE *CONTINUED*

- [36]Energy Consumption—Manufacturing and using products requires energy. [37]An increase in energy demand leads to the extraction, processing, delivery, and combustion of more fossil fuels. [38]This process leads to the release of more GHGs into the atmosphere.
- [39]Raw Material Use—Harvesting, extracting, and transporting raw materials releases GHGs. [40]In addition, harvesting trees and other plants decreases carbon storage. [41]Plants absorb CO_2 from the atmosphere and store the carbon.
- [42]Waste Disposal/Incineration—Disposing of organic materials, such as food, paper, and yard trimmings, increases CH_4 levels during decomposition that occurs in landfills. [43]Also, the collection, transportation, and processing of wastes release GHG emissions.

Life Cycle Stages and Opportunities to Reduce GHG Emissions

[44]The term "life cycle" is made up of all activities included in the product's lifetime. [45]This cycle goes from manufacturing, to use, to maintenance, to disposal. [46]This life cycle is also known as "cradle to grave." [47]Companies can analyze a product's life cycle to determine where they can make changes. [48]Changes may include preventing waste, reducing amounts of materials used, reusing products, recycling, or using recycled materials in a product. [49]Because GHGs are released during each stage of a product's life cycle, there are many opportunities to decrease a product's impact on climate change.

The Link Between Waste Management and Greenhouse Gases

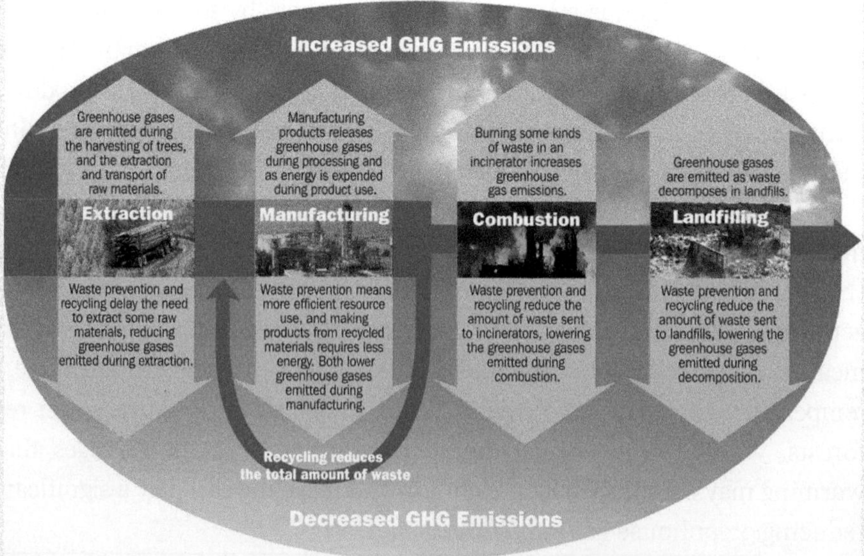

Logical Order: The writer provides a conclusion to emphasize the central point of the passage. **Underline the sentence that best restates the central point.**

[50]Human activity has intensified the greenhouse effect. [51]Human activity has affected global climate change. [52]Companies can and should take steps to reduce their climate footprints.

—Adapted from "Don't 'Waste Your Chance to Do Your Share: How to Reduce Your Climate Footprint." U.S. Environmental Protection Agency. 20 March 2014.

I. Introduction

A. ______________________________

1. Greenhouse gases include water vapor, carbon dioxide, methane, nitrous oxide, hydrofluorocarbons, perfluorocarbons, and sulfur hexafluoride.

2. Greenhouse effect is ______________________________

____

B. ______________________________

1. Humans began altering the climate and environment through changing agricultural and industrial practices.

2. These activities have changed the makeup of the Earth's atmosphere by increasing the levels of GHGs, primarily CO_2, CH_4, and N_2O.

3. Thesis Statement: ______________________________

____

II. Body

A. ______________________________

1. ______________ requires energy and releases GHGs into the atmosphere.

2. ______________ releases GHGs and decreases carbon storage.

3. ______________ increases GHG emissions in landfills and in the collection, transportation, and processing of wastes.

B. ______________________________

1. ______________ is made up of all activities included in the product's lifetime.

2. This cycle goes from ______________________________

____

3. Changes may include preventing waste, reducing amounts of materials used, reusing products, recycling, or using recycled materials in a product.

III. __________

A. Human activity has intensified the greenhouse effect.

B. Human activity has affected global climate change.

C. ______________________________

____

CONTINUED

EXAMPLE *CONTINUED*

Explanation

Compare your answers to the following think-aloud.

The guided annotations helped me locate answers to the before and during reading questions. The following journal entry records what I annotated and my answers to the questions.

1. Logical order. The writer gave a long introduction made up of several paragraphs. These paragraphs gave information that strengthened my prior knowledge so I could better understand the writer's point. The writer also gave a conclusion. I underlined sentence 52 as the sentence that best restated the central idea. This sentence is a call for action that is based on all the information in the passage.
2. Central idea. The point the writer is making about the topic "reducing greenhouse emissions" is "waste prevention and recycling can play a significant role." All the details in the passage support this controlling point.
3. Relevant details. The details I underlined are the very details that I gave to complete the outline.
4. Effective language: I circled the phrase "cradle to the grave" as vivid words. This phrase helped me clearly see and remember the life cycle of a product. I completed the outline with the following information.

    A. Greenhouse Gases and the Greenhouse Effect

      2. the warming of the Earth's surface and lower atmosphere by these gases.

    B. Climate Change—The Basics

      3. Thesis statement: Waste prevention and recycling can play a significant role in reducing greenhouse emissions.

    A. Waste Generation and Climate Change

      1. Energy consumption. 2. Raw material. 3. Waste disposal/incineration.

    B. Life Cycle Stages and Opportunities to Reduce GHG emissions

      1. Life cycle. 2. manufacturing, to use, to maintenance, to disposal.

III. Conclusion.

  C. Companies can and should take steps to reduce their climate footprints.

Practice 1

Question, Read, Annotate, and Review an Essay

Assume the following two passages are the next assigned readings on the theme "protecting the environment." Your professor has provided a few questions to guide your thinking. Before reading each passage, survey the questions and skim the passage for possible answers. Then read the passage. As you read, annotate the details in the passage that answer the questions. After reading, respond to the prompts that follow each passage.

Before and During Reading Questions:
Logical Order: Does the writer provide an introduction, body, and conclusion?
Central Idea: What is the writer's central point?
Relevant Details: How does climate change affect agriculture, forestry, health, and economics?
Effective Language: What vivid words does the writer use to create mental images in the reader's mind?

The Dangers of Climate Change

1 Drought, flooding, storm surges, and sea level rise have already taken a toll on the lives and livelihoods of millions of people. 2 However, climate change will have still more consequences. 3 These include impacts on agriculture, forestry, health, and economics.

CONTINUED

PRACTICE 1 *CONTINUED*

Agriculture [4]For some crops in the temperate zones, moderate warming may slightly increase production because growing seasons become longer. [5]The availability of additional carbon dioxide to plants for photosynthesis may also increase yields. [6]However, some research shows that crops become less nutritious when supplied with more carbon dioxide. [7]And if rainfall shifts in space and time, intensified droughts and floods will likely cut into agricultural productivity. [8]Considering all factors together, experts expect crop yields to decline. [9]In seasonally dry tropical and subtropical regions, growing seasons may be shortened and harvests may be more susceptible to drought. [10]Thus, scientists predict that crop production will fall in these regions even with minor warming. [11]This would worsen hunger in many of the world's developing nations.

Forestry [12]In the forests that provide our timber and paper products, enriched atmospheric CO_2 may spur greater growth in the near term, but other climatic effects such as drought, fire, and disease may eliminate these gains. [13]For example, droughts brought about by a strong El Nino in 1997–1998 allowed immense forest fires to destroy vast areas of rainforest in Indonesia, Brazil, and Mexico. [14]In North America, forest managers increasingly find themselves battling catastrophic fires, invasive species, and insect and disease outbreaks. [15]Catastrophic fires are caused in part by decades of fire suppression but are also promoted by longer, warmer, drier fire seasons. [16]Milder winters and hotter, drier summers are promoting outbreaks of bark beetles that are destroying millions of acres of trees.

Health [17]As climate change proceeds, we will face more heat waves—and heat stress can cause death, especially among older adults. [18]A 1995 heat wave in Chicago killed at least 485 people, and a 2003 heat wave in Europe killed 35,000 people. [19]A warmer climate also exposes us to other health problems:

- [20]Respiratory ailments from air pollution, as hotter temperatures promote formation of photochemical smog,
- [21]Expansion of tropical diseases, such as dengue fever, into temperate regions as vectors of infectious disease (such as mosquitoes) move toward the poles,
- [22]Disease and sanitation problems when floods overcome sewage treatment systems,
- [23]Injuries and drowning if storms become more frequent or intense.

[24]Health hazards from cold weather will decrease, but most researchers feel that the increase in warm-weather hazards will more than offset these gains.

Economics [25]People will experience a variety of economic costs and benefits from the many impacts of climate change, but on the whole researchers predict that costs will outweigh benefits, especially as climate change grows more severe. [26]Climate change is also expected to widen the gap between rich and poor, both within and among nations. [27]Poorer people have less wealth and technology with which to adapt to climate change, and they rely more on resources (such as local food and water) that are sensitive to climatic conditions.

—Adapted from Withgott and Laposata. *Environment: The Science Behind the Stories*, 5th ed., 2014. pp. 432–433, 502–503.

After Reading Response: Respond to the following prompts in your reading/writing journal:

- Write a summary of the passage (for more about writing a summary, see Module 1, page 34).
- Create an outline that answers the following prompt:
    - How may waste generation and the life cycle of a product (see "Climate Change: Reducing the Climate Footprint" on pages 222–224) harm the environment as described in the essay "The Dangers of Climate Change"?

CONTINUED

PRACTICE 1 *CONTINUED*

Before and During Reading Questions:
Logical Order: Does the writer provide an introduction, body, and conclusion?
Central Idea: What is the writer's central point?
Relevant Details: What was the town like when it was in harmony with its surroundings? In what ways did everything change?
Effective Language: What vivid words does the writer use to create mental images in the reader's mind?

A Fable for Tomorrow

by Rachel Carson

[1]There was once a town in the heart of America where all life seemed to live in harmony with its surroundings. [2]The town lay in the midst of a checkerboard of prosperous farms, with fields of grain and hillsides of orchards where, in spring, white clouds of bloom drifted above the green fields. [3]In autumn, oak and maple and birch set up a blaze of color that flamed and flickered across a backdrop of pines. [4]Then foxes barked in the hills and deer silently crossed the fields, half hidden in the mists of the fall mornings.

[5]Along the roads, laurel, viburnum and alder, great ferns and wildflowers delighted the traveler's eye through much of the year. [6]Even in winter the roadsides were places of beauty, where countless birds came to feed on the berries and on the seed heads of the dried weeds rising above the snow. [7]The countryside was, in fact, famous for the abundance and variety of its bird life, and when the flood of migrants was pouring through in spring and fall people traveled from great distances to observe them. [8]Others came to fish the streams, which flowed clear and cold out of the hills and contained shady pools where trout lay. [9]So it had been from the days many years ago when the first settlers raised their houses, sank their wells, and built their barns.

[10]Then a strange blight crept over the area and everything began to change. [11]Some evil spell had settled on the community: mysterious maladies swept the flocks of chickens; the cattle and sheep sickened and died. [12]Everywhere was a shadow of death. [13]The farmers spoke of much illness among their families. [14]In the town the doctors had become more and more puzzled by new kinds of sickness appearing among their patients. [15]There had been several sudden and unexplained deaths, not only among adults but even among children, who would be stricken suddenly while at play and die within a few hours.

[16]There was a strange stillness. [17]The birds, for example—where had they gone? [18]Many people spoke of them, puzzled and disturbed. [19]The feeding stations in the backyards were deserted. [20]The few birds seen anywhere were moribund; they trembled violently and could not fly. [21]It was a spring without voices. [22]On the mornings that had once throbbed with the dawn chorus of robins, catbirds, doves, jays, wrens, and scores of other bird voices there was now no sound; only silence lay over the fields and woods and marsh.

[23]On the farms the hens brooded, but no chicks hatched. [24]The farmers complained that they were unable to raise any pigs—the litters were small and the young survived only a few days. [25]The apple trees were coming into bloom but no bees droned among the blossoms, so there was no pollination and there would be no fruit.

[26]The roadsides, once so attractive, were now lined with browned and withered vegetation as though swept by fire. [27]These, too, were silent, deserted by all living things. [28]Even the streams were now lifeless. [29]Anglers no longer visited them, for all the fish had died.

[30]In the gutters under the eaves and between the shingles of the roofs, a white granular powder still showed a few patches; some weeks before it had fallen like snow upon the roofs and the lawns, the fields and streams.

[31]No witchcraft, no enemy action had silenced the rebirth of new life in this stricken world. [32]The people had done it themselves.

[33]This town does not actually exist, but it might easily have a thousand counterparts in America or elsewhere in the world. [34]I know of no community that has experienced all the misfortunes I describe. [35]Yet every one of these disasters has actually happened somewhere, and many real communities have already suffered a substantial number of them. [36]A grim specter has crept upon us almost unnoticed, and this imagined tragedy may easily become a stark reality we all shall know.

?

After Reading Response: Respond to the following prompts in your reading/writing journal:

- Write a summary of the passage (see Module 1, page 34).
- Create an outline that answers the following prompt:
  - How does "A Fable for Tomorrow" illustrate the facts and theories stated in "The Dangers of Climate Change" (see page 227) and "Climate Change: Reducing the Climate Footprint" (see page 222)?

L3 Prewrite a Draft of a Central Idea: Thesis Statement

PREWRITE: RECITE/REVIEW/ BRAINSTORM

A thesis statement answers the question "What's the point?" This point is the writer's opinion about the topic that is explained and supported in the essay. In fact, this point further narrows the topic. The writer's point or opinion is often referred to as the **controlling point**. The controlling point often includes a pattern of organization (see Modules 8–12) as well as the writer's opinion. The following graphic illustrates an effective thesis statement.

Controlling point limits or focuses the development of a topic through an opinion or a pattern of organization.

TOPIC — WRITER'S OPINION

Climate change occurs for several key reasons.

PATTERN OF ORGANIZATION SIGNAL WORDS

The topic is *climate change*. The writer's controlling point offers an opinion and suggests a pattern of organization. The words *occurs* and *reasons* suggest that the essay will focus on the causes of climate change. The word *several* suggests that the writer will identify more than one cause. *Key* states the writer's opinion about the importance of those causes. While you may not always indicate the pattern of organization in your thesis statement, doing so may help you organize the ideas you want to develop in your essay. The following chart offers a few examples of patterns of organization and signal words, which may be helpful as you draft your thesis statement.

Pattern of Organization	Signal Words	Pattern of Organization	Signal Words
Time	*events, occurrence, process, sequence, steps*	**Example**	*illustration, including, such as*
Space	*depict, describe, portray*	**Comparison/ Contrast**	*although, just as, compares, differs, while*
Listing	*a few, numerous, several, some*	**Cause/Effect**	*because, therefore*
Classification	*kinds, levels, roles, types*	**Argument**	*must, must not, should, should not*

Keep in mind that a thesis statement asserts a clear and focused point. It does not ask a question, nor does it directly announce your topic. The following chart offers several additional hints for drafting a thesis statement.

Hints for Drafting a Thesis Statement
Use specific statements. Replace vague, general words with vivid, exact words. *"Football is a dumb game"* is too vague and general. *"Football glorifies violence"* is specific and vivid.
Always state your thesis statement as a complete sentence.
Avoid asking a question. A question may introduce a topic or thesis statement, but it may never be a thesis statement. Does football glorify violence?
Avoid announcing your topic. Never say, *"I am going to write about football and violence,"* or *"My essay is about football and violence,"* or *"My topic is football violence."*
Review and, if necessary, revise your thesis statement after you have written a rough draft. As you think about a topic, the point you want to make often becomes clearer.

Example

Your instructor has asked you to use the readings on pages 222–231 to write an essay that addresses the following prompt: "What are the dangers to the environment, and what should we do to protect it?" The first part of the assignment is to generate a central idea or thesis statement for the essay. Use the following steps to brainstorm your thesis statement.

1. Narrow Topic: ______________________

2. Identify Pattern of Organization Signal Words: ______________________

____

____

3. Identify Opinion: ______________________

____

____

4. Combine into a Draft of Thesis Statement: ______________________

____

____

EXAMPLE *CONTINUED*

Explanation

Compare your responses to the following think-aloud.

The question "What are the dangers to the environment, and what should we do to protect it?" has two parts. So I decided to break my essay response into two sections. In the first section I am going to describe the types of threats to the environment. In the second section, I am going to talk about the steps we could take to protect the environment. Brainstorming my thesis statement has already made me think about the specific details I will use to support my central point. It also made me think about how I would organize those details. Here are the steps I took to brainstorm my thesis statement.

1. Narrow Topic: Types of dangers to environment and steps to take to protect it.
2. Pattern of Organization Signal Words: **types** and **steps.**
3. Opinion Words: **needless dangers, must take necessary steps.**
4. We must take the necessary steps to deal with the needless dangers to our environment.

Practice 2

Prewrite a Draft of a Central Idea

In your reading/writing journal, identify the steps you used to draft your thesis statement for your essay. How did your thesis statement differ from the thesis statement in the Example's think-aloud? Did your brainstorming process differ from the process described in the think-aloud? If so, how and why?

Prewrite to Generate and Organize Relevant Details

LO4

Most writers generate details during the prewriting stage by listing or freewriting. Then they organize the details into a writing plan. Many writers use concept mapping or outlining to help create a plan for the essay. Mapping and outlining are excellent ways to see if there are enough details to support the point of the essay. When master writers compose an essay in response to what they have read, they often rely on details that they annotated in the passages they have read. They then either respond to those details or use them to support their own views.

Example

Assume your class is continuing to work on the essay addressing the question "What are the dangers to the environment, and what should we do to protect it?" Now your assignment is to return to the texts to identify details that you will use in your essay. You may use the following outline to prewrite and organize details for your essay.

Title: ____________________

I. Introduction [Details from readings to establish background and importance of topic]

A. ____________________

____

B. Thesis Statement: ____________________

____

II. Body [Details from readings and explanations that support your thesis statement]

A. ____________________

____

B. ____________________

____

C. ____________________

____

III. Conclusion [Details that reinforce your or restate your central point]

A. ____________________

____

B. ____________________

____

EXAMPLE *CONTINUED*

Explanation

Compare your answers to the following think-aloud.

I completed this outline by using the details I had annotated in the passages that I had read. I indicated which passage each detail came from by giving the title of the passage in parentheses after each one.

Title: Avoiding Needless Dangers to the Environment

I. Introduction
   A. Human activity increases the greenhouse effect. ("Climate Change: Reducing the Climate Footprint")
   B. Human activity causes needless dangers to agriculture, forests, and human health. ("The Dangers of Climate Change")
   C. We must take the necessary steps to deal with the needless dangers to our environment.

II. Body
   A. First step is to recognize the problem. ("The Dangers of Climate Change")
   B. Second step is to prevent waste. ("Climate Change: Reducing the Climate Footprint")
   C. Third step is to reduce amounts of materials used. ("Climate Change: Reducing the Climate Footprint")
   D. Fourth step is to recycle products and materials. ("Climate Change: Reducing the Climate Footprint")

III. Conclusion
   A. Let us exist in accord with our environment. (Carson, "A Fable for Tomorrow")
   B. Avoid the tragedy of a needless and bleak future. (Carson, "A Fable for Tomorrow")

Practice 3

Prewrite to Generate and Organize Relevant Details

In your reading/writing journal, identify the steps needed to generate relevant details to support a thesis statement. Identify the steps the writer of the outline in the example went through as he annotated the texts and created his outline. How did your prewrites differ?

Compose a Draft Using Logical Order LO5

Once you have brainstormed details to compose an essay, you are ready to begin the drafting process. First, review the concept map or outline you completed with the details from the readings and your own insights or responses. As you review your prewrite, rearrange details into the most logical order. Add details if needed. Once the paragraphs are ordered logically, use **transitions** to connect each paragraph to the next so that readers can follow your chain of thought. The following chart lists and illustrates several options to connect paragraphs to each other.

Transitions are linking words or phrases that signal a specific pattern of organization or the logical order of ideas.

Connect Paragraphs	
Echo or repeat important words or phrases from the thesis statement in body paragraphs to support the thesis statement with relevant details.	
I. Thesis statement:	We can *ease* the *pain* that occurs from illness or injury in several different ways.
II. Topic sentence:	*Pain* can be *eased* by deep breathing.
III. Topic sentence:	Visualization and imagery *ease pain.*
Refer to the main idea of the previous paragraph in the topic sentence of the present paragraph.	
I. Thesis statement:	Applying the principles of computer ergonomics reduces the chances of injury and fatigue.
II. Topic sentence:	The *computer screen* should be *placed properly* to avoid painful injuries to the neck.
III. Topic sentence:	*Proper placement* of the *monitor* not only *reduces* the possibility of *neck injury* but also eases eye fatigue.
Use transitional words, phrases, or sentences to link paragraphs that follow.	
I. Thesis statement:	Sleep disorders can deprive sufferers of much needed rest and complicate their lives.
II. Topic sentence:	*One type* of sleep disorder is known as night terrors.
III. Topic sentence:	*Another type* of sleep disorder, nightmares, torments many people.
IV. Transition sentence and topic sentence:	*At least the previous two disorders occur in the privacy of one's home.* Narcolepsy, a *third kind* of sleep disorder, can occur suddenly anywhere, and at any time without warning.
Tie the last idea in one paragraph to the opening of the next paragraph.	
I. Thesis statement:	Hurricane activity is on the rise, is likely to increase, and calls for new methods of preparation.
II. Topic sentence and ending idea of paragraph:	Hurricane activity is on the rise because of higher ocean temperatures and lower vertical wind shear. Therefore, these *climate changes* are likely to continue for as many as 10 to 40 years.
III. Topic sentence:	*These shifts in climate* call for new methods of hurricane preparation.

Master writers create several drafts to achieve a logical order and smooth flow of ideas.

Example

Assume you are still working toward writing an essay that answers the prompt "What are the dangers to the environment, and what should we do to protect it?" On your own paper, write a draft of your essay.

Explanation

Compare your answers to the following think-aloud and essay.

I followed my outline without having to make any changes to the logical order. I included signal words to connect paragraphs, such as **first step**, **second step**, and so on. Each body paragraph starts with a detail from a reading passage followed by the name of the passage it came from in parentheses. I then gave examples based on my observations and personal experiences.

Avoiding Needless Dangers to the Environment

The greenhouse effect has long occurred naturally due to gases that are essential parts of Earth's atmosphere such as water vapor and carbon dioxide. However, recent human activity has introduced gases that are not natural but are the result of newer industrial and farming practices ("Climate Change: Reducing the Climate Footprint"). As a result, human activity threatens our agriculture, our forests, and our health ("The Dangers of Climate Change"). We must take the necessary steps to deal with the needless dangers to our environment.

The first step we must take is to recognize the problem. We must see that global warming will lead to terrible droughts, reduced food production, and worldwide hunger ("The Dangers of Climate Change"). Much of global warming can be linked to the emissions of gases from the use of fossil fuels such as gasoline and coal. We must realize that if we caused this problem, we can also correct this problem. The first step is taking responsibility. Then we can change our actions.

The second step is to prevent waste ("Climate Change: Reducing the Climate Footprint"). Think of how much we waste our resources. We leave lights on in rooms we aren't in. We drive our cars when we could walk or bike or share rides with others. We use paper and plastic bags instead of cloth shopping bags. Lighting, gasoline, and paper and plastic bags all use fossil fuels and emit harmful gases in their production, use, and even disposal. We need to stop being so wasteful.

The third step is to reduce amounts of materials we use ("Climate Change: Reducing the Climate Footprint"). Reducing means using less of something. For example, we can use fewer paper napkins at a fast food restaurant. We can also use cloth napkins and ceramic plates at home instead of paper napkins and plates. We can buy products with less packaging. We can compost food waste instead of throwing it in the garbage. The ways to reduce waste are numerous. It just requires us to think and act responsibly.

The fourth step is to recycle products and materials ("Climate Change: Reducing the Climate Footprint"). Recycling actually helps with reducing and preventing waste. Paper, plastic, metal, and glass can all be recycled. Many cities and companies provide recycling bins to sort products so they can be easily recycled. However, other items can also be recycled, such as electronic equipment, furniture, clothing, and even vehicles. In addition, we should buy products that use recycled materials. Recycling reduces harmful emissions from landfills and fossil fuels used to produce and transport new goods.

We must listen to Rachel Carson's plea in "A Fable for Tomorrow" and choose to exist in accord with our environment. We must heed her warning and avoid the needless catastrophe of a bleak future in a damaged environment.

Practice 4

Compose a Draft of an Essay

In your reading/writing journal, identify the steps you took to write your draft. Identify the steps the writer of "Avoiding Needless Dangers to the Environment" took as he wrote his draft. How are your drafts different? How are they similar? What can you apply from this writer's method to your own writing in the future?

L6 Revise and Proofread for Effective Language: Word Choice

Both readers and writers use introductions and conclusions to comprehend meaning and make a point in their writing. An effective introduction serves several purposes: It introduces the essay topic, explains the importance of this topic, and/or gives necessary background information about it. An effective introduction also hooks the reader's interest. It presents the essay's main idea in a thesis statement. An effective conclusion fulfills the following purposes: It restates the essay's main idea and sums up the major points in the essay. It brings the essay to an end.

The following chart describes and illustrates ten of the most common types of introductions and conclusions. Many of these types may be used as either an introduction or a conclusion. Others are best used only as an introduction. The chart suggests the appropriate use of each type.

Ten Types of Introductions and Conclusions	
A question **Introduction or conclusion**	**EXAMPLE:** Don't you want to experience the well-being that results from a healthful diet and regular exercise?
A quotation **Introduction or conclusion**	**EXAMPLE:** Just as renowned coach of the Green Bay Packers Vince Lombardi said, "The difference between a successful person and others is not a lack of strength, not a lack of knowledge, but rather in a lack of will."
A definition **Introduction**	**EXAMPLE:** Hope is belief that the impossible is possible. Hope is the future counted in the present. Hope is a light, a map, and a compass. Hope gave me the will to fight and survive cancer.
A call to action **Introduction or conclusion**	**EXAMPLE:** This is not a time for indecision or hesitation. This is a time for commitment and action. Tell your federal, state, and local governments that you demand a coordinated response plan for natural disasters.
A suggestion **Introduction or conclusion**	**EXAMPLE:** Your best friend is the one who will tell you a hard truth for your own good.

Ten Types of Introductions and Conclusions *continued*	
A warning about consequences **Introduction or conclusion**	**EXAMPLE:** If instruments used for ear and body piercing are not properly cleaned and sterilized between clients, then you could contract HIV, hepatitis B, or hepatitis C.
A vivid image **Introduction or conclusion**	**EXAMPLE:** Two gas stations. A car repair shop barely visible through the rusty open hoods of dismantled racecars. A man clad in overalls selling roasted peanuts from the back of his truck. These are a few sights at the unpretentious intersection that is the small town of Barberville in Northwest Volusia. To some, the settlement along the corner of U.S. 17 and State Road 40 represents one of the area's last strongholds of unspoiled country life. Maria Herrera, "Rural Residents Wary of Road Project"
A surprising fact or statement **Introduction**	**EXAMPLE:** Nearly one in seven Americans has key clinical data missing from their medical files, according to a report in *The Journal of the American Medical Association* (JAMA). And in 44 percent of cases the absent information would have impacted a doctor's diagnosis, potentially putting patients' health at risk. You can take a few simple steps to maintain accurate and accessible personal-health records and safeguard your well-being. Adapted from "Read This Before Your Next Doctor's Appointment," *First Magazine*
A contradiction or an opposing view **Introduction**	**EXAMPLE:** Many wanna-be runners don't even try because they believe they don't have the right physique. Their legs are too short. Their stomach is too big. Their shoulders are too broad. Their body weight is too much. These people are wrong. The body is unimportant. The mind is everything. Running is not a physical sport. It's mental. "Mind Over Body," *Running Fit Prevention Guide*
Context information or a summary **Introduction or conclusion**	**EXAMPLE:** It is especially important to wash your hands before, during, and after you prepare food, before you eat, after you use the bathroom, after handling animals or animal waste, when your hands are dirty, and more frequently when someone in your home is sick. National Center for Infectious Diseases, "Wash Your Hands Often"

Example

Use suggestions from the chart "Ten Types of Introductions and Conclusions" to revise the introduction and conclusion of the essay you composed in response to the question "What are the dangers to the environment, and what should we do to protect it?" Use your own paper.

Explanation

Compare your answers to the following think-aloud and revised introduction and conclusion.

As I reviewed my draft to revise my introduction and conclusion, I decided to revise both.

It was clear that I needed to begin my essay with a definition of "the greenhouse effect." Beginning with this definition gives the reader the background information needed to understand the danger to the environment. Also, the essay seemed to begin in the middle of a thought, but giving the definition offers a good place to begin the discussion. My definition is a paraphrase and summary of the long explanation of the greenhouse effect given in the essay "Climate Change: Reducing the Climate Footprint." So I put the title in parentheses after the definition. I also found a photograph to illustrate my introduction.

As I thought about my conclusion, it seemed that I had used a combination of a warning and a call to action by paraphrasing Rachel Carson's warnings. But the call to action seemed vague. So I added two sentences to make the need for action sound urgent and to give specific actions to take. I wanted to include a photograph for my conclusion, too. These pictures drive my central point home and make it memorable. Here are my revisions:

Revised Introduction: The greenhouse effect is the warming of the earth's temperature on land and in the oceans. ("Climate Change: Reducing the Climate Footprint"). The greenhouse effect has long occurred naturally due to gases that are

essential parts of Earth's atmosphere such as water vapor and carbon dioxide. However, recent human activity has introduced gases that are not natural but are the result of newer industrial and farming practices ("Climate Change: Reducing the Climate Footprint"). As a result, human activity threatens our agriculture, our forests, and our health ("The Dangers of Climate Change"). We must take the necessary steps to deal with the needless dangers to our environment.

Revised Conclusion: We must listen to Rachel Carson's plea in "A Fable for Tomorrow" and choose to exist in accord with our environment. We must heed her warning and avoid the needless catastrophe of a bleak future in a damaged environment. There is no time for delay. Today each of us must do our part to prevent waste, recycle, and reduce GHG emissions.

Practice 5

Revise and Proofread for Effective Language

In your reading/writing journal, identify the types of introduction and conclusion you used in the revision of your essay. Explain your choices. Identify the type of introduction and conclusion the writer used in his revision of "Avoiding Needless Dangers to the Environment." How are your revisions different? How are they similar? What can you apply from this writer's method to your own writing in the future?

Workshop: Understanding the Essay

Assume you are continuing your study of the theme of protecting the environment in your college earth science class. The following passage from the Website of the National Oceanic and Atmospheric Administration (NOAA) is your capstone reading assignment. Your capstone writing assignment is to write an essay responding to the question "What are the dangers to the environment, and what should we do to protect it?" To complete your writing assignment, skim the prereading questions to guide your reading, read the passage, and then complete the activities that follow.

MARINE DEBRIS AND THE ENVIRONMENT

What Is Marine Debris?

[1]Our oceans are filled with items that do not belong there. Huge amounts of consumer plastics, metals, rubber, paper, textiles, derelict fishing gear, vessels, and other lost or discarded items enter the marine environment every day, making marine debris one of the most widespread pollution problems facing the world's oceans and waterways. Marine debris is defined as any persistent solid material that is manufactured or processed and directly or indirectly, intentionally or unintentionally, disposed of or abandoned into the marine environment or the Great Lakes. It is a global problem, and it is an everyday problem. There is no part of the world left untouched by debris and its impacts. Marine debris is a threat to our environment, navigation safety, the economy, and human health. Most of all, marine debris is preventable.

Types and Sources

[2]Anything man-made, including litter and fishing gear, can become marine debris once lost or thrown into the marine environment. The most common materials that make up marine debris are plastics, glass, metal, paper, cloth, rubber, and wood. Glass, metal, and rubber are similar to plastic in that they are used for a wide range of products. While they can be worn away—broken down into smaller and smaller fragments, they generally do not biodegrade entirely. As these materials are used commonly in our society, their occurrence as marine debris is overwhelming. Debris typically comes from both land-based and ocean-based sources.

Marine debris from below, Hawaii

Plastics

[3]One of the main types of marine debris that you hear about today is plastic marine debris. In many places, it is the main type of debris that you will see as you walk along a beach, though perhaps not underwater. As common as they are on our beaches and in our homes, how much do you really know about plastics? As society has developed new uses for plastics, the variety and quantity of plastic items found in the marine environment has increased dramatically. These products range from common domestic material (bags, Styrofoam cups, bottles, balloons) to industrial products (strapping bands, plastic sheeting, hard hats, resin pellets) to lost or discarded fishing gear (nets, buoys, traps, lines).

[4]Plastics can enter into the marine environment a number of ways: through ineffective or improper waste management, intentional or accidental dumping and littering on shorelines or at sea, or through storm water runoff. Eventually, these plastics will degrade into smaller and smaller pieces.

[5]Plastics are used in many aspects of daily life and are a big part of our waste stream. Many plastics are colorful and will float in water, which makes plastic debris a very visible part of the

marine debris problem. However, an accurate estimate does not yet exist for how much debris is composed of plastic materials.

Derelict Fishing Gear

6Derelict fishing gear (DFG) refers to nets, lines, crab/shrimp pots, and other recreational or commercial fishing equipment that has been lost, abandoned, or discarded in the marine environment. Modern gear is generally made of synthetic materials and metal, and lost gear can persist for a very long time.

Movement

7How does marine debris move and where does it go? Wind, gyres, and ocean currents all impact how marine debris gets around. Floatable marine debris items, once they enter the ocean, are carried via oceanic currents and atmospheric winds. Factors that impact currents and winds, such as El Niño and seasons, also affect the movement of marine debris in the ocean. Debris items can be carried far from their origin, which makes it difficult to determine exactly where an item came from. Oceanic features can also help trap items in debris accumulation zones, often referred to in the media and marine debris community as "garbage patches."

Great Pacific Garbage Patch

8The name "Pacific Garbage Patch" has led many to believe that this area is a large and continuous patch of easily visible marine debris items such as bottles and other litter—akin to a literal island of trash that should be visible with satellite or aerial photographs. While higher concentrations of litter items can be found in this area, along with other debris such as derelict fishing nets, much of the debris is actually small pieces of floating plastic that are not immediately evident to the naked eye.

9The debris is continuously mixed by wind and wave action and widely dispersed both over huge surface areas and throughout the top portion of the water column. It is possible to sail through the "garbage patch" area and see very little or no debris on the water's surface. It is also difficult to estimate the size of these "patches," because the borders and content constantly change with ocean currents and winds. Regardless of the exact size, mass, and location of the "garbage patch," man-made debris does not belong in our oceans and waterways and must be addressed.

Impacts

10The impact of marine debris is wide ranging and devastating. Economic loss, wildlife entanglement and ingestion, and habitat damage, navigation hazards, and alien species transport are just some of impacts of marine debris.

- **Economic loss** Marine debris is an eyesore along shorelines around the world. It degrades the beauty of the coastal environment and, in many cases, may cause economic loss if an area is a popular tourist destination. Would you want to swim at a beach littered in trash? Coastal communities may not have the resources to continually clean up debris.
- **Habitat Damage** Marine debris can scour, break, smother, and otherwise damage important marine habitat, such as coral reefs. Many of these habitats serve as the basis of marine ecosystems and are critical to the survival of many other species.

CONTINUED

- **Wildlife Entanglement and Ghost Fishing** One of the most notable types of impacts from marine debris is wildlife entanglement. Derelict nets, ropes, line, or other fishing gear, packing bands, rubber bands, balloon string, six-pack rings, and a variety of marine debris can wrap around marine life. Entanglement can lead to injury, illness, suffocation, starvation, and even death.
- **Ingestion** Many animals, such as sea turtles, seabirds, and marine mammals have been known to ingest marine debris. The debris item may be mistaken for food and ingested, an animal's natural food (e.g. fish eggs) may be attached to the debris, or the debris item may have been ingested accidentally with other food. Debris ingestion may lead to loss of nutrition, internal injury, intestinal blockage, starvation, and even death. Once marine debris, such as microplastic, is ingested, their chemicals transfer through the food web.
- **Vessel Damage and Navigation Hazards** Marine debris can be quite large and difficult to see in the ocean, if it's floating below the water surface. Encounters with marine debris at sea can result in costly vessel damage, either to its structure or through a tangled propeller or clogged intake.
- **Alien Species Transport** If a marine organism attaches to debris, it can travel hundreds of miles and land on a shoreline where it is non-native. Invasive species can have a devastating impact on fisheries and local ecosystems and can be costly to eradicate.

Solutions

11 Marine debris is one of the most widespread pollution problems facing the world's oceans and waterways. There are many ways people can prevent and reduce marine debris—from government action to individual lifestyle changes. For example, states are considering plastic microbead bans. Many face washes and body scrubs contain tiny plastic spheres—sometimes labeled "microscrubbers"—meant to exfoliate skin. Take a look at the ingredient lists on personal care bottles; if they say polyethylene and polypropylene, then there is plastic in them. Once rinsed off, the beads go down the drain. In most cases, they are so tiny that they slip through wastewater treatment plants and into nearby waterways. State legislatures in California, Minnesota, New York, and Ohio are considering bans or other legislation on plastic microbeads, citing concern over how these plastic pieces will impact fish and other wildlife. Some major manufacturers, including Unilever, Johnson & Johnson, and L'Oreal have also pledged to phase plastic microbeads out of their products and search for alternatives. In June 2014, Illinois became the first state to ban the production, manufacture, or sale of personal care products containing plastic microbeads.

12 Individuals can also help prevent marine debris. We can join or lead a cleanup. We can volunteer to pick up marine litter in our local communities. We can read labels and purchase products that don't turn into marine debris. We can properly dispose of our trash so it doesn't end up in the ocean or waterways. We can help keep our coastlines clear!

–Adapted from "Marine Debris." NOAA 28 August 2014. http://marinedebris.noaa.gov/marinedebris101. Copyright © by 2004 NOAA.

Preread: Survey and Question

PREREAD: SURVEY/ QUESTION

1. What is your prior knowledge about marine debris?

2. What is marine debris?

3. What are the types and sources of marine debris?

4. What are the impacts of marine debris?

5. What are some solutions to marine debris?

6. How does marine debris fit into the "life cycle" of a product (See "Climate Change: Reducing the Climate Footprint" page 222.)

7. What role may marine debris play in the greenhouse effect? (See "Climate Change: Reducing the Climate Footprint" page 222.)

8. How are the impacts of marine debris on the environment and society similar to the impacts discussed in the article "The Dangers of Climate Change" on page 227?

9. In her essay "A Fable for Tomorrow" (page 230), Rachel Carson describes two views of a town's environment: unspoiled and thriving versus damaged and dying. How would you describe two views of an ocean: unspoiled and thriving versus damaged and dying?

Read and Annotate

As you read, annotate key ideas, particularly those details that answer your Prereading questions.

Recite, Review, and Brainstorm

Recite and **Review** the information. Paraphrase ideas. Summarize the most important parts. **Brainstorm** ideas for your written response to the passage. Answer your Prereading questions. *Freewrite* or *map* the relationship among answers to questions or ideas you have annotated in the text. *Outline* or *list* key ideas and details in blocks of thought. Identify the central point you want to make. Use your own paper.

Write a Draft of Your Response

Using the ideas you generated by brainstorming, compose a draft of your response. Use your own paper.

Revise Your Draft

Once you have created a draft of your essay, read it over to answer the questions in the "Questions for Revising an Essay" box that follows. Indicate your answers by annotating your paper. If you answer "yes" to a question, underline, check, or circle examples. If you answer "no" to a question, write needed information in margins and draw lines to indicate placement of additional details. Revise your essay based on your reflection. (*Hint:* Experienced writers create several drafts as they focus on one or two questions per draft.)

Step by Step: Questions for Revising an Essay

- ☐ Have I stated or implied a focused main idea?
- ☐ Have I made my purpose clear?
- ☐ Is my tone appropriate for my audience and purpose?
- ☐ Is the logical order of ideas clear? Have I used words to clearly guide my reader, such as *first, second, next,* etc.?
- ☐ Have I used concrete details to make my point?
- ☐ Have I made my point with adequate details?
- ☐ Do all the details support my point?
- ☐ Have I used proper attribution styles for quotes and reported speech?

Proofread Your Draft

Once you have made any revisions to your essay that may be needed, proofread your essay to eliminate careless errors.

MySkillsLab™
Complete this Exercise
on myskillslab.com

Reading and Writing for Everyday Life

Assume you are a parent of a child in an elementary public school, and you serve on the Parent-Teachers Association (PTA). You are the chairperson of a committee looking into expanding the school's free lunch program. Read the following article. Write a letter to the principal of the school making your recommendation. Explain your reasons.

School Lunches and Lunches Brought from Home: A Comparative Analysis

BACKGROUND: Considerable effort has been put forth to improve the nutritional quality of school meals by the National School Lunch Program (NSLP). However, a large percentage of children do not obtain their meals from school and instead bring lunch from home. Little research has focused on the content of these lunches. The purpose of the current study was to examine differences between school lunch and lunch brought from home.

METHODS: Children in the 2nd grade from seven schools in a large suburban school district were observed on three separate days. A total of 2107 observations were made, with 38.5% of these being lunches brought from home. Chi-squared analyses evaluated differences in the presence of specific food items between school lunch and lunch brought from home.

RESULTS: Compared to children with a school lunch, children with a lunch brought from home were significantly less likely to have fruits (75.9% vs. 45.3%), vegetables (29.1% vs. 13.2%), and dairy (70.0% vs. 41.8%) ($p < 0.001$). Children with a lunch from home were more likely to have snacks high in sugar and/or fat (17.5% vs. 60.0%) and non 100% fruit juice/fruit drink (0.3% vs. 47.2%) ($p < 0.001$) than children with a school lunch.

CONCLUSIONS: The NSLP has been widely criticized; however, conducting a comparison in this manner demonstrates advantages to children obtaining school lunches. Although it was beyond the scope of this study to examine diet quality (e.g., actual intake and nutrient/caloric density), these results provide compelling evidence that lunches brought from home should be an area of emphasis for research and intervention.

—US National Library of Medicine, National Institutes of Health, August 26, 2014
http://www.ncbi.nlm.nih.gov/pubmed/22867076

Reading and Writing for College Life

Assume you are taking a college course in student success. You are to give a speech to your class about a way to improve learning. Read the following textbook selection. Compose a speech that explains the need for sleep, the types of sleep, and how to get enough sleep.

176 NAVIGATING YOUR FUTURE SUCCESS

■ QUALITY SLEEP

Sleep is needed for the body to repair and recharge. Poor sleep leads to less energy, lack of focus, illness, irritability, forgetfulness, and a decreased reaction time. It also means you are most likely wasting precious study time, not reading effectively, and making more mistakes. Naturally, your academic and personal life will suffer.

In ancient times, sleep was based on the natural cycle of light and darkness. The invention of light bulbs, TVs, and computers has changed this cycle. Most studies still show we need between 7 and 8 hours of quality sleep each night. Quality sleep means that we spend most of our time in the deeper stage of sleep, non-rapid eye movement (NREM) sleep, and a smaller portion in the lighter stage, or rapid eye movement (REM) sleep. NREM is the longer period of sleep, during which brain and body activity really slows down to regenerate. REM, which occurs when we dream, normally occurs in brief spurts.

Healthy sleep includes both stages of sleep, but usually 80 minutes of NREM is followed by 10 minutes of REM cycled throughout the night. If this cycle is interrupted, your sleep quality is affected. If you spend more time in the lighter stage of sleep (REM), your body doesn't recharge even if you get 10 hours of sleep. Quantity (7 to 8 hours) and quality (most time spent in deeper sleep stage) are required for healthy sleep. These tips help ensure a healthy sleep:

- Keeping a steady schedule can classically condition your body to connect sleep to a certain time. Get 7 to 8 hours of sleep, even on weekends.
- Reduce noise or, if necessary, reduce distracting noise by substituting with soothing noise.
- Avoid naps because they may disrupt your normal sleep cycle.
- Lights out: Even when you get to sleep, light can keep you in the lighter stages of sleep.
- Avoid all night study sessions.
- Wind down, not up, before bedtime. Listen to soothing music, meditate, or take a hot bath. Reduce consumption of alcohol and caffeine (coffee, tea, chocolate, and cola). Also, exercise regularly (but not within 3 hours of sleep).
- Make sure your sleeping area is comfortable.
- Don't lie in bed and worry about not sleeping. Get up and do something boring until you get tired.

—Colbert, *Navigating Your Future Success*. 2nd ed. Pearson, 2015, pp. 176–17.

Reading and Writing for Working Life

Assume you are an assistant manager of a baseball stadium. Your senior manager has asked you to research ways to set up a recycling program to manage the stadium's waste. Read the following pamphlet that offers advice about how to set up a recycling program. Then compose a memo to send to your manager in which you make recommendations. Explain your reasons.

HOW TO SET UP A RECYCLING PROGRAM

STEP 1: Select a Recycling Coordinator

Select a recycling coordinator to oversee the entire operation. This individual is responsible for designing the collection program, selecting a hauler or arranging in-house transportation of materials, facilitating education and outreach, and tracking progress. In addition, the recycling coordinator will address questions and concerns from venue managers, concessionaires, staff, and the public.

STEP 2: Determine the Waste Stream

Determine which materials are going to be recycled. Conduct a waste assessment to figure out what is currently being thrown away and identify how much of each material is tossed. This will provide baseline data for the amount of materials that can be recycled compared to the total amount of waste generated. Many venues will generate predominantly bottles, cans, and cardboard from concessionaires' packaging. Consider donating surplus food or composting food waste if feasible. Recyclables are marketed by weight. You'll need to estimate this for each material you plan to recycle. Prices for recyclables, like all commodities, fluctuate with supply and demand. Some of the materials that you should consider including are: aluminum, plastics, glass, food scraps, cardboard, and newspaper.

STEP 3: Practice Waste Prevention

Waste prevention means using less material to get a job done—and ending up with less waste to manage. In addition to environmental benefits, waste prevention saves money. Take a good look at your recycling collection data to see ways to reduce waste first. The most common forms of waste prevention are reducing, reusing, and donating.

STEP 4: Include Concessionaires, Staff, and Volunteers

You've researched the options and have developed your recycling program. Who at the venue knows about the program? Support from concessionaires, venue staff, and volunteers is essential when it comes to achieving a positive outcome.

STEP 5: Select a Contractor/Hauler

The first step in transporting recyclables from your program site to a recycler is to decide if you will contract out or haul recyclables using in-house staff. If your venue chooses to contract with a hauler, your current trash hauler may offer recycling pickup. Economically, this may be your best option. If your trash hauler does not provide recycling services, contact local recycling companies—they should be listed in your

CONTINUED

phone book. Some contractors only accept single stream or multi-stream recycling collection. You need to select a collection method before choosing a contractor.

- Single stream collection uses one bin to collect all of the various types of recyclables.
- Multi-stream collection separates the various recyclables into different bins.

STEP 6: Set Up the Collection Program Collection Bins and Liners

Making recycling easy and convenient will greatly boost levels of public and vendor participation. Collection bins should be placed where they are most convenient and close to where the recyclables are generated. Ideally, place collection bins next to each trash can. Make sure that it's just as easy for the public to recycle as it is to throw something away. Avoid confusion. The recycling bins should look different from trashcans and be easy to identify. Lids with round holes on recycling bins for bottles and cans will reduce contamination. The labels on the bins should be large and clear with both words and pictures indicating what is being collected. Make sure to clearly label the trashcans too. You also will need appropriate plastic liners (bags) for the bins. If a single stream collection system is being used, consider using clear bags so the contents can be easily identified once filled.

Storage and Pickup

Once the materials have been removed from the collection bins, they need to be stored on-site until picked up by a hauler or delivered to a transfer station or materials recovery facility.

- Will the materials be stored on-site in a shed or a dumpster?
- Will the hauler provide a compactor as part of its contract?

STEP 7: Facilitate Outreach and Education

Education is the best way to encourage the public and concessionaires to recycle. Use signs, displays, loudspeaker announcements, and/or text to teach them:

- WHY they should recycle.
- WHAT they should recycle.
- WHERE they can recycle.
- HOW they can recycle.

—"How to Set Up a Recycling Program" from U.S. Environmental Protection Agency website, 3 April, 2014.

Review Test

MySkillsLab™
Complete this Exercise on myskillslab.com

Score (number correct) _____ x 10 = _____%

Understanding the Essay

Read the following passage from a college sociology textbook. Answer the questions that follow.

Glossary

incompatible (sentence 1): mismatched, opposed
fragile (sentence 10): weak, unstable, breakable
interpersonal (sentence 19): between people

Conflict Defined

[1]Conflict is the interaction of interdependent people who perceive **incompatible** goals and interference from each other in achieving those goals. [2]This definition has the advantage of providing a much clearer focus than definitions that view conflict simply as disagreement, as competition, or as the presence of opposing interests.

[3]The most important feature of conflict is that it is based in interaction. [4]Conflicts are formed and sustained by the behaviors of the parties involved and their verbal and nonverbal reactions to one another. [5]Conflict interaction takes many forms, and each form presents special problems and requires special handling. [6]The most familiar type of conflict interaction is marked by shouting matches or open competition in which each party tries to defeat the other. [7]But conflicts may also be more subtle. [8]People may react to conflict by suppressing it. [9]A husband and wife may communicate in ways that allow them to avoid confrontation. [10]Either they are afraid the conflict may damage a **fragile** relationship, or they convince themselves that the issue "isn't worth fighting over." [11]This response is as much a part of the conflict process as fights and shouting matches.

[12]People in conflict perceive that they have incompatible goals or interests; they also believe that others are a barrier to achieving their goals. [13]The key word here is ***perceive***. [14]Regardless of whether goals are actually incompatible, if the parties believe them to be incompatible, then conditions are ripe for conflict. [15]Regardless of whether one employee really stands in the way of a co-worker's promotion, if the co-worker interprets the employee's behavior as interfering with his promotion, then a conflict is likely to occur. [16]Communication is important; it is the key to shaping and maintaining the perceptions that guide conflict behavior.

[17]Communication problems can be an important cause of conflict. [18]Conflict may result from misunderstandings that occur when people have different communication styles. [19]For example, Tannen argues that men and women have different approaches to **interpersonal** communication. [20]Men are mostly task-oriented; they are concerned with establishing their position relative to others in conversations. [21]In contrast, women use conversations to build relationships and establish connections with others. [22]As a result, men and women may interpret the same act in very different ways. [23]When a man makes a demand during a conflict, he might mean to signal that he is strong and has a definite position. [24]A woman hearing this demand is likely to focus more on its **implications** for their relationship. [25]Thus she may interpret it as a signal that it will be very difficult to deal with this man. [26]As a result, the woman may become more competitive toward her male partner than she would have had she seen his demand in the man's terms. [27]According to Tannen, stylistic differences of this sort create communication barriers that make misunderstanding—and the conflict that results from it—inevitable in male-female relationships. [28]Similar communication problems can occur across almost any social divide, such as those between people of different cultures, ages, educational backgrounds, and socioeconomic classes.

—Adapted from Folger, Poole, and Stutman, *Working Through Conflict*, 4th ed., pp. 5–6.

Vocabulary in Context

1. What does the word **implications** mean in sentence 24?

a. conflicts
b. meaning
c. accusations
d. levels

Inference

2. Based on the information in the passage, the reader may infer that

a. conflict only occurs between dependent, insecure people.
b. men are more prone to conflict than women.
c. lack of communication is the only reason conflict occurs.
d. people can learn to effectively manage conflict.

Tone

3. The tone of sentence 1 is

a. matter-of-fact.
b. condemning.
c. bitter.
d. understanding.

Purpose

5. The writer's purpose is to
   a. argue against conflict.
   b. entertain the reader with little known facts about conflict.
   c. inform the reader about the nature of conflict.

Fact and Opinion

6. Sentence 3 is
   a. a fact.
   b. an opinion.
   c. a mixture of fact and opinion.

Central or Main Idea

7. Which sentence states the central idea of the passage?
   a. sentence 1
   b. sentence 2
   c. sentence 3
   d. sentence 4

Central or Main Idea

8. Which sentence is the topic sentence of the fourth paragraph (sentences 17–28)?
   a. sentence 17
   b. sentence 18
   c. sentence 20
   d. sentence 27

Supporting Details

9. Sentence 7 is
   a. a major supporting detail.
   b. a minor supporting detail.

Supporting Details

10. Sentence 9 is
    a. a major supporting detail.
    b. a minor supporting detail.

Summary Response

Restate the authors' central idea in your own words. In your summary, follow the thought pattern used by the authors. Begin your summary response with the following: *The central idea of "Conflict Defined" by Folger, Poole, and Stutman is. . . .*

Reader Response

Assume you are a supervisor of a sales staff at a local retail store, and two employees under your supervision are in conflict with each other. Assume you have met with them both privately and individually to understand and resolve the conflict. Write a memo to be sent to both employees and placed in their personnel files. Consider the following:

Describe the conflict.
Suggest steps that you expect both people to take to resolve the issue.

Academic Learning Log: Module Review

MySkillsLab™
Complete this Exercise
on myskillslab.com

Summary of Key Concepts of Understanding the Essay

Assess your comprehension of the essay.

LO 1

1. An ________________ expresses a writer's point about a topic in a series of closely connected paragraphs. Four levels of information in an essay are ________________, ________________, ________________, and ________________.
2. The introduction of an essay often includes a ________________, a sentence that states the writer's central point.
3. A ________________ is a series of closely related sentences that develop and support one point or subtopic within a piece of writing. Four levels of information in a paragraph are ________________, ________________, ________________, and ________________.
4. The main idea of a paragraph is often stated in a ________________.
5. ________________ are the specific ideas that develop, explain, or support a central or main idea. A ________________ directly explains, develops, or illustrates a main idea in a paragraph or the central point in an essay. A ________________ directly explains, develops, or illustrates a major detail.
6. ________________ is the pattern of organization that controls the flow of ideas within a paragraph or essay: examples include narration, description, and classification.
7. Effective expression is the writer's use of ________________.

LO 1 LO 4

8. Four ways to connect paragraphs are: **A.** Echo or repeat words or phrases from the ________________. **B.** Refer to the main idea of the previous paragraph in the ________________ of the next paragraph. **C.** Use ________________ words and phrases. **D.** Tie the ________________ idea in one paragraph to the ________________ of the next paragraph.

LO1 LO6

9. Ten types of conclusions and introductions are a ______________, a ______________, a ______________, a call to ______________, a ______________, a ______________ about consequences, a ______________ image, a surprising ______________ or statement, a ______________ or opposing view, context information or a ______________.

Test Your Comprehension of the Essay

Respond in your own words to the following questions and prompts.

LO1 LO2 LO3 LO4 LO5 LO6

In your own words, explain your reading/writing strategy for comprehending, responding to, and composing an essay.

1. **How will I use what I have learned?** In your notebook, discuss how you will apply to your own reading/writing strategy what you have learned about the essay. When will you apply this knowledge to your reading/writing strategy?
2. **What do I still need to study about the essay?** In your notebook, discuss your ongoing study needs. Describe what, when, and how you will continue studying and using the essay.

MySkillsLab™

Complete the Post-test for Module 6 in MySkillsLab.

7

A Reading/Writing Strategy for Research

LEARNING OUTCOMES

After studying this module you should be able to:

- LO 1 Answer the Question "What's the Point of Developing a Reading/Writing Strategy for Research?"
- LO 2 Develop Your Reading/Writing Strategy for Research
- LO 3 Choose a Topic to Research
- LO 4 Find and Evaluate Sources of Research Information
- LO 5 Avoid Plagiarism Throughout the Research Process
- LO 6 Master the Basics of Documentation Styles: MLA and APA

Research is an act of investigation. Research is a thoughtful, focused study that entails a search for facts, the interpretation of these facts, the revision of ideas in the light of new facts, and the practical application of information. Through research, we learn a new concept, clarify an idea, support a viewpoint, or make a sound decision. Research gives power to your decisions, studies, and viewpoints.

Research is the process of gathering, reading, evaluating, synthesizing, writing, documenting, and publishing information for a specific purpose.

Most research occurs in response to a specific situation that prompts the need to learn more about a topic. For example, in everyday life, we often research a product before we buy it. In our academic life, we use research to learn independently about a particular topic. In our work life, employers research the background of job seekers to determine which candidate is best suited to the job. Retailers conduct market research to determine which products to sell to whom and where.

Knowing the best research strategies and resources will help you find and use the information you need in your everyday life, academic life, and work life.

WHAT'S THE POINT of Developing a Reading/Writing Strategy for Research?

LO1

The following photographs illustrate several research situations in everyday life, academic life, and work life. Study each photograph and its caption. In the spaces provided, state the need for research in each situation. Then state the overall point of research.

Photographic Organizer: What Is the Point of Developing a Reading/Writing Strategy for Research?

EVERYDAY LIFE

ACADEMIC LIFE

WORK LIFE

What's the point of developing a reading/writing strategy for research?

L2 Develop Your Reading/Writing Strategy for Research

Effective research is based on all that you have learned about the reading/writing strategy. You have learned how to survey information to question and annotate text. You have learned how to distinguish between fact and opinion. You have learned to comprehend the writer's point by reciting and reviewing main ideas and supporting details. You have learned to brainstorm and organize details in response to what you have read. You have thought

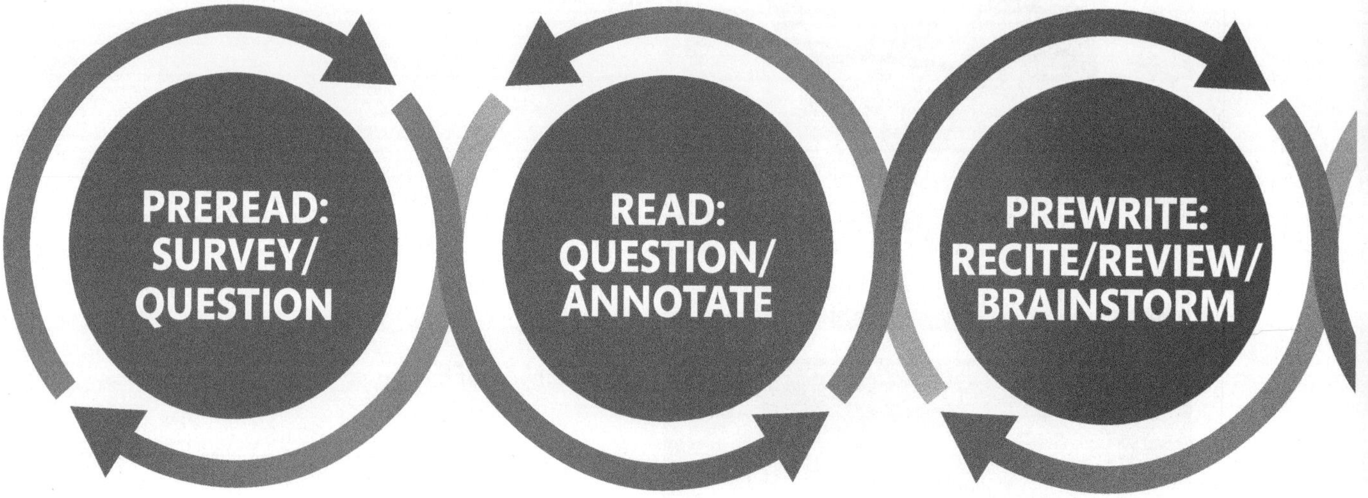

PREREAD: SURVEY/ QUESTION

READ: QUESTION/ ANNOTATE

PREWRITE: RECITE/REVIEW/ BRAINSTORM

Preread:

- Choose a topic to research.
- Create questions based on titles, headings, bold/italic terms, and visuals.
- What is my prior knowledge?
- What is my purpose for researching?
- Who is the intended audience for my research?
- Is this information relevant to my research?
- What kind of information is needed? Where can I find information? Is the information reliable?
- Find and evaluate sources.

Read:

- Ask/record questions.
- Annotate text.
- Underline main ideas.
- Circle new/key words.
- Highlight key details.
- Restate ideas out loud.
- Take notes. Record attribution of sources.

Prewrite:

- Organize notes taken.
- List, cluster, outline topics based on survey; leave room to fill in details during reading.
- Take notes. Restate ideas.
- Record quotes.
- Narrow writing topic based on reading/notes.
- Generate details based on narrowed topic, audience, and purpose for research.
- Freewrite a first response.
- Outline or map out details.

carefully about the use of effective expression to make your point clear to your own readers. All of these steps are vital to the research process.

Developing your own reading/writing strategy for research enables you to find and use the information you need in your everyday life, college life, and work life. A reading/writing strategy integrates the steps of reading and writing in order for a researcher to investigate a topic, comprehend information, and compose a written report of the findings of the research. Just as it is with any reading/writing situation, the strategy for research is recursive; the steps are repeated as needed.

Draft:

- Refer to notes.
- Write a thesis statement.
- Write the body, introduction, and conclusion of your research.
- Include quotes, paraphrases of expert opinions.
- Include facts from reliable sources.
- Avoid plagiarism.

Review/Revise:

- Refine ideas.
- Review draft for clear use of wording, details, and organization.
- Annotate draft with needed revisions.
- Rewrite draft based on review and annotations.
- Apply proper documentation style: MLA or APA.
- Avoid plagiarism.

Proofread:

- Polish ideas.
- Reread draft to identify/correct errors in grammar, spelling, usage, style of documentation.

Practice 1

Develop Your Reading/Writing Strategy For Research

In your reading/writing journal, reflect on your research process. Describe your prior experiences with research. Then, predict how your research process may change as you develop your reading/writing strategy for research.

L3 Choose a Topic to Research

Research is an orderly process best accomplished in a logical order of steps. The box "Discover a Research Topic" describes five steps to take to discover and narrow down a research topic. Master researchers may repeat this strategy several times as they gather more information until they discover a workable topic. The length of the final research report plays a significant role in choosing and narrowing a topic. The shorter the report is, the narrower the focus will be; in addition, fewer subtopics will be developed. The longer the report is, the greater is your ability to develop more subtopics.

Step by Step: Discover a Research Topic

1. Describe the research situation:
   - ❑ What is the general topic or subject area of the research?
   - ❑ What is the purpose of the research?
   - ❑ What is the length of the final research report?
   - ❑ Who is the audience of the research?
2. Identify possible sources for topics and subjects:
   - ❑ What are key problems, concepts, or issues suggested by a professor, lecture notes, or a textbook?
   - ❑ What are some relevant current events or issues covered in newspapers, magazines, or online news sources?
3. Explore background information about a key problem, issue, or concept. Skim relevant information in sources (such as general and subject encyclopedias, research guides, or yearbook reviews) to answer the following questions:
   - ❑ What are the keywords and terms used to discuss this topic?
   - ❑ How has the issue developed or changed over time?
   - ❑ What is debatable or controversial about the topic?
   - ❑ Who are the accepted or well-known experts about the topic?
   - ❑ What are the publications that cover this topic?
4. Focus your topic. A topic that is too narrow makes it difficult to find adequate information to conduct reasonable research. A topic that is too broad becomes overwhelming and difficult to manage. Narrow your topic by applying one or more of the following focuses:
   - ❑ Content focus: biological, economic, ethical, legal, psychological, political, social, etc.
   - ❑ The timeframe for the research: historical? recent past? current? and so on.
   - ❑ Traits of the population being researched: age, culture, education, gender, nationality, occupation, social/economic class, etc.
   - ❑ Place or region being researched: neighborhood, city, county, state, nation, international region, etc.

5. State your topic as a research question. Use signal words for patterns of organization along with the focus of your topic to form a question that you can answer through research. The questions "Why?" and "How?" form the best basis of research questions, as in the following examples (subject areas listed in parentheses):
   - ❑ How does corporal punishment affect children's emotional development? (psychology, sociology, health)
   - ❑ How does plastic trash impact the environment? (biology, ecology, health, physical sciences)
   - ❑ How do violent video games affect regular players? (psychology, sociology, health)
   - ❑ How should the NFL respond to the problem of concussions suffered by players? (economics, physical fitness, health, team sports medicine)
   - ❑ Why do so many NFL players suffer from concussions? (physical fitness, health, team sports medicine)
   - ❑ Why should the national minimum wage be raised? (economics, political science, sociology)
   - ❑ Why does the cost of gas go up during certain times of the year? (economics, business)

Practice 2

Choose a Research Topic

Begin a research journal to record the steps of your research. Gather the following supplies: a 3-prong folder with pockets, looseleaf paper for handwritten notes, a 3-hole punch for printed material, and a stack of 3" x 5" index cards. In this journal, complete the five steps to discover a research topic. Use one of the following general topics or one of your own choosing. After completing all the steps, share your work and your reasoning in a think-aloud discussion with a peer or a small group of classmates.

General Topics:

Bullying	Obesity	Legal Drinking Age
Drones	Sleep	Significant Historical Event or Person

L4 Find and Evaluate Sources of Research Information

One of the most basic and early steps in the research process is finding useful and trustworthy information. A good way to begin your research is to ask the following three questions:

- What kind of information do I need?
- Where can I find the information I need?
- How do I know the information I find is reliable or trustworthy?

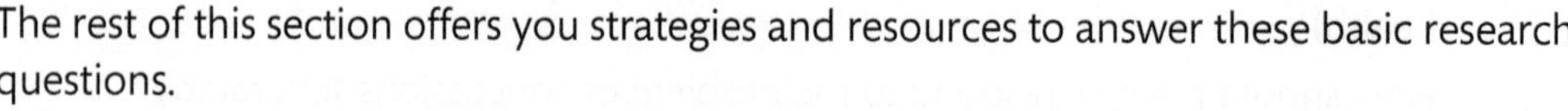

The rest of this section offers you strategies and resources to answer these basic research questions.

What Kind of Information Do I Need?

Basically, two types of information guide our thinking and writing: facts and opinions. The skills you developed in Module 5 to distinguish between fact and opinion are essential to you as a researcher. Remember:

- A fact is something that can be shown to be true, to exist, or to have happened based on evidence. The following statistic is an example of a fact: "About one-third of U.S. adults (33.8%) are obese." The source of this fact is the government agency the Centers for Disease Control and Prevention (CDC).
- An opinion is a personal view somebody takes about an issue. The following statement is an example of an expert opinion given by Dr. Oz, a heart surgeon and author—a medical expert. "You can control your health destiny." This quote is his expert opinion as stated on page 2 of his best-selling book about health, *You: The Owner's Manual.*

An undeniable fact or an expert opinion is a convincing research detail. Master researchers identify sources for facts and opinions.

Where Can I Find the Information I Need?

Identifying the type of information you need helps you know where to look for it. The two main storehouses of information are the library and the Internet. Both offer a variety of resources for help in locating information as well as sources of information.

Library Resources and Sources

- Seek out your library's **reference librarian**. These professionals are trained to teach you how to use the library and its resources. They can answer queries about specific information and also can recommend good sources for specific topics. Reference librarians have to stay up to date with technology and customer needs; thus they are able to assist your use of all types of research resources.

A **reference librarian** is trained in library work and is responsible for a collection of specialized or technical information or materials.

- Search the **library's online catalogue**. Easily reached from the Internet, the catalogue is used mainly to find books and other material physically located at a library. You can search for a source by author, title, subject, or keywords. As you find a source you think you may use, write down the title, author, and call number (or other reference information) so you can find the item on its library shelf.

The **library's online catalogue** is an index of materials held by the library.

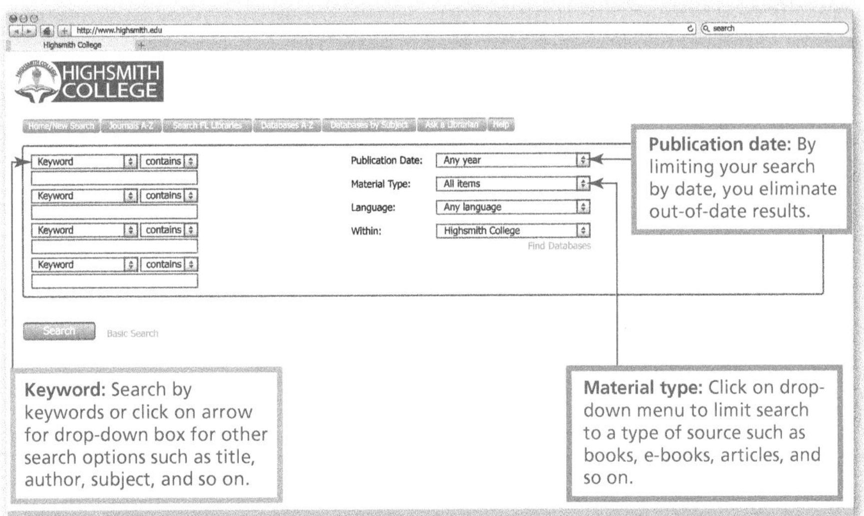

- Search the **library's electronic database collection**. This information is organized by searchable fields, such as author, title, subject, or keywords. A library's electronic database collection gives you access to thousands of sources such as magazine, journal, and newspaper articles, as well as essays and e-books.

The **library's electronic database collection** is a computer-based collection of records or listings of a wide variety of information.

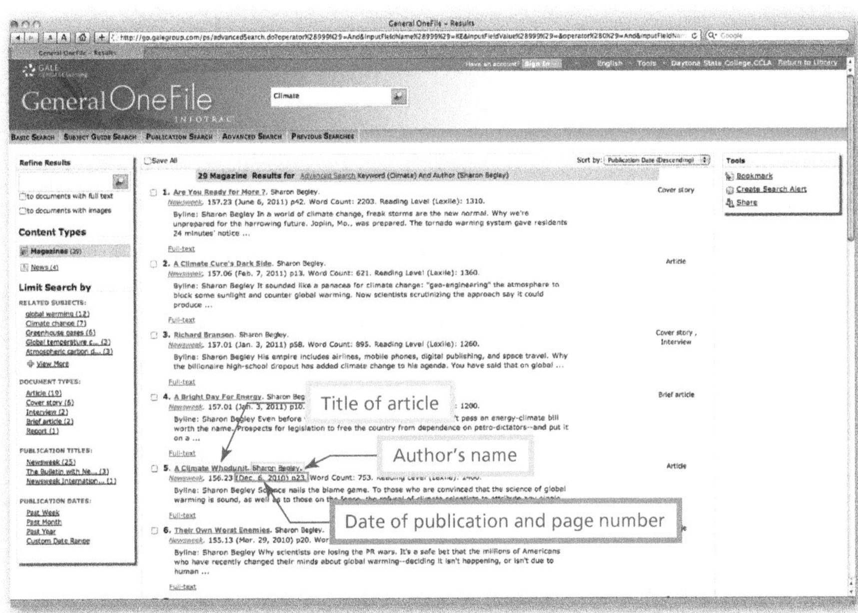

—Screenshot from General OneFile. © Gale, a part of Cengage Learning, Inc. Reproduced by permission.

Practice 3

Find Sources: Keep a Research Journal

Practice using your college's library as a resource to find information about the topic you chose in Practice 2. On each index card, record the following information for each type of source. Store completed cards in your research journal. Ask a reference librarian for assistance as needed. After completing your index cards, share your work and your reasoning in a think-aloud discussion with a peer or small group of classmates.

1. Find a book using your college's online catalogue. Record the following information about the book:

   Title ______________________________

   Author(s) or Editor(s) ______________________________

   City of publication ______________________________

   Publisher ______________ Year published ______________

   Call # ______________ Available ______________ or checked out ______________

   Print ______________ or e-book ______________

2. Find a magazine or journal article using your college library's electronic database collection. Record the following information about the article:

   Title of article ______________________________

   Author(s) if given ______________________________

   Magazine/journal title (Source) ______________________________

   Date published ______________ Page # ______________

   Name of database ______________________________

3. Find a newspaper article using your college library's electronic database collection. Record the following information about the article:

   Title of article ______________________________

   Author(s) if given ______________________________

   Newspaper title (Source) ______________________________

   Date published ______________ Page # ______________

   Name of database ______________________________

Internet Resources and Sources

A **search engine** looks for and retrieves information from millions of sites on the Internet. The search engine records each word within a document on the Internet. When you conduct a search, it matches your keywords to the records it has in its databases and retrieves a list of links that match your request. Examples of search engines are Yahoo!, Google, Ask.com, and Bing.

A **search engine** is a computer software program that uses keywords to search for and locate text, data, or any specific information on the Internet.

- Search by **keywords**. A keyword is a term used to indicate a word (or series of words) a researcher types into a search engine to locate specific information on the Internet. If a keyword is too broad, then too many results are returned. If a keyword is too narrow, then too few results are returned.

A **keyword** is a word used as a query or point of reference for seeking more information about a topic.

- Use quotation marks or Boolean (NOT, OR) operators to group words together. Enclosing words in quotation marks tells the search engine to search for the complete phrase, not the individual words. Searches that use the Boolean operator "NOT" tell the search engine to search for sites that mention the first item, but not the second. Finally, searches that use the Boolean operator "OR" tell the search engine to search for one term or the other. For example, a search for *"green energy" NOT nuclear* will find sites on green energy that do not mention nuclear power. Searches for *"green energy" OR nuclear* will find sources that discuss either green energy or nuclear power. Spell your keywords carefully, and consider alternate spellings.
- Investigate your search engine's Advanced Search options. Most sites allow you to limit results by date, type of site, or many other options.
- Search by website domains. To search by domains, you need to understand a website's **URL**.

  Basically, a URL has three main parts:

A **URL** is a site's universal resource locator, also referred to as the website's address.

PROTOCOL SERVER OR HOST NAME RESOURCE INFORMATION

http://www.nlm.nih.gov/**medlineplus/bullying.html**

Notice the three letters at the end of the host name; these letters identify the type of organization that provides the information. To search a topic by a domain, think about which domain is most likely to host the type of information you need. Then include the domain in your query by leaving a space after the last word and typing a period and the three letters of the domain.

Types of Domains That Host Websites with Examples		
.com	companies and commercial sites	msnbc.com
.edu	educational institutions	http://owl.english.purdue.edu
.gov	government organizations	http://www.usa.gov
.org	nonprofit organizations	http://redcross.org

- Use an Internet bookmark. An **Internet bookmark** acts as a marker for a website. Once you find a website as a source of information, you can save it for easy and quick access. Look in the toolbar of your web browser for the Favorites or Bookmark option.

An **Internet bookmark** is a link or URL stored in a Web browser for future access.

- Document sources you may use as soon as you locate them:
  - Write in a log or cut and paste into a Word file the source's publication information.
  - Send to your e-mail account the record of the link to the source.
  - Download the document, or create a copy of the document by cutting and pasting it into a Word file.
  - Store hard copies of the article or passage in your research journal.

Practice 4

Find Sources: Keep a Research Journal

Find two Internet sources for the topic you chose in Practice 2. In your research journal, record the information needed to track and document each Internet source. Ask a reference librarian for assistance as needed. After completing this step, share your work and your reasoning in a think-aloud discussion with a peer or small group of classmates.

1. Website name ______________________________

Website address (URL) ______________________________

Title of Article ______________________________

Article's author(s) if given ______________________________

Website sponsor ______________________________

Date of last update ______________ Date of your access ______________

2. Website name ______________________________

Website address (URL) ______________________________

Title of Article ______________________________

Article's author(s) if given ______________________________

Website sponsor ______________________________

Date of last update ______________ Date of your access ______________

How Can I Know the Information I Find Is Reliable or Trustworthy?

Before publishing material in books, newspapers, magazines, and scholarly journals, editors and peers carefully evaluate sources and review information to ensure they are reliable and accurate. But even then, print materials may reveal a bias or share incomplete or misleading information. The Internet, on the other hand, allows anyone to publish information without any screening of the information for reliability or accuracy. Thus, more than ever before, we must carefully evaluate information to determine how reliable and accurate it is. The following chart offers a guide for evaluating sources from the library and the Internet. If a source qualifies as usable based on this guide, then use that source as **PAART** of your research.

PAART: A Guide to Evaluating Sources		
P	**P**urpose Why did the author write?	Identify the purpose of the information: to inform, to argue, to entertain. Identify the type of information: fact, opinion, expert opinion. Identify any specific bias: cultural, personal, political, religious viewpoints.
A	**A**uthority Who is the author or host?	Identify the author, publisher, source, or sponsor. Identify contact information: e-mail or street address. Identify the qualifications of the author: education, experience. For a website: Identify the type of domain that hosts the site.
A	**A**ccuracy How correct is the information?	Note errors: grammar, spelling, typographical (typos). Verify the information in another source. Identify the source of the information. Look for reviewers or editors of the publication.
R	**R**elevance How does the information relate to the topic of the research?	Identify the intended audience for the publication. Evaluate how the information relates to your topic of research. Review a variety of sources before making a final choice to use a particular source.
T	**T**imeliness When was the information written?	Evaluate the need for current or historical information. Note the date of the publication. Note if the information has been updated or revised. For a website: Test the hyperlinks to make sure they still work.

The PAART guide can be used to quickly evaluate a source for research in everyday, college, and work life. We need to test information before we accept it as useful to our thinking or decision-making process.

Practice 5

Evaluate Sources: Keep a Research Journal

Use the following guide to evaluate each of the sources you located in Practices 3 and 4. For each source, answer every question with a score of 5 to 1. A score of 5 means excellent, and a score of 1 means unacceptable. Then add up the total score. After evaluating your sources, share your work and your reasoning in a think-aloud discussion with a peer or small group of classmates. What makes a source excellent?

PAART: A Guide to Evaluating Sources						
Title of Source:						
Criteria	**Questions to Evaluate Source**	**Rating of Source**				
Purpose What?	Is the purpose of the publication made clear?	5	4	3	2	1
	Is the type of information appropriate for the research topic?	5	4	3	2	1
	Does a specific bias influence the information?	5	4	3	2	1
Authority Who?	Is the author, publisher, source, or sponsor of the publication stated?	5	4	3	2	1
	Is contact information available?	5	4	3	2	1
	Is the author qualified to address the topic?	5	4	3	2	1
	For a website: Is the domain that hosts the site appropriate for the topic?	5	4	3	2	1
Accuracy How?	Are there errors: grammar, spelling, typographical (typos)?	5	4	3	2	1
	Can the information be verified in another source?	5	4	3	2	1
	Is the source of information reliable?	5	4	3	2	1
	Has the information been reviewed by peers or editors in the field?	5	4	3	2	1
Relevance How?	Is the intended audience for the publication made clear?	5	4	3	2	1
	Does the information relate to the topic of research?	5	4	3	2	1
	Is the information at the appropriate level?	5	4	3	2	1
	Have a variety of sources been reviewed before making a final choice to use a particular source?	5	4	3	2	1
Timeliness When?	Does the topic of research call for current or historical information?	5	4	3	2	1
	Is the date of publication given?	5	4	3	2	1
	Is the date of publication appropriate for the need of current historical information?	5	4	3	2	1
	Has the information been updated or revised?	5	4	3	2	1
	For a website: Do the hyperlinks still work?	5	4	3	2	1
	Total score					

Score Range	**Excellent** 100–81	80–61	60–41	40–21	**Unacceptable** 20–0

Avoid Plagiarism Throughout the Research Process

L5

Plagiarism is a form of stealing that leads to serious consequences in both the classroom and the workplace. The penalties for plagiarism in the classroom range from failing the assignment to expulsion. Likewise, plagiarism in the workplace may result in demotion, lack of opportunity for promotion, or job loss. Plagiarism is not only unethical, but also illegal. Original work is protected by copyright law. Thus, plagiarism can result in legal action. Many times, plagiarism is not a deliberate act. Instead, it may occur from a lack of knowledge about how to use the work of others or how to give them proper credit for their work. You can avoid plagiarism by properly paraphrasing, **quoting**, and summarizing and citing the words and ideas of other people.

Plagiarism is the act of presenting the words or ideas of another author as one's own or using information without giving credit to its original source.

Quoting is reciting the exact words of the author or speaker.

The following chart outlines five steps for paraphrasing.

The Five R's of Paraphrasing: Read, Restate, Revise, Revisit, Repeat	
Read	Read the text to understand the author's meaning. Highlight key ideas. Look up words you don't know.
Restate	Put the original text out of sight. Recall in writing the author's ideas using your own words.
Revise	Wait for a space of time (from a few minutes to a few days) to create an opportunity to see your paraphrase with fresh eyes. Then revise your paraphrase for clear wording and smooth flow of ideas.
Revisit	After drafting your paraphrase, revisit the original text. Compare your paraphrase to the author's wording. Change any wording that is too close to the author's words. Double check to make sure your paraphrase correctly restates the author's message.
Repeat	Complete the preceding steps as many times as needed to draft a sound paraphrase.

With a peer or small group of classmates, study the following example of a paraphrase. Read the original text and the paraphrase. Then discuss how the paraphrase differs from the original text. Finally, discuss how the paraphrase is similar to the original text.

Original Text:

"Health and safety procedures for body artists may be regulated by city, county, or state agencies. Reputable shops and tattoo parlors govern themselves and follow strict safety procedures to protect their clients—and their body artists."

Source of Text:

"Body Art: Tattoos and Piercings." Centers for Disease Control and Prevention (CDC), 29 Aug. 2011. Web.

Paraphrase:

Trustworthy tattooists and body piercers are rigorous in hygiene. They are also faithful to the laws set in place by different levels of government. Responsible "body artists" take steps to ensure the physical well-being of their customer and themselves ("Body Art: Tattoos and Piercings").

Notice that the paraphrase is about the same length as the original text. Also notice that in the paraphrase, any exact words taken from the original text are placed in quotation marks. Finally, the source of the paraphrase is cited in the text to avoid plagiarism. Since the source does not have an author, the title is used in the citation. Also, since this information is from the Internet, no page number is given. However, the page numbers where information appears in a print source should be included in the citation. The complete publication information will also be provided in the Works Cited page.

Quoting, using the exact words of a text, is another way to avoid plagiarism. Quoting a text entails repeating the exact words of the author. When you use the exact words of another person, you enclose that exact wording within a pair of quotation marks. You should use quotes rarely and purposefully in your writing. A well-placed quote adds interest, emphasis, and authority to an important point. Too many quotes make it look like you didn't take time to understand the text well enough to offer a fresh view of the topic.

With a peer or a small group of classmates, review your understanding of quoting information. Study the following use of a quote in a piece of writing. Annotate the following: Underline the information that gives the context of the quote. Double underline the attribution of the quote. Circle the publication information. Underline the quote with a squiggly line.

Example of Quoting:

On a cold, snowy day, January 21, 1961, John F. Kennedy at the age of 43 took the oath of office as the youngest man elected to be President of the United States of America. Kennedy exclaimed, "And so, my fellow Americans, ask not what your country can do for you; ask what you can do for your country" (American Rhetoric: Top 100 Speeches). Kennedy effectively beckoned an entire generation into public service with this moving call to action.

Notice several aspects of this example of proper quoting that apply as general rules for quoting text. First, a comma follows the attribution verb *exclaimed* to introduce the quote. Second, a pair of quotation marks enclose the exact words of President Kennedy. Third, the source or publication information is placed inside a pair of parentheses and immediately follows the quote. Finally, the end sentence punctuation is placed outside the closing parenthesis.

Summarizing is a third way to avoid plagiarism. You have already been using the summary skills you learned in Module 1 as you have responded to passages you have read in previous modules. As you learned, summarizing a text entails reducing a section of text to its main points and key details. Since you paraphrase ideas in a summary, any exact words quoted from the original text are placed in quotation marks. Just as with a paraphrase, the source of the summary is cited in the text and Works Cited or References page to avoid plagiarism.

To avoid plagiarism, master researchers record information in the form of notes, often on index cards. Each note is labeled as a paraphrase, a quote, or a summary, and each note is clearly linked to its source.

Practice 6

Avoid Plagiarism: Keep a Research Journal

Begin taking notes from the sources you located in Practices 3 and 4. Paraphrase, quote, and summarize three ideas from your sources. Link each note to its source. After writing your notes, share your work and your reasoning in a think-aloud discussion with a peer or small group of classmates.

1. **Paraphrase**: ______________________________

   ____

   ____

   ____

   Source: ______________________________

2. **Quote**: ______________________________

   ____

   ____

   ____

   Source: ______________________________

3. **Summary**: ______________________________

   ____

   ____

   ____

   Source: ______________________________

LO6 Master the Basics of Documentation Styles: MLA and APA

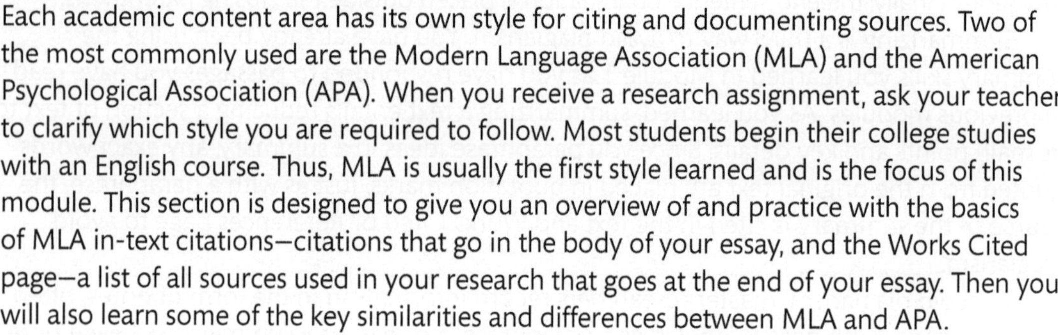

PROOFREAD

Each academic content area has its own style for citing and documenting sources. Two of the most commonly used are the Modern Language Association (MLA) and the American Psychological Association (APA). When you receive a research assignment, ask your teacher to clarify which style you are required to follow. Most students begin their college studies with an English course. Thus, MLA is usually the first style learned and is the focus of this module. This section is designed to give you an overview of and practice with the basics of MLA in-text citations—citations that go in the body of your essay, and the Works Cited page—a list of all sources used in your research that goes at the end of your essay. Then you will also learn some of the key similarities and differences between MLA and APA.

The Basics of MLA

MLA is used primarily in the humanities. Courses of study in the humanities include ancient and modern languages, literature, philosophy, religion, music, communication, and cultural studies.

MLA IN-TEXT CITATIONS

Each paraphrase, summary, or quote of an original source that you include in your writing must be noted in the body of your essay where it appears. This notation is called an "in-text citation" or "parenthetical notation." The following annotated examples show the basic forms of in-text citations for non-Web and Web sources. Note the use of commas, italics, quotation marks, parentheses, and periods.

Non-Web Source Stated in Sentence:

Source Stated in Sentence to Introduce

In their book *Anybody's Business*, Barbara Van Syckle and Brian Tietje claim, "Democratic leaders empower others" (136).

Quote — Page Number in Parentheses before Period

Non-Web Source Stated at End of Sentence:

Quote — Author(s) Name(s) and Page Number in Parentheses before Period

"Democratic leaders empower others" (Van Syckle and Tietje 136).

Web Source Stated in Sentence:

Source Stated in Sentence to Introduce — Paraphrase

The CDC identifies "heavy drinking" as two or more daily servings of alcohol for men and one or more daily servings for women.

No Parenthetical Notation Due to No Need for Page Numbers of Web Sources

Web Source Stated at End of Sentence:

Paraphrase

"Heavy drinking" is defined as two or more daily servings of alcohol for men and one or more daily servings for women (CDC).

Source in Parentheses before Period
(No Page numbers for Web Sources)

MLA WORKS CITED PAGE

A Works Cited page is a complete listing of all the sources you used in your writing, including in paraphrases, summaries, and quotes. The following section offers you an overview of the general guidelines for formatting a Works Cited page and a few basic models of common types of entries.

Tips for Formatting a Works Cited Page: MLA Style	
General Format	Start the Works Cited page as a separate page at the end of your research paper.
	Continue using the format of the entire paper: one-inch margins, last name heading, and page numbering.
	Center the words Works Cited at the top of the page. Do not italicize the words Works Cited or place them in quotation marks. Double space the entire page. Do not skip spaces between entries.
	Create a hanging indent by indenting by five spaces the second and subsequent lines of each citation.
	Identify the medium of publication for each entry such as Print, Web, Film, CD-Rom, DVD, or Personal Interview.
	URLs are no longer required by MLA, but if requested by a teacher or employer, place URLs in <angle brackets> at the end of the entry before the period. For long URLs, break lines before the slashes.
Order of Listing for Entries	List entries alphabetically by the authors' last names. Authors' names are given in the following order: last name first, then first name, followed by middle name or initials. If there are multiple authors, list only the first author's name in this order; list the later authors in standard (first, middle, last) order.
	Do not include titles such as Dr., Sir, Mr., or Ph.D.
	Do include identifiers such as Jr. or II. **Example:** King, Martin Luther, Jr.
	When no author is given, begin the entry with and alphabetize by the title of article, book, or website.
Grammar Rules	Use italics for titles of longer works such as books and magazines, and quotation marks for short works such as poems and articles.
	Capitalize each word in the titles of articles, books, and magazines except for articles (*a, an, the*), prepositions (*of, for, in*) or conjunctions (*and, but*) unless one appears as the first word in the title. Example: *Death of a Salesman.*

Compare these tips to the format of the Works Cited page in the student research essay on page 286. Now that you have an idea about the general format of a Works Cited page, the following sections offer annotated examples to model common types of entries. These models show how to format non-Web and Web sources as entries in a Works Cited page.

Basic MLA Format for Works Cited entries call for four broad categories of information that are presented in the citation in the following order.

Name of author(s): The name of whoever wrote the information: Last name, First name. For an anthology, name of editor(s) are also given.

Title of Source: The name of the book, article, or website you are citing. Use quotes for smaller works such as poems and articles. Use italics for larger works such as books and magazines. Include both when you are citing a small part of something larger like an article in a newspaper.

Publication Information: Any information about where and when the source was created. Information may include the city of publication, the publishing company, the year published, issue number, volume number, edition, and page numbers.

Medium: The format of the source such as Print, Web, Video, DVD, CD-Rom, etc.

For each of the following models for non-Web and Web sources alike, the type of entry is given, along with the specific pattern of information required for the type of entry, and is followed by an annotated illustration. Note the use of indenting, commas, italics, quotation marks, parentheses, and periods.

Book:

Author. *Title of Book*. City of publication: Publisher, Year. Medium.

Author. — **Title of Book.** — **City of publication: Publisher,**

Angelou, Maya. *I Know Why the Caged Bird Sings*. New York: Random House, 1970. Print.

Year. — **Medium.**

Book by two or three authors: Format is the same as a book with one author except for treatment of the second author's name. List authors in the order that they appear on the title page of publication. Use natural order for the name of the second author. Note the hanging indent of the second line of the entry.

Powers, Scott K., Stephen L. Dodd, and Erica M. Jackson. *Total Fitness & Wellness*, 6th ed. Glenview, IL: Pearson, 2014. Print.

Book by four or more authors: Format is the same as for other books except only the name of the first author listed on title page is used followed by "et al." which means "and others."

Carlson, Neil R., et al. *Psychology: The Science of Behavior*. Boston: Allyn & Bacon, 2010. Print.

Article from a reference book:

Author(s). "Title of Article." *Title of Reference Book*. Year. Medium.

If no author is listed, start with the title of the article.

"Terrorism." *The World Book Encyclopedia*. 2009 ed. Print.

Selection from an Anthology:

Author(s). "Title of Selection." *Title of Anthology*. Ed. Editor(s) name(s). City of Publication: Publisher, Year. Page numbers. Medium.

Sheehan, George. "Running." *Runners on Running*. Ed. Richard Elliot. Champaign: Human Kinetics, 2011. 2-8. Print.

Article from a Magazine:

Author(s). "Title of Article." *Title of Magazine* Day Month Year: Page numbers. Medium.

Author. "Title of Article." *Title of Magazine* Month Year:

Boerner, Heather. "Better Health." *Better Homes and Gardens* Sept. 2011: 224-30. Print.

page numbers. Medium.

Article from a Newspaper:

Author(s). "Title of Article." *Title of Newspaper* Day Month Year: Section Page numbers. Medium.

Author. "Title of Article."

Harper, Marc. "Low Cost Food Helps Families in Hard Times." *The Daytona Beach News-Journal* 20 Aug. 2011: C1. Print.

Title of Newspaper Day Month Year: Section Page number. Medium.

DVD:

Title. Dir. Director's Name. Company, Release year. DVD.

Title. Director.

The Hunger Games: Mockingjay—Part 1. Dir. Francis Lawrence. Lionsgate, 2015. DVD.

Company, Year. Medium.

Sound Recording:

Name of Performer(s). "Title of Song." *Title of Album.* Name of Recording Company, Year of release. File Type.

Performer. "Title of Song." *Title of Album.* Name of Recording Company,

Maroon 5. "Maps." *V*. Interscope, 2014. MP3.

Year. Medium.

Television or Radio Program:

Authors. "Title of Episode." *Title of Program.* Network or Station. Date of broadcast. Medium.

Authors. "Title of Episode." *Title of Program.*

Brewster, Joe, and Michele Stephenson. "American Promise." *POV*. PBS. 3 Feb. 2013. Television.

Network. Date of broadcast. Medium.

Personal Interview:

Interviewee. Personal Interview. Day Month Year.

Interviewee. Day Month Year

White, Frank. Personal Interview. 8 Nov. 2015.

Article or Page within a Website:

Author(s). "Article/Page Title." *Site Name*. Publisher or Sponsor of Site, Date of last update or copyright. Medium. Date of Access.

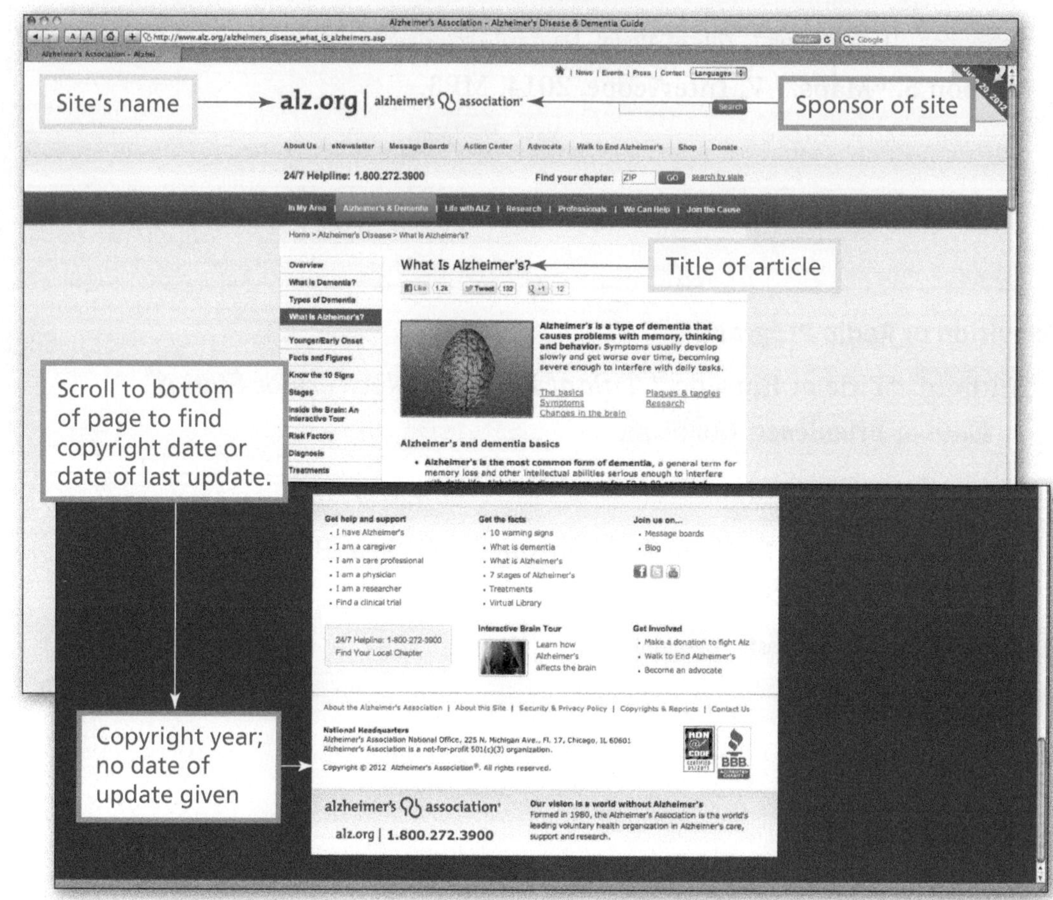

"Title." *Site Name.* Sponsor of Site.

"What is Alzheimer's?" *Alz.org*. The Alzheimer's Association. 27 Dec. 2013. Web.

Date of last update. Medium.

Picture from the Web:

Name(s) of Artist(s). *Title*. Date of Composition. Medium. Host Institution, City. *Site Name*. Date of Access.

Creator. *Title.* Medium. Date of Access.

NASA. *Night Flight*. 1983. JPEG Image. *Nasa.gov*. 30 Aug. 2011.

Date of Composition. *Site Name.*

Magazine Article from a Library Database:

Author(s). "Article Title." *Magazine Title* Day Month Year: Page numbers. *Name of Database*. Medium. Date of Access.

Author. "Article Title." *Magazine Title* Day Month Year: Page number.

Begley, Sharon. "A Climate Whodunit." *Newsweek* 6 Dec. 2010: 23. *General OneFile*. Web. 31 Aug. 2011.

Database. Medium. Date of Access.

Newspaper Article from a Library Database:

Author(s). "Article Title." *Newspaper Title* Day Month Year, edition. *Name of Database*. Medium. Date of Access.

Author. "Article Title."

Hellmich, Nanci. "Outlook on Obesity is Pretty Grim—U. S. Could Hit 50% by 2030." *USA Today*. 30 Aug. 2011, Final. *NewsBank*. Web. 31 Aug. 2011.

Date of Access. *Title of Newspaper*. Publication Date, Edition. *Database.* Medium.

Scholarly Journal Article:

Author(s). "Article Title." *Journal Title*. Volume (Year): page. *Name of Database*. Medium. Date of Access.

Author. "Article Title."

Anstey, Matthew H. R. "Climate Change and Health—What's the Problem?" *Globalization and Health* 9 (2013): 4. *Academic OneFile*. Web. 28 Dec. 2013.

Journal Title. Volume (Year): page. Database. Medium. Date of Access.

Key Differences between MLA and APA

While MLA is used mostly in the humanities, APA is used in the social sciences. Courses of study in the social sciences include anthropology, economics, political science, psychology, and sociology. Both MLA and APA document the same types of information about a source. For example, both styles require the page number where the information appears in print sources such as books and magazines, but do not require page numbers for Web sources. However, key differences in format and punctuation exist. The following chart outlines these differences.

Key Differences Between MLA and APA		
Format Type of Information	**MLA**	**APA**
Author's name	Spell out the author's first and last name (full name)	Spell out author's last name. Give only the initial of first name.
Titles	Capitalize all major words in the title. Place a pair of quotation marks around titles of shorter publications, such as an article.	Capitalize only the first word of the title, the first word of a subtitle, and proper nouns, such as names. Use lowercase for all other words. Do not use quotation marks around titles of shorter publications such as an article.
In-text Citations	Enclose in parentheses the last name of the author and the page number. Do not use commas to separate author and page number.	Enclose in parentheses the last name of the author, the year, and page numbers. Use commas to separate author, year, and page numbers. Use p. and pp. to refer to page numbers.
Examples: In-text Citations	(Chretien A9)	(Chretien, 2012, p. A9)
Order of Information in Source Citation	Author's last name, first name. Title of Publication. Place of Publication. Publisher. Date of Publication. Medium of publication.	Author's last name, initial of author's first name. (Date of publication). Title of publication. Place of publication, including state abbreviation. Publisher.
Source Page	Label source page "Works Cited." Give the medium of the publication.	Label source page "References." Do not give the medium of the publication.
Example: Source Page Citations: Newspaper	Chretien, Katherine. "Living with Combat Stress." *USA Today* 17 April 2012: A9. Print.	Chretien, K. (2012, April 17). Living with combat stress. *USA Today*, p. A9.
Book	Posen, David B. *The Little Book of Stress Relief*. New York: Firefly Books, 2012. Print.	Posen, D. B. (2012). *The little book of stress relief*. New York, NY: Firefly Books.
Magazine (online)	Goad, Kimberly. "Stop Stress for Good: Exercise to Fight Stress." *Fitness*. 4 March 2011. Web.	Goad, K. (2011, March 4). Stop stress for good: Exercise to fight stress. *Fitness*. Retrieved from http://www.womenshealthmag.com/health/stress-help

Practice 6

Master the Basics of Documentation: MLA and APA

Continue working with the topic you used in Practice 2. Select one of the sources you identified and evaluated for your topic. In your research journal, create two citations for this source. Format the source information into both an MLA citation and an APA citation.

Sample Student Research Essay: MLA

The following essay is a model of the use of the MLA style for citing and documenting sources in a research essay. The annotations point out and explain a few examples of the application of MLA style.

General Format: 1-inch margins. Double spaced. Each page has header of writer's last name and page number.

Powell 1

Flush with left margin, list writer's name, professor's name, course number, and date.

Jean Powell

Professor Henry

History 101

10 September 2014

Center title without use of quotation marks, bold font, or italicized font.

The History of Black Police Officers in Miami, Florida

When the United States entered the Second World War, the U.S. armed forces aggressively sought African American recruits for active duty; however, these new recruits were allowed to carry out only unskilled jobs and tasks. Following the war, many Black soldiers decided to settle in Miami, Florida, and as a result, the Black population in the City of Miami greatly and rapidly increased (Uguccioni and Eaton). This growth in population gave rise to unprecedented law enforcement opportunities in the historically Black neighborhoods in the City of Miami. The history of Black police officers in Miami, Florida illustrates a separate but unequal path in the civil rights journey.

Note that the writer chose to state the central point of the essay in a thesis statement at the end of the introductory paragraph.

By 1944, the city's Black population had reached 43,187. Most of these people lived in the "Central Negro District," once known as "Colored Town" ("The First Five"). The newly created Negro Citizens League insistently lobbied public officials, asserting that the presence of a Black police force was vitally necessary. Finally, the City of Miami bowed to the pressure, and

Powell 2

Don D. Rosenfelder, Director of the Public Safety Department responsible for police services, began recruiting the men who would become the first Black policemen in Miami. His method of recruitment was to ask Black leaders to nominate appropriate candidates. However, the White community greatly opposed the idea of a Black police force. Therefore, Black officers were trained "under extreme secrecy" (Uguccioni and Eaton). The newly created Black police force became a division independent of the White police force.

Note this example of a summary correctly cited in-text.

Finally, the Miami Police Department (MPD) began hiring Black police officers ("History"). On September 1, 1944, five African American men took the oath to serve as the City of Miami's first Black police officers (Uguccioni and Eaton). These men who made history included Ralph White, Moody Hall, Clyde Lee, Edward Kimball, and John Milledge ("The First Five"). While the hiring of these five Black officers was celebrated as "an exciting innovation" in fact, the program proved to be a "separate and unequal" approach to law enforcement in the Black community (Dulaney 58).

These brave pioneers did not have the same respect or power given to White policemen. Black officers were referred to as mere "patrolmen" instead of the seemingly more lofty designation of "officers" given to the White officers ("The First Five"). They were forced to wear black shirts while White officers wore white shirts (Dulaney 58). The Black patrolmen could arrest only African Americans and had no authority over Whites. Black officers could only patrol Black communities and only during the specific "black watch" from 6:00 in the evening until 2:00 in the morning (Dulaney 58). In addition, they had no job security or retirement benefits, nor were they classified as civil service personnel like their White counterparts (Uguccioni and Eaton). Black officers were given little in the way of resources. They had no headquarters, no patrol cars, and no radio communication. They patrolled on foot or on bicycles. As documented on the "History" page of the *Black Police Precinct Courthouse and Museum*

Website, "There are many stories of arrested prisoners being taken to jail on bicycle handlebars, or by walking, or, sometimes, by hailing a Black citizen's car as the citizen was driving by." The purpose and effect of all these measures was to underscore to "the public as well as to black police officers themselves that they were not equal to white officers in authority or prestige" (Dulaney 58).

Note this example of a quotation correctly punctuated and cited in-text.

These patrolmen were assigned to the Central Negro District, which included parts of Liberty City and Colored Town, also called Overtown. Their first headquarters was located in the office of Ira P. Davis, a Black dentist, at 1036 SW 2nd Avenue. Later they used a one-bedroom apartment in the Central Negro District ("History"). One year later, the number of Black patrolmen had grown to 15 and by 1950 their number had increased to 41 (Dulaney 58). Their assignment was limited to the historically Black areas of Coconut Grove. The men had to travel a specified route between Overtown and Coconut Grove to limit any mingling with Whites. These patrolmen "were directed to clear crowded sidewalks, stop all gambling and profanity, confiscate weapons, as well as stop and frisk suspicious people or known trouble makers" ("The First Five"). Quickly they became known for their great success, making 4,326 arrests and taking in $56,321 in fines (Dulaney 58). Additionally, violent crimes in Black areas were greatly reduced—to around fifty percent ("History").

In May of 1950, a police precinct was established at 480 NW 11 Street to provide a headquarters for African American policemen and a courtroom for African American judges in which to try African American defendants (Dulaney 58). This building was exceptional in that there was no other known structure in the nation that was designed, devoted to, and operated as a separate station house and city court for Blacks ("History"). The idea was that Black judges were best suited to try Black defendants (Dulaney 60).

Note this example of a paraphrase correctly punctuated and cited in-text.

Highly respected and widely known Miami architect Walter G. DeGarmo designed and built the building (Uguccioni and Eaton). Since the

Powell 4

Black Precinct was the first and only of its kind built in the United States, the City of Miami gained fame as a trailblazer in clearing a path to equal opportunity for African Americans (Dulaney 58). By the time the Black Precinct moved into their new building in 1950, there were over 40 Black officers on the force (Uguccioni and Eaton).

Segregation remained in effect in the MPD for nearly 20 years after the hiring of those first five Black officers. Racial discrimination and segregation plagued the Miami police force into the 1960s, greatly hindering the careers of Black police officers ("History"). The precinct closed in 1963, and the police department was integrated at the main MPD police station (Dulaney 61). The original building now serves as a museum.

The title "Works Cited" is centered and capitalized.

Note the alphabetical order of citations, the first line of each entry flush with left margin, and the hanging indentation of subsequent lines of an entry.

Powell 5

Works Cited

Dulaney, W. Marvin. *Black Police in America*. Bloomington: Indiana University Press, 1996. Print.

"History." *Black Police Precinct Courthouse and Museum*. Historicalblackprecinct.org. 3 Sept. 2014. Web.

"The First Five." *Black Police Precinct Courthouse and Museum*. Historicalblackprecinct.org. 3 Sept. 2014. Web.

Uguccioni, Ellen J., and Sarah E. Eaton. "Black Police Precinct and Courthouse 1009 NW 5th Avenue: Designation Report." Historicpreservationmiami.com. City of Miami. 17 Sept. 2002. Web.

Sample Student Research Essay: APA

The following essay serves as a model of the use of the APA style for citing and documenting sources in a research essay. The annotations point out and explain examples of the application of APA style. APA requires a title page.

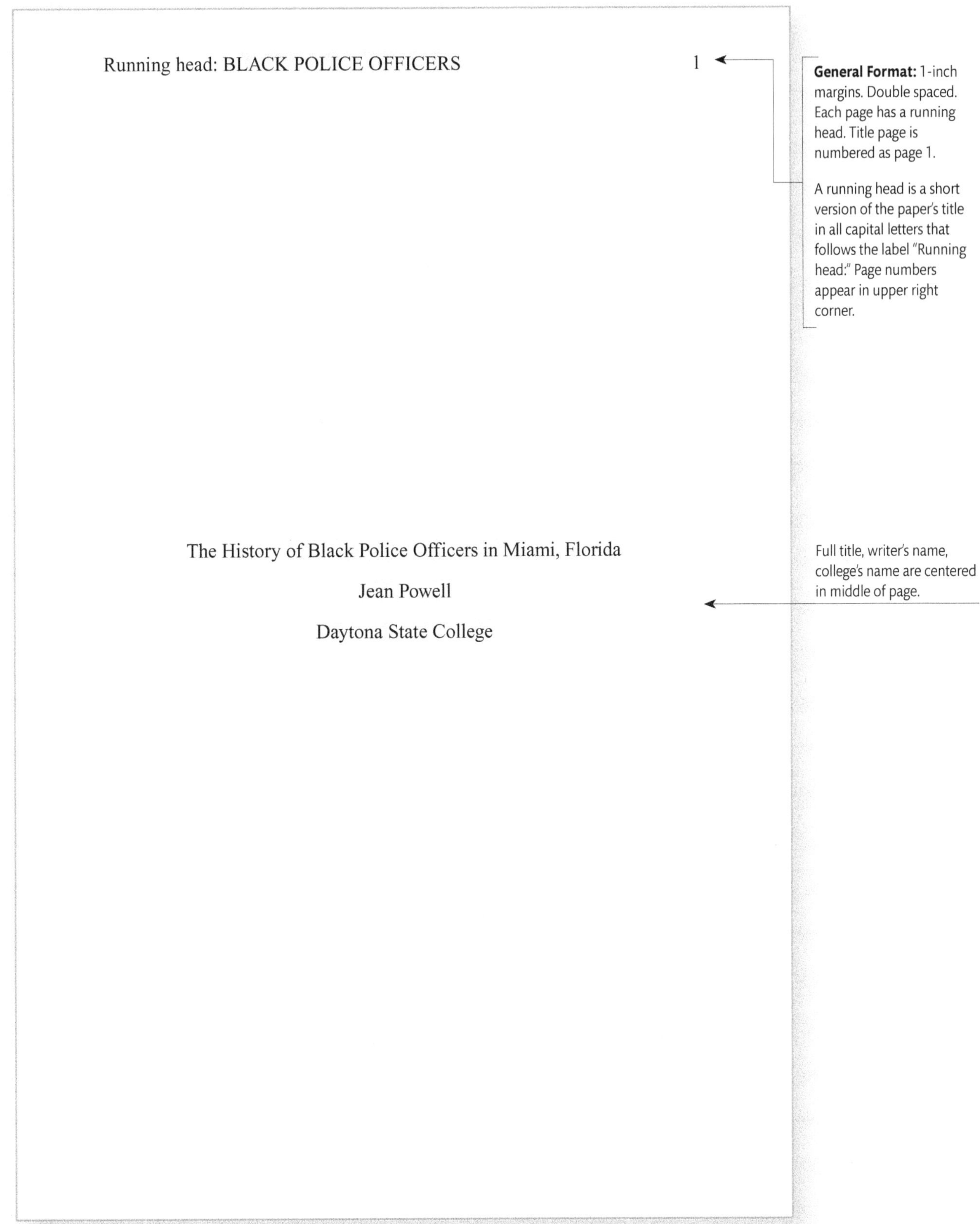

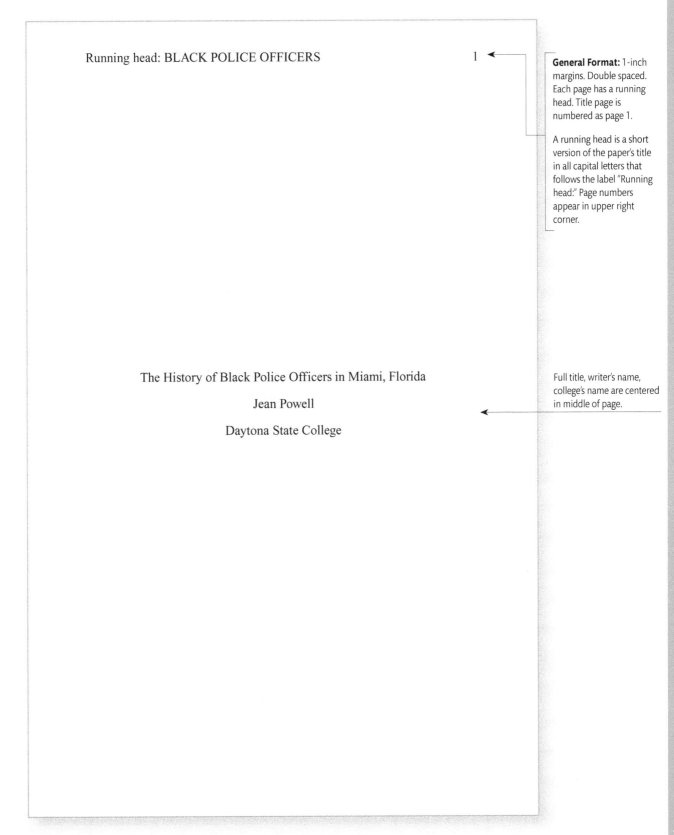

Running head: BLACK POLICE OFFICERS 1

The History of Black Police Officers in Miami, Florida

Jean Powell

Daytona State College

General Format: 1-inch margins. Double spaced. Each page has a running head. Title page is numbered as page 1.

A running head is a short version of the paper's title in all capital letters that follows the label "Running head:" Page numbers appear in upper right corner.

Full title, writer's name, college's name are centered in middle of page.

Full title is centered on this page.

BLACK POLICE OFFICERS 2

The History of Black Police Officers in Miami, Florida

When the United States entered the Second World War, the U.S. armed forces aggressively sought African American recruits for active duty; however, these new recruits were allowed to carry out only unskilled jobs and tasks. Following the war, many Black soldiers decided to settle in Miami, Florida, and as a result, the Black population in the City of Miami greatly and rapidly increased (Uguccioni & Eaton, 2002, p. 7). This growth in population gave rise to unprecedented law enforcement opportunities in the historically Black neighborhoods in the City of Miami. The history of Black police officers in Miami, Florida illustrates a separate but unequal path in the civil rights journey.

Use quotations and capitals for in-text citations.

By 1944, the city's Black population had reached 43,187. Most of these people lived in the "Central Negro District," once known as "Colored Town" ("The First Five," 2014). The newly created Negro Citizens League insistently lobbied public officials, asserting that the presence of a Black police force was vitally necessary. Finally, the City of Miami bowed to the pressure, and Don D. Rosenfelder, Director of the Public Safety Department responsible for police services, began recruiting the men who would become the first Black policemen in Miami. His method of recruitment was to ask Black leaders to nominate appropriate candidates. However, the White community greatly opposed the idea of a Black police force. Therefore, Black officers were trained "under extreme secrecy" (Uguccioni & Eaton, 2002, p. 8). The newly created Black police force became a division independent of the White police force.

Note this summary is correctly punctuated and cited in-text using APA.

Finally, the Miami Police Department (MPD) began hiring Black police officers ("History," 2014). On September 1, 1944, five African American men took the oath to serve as the City of Miami's fist Black police officers (Uguccioni & Eaton, 2002, p. 8). These men who made history included Ralph White, Moody Hall, Clyde Lee, Edward Kimball, and John Milledge ("The First Five," 2014). While the hiring of these five Black officers was celebrated as "an exciting innovation" in fact, the program proved to be a "separate and unequal" approach to law enforcement in the Black community (Dulaney, 1996, p. 58).

These brave pioneers did not have the same respect or power given to White policemen. Black officers were referred to as mere "patrolmen" instead of the seemingly more lofty designation of "officers" given to the White officers ("The First Five," 2014). They were forced to wear black shirts while White officers wore white shirts (Dulaney, 1996, p. 58). The Black patrolmen could arrest only African Americans and had no authority over Whites. Black officers could only patrol Black communities and only during the specific "black watch" from 6:00 in the evening until 2:00 in the morning (Dulaney, 1996, p. 58). In addition, they had no job security or retirement benefits, nor were they classified as civil service personnel like their White counterparts (Uguccioni & Eaton, 2002, p. 8). Black officers were given little in the way of resources. They had no headquarters, no patrol cars, and no radio communication. They patrolled on foot or on bicycles. As documented on the History page of the *Black Police Precinct Courthouse and Museum* Website, "There are many stories of arrested prisoners being taken to jail on bicycle handlebars, or by walking, or, sometimes, by hailing a Black citizen's car as the citizen was driving by." The purpose and effect of all these measures was to underscore to "the public as well as to black police officers themselves that they were not equal to white officers in authority or prestige" (Dulaney, 1996, p. 58).

Note this example of a quotation correctly punctuated and cited in-text using APA.

These patrolmen were assigned to the Central Negro District, which included parts of Liberty City and Colored Town, also called Overtown. Their first headquarters was located in the office of Ira P. Davis, a Black dentist, at 1036 SW 2nd Avenue. Later they used a one-bedroom apartment in the Central Negro District ("History," 2014). One year later, the number of Black patrolmen had grown to 15 and by 1950 their number had increased to 41 (Dulaney, 1996, p. 58). Their assignment was limited to the historically Black areas of Coconut Grove. The men had to travel a specified route between Overtown and Coconut Grove to limit any mingling with Whites. These patrolmen "were directed to clear crowded sidewalks, stop all gambling and profanity, confiscate weapons, as well as stop and frisk suspicious people or known trouble makers" ("The First Five," 2014). Quickly they became known for their great success, making 4,326 arrests and taking in $56,321 in fines (Dulaney, 1996, p. 58). Additionally, violent crimes in Black areas were greatly reduced—to around 50% ("History," 2014).

In May of 1950, a police precinct was established at 480 NW 11 Street to provide a headquarters for African American policemen and a courtroom for African American judges in which to try African American defendants (Dulaney, 1996, p. 58). This building was unique in that there was no other known structure in the nation that was designed, devoted to, and operated as a separate station house and city court for Blacks ("History," 2014). The idea was that Black judges were best suited to try Black defendants (Dulaney, 1996, p. 60).

Note this example of a paraphrase correctly punctuated and cited in-text using APA.

Highly respected and widely known Miami architect Walter G. DeGarmo designed and built the building (Uguccioni & Eaton, 2002, p. 9). Since the Black Precinct was the first and only of its kind built in the United States, the City of Miami gained fame as a trailblazer in clearing a path to equal opportunity for African Americans (Dulaney, 1996, p. 58). By the time the Black Precinct moved into their new building in 1950, there were over 40 Black officers on the force (Uguccioni & Eaton, 2002).

Segregation remained in effect in the MPD for nearly 20 years after the hiring of those first five Black officers. Racial discrimination and segregation plagued the Miami police force into the 1960s, greatly hindering the careers of Black police officers ("History," 2014). The precinct closed in 1963, and the police department was integrated at the main MPD police station (Dulaney, 1996, p. 61). The original building now serves as a museum.

References

Dulaney, W. (1996). *Black police in America.* (pp. 58–61). Bloomington, IN: Indiana University Press.

History. (2014). *Black police precinct courthouse and museum.* Retrieved September 3, 2014, from www.historicalblackprecinct.org

The first five. (2014). *Black police precinct courthouse and museum.* Retrieved September 4, 2014, from www.historicalblackprecinct.org

Uguccioni, E., & Eaton, S. (2002, September 17). Black police precinct and courthouse 1009 NW 5th avenue: Designation report [PDF]. (pp. 7–9). Retrieved from http://www.historicpreservationmiami.com/pdfs/Black%20Police%20Precinct.pdf

The source page is labeled "References." Compare and contrast the APA format of these sources to the MLA format used in the Works Cited on page 286.

Workshop: Applying the Reading/ Writing Strategy to Research

You are now ready to conduct independent research. You may select one of the topics suggested in Practice 2 with which you have not already worked, you may use a topic from the Reading and Writing Assignments on page 294, or you may research a topic of your own choosing. Use the following steps of the reading/writing strategy to guide your research process and to write a research paper.

Preread: Survey and Question

What is my general topic or subject area of research?

____

____

What are key problems, concepts, or issues related to my topic?

____

____

What are the keywords and terms I can use to locate information?

____

____

How has the issue changed or developed over time?

____

____

What is debatable or controversial about the topic?

____

____

What is my research question?

____

____

What kind of information do I need, and where can I locate reliable sources?

____

____

Read and Annotate

As you read, annotate key ideas, particularly those details you will record as notes in your research journal.

Recite, Review, and Brainstorm

Recite and **Review** the information. Paraphrase ideas. Summarize the most important parts. **Brainstorm** ideas for your written response to the passage. Answer your prereading questions. *Freewrite* or *map* the relationship among answers to questions or ideas you have annotated in the text. *Outline* or *list* key ideas and details in blocks of thought. Identify the central point you want to make. Use your own paper.

Write a Draft of Your Response

Using the ideas you generated by brainstorming, compose a draft of your response. Use your own paper.

Revise Your Draft

Once you have created a draft of your research paper, read it over to answer the questions in the "Questions for Revising Research" box that follows. Indicate your answers by annotating your paper. If you answer "yes" to a question, underline, check, or circle examples. If you answer "no" to a question, write needed information in margins and draw lines to indicate placement of additional details. Revise your essay based on your reflection. (*Hint:* Experienced writers create several drafts as they focus on one or two questions per draft.)

Step by Step: Questions for Revising Research

- ❑ Have I stated or implied a focused main idea?
- ❑ Is the order of the ideas clear?
- ❑ Have I used concrete details to make my point?
- ❑ Have I made my point with adequate details?
- ❑ Have I included only the details that are relevant to my thesis statement?
- ❑ Have I appropriately paraphrased, quoted, or summarized ideas?
- ❑ Have I effectively used the appropriate documentation style?

Proofread Your Draft

Once you have made any revisions to your essay that may be needed, proofread your essay to eliminate careless errors.

Reading and Writing Assignments

MySkillsLab™ Complete this Exercise on myskillslab.com

Reading and Writing for Everyday Life

Assume your state is considering legalizing medical marijuana or has recently legalized it. As a concerned citizen, you want to clarify your stand on this issue. Find three sources that discuss the benefits or dangers of medical marijuana use. Then, write a letter to an elected official representing your district in your state. In your letter, support or oppose the legalization of medical marijuana. Appropriately paraphrase, quote, or summarize ideas in your letter. Track and appropriately document your sources.

Reading and Writing for College Life

Assume you are taking a college course in student success. Your professor requires a research essay between 750 and 1000 words on a topic related to student success. Since group work is often expected in academic classes, you have decided to research how to be an effective member of a small group. Find three sources that explain the roles of members of small groups and behaviors to model or avoid as a group member. Appropriately paraphrase, quote, or summarize ideas in your research essay. Track and appropriately document your sources.

Reading and Writing for Working Life

Assume you are the manager of a local branch of a business that has several regional stores. You have noticed that the company does not recycle. At a recent management meeting, you raised recycling as a concern, stating that the company should be socially responsible about this issue. Upper management responded with interest and asked you to explain your concerns and make suggestions in a written report. Find three sources on how a corporation or business may efficiently recycle. Appropriately paraphrase, quote, or summarize ideas in your report. Track and appropriately document your sources.

Review Test

MySkillsLab™
Complete this Exercise
on myskillslab.com

Score (number correct) _____ x 10 = _____%

Read the following passage from a college social science textbook. Then answer the questions.

Glossary

spectrum (sentence 9): range, field, variety
persona (sentence 18): role, character, image

DATING IN CYBERSPACE

[1]There seems little doubt that the dating industry has changed dramatically as a result of new and increasing computer technology. [2]Some observers say that a quiet revolution has overtaken the world of romance as the increasingly popular electronic bulletin boards have transformed into what some call "online pickup joints." [3]One thing for sure, there is now relatively broad public contact with the online dating world. [4]Some 31 percent of American adults say they know someone who has used a dating Web site and 15 percent of American adults—about 30 million people—say they know someone who has been in a long-term relationship or married someone she or he met online (Madden & Lenhart, 2006). [5]Mate selection, by way of the computer and the Internet, has become pretty routine for a wide range of dating and dating-related behaviors among a variety of today's singles.

[6]For example, many single professionals are looking for a mate in cyberspace. [7]Modern life for the unmarried professional today is increasingly complicated and full, making finding a partner difficult, if not impossible, for those who are interested. [8]Today's professionals are marrying later; they travel thousands of miles each year for business reasons; they relocate frequently as they climb the corporate ladder; they run in and out of health and other exercise clubs on a tight schedule on their way to the office; they rarely date colleagues on the job; and many of them are fed up with singles' bars, blind dates, and family and friend fix-ups (rarely does what they want in a partner coincide with what family and friends think they need). [9]In addition, at both ends of the dating age **spectrum**, an increasing number of teenagers and people 50 years of age and older are growing segments of online daters.

[10]In this regard, some relationship experts predict that "niche dating sites" are the wave of the future for online dating. [11]They say that as more new dating sites come online, the best chance for success is to focus on a particular niche. [12]In fact, there are already hundreds of such niche dating sites currently online. [13]These sites run the **gamut** from sites specifically for Seventh Day Adventists, Big, Beautiful Women, Christians, Singles who are Deaf, Military Singles and their Admirers, and Singles over 40 to Single Parents, Single and Widowed Seniors, and one for every possible racial/ethnic and religious group. [14]Ironically, it is the same technology that some people feel isolates us and is too invasive that is also responsible for bringing people together.

CONTINUED

REVIEW TEST *CONTINUED*

[15]Online dating has advantages as well as pitfalls. [16]Some of the advantages of online dating are its accessibility, **autonomy**, and increasingly low cost. [17]Subscribers can sit in the privacy of their homes and access tens of thousands of eligible mates, sifting through them as often as they like by specific "niche" characteristics such as age, race/ethnicity, religion, or body type. [18]They can also remain anonymous as long as they like, thus allowing people to portray the **persona** they choose until they are ready to get involved. [19]This can lead to more open expression because people do not have to worry about seeing or running into each other if the online relationship does not work. [20]It also saves the time and expense that might be spent on a bad blind or fix-up date, and it cuts out the need for barhopping. [21]A pitfall is the potential for dishonesty and even harassment or violence if, for example, the online relationship does not work out (Madden & Lenhart, 2006; Nichcolas and Milewski, 1999). [22]When it does work, it can lead a couple to the altar. [23]Online Dating Magazine estimates that there are more than 280,000 marriages a year as a direct result of people meeting on an online dating service (Online Dating Magazine – January 2011).

—Schwartz and Scott, *Marriages and Families: Diversity and Change*, 2010, Census Update, p. 136.

Vocabulary

1. The best meaning of the word **gamut** as used in sentence 13 is

a. range.
b. confines.
c. route.
d. limits.

Vocabulary

2. The best meaning of the word **autonomy** as used in sentence 16 is

a. ease of use.
b. quickness.
c. success rate.
d. independent control.

Inference

3. Based on the information in the passage, we may infer that

a. only young professionals go online to find dates.
b. online dating will continue to grow in popularity.
c. the dangers outweigh the benefits of finding a date online.

Main Idea/ Details

4. Sentence 3 states a

a. main idea.
b. major supporting detail.
c. minor supporting detail.

Central Idea

5. Which sentence best states the authors' central idea?

a. sentence 1
b. sentence 5
c. sentence 6
d. sentence 23

Supporting Details

6. About how many adults know someone who has used a dating website?

a. 15 percent
b. 30 percent
c. 31 percent
d. 50 percent

Purpose

7. The author's main purpose is

a. to entertain the reader with stories of online dating.
b. to inform the reader about online dating.
c. to persuade the reader to use online dating.

Tone

8. The tone of the passage is

a. cynical.
b. amused.
c. objective.
d. disapproving.

Fact and Opinion

9. Sentence 15 is a statement of

a. fact.
b. opinion.
c. fact and opinion.

Fact and Opinion

10. Sentence 23 is a statement of

a. fact.
b. opinion.
c. fact and opinion.

Summary Response

Restate the authors' central idea in your own words. Begin your summary response with the following: *The central idea of "Dating in Cyberspace" by Schwartz and Scott is. . . .*

Reader Response

Assume you write a blog about issues of concern to people your age, and you have several hundred followers. Write a blog entry that discusses the advantages and disadvantages of meeting potential dates online. Summarize, paraphrase, or quote ideas from the passage.

Academic Learning Log: Module Review

MySkillsLab™
Complete this Exercise
on myskillslab.com

Summary of Key Concepts of a Reading/Writing Strategy for Research

Assess your comprehension of a reading/writing strategy for research.

LO1 LO2 LO3 LO4

1. What are two kinds of information that inform our thinking and writing? ____

2. What are the two storehouses of information? ____

3. What is PAART? ____.

LO1 LO2 LO3 LO4 LO5

4. Plagiarism is ____.

   Four ways to avoid plagiarism include: ______________, ______________, ______________, and ______________.

5. What are the five Rs of paraphrasing? ______________, ______________, ______________, ______________, and ______________.

Test Your Comprehension of a Reading/Writing Strategy for Research

Respond in your own words to the following questions and prompts.

LO1 LO2 LO3 LO4 LO5

In your own words, explain the differences among paraphrasing, summarizing, and quoting.

In your own words, explain how a researcher avoids plagiarism throughout the research process.

LO1 LO2 LO3 LO4 LO5

1. **How will I use what I have learned?** In your notebook, discuss how you will apply to your own reading/writing strategy what you have learned about developing a reading/writing strategy for research. When will you apply this knowledge to your reading/writing strategy?

2. **What do I still need to study about the reading/writing strategy for research?** In your notebook, discuss your ongoing study needs. Describe what, when, and how you will continue studying and using a reading/writing strategy for research.

MySkillsLab™

Complete the Post-test for Module 7 in MySkillsLab.

8

LEARNING OUTCOMES

After studying this module you should be able to:

- **LO 1** Answer the Question "What's the Point of Time and Space Order?"
- **LO 2** Question, Read, Annotate, and Review Passages Using Time and Space Order
- **LO 3** Prewrite a Draft of a Thesis Statement Using Time and Space Order
- **LO 4** Prewrite to Generate Relevant Details Using Time and Space Order
- **LO 5** Compose a Draft Using Logical Order: Time and Space Order
- **LO 6** Revise and Proofread for Effective Language with Time and Space Order

Time and Space Order Patterns: *Narration, Process,* and *Description*

Clear communication between a writer and a reader comes from clear organization. Clear organization is based on logical connections between ideas. **Transitions** and **patterns of organization** are used to organize and express these logical connections.

Transitions are words or phrases connecting one idea to another.

A **pattern of organization** is the arrangement of ideas in a logical order to make a specific point.

Time order, also known as *chronological order*, presents ideas based on the time in which they occurred. Time order enables us to tell about and understand an event, a series of actions, or a process. Space order tells where something occurs. Space order creates a clear visual image of a person, place, object, or scene. Time and space are closely linked in our thinking. Action occurs in both time and space.

WHAT'S THE POINT of Time and Space Order? LO1

Before you study this module, predict the importance of the time order and space order patterns of organization. Study each photograph in the following series. Think about how a writer would use time order to make a point about this sequence of events. Would the writer tell a story or describe a series of steps? Would the writer also need to describe the place in which the actions occur? Also think about how a reader would use time order and space order to comprehend the writer's point. Write a caption for each image by answering the questions in the spaces given. Next, write a sentence to state the central point of the sequence of photographs. Finally, predict an answer to the question "What's the point of time order and space order?"

Photographic Organizer: How Do We Learn to Communicate?

How, where, and what do infants learn about language?

How, where, and what do toddlers learn about language?

How, where, and what have five- and six-year-olds learned?

Central point of photographs: ______

What's the point of time and space order? ______

L2 Question, Read, Annotate, and Review Passages Using Time and Space Order

Two types of **time order** are narration and process.

The **time order** or *chronological* pattern of organization relays a chain of actions or events in the order in which they occur.

1. *Narration* conveys an event or story. For example, narration records the important events in the life of a famous person or the details of a significant event in history. Narration is also used to organize a piece of fiction.
2. *Process* gives directions to perform a task or lists stages of a task in time order. For example, process describes how to change a tire or lists the phases of development of a living being.

Space order offers descriptive details to help readers create vivid mental pictures of what the writer is describing.

The same transitions and signal words are used to indicate narration and process. The following chart lists a few examples of time order transitions or signal words.

Space order, also known as *spatial order* or *description*, describes details based on their physical location in a given area.

Time Order Transitions and Signal Words for Narration and Process				
after	currently	last	once	soon
afterward	during	later	over (time)	then
ago	eventually	meanwhile	previously	ultimately
as	finally	next	quickly	until
around	first	now	second	when
before	formerly	often	since	while

Transitions or signal words of space order indicate a logical order based on two elements: (1) how the object, place, or person is arranged or occurs in space, and (2) the starting point from which the writer chooses to begin the description. The following chart lists just a few of the many transition and signal words writers use to establish space order.

Space Order Transitions or Signal Words for Description				
above	back	center	in	outside
across	behind	close to	inside	over
adjacent	below	down	into	right
around	beneath	far away	left	there
at the bottom	beside	farther	middle	under
at the side	beyond	front	nearby	underneath
at the top	by	here	next to	within

Most often, we explain events and actions in terms of *when* and *where* they occur. Thus, writers often use space order along with time order to narrate an event or describe a process. Master readers question, annotate, and review the writer's use of time and space order to comprehend the point of a narrative or process. Often, master readers complete a concept map or graphic organizer to see the flow of the writer's ideas and deepen comprehension.

For Module 8, assume you are taking a college course in communication, and your class is beginning a study on the theme of barriers to communication. Each reading in this module follows this theme. After completing all assigned readings, you will write an essay in response to the following guiding question: "How do we overcome barriers in communication?"

Example

Assume the following passage is your first assigned reading on the theme "barriers to communication." Your professor has provided before and during reading questions and guided annotations to prepare you to read about and respond to the theme. Before reading, survey the questions and skim the passage for possible answers. Then read the passage and the annotations. As your read, add your own annotations by completing the prompts in **bold** print in the annotations. After reading, use your own words to answer the questions about relevant details. Record your answers in your reading/writing journal. Finally, complete the concept map with information from the passage.

Before and During Reading Questions:

Logical Order: Is this passage a narration or a process? Which transitions/signal words did the writer use?

Central Idea: What is the writer's central point?

Relevant Details: What is language? What are Piaget's and Vygotsky's theories about language and thought? What is linguistic relativity hypothesis? What is the receptive-productive lag? What is child-directed speech? What are the stages of language development?

Effective Language: What vivid words does the writer use to create images in the reader's mind?

Language

[1]Language is a system for combining symbols (such as words) so that an infinite number of meaningful statements can be made for the purpose of communicating with others. [2]Language allows people not only to communicate with one another but also to represent their own internal mental activity. [3]In other words, language is a very important part of how people think.

Relevant Details: This detail answers the first prereading question "What is language?" **Underline details that answer the remaining prereading questions.**

CONTINUED

EXAMPLE *CONTINUED*

Central Idea: The central idea is the point the writer makes about the topic of the passage. The topic is "the development of language." **Underline the writer's point about the topic.**

Chronological Order: Time order is established with the word *before*. **Circle two more words that indicate time order.**

Effective Language: Vivid phrases such as "'pegs upon which words are hung'" create a mental picture and deepen meaning. **Double underline one more vivid word or phrase.**

[4]As with the controversy of nature versus nurture, researchers have long debated the relationship between the development of language and thought. [5]*Does language actually influence thought, or thinking influence language?*

[6]Two very influential developmental psychologists, Jean Piaget and Lev Vygotsky, often debated the relationship of language and thought (Duncan, 1995). [7]Piaget (1926, 1962) theorized that concepts preceded and aided the development of language. [8]For example, a child would have to have a concept or mental schema for "mother" before being able to learn word "mama." [9]In a sense, concepts become the "pegs" upon which words are "hung." [10]Piaget also noticed that preschool children seemed to spend a great deal of time talking to themselves—even when playing with another child. [11]Each child would be talking about something totally unrelated to the speech of the other, in a process Piaget called *collective monologue*. [12]Piaget believed that this kind of nonsocial speech was very egocentric (from the child's point of view only, with no regard for the listener), and that as the child became more socially involved and less egocentric, these nonsocial speech patterns would reduce.

[13]Vygotsky, however, believed almost the opposite. [14]He theorized that language actually helped develop concepts and that language could also help the child learn to control behavior—including social behavior (Vygotsky, 1962, 1978, 1987). [15]For Vygotsky, the word helped form the concept. [16]Once a child had learned the word "mama," the various elements of "mama-ness"—*warm, soft, food, safety*, and so on—could come together around that word. [17]Vygotsky also believed that the "egocentric" speech of the preschool child was actually a way for the child to form thoughts and control actions. [18]This "private speech" was a way for children to plan their behavior and organize actions so that their goals could be obtained. [19]Since socializing with other children would demand much more self-control and behavioral regulation on the part of the preschool child, Vygotsky believed that private speech would actually increase as children became more socially active during the preschool years. [20]This was, of course, the opposite of Piaget's assumption, and the evidence seems to bear out Vygotsky's view. [21]Children, especially bright children, do tend to use more private speech when learning how to socialize with other children or when working on a difficult task (Berk, 1992; Berk & Spuhl, 1995; Bivens & Berk, 1990).

Linguistic Relativity Hypothesis

Spatial Order: Space order is established with the word *within*. This tells us where words determine thought processes and concepts. **Circle one more word that establishes space order.**

[22]The hypothesis that language shapes and influences thoughts was accepted by many theorists, with a few notable exceptions, such as Piaget. [23]One of the best-known versions of this view is the Sapir-Whorf hypothesis (named for the two theorists who developed it, Edward Sapir and his student, Benjamin Lee Whorf). [24]This hypothesis assumes that the thought processes and concepts within any culture are determined by the words of the culture (Sapir, 1921; Whorf, 1956). [25]It has come to be known as the **linguistic relativity hypothesis**, meaning that thought processes and concepts are controlled by (relative to) language. [26]That is, the words people use determine much of the way in which they think about the world around them. [27]Neither Sapir nor Whorf provided any scientific studies that would support their proposition.

[28]There have been numerous studies by other researchers, however, and the ongoing investigation appears to support linguistic relativity and how language can shape our thoughts about space, time, colors, and objects.

Stages of Language Development

[29]The development of language is a very important milestone in the cognitive development of a child because language allows children to think in words rather than just images, to ask questions, to communicate their needs and wants to others, and to form concepts (L. Bloom, 1974; P. Bloom, 2000). [30]Language development in infancy is influenced by the language they hear, a style of speaking known as *child-directed speech* (the way adults and older children talk to infants and very young children, with higher pitched, repetitious, sing-song speech patterns). [31]Infants and toddlers attend more closely to this kind of speech, which creates a learning opportunity in the dialogue between caregiver and infant (Dominey & Dodane, 2004; Fernald, 1984, 1992; Kuntay & Slobin, 2002). [32]Other researchers are looking at the infant's use of gestures and signs (Behne et al., 2005; Lizskowski et al., 2006; Moll & Tomasello, 2007; Tomasello et al., 2007).

[33]Infants also seem to understand far more than they can produce, a phenomenon known as the *receptive-productive lag* (Stevenson et al., 1988). [34]They may be able to only produce one or two words, but they understand much longer sentences from their parents and others. [35]There are several stages of language development that all children experience, no matter what culture they live in or what language they will learn to speak (Brown, 1973):

1. [36]**Cooing:** At around 2 months of age, babies begin to make vowel-like sounds.
2. [37]**Babbling:** At about 6 months, infants add consonant sounds to the vowels to make a babbling sound, which at times can almost sound like real speech. [38]Deaf children actually decrease their babbling after 6 months while increasing their use of primitive hand signs and gestures (Petitto & Marentette, 1991; Petitto et al., 2001).
3. [39]**One-word speech:** Somewhere just before or around age 1, most children begin to say actual words. [40]These words are typically nouns and may seem to represent an entire phrase of meaning. [41]They are called *holophrases* (whole phrases in one word) for that reason. [42]For example, a child might say "Milk!" and mean "I want some milk!" or "I drank my milk!"
4. [43]**Telegraphic speech:** At around a year and a half, toddlers begin to string words together to form short, simple sentences using nouns, verbs, and adjectives. [44]"Baby eat," "Mommy go," and "Doggie go bye-bye" are examples of telegraphic speech. [45]Only the words that carry the meaning of the sentence are used.
5. [46]**Whole sentences:** As children move through the preschool years, they learn to use grammatical terms and increase the number of words in their sentences, until by age 6 or so they are nearly as fluent as an adult, although the number of words they know is still limited when compared to adult vocabulary.

—Adapted Ciccarelli and White. *Psychology*, 4th ed., Pearson, 2015, pp. 294–297, 325.

CONTINUED

EXAMPLE *CONTINUED*

of Language Development			
When	**Who**	**What**	**Where**
			all cultures
			all cultures
			all cultures
			all cultures
			all cultures

Explanation

Compare your answers to the following think-aloud, completed by Reagan, another student in your class.

The guided annotations helped me find the answers to the before and during reading questions. This passage is a process that describes the phases humans go through to learn how to communicate. The two time order words I circled are **Once** in sentence 15 and **begin** in sentence 43. The space order word I circled is **upon** in sentence 9. The writer's central point about the development of language is the relationship between language and thought. I underlined the following details that supported the writer's central idea. First, I underlined sentence 1 because it answered the question "What is language?" Sentence 7 stated Piaget's theory, and sentence 14 stated Vygotsky's theory. In sentence 25, I underlined "thought processes and concepts are controlled by (relative to) language" as the meaning of "linguistic relativity hypothesis." In sentence 30, I underlined "a style of speaking," "child directed speech," and "the way adults and older children talk to infants and very young children." I underlined sentence 33 because it defined "receptive-productive lag." Finally, I underlined the following words to answer the question "What are the stages of language development?" I double underlined the words **warm, soft** because they create a vivid mental image of how a baby thinks of its mother. Here are the details I used to fill in the concept map: **2 months, babies, cooing; 6 months, infants, babbling; age 1, children, one-word speech; around a year and a half, toddlers, telegraphic speech; preschool, by age 6, children, whole sentences.**

Practice 1

Question, Read, Annotate, and Review Passages Using Time and Space Order

Assume the following two passages are the next assigned readings on the theme "barriers to communication." Your professor has provided a few questions to guide your thinking. Before reading each passage, survey the questions and skim the passage for possible answers. Then read the passage. As you read, annotate the details in the passage that answer the questions. After reading, respond to the prompts that follow each passage.

Before and During Reading Questions:

Logical Order: Is this passage a narration or a process? Which transitions/signal words did the writer use?

Central Idea: What is the writer's central point?

Relevant Details: What are the "different Englishes" Amy Tan uses?
How does the linguistic relativity hypothesis apply to Tan's experience with language?
How does Tan's mother illustrate the receptive-productive lag?
What stage of language development does the English of Tan's mother reflect?
How did Tan overcome barriers in her English language development?

Effective Language: What vivid words does the writer use to create images in the reader's mind?

Mother Tongue

by Amy Tan

[1]I am not a scholar of English or literature. [2]I cannot give you much more than personal opinions on the English language and variations in this country or others.

[3]I am a writer. [4]And by that definition, I am someone who has always loved language. [5]I am fascinated by language in daily life. [6]I spend a great deal of my time thinking about the power of language—the way it can evoke an emotion, a visual image, a complex idea, or a simple truth. [7]Language is the tool of my trade. [8]And I use them all—all the Englishes I grew up with.

Amy Tan

CONTINUED

PRACTICE 1 *CONTINUED*

[9]Recently, I was made keenly aware of the different Englishes I do use. [10]I was giving a talk to a large group of people, the same talk I had already given to half a dozen other groups. [11]The nature of the talk was about my writing, my life, and my book, *The Joy Luck Club*. [12]The talk was going along well enough, until I remembered one major difference that made the whole talk sound wrong. [13]My mother was in the room. [14]And it was perhaps the first time she had heard me give a lengthy speech, using the kind of English I have never used with her. [15]I was saying things like, "The intersection of memory upon imagination" and "There is an aspect of my fiction that relates to thus-and-thus—a speech filled with carefully wrought grammatical phrases, burdened, it suddenly seemed to me, with nominalized forms, past perfect tenses, conditional phrases, all the forms of standard English that I had learned in school and through books, the forms of English I did not use at home with my mother.

[16]Just last week, I was walking down the street with my mother, and I again found myself conscious of the English I was using, the English I do use with her. [17]We were talking about the price of new and used furniture and I heard myself saying this: "Not waste money that way." [18]My husband was with us as well, and he didn't notice any switch in my English. [19]And then I realized why. [20]It's because over the twenty years we've been together I've often used the same kind of English with him, and sometimes he even uses it with me. [21]It has become our language of intimacy, a different sort of English that relates to family talk, the language I grew up with.

[22]So you'll have some idea of what this family talk I heard sounds like, I'll quote what my mother said during a recent conversation which I videotaped and then transcribed.

[23]During this conversation, my mother was talking about a political gangster in Shanghai who had the same last name as her family's, Du, and how the gangster in his early years wanted to be adopted by her family, which was rich by comparison. [24]Later, the gangster became more powerful, far richer than my mother's family, and one day showed up at my mother's wedding to pay his respects. [25]Here's what she said in part:

[26]"Du Yusong having business like fruit stand. [27]Like off the street kind. [28]He is Du like Du Zong—but not Tsung-ming Island people. [29]The local people call putong, the river east side, he belong to that side local people. [30]That man want to ask Du Zong father take him in like become own family. [31]Du Zong father wasn't look down on him, but didn't take seriously, until that man big like become a mafia.

[32]Now important person, very hard to inviting him. [33]Chinese way, come only to show respect, don't stay for dinner. [34]Respect for making big celebration, he shows up. [35]Mean gives lots of respect. [36]Chinese custom, Chinese social life that way. [37]If too important won't have to stay too long. [38]He come to my wedding. [39]I didn't see, I heard it. [40]I gone to boy's side, they have YMCA dinner. [41]Chinese age I was nineteen."

[42]You should know that my mother's expressive command of English belies how much she actually understands. [43]She reads the Forbes report, listens to Wall Street Week, converses daily with her stockbroker, reads all of Shirley MacLaine's books with ease—all kinds of things I can't begin to understand. [44]Yet some of my friends tell me they understand 50 percent of what my mother says. [45]Some say they understand 80 to 90 percent. [46]Some say they understand none of it, as if she were speaking pure Chinese. [47]But to me, my mother's English is perfectly clear, perfectly natural. [48]It's my mother tongue. [49]Her language, as I hear it, is vivid, direct, full of observation and imagery. [50]That was the language that helped shape the way I saw things, expressed things, made sense of the world.

[51]Lately, I've been giving more thought to the kind of English my mother speaks. [52]Like others, I have described it to people as "broken," or "fractured" English. [53]But I wince when I say that. [54]It has always bothered me that I can think of no way to describe it other than "broken," as if it were damaged and needed to be fixed, as if it lacked a certain wholeness and soundness. [55]I've heard other terms used, "limited English," for example. [56]But they seem just as bad, as if everything is limited, including people's perceptions of the limited English speaker.

[57]I know this for a fact, because when I was growing up, my mother's "limited" English limited my perception of her. [58]I was ashamed of her English. [59]I believed that her English reflected the quality of what she had to say. [60]That is, because she expressed them imperfectly her thoughts were imperfect. [61]And I had plenty of empirical evidence to support me: the fact that people in department stores, at banks, and at restaurants did not take her seriously, did not give her good service, pretended not to understand her, or even acted as if they did not hear her.

. . .

[62]I think my mother's English almost had an effect on limiting my possibilities in life as well. [63]Sociologists and linguists probably will tell you that a person's developing language skills are more

CONTINUED

PRACTICE 1 *CONTINUED*

influenced by peers. [64]But I do think that the language spoken in the family, especially in immigrant families which are more insular, plays a large role in shaping the language of the child. [65]And I believe that it affected my results on achievement tests, IQ tests, and the SAT. [66]While my English skills were never judged as poor, compared to math, English could not be considered my strong suit. [67]In grade school I did moderately well, getting perhaps B's, sometimes B-pluses, in English and scoring perhaps in the sixtieth or seventieth percentile on achievement tests. [68]But those scores were not good enough to override the opinion that my true abilities lay in math and science, because in those areas I achieved A's and scored in the ninetieth percentile or higher.

[69]This was understandable. [70]Math is precise; there is only one correct answer. [71]Whereas, for me at least, the answers on English tests were always a judgment call, a matter of opinion and personal experience. [72]Those tests were constructed around items like fill-in-the-blank sentence completion, such as, "Even though Tom was ______, Mary thought he was ______." [73]And the correct answer always seemed to be the most bland combinations of thoughts, for example, "Even though Tom was shy, Mary thought he was charming," with the grammatical structure *even though* limiting the correct answer to some sort of semantic opposites, so you wouldn't get answers like, "Even though Tom was foolish, Mary thought he was ridiculous." [74]Well, according to my mother, there were very few limitations as to what Tom could have been and what Mary might have thought of him. [75]So I never did well on tests like that.

[76]The same was true with word analogies, pairs of words in which you were supposed to find some sort of logical, semantic relationship—for example, "*Sunset* is to *nightfall* as_____is to ______." [77]And here you would be presented with a list of four possible pairs, one of which showed the same kind of relationship: *red* is to *stoplight, bus* is to *arrival, chills* is to *fever, yawn* is to *boring.* [78]Well, I could never think that way. [79]I knew what the tests were asking, but I could not block out of my mind the images already created by the first pair, "*sunset* is to *nightfall*—and I would see a burst of colors against a darkening sky, the moon rising, the lowering of a curtain of stars. [80]And all the other pairs of words—*red, bus, stoplight, boring*—just threw up a mass of confusing images, making it impossible for me to sort out some thing as logical as saying: "A sunset precedes nightfall" is the same as "a chill precedes a fever." [81]The only way I would have gotten that answer right would have been to imagine an associative situation, for

example, my being disobedient and staying out past sunset, catching a chill at night, which turns into feverish pneumonia as punishment, which indeed did happen to me.

. . .

[82]Fortunately, I happen to be rebellious in nature and enjoy the challenge of disproving assumptions made about me. [83]I became an English major my first year in college, after being enrolled as pre-med. [84]I started writing nonfiction as a freelancer the week after I was told by my former boss that writing was my worst skill and I should hone my talents toward account management.

[85]But it wasn't until 1985 that I finally began to write fiction. [86]And at first I wrote using what I thought to be wittily crafted sentences, sentences that would finally prove I had mastery over the English language. [87]Here's an example from the first draft of a story that later made its way into *The Joy Luck Club*, but without this line: "That was my mental quandary in its nascent state." [88]A terrible line, which I can barely pronounce.

[89]Fortunately, for reasons I won't get into today, I later decided I should envision a reader for the stories I would write. [90]And the reader I decided upon was my mother, because these were stories about mothers. [91]So with this reader in mind—and in fact she did read my early drafts—I began to write stories using all the Englishes I grew up with: the English I spoke to my mother, which for lack of a better term might be described as "simple"; the English she used with me, which for lack of a better term might be described as "broken"; my translation of her Chinese, which could certainly be described as "watered down"; and what I imagined to be her translation of her Chinese if she could speak in perfect English, her internal language, and for that I sought to preserve the essence, but neither an English nor a Chinese structure. [92]I wanted to capture what language ability tests can never reveal: her intent, her passion, her imagery, the rhythms of her speech and the nature of her thoughts.

[93]Apart from what any critic had to say about my writing, I knew I had succeeded where it counted when my mother finished reading my book and gave me her verdict: "So easy to read."

After Reading Response: Respond to the following prompts in your reading/writing journal:

- Write a summary of the passage (see Module 1, page 34).
- Create a time/space order concept map that answers the following question: "How did Tan overcome barriers in her English language development?"

CONTINUED

PRACTICE 1 *CONTINUED*

Before and During Reading Questions:

Logical Order: Is this passage a narration or a process? Which transitions/signal words did the writer use?

Central Idea: What is the writer's central point?

Relevant Details: How does the linguistic relativity hypothesis apply to Keller's experience with language?

How does Keller illustrate the receptive-productive lag?

How do the stages of language development apply to Keller's experience?

What communication barriers did Keller face during her language development?

How did Keller overcome her barriers to language development?

Effective Language: What vivid words does the writer use to create images in the reader's mind?

Annie Sullivan's Letters about Educating Helen Keller

The following letters were written to Mrs. Sophia C. Hopkins, a matron at the Perkins Institute at which Miss Sullivan was a student before becoming Helen Keller's teacher.

March 6, 1887, Tuscumbia, Alabama [1]There's nothing pale or delicate about Helen. [2]She is large, strong, and ruddy, and as unrestrained in her movements as a young colt. [3]She has none of those nervous habits that are so noticeable and so distressing in blind children. [4]Her body is well formed and vigorous, and Mrs. Keller says she has not been ill a day since the illness that deprived her of her sight and hearing. [5]She has a fine head, and it is set on her shoulders just right. [6]Her face is hard to describe. [7]It is intelligent, but lacks mobility, or soul, or something. [8]Her mouth is large and finely shaped. [9]You see at a glance that she is blind. [10]One eye is larger than the other, and protrudes noticeably. [11]She rarely smiles; indeed, I have seen her smile only once or twice since I came. [12]She is unresponsive and even impatient of caresses from any one except her mother. [13]She is very quick-tempered and willful, and nobody, except her brother James, has attempted to control her. [14]The greatest problem I shall have to solve is how to discipline and control her without breaking her spirit. [15]I shall go rather slowly at first and try to win her love. [16]I shall not attempt to conquer her by force alone; but I shall insist on reasonable obedience from the start. [17]One thing that impresses everybody is Helen's tireless activity. [18]She is never still a moment. [19]She is here, there, and everywhere. [20]Her hands are in everything; but nothing holds her attention for long. [21]Dear child, her restless spirit gropes in the dark. [22]Her untaught, unsatisfied hands destroy whatever they touch because they do not know what else to do with things. [23]She helped me unpack my trunk when it came, and was delighted when she found the doll the little girls sent her. [24]I thought it a good opportunity to teach her her first word. [25]I spelled "d-o-l-l" slowly in her hand and pointed to the doll and nodded my head, which seems to be her sign for possession. [26]Whenever anybody gives her anything, she points to it, then to herself, and nods her head. [27]She looked puzzled and felt my hand, and I repeated the letters. [28]She imitated them very well and pointed to the doll. [29]Then I took the doll, meaning to give it back to her when she had made the letters; but she thought I meant to take it from her, and in an instant she was in a temper, and tried to seize the doll. [30]I shook my head and tried to form the letters with her fingers; but she got more and more angry. [31]I forced her into a chair and held her there until I was nearly exhausted. [32]Then it occurred to me that it was useless to continue the struggle—I must do something to turn the current of her thoughts. [33]I let her go, but refused to give up the doll. [34]I went downstairs and got some cake (she is very fond of sweets). [35]I showed Helen the cake and spelled "c-a-k-e" in her hand, holding the cake toward her. [36]Of course she wanted it and tried to take it; but I spelled the word again and patted her hand. [37]She made the letters rapidly, and I gave her the cake, which she ate in a great hurry, thinking, I suppose, that I might take it from her. [38]Then I showed her the doll and spelled the word again, holding the doll toward her as I held the cake. [39]She made the letters "d-o-l" and I made the other "l" and gave her the doll. [40]She ran downstairs with it and could not be induced to return to my room all day. [41]Yesterday I gave her a sewing-card to do. [42]I made the first row of vertical lines and let her feel it and notice that there were several rows of little holes. [43]She began to work delightedly and finished the card in a few minutes, and did it very neatly indeed. [44]I thought I would try another word; so I spelled "c-a-r-d" She made the "c-a," then stopped and thought, and making the sign for eating and pointing downward she pushed me toward the door, meaning that I must go downstairs for some cake. [45]The two letters "c-a," you see, had reminded her of Friday's "lesson"—not that she had any idea that cake was the name of the thing, but it was simply a matter of association, I suppose. [46]I finished the word "c-a-k-e" and obeyed her command. [47]She was delighted. [48]Then I spelled "d-o-l-l" and began to hunt for it. [49]She follows with her hands every motion you make, and she knew that I was looking for the doll. [50]She pointed down, meaning that the doll was downstairs. [51]I made the signs that she had used when she wished me to go for the cake, and pushed her toward the door. [52]She started forward, then hesitated a moment, evidently debating within herself whether she would go or not. [53]She decided to send me instead. [54]I shook my head and spelled "d-o-l-l" more emphatically, and opened the door for her; but she

CONTINUED

obstinately refused to obey. [55]She had not finished the cake she was eating, and I took it away, indicating that if she brought the doll I would give her back the cake. [56]She stood perfectly still for one long moment, her face crimson; then her desire for the cake triumphed, and she ran downstairs and brought the doll, and of course I gave her the cake, but could not persuade her to enter the room again.

March 20, 1887. [57]My heart is singing for joy this morning. [58]A miracle has happened! [59]The light of understanding has shone upon my little pupil's mind, and behold, all things are changed! [60]The wild little creature of two weeks ago has been transformed into a gentle child. [61]She is sitting by me as I write, her face serene and happy, crocheting a long red chain of Scotch wool. [62]She learned the stitch this week, and is very proud of the achievement. [63]When she succeeded in making a chain that would reach across the room, she patted herself on the arm and put the first work of her hands lovingly against her cheek. [64]She lets me kiss her now, and when she is in a particularly gentle mood, she will sit in my lap for a minute or two; but she does not return my caresses. [65]The great step—the step that counts—has been taken. [66] The little savage has learned her first lesson in obedience, and finds the yoke easy. [67]It now remains my pleasant task to direct and mold the beautiful intelligence that is beginning to stir in the child-soul. [68]Already people remark the change in Helen. [69]Her father looks in at us morning and evening as he goes to and from his office, and sees her contentedly stringing her beads or making horizontal lines on her sewing-card, and exclaims, "How quiet she is!" [70]When I came, her movements were so insistent that one always felt there was something unnatural and almost weird about her. [71]I have noticed also that she eats much less, a fact which troubles her father so much that he is anxious to get her home. [72]Helen has learned several nouns this week. [73]"M-u-g" and "m-i-l-k," have given her more trouble than other words. [74]When she spells "milk," she points to the mug, and when she spells "mug," she makes the sign for pouring or drinking, which shows that she has confused the words. [75]She has no idea yet that everything has a name. [76]Yesterday I had the little Negro boy come in when Helen was having her lesson, and learn the letters, too. [77]This pleased her very much and stimulated her ambition to excel Percy. [78]She was delighted if he made a mistake, and made him form the letter over several times. [79]When he succeeded in forming it to suit her, she patted him on his woolly head so vigorously that I thought some of his slips were intentional. [80]One day this week Captain Keller brought Belle, a setter of which he is very proud, to see us. [81]He wondered if Helen would recognize her old playmate. [82]Helen was giving Nancy a bath, and didn't notice the dog at first. [83]She usually feels the softest step and throws out her arms to ascertain if any one is near her. [84]Belle didn't seem very anxious to attract her attention. [85]I imagine she has been rather roughly handled sometimes by her little mistress. [86]The dog hadn't been in the room more than half a minute, however, before Helen began to sniff, and dumped the doll into the washbowl and felt about the room. [87]She stumbled upon Belle, who was crouching near the window where Captain Keller was standing. [88]It was evident that she recognized the dog; for she put her arms round her neck and squeezed her. [89]Then Helen sat down by her and began to manipulate her claws. [90]We couldn't think for a second what she was doing; but when we saw her make the letters "d-o-l-l" on her own fingers, we knew that she was trying to teach Belle to spell.

April 5, 1887. [91]I must write you a line this morning because something very important has happened. [92]Helen has taken the second great step in her education. [93]She has learned that everything has a name, and that the manual alphabet is the key to everything she wants to know. [94]In a previous letter I think I wrote you that "mug" and "milk" had given Helen more trouble than all the rest. [95]She confused the nouns with the verb "drink." [96]She didn't know the word for "drink," but went through the pantomime of drinking whenever she spelled "mug" or "milk." [97]This morning, while she was washing, she wanted to know the name for "water." [98]When she wants to know the name of anything, she points to it and pats my hand. [99]I spelled "w-a-t-e-r" and thought no more about it until after breakfast. [100]Then it occurred to me that with the help of this new word I might succeed in straightening out the "mug-milk" difficulty. [101]We went out to the pump-house, and I made Helen hold her mug under the spout while I pumped. [102]As the cold water gushed forth, filling the mug, I spelled "w-a-t-e-r" in Helen's free hand. [103]The word coming so close upon the sensation of cold water rushing over her hand seemed to startle her. [104]She dropped the mug and stood as one transfixed. [105]A new light came into her face. [106]She spelled "water" several times. [107]Then she dropped on the ground and asked for its name and pointed to the pump and the trellis, and suddenly turning round she asked for my name. [108]I spelled "Teacher." [109]Just then the nurse brought Helen's little sister into the pump-house, and Helen spelled "baby" and pointed to the nurse. [110]All the way back to the house she was highly excited, and learned the name of every object she touched, so that in a few hours she had added thirty new words to her vocabulary. [111]Here are some of them: *Door, open, shut, give, go, come,* and a great many more. [112]P. S.—I didn't finish my letter in time to get it posted last night; so I shall add a line. [113]Helen got up this morning like a radiant fairy. [114]She has flitted from object to object, asking the name of everything and kissing me for very gladness. [115]Last night when I got in bed, she stole into my arms of her own accord and kissed me for the first time, and I thought my heart would burst, so full was it of joy.

–*The Story of My Life: Helen Keller, Annie Sullivan.* New York: Grosset & Dunlap. 1905.

After Reading Response: Respond to the following prompts in your journal.

- Write a summary of the passage (see Module 1, page 34).
- Create a time/space order concept map that answers the following prereading questions:
    - How do the stages of language development apply to Keller's experience?
    - What communication barriers did Keller face during her language development?
    - How did Keller overcome her barriers to language development?

L3 Prewrite a Draft of a Thesis Statement Using Time and Space Order

Writers use time and space order to convey the central idea of a narration or a process.

To write a narration, limit your topic to an event that occurred during a specific time and in a particular place. Most likely, a writer has an opinion or attitude about the event. This attitude or opinion shapes the controlling point about the event. A writer also reveals an opinion in the description of the event and the place where the event takes place. The following topic sentence illustrates the use of time and space order to state a thesis statement for a narrative.

Narrative Thesis Statement:

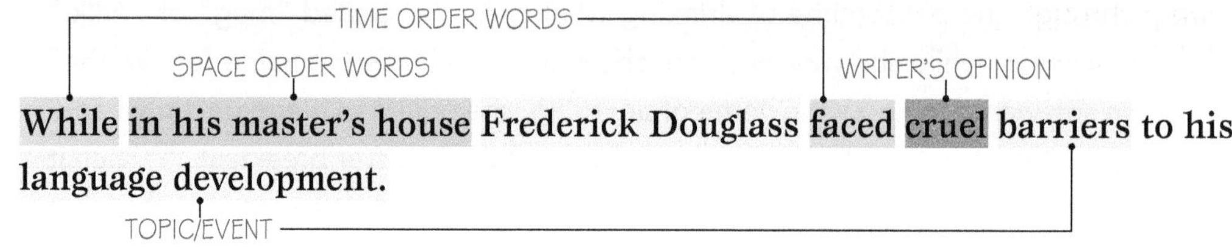

To write a process, limit your topic to a series of steps, phases, or directions. Many times, a step or phase of a process is closely tied to where it occurs. Most likely, a writer has an opinion or attitude about the process. This attitude or opinion shapes the controlling point of your main idea. A writer also reveals an opinion in the description of how or why the process unfolds or develops.

Process Thesis Statement:

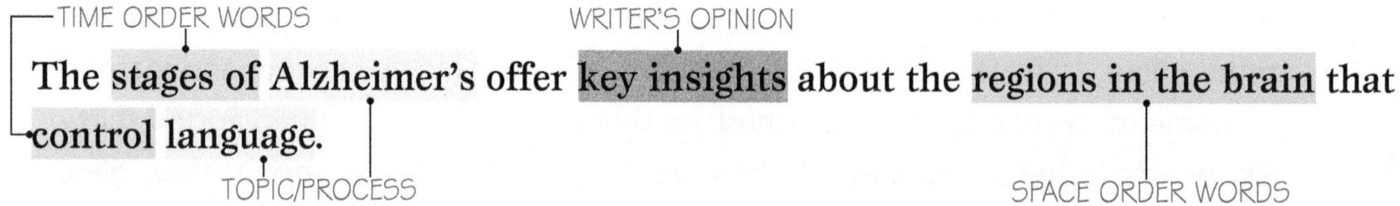

To draft a central idea, a writer may brainstorm key words that signal time and space, and reflect an opinion. These words narrow the topic into a logical narrative or process. The writer then combines these words to compose a thesis statement. Consider the preceding examples. Both deal with the general topic "barriers to language development." However, the narrative thesis statement focuses on Frederick Douglass while the process thesis statement focuses on the stages of Alzheimer's.

Example

Your instructor has asked you to respond to the readings on pages 303–315. You are to write an essay that addresses the guiding question: "How do we overcome barriers to communication?" The first part of the assignment is to generate a thesis statement for the essay. You need to decide whether you will use narration or process to make your point. Use the following steps to brainstorm your thesis statement.

Topic: Ways to overcome barriers in communication

1. Narrow Topic: ______

2. Choose Narration or Process: ______

3. Identify Time or Space Order Signal Words: ______

5. Combine into a Draft of Thesis Statement: ______

Explanation

Compare your answers to Reagan's think-aloud.

Annotating the passages helped me focus my topic. I don't want to just retell how Keller and Tan learned language. I want to show that specific steps can help anyone with any barrier learn language. So my narrowed topic is the process or ways people overcome their own barriers. The time order word in my thesis statement is **steps.** I did not use a space order signal word because these steps can be taken anywhere by anyone. My thesis statement: There are steps people have taken to overcome their own barriers in communication.

Practice 2

Prewrite a Draft of a Thesis Statement Using Time and Space Order

In your reading/writing journal, identify the steps you used to write a thesis statement using time or space order. How did your thesis statement differ from Reagan's?

LO 4 Prewrite to Generate Relevant Details Using Time and Space Order

To generate details based on time and space, writers often ask the reporter's questions *who, what, when, where, why*, and *how*. Who is the person or people involved in a narrative? Who is carrying out the steps of a process? What are the specific actions that occur? What sensory details (such as sight, sound, smell, taste, or touch) are involved? When does each action occur? Where does the action occur? Why is this step or event important? How does the event unfold, or how are specific steps accomplished? Asking and answering these questions generates details that help a writer to narrate an event or explain a process. Usually, time order and space order transitions and signal words introduce these details. Some major and minor details may also explain the writer's opinion about the event or process. Master readers and writers often use a concept map to organize answers to the reporter's questions. A time and space order graphic organizer helps a writer create or access vivid details to make or support a point. At this point in the reading/writing process, a writer focuses on brainstorming details. In the next step, those details can be organized into a smooth and logical flow of ideas

Example

Assume your class is continuing to work on the essay addressing the guiding question "How do we overcome obstacles in order to communicate?" Now your assignment is to return to the texts to identify details that you will use to support your thesis statement and create a concept map to organize your ideas for the essay. Fill in the title with your narrowed topic and the columns with key details. Be sure to include relevant sensory details in each column.

Time/Space Order Concept Map: ______________________					
When	**Who**	**What**	**Where**	**How**	**Why**

Explanation

Compare your responses to Reagan's think-aloud.

Completing this chart helped me pull the specific details from the reading passages that I wanted to refer to in my own essay. Also, the chart made me think about which words to choose for vivid sensory details as I draft my essay. While I didn't really choose to list **where** or space order words separately in the chart, I noticed that space order words are a part of the process. For example, Annie Sullivan spelled words "in" or "on" Helen Keller's palm. And Amy Tan heard broken English "in" her home, and learned Standard English in her studies "in" school. Here are the details I generated using the concept map.

When	Who	What	Sensory Details
First	babies and those like Keller	learn words	blind and deaf spelling in palms
Second		recognize and name things	cold water flowing over hand while word **water** spelled in her hand
Third	Not native speaking, like Tan	learn sentences and proper grammar	Standard and broken English

Practice 3

Prewrite to Generate Relevant Details Using Time and Space Order

In your reading/writing journal, identify the steps needed to create relevant details to support a thesis statement. Identify the steps Reagan went through as she annotated the texts and created her graphic organizer. How did your concept maps differ?

L5 Compose a Draft Using Logical Order: Time and Space Order

Once you have brainstormed details based on time and space order to compose a narration or a process, you are ready to begin the drafting process. First, review the concept map you completed with the details from the reading and your own insights or response. As you review your concept map, move details as needed into the most logical order. Add details if needed. Also, include time and space order signal words to guide your reader through the narration or process. Master writers create several drafts to achieve a logical order and smooth flow of ideas.

Example

Assume you are still working toward writing an essay that answers the guiding question "How do we overcome barriers to communication?" On your own paper, write a draft of your essay.

Explanation

Compare your answer to Reagan's essay and think-aloud.

As I began to draft my essay, I discovered that the details I generated in my concept map made up the body of my essay. However, I decided that I needed to give my reader some background information. So I drafted a short paragraph to introduce my topic. Then, the second paragraph offered some background about the types of barriers people face using Helen Keller and Amy Tan as examples. Then, the third paragraph gives the specific steps people can take to overcome these types of barriers. The first sentence of the third paragraph is my thesis sentence. I also included transitions such as **first, second step,** and **third.** I generated these transitions when I brainstormed details using the concept map.

Reagan Earnest
Professor Powell
Interpersonal Communication 101
20 Sept. 2015

Overcoming Communication Barriers

Language is a major part of communication between people. As children, we learn to speak slowly—first with noises, then with simple words, and eventually with sentences. It is not known for certain whether language precedes mental development or whether mental development takes place first.

Sometimes, it is difficult for very young children to make themselves understood because of their lack of ability to speak well. Young children are not the only people who struggle with this: often people who are not native English speakers, or whose parents are not, also have difficulty with language. As Amy Tan describes in her essay "Mother Tongue," non-native speakers of English actually have to master several forms of the language—Standard English and the simple or broken English spoken at home. There are also people who, whether because they are mute, deaf—or both, like Helen Keller—or in some other way kept from being able to speak properly, do not have the physical ability to communicate using words.

There are steps people have taken to overcome their own barriers in communication. First, they learn to use words. In the textbook selection "Language," Ciccarelli and White describe the stages we go through from birth to age 6 to learn to use words correctly by interacting with others. However, people who struggle with language barriers for various reasons have to take other steps: Annie Sullivan, for example, taught Helen Keller—because

CONTINUED

EXPLANATION *CONTINUED*

she was deaf, blind, and therefore, unable to speak—how to use the method of "spelling" on the palms of hands. The second step in the process outlined by Ciccarelli and White is learning how to recognize things and give them their proper names. Keller's breakthrough moment with language came when she understood that the letters tapped into her hand by Sullivan represented the word *water* to name the object that was flowing over her hands. Third, they learn how to use complete sentences and proper grammar, as in the case of Amy Tan, who worked hard to excel in her English studies and overcome her difficulties with it.

People have discovered ways to "bridge" these "gaps" in communication as did Keller and Tan. These women prove that a lack of ability to communicate does not indicate that a person is not well developed mentally, but that an individual may have an obstacle that has kept him or her from learning to effectively communicate. Their struggles also illustrate that people are able to overcome their difficulties and learn how to communicate in a way that allows them to be not only understood, but esteemed.

Practice 4

Compose a Draft Using Logical Order: Time and Space Order

In your reading/writing journal, identify the steps you took to write your draft. Identify the steps Reagan took as she wrote her draft. How are your drafts different? How are they similar? What can you apply from Reagan's method to your own writing in the future?

Revise and Proofread for Effective Language with Time and Space Order

Precise word choice communicates exact meaning. Words chosen for a specific emotional or visual impact create strong images in the reader's mind and carry out the writer's purpose. Master readers and writers understand and use the **denotative** and **connotative** meanings of words to grasp and create vivid images and impressions.

> **Denotation** refers to the exact, literal, or neutral meaning of a word—the dictionary meaning.
>
> **Connotation** refers to the associations or emotional connections implied by a word.
>
> A **figure of speech** is a word or phrase that departs from literal meaning to create a special effect or fresh meaning.

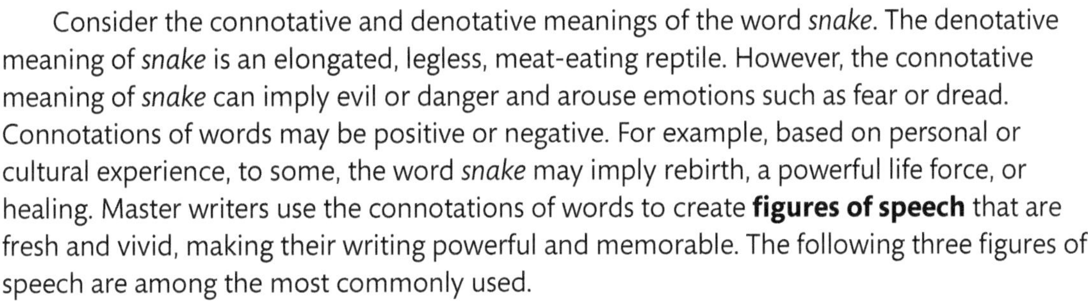

Consider the connotative and denotative meanings of the word *snake*. The denotative meaning of *snake* is an elongated, legless, meat-eating reptile. However, the connotative meaning of *snake* can imply evil or danger and arouse emotions such as fear or dread. Connotations of words may be positive or negative. For example, based on personal or cultural experience, to some, the word *snake* may imply rebirth, a powerful life force, or healing. Master writers use the connotations of words to create **figures of speech** that are fresh and vivid, making their writing powerful and memorable. The following three figures of speech are among the most commonly used.

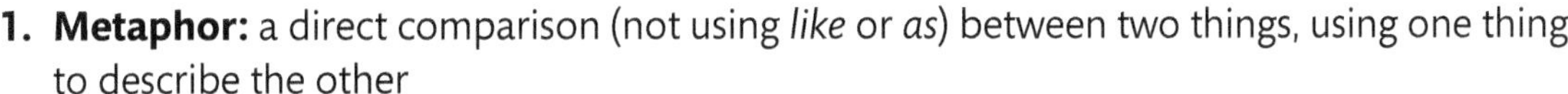

1. **Metaphor:** a direct comparison (not using *like* or *as*) between two things, using one thing to describe the other

   Forgiveness is a well of water.

   A wave of grief swept over him.

2. **Simile:** an indirect comparison between two things, usually using *like, as,* or *than*

   Daniel, like a giant oak, stands firm and tall.

   Life blooms and fades as quickly as a flower.

3. **Onomatopoeia:** a word that imitates the sound it represents

   The car zoomed around the racetrack.

   The motor purred with power.

   The water hissed as it splashed on the hot burner.

Example

A. Review the readings "Language" (page 303), "Mother Tongue" by Amy Tan (page 307), and "Annie Sullivan's Letters about Educating Helen Keller" (page 312). Choose one passage. Identify an expression that uses connotative meanings or figures of speech. Then discuss the effect of each figure of speech on you as a reader.

Essay Title: ____________________

Words/Connotative Meanings: ____________________

____

____

Figure of Speech: ____________________

____

____

Effect: ____________________

____

____

B. Review the draft of the essay you composed in response to the guiding question "How do we overcome barriers in communication?" Choose two words or expressions to revise using connotative meaning or a figure of speech.

Original Expression: ____________________

____

____

____

____

____

____

Revised for Connotative Meaning or Figure of Speech: ____________________

____

____

____

____

____

____

Explanation

Compare your answers to Reagan's think-aloud.

In the last paragraph of my essay, I used the phrase "bridge these gaps in communication." I now see that this is a metaphor. So I decided to revise another expression to continue the use of the bridge metaphor. In the last sentence I revised the phrase "able to overcome their difficulties" to "able to build new foundations that allow them to span their difficulties." I liked this metaphor so much that I wanted to use it earlier all through the essay, too. So I revised the following sentences:

In the first paragraph, I revised the first sentence from "Language is a major part of communication between people" to "Language is the main bridge of communication between people."

In the second paragraph, I revised the last sentence from "...do not have the physical ability to communicate using words" to "do not have the physical ability to build a bridge with words to communicate."

In the third paragraph, I also revised the following sentence "First, they learn to use words" to "First, they build up their knowledge about words and how to use them."

I could have made more revisions to create more figures of speech about building communication bridges, but I didn't want to include so many that my reader became bored with the metaphor.

Practice 5

Revise and Proofread for Effective Language with Time and Space Order

In your reading/writing journal, list the steps needed to revise, edit, and proofread an essay. What did Reagan do as part of her revision process? How did your processes differ? What can you learn from Reagan's revision that you can apply to your own editing process in the future?

Workshop: Comprehend and Create Time and Space Order

Assume you are continuing your study of the theme "barriers to communication" in your college communication course. The following passages make up a capstone reading assignment. Your capstone writing assignment is to write an essay in response to the same guiding question, "How do we overcome barriers to communication?" You may also be asked to make connections among these passages and the ones you have already read in this module. To complete this assignment, skim the prereading questions, read the following passages, and complete the writing activities that follow.

Do Women and Men Speak Different Languages?

[1]Linguist Deborah Tannen (1990, 1994a, 1994b, 2010) argues that women and men are members of different speech communities. According to Tannen, women and men have different communication styles and different communication goals. Just as people from different cultures speak different dialects, women and men speak different *genderlects*. Women, maintains Tannen, speak and hear a language of intimacy and connection, whereas men speak and hear a language of status and independence. As a result, conversations between men and women are often like conversations between two people from different cultures and they produce a similar result: a great deal of misunderstanding (see also Shem & Surrey, 1998). But while Tannen's stories about miscommunications between women and men frequently bring smiles of recognition to people's faces, there are other researchers who question the extent to which women and men communicate differently (Smith, 2007). For example, some studies show few communication differences between women and men. Instead, they found that for both women and men, communication patterns and styles were influenced by a number of situational factors, including the sex of the person with whom they were speaking, the context of the conversation, and the perceived status of both the speaker and the listener (Holmstrom, 2009; MacGeorge et al., 1999). Similarly, in a study of listeners' reactions to friends' self-disclosures, Leaper and colleagues (1995) found few differences between female and male listeners, with the exception that female listeners gave more "active understanding" responses (e.g., explicit acknowledgment of the speaker's feelings or opinions) when the speaker was a female friend (see also Ridgeway & Smith-Lovin, 1999). Findings such as these remind us that communication is an *interactive* process affected by a variety of factors, of which gender is only one.

[2]Nevertheless, many researchers have observed that gender inequality characterizes much everyday communication, reflecting differences in men's and women's life experiences, social status, and power (Henley, Hamilton, & Thorne,

1985; Lakoff, 1990; Nichols, 1986). For example, in cross-sex conversations, researchers have found that men often do more of the talking, which is a direct result of the fact that in many situations (e.g., business meetings), they have more opportunity to express their opinions. Men also have more success than women in getting a conversation focused on topics they introduce. Moreover, when men speak, listeners of both sexes more actively attend to them than to women speakers (McConnell-Ginet, 1989; Ridgeway & Smith-Levin, 1999). Research suggests that this may be due to the fact that men are more likely than women to use assertive speech (Leaper & Ayres, 2007), and men interrupt women more than women interrupt men (Leaper & Ayres, 2007). Women, though, are more likely than men to use intensifiers such as "really" and "very" (Mulac, 2006), and they are less likely than men to use profanity (Jay, 2009). The nonverbal communication of men in cross-sex interaction can also best be described as dominant. For instance, men control more space than women, and they touch and stare at women more. Women, in contrast, tend to avert their eyes when stared at by men, but they also smile and laugh more than men whether they are happy or not, a gesture that can be viewed as both social and submissive (McQuiston & Morris, 2009; Ridgeway & Smith-Lovin, 1999).

[3]These findings fly in the face of the common stereotype that women are more talkative than men. Research on same-sex conversation, however, does show that in all female groups, women talk more than men do in all-male groups. While men prefer to talk to one another about work, sports, or activities they have in common, women tend to prefer to talk to one another about more personal topics (Bischoping, 1993). In addition, studies of same-sex talk indicate that women's conversations are less individualistic and more dynamic than men's conversations, with women attempting to introduce topics and signaling active listening (nodding, making noise such as *"mmbmm"*) (Helweg-Larsen et al., 2004; McConnell-Ginet, 1989; Ridgeway & Smith-Lovin, 1999). Interestingly, interruptions are frequent in women's conversations, but researchers have found that these interruptions are typically supportive rather than aggressive or hostile and often function to help the speaker put into words something she is having difficulty expressing (DeVault, 1986; Hayden, 1994; Ridgeway & Smith-Lovin, 1999).

[4]Unfortunately, women's conversations have traditionally been negatively stereotyped and parodied. It is commonly believed, for example, that women devote the majority of their communications with one another to gossip and other frivolous matters, whereas men's communications with one another are more serious and, therefore, "important." Indeed, any negative traits and consequences of communication differences have been associated almost exclusively with women, in large part because men have had greater power to define acceptable standards of communication. In this way, women's communications have been considered not only different from men's, but also typically inferior.

—Renzetti, *Women, Men, and Society*, 6th ed., 2012 Pearson Education, Inc., pp. 147–149.

CONTINUED

Sex, Lies, and Conversation: Why Is It So Hard for Men and Women to Talk to Each Other?

Deborah Tannen

[1]I was addressing a small gathering in a suburban Virginia living room—a women's group that had invited men to join them. Throughout the evening, one man had been particularly talkative, frequently offering ideas and anecdotes, while his wife sat silently beside him on the couch. Toward the end of the evening, I commented that women frequently complain that their husbands don't talk to them. This man quickly concurred. He gestured toward his wife and said, "She's the talker in our family." The room burst into laughter; the man looked puzzled and hurt. "It's true," he explained. "When I come home from work I have nothing to say. If she didn't keep the conversation going, we'd spend the whole evening in silence."

[2]This episode crystallizes the irony that although American men tend to talk more than women in public situations, they often talk less at home. And this pattern is wreaking havoc with marriage.

[3]The pattern was observed by political scientist Andrew Hacker in the late '70s. Sociologist Catherine Kohler Riessman reports in her new book "Divorce Talk" that most of the women she interviewed—but only a few of the men—gave lack of communication as the reason for their divorces. Given the current divorce rate of nearly 50 percent, that amounts to millions of cases in the United States every year—a virtual epidemic of failed conversation.

[4]In my own research, complaints from women about their husbands most often focused not on tangible inequities such as having given up the chance for a career to accompany a husband to his, or doing far more than their share of daily life-support work like cleaning, cooking, social arrangements and errands. Instead, they focused on communication: "He doesn't listen to me," "He doesn't talk to me." I found, as Hacker observed years before, that most wives want their husbands to be, first and foremost, conversational partners, but few husbands share this expectation of their wives.

[5]In short, the image that best represents the current crisis is the stereotypical cartoon scene of a man sitting at the breakfast table with a newspaper held up in front of his face, while a woman glares at the back of it, wanting to talk.

Linguistic Battle of the Sexes

[6]How can women and men have such different impressions of communication in marriage? Why the widespread imbalance in their interests and expectations?

[7]In the April issue of *American Psychologist*, Stanford University's Eleanor Maccoby reports the results of her own and others' research showing that children's

development is most influenced by the social structure of peer interactions. Boys and girls tend to play with children of their own gender, and their sex-separate groups have different organizational structures and interactive norms.

[8]I believe these systematic differences in childhood socialization make talk between women and men like cross-cultural communication, heir to all the attraction and pitfalls of that enticing but difficult enterprise. My research on men's and women's conversations uncovered patterns similar to those described for children's groups.

from My English

Julia Alvarez

. . . [1]Soon, I was talking up an English storm. "Did you eat English parrot?" my grandfather asked one Sunday. I had just enlisted yet one more patient servant to listen to my rendition of "Peter Piper picked a peck of pickled peppers" at breakneck pace. "Huh?" I asked impolitely in English, putting him in his place. *Cat got your tongue? No big deal! So there! Take that! Holy Toledo!* (Our teacher's favorite "curse word.") *Go jump in the lake! Really dumb. Golly. Gosh.* Slang, clichés, sayings, hotshot language that our teacher called, ponderously, idiomatic expressions. Riddles, jokes, puns, conundrums. *What is yellow and goes click-click? Why did the chicken cross the road? See you later, alligator.* How wonderful to call someone an alligator and not be scolded for being disrespectful. In fact, they were supposed to say back, *In a while, crocodile.*

[2]There was also a neat little trick I wanted to try on an English-speaking adult back home. I had learned it from Elizabeth, my smart-alecky friend in the fourth grade, whom I alternately worshiped and resented. I'd ask her a question that required an explanation, and she'd answer, "Because…" "Elizabeth, how come you didn't go to Isabel's birthday party?" "Because…" "Why didn't you put your name in your reader?" "Because…" I thought that was such a cool way to get around having to come up with answers. So, I practiced saying it under my breath, planning for the day I could use it on an unsuspecting English-speaking adult.

[3]One Sunday at our extended family dinner, my grandfather sat down at the children's table to chat with us. He was famous, in fact, for the way he could

CONTINUED

carry on adult conversations with his grandchildren. He often spoke to us in English so that we could practice speaking it outside the classroom. He was a Cornell man, a United Nations representative from our country. He gave speeches in English. Perfect English, my mother's phrase. That Sunday, he asked me a question. I can't even remember what it was because I wasn't really listening but lying in wait for my chance. "Because...," I answered him. Papito wanted for a second for the rest of my sentence and then gave me a thumbnail grammar lesson. "Because has to be followed by a clause."

4"Why's that?" I asked, nonplussed.

5"Because," he winked. "Just because."

6A beginning wordsmith, I had so much left to learn: sometimes it was disheartening. Once Tío Gus, the family intellectual, put a speck of salt on my grandparents' big dining table during Sunday dinner. He said, "Imagine that this whole table is the human brain. Then this teensy grain is all we ever use of our own intelligence." He enumerated geniuses who had perhaps two grains, maybe three: Einstein, Michelangelo, da Vinci, Beethoven. We children believed him. It was the kind of impossible fact we thrived on, proving as it did that the world out there was not drastically different from the one we were making up in our heads.

7Later, at home, Mami said that you had to take what her younger brother said "with a grain of salt." I thought she was still referring to Tío Gus's demonstration, and I tried to puzzle out what she was saying. Finally, I asked what she meant. "Taking what someone says with a grain of salt is an idiomatic expression in English," she explained. It was pure voodoo is what it was—what I later learned poetry could also do: a grain of salt could symbolize both the human brain and a condiment for human nonsense. And it could be itself, too: a grain of salt to flavor a bland plate of American food.

8When we arrived in New York, I was shocked. A country where everyone spoke English! These people must be smarter, I thought. Maids, waiters, taxi drivers, doormen, bums on the street, all spoke this difficult language. It took some time before I understood that Americans were not necessarily a smarter, superior race. It was as natural for them to learn their mother tongue as it was for a little Dominican baby to learn Spanish. It came with "mother's milk," my mother explained, and for a while I thought a mother tongue was a mother tongue because you got it from your mother's milk along with the protein and vitamins.

9Soon it wasn't so strange that everyone was speaking English instead of Spanish. I learned not to hear it as English, but as sense. I no longer strained to understand, I understood. I relaxed in this second language. Only when someone with a heavy southern or British accent spoke in a movie, or at church when the priest droned his sermon—only then did I experience that little catch of anxiety. I worried that I would not be able to understand, that I wouldn't be able to "keep up" with the voice speaking in this acquired language. I would be like those people from the Bible we had studied in religion class, whom I imagined standing at the foot of an enormous tower that looked just like the skyscrapers around me. They had been punished for their pride by being made to speak different languages so that they didn't understand what anyone was saying.

10But at the foot of those towering New York skyscrapers, I began to understand more and more—not less and less—English. In sixth grade, I had one of the first in a lucky line of great English teachers who began to nurture in me a love of language, a love that had been there since my childhood of listening closely to words. Sister Maria Generosa did not make our class interminably diagram sentences from a workbook or learn a catechism of grammar rules. Instead, she asked us to write little stories imagining we were snowflakes, birds, pianos, a stone in the pavement, a star in the sky. What would it feel like to be a flower with roots in the ground? If the clouds could talk, what would they say? She had an expressive, dreamy look that was accentuated by the wimple that framed her face.

11Supposing, just supposing...My mind would take off, soaring into possibilities, a flower with roots, a star in the sky, a cloud full of sad, sad tears, a piano crying out each time its back was tapped, music only to our ears.

12Sister Maria stood at the chalkboard. Her chalk was always snapping in two because she wrote with such energy, her whole habit shaking with the swing of her arm, her hand tap-tap-tapping on the board. "Here's a simple sentence: 'The snow fell.'" Sister pointed with her chalk, her eyebrows lifted, her wimple poked up. Sometimes I could see wisps of gray hair that strayed from under her headdress. "But watch what happens if we put an adverb at the beginning and a prepositional phrase at the end: 'Gently, the snow fell on the bare hills.'"

13I thought about the snow. I saw how it might fall on the hills, tapping lightly on the bare branches of trees. Softly, it would fall on the cold, bare fields. On toys children had left out in the yard, and on cars and on little birds and on people out late walking on the streets. Sister Marie filled the chalkboard with snowy print, on and on, handling and shaping and moving the language, scribbling all over the board until English, those verbal gadgets, those tricks and turns of phrases, those little fixed units and counters, became a charged, fluid mass that carried me in its great fluent waves, rolling and moving onward, to deposit me on the shores of my new homeland. I was no longer a foreigner with no ground to stand on. I had landed in the English language.

—"My English" by Julia Alvarez, from *Something to Declare*, published by Plume, an imprint of Penguin Random House, in 1999, and originally in hardcover by Algonquin Books of Chapel Hill.

Preread: Survey and Question

What does the term *genderlects* mean?

How do men hear and speak? (See "Do Men and Women Speak Different Languages?")

How do women hear and speak? (See "Do Men and Women Speak Different Languages?")

How do men and women speak in "cross-sex" conversations?

According to Tannen, in the passage from "Sex, Lies, and Conversation," how do men communicate in private? How do they communicate in public?

How do Tannen's observations of children communicating fit into the stages of language development? (See "Language," page 303.)

How is Julia Alvarez's experience in learning language similar to or different from Amy Tan's?

How were the teaching methods of Helen Keller's teacher Annie Sullivan similar to or different from the teaching methods of Julia Alvarez's teacher Sister Maria Generosa?

What are the various barriers to learning language that you have read about in this module?

In what ways are the solutions to these barriers common?

What steps could be taken to overcome any barrier in communication?

Read and Annotate

As you read, annotate key ideas, particularly those details that answer your prereading questions.

Recite, Review, and Brainstorm

Recite and **Review** the information. Paraphrase ideas. Summarize the most important parts. **Brainstorm** ideas for your written response to the passage. Answer your prereading questions. *Freewrite* or *map* the relationship among answers to questions or ideas you have annotated in the text. *Outline* or *list* key ideas and details in blocks of thought. Identify the central point you want to make. Use your own paper.

Write a Draft of Your Response

Using the ideas you generated by brainstorming, compose a draft of your response. Use your own paper.

Revise Your Draft

Once you have created a draft of a time/space order response, read it over to answer the questions in the "Questions for Revising a Time/Space Order Essay" box that follows. Indicate your answers by annotating your paper. If you answer "yes" to a question, underline, check, or circle examples. If you answer "no" to a question, write needed information in the margins and draw lines to indicate the placement of additional details. Revise your essay based on your reflection. (*Hint:* Experienced writers create several drafts as they focus on one or two questions per draft.)

Step by Step: Questions for Revising a Time/Space Order Essay

- ☐ Have I stated or implied a focused central idea?
- ☐ Have I stated or implied the specific points of time and space order?
- ☐ Is the order of the specific points clear? Have I used strong transitions of time and space order?
- ☐ Have I used concrete details to make my point?
- ☐ Have I made my point with adequate details?
- ☐ Have I included only the details that are relevant to my topic sentence?
- ☐ Have I used figurative language to make my point clear to my readers?

Proofread Your Draft

Once you have made any revisions to your essay that may be needed, proofread your essay to eliminate careless errors.

Reading and Writing Assignments

MySkillsLab™
Complete this Exercise
on myskillslab.com

Reading and Writing for Everyday Life

Assume you are the leader of a youth group such as Girl Scouts, Boy Scouts, or a YMCA program and you host a blog to share information with your group. You plan on sharing the following information from a government Website with your youth group. Read the information and write an article for your blog about the steps youth can take to safely socialize online.

KIDS AND SOCIALIZING ONLINE

Among the pitfalls that come with online socializing are sharing too much information or posting comments, photos, or videos that can damage a reputation or hurt someone's feelings. Applying real-world judgment can help minimize those risks.

Kids should post only what they're comfortable with others seeing. Some of your child's profile may be seen by a broader audience than you—or they—are comfortable with, even if privacy settings are high. Encourage your child to think about the language they use online, and to think before posting pictures and videos, or altering photos posted by someone else. Employers, college admissions officers, coaches, teachers, and the police may view your child's posts.

Remind kids that once they post it, they can't take it back. Even if you delete the information from a site, you have little control over older versions that may exist on other people's computers and may circulate online.

Tell your kids not to impersonate someone else. Let your kids know that it's wrong to create sites, pages, or posts that seem to come from someone else, like a teacher, a classmate, or someone they made up.

Help your kids understand what information should stay private. Tell your kids why it's important to keep some things—about themselves, family members, and friends—to themselves. Information like their Social Security number, street address, phone number, and family financial information—say, bank account or credit card numbers—is private and should stay that way.

Talk to your teens about avoiding sex talk online. Research shows that teens who don't talk about sex with strangers online are less likely to come in contact with predators. In fact, researchers have found that predators usually don't pose as children or teens, and most teens who are contacted by adults they don't know find it creepy. Teens should not hesitate to ignore or block them.

Encourage Online Manners: Politeness counts. You teach your kids to be polite offline; talk to them about being courteous online as well. Texting may seem fast and impersonal, yet courtesies like "pls" and "ty" (for *please* and *thank you*) are common text terms.

Tone it down. Using all caps, long rows of exclamation points, or large bolded fonts are the online equivalent of yelling. Most people don't appreciate a rant.

Cc: and Reply all: with care. Suggest that your kids resist the temptation to send a message to everyone on their contact list.

Limit Access to Your Kids' Profiles: Use privacy settings. Many social networking sites and chat rooms have adjustable privacy settings, so you can restrict who has access to your kids' profiles. Talk to your kids about the importance of these settings, and your expectations for who should be allowed to view their profile.

Set high privacy preferences on your kids' chat and video chat accounts, as well. Most chat programs allow parents to control whether people on their kids' contact list can see their status, including whether they're online. Some chat and email accounts allow parents to determine who can send messages to their kids, and block anyone not on the list.

Create a safe screen name. Encourage your kids to think about the impression that screen names can make. A good screen name won't reveal much about how old they are, where they live, or their gender. For privacy purposes, your kids' screen names should not be the same as their email addresses.

Review your child's friends list. You may want to limit your children's online "friends" to people they actually know.

Know what your kids are doing. Get to know the social networking sites your kids use so you understand their activities. If you're concerned about risky online behavior, you may want to search the social sites they use to see what information they're posting. Are they pretending to be someone else? Try searching by their name, nickname, school, hobbies, grade, or community.

Ask your kids who they're in touch with online. Just as you want to know who your kids' friends are offline, it's a good idea to know who they're talking to online.

Encourage your kids to trust their guts if they have suspicions. Encourage them to tell you if they feel threatened by someone or uncomfortable because of something online. You can then help them report concerns to the police and to the social networking site. Most of these sites have links for users to report abusive, suspicious, or inappropriate behavior.

—Kids and Socializing Online, OnGuardOnline.gov, Homeland Security, August 26, 2014

Reading and Writing for College Life

Assume you are taking a college sociology class. You are expected to respond in writing to a passage in your textbook about group behavior. You have decided to analyze the way people in small groups engage in meaningful discussions. Read the following passage, and write an essay that describes how to best make a discussion meaningful.

12 The Art of Thinking: a Guide to Critical Thought

MAKING DISCUSSION MEANINGFUL

At its best, discussion deepens understanding and promotes problem solving and decision-making. At its worst, it frays nerves, creates animosity, and leaves important issues unresolved. Unfortunately, the most prominent models for discussion in contemporary culture—radio and TV talk shows—often produce the latter effects. Many hosts demand that their guests answer complex questions with simple "yes" or "no" answers. If the guests respond that way, they are attacked for oversimplifying. If, instead, they try to offer a balanced answer, the host shouts, "You're not answering the question." Guests who agree with the host are treated warmly; others are dismissed as ignorant or dishonest. As often as not, when two guests are debating, each takes a turn interrupting while the other shouts, "Let me finish." Neither shows any desire to learn from the other. Typically, as the show draws to a close, the host thanks the participants for a "vigorous debate."

In contrast, here is a simple guideline for ensuring that the discussions you engage in—in the classroom, on the job, or at home—are more civil, meaningful, and productive. When the participants don't listen to one another, discussion becomes little more than serial monologue—each person taking a turn at speaking while the rest ignore what is being said. This can happen quite unintentionally because the mind can process ideas faster than the fastest speaker can deliver them. Your mind may get tired of waiting and wander about aimlessly like a dog off its leash. In such cases, instead of listening to what is being said, you may think about the speaker's clothing or hairstyle or look outside the window and observe what is happening there. Even when you are making a serious effort to listen, it is easy to lose focus. If the speaker's words trigger an unrelated memory, you may slip away to that earlier time and place. If the speaker says something you disagree with, you may begin framing a reply. The best way to maintain your attention is to be alert for such distractions and to resist them. Strive to enter the speaker's fame of mind and understand each sentence as it is spoken and to connect it with previous sentences. Whenever you realize your mind is wandering, drag it back to the task.

—Adapted from Ruggiero, *The Art of Thinking: a Guide to Critical Thought*, 10th ed. Pearson Education, 2012, pp. 12–14.

Reading and Writing for Working Life

Assume you are a member of a human resource team at a local business. You are writing a piece that will appear in next month's company newsletter. Read the following text. Then write an article that explains the importance of conflict management and applies the process to the following situations: (1) A customer dissatisfied with service; (2) An employee dissatisfied with his or her performance review by management; (3) A dispute between employees about shared office space.

Managing CONFLICT through COMMUNICATION

A conflict is an emotional state that arises when the behavior of one person interferes with that of another. Conflict is inevitable whenever people live or work together. Not all conflict is bad; in fact, airing feelings and coming to some form of resolution over differences can sometimes strengthen relationships. Conflict resolution and successful conflict management form a systematic approach to resolving differences fairly and constructively, rather than allowing them to fester. The goal of conflict resolution is to solve differences peacefully and creatively. Here are some strategies for conflict resolution.

1 Identify the problem or issues. Talk with each other to clarify exactly what the conflict or problem is. Try to understand both sides of the problem. In this first stage, you must say what you want and listen to what the other person wants. Focus on using "I" messages and avoid using any blaming "you" messages. Be an active listener—repeat what the other person has said and ask questions for clarification or additional information.

2 Generate several possible solutions. Base your search for solutions on the goals and interests identified in the first step. Come up with several different alternatives, and avoid evaluating any of them until you have finished brainstorming.

3 Evaluate the alternative solutions. Discard any that are unacceptable to either of you, and keep narrowing down the solutions to one or two that seem to work for both parties. Be honest about your concerns, but also be open to compromise.

4 Decide on the best solution. Choose an alternative that is acceptable to both parties. You both need to be committed to the decision for this solution to be effective.

5 Implement the solution. Discuss how the decision will be carried out. Establish who is responsible to do what and when. The solution stands a better chance of working if you agree on the plans for implementing it.

6 Follow up. Evaluate whether the solution is working. Gather feedback from those involved. If something is not working as planned, or if circumstances have changed, discuss revising the plan. Remember that both parties must agree to any changes to the plan, as they did with the original.

–Adapted from Donatelle, *Health: The Basics*, 11th ed. Pearson Education, Inc. 2015, p. 143.

Review Test

MySkillsLab™
Complete this Exercise on myskillslab.com

Score (Number Correct) _____ × 10 = _____%

Time and Space Orders: Narration, Process, and Description

Read the following passage from a college communication textbook. Then answer the questions.

Glossary
auditory (sentence 10): related to hearing
reconstructive (sentence 25): rebuilding, recreating

Listening in Public Speaking

[1]Effective listening will help you increase the amount of information you learn and will decrease the time you need to learn it. [2]It will help you distinguish logical from illogical appeals and thus decrease your chances of getting duped. [3]And, not surprisingly, effective listening will help you become a better public speaker. [4]Listening is a collection of skills involving attention and concentration (*receiving*), learning (*understanding*), memory (*remembering*), critical thinking (*evaluation*), and feedback (*responding*). [5]You can enhance your listening ability by strengthening these skills, which make up the five steps of the listening process.

[6]First, unlike listening, hearing begins and ends with the first stage: **receiving**. [7]Hearing is something that just happens when you get within earshot of some auditory stimulus. [8]Listening is quite different; it begins (but does not end) with receiving a speaker's message. [9]Receiving messages is a highly selective process. [10]You don't listen to all the available **auditory** stimuli. [11]Rather, you selectively tune in to certain messages and tune out others. [12]Generally, you listen most carefully to messages that you feel will prove of value to you or that you find particularly interesting. [13]To improve your receiving skills:

- [14]**Look at the speaker**; make your mind follow your body and focus attention on the person speaking.
- [15]**Focus your attention** on the speaker's verbal and nonverbal messages, on what is said and on what isn't said.
- [16]**Avoid attending to distractions** in the environment.
- [17]**Focus your attention on what the speaker is saying** rather than on any questions or objections *you* may have to what the speaker is saying.

[18]Second, **understanding** a speaker means grasping not only the thoughts that are expressed but also the emotional tone that accompanies these thoughts; for example, the urgency or the joy or sorrow expressed in the message. [19]To enhance understanding:

- [20]**Relate the new to the old**; relate the information the speaker is giving to what you already know.
- [21]**See the speaker's messages from the speaker's point of view**; avoid judging the message until you fully understand it as the speaker intended.
- [22]**Rephrase (paraphrase)** the speaker's ideas into your own words as *you* continue to listen.

[23]Third, messages that you receive and understand need to be retained for at least some period of time. [24]In public speaking situations you can enhance the process of **remembering** by taking notes or by taping the messages. [25]Memory is **reconstructive**; you actually reconstruct the messages you hear into a system that seems to make sense to you. [26]In remembering:

- [27]**Identify** the thesis or central idea and the main points.
- [28]**Summarize** the message in a more easily retainable form, being careful not to ignore crucial details or important qualifications.
- [29]**Repeat** names and key concepts to yourself.
- [30]**Identify** the organizational pattern and use it (visualize it) to organize what the speaker is saying.

[31]Fourth, **evaluating** consists of judging the message and the speaker's credibility, truthfulness, or usefulness in some way. [32]At this stage your own biases and prejudices become especially influential. [33]They will affect what you single out for evaluation and what you'll just let pass. [34]They will influence what you judge to be good and what you judge to be bad. [35]When evaluating:

- [36]**Resist** evaluation until you feel you understand (at least reasonably well) the speaker's point of view.
- [37]**Distinguish** facts from inferences, opinions, and personal interpretations that you're making as well as those made by the speaker.
- [38]**Identify** any speaker biases, self-interests, or prejudices that may lead the speaker to slant unfairly what he or she is presenting.
- [39]**Identify** any of your own biases that may lead you to remember what supports your attitudes and beliefs and to forget what contradicts them.

[40]Fifth, **responding** occurs in two phases: (1) nonverbal (and occasionally verbal) responses you make while the speaker is talking and (2) responses you make after the speaker has stopped talking. [41]Responses made while the speaker is talking should support the speaker and show that you're listening. [42]These include what nonverbal researchers call ***backchannel*** *cues*—gestures that let the speaker know that you're listening, such as nodding your head, smiling, and leaning forward (Burgoon, Guerrero, & Floyd, 2010). [43]Responses you make to the speaker after he or she has stopped talking are generally more elaborate and might include questions of clarification ("I wasn't sure what you meant by reclassification"); expressions of agreement ("I'll support your proposal when it comes up for a vote"); and expressions of disagreement ("I disagree that Japanese products are superior to those produced in the United States"). [44]In responding:

- [45]**Backchannel**. Use a variety of backchanneling cues to support the speaker. [46]Using only one cue—for example, nodding constantly—will make it appear that you're not listening but are on automatic pilot.

CONTINUED

REVIEW TEST *CONTINUED*

- [47]**Support** the speaker in your final responses by saying something positive.
- [48]**Own** your own responses: State your thoughts and feelings as your own, and use I-messages. [49]For example, say, "I think the new proposal will entail greater expense than you outlined" rather than "Everyone will object to the plan because it will cost too much."

—DeVito, *Essential Elements of Public Speaking*, 5th ed., Pearson, 2015, pp. 19–22.

Vocabulary

1. The best synonym for the word **backchannel** (sentence 45) is

a. delay.
b. verbalization.
c. rejection.
d. affirmation.

Inference

2. Based on information in the passage, we may infer that

a. listening comes naturally and easily.
b. listening is to speaking like reading is to writing.
c. listening and hearing are the same.

Central Idea

3. Which sentence best states the author's central idea?

a. sentence 1
b. sentence 4
c. sentence 5
d. sentence 6

Purpose/Tone

4. The author's main purpose and tone is

a. to amuse the reader with details about listening in public speaking.
b. to instruct the reader about the process of listening to a public speaker and how to improve listening skills.
c. to convince the reader that listening to a public speaker always occurs in phases.

Fact and Opinion

5. Overall the writer offers

a. facts.
b. personal opinion.
c. facts and expert opinions.

Supporting Details/Patterns of Organization

6–10. Complete the following concept map with details from the passage.

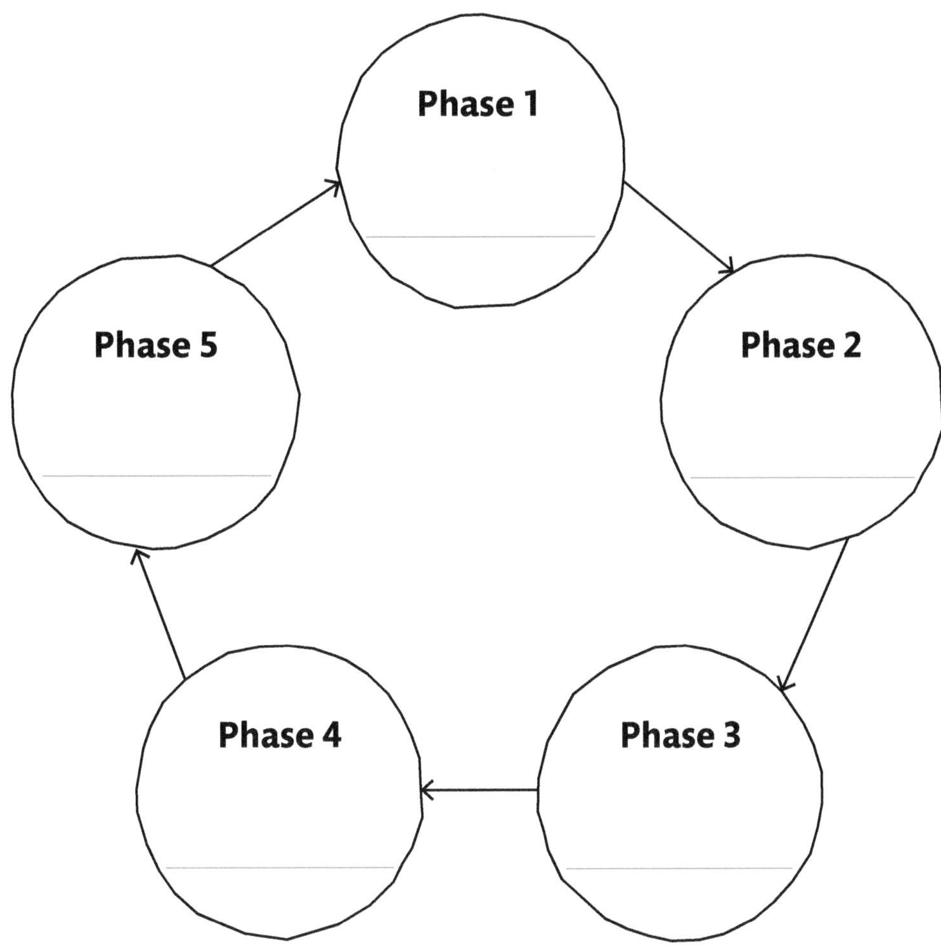

Summary Response

Restate the author's central idea in your own words. Begin your summary response with the following: *The central idea of "Listening in Public Speaking" by DeVito is . . . .*

Reader Response

Assume you are preparing for an essay exam on the elements of listening in public speaking in your college speech class. Your professor has supplied you with the following study question. Draft an essay in response to prepare for the exam.

In your own words, define *listening* by explaining its five steps, and identify the suggestions for improvement at each stage.

MySkillsLab™
Complete this Exercise
on myskillslab.com

Academic Learning Log: Module Review

Summary of Key Concepts of the Time and Space Order Patterns

Assess your comprehension of the time and space order patterns.

LO1 LO2

1. The two time order patterns of organization are __________ and __________.
2. __________ relays a series of __________ by describing __________ they occur and __________.
3. __________ describes the __________, __________, or __________ that can be repeated with similar results.
4. Space order is __________.
5. Signal words for time order include __________, __________, __________, __________, __________.
6. Signal words for space order include __________, __________, __________, __________, __________.

LO3 LO4 LO5 LO6

7. To draft a thesis statement, a writer may brainstorm key words that signal __________, __________, and reflect an __________.
8. To identify and generate details based on time and space order, readers and writers may ask the reporter's questions __________, __________, __________, __________, __________, and __________.
9. __________ is the exact or literal meaning of a word; __________ refers to the associations or emotional connections suggested by the word.
10. Three types of figures of speech are __________, __________, and __________.

Test Your Comprehension of the Time Order and Space Order Patterns

Respond in your own words to the following questions and prompts.

L2 L3 L6

1. In your own words, explain the similarity and difference between narration and process.

2. In your own words, explain the difference between denotative and connotative meanings.

3. In your own words, define the term *figure of speech*.

L1 L2 L3 L4 L5 L6

1. **How will I use what I have learned?** In your notebook, discuss how you will apply to your own reading/writing strategy what you have learned about the time and space order patterns. When will you apply this knowledge to your reading/writing strategy?
2. **What do I still need to study about the time and space order patterns?** In your notebook, discuss your ongoing study needs. Describe what, when, and how you will continue studying and using the time and space order patterns.

MySkillsLab™

Complete the Post-test for Module 8 in MySkillsLab.

9 The Cause and Effect Pattern

LEARNING OUTCOMES

After studying this module you should be able to:

- LO 1 Answer the Question "What's the Point of Cause and Effect?"
- LO 2 Question, Read, and Annotate Passages Using Cause and Effect
- LO 3 Prewrite a Draft of a Thesis Statement Using Cause and Effect
- LO 4 Prewrite to Generate Relevant Details Using Cause and Effect
- LO 5 Compose a Draft Using Logical Order: Cause and Effect
- LO 6 Revise and Proofread for Effective Language with Cause and Effect

Understanding the relationship between cause and effect is a vital critical thinking skill used in all aspects of life. Consider the following examples. In everyday life, we consider the sources of pollution and the benefits of recycling garbage in our environment. In college classes, we analyze the causes and effects of historical events and scientific phenomena. In working life, we acquire skills that will lead to better jobs. Thinking about cause and effect points out the relationship between events based on reasons and results. The focus may be only on the causes or only on the effects, or it may include both. As a reader, you identify the writer's focus, list the given causes or effects, and comprehend the central idea supported by the writer's explanation of causes or effects. As a writer, you must choose the causes or effects on which to focus. Often, there are too many causes or effects to explain in one essay. So the writer decides which are the key causes or effects, and then establishes and explains the flow between cause and effect. A master writer presents details in a logical order that explains why each cause leads to a specific effect. Both readers and writers test the truth of each cause.

WHAT'S THE POINT of Cause and Effect? 

Before you study this module, predict the purpose of using cause and effect. The following photographs document a set of causes and effects. Study the images and write captions that identify the appropriate causes and effects illustrated. Answer the following question: What are the causes and effects of human motivation and achievement? Then answer the question "What's the point of cause and effect?" with a one-sentence statement of the overall main idea.

Photographic Organizer: What Are the Causes and Effects of Human Motivation and Achievement?

Scientist or doctor using a microscope

Astronauts work outside the International Space Station

Detail from a painting in the U.S. Capitol depicting settlers arriving at the Pacific Ocean

What are the causes and effects of human motivation and achievement?

What's the point of cause and effect?

L2 Question, Read, and Annotate Passages Using Cause and Effect

A **cause** states why something happens. An **effect** states a result or outcome. At times, a single cause leads to several effects. For example, "Stress leads to both short-term and long-term effects." Other times, several causes contribute to a single effect. For example, "Several factors contribute to success on the job." Still other times, a chain of causes and effects occurs in a series of events known as a *causal chain*. A **causal chain** is a sequence of events in which any one event in the chain causes the next one, leading up to a final effect. For example, "A series of events led to the current conflict in Syria." Master readers question, read, and annotate a text for use of cause and effect signal words to identify the writer's focus and central idea. To ensure that readers grasp their focus and point, master writers often use cause and effect transitions and signal words in order to state the central point and introduce supporting details.

A **cause** is something or someone that creates an effect, brings about a result, has a consequence, or is the reason for a condition.

An **effect** is a result, condition, or consequence brought about by something or someone.

A **causal chain** is a linked sequence of events in which one event leads to the next event and continues up to a final outcome.

Transitions That Signal Cause and Effect				
accordingly	consequently	hence	on account of	so
as a result	due to	if . . . then	results in	therefore
because of	for that reason	leads to	since	thus

Verbs That Signal Cause and Effect (sample list)					
affect	constitute	create	force	initiate	restrain
benefit	construct	damage	harm	institute	stop
cause	contribute	determine	induce	preclude	
compose	control	facilitate	influence	prevent	

Nouns That Signal Cause and Effect (sample list)				
actor	consequence	end	impact	product
agent	creation	event	influence	result
author	creator	factor	issue	source
benefit	damage	grounds	outcome	
condition	effect	harm	outgrowth	

For Module 9, assume you are taking a college course in sociology, and your class is beginning a study on the theme of human motivation and achievement. Each reading in this module follows this theme. After completing all assigned readings, you will write an essay in response to the following guiding question: "What are the causes and effects of human motivation and achievement?"

Example

Assume the following passage is your first assigned reading on the theme "human motivation and achievement." Your professor has provided before and during reading questions and guided annotations to prepare you to read about and respond to the theme. Before reading, survey the questions and skim the passage for possible answers. Next, read the passage and the annotations. As your read, add your own annotations by completing the prompts in **bold** print in the annotations. After reading, use your own words to answer the questions. Record your answers in your reading/writing journal. Finally, complete the concept maps with information from the passage.

Before and During Reading Questions:
Logical Order: Does this passage mostly focus on causes, effects, or causes and effects?
Central Idea: What is the writer's central point?
Relevant Details: How does extrinsic motivation affect human achievement?
How does intrinsic motivation influence human achievement?
How do needs and drives influence human achievement?
How does drive-reduction theory influence human achievement?
What roles do primary drives, secondary drives, and homeostasis play in drive-reduction theory?
How do the need for affiliation, the need for power, and the need for achievement influence human achievement?
Effective Language: What is the difference in meaning of *affect* and *effect* based on the writer's use of these words?

UNDERSTANDING MOTIVATION

[1]The study of motivation explores reasons behind our actions. [2]Motivation is the process by which activities are started, directed, and continued so that physical or psychological needs or wants are met (Petri, 1996). [3]The word itself comes from the Latin word *mouere,* which means "to move." [4]Motivation is what affects or "moves" people to do the things they do. [5]For example, when a person is relaxing in front of the television and begins to feel hungry, the physical need for food might cause the person to get up, go into the kitchen, and search for something to eat. [6]The physical need of hunger affected the action (getting up), directed it (going to the kitchen), and sustained the search (finding or preparing something to eat). [7]Hunger is only one example, of

Central Idea: The central idea is the point the writer makes about the topic of the passage. The topic is *motivation.* **Underline the writer's point about the topic.**

Logical Order: The verb *cause* signals that the writer is using cause and effects. **Circle three more transitional phrases or signal words that indicate cause and effect.**

CONTINUED

EXAMPLE *CONTINUED*

course. [8]Loneliness may lead to calling a friend or going to a place where there are people. [9]The desire to get ahead in life motivates many people to go to college. [10]Just getting out of bed in the morning is motivated by the need to keep a roof over one's head and food on the table by going to work.

[11]There are different types of motivation. [12]Sometimes people are driven to do something because of an external reward of some sort (or the avoidance of an unpleasant consequence, as when someone goes to work at a job to make money and avoid losing possessions such as a house or a car). [13]In **extrinsic motivation**, a person performs an action because it leads to an effect or outcome that is separate from the person (Ryan & Deci, 2000). [14]Other examples would be giving a child money for every A received on a report card, offering a bonus to an employee for increased performance, or tipping a server in a restaurant for good service. [15]The child, employee, and server are motivated to work for the external or extrinsic rewards. [16]In contrast, **intrinsic motivation** is the type of motivation in which a person performs an action because the act itself is fun, rewarding, challenging, or satisfying in some internal manner. [17]Both outcome and level of effort can vary depending on the type of motivation. [18]Psychologist Teresa Amabile (Amabile et al. 1976) found that children's creativity was affected by the kind of motivation for which they worked. [19]Extrinsic motivation decreased the degree of creativity shown in an experimental group's artwork when compared to the creativity levels of the children in an intrinsically motivated control group.

Relevant Details: This detail answers the first prereading question about relevant details: *"How does extrinsic motivation affect human achievement?"* **Underline details that answer the remaining prereading questions about relevant details.**

APPROACHES BASED ON NEEDS AND DRIVES

[20]The next approach to understanding motivation focuses on the concepts of needs and drives. [21]A **need** is a requirement of some material (such as food or water) that is essential for survival of the organism. [22]When an organism has a need, it leads to a psychological tension as well as a physical arousal that motivates the organism to act in order to fulfill the need and reduce the tension. [23]This tension is called a **drive** (Hull, 1943).

[24]**Drive-Reduction Theory** proposes just this connection between internal physiological states and outward behavior; in this theory, there are two kinds of drives. [25]**Primary drives** are those that involve survival needs of the body such as hunger and thirst, whereas **acquired (secondary) drives** are those that are learned through experience or conditioning, such as the need for money or social approval, or the need of recent former smokers to have something to put in their mouths.

[26]This theory also includes the concept of **homeostasis**, or the tendency of the body to maintain a steady state. [27]One could think of homeostasis as the body's version of a thermostat—thermostats keep the temperature of a house at a constant level, and homeostasis does the same thing for the body's functions. [28]When there is a primary drive need, the body is in a state of imbalance. [29]This stimulates behavior that brings the body back into balance, or homeostasis. [30]For example, if Jarrod's body needs food, he feels hunger and the state of tension/arousal associated with that need. [31]He

will then seek to restore his homeostasis by eating something, which is the behavior stimulated to reduce the hunger drive.

[32]Although drive-reduction theory works well to explain the actions people take to reduce tension created by needs, it does not explain all human motivation.

[33]Why do people eat when they are not really hungry? [34]People don't always seek to reduce their inner arousal either—sometimes they seek to increase it. [35]Bungee-jumping, parachuting as a recreation, rock climbing, and watching horror movies are all activities that increase the inner state of tension and arousal, and many people love doing these activities. [36]Why would people do such things if they don't reduce some need or restore homeostasis? [37]The answer is complex. [38]There are different types of needs, different effects of arousal, different incentives, and different levels of importance attached to many forms of behavior. [39]The following theories explore some of these factors in motivation.

Effective Language: The words *effect* and *affect* are often confused. Though they both signal a cause/effect relationship, they express different meanings. **Double underline the writer's use of *affect* and *effect*. Predict the difference in the meanings of *effect* and *affect*.**

DIFFERENT STROKES FOR DIFFERENT FOLKS: PSYCHOLOGICAL NEEDS • WHAT ARE THE CHARACTERISTICS OF THE THREE TYPES OF NEEDS?

[40]Obviously, motivation is about needs. [41]Drive-reduction theory talks about needs, and other theories of motivation include the concept of needs. [42]In many of these theories, most needs are the effect or result of some inner physical drive (such as hunger or thirst) that demands to be satisfied, but other theories examine our psychological needs.

McClelland's Theory: Affiliation, Power, and Achievement Needs [43]Harvard University psychologist David C. McClelland (1961, 1987) proposed a theory of motivation that highlights the importance of three psychological needs not typically considered by the other theories: affiliation, power, and achievement.

[44]According to McClelland, human beings have a psychological need for friendly social interactions and relationships with others. [45]Called the **need for affiliation** (abbreviated as **nAff** in McClelland's writings), people high in this need seek to be liked by others and to be held in high regard by those around them. [46]This makes high affiliation people good team players, whereas a person high in achievement just might run over a few team members on the way to the top.

[47]A second psychological need proposed by McClelland is the **need for power (nPow)**. [48]Power is not about reaching a goal but about having control over other people. [49]People high in this need would want to have influence over others and make an impact on them. [50]They want their ideas to be the ones that are used, regardless of whether or not their ideas will lead to success. [51]Status and prestige are important, so these people wear expensive clothes, live in expensive houses, drive fancy cars, and dine in the best restaurants. [52]Whereas someone who is a high achiever may not need a lot of money to validate the achievement, someone who is high in the need for power typically sees the money (and cars, houses, jewelry, and other "toys") as the achievement.

CONTINUED

EXAMPLE *CONTINUED*

[53]The **need for achievement (nAch)** involves a strong desire to succeed in attaining goals, not only realistic ones but also challenging ones. [54]People who are high in nAch look for careers and hobbies that allow others to evaluate them because these high achievers also need to have feedback about their performance in addition to the achievement of reaching the goal. [55]Although many of these people do become wealthy, famous, and publicly successful, others fulfill their need to achieve in ways that lead only to their own personal success, not material riches—they just want the challenge. [56]Achievement motivation appears to be strongly related to success in school, occupational success, and the quality and amount of what a person produces (Collins et al., 2004; Gillespie et al., 2002; Spangler, 1992).

—Adapted from Ciccarelli and White. *Psychology* 4th ed. Pearson, 2015, pp. 354–358.

The Causal Chain of Homeostasis

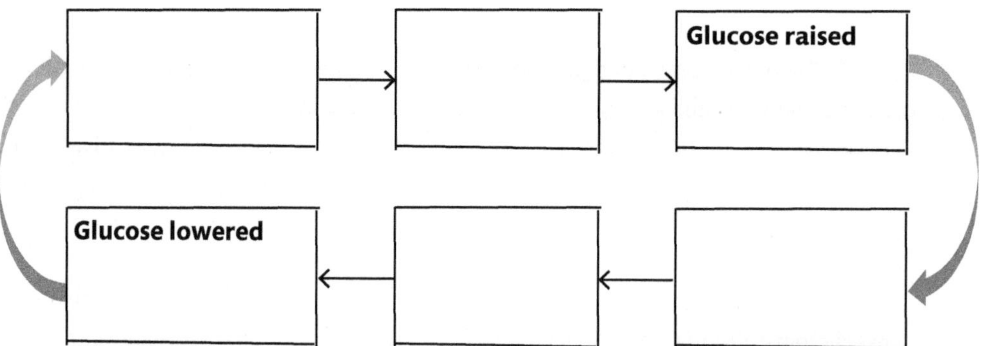

McClelland's Theory of Psychological Needs

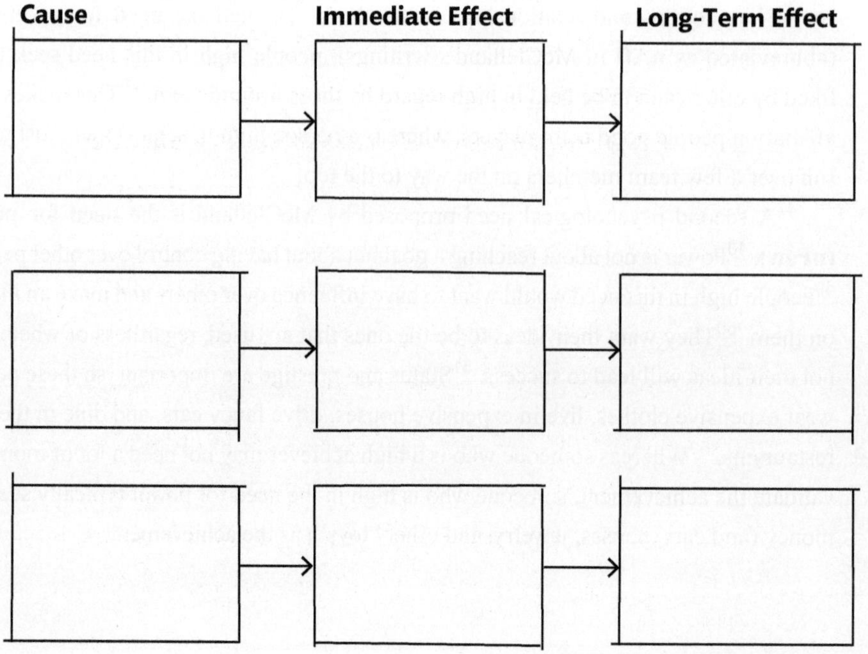

Explanation

Compare your answers to the following think-aloud, completed by Alex, another student in your class.

This passage discusses both causes and effects. The writer identifies several reasons behind human motivation and also explains the effects of each reason or motivation for human behavior. The writer used cause and effect signal words such as **cause**, **effect**, **reason**, and **motivation**. In addition, the writer used verbs to indicate the cause and effect relationship, such as **lead to** and **make**. The writer's controlling point about motivation is "the study of" motivation "explores reasons behind our actions." I underlined the following details that answered the before and during reading questions:

I underlined sentence 16, which explains intrinsic motivation and its influence on human achievement.

To answer the question about needs and drives, I underlined the following key details in sentences 21–23: "A need is a requirement of some material (such as food or water) that is essential for survival; it leads to a psychological tension, physical arousal called a drive."

I underlined sentences 24 and 25, which explain the drive-reduction theory as well as primary and secondary drives. Homeostasis is an example of the primary/secondary drives, so I underlined the following ideas in sentence 29: Homeostasis stimulates behavior that brings the body back into balance. To answer the question about the needs for affiliation, power, and achievement, I underlined the following sentences: 44–45, 47, 51, 53, and 56. I also used details from these sentences to fill in the concept map.

The first time the writer uses **affects**, the word **moves** appeared as a synonym. Other times **affect** could be easily replaced with the word **influence**. The word **effect** was used with the synonym **result**. So **affect** is an action that influences and **effect** is a consequence.

Practice 1

Question, Read, and Annotate Passages Using Cause and Effect

Assume the following two passages are the next assigned readings on the theme "human motivation and achievement." Your professor has provided a few questions to guide your thinking. Before reading each passage, survey the questions and skim the passage for possible answers. Then read the passage. As you read, annotate the details in the passage that answer the prereading questions. After reading, respond to the prompts that follow each passage.

Before and During Reading Questions:
Logical Order: Does this passage mostly focus on causes, effects, or causes and effects? Which transitions/signal words did the writer use?
Central Idea: What is the writer's central point?
Relevant Details: What human needs or drives motivate space exploration? What are past achievements of space exploration? What are the current benefits of space exploration? What are the future benefits anticipated from space exploration?
Effective Language: The writer uses synonyms for cause and effect such as *create*, *inspire*, and *benefits*. What other synonyms does the writer use for cause and effect?

from *The Space Economy*

Michael D. Griffin

[1]NASA opens new frontiers and creates new opportunities, and because of that is a critical driver of innovation. [2]We don't just create new jobs, we create entirely new markets and possibilities for economic growth that didn't previously exist. [3]This is the emerging Space Economy, an economy that is transforming our lives here on Earth in ways that are not yet fully understood or appreciated. [4]It is not an economy in space. [5]Not yet. [6]But space activities create products and markets that provide benefits right here on Earth, benefits that have arisen from our efforts to explore, understand, and utilize this new medium.

...

[7]We want better lives for our children. [8]We want to be able to compete in the world. [9]But economic growth and competitive success result primarily from the introduction of new products and services, or from finding more efficient ways to produce existing ones. [10]Economic growth is driven by technological innovation. [11]Societies that foster it lead the pack, while others lag behind.

[12]But if technological innovation drives competitiveness and growth, what drives innovation? [13]There are many factors, but the exploration and exploitation of the space frontier is one of them. [14]The money we spend—half a cent of the Federal budget dollar—and the impact of what we do with it, doesn't happen "out there." [15]It happens here, and

the result has been the Space Economy. [16]So if America is to remain a leader in the face of burgeoning global competition, we must continue to innovate, and we must continue to innovate in space.

•••

[17]In celebration of its 25th birthday, *USA Today* recently offered a list of the "Top 25 Scientific Breakthroughs" which have occurred since its founding. [18]Nine of them come from space, eight of them directly from NASA.

[19]We see the transformative effects of the Space Economy all around us through numerous technologies and life-saving capabilities. [20]We see the Space Economy in the lives saved when advanced breast cancer screening catches tumors in time for treatment, or when a heart defibrillator restores the proper rhythm of a patient's heart. [21]We see it when GPS—the Global Positioning System—developed by the Air Force for military applications—helps guide a traveler to his or her destination. [22]We see it when weather satellites warn us of coming hurricanes, or when satellites provide information critical to understanding our environment and the effects of climate change. [23]We see it when we use an ATM or pay for gas at the pump with an immediate electronic response via satellite. [24]Technologies developed for exploring space are being used to increase crop yields and to search for good fishing regions at sea.

[25]Sometimes a personal example carries more weight than the most comprehensive factual data. [26]So consider the case of Sarah Moody and her young nephew, Steve, who was born with a rare disorder. [27]He had no sweat glands to cool down during the summer, and his body would overheat dangerously. [28]After one too many close calls, Sarah thought to herself what many have thought before: if we can put a man on the Moon, why can't someone figure out a solution to Steve's problem? [29]So she called NASA, and was put through to what is now our Innovative Partnerships Program.

[30]NASA scientists were able to adapt cooling technologies developed for the Apollo astronauts to create a cooling vest for Steve. [31]It worked. [32]Sarah started a foundation that has delivered some 650 such vests to people suffering similar disorders. [33]Her foundation also turned to NASA for help with kids who had to live in dark rooms to avoid suffering tumors when exposed to ultraviolet light. [34]NASA's contractors helped create suits that blocked it, allowing these kids to go outside. [35]Sarah Moody died a few years ago, but her legacy lives on.

[36]Gary Thompson, an athletic 50-year-old man with a family history of heart disease, was given a clean bill of health in a series of tests with several doctors a few years ago, then had a heart attack while running a marathon. [37]He survived, and subsequently heard of a new ultrasound imaging technology derived from algorithms used to process images of Mars at the NASA Jet Propulsion Laboratory. [38]He was diagnosed correctly with this new technology, something all the other tests had failed to do. [39]He was so impressed, he started a company, Medical Technologies International Inc., to make this new technology more widely available. [40]It is now in use across the country.

CONTINUED

[41]These examples only begin to tell the story. [42]All of us can be proud that they exist, but equally we recognize that we wouldn't create a space program in order to get these collateral benefits. [43]But NASA is transformative. [44]We don't just help develop new technologies, we inspire whole new industries, revolutionize existing ones, and create new possibilities.

[45]I often wonder if it might be possible to quantify the value to society of upgrading the standards of precision to which the entire industrial base of that society operates. [46]Any company bidding on space projects—anyone who wants to be a subcontractor or supplier, who even wants to supply nuts, bolts and screws to the space industry—must work to a higher level of precision than human beings have ever had to do before. [47]How do we value that asset? [48]I don't know, but I know that it is real.

[49]In a related vein, another benefit of space to the economy is the way it inspires people to go into the technology sector. [50]People like Steve Jobs, Bill Gates, and Burt Rutan immediately come to mind, but it is more important to realize that a large number of technical professionals, in all fields, first got hooked on space and were then inspired to pursue technical careers. [51]This is truly one of the best "spinoffs" we have, and the space exploration enterprise should receive due credit for it. [52]At a time when we are concerned about declining enrollments in engineering, science, and mathematics, this should be no small factor in our thinking.

[53]Most of you know how the demands of spaceflight sparked the revolution in integrated circuitry. [54]But we didn't only get integrated circuits from the effort to master spaceflight, we got all of the other technologies that made them possible. [55]These capabilities now permeate our entire industrial base, and the use of integrated circuits is so ubiquitous, in devices whose very existence would have been almost unimaginable only a few years ago, that we no longer even notice it. [56]Cellphones are given away as a competitive inducement to select one wireless provider or rate plan over another. [57]Devices that can store gigabytes of information, a capability once beyond price, are given away as keychain fobs in promotional advertising. [58]Built into your checkbook can be a calculator that Newton or Gauss would have given years of their careers to have. [59]For a few hundred dollars, you can buy a device that will allow you to navigate to any address in the country over any road on the map. [60]And who even notices?

[61]Today, NASA is again among those at the forefront of microprocessor development, as evidenced by the recent demonstration of a Quantum Computer Chip—a device that operates at the limits of our understanding of the physical universe and makes use of the strange and elusive properties of quantum mechanics. [62]Quantum computing won't be just one more incremental improvement on present-day computing—it will revolutionize it. [63]It's the kind of breakthrough you get when you set the bar impossibly high, simply because the rigors of space exploration demand it.

...

[64]Fifty years into the Space Age, the greatest obstacle to the exploration and utilization of our solar system is the very high cost of space transportation. [65]No government effort has yet made a successful attack on this problem. [66]But when we do have it, we will find that commercially viable, low-cost space transportation will be as transformative to the economy as the transition from steam to diesel power, or the achievement of powered flight. [67]It will open up possibilities that now appear impractical, if not outlandish.

[68]This takes us to the Vision for Space Exploration, laid out by the President in 2004 and enacted in the NASA Authorization Act of 2005. [69]In the wake of the Columbia tragedy, it calls for NASA to extend human and robotic presence to the Moon, Mars and beyond. [70]As the President's Science Advisor, Dr. Jack Marburger, stated in his March, 2006 speech at the Goddard Symposium, "As I see it, questions about the Vision boil down to whether we want to incorporate the Solar System into our economic sphere, or not." [71]Precisely so. [72]Every aspect of human knowledge will be tested and advanced: physics, chemistry, biology and their practical applications in engineering, medicine, materials science, computer science, robotics, artificial intelligence, power, and many other fields—and we haven't even mentioned rocket science. [73]This is a legacy the crew of Columbia would be proud to know we had carried forward.

[74]Reaching for the unknown, making our lives bigger and our horizons broader, achieving things never before possible, are the heart and soul of what we do at NASA. [75]By pushing beyond the frontier, by setting for ourselves seemingly impossible challenges, we are transforming our lives for the better here on Earth even as we explore new worlds in space. [76]If, as Shakespeare said, life is but a stage, then NASA takes the play to the grandest possible stage. [77]And in doing so, we create the Space Economy. [78]At NASA, we are making the future happen—now.

–Griffin, Michael D. "The Space Economy." 17 Sept. 2007. NASA.

After Reading Response: Respond to the following prompts in your reading/writing journal:

- Write a summary of the passage (see Module 1, page 34).
- Create a cause and effect concept map that answers the following prompt:

  Discuss how one or more achievements of NASA's space program illustrate needs and drives (such as the need for affiliation, power, or achievement) as discussed in the passage "Understanding Motivation" on page 347.

CONTINUED

PRACTICE 1 *CONTINUED*

Before and During Reading Questions:
Logical Order: Does this passage mostly focus on causes, effects, or causes and effects?
Central Idea: What is the writer's central point?
Relevant Details: What human achievement does the writer seek? What needs or drives motivate the writer to take action?
Effective Language: Why does the writer use so few cause and effect signal words such as *effect, affect, result,* or *therefore*? How does she establish cause and effect?

from *Around the World in 72 Days*

Nellie Bly, New York City, 1890

[1]What gave me the idea?

[2]It is sometimes difficult to tell exactly what gives birth to an idea. [3]Ideas are the chief stock in trade of newspaper writers and generally they are the scarcest stock in market, but they do come occasionally,

[4]This idea came to me one Sunday. [5]I had spent a greater part of the day and half the night vainly trying to fasten on some idea for a newspaper article. [6]It was my custom to think up ideas on Sunday and lay them before my editor for his approval or disapproval on Monday. [7]But ideas did not come that day and three o'clock in the morning found me weary and with an aching head tossing about in my bed. [8]At last tired and provoked at my slowness in finding a subject, something for the week's work, I thought fretfully:

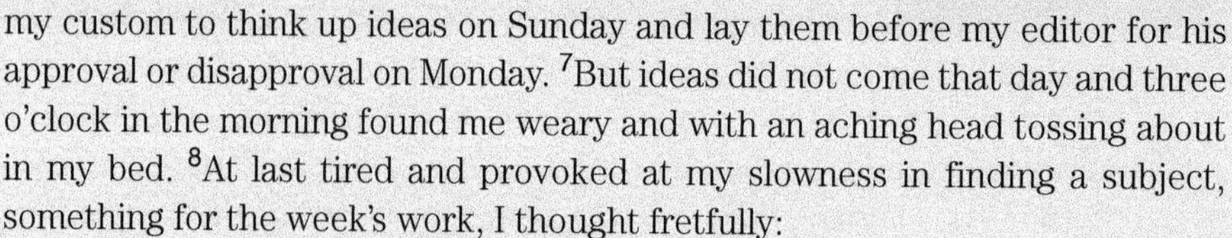

[9]"I wish I was at the other end of the earth!"

[10]"And why not?" the thought came: "I need a vacation; why not take a trip around the world?"

[11]It is easy to see how one thought followed another. [12]The idea of a trip around the world pleased me and I added: "If I could do it as quickly as Phileas Fogg did, I should go."

[13]Then I wondered if it were possible to do the trip in eighty days and afterwards I went easily off to sleep with the determination to know before I saw my bed again if Phileas Fogg's record could be broken.

[14]I went to a steamship company's office that day and made a selection of time tables. [15]Anxiously I sat down and went over them and if I had found the elixir of life I should not have felt better than I did when I conceived a hope that a tour of the world might be made in even less than eighty days.

[16]I approached my editor rather timidly on the subject. [17]I was afraid that he would think the idea too wild and visionary.

[18]"Have you any ideas?" he asked, as I sat down by his desk.

[19]"One," I answered quietly.

[20]He sat toying with his pens, waiting for me to continue, so I blurted out:

[21]"I want to go around the world!"

[22]"Well?" he said, inquiringly looking up with a faint smile in his kind eyes.

[23]"I want to go around in eighty days or less. [24]I think I can beat Phileas Fogg's record. [25]May I try it?"

[26]To my dismay he told me that in the office they had thought of this same idea before and the intention was to send a man. [27]However he offered me the consolation that he would favor my going, and then we went to talk with the business manager about it.

[28]"It is impossible for you to do it," was the terrible verdict. [29]"In the first place you are a woman and would need a protector, and even if it were possible for you to travel alone you would need to carry so much baggage that it would detain you in making rapid changes. [30]Besides you speak nothing but English, so there is no use talking about it; no one but a man can do this."

[31]"Very well," I said angrily, "Start the man, and I'll start the same day for some other newspaper and beat him."

[32]"I believe you would," he said slowly. [33]I would not say that this had any influence on their decision, but I do know that before we parted I was made happy by the promise that if any one was commissioned to make the trip, I should be that one.

[34]After I had made my arrangements to go, other important projects for gathering news came up, and this rather visionary idea was put aside for a while.

[35]One cold, wet evening, a year after this discussion, I received a little note asking me to come to the office at once. [36]A summons, late in the afternoon, was such an unusual thing to me that I was to be excused if I spent all my time on the way to the office wondering what I was to be scolded for.

[37]I went in and sat down beside the editor waiting for him to speak. [38]He looked up from the paper on which he was writing and asked quietly: "Can you start around the world day after tomorrow?"

[39]"I can start this minute," I answered, quickly trying to stop the rapid beating of my heart.

...

[40]I always have a comfortable feeling that nothing is impossible if one applies a certain amount of energy in the right direction. [41]When I want things done, which is always at the last moment, and I am met with such an answer: "It's too late. I hardly think it can be done;" I simply say:

[42]"Nonsense! [43]If you want to do it, you can do it. [44]The question is, do you want to do it?"

[45]I have never met the man or woman yet who was not aroused by that answer into doing their very best.

[46]If we want good work from others or wish to accomplish anything ourselves, it will never do to harbor a doubt as to the result of an enterprise.

—From *Around the World in 72 Days* by Nellie Bly, New York City, 1890.

After Reading Response: Respond to the following prompts in your reading/writing journal:

- Write a summary of the passage (see Module 1, page 34).
- Create a cause and effect concept map that answers the following prompt: What motivations drive both Bly's actions and NASA's exploration of space? (See "Understanding Motivation," page 347 and "The Space Economy," page 352.)

L3 Prewrite a Draft of a Thesis Statement Using Cause and Effect

PREWRITE: RECITE/REVIEW/ BRAINSTORM

To write a cause and effect passage, limit your topic to the reasons and/or results of an action, event, condition, decision, or belief. Most likely you have an opinion or belief about this narrowed topic. Your opinion is your point or main idea. However, you also reveal your opinion by the value or importance you assign to each cause or effect you discuss. A thesis sentence states your central point. For example, the following thesis statement contains (1) a topic, (2) the writer's opinion about the topic, and (3) cause/ effect signal words.

TOPIC — CAUSE/EFFECT SIGNAL WORDS

Positive thinking leads to unquestionable benefits.

WRITER'S OPINION

Example

Your instructor has asked you to use the readings on pages 347 and 352 to write an essay that addresses the guiding question "What are the causes and effects of human motivation and achievement?" First, you need to generate a thesis statement. Use the following steps to brainstorm your thesis statement.

Topic: Human Motivation and Achievement

1. Narrow Topic: ____________________

2. Identify Cause and Effect Order Signal Words: ____________________

3. Identify Opinion: ____________________

4. Combine into a Draft of Thesis Statement: ____________________

Explanation

Compare your answers to Alex's think-aloud.

The passages about human motivation and achievement made me think about what motivates me. The passage by Nellie Bly and her decision-making process inspired me to think about what motivates my decisions and actions. So I narrowed my topic to focus on a self-analysis that answers the question "What causes me to do things in my life?" I used the steps in the example to brainstorm my thesis statement. My narrow topic is "me." So I plan to use the first person pronoun **I** as the subject. I chose to use the terms **internal motivations** and **external motivations** from the first reading, "Understanding Motivation." In addition, I chose to include the cause and effect signal word **result** to state the link between motivation and action. I also chose to use the opinion word **seem** since one of my purposes for writing this essay is to discover something new about myself. My thesis statement is "My actions seem to be a combined result of internal and external motivations."

Practice 2

Prewrite a Draft of a Thesis Statement Using Cause and Effect

In your reading/writing journal, identify the steps you used to write a thesis statement using cause and effect. How did your thesis statement differ from Alex's? Did he use any methods you didn't?

L4 Prewrite to Generate Relevant Details Using Cause and Effect

PREWRITE: RECITE/REVIEW/ BRAINSTORM

To identify and generate details based on cause and effect, readers and writers may ask the reporter's questions *why* and *what*. Why has this occurred? What are the causes? What are the effects? These questions may also focus on one or more of the following traits of causes and effects: major or minor, long term or short term, obvious or subtle. What are the major causes? What are the major effects? What are the minor causes or effects? What are the long-term causes or effects? What are the short-term or immediate causes or effects? What are the obvious or clear causes or effects? What are the subtle, unseen, or indirect causes or effects? Answers to these questions enable readers to identify and writers to generate details to explain the causes or effects of an action, event, condition, decision, or belief. Usually, cause and effect transitions and signal words introduce these details. Since causes and effects are often listed or occur in time, transitions such as *first*, *next*, and *ultimately* are also used to identify or introduce a cause or effect. Many readers and writers use a cause and effect flow chart or concept map to identify and generate details.

Example

Assume your class is continuing to work on the essay addressing the guiding question "What are the causes and effects of human motivation and achievement?" Now your assignment is to return to the texts to identify details that you will use in your paper and create a concept map to organize your ideas for the essay. The following graphic organizers offer you a few options for generating cause and effect details. Choose one that best suits your topic. Then, create your concept map in your journal. Finally, share and discuss your completed map with a peer or small group of classmates.

A Causal Chain

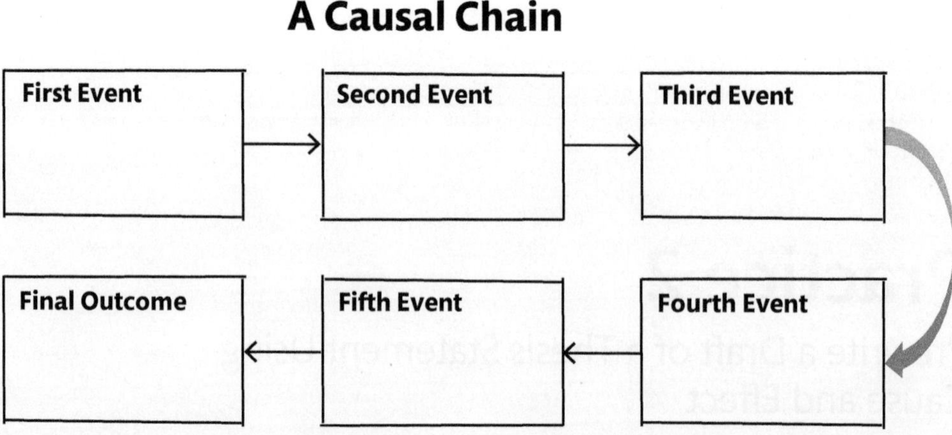

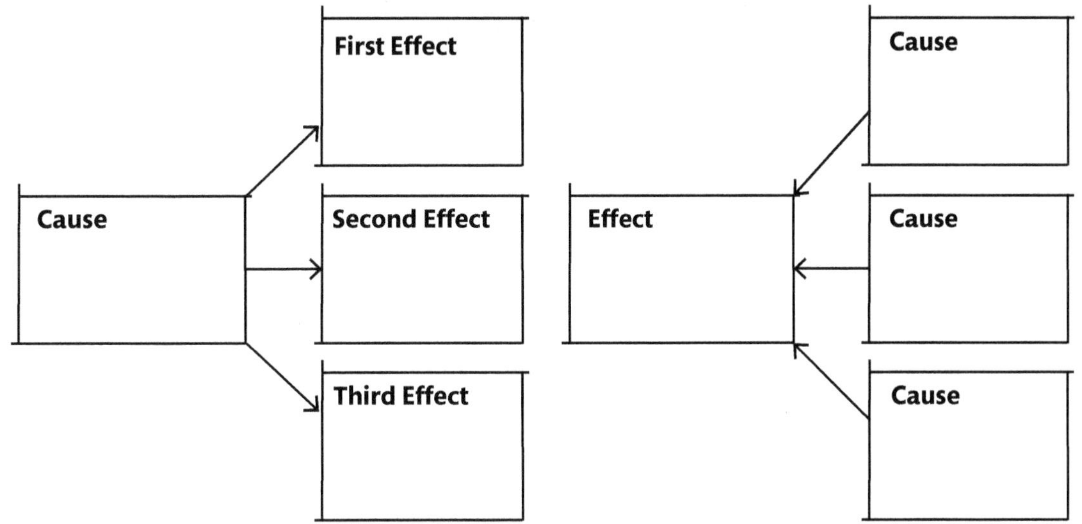

Explanation

Compare your responses to Alex's think-aloud.

I chose to generate details using the causal chain of events to show how intrinsic and extrinsic motivations combine to affect decisions and outcomes. To make this causal chain of decisions clear, I also decided to contrast my motivations and decisions with my brother's motivations and decisions. I used the following map as a general guide.

My brother's goal: Take right classes > study, pass MCAT > go to med. school > become doctor.

My brother's possible motivations: Make money > live doctor's lifestyle; or fulfill father's dream or prove others wrong.

My goal: Live life fully: In the past, Road trips > world travel > odd jobs > no money. My possible motivations: Easily bored, rebellion against my father and the "ordinary life." Recently: Desire to settle down > to have money to have opportunities > returned to school > entered conservative corporate job force.

Practice 3

Prewrite to Generate Relevant Details Using Cause and Effect

In your reading/writing journal, identify the steps needed to create relevant details to support a thesis statement. Identify the steps Alex went through as he annotated the texts and generated details. How did your steps differ?

L5 Compose a Draft Using Logical Order: Cause and Effect

Once you have brainstormed details to compose a passage using cause and effect, you are ready to begin the drafting process. First, review the concept map you completed with the details from the readings, along with your own insights or response. As you review your concept map, move details into the most logical order. Add details, if needed. Also, provide appropriate signal words and transitions to guide your reader through the cause and effect process. Many writers create several drafts to achieve a logical order and smooth flow of ideas.

Example

Assume you are still working toward writing an essay for a college course in psychology. Your essay answers the guiding question "What are the causes and effects of human motivation and achievement?" On your own paper, write a draft of your essay.

Explanation

Compare your answer to Alex's think-aloud and essay.

I decided that to fully answer the question, I needed to examine intrinsic and extrinsic motivations of my own. My essay illustrates the complex relationship between those motivations, but I decided not to use those terms to support my point. Instead, I modeled my essay on Nellie Bly's, choosing to tell my own story and let my decisions illustrate the concepts of inner drives and the external results. Drafting a thesis statement before writing a draft kept me focused on my central point, but I chose to imply my central point rather than include the thesis statement directly.

Alex Obed
Professor Staller
Psychology 101
May 20, 2015

Let Your Life Speak

What causes some people to get up every day and go to a job, while other people choose to become entrepreneurs? Some people to go to medical school and become doctors, while others steal and end up in jail? Sometimes, the motivation or "cause" appears planned; other times it appears unplanned.

Let's take my family, for example. My brother and I lived almost opposite lives growing up. From an early age, he knew that what he wanted most in life was to become a doctor. Alternatively, I had no idea what I wanted to do with my life! His path was laid out before him: take all the right classes, do well on the MCAT exam, go to medical school, complete a residency program and—voila—become a doctor! You could say that it was all planned out. He *knew* his goal, and he took the necessary steps to achieve it.

What *caused* him to want to be a doctor, though? What caused him to study practically non-stop for the past twenty years? Where did his *drive* come from?

I remember our dad telling us at an early age that if he could do it all over again he would become a doctor. He grew up poor, though, so he never was able to go to college. Is it possible that my brother was seeking to fulfill the unfulfilled dream of our father by becoming a doctor? Did my dad's words plant the seed in my brother's mind to want to become a doctor?

Maybe. But perhaps there were other extrinsic motivations at play: to become someone important in the world; to make a lot of money and have the lifestyle of a doctor (he owns a black 911 Porsche convertible). Maybe he also wanted to prove the "haters"—which included some of his teachers—wrong. Since he didn't make very good grades growing up, and learning didn't come easily to him, he may have had something to prove. In the end, I'm not sure that even my brother knows exactly why he chose to become a doctor, but a doctor he became.

I, on the other hand, didn't have to work very hard in school. I would pull "all-nighters" or do cram sessions to prepare for an exam or paper—and somehow I still seemed to always end up with great grades. Unlike my brother, I didn't have a clear sense of what I wanted to do with my life. I studied Engineering for a semester in college, but I quit that idea once I took chemistry and calculus. I thought I might want to become a school teacher, but I didn't end up doing that, either. I had a lot of *ideas* of what I might want to do, but the truth is that I got bored of them very quickly!

Although I didn't know what I wanted to *be*, I always knew that one day I would go back to school and get my Master's degree in Psychology. Every year or so I would look at the graduate programs across the country and occasionally ask a school to send me an application. However, the timing never seemed quite right. One year I tossed the application in the trash and found something else to do—ROAD TRIP!

CONTINUED

EXPLANATION *CONTINUED*

I traveled around the entire United States with a good friend for six months. We took his Honda CRV and camped at parks and worked odd jobs all along the way for gas and food money. We worked at Ben & Jerry's "Scoop Shop" in Burlington, Vermont; we volunteered at a yoga center in Massachusetts for three weeks in exchange for room and board; we hiked "The Badlands" in South Dakota in the beginning of winter, sleeping in the car during freezing temperatures, wearing every piece of clothing we had just to stay warm to save money on a motel; we worked at Peet's Coffee Shop in Marin, California and hung out with his uncle who owned a recording studio; and we made friends with complete strangers throughout our trip, many of whom invited us into their homes, fed us and let us do a load of laundry. We traveled in part because we wanted to see and hike every beautiful place in this country, but also because we really didn't know what else to do with our lives. An ordinary life seemed, well . . . boring. Intrinsically, we wanted adventure! As my friend and filmmaker, Eric Saperston, who produced *The Journey* film said, "Sometimes you take a trip, and sometimes the trip takes you." For us, it was definitely a lot of both.

After our epic road trip, I traveled to Israel where I studied religion and Jewish mysticism. It wasn't my plan; it just kind of *happened*. I then moved to New York City and lived without a car, sleeping in my friend's converted closet with a bunk-bed in it (again to save money); worked as a carpenter's apprentice in beautiful Connecticut; and taught environmental education to middle school students. However, after years of constant traveling, moving from place to place to place and leaving good friends behind, I was finally ready to settle down a bit. It was time to pursue my dream of going back to school to study Psychology. I really didn't know what I was going to do with the degree, but that didn't stop me.

After finishing my program, I decided to become a Life Coach. I hadn't even heard of Life Coaches before entering the program. I started a semi-successful business as a Life Coach, while I taught Hebrew on the side to pay the bills.

Here's my point: my brother and I took radically different paths in life. He was motivated to become a doctor. He stuck to a path—and he never wavered. I floated around in life, letting the wind—and my passions—blow me from place to place. I was motivated primarily by a desire *not* to get stuck doing something that I would hate for the rest of my life—which it seemed like everyone else was doing. I grew up watching my dad work seven days a week, serving breakfast, lunch and dinner for years in our family restaurant business. As Thoreau challenged, why spend the best years of your life preparing for your worst? I didn't want to come to the end of my life regretting that I hadn't really lived life on my terms.

Just as my brother was partially motivated by my dad's desire to become a doctor, I realized that I was partially motivated by watching my dad work. At the time, I couldn't understand why he would choose to work so much. And it hurt because it felt like he was choosing work over spending time with me. I vowed that I would never be like him. I would never trade freedom for money, and I eschewed the idea of owning my own business because I didn't want to be owned by it. So as you can probably see, our childhood experiences—my own and that of my brother's—greatly affected both of our lives, but in completely different trajectories. Same family. Same parents. Very different outcomes. Why? To sum up, I would say it's because life and human beings are complex!

If I told you what I'm doing now (and I will), many of you would laugh. I work a corporate job, sitting behind a computer from 9am-6pm. In the evening and on weekends I'm working on my own financial advising business. I can hear you saying it—*kinda boring, right?*

How *on Earth* did I get here? I've wondered that *a lot* recently.

At some point I realized that it takes more energy to resist life than it does to say, "*YES*" (remember, "Yes, Man!"). I thought I was so much better than everyone who lived "ordinary" lives. I had all the freedom you could imagine, but every winter when my brother invited me to go snowboarding in Colorado, I had to say no because I couldn't afford it. I got tired of continually having to say no to opportunities because I couldn't afford them. Now, I'm working my butt off because I want to create the kind of future where I can have the time *and* the freedom to do exactly what I want in the near future. I now have a plan. I guess I'm becoming more like my brother and my father. Indeed, life seems to have a sense of humor—which apparently is not so evident until we get one ourselves. I was always worried I would become a "sell-out," like everyone else. Now, I realize that I've actually *sold-in*, as I follow my own dreams and goals.

As one of my favorite authors and educators, Parker Palmer, says in *Let Your Life Speak*, "Before you tell your life what you intend to do with it, listen for what it intends to do with you." Quite imperfectly, that's how I have tried to live my life—and it has made all the difference.

Practice 4

Compose a Draft Using Logical Order: Cause and Effect

In your reading/writing journal, identify the steps you took to write your draft. Identify the steps Alex took as he wrote his draft. How are your drafts different? How are they similar? What can you apply from Alex's method to your own writing in the future?

LO6 Revise and Proofread for Effective Language with Cause and Effect

Effective expression reflects a writer's thoughtful choice of words to make the biggest impact on the reader. Some words, such as *affect* and *effect*, seem closely related because they are similar in their sounds and spellings. These similarities often cause confusion and lead to the misuse of the words. However, their meanings are clearly distinct, so thoughtful writers use the correct word for effective expression.

Affect is a **verb** that means **to influence** or **to cause**.

Example

Video games **affect** learning by improving concentration and visual skills.

Effect is a **noun** that means **result**.

Example

Video games have a positive **effect** on learning by improving concentration and visual skills.

Effect is a **verb** that means **to bring about** or **cause**.

Example

The new law will **effect** a change in the sentencing of sex offenders.

Master writers also avoid relying too much on the words *cause* or *effect* to avoid sounding repetitive. As you have seen in the essays, writers often use vivid synonyms for *cause* and *effect*, such as *create, inspire, benefits*, or *outcomes* to engage their readers.

Example

Assume the role of peer editor for Alex's essay, "Let Your Life Speak." Identify two sentences that would benefit from revising for proper use of *affect* and *effect* or with the use of vivid synonyms for *cause* and *effect*. Suggest possible revisions.

1. **Original sentence:** ______________________________

____

Revised sentence: ______________________________

____

2. **Original sentence:** ______________________

____

Revised sentence: ______________________

____

Explanation

Compare your answers to the following think-aloud.

Alex did not use the word **effect** in his essay. Instead, he listed or described the effects of his decisions. He did use the word **cause** often, and a variety of synonyms for **cause**. The one he used most often was **motivated**. So I chose one sentence to revise **motivated** to **affected**. I also would revise one of his uses of **caused** to **affected** in the third paragraph. Here are my suggestions: 1. What affected him to study practically nonstop for the past twenty years? 2. our childhood experiences in our family–that of my own and my brother–affected both of our lives"

Practice 5

Revise and Proofread for Effective Language with Cause and Effect

Work with the rough draft of the passage you composed in response to the question "What are the causes and effects of human motivation and achievement?" Choose two sentences and revise each one to create effective expression through the thoughtful and proper use of *affect* and *effect*. Use the following space to record your original and revised sentences.

1. **Original sentence:** ______________________

____

Revised sentence: ______________________

____

2. **Original sentence:** ______________________

____

Revised sentence: ______________________

____

Workshop: Comprehend and Create a Cause and Effect Essay

Assume you are continuing your study of human motivation and achievement. The following passages make up a capstone reading assignment. Your capstone writing assignment is to write an essay in response to the same guiding question "What are the causes and effects of human motivation and achievement?" Skim through the prereading questions and then read the following passages. You may be asked to make connections among these passages and the ones you have already read in this module. To complete this assignment, read the following passages and complete the writing activities that follow.

Remarks by President Obama on the BRAIN Initiative and American Innovation

[1]Today I've invited some of the smartest people in the country, some of the most imaginative and effective researchers in the country—some very smart people to talk about the challenge that I issued in my State of the Union address: to grow our economy, to create new jobs, to reignite a rising, thriving middle class by investing in one of our core strengths, and that's American innovation.

[2]Ideas are what power our economy. It's what sets us apart. It's what America has been all about. We have been a nation of dreamers and risk-takers; people who see what nobody else sees sooner than anybody else sees it. We do innovation better than anybody else—and that makes our economy stronger. When we invest in the best ideas before anybody else does, our businesses and our workers can make the best products and deliver the best services before anybody else.

[3]And because of that incredible dynamism, we don't just attract the best scientists or the best entrepreneurs—we also continually invest in their success. We support labs and universities to help them learn and explore. And we fund grants to help them turn a dream into a reality. And we have a patent system to protect their inventions. And we offer loans to help them turn those inventions into successful businesses.

[4]And the investments don't always pay off. But when they do, they change our lives in ways that we could never have imagined. Computer chips and GPS technology, the Internet—all these things grew out of government investments

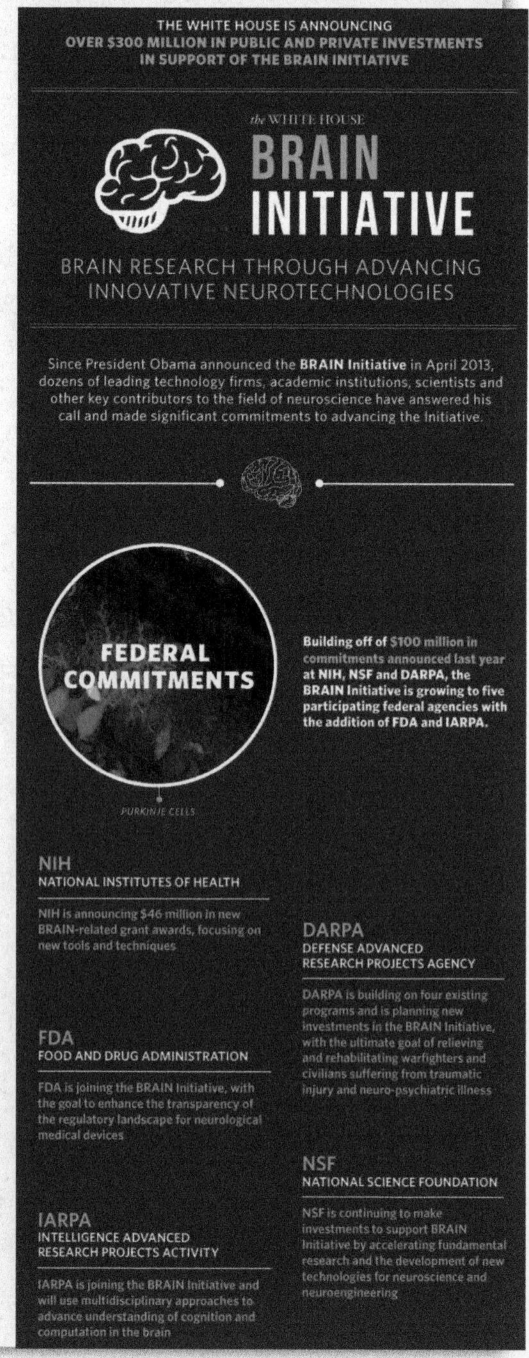

in basic research. And sometimes, in fact, some of the best products and services spin off completely from unintended research that nobody expected to have certain applications. Businesses then used that technology to create countless new jobs.

5So the founders of Google got their early support from the National Science Foundation. The Apollo project that put a man on the moon also gave us eventually CAT scans. And every dollar we spent to map the human genome has returned \$140 to our economy—\$1 of investment, \$140 in return. Dr. Collins helped lead that genome effort, and that's why we thought it was appropriate to have him here to announce the next great American project, and that's what we're calling the BRAIN Initiative.

6As humans, we can identify galaxies light years away, we can study particles smaller than an atom. But we still haven't unlocked the mystery of the three pounds of matter that sits between our ears. (Laughter.) But today, scientists possess the capability to study individual neurons and figure out the main functions of certain areas of the brain. But a human brain contains almost 100 billion neurons making trillions of connections. So Dr. Collins says it's like listening to the strings section and trying to figure out what the whole orchestra sounds like. So as a result, we're still unable to cure diseases like Alzheimer's or autism, or fully reverse the effects of a stroke. And the most powerful computer in the world isn't nearly as intuitive as the one we're born with.

7So there is this enormous mystery waiting to be unlocked, and the BRAIN Initiative will change that by giving scientists the tools they need to get a dynamic picture of the brain in action and better understand how we think and how we learn and how we remember. And that knowledge could be—will be—transformative.

...

8We have a chance to improve the lives of not just millions, but billions of people on this planet through the research that's done in this BRAIN Initiative alone. But it's going to require a serious effort, a sustained effort. And it's going to require us as a country to embody and embrace that spirit of discovery that is what made America, America.

9The year before I was born, an American company came out with one of the earliest mini-computers. It was a revolutionary machine, didn't require its own air conditioning system. That was a big deal. It took only one person to operate, but each computer was eight feet tall, weighed 1,200

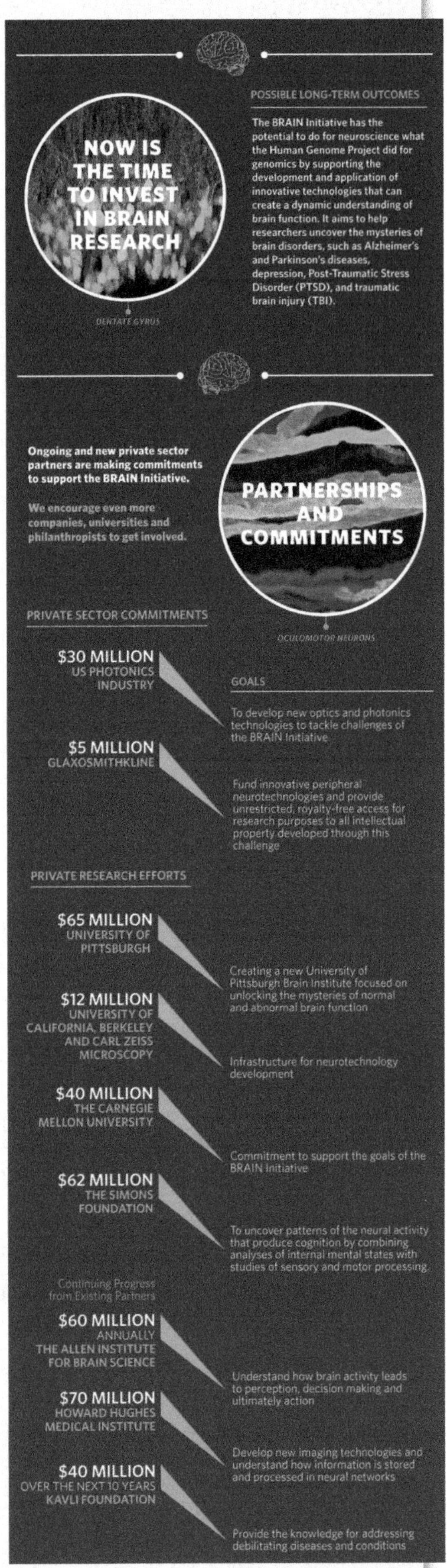

NOW IS THE TIME TO INVEST IN BRAIN RESEARCH
DENTATE GYRUS
POSSIBLE LONG-TERM OUTCOMES
The BRAIN Initiative has the potential to do for neuroscience what the Human Genome Project did for genomics by supporting the development and application of innovative technologies that can create a dynamic understanding of brain function. It aims to help researchers uncover the mysteries of brain disorders, such as Alzheimer's and Parkinson's diseases, depression, Post-Traumatic Stress Disorder (PTSD), and traumatic brain injury (TBI).
Ongoing and new private sector partners are making commitments to support the BRAIN Initiative.
We encourage even more companies, universities and philanthropists to get involved.
PARTNERSHIPS AND COMMITMENTS
OCULOMOTOR NEURONS
PRIVATE SECTOR COMMITMENTS
GOALS
\$30 MILLION US PHOTONICS INDUSTRY
To develop new optics and photonics technologies to tackle challenges of the BRAIN Initiative
\$5 MILLION GLAXOSMITHKLINE
Fund innovative peripheral neurotechnologies and provide unrestricted, royalty-free access for research purposes to all intellectual property developed through this challenge
PRIVATE RESEARCH EFFORTS
\$65 MILLION UNIVERSITY OF PITTSBURGH
Creating a new University of Pittsburgh Brain Institute focused on unlocking the mysteries of normal and abnormal brain function
\$12 MILLION UNIVERSITY OF CALIFORNIA, BERKELEY AND CARL ZEISS MICROSCOPY
Infrastructure for neurotechnology development
\$40 MILLION THE CARNEGIE MELLON UNIVERSITY
Commitment to support the goals of the BRAIN Initiative
\$62 MILLION THE SIMONS FOUNDATION
To uncover patterns of the neural activity that produce cognition by combining analyses of internal mental states with studies of sensory and motor processing.
Continuing Progress from Existing Partners
\$60 MILLION ANNUALLY THE ALLEN INSTITUTE FOR BRAIN SCIENCE
Understand how brain activity leads to perception, decision making and ultimately action
\$70 MILLION HOWARD HUGHES MEDICAL INSTITUTE
Develop new imaging technologies and understand how information is stored and processed in neural networks
\$40 MILLION OVER THE NEXT 10 YEARS KAVLI FOUNDATION
Provide the knowledge for addressing debilitating diseases and conditions

CONTINUED

pounds, and cost more than $100,000. And today, most of the people in this room, including the person whose cell phone just rang—(laughter)—have a far more powerful computer in their pocket. Computers have become so small, so universal, so ubiquitous, most of us can't imagine life without them—certainly, my kids can't.

10And, as a consequence, millions of Americans work in fields that didn't exist before their parents were born. Watson, the computer that won "Jeopardy," is now being used in hospitals across the country to diagnose diseases like cancer. That's how much progress has been made in my lifetime and in many of yours. That's how fast we can move when we make the investments.

11But we can't predict what that next big thing will be. We don't know what life will be like 20 years from now, or 50 years, or 100 years down the road. What we do know is if we keep investing in the most prominent, promising solutions to our toughest problems, then things will get better.

MAINTAINING OUR HIGHEST ETHICAL STANDARDS

In May 2014, at the President's request, the Presidential Commission for the Study of Bioethical Issues released the first of two reports exploring core ethical standards to guide the BRAIN Initiative and other recent advances in neuroscience.

DENTATE GYRUS - HILUS

The Human Genome Project demonstrates the potential impact that ambitious research programs like the BRAIN initiative can have. From 1988-2003, the Federal Government invested $3.8 billion in the Human Genome Project, which has since generated an economic output of $796 billion —a return of $141 for every $1 invested.

LEARN MORE AT WHITEHOUSE.GOV/BRAIN

All images from: cbs.fas.harvard.edu/science/connectome-project/brainbow

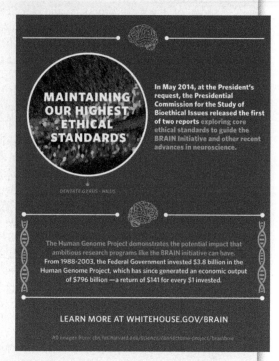

12I don't want our children or grandchildren to look back on this day and wish we had done more to keep America at the cutting edge. I want them to look back and be proud that we took some risks, that we seized this opportunity. That's what the American story is about. That's who we are. That's why this BRAIN Initiative is so important. And if we keep taking bold steps like the one we're talking about to learn about the brain, then I'm confident America will continue to lead the world in the next frontiers of human understanding. And all of you are going to help us get there.

—http://www.whitehouse.gov/the-press-office/2013/04/02/remarks-president-brain-initiative-and-american-innovation

Explosion of the Space Shuttle *Challenger* Address to the Nation, January 28, 1986

President Ronald Reagan

1Ladies and gentlemen, I'd planned to speak to you tonight to report on the state of the Union, but the events of earlier today have led me to change those plans. Today is a day for mourning and remembering.

2Nancy and I are pained to the core by the tragedy of the shuttle Challenger. We know we share this pain with all of the people of our country. This is truly a national loss.

3Nineteen years ago, almost to the day, we lost three astronauts in a terrible accident on the ground. But we've never lost an astronaut in flight; we've never had a tragedy like this. And perhaps we've forgotten the courage it took for the crew of the shuttle; but they, the Challenger Seven, were aware of the dangers, but overcame them and did their jobs brilliantly. We mourn seven heroes: Michael Smith, Dick Scobee, Judith Resnik, Ronald McNair, Ellison Onizuka,

Gregory Jarvis, and Christa McAuliffe. We mourn their loss as a nation together.

[4]For the families of the seven, we cannot bear, as you do, the full impact of this tragedy. But we feel the loss, and we're thinking about you so very much. Your loved ones were daring and brave, and they had that special grace, that special spirit that says, "Give me a challenge and I'll meet it with joy." They had a hunger to explore the universe and discover its truths. They wished to serve, and they did. They served all of us.

[5]We've grown used to wonders in this century. It's hard to dazzle us. But for 25 years the United States space program has been doing just that. We've grown used to the idea of space, and perhaps we forget that we've only just begun. We're still pioneers. They, the members of the Challenger crew, were pioneers.

[6]And I want to say something to the schoolchildren of America who were watching the live coverage of the shuttle's takeoff. I know it is hard to understand, but sometimes painful things like this happen. It's all part of the process of exploration and discovery. It's all part of taking a chance and expanding man's horizons. The future doesn't belong to the fainthearted; it belongs to the brave. The Challenger crew was pulling us into the future, and we'll continue to follow them.

[7]I've always had great faith in and respect for our space program, and what happened today does nothing to diminish it. We don't hide our space program. We don't keep secrets and cover things up. We do it all up front and in public. That's the way freedom is, and we wouldn't change it for a minute.

[8]We'll continue our quest in space. There will be more shuttle flights and more shuttle crews and, yes, more volunteers, more civilians, more teachers in space. Nothing ends here; our hopes and our journeys continue.

[9]I want to add that I wish I could talk to every man and woman who works for NASA or who worked on this mission and tell them: "Your dedication and professionalism have moved and impressed us for decades. And we know of your anguish. We share it."

[10]There's a coincidence today. On this day 390 years ago, the great explorer Sir Francis Drake died aboard ship off the coast of Panama. In his lifetime the great frontiers were the oceans, and an historian later said, "He lived by the sea, died on it, and was buried in it." Well, today we can say of the Challenger crew: Their dedication was, like Drake's, complete.

[11]The crew of the space shuttle Challenger honored us by the manner in which they lived their lives. We will never forget them, nor the last time we saw them, this morning, as they prepared for their journey and waved goodbye and "slipped the surly bonds of earth" to "touch the face of God."

<http://history.nasa.gov/reagan12886.html>

NEW AMERICA

by Robert D. Ballard

[1]America has had two great ages of exploration. The one that every schoolchild learns about began in 1804, when Thomas Jefferson sent Meriwether Lewis and William Clark on their epic journey across North America. The other one is just beginning. During this new age of exploration we will go farther than Lewis and Clark and learn the secrets of territories beyond even Jefferson's wildest imagination. Yet it seems safe to say that most Americans don't know anything about it.

[2]Few realize that the single largest addition to the American domain came on March 10, 1983, when President Ronald Reagan, with the stroke of a pen, expanded the country's sovereign rights 200 nautical miles from its shores "for the purpose of exploring, exploiting, conserving, and

CONTINUED

managing natural resources." By establishing an exclusive economic zone (EEZ), Reagan roughly doubled the area within United States boundaries, as Jefferson had with the Louisiana Purchase.

[3]Other countries have increased their jurisdiction over natural resources through EEZs and are eager to add more. Under the 1982 UN Convention on the Law of the Sea, which the United States has not joined, countries can claim sovereign rights over a larger region if they can prove that the continental shelf—the submerged portion of a continent—extends beyond their EEZ and meets certain other conditions. The United States potentially has one of the largest continental shelves in the world.

[4]A lot is at stake. Just like the land that Lewis and Clark explored, the ocean floor contains natural resources, many of them untapped. Vast oil and gas deposits lie under the waves. So do hydrothermal vents, where copper, lead, silver, zinc, and gold have been accumulating for hundreds of millions of years. By some estimates there are more than 100,000 seamounts containing minerals critical for national defense. That's not all that lies beneath. These watery zones encompass fisheries that nations rely on for sustenance, shipwrecks that may reveal lost chapters of history, and habitats that need to be preserved as marine sanctuaries.

[5]Most of the U.S. EEZ hasn't been explored. In 1803, with the territory from the Louisiana Purchase newly in hand, Jefferson instructed expedition leader Lewis to "take observations on . . . the soil & face of the country, its growth & vegetable productions . . . the mineral productions of every kind . . . volcanic appearances [and] climate as characterized by the thermometer."

[6]Reagan did not follow Jefferson's example. To this day we have better maps of Venus, Mars, and the far side of the moon than we do of much of underwater America. But now it's time for a new epic journey. Last June the United States' only dedicated ships of exploration launched a joint, concentrated effort to find out what lies within the country's EEZ. The National Oceanic and Atmospheric Administration's *Okeanos Explorer* mapped some of the New England Seamount chain near Rhode Island, among other places, while my vessel—the Ocean Exploration Trust's *Nautilus*—mapped portions of the Gulf of Mexico and the Caribbean. Both ships use multibeam sonars mounted on their hulls, which enable the creation of maps in three dimensions.

[7]Lewis and Clark traveled for more than two years and had to wait until their return home to share their discoveries with an expectant nation. Although the ocean depths plumbed by these modern expeditions are more remote than the land Lewis and Clark charted, we are in constant communication with oceanographers and other experts on shore. The moment a discovery is made, scientists can step aboard either of the two ships virtually, take over operations, and share findings in real time with a plugged-in world. This is a voyage of discovery everyone can make.

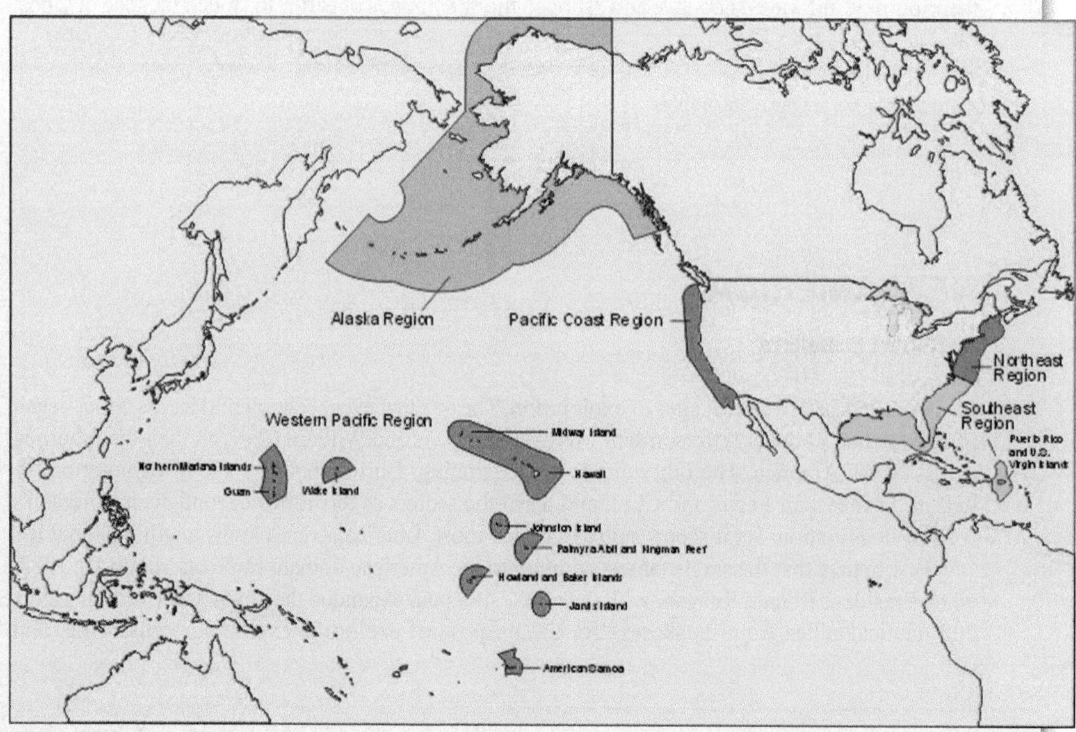

—Robert D. Ballard, "New America" *National Geographic Magazine*, Nov. 2013.

Preread: Survey and Question

PREREAD: SURVEY/ QUESTION

According to President Obama, how have government initiatives affected the economy?

How do the details in the article "The Space Economy" (page 352) support Obama's assertion about the impact of scientific exploration?

Why does President Obama support the BRAIN Initiative? What are the proposed benefits?

How does the BRAIN Initiative illustrate a primary drive as described in "Understanding Motivation" (page 347)?

How is Nellie Bly's motivation to go around the world in 72 days similar to or different from an astronaut's desire to explore space?

In his address to the nation about the explosion of the *Challenger*, President Reagan speaks of the "hunger to explore." How does McClelland's theory of needs (page 347) explain this hunger?

How is this "hunger to explore" illustrated by the BRAIN Initiative?

What is the exclusive economic zone (EEZ), and why did Reagan establish this zone?

How is the "hunger to explore" illustrated by Ballard's desire to map the ocean floor in the EEZ?

What are possible benefits of exploring the EEZ?

Read and Annotate

As you read, annotate key ideas, particularly those details that answer your prereading questions.

Recite, Review, and Brainstorm

Recite and **Review** the information. Paraphrase ideas. Summarize the most important parts. **Brainstorm** ideas for your written response to the passage. Answer your prereading questions. *Freewrite* or *map* the relationship among answers to questions or ideas you have annotated in the text. *Outline* or *list* key ideas and details in blocks of thought. Identify the central point you want to make. Use your own paper.

Write a Draft of Your Response

Using the ideas you generated by brainstorming, compose a draft of your response. Use your own paper.

Revise Your Draft

Once you have created a draft of a cause and effect essay, read the draft to answer the questions in the "Questions for Revising a Cause and Effect Essay" box that follows. Indicate your answers by annotating your paper. If you answer "yes" to a question, underline, check, or circle examples. If you answer "no" to a question, write needed information in the margins and draw lines to indicate the placement of additional details. Revise your essay based on your reflection. (*Hint:* Experienced writers create several drafts as they focus on one or two questions per draft.)

Step by Step: Questions for Revising a Cause and Effect Essay

- ☐ Have I stated or implied a focused main idea?
- ☐ Have I stated or implied the specific points of cause and effect?
- ☐ Is the order of specific points clear? Have I used strong transitions of cause and effect?
- ☐ Have I used concrete details to make my point?
- ☐ Have I made my point with adequate details?
- ☐ Have I included only the details that are relevant to my thesis statement?
- ☐ Have I correctly used *affect* and *effect*?

Proofread Your Draft

Once you have made any revisions to your essay that may be needed, proofread your essay to eliminate careless errors.

Reading and Writing Assignments

MySkillsLab™
Complete this Exercise
on myskillslab.com

Reading and Writing for Everyday Life

Assume you write a blog that has a following of several hundred people from all walks of life. Read the following passage and write an entry to motivate your readers to set realistic goals.

THE POWER OF SETTING GOALS

Why Set Goals? If you can learn the best way to set goals, you can map out your personal and professional success. Research shows that people who effectively set goals concentrate better, show more self-confidence, feel more motivated, and focus on tasks better. To turn your dreams into reality, goals will help you by giving you an action plan with specific deadlines.

What Are Goals? Goals are what we aim for, the things we want to achieve in our lives. Goals motivate us and help navigate our journey to success. You may have already chosen your educational goal and can use goal setting to help you achieve it. If you haven't yet chosen your educational program, you can use goal setting to help you determine your career path. Developing goals will help you to decide where you want to go and actually get you there. The key factor on your journey to success is to set *SMART* goals: **S**pecific, **M**easurable, **A**chievable, **R**ealistic, **T**ime frame. Let's look at each of these characteristics in a little more depth.

SPECIFIC. Your goal must be to the point, as if you are aiming at the bulls-eye of a target, as opposed to just getting your dart to stick. For example, let's say your goal is to "to lose weight." This is too vague. How much weight? If you say "I want to lose 10 pounds this month," you now have a specific goal to reach for. You will know for sure if you achieved the goal or not by the end of the month. The more specific your goal, the easier it is to measure.

MEASURABLE. When you can measure something it becomes concrete. Being able to do this with your goal aids in bringing it to life, making it more real rather than keeping it an abstract concept in your mind. Measuring means you are taking responsibility for its *progress* by asking the question "How?" How will your goal come to life? How will you choose the steps to take and what will they be? How will you chart its progress and how often? Finding ways to measure your goal every step along the way will certainly keep you on track toward its success.

ACHIEVABLE. You must be able to see yourself achieving this goal, and therefore it must be within your reach. This does not mean you should set easy goals. In fact, every goal you set should be a challenge to a certain degree. If your goal is simply living up to your current standard, then you are limiting your own growth. For example, in sports it is easier to play against weak competition and look really good. However, to improve,

CONTINUED

you should play against people who are actually better than you. Many coaches say, "You're only as good as your competition." Become your own competition by choosing a goal that will challenge you.

REALISTIC. On the other hand, if you create goals that are unrealistic and simply out of your reach, you may be setting yourself up for disappointment. You must be able to *believe* you can achieve it and have the resources available to help you. Remember, each time you accomplish a new goal, you are setting the bar a little higher and therefore expanding on what is achievable and realistic for you. You have to determine where that bar will be placed. If you *do* try to jump too high and end up on the ground, simply get back up and readjust!

TIME FRAME. Many of us need deadlines in order to accomplish a task. Goals are no different. When a time frame is deliberately chosen for your goal, it becomes set in motion. Ask yourself when, realistically, you want to complete your goal. Which of the following categories does it fall under?

- Short-range goal: tomorrow, next week, next month
- Medium-range goal: 1 to 6 months or so
- Long-term goal: 1 year or more

Although the time frame of *completion* is key, you will also want to set checkpoints along the way, as a form of *measuring* your progress. For instance, if you have a medium-range goal of being able to run a half-marathon in 6 months, you must certainly check in with your progress at least every month to make sure you are on track. Creating a schedule of mini-deadlines within your ultimate time frame can combat procrastination by keeping you motivated along the way.

Consider the Following When Setting Goals. Always use *positive language* when stating a goal. For example, stating, "I will plan healthy menus each week," is much better than "I will not eat junk food anymore." It is better to say what you *will* do than to focus on what you will *avoid* doing. Along with being positive, affirm your goal by stating it firmly: "I *will* exercise three times a week" rather than hedging by saying "I will *try* to exercise."

Be sure the goals you set are *self-chosen*. Do you think you will better commit to a goal someone else sets for you or one you create that is in line with your own *values*? Several well-meaning people in your life may have your best interests at heart and attempt to set goals for you. Although you should consider their thoughts, your ultimate goals must be chosen by you. This gives you ownership and responsibility for your goals.

Often we forget to use our past successes as motivation to continue our personal progress. When coming up with new goals it may be helpful to take a minute and reflect upon what you have already accomplished. Remember and visualize that feeling of success and use it as inspiration.

—Adapted from Colbert, *Navigating Your Future Success*, 2nd ed., Pearson, 2015. pp. 29–31.

Reading and Writing for College Life

Assume your academic counselor has suggested that you consider applying to a study abroad program. To be accepted and gain funding for the program, you must write an essay that explains why you want to study abroad. Read the following passage. Then draft an essay that explains what you hope to get from studying abroad.

WHY STUDY ABROAD

The number of study abroad programs, particularly in currently under-served areas of the world including most of Africa, most of Asia, and most of Latin America is expanding and offers exciting opportunities for undergraduate and graduate students to study abroad. Moreover, significant funding opportunities exist through the Fulbright-Hays Group Projects Abroad programs and other Title VI grants to fund support for students to study abroad. The importance of study abroad experience for our students, our colleges and universities, and our nation can be summarized with four widely recognized benefits:

- Study abroad programs provide young citizens with cognitive and affective competencies necessary for them to thrive in a global economy, while concurrently providing the nation with a citizenry that is economically competitive and politically savvy; necessary skills for the maintenance of national interests, security, and the ability to effectively respond to political instability, including threats of terrorism.
- International experience and competency contributes to a comprehensive liberal arts education. There is a substantive research literature that demonstrates that some of the core values and skills of a liberal arts education are enhanced by participation in study abroad programs. These values and skills include:
  - Critical thinking skills;
  - Ability to communicate in more than one language;
  - Ability to communicate across cultural and national boundaries;
  - Ability to make informed judgments on major personal and social issues based on the analysis of various perspectives.
- Study abroad programs can provide specialized training not available at home institutions such as:
  - Advanced level foreign language competency courses;
  - Specialized courses in disciplines such as archeology, art, international business, development studies, education, engineering, nursing/allied health, performance, and world music.
- Study abroad experiences promote personal growth, development and maturity among participating students.

—U.S. Department of Education, Office of Postsecondary Education.

Reading and Writing for Working Life

Assume you are the manager of a sales team at a local car dealer, and you have noticed that several team members engage in negative self-talk that is affecting morale and sales. You are facilitating a workshop to identify the negative effects of self-talk and ways to reduce its impact. Read the passage and create a multimedia presentation about the causes and effects of self-talk.

THE EFFECT OF SELF-TALK

So, how can you control your thoughts so as to reduce your stress? The first step is to discover the ways in which your "self-talk" contributes to your stress. Self-talk is verbalizing, either out loud or to ourselves, inner messages. We can use self-talk to improve the way we think about other potentially stressful events. Consider how these different ways of thinking about the same event, shown in the table, can increase or reduce stress.

Situation	Self-Talk Increasing Stress	Self-Talk Decreasing Stress
Romantic	I'll never find someone like him or her again.	I enjoyed my time with him or her and I know there's someone else out there.
Failing a test	I'm so stupid. I won't pass.	I can take other actions to bring up my class grade. I can study differently next time.
Getting a speeding ticket	Everyone was speeding. Why me?	I was going over the speed limit. I intend to concentrate more on my driving.

Helpful self-talk is rational. Three unhelpful kinds of statements are "shoulds," "awfuls," and "overgeneralizations." "Shoulds" have to do with the expectations we have for ourselves, for others close to us, and for the world in general. "Should" statements also contain words like "ought," "must," and "have." Some of the shoulds are unreasonable, and create expectations that are impossible to meet. Another kind of negative self-talk includes "awful" statements. When people talk about how horrible their circumstances are, or the fact that it is simply unbearable, it is pretty easy to start thinking that nothing can change. Continuing self-talk that makes change seem unlikely probably results in situations that do not change. The final means of negative self-talk, "overgeneralizations" contains words like "always," "never," "everyone," and "no one." Overgeneralizations happen when people think one event is indicative of their entire life. You failed a test, so you're a complete failure. Someone didn't listen to you in this one instance, and that person never listens to you, and so on. Negative self-talk is a poor means of controlling your thoughts in a situation. It leads to stress, and the need for more self-talk. Recognize that you have control over your responses.

—Cahn, *Managing Conflict through Communication*, 5th ed., Pearson, 2014, pp. 813–184.

Review Test

MySkillsLab™
Complete this Exercise
on myskillslab.com

Cause and Effect

Score (number correct) _____ x 10 = _____%

Read the following passage, and then answer the questions.

What Risks are Involved in Tattooing?

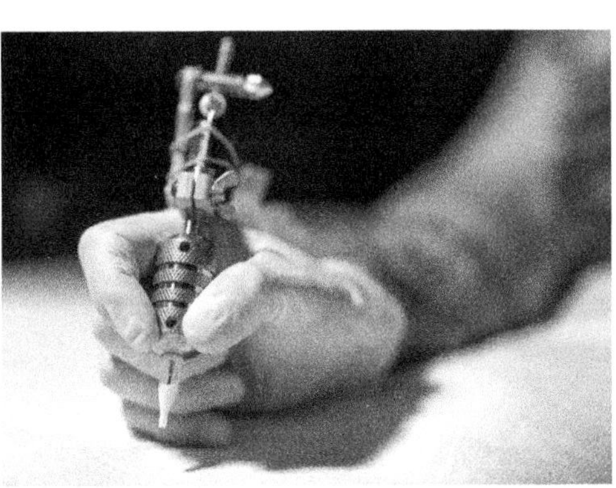

[1]Despite the obvious popularity of body art, several complications can result from tattooing. [2]Tattooing can cause infections. [3]Unsterile tattooing equipment and needles can transmit infectious diseases, such as hepatitis; thus the American Association of Blood Banks requires a one-year wait between getting a tattoo and donating blood. [4]Even if the needles are sterilized or never have been used, the equipment that holds the needles may not be sterilized reliably due to its design. [5]In addition, a tattoo must be cared for properly during the first week or so after the **pigments** are injected.

[6]Tattooing involves removal problems. [7]Despite advances in laser technology, removing a tattoo is a painstaking process, usually involving several treatments and considerable expense. [8]Complete removal without scarring may be impossible.

[9]Although allergic reactions to tattoo pigments are rare, when they happen they may be particularly troublesome because the pigments can be hard to remove. [10]Occasionally, people may develop an allergic reaction to tattoos they have had for years.

[11]Tattoos may also result in granulomas and keloids. [12]Granulomas are nodules that may form around material that the body perceives as foreign, such as particles of tattoo pigment. [13]If you are prone to developing keloids—scars that grow beyond normal boundaries—you are at risk of keloid formation from a tattoo. [14]Keloids may form any time you injure or traumatize your skin. [15]According to experts, tattooing or micropigmentation is a form of trauma, and keloids occur more frequently as a consequence of tattoo removal.

—Adapted from "Tattoos and Permanent Makeup." U.S. Food and Drug Administration Center for Food Safety and Applied Nutrition Office of Cosmetics and Colors Fact Sheet. 29 November 2000; Updated 22 August 2012.

Vocabulary

1. The best meaning of the word **pigments** as used in sentence 5 is
   a. infections.
   b. protections.
   c. dyes.
   d. skin.

Inference

2. Based on information in the passage, we may infer that
   a. most tattoo artists do not properly sterilize their instruments.
   b. the government certifies tattoo artists.
   c. clients should question tattoo artists about their procedures.

Central Idea

3. The sentence that best states the central idea of the passage is
   a. sentence 1.
   b. sentence 2.
   c. sentence 5.
   d. sentence 12.

Transitions

4. The relationship between sentences 11 and 12 is one of
   a. definition.
   b. cause and effect.
   c. time order.
   d. addition.

Transitions

5. The relationship of the ideas within sentence 3 is
   a. definition.
   b. cause and effect.
   c. time order.
   d. comparison and contrast.

Thought Patterns

6. What is the overall thought pattern of the passage?
   a. comparison and contrast
   b. cause and effect
   c. time order
   d. definition

Supporting Details

7. Sentence 6 is a

a. main idea.

b. major supporting detail.

c. minor supporting detail.

Purpose/Tone

8. The author's main purpose in the passage is

a. to inform with objective details.

b. to entertain with graphic details.

c. to persuade with pessimistic details.

9–10. Complete the outline below with information from the passage.

Central idea: ______________________________

I. Tattooing can cause infections.

II. Tattooing involves removal problems.

III. ______________________________

IV. Tattooing may result in granulomas and keloids.

Summary Response

Restate the author's central idea in your own words. Begin your summary response with the following: *The central idea of "What Risks Are Involved in Tattooing?" is. . . .*

What Do You Think?

The passage above details some of the causes and effects of health risks associated with tattooing. In your experience, what are some of the social causes and effects of body modification, such as tattooing and piercing? Do you have tattoos or piercings, and if so, why did you get them? If not, why did you choose not to?

MySkillsLab™
Complete this Exercise
on myskillslab.com

Academic Learning Log: Module Review

Summary of Key Concepts of Cause and Effect

Assess your comprehension of the cause and effect pattern.

L1 L2 L3 L4

1. To read or write a cause and effect essay, you analyze the ____________ for the ____________ of an ____________, ____________, ____________, ____________, or ____________.
2. The focus of the essay may only be on the ____________, only on the ____________ or may include ____________.
3. A cause states ____________ something occurs.
4. An effect states the ____________ or ____________.
5. A causal chain is a ____________ of ____________ in which any one event in the chain causes the next one, leading up to a final ____________.
6. Signal words for cause and effect may be transitions, ____________, or ____________.
7. Transitions for cause and effect include ____________, ____________, ____________, ____________, and ____________.
8. Verbs that signal cause and effect include ____________, ____________, ____________, ____________, and ____________.
9. To identify and generate details based on cause and effect, readers and writers may primarily ask the reporter's questions ____________ and ____________.

L5

10. *Affect* is a verb that means ____________ or ____________. *Effect* is a noun that means ____________. *Effect* may also be a ____________ that means to bring about or ____________.

Test Your Comprehension of the Cause and Effect Pattern

Respond in your own words to the following questions and prompts.

LO1 LO2

In your own words, answer the following questions. Give examples from readings or your observations as supporting details.

1. What is the difference between cause and effect?

2. What is a causal chain?

LO1 LO2 LO3 LO4 LO5 LO6

1. **How will I use what I have learned?** In your notebook, discuss how you will apply to your own reading/writing strategy what you have learned about the cause and effect pattern. When will you apply this knowledge to your reading/writing strategy?
2. **What do I still need to study about the cause and effect pattern?** In your notebook, discuss your ongoing study needs. Describe what, when, and how you will continue studying and using the cause and effect pattern.

MySkillsLab™

Complete the Post-test for Module 9 in MySkillsLab.

10 The Example Patterns

LEARNING OUTCOMES

After studying this module you should be able to:

LO 1 Answer the Question "What's the Point of the Example Patterns?"

LO 2 Question, Read, Annotate, and Review Passages Using Examples

LO 3 Prewrite a Draft of a Thesis Statement Using Examples

LO 4 Prewrite to Generate Relevant Details Using Examples

LO 5 Compose a Draft Using Logical Order: Examples

LO 6 Revise and Proofread for Effective Language with Examples

When we communicate—with family members, employers, teachers, or friends—we often use **examples** to clarify a general idea or define a new word or concept. Think of a situation you were in recently where you used examples to make a point. What makes an example effective?

An **example**, also called *exemplification*, is a specific illustration or representation of a more general idea.

In everyday life, we illustrate our decorating ideas with paint chips and swatches of fabric, or we define our values using illustrations. In college life, professors and textbook writers use examples to teach new words and concepts in every discipline. In working life, we offer examples of our hard work and successes when we apply for jobs and promotions.

To effectively use examples, a writer moves from a general idea to specific examples that support and clarify the main point or define a key term. Sometimes, as in a science lab report, a writer may present the specific examples first and then come to a general conclusion based on the examples.

WHAT'S THE POINT of the Example Patterns?

LO1

Identifying and analyzing examples help a reader to understand a writer's central idea. Generating and organizing examples help a writer to discover his or her point about a particular topic. The following photographs offer three examples of life in the digital age. Study each photograph. Write captions that briefly describe each photograph. Then answer the question "What's the point of examples?"

Photographic Organizer: What Are Examples of the Pros and Cons of Living in the Digital Age?

A virtual screen with many choices

Surveillance cameras at public corner

You Loser

Social media

What are examples of the pros and cons of living in the digital age?

What's the point of examples?

L2 Question, Read, Annotate, and Review Passages Using Examples

Readers and writers rely on examples to support generalizations such as a main idea, or to define new or difficult words. Master readers often skim for key examples as a way to locate, confirm, or infer a main idea, or to comprehend the definition of a new or difficult word or concept. Master writers often include key words in the topic sentence and paragraph body to signal the use of either the generalization-example pattern or the definition-example pattern.

In the **generalization-example pattern**, the writer makes a general statement and then offers an example or a series of examples to clarify the generalization.

The **generalization-example pattern** first states an overall idea and then gives examples to illustrate, represent, or explain that idea.

The Generalization-Example Pattern

Statement of a general idea

Example

Example

Key words may introduce the example pattern in the topic sentence (general statement), and key words along with transition words may signal specific examples (supporting details) as they occur throughout the paragraph. The following charts list a few of the key words and transition words used to signal examples.

Key Words Used to Signal Examples			
an illustration	for instance	once	to illustrate
for example	include/including	such as	typical, typically

Transition Words Used to Signal Examples				
also	certain	first of all	last	one
and	final	for one thing	last of all	second
another	finally	furthermore	moreover	specifically
besides	first	in addition	next	third

The definition-example pattern is similar to the generalization-example pattern. Both offer general statements followed by specific examples. However, the definition-example pattern serves a very specific purpose. A **definition-example pattern** clarifies the meaning of a word or concept. Writers may use either a simple definition example or an extended definition example.

In the **simple definition-example pattern**, the writer makes a general statement that introduces and gives the meaning of a new, specialized, or difficult term. Definition statements often include words such as

The **definition-example pattern** introduces a new word or specialized term, gives its definition, and provides examples to illustrate or explain the word.

The **simple definition-example pattern** defines and exemplifies a word or term in one sentence or a few sentences.

is, are, and *means.* The writer then offers one or more examples to show how the word and its meaning are used or applied in a specific context or situation. Simple definitions are often short—no more than just a few sentences.

The Simple Definition-Example Pattern

Term and definition

Example

Example

In the **extended definition-example pattern**, the writer makes a general statement introducing a term that represents a more difficult concept. To define the concept, the writer identifies and explains its traits, describes what the concept is like or similar to, and offers examples. Often, to clarify meaning, a writer may also include an explanation and example of what the term is *not*. The extended definition is sometimes developed as a supporting paragraph within an essay. However, extended definitions are often the basis of an entire essay.

The **extended definition-example pattern** develops a deeper meaning of a word or term by using classification, comparison, contrast, and examples or illustrations in one or more paragraphs.

The Extended Definition-Example Pattern

Concept and definition

Traits	Example
What it is similar to	Example
What it is *not*	Example

Both the simple and extended definition-example patterns use many of the same key words and transition words used in the generalization-example pattern. However, master writers use additional words to signal the use of definitions. The following chart includes just a few of the key words that signal definition.

Key Words That Signal Definition			
as	consists of	i.e. (that is to say)	means
are	constitutes	in particular	suggests
category	defined as	indicates	trait
characteristics	denotes	is, is called, is known as	unlike
characterized by	differs	is not	
connotes	distinguished from	like	

For Module 10, assume you are taking a college course in technology, and your class is beginning a study on the theme of "living in the digital age." Each reading in this module follows this theme. After completing all assigned readings, you will write in response to the following guiding question: "What are the pros and cons of living in the digital age?"

Example

Assume the following passage is your first assigned reading on the theme "living in the digital age." Your professor has provided before and during reading questions and guided annotations to prepare you to read about and respond to the theme. Before reading, survey the questions and skim the passage for possible answers. Next, read the passage and note the annotations. As you read, add your own annotations by completing the prompts in **bold** print in the annotations. After reading, use your own words to answer the questions about relevant details. Record your answers in your reading/writing journal. Finally, complete the concept map with information from the passage.

Before and During Reading Questions:

Logical Order: How does this passage use the various example patterns? Which transitions/signal words do the writers use?

Central Idea: What is the writers' central point?

Relevant Details: What are the definitions and examples of the following terms: *relativism, situational ethics, societal ethics, rule utilitarianism*, and *unethical behavior*?

What are the pros and cons of personal privacy in the digital age? What are the pros and cons of the opportunities technology provides?

Effective Language: What vivid words do the writers use to create images in the reader's mind?

ETHICS IN COMPUTING

[1]You just bought a new notebook computer. [2]You know you can go to BitTorrent or LimeWire to download the latest summer blockbuster movie and its soundtrack. [3]You also probably know this is unethical. [4]Although pirating music and videos is a valid example of unethical behavior, it has been overused as an illustration of the ethical challenges of technology. [5]There are key ethical issues surrounding technology.

Central Idea: The central idea is the point the writer makes about the topic of the passage. The topic is "ethics and technology." **Underline the writer's point about the topic.**

What Is Ethics?

[6]Ethics is the study of the general nature of morals and of the specific moral choices made by individuals. [7]Morals involve conforming to established or accepted ideas of right and wrong (as generally dictated by society), and are usually viewed as black and white. [8]Ethical issues often involve subtle distinctions, such as the difference between fairness and equity. [9]Ethical values are the guidelines you use to make decisions each day. [10]For example, the person in front of you at the coffee shop drops a dollar on the floor and doesn't notice it. [11]Do you tell him or her about it, or do you pick up the dollar and use it to pay for your coffee?

[12]**Doesn't everyone have the same basic ethics?** [13]There are many systems of ethical conduct. [14]**Relativism** is a theory that holds that there is no universal moral truth and that instead there are only beliefs,

Relevant Details: This detail answers the first prereading question about relevant details: "What is the definition of relativism?" **Underline details that answer the remaining prereading questions about relevant details.**

perspectives, and values. [15]Everyone has his or her own ideas of right and wrong, and so who are we to judge anyone else? [16]Another ethical philosophy is **situational ethics**, which states that decision-making should be based on the circumstances of a particular situation and not on fixed laws.

[17]Many other ethical systems have been proposed over time, some of which are defined by religious traditions. [18]For example, the expression "Judeo-Christian ethics" refers to the common set of basic values shared across the Jewish and Christian religious traditions. [19]These include behaviors such as respecting property and relationships, honoring one's parents, and being kind to others.

Logical Order: The transitional phrase "For example" signals that the writer is using examples. **Circle two more transitional phrases that indicate examples.**

[20]**Are laws established to guide people's ethical actions?** [21]Laws are formal, written standards designed to apply to everyone. [22]Laws are enforced by government agencies (such as the police, the Federal Bureau of Investigation, the Food and Drug Administration, and so on) and interpreted by the courts. [23]It is not possible to pass laws that cover every possible behavior that human beings can engage in. [24]Therefore, **societal ethics** provides a general set of unwritten guidelines for people to follow. [25]**Rule utilitarianism** is an ethical theory that espouses establishing moral guidelines through specific rules. [26]The idea behind this system is that if everyone adheres to the same moral code, society as a whole will improve and people will be happier. [27]Many societies follow this system in general terms, including the United States. [28]For instance, laws against nudity in public places (except for a few nude beaches) in the United States help define public nudity as immoral.

[29]**Don't some people behave unethically?** [30]Although many valid systems of ethical conduct exist, sometimes people act in a manner that violates the beliefs they hold or the beliefs of the ethical system they say they follow. [31]**Unethical behavior** can be defined as not conforming to a set of approved standards of social or professional behavior. [32] For instance, using your phone to text message your friend during an exam is prohibited by most colleges' rules of student conduct. [33]This behavior is different from amoral behavior, in which a person has no sense or right and wrong—and no interest in the moral consequences of his or her actions.

Technology and Ethics: How One Affects the Other

[34]In both good and bad ways, technology affects our community life, family life, work environment, education, and medical research. [35]How technology is used is often left up to the individual and the guidance of his or her personal ethics. [36]Ethical considerations are never black and white. [37]They are complex, and reasonable people can have different yet equally valid views. [38]We present alternative viewpoints in each setting for you to consider and discuss.

CONTINUED

Using Computers to Support Ethical Conduct

[39]Although there are many opportunities to use computers and the Internet unethically, many more ways are available to use technology to support ethical conduct.

[40]Many charitable organizations use the Internet for fund-raising. [41]When the Sichuan earthquake struck China in 2008, organizations such as the American Red Cross and other charities supporting relief efforts used their Web pages to help donors quickly, easily, and securely make contributions to aid earthquake victims. [42]Using technology to garner contributions enables charities to raise billions of dollars quickly for relief efforts.

[43]When you spot unethical behavior at your company, you need a fast, secure way to report it to the appropriate members of management. [44]The Sarbanes-Oxley Act of 2002 requires companies to provide mechanisms for employees and third parties to report complaints, including ethics violations. [45]These mechanisms are required to provide the employees with anonymity. [46]In addition, many businesses are using their Web sites to allow whistle-blowers to report wrongdoing anonymously, replacing previous e-mail and telephone hotline systems, which did not shield employees from being identified. [47]With an electronic system, it is easier for a company to sort and classify complaints and designate them for appropriate action.

[48]Electronic systems such as intranets and e-mail are also excellent mechanisms for informing employees about ethics policies. [49]Storing ethics guidelines electronically on a company intranet ensures that employees have access to information whenever they need it. [50]By using e-mail, a company can communicate new policies, or changes to existing policies, to employees quickly and efficiently.

[51]Throughout your life, you will encounter many ethical challenges relating to information technology. [52]Your personal ethics—combined with the ethical guidelines your company provides and the general ethical environment of society—will guide your decisions.

[53]Technology constantly challenges our ethics as individuals and as a society. [54]Some issues involving the relationship between technology and ethics require us to examine situations in which ethics and technology touch each other such as intellectual property (fair use), privacy (personal privacy and access) and social justice (benefits of technology). [55]For example, let's take a deeper look at two issues: privacy and social justice.

Is Personal Privacy a Casualty of the Modern Age?

Summary of the Issue

[56]Like respect and dignity, privacy is a basic human right. [57]What, exactly, is privacy? [58]Simply stated, privacy is the right to be left alone to do as one pleases. [59]The idea of privacy is often associated with hiding something (a

behavior, a relationship, or a secret). 60However, privacy really means not being required to explain your behavior to others. 61With the advent of the digital society, is there any such thing as personal privacy? 62Like Hansel and Gretel, we leave a trail of electronic breadcrumbs almost everywhere we go.

Effective Language: Using a figure of speech such as "Like Hansel and Gretel" creates a mental picture and deepens meaning. **Double underline one more vivid word or phrase.**

63Debit and credit cards are fast replacing cash, and they leave records of our purchases at merchants and our transactions at the bank. 64E-mail is fast replacing snail mail, so now your correspondence (and your secrets) may live on indefinitely in Web servers around the world. 65Have you visited a Web site lately? 66Chances are that the owner of that site kept track of what you looked at while you were visiting the site.

67Can't we just modify our behavior to protect our privacy? 68We could, but a survey by the Ponemon Institute revealed that only about 7 percent of Americans are willing to change their behavior to protect privacy. 69Many people freely give personal information (such as their name, address, and phone number) to obtain buyer loyalty cards that qualify them for discounts at supermarkets and pharmacies. 70In addition, to obtain a discount on tolls and speed up their trips, many people sign up for electronic toll passes, which are actually radio frequency identification (RFID) devices that can be used to track where a driver was at a specific point in time. 71Information gathered by these programs could be used against you in a divorce case to prove you were a bad parent because you were routinely out in your car at 2 A.M. on school nights, or because you bought mostly junk food at the supermarket. 72Although many Americans say they are concerned about a loss of privacy, they have made few moves to preserve privacy rights in the United States.

POINT: Protect Personal Privacy

73The advocates of protecting privacy in the United States argue that the right to privacy is a basic human right that should be afforded to everyone. 74As long as individuals aren't hurting anyone or breaking any laws, people should be entitled to do what they want without fear of being monitored.

1. 75If I'm not doing anything wrong, then you have no reason to watch me.
2. 76If the government is collecting information by watching citizens, it might misuse or lose control of the data.
3. 77By allowing the government to determine what behaviors are right and wrong, we open ourselves to uncertainty because the government may arbitrarily change the definition of which behaviors are unacceptable.

CONTINUED

EXAMPLE *CONTINUED*

4. [78]Requiring national ID cards is reminiscent of the former Nazi and Soviet regimes.
5. [79]Implementing privacy controls (such as national ID cards) or requiring passports for travel to Canada and Mexico is extremely expensive and a waste of taxpayer funds.

COUNTERPOINT: Reduced Privacy Is a Fact of Modern Life

[80]Advocates for stronger monitoring of private citizens usually cite national security concerns and the prevention of terrorist activities. [81]Inconvenience to ordinary people who are doing nothing wrong is just a price that everyone must pay to ensure that society is free from the malicious acts of a few malcontents.

1. [82]If you aren't doing anything wrong, then you don't have anything to hide.
2. [83]Electronic enhancements to identification documents are essential in the digital world we live in so that government agencies can more efficiently exchange information, thus facilitating the detection and apprehension of suspected terrorists.
3. [84]Laws protect citizens from being abused or taken advantage of by overzealous government officials who are involved in monitoring activities.
4. [85]It is not possible to put a price on freedom or security; therefore, projects such as a national ID system are worth the cost of implementation.

Can Technology Be Used to Benefit Everyone?

Summary of the Issue

[86]Does our society have a responsibility to use technology to help achieve social justice? [87]Freeman Dyson, an American physicist and mathematician, sparked discussion about this issue by saying that science is concentrating *too* much on "making toys for the rich" instead of addressing the needs of the poor. [88]There is great promise for financial reward from creating an even smaller cellular phone, but there is little incentive to find solar energy solutions that will help struggling rural communities. [89]Dyson proposes the application of three technologies to turn poor rural areas into sources of wealth: solar energy, genetic engineering, and Internet access.

[90]Solar energy is available virtually everywhere in the world. [91]It could become cheap enough to compete with oil. [92]The spiraling price of oil, which has been caused primarily by increased worldwide demand, has created a barrier to elevating poor rural communities above the poverty level.

[93]Through genetic engineering, it might be possible to design new plants (or modify existing plants) to achieve novel biological processes such as converting sunlight into fuel efficiently. [94]If plants could be engineered to

improve their efficiency as sources of energy, or to provide other qualities that are in demand (such as making them better sources of protein and fiber when consumed), rural residents would be able to produce items with high market demand and would have greater opportunities to increase their standard of living.

[95]The Internet can help businesses and farms in remote areas become part of the modem economy. [96]Currently, it is difficult for rural farmers in Third World countries to determine the best place to take their crops to market. [97]By consulting the Internet, however, they could obtain price quotes for markets within their reach and determine which ones would provide the best prices for their crops.

POINT: Technology Provides Economic Opportunity for All

[98]The advocates of Dyson's position maintain that a lack of technology or resources is not what keeps the majority of the world's population in poverty. [99]Instead, they argue, it is a lack of commitment to (and focus on) the problems of social justice that allows poverty to continue.

1. [100]If people all agree that poverty is unacceptable, the world possesses the technology and resources to eliminate it.
2. [101]Technology can improve the quality of life of poor countries (and poor people in rich countries) if scientists and business leaders join together.
3. [102]Technology can be an ethical force to humanize us, giving us the ability to affect deeply the lives of all. [103]Francis Bacon, the 16th- and 17th-century English philosopher, once wrote that science can "endow the human family with new mercies."

COUNTERPOINT: Technology Doesn't Provide Economic Opportunity for All

[104]Dyson's critics maintain that his suggestions on using technology for social change are impractical and cannot be achieved with the current resources. [105]They even feel his plan might be dangerous, inasmuch as it may have unforeseen scientific and political results.

1. [106]No one can solve the problems of poverty. [107]The proof is that it has never been done.
2. [108]The problem of poverty is not an issue for technologists. [109]It should be addressed by religious leaders, education experts, and politicians.
3. [110]Genetic engineering may hold the promise of great benefits, but it should not be explored because of its potential risks.
4. [111]Any move away from an oil-centered energy plan threatens the stability of the world's economies.

—Adapted from Evans, Martin, and Poatsy. *Introductory Technology in Action*, 7th ed., Pearson, 2011, pp. 142–149.

CONTINUED

EXAMPLE *CONTINUED*

Term	Definition	Trait	What It Is Not	Examples
Relativism			Judeo-Christian ethics	None given
Situational ethics		None given	Judeo-Christian ethics	None given
Societal ethics		None given		None given
Rule utilitarianism			Situational ethics	
Unethical behavior		None given	Amoral behavior—no sense of right or wrong	

Explanation

Compare your answers to the following think-aloud, completed by Madelyn, another student in your class.

The writers of this passage used both the generalization-example and the definition-example patterns. Almost every paragraph begins with a general statement followed by examples as supporting details. For example, sentence 61 makes a general statement, and sentences 62–65 give examples to support it. The writer also defines several ethics terms used. For example, sentence 25 defines the term **rule utilitarianism**. Sentences 26 and 27 give an extended definition of the term, and sentence 28 gives examples. To answer the prereading questions, I underlined all the terms in bold print and their definitions in sentences 16, 24, 25, and 31. I underlined examples in sentences 28 and 32. The writers' controlling point about the topic "ethics and technology" was stated as "key issues surrounding." I circled the transition phrase "For instance," in sentence 32. I double underlined "is reminiscent of the former Nazi and Soviet regimes" in sentence 78. This is a startling comparison aimed at clarifying the depth of unethical behavior. I completed the concept map with the following details from the passage:

- Relativism: A theory asserting that there are no universal truths, only beliefs, perspectives, and values. Everyone has his or her own ideas of right and wrong; nonjudgmental
- Situational ethics: Decision making based on the circumstances, not fixed laws
- Societal ethic: General set of unwritten guidelines
- Rule utilitarianism: Moral guidelines through specific rules. Improved society; happier people. Laws against public nudity.
- Unethical behavior: Not conforming to a set of approved standards or professional behavior. Using phone to text a friend during an exam.

Practice 1

Question, Read, Annotate, and Review Passages Using Examples

Assume the following two passages are the next assigned readings on the theme "living in the digital age." Your professor has provided a few questions to guide your thinking. Before reading each passage, survey the prereading questions and skim the passage for possible answers. Then read the passage. As you read, annotate the details in the passage that answer the prereading question. After reading, respond to the prompts that follow.

Before and After Reading Questions:

Logical Order: Does this passage use the generalization-example or the definition-example pattern? Which transitions/signal words does the writer use?

Central Idea: What is the writer's central point?

Relevant Details: What are the definitions of *cyberbullying*? How is cyberbullying different from being bullied in person? What are the effects of cyberbullying? How frequently does cyberbullying occur?

Effective Language: What vivid words does the writer use to create images in the reader's mind?

PRACTICE 1 *CONTINUED*

WHAT IS CYBERBULLYING?

[1]Cyberbullying is bullying that takes place using electronic technology. [2]Electronic technology includes devices and equipment such as cell phones, computers, and tablets as well as communication tools including social media sites, text messages, chat, and websites.

[3]Examples of cyberbullying include mean text messages or emails, rumors sent by email or posted on social networking sites, and embarrassing pictures, videos, websites, or fake profiles.

WHY CYBERBULLYING IS DIFFERENT

[4]Kids who are being cyberbullied are often bullied in person as well. [5]Additionally, kids who are cyberbullied have a harder time getting away from the behavior.

- [6]Cyberbullying can happen 24 hours a day, 7 days a week, and reach a kid even when he or she is alone. [7]It can happen any time of the day or night.
- [8]Cyberbullying messages and images can be posted anonymously and distributed quickly to a very wide audience. [9]It can be difficult and sometimes impossible to trace the source.
- [10]Deleting inappropriate or harassing messages, texts, and pictures is extremely difficult after they have been posted or sent.

EFFECTS OF CYBERBULLYING

[11]Cell phones and computers themselves are not to blame for cyberbullying. [12]Social media sites can be used for positive activities, like connecting kids with friends and family, helping students with school, and for entertainment. [13]But these tools can also be used to hurt other people. [14]Whether done in person or through technology, the effects of bullying are similar.

- [15]Kids who are cyberbullied are more likely to:
- [16]Use alcohol and drugs
- [17]Skip school
- [18]Experience in-person bullying
- [19]Be unwilling to attend school
- [20]Receive poor grades
- [21]Have lower self-esteem
- [22]Have more health problems

FREQUENCY OF CYBERBULLYING

[23]The 2008–2009 School Crime Supplement (National Center for Education Statistics and Bureau of Justice Statistics) indicates that 6% of students in grades 6–12 experienced cyberbullying.

[24]The 2011 Youth Risk Behavior Surveillance Survey finds that 16% of high school students (grades 9–12) were electronically bullied in the past year.

[25]Research on cyberbullying is growing. [26]However, because kids' technology use changes rapidly, it is difficult to design surveys that accurately capture trends.

—"What is Cyberbullying?" 11 Sept. 2014. http://www.stopbullying.gov/cyberbullying/what-is-it/index.html

After Reading Response: Respond to the following prompts in your journal:

- Write a summary of the passage (see Module 1, page 34).
- Create an example concept map that answers the following prereading questions:
  - How is cyberbullying an illustration of ethics and technology?
  - Do parents, school officials, or police have the right to monitor the online behavior of those suspected of cyberbullying?
  - In what ways could the behaviors of a cyberbully negatively affect him or her in the future?

Before and After Reading Questions:

Logical Order: Does this passage use the generalization-example or the definition-example pattern? Which transitions/signal words does the writer use?
Central Idea: What is the writer's central point?
Relevant Details: What are key examples of barriers to literacy in the developing world? What are examples of the positive impact of the Worldreader program in the developing world?
Effective Language: What vivid words does the writer use to create images in the reader's mind?

E-READERS MARK A NEW CHAPTER IN THE DEVELOPING WORLD

Lynn Neary

[1]A former Amazon executive who helped Jeff Bezos turn shopping into a digital experience has set out to end illiteracy. [2]David Risher is now the head of Worldreader, a nonprofit organization that brings e-books to kids in developing countries through Kindles and cellphones.

[3]Risher was traveling around the world with his family when he got the idea for Worldreader. [4]They were doing volunteer work at an orphanage in Ecuador when he saw a building with a big padlock on the door. [5]He asked a woman who worked there what was inside, and she said, "It's the library."

[6]"I asked, 'Why is it locked up?' [7]And she said it took too long for books to get there," says Risher. [8]"[The books] came by boat and by the time they got there, they were uninteresting to the kids. [9]And I said, 'Well, can we take a look inside? [10]I'd like to see this.' [11]And she said, 'I think I've lost the key.'"

[12]This, Risher thought, can be fixed. [13]If it's so hard to give kids access to physical books, why not give them e-books and the digital devices they would need to read them? [14]Risher had joined Amazon at its beginning, helping it grow into the dominant online

CONTINUED

PRACTICE 1 *CONTINUED*

retailer it is today. [15]He felt he could apply some of the lessons he had learned at Amazon to the problem of illiteracy.

[16]"We were really trying to change people's behavior, but once that started to happen, of course it took off because it was convenient and because the prices were lower," says Risher. [17]"In a way, we are trying to do something very similar here. ... [18]Here's a culture where reading has never really gotten a chance to take off because the access to books is so limited. [19]So we make it easy for people to get access to books and we try to put books on the e-readers that are appealing to kids and interesting to teachers so that we can, over time, help people shift a little in their behavior and their mindset."

[20]Working through schools and local governments, Worldreader launched its first program in Ghana and is now in nine African countries. [21]As of last month, Worldreader says, it has put more than 700,000 e-books in the hands of some 12,000 children.

[22]Donations from corporate partners and individuals help pay for the Kindles. [23]E-books are donated by authors and publishers in both Western countries and the countries where the schools are located. [24]Risher says it may seem counterintuitive to use e-readers in schools in poor, developing countries, but it actually makes a lot of sense.

[25]"[E-readers] turn out to be remarkably well-adapted to the developing world, in part because they don't take very much power, they are very portable. [26]It's almost like having an entire library in your hand and, like all technology, they get less and less expensive over time," Risher says.

[27]A study of the Worldreaders pilot program in Ghana was funded by the U.S. Agency for International Development. [28]Tony Bloome, a senior education technology specialist with USAID, says the initial results were mostly positive.

[29]"We definitely found that it provided more access to materials. [30]That wasn't surprising at all," says Bloome. [31]"I think kids' appreciation and use of technology is somewhat universal in terms of the excitement—so much so [that] the kids would sit on their devices because they were concerned they would be stolen. [32]And that led to one of the challenges we had in terms of breakage."

[33]Worldreader has responded to the breakage problem with tougher e-readers and training for students and teachers in how to handle them. [34]Even with the breakage problem, though, the USAID study found the program to be cost effective. [35]It also found that kids who had never used a computer before learned to use e-readers quickly and it didn't take them long to find games and music. [36]But Bloome says that their excitement was contagious.

[37]"Especially with the group that was able to take the e-readers home, basically the young people became rock stars in regards to being able to introduce their parents or other kids in the community to e-readers," he says. [38]"But really focused on content, which is really exciting. [39]It's about the provision of reading materials."

[40]Bloome says USAID is still assessing how the access to books is affecting learning in primary grades. [41]In the meantime, Worldreader is moving on to smaller devices with a program that created an e-reader app for cellphones used in developing countries. [42]Risher says the potential for getting access to books on cellphones is huge.

[43]"It really is the best way to get books into people's hands where the physical infrastructure isn't very good, the roads are bad, gas costs too much ... but you can beam

books through the cellphone network just like you can make a phone call—and that's really the thing that changes kids' lives."

44Risher says he knows Worldreader alone won't solve illiteracy, but he hopes it can be a catalyst for change.

—Neary, Lynn. "E-Readers Mark a NEW Chapter in the Developing World." 2 Dec. 2013. http://www.npr.org/blogs/parallels/2013/12/02/248194408/e-readers-mark-a-new-chapter-in-the-developing-world.

After Reading Response: Respond to the following prompts in your journal.

- Write a summary of the passage (see Module 1, page 34).
- Create an example concept map that answers the following question:
  How does Risher's Worldreader exemplify ethics and technology?

Prewrite a Draft of a Thesis Statement Using Examples

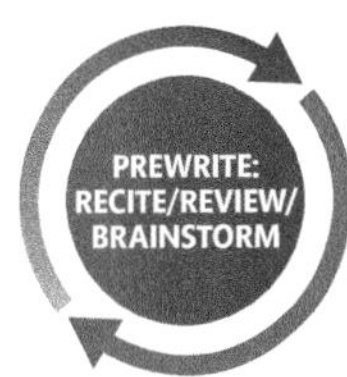

When you write using the generalization-example pattern, you limit the development of your topic to a set of specific examples, instances, or cases. Most likely, you have an opinion or point of view about the topic and its examples, and this opinion or attitude is your point or central idea. You may reveal your opinion by listing the examples in a particular order of importance. A thesis sentence states the point or purpose of the examples. However, at times, the example pattern is only implied in the thesis statement.

When you write an extended definition example, most likely you have an opinion or belief about the word or concept you are defining. Your opinion is your point or main idea. A topic sentence states the overall point of the definition. For example, each of the following two topic sentences contains (1) a concept, (2) the writer's attitude about the concept, and (3) the signal word indicating the definition-example pattern of organization.

Generalization-Example Thesis Statement:

TOPIC — WRITER'S OPINION — EXAMPLES

Computer literacy benefits everyday, college, and working life.

Definition-Example Thesis Statement:

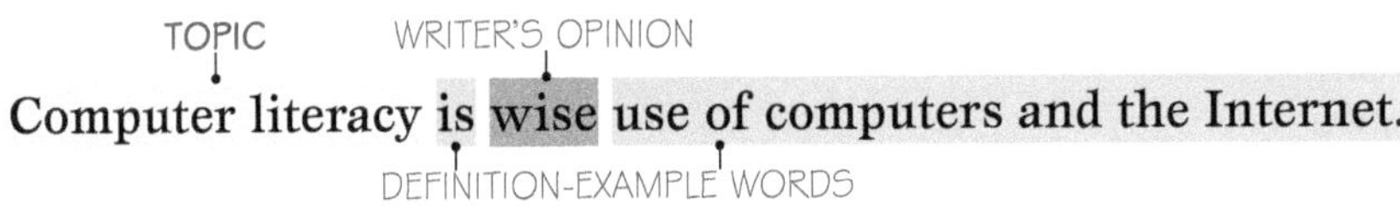

To draft a central idea, a writer may brainstorm key words that signal examples and reflect an opinion. These words narrow the topic to focus on exemplification. The writer then combines these words to compose a thesis statement. Consider the preceding examples. Both deal with the general topic "computer literacy." However, the generalization-example thesis statement focuses on benefits in three areas of life. In contrast, the definition-example thesis statement focuses on defining the term.

Example

Your instructor has asked you to respond to the ideas in the readings on pages 388-399. You are to write an essay that addresses the guiding question "What are the pros and cons of living in the digital age?" The first part of the assignment is to generate a central idea or thesis statement for the essay. Your next step is to decide whether you will use generalization example or definition example, or a combination of the two to make your point. Use the following steps to brainstorm your thesis statement.

Topic: Pros and Cons of Living in Digital Age

1. Narrow Topic: ______________________________
2. Choose Type of Exemplification: ______________________________
3. Identify Example Signal Words: ______________________________

   ____
4. Identify Opinion Words: ______________________________

   ____
5. Combine into a Draft of Thesis Statement: ______________________________

   ____

Explanation

Compare your answers to Madelyn's think-aloud.

I wanted to state a general thought and then use examples throughout the essay to support it. So my pattern of organization is generalization and example. I gave examples to illustrate the opinion words **positives** and **negatives**. I also used the wording "both sides of the argument" to signal to my reader that I would offer examples of both. My thesis statement is "There are positives and negatives to each side of the argument."

Practice 2

Prewrite a Draft of a Thesis Statement Using Examples

In your reading/writing journal, identify the steps you used to write a thesis statement using examples. How did your thesis statement differ from Madelyn's? Did she use any methods you didn't?

Prewrite to Generate Relevant Details Using Examples

LO4

During the prewriting phase of the writing process, use an example concept map to generate details to clarify a generalization or define a key word or concept. To generate details based on the example patterns of organization, writers may use some of the reporter's questions such as *who, what, when,* and *how*. The following chart lists some questions you may ask to identify key details as you brainstorm.

Ask Questions to Identify Key Details

What is the general idea being illustrated?
What is the term or concept being defined?
Who or what serves as an example of this idea?
What examples are given?
How do the examples illustrate the general idea or specific word or concept?

The generalization-example concept map usually flows from the main or general idea to key examples that are the major supporting details. Often, you will also provide minor details that describe or further explain an example.

The definition-example concept map also usually flows from the central idea to key examples that are the major supporting details. However, the extended definition-example concept map also prompts you to generate additional details. To define a word or concept, you may generate details that explain the traits of the concept, what it is, and what it is *not*, as well as examples.

General (Central) Idea
Example
    Explanation
Example
    Explanation
Example
    Explanation

Definition
What it is like
What it is not
Traits
Examples

Example

Assume your class is continuing to work on the essay addressing the guiding question "What are examples of the pros and cons of living in the digital age?" Now your assignment is to return to the texts to identify details that you will use in your paper and create a concept map to organize your ideas for the essay. Use one or both of the following concept maps to generate relevant details.

Generalization-Example Concept Map

General Idea:

Major Detail: Example 1

Major Detail: Example 2

Minor Details: Explanation

Minor Details: Explanation

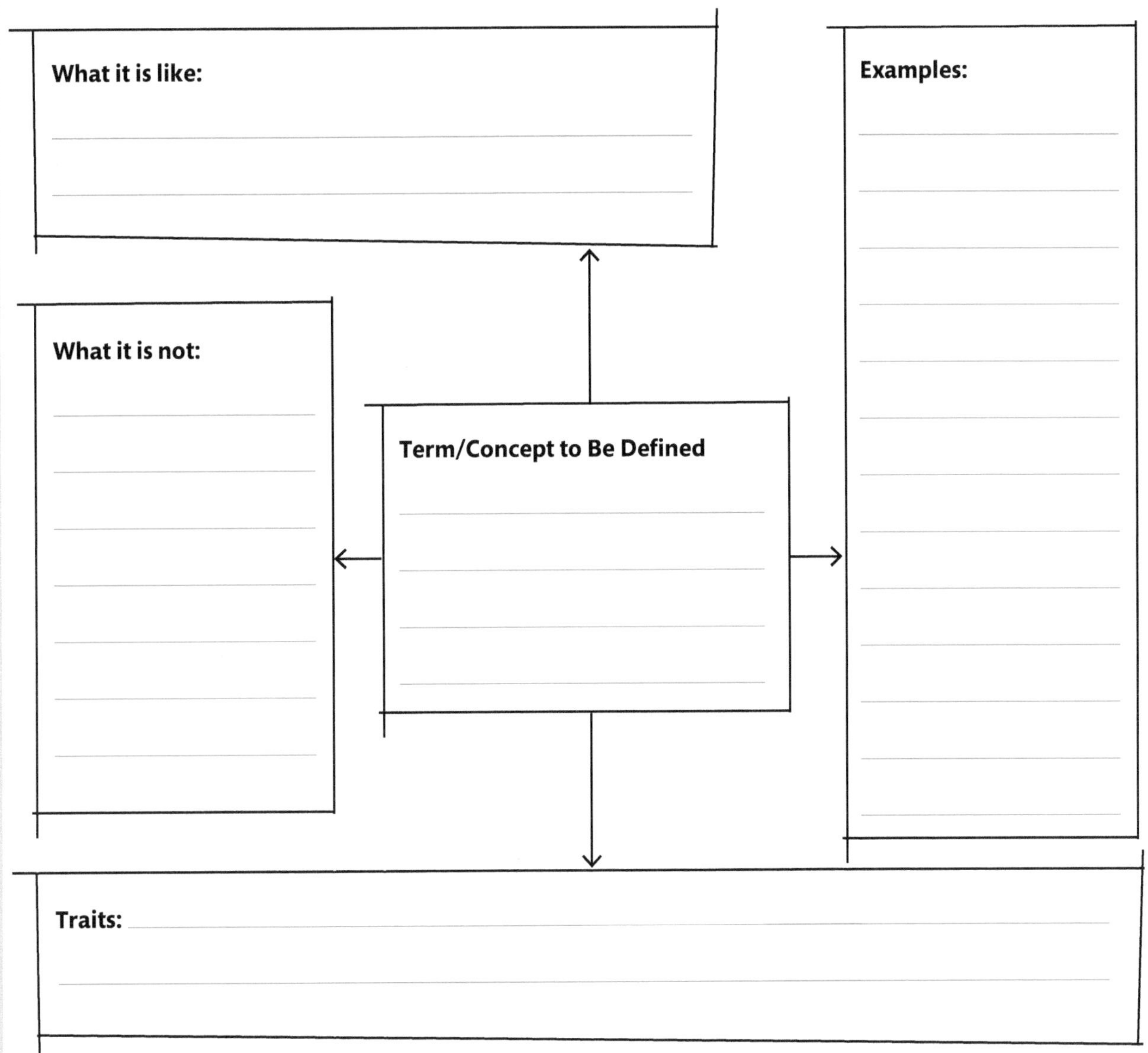

Explanation

Compare your responses to Madelyn's think-aloud.

After reading the articles, I did a freewrite to get my first thoughts on paper. Then, I filled in the generalization-example concept map with details from my freewrite. I saw that I had come up with enough examples, but needed to explain how some of my examples supported my thesis. So I went back to my Word document and expanded my explanations where necessary. Here is an outline based on my concept map.

Thesis: There are positives and negatives to each side of the argument.

CONTINUED

EXAMPLE *CONTINUED*

A. Pros of digital age
  1. Instantaneous communication
    a. Emergency phone calls to 9-1-1
    b. Company e-mails employees about policy changes or meetings
    c. Company advertises with mass e-mails or texts
    d. Google searches for quick answers to questions
  2. Increased literacy
    a. E-Readers on Kindles and cellphones promote literacy in developing countries
B. Cons of digital age
  1. Cyberbullying
  2. Loss of privacy

Practice 3

Prewrite to Generate Relevant Details Using Examples

In your reading/writing journal, identify the steps needed to create relevant details to support a thesis statement. Identify the steps Madelyn went through as she annotated the texts and created her graphic organizer. How did your concept maps differ from hers?

L5 Compose a Draft Using Logical Order: Examples

READ: QUESTION/ ANNOTATE

PREWRITE: RECITE/REVIEW/ BRAINSTORM

DRAFT YOUR RESPONSE

Once you have brainstormed details for an example pattern, you are ready to begin the drafting process. First, review the concept map you completed with the details from the reading and your own insights or response. As you review your concept map, move details as needed into the most logical order. Add details if needed. Also, include example order signal words to guide your reader through your essay. Master writers create several drafts to achieve a logical order and smooth flow of ideas.

Example

Assume you are still working toward writing an essay that answers the guiding question "What are the pros and cons of living in the digital age?" On your own paper, write a draft of your essay.

Explanation

Compare your answer to Madelyn's think-aloud and essay.

Since I spent so much time prewriting, using a freewrite, concept map, and outline, drafting the essay came easily. I did create several drafts. As I reread each draft, I found places to add more explanations or change wording so it made sense.

The Pros and Cons of Living in a Digital Age
by Madelyn Miller

Technology: teens love technology, while adults hate it. Looking back at society and how it has transformed over the last couple of decades is evidence enough to see that the culture of today's society has made a complete 360. What humanity prioritized 50 years ago and what it values now are drastically different. Some may see the invention and continuous upgrades to the numerous technological devices as a blessing to the world, but of course there are two sides to every coin. The other half of the population will always find fault with technology and see how it is causing humanity to regress in its social and intellectual capabilities. There are positives and negatives to each side of the argument. It just depends on how you view it.

Living in a digital age comes with many plusses. Technology has the ability to open so many doors that have previously been left closed and untouched. For centuries, communication meant handwriting letters, entrusting them to the hands of messengers, and then relying on horses and boats to carry the messages to their intended receivers. It could take days, weeks, or even months to carry out a conversation with someone who didn't live in the same town as you. If your message was urgent, then you were out of luck, because there was no faster way of travel until the steam engine was invented. Fast forward to present day and it is easy to see how communication has evolved. Communication between two people can happen in a matter of seconds due to texting and calling. When there is an emergency, dial 9-1-1 and

CONTINUED

EXAMPLE *CONTINUED*

assistance will arrive in minutes. Instantaneous communication also comes in handy when it comes to businesses. Companies use e-mail to alert their employees of policy changes or when meetings will be. Companies that sell direct to the consumer use e-mail or mass text messages to offer discounts or to advertise sales.

When a question comes up and no one knows the answer, what is the first solution that comes to mind? Google it. Search it on the Internet; there is no need to waste any more time thinking about it, right? The answer is only seconds away. If Google disappeared for even just a week, today's society, especially the younger generations, would be hard pressed to know how to find answers to their questions. With unlimited knowledge at the fingertips of smart and inventive and creative people, it is easy to observe how this generation has become so advanced.

In under-developed countries where the illiteracy rate is astoundingly high, technology has assisted in decreasing that trend. While importing hard copies of books is expensive, downloading digital copies is affordable. The absence of books and school reading materials has prevented children from having the opportunity to learn to read. By donating e-readers to third-world countries, kids and teachers are able to access hundreds of books that normally would not be available to them. Due to this, children are able to learn to read faster and more efficiently.

While it is not hard to see that technology had made some vast, significant changes in the lives of everyone, it is also easy to spot the downside of living in a digital age as well. The word *bullying* makes a person automatically picture the giant upperclassman taking lunch money from the little freshman. That's not the case anymore, though. The social media revolution has brought with it a new era of bullying. Bullies, while they may not be able to physically harm someone over the Internet, can do just as much damage with their words, pictures, and rumors. This new type of bullying is known as *cyberbullying*. Kids cannot escape their tormenters by going home. Even if the person being bullied is not actively engaging on social media websites, the information is still out there for anyone to see. Once it's out there, you can never get it back. Cyberbullying has the potential to affect a child for the rest of his or her life; it can cause health problems, truancy, alcohol and drug use, and mental states that many may never be able to understand.

The Internet stores information forever. Everything that enters into it is held there and never released. No matter how hard someone tries, nothing can ever be truly removed once the information has been submitted. While this can be viewed as helpful, it is mostly seen as our privacy slowly being chipped away. The government has the ability to access any information about you. When the government has more and more access into the lives of the citizens, they are able to pull tighter and tighter on the reins they have around their people. Some people may say the government's capability to access this information is strictly for safety and legal purposes and that it is constitutional. Others may say that this power of the government is violating the rights of the American citizen. The line between the two opinions on this subject is fuzzy and grey, so it is up to each individual to decide what he or she thinks.

There are pros and cons to living life in a digital age. There are facts and evidence for both sides of the case. Does the positive side of this new life outweigh the negative? Everyone is entitled to his or her own opinion, and no one can be right or wrong on a matter like this. However, the people who are against this "new technological age" are sadly out of luck; the future is quickly approaching and nothing is going to be able to turn back the technological clock.

Practice 4

Compose a Draft Using Logical Order: Examples

In your reading/writing journal, identify the steps you took to write your draft. Identify the steps Madelyn took as she wrote her draft. How are your drafts different? How are they similar? What can you apply from Madelyn's method to your own writing in the future?

L6 Revise and Proofread for Effective Language with Examples

Master writers may rely on descriptive language to clearly exemplify a general idea or define a key word. Sensory details and figures of speech such as metaphors and similes create vivid images in the reader's mind that can clarify the main idea. Often, a writer uses figurative language to state a generalization as the main idea and then provides examples and illustrations as supporting details that clarify the point. Likewise, writers may use figurative language to compare a key term to concepts more familiar to the reader.

Example

Assume the role of peer editor for Madelyn's essay "The Pros and Cons of Living in a Digital Age." Identify two expressions or details that would benefit by revising using sensory details or figures of speech. Suggest possible revisions.

Original Expression or Detail: ______________________________

____

Revised for Sensory Details or Figures of Speech: ______________________________

____

Original Expression or Detail: ______________________________

____

Revised for Sensory Details or Figures of Speech: ______________________________

____

Explanation

Compare your answers to Madelyn's think-aloud.

When I was drafting my essay, I remembered that we had learned about figurative language in an earlier module. So I looked for ways to use figurative language to add interest to my ideas and make them memorable. The first sentence I wanted to revise was, "Teens love technology, while adults hate it." I revised the sentence to "Teens are clinging to it like a lifeline, while at the other end of the spectrum, adults are avoiding it like the plague." I really like the way these similes contrast a positive with a negative view, between life and death. The second sentence I chose to revise was "The internet stores information forever." I revised the sentence to "The internet is a vault." I like this metaphor because a vault holds treasures. And we think a vault is secure. But a vault can be broken into and treasures stolen. That's the danger of the internet. Personal information can be stolen and shared for someone else's gain. I also decided to revise my thesis sentence, "There are positives and negatives to each side of the argument" into a shorter, stronger statement: "There are pros and cons to living in the digital age."

Practice 6

Revise and Proofread for Effective Language with Examples

Identify three expressions or details in the latest draft of your essay to revise using sensory details or figures of speech. Create a new draft of your essay that includes your revisions.

Workshop: Comprehend and Create an Essay Using Examples

Assume you are continuing your study of the theme "living in the digital age" in your college technology course. The following passages make up a capstone reading assignment. Your capstone writing assignment is to write an essay in response to the same guiding question, "What are the pros and cons of living in the digital age?" You may also be asked to make connections among these passages and the ones you have already read in this module. Read the following passages and complete the writing activities that follow.

THE HIVE

D. J. Henry

[1]Eta Pother hated the HIVE. She hated the Five Words of Wisdom. She hated all the Boxes, particularly the Brood Box. Most of all, she hated MAMA.

[2]Everywhere Eta Pother looked she saw those eyes. MAMA's eyes. MAMA's mesmerizing eyes. Eyes set in the image of a woman around thirty, with a smooth brown face, thick, shiny-black hair, and photogenic good looks. An omnipresent hologram, she

CONTINUED

appeared cordial and threatening at the same time. Always crowning her head, like an arched ribbon of ticker tape, these words continuously flowed: "Message from MAMA: ***M**easures of **A**nthropological **M**ediation **A**gency*."

[3]Those eyes greeted Eta every morning from the monitoring walls in her bedroom as she awoke. They looked up at her from the kitchen's counter top as she prepared and ate meals. They gazed at her from the yellowed walls in the halls and landings of Paradise East, her housing unit. They accosted her from billboards in open spaces, from sidewalks, office and elevator walls—outside, inside, high, low, always, everywhere; those eyes could and did appear on any surface at any time. Those startling-blue orbs followed Eta's every movement. Eta was only one of 5.23 million souls in the HIVE; MAMA watched them all. As those eyes watched, MAMA tenderly spoke the Five Words of Wisdom:

> [4]Know you are not special.
> [5]Know you are not good.
> [6]Know you are not smart.
> [7]Know you are not loved.
> [8]Know MAMA knows all.

[9]This morning, Eta's stomach roiled as she lay beneath the covers listening to the Five Words. And beneath those covers, hidden from MAMA's eyes, Eta breathed rebellion. After each Word, Eta countered, "I know I am special. I know I am good. I know I am smart. I know I am loved. I love me. MAMA can't know all."

[10]Once, she had made the mistake of speaking rebellion openly—in the kitchen. A Freedom Rider had instantly materialized and commanded that she speak only Clean Thoughts. Clear Thoughts. To purify her thoughts, he stunned her with the Instructor, a Taser that set afire her every nerve. For days, her thoughts scrambled to find sense, and time warped into slow motion. After, she only whispered rebellion in quiet thoughts beneath the covers of her bedding.

[11]On this day, Eta's queasiness did not come from the Five Words or MAMA's eyes. This day she had dreaded from her first moment of understanding. This day was the day of Eta's New Birth.

[12]In the HIVE, a child was separated from bio-mother at the moment of inception to be reared in the Brood Box, until age 6 at which time he or she was assigned to a Forever Family more suited to the child's predetermined function in the HIVE. At age 12, the Age of Accountability, every child went through the New Birth.

[13]Eta had been placed with the Taylor family who made and supplied clothing goods to the Produce Boxes for distribution among the HIVE. Eta hated the SmartClothes she had learned to make—all following the same nondescript pattern cut from the same dull grey cloth best suited for weaving in the specialized components of wearable technology that connected each wearer to the HIVE. For six years, Eta had apprenticed with the Taylors. After her New Birth, she would be promoted to Skilled Weaver and work the daily 15-hour shift of an adult.

[14]Eta had no intention of enduring the New Birth. She had watched as older children had gone through the ritual. She had watched her best friend Lambda instantly morph from a playful, loving spirit into a slavish HIVE worker. Eta would have never believed that Lambda could love MAMA or the HIVE more than her. After Lambda went through the New Birth, he loved MAMA best.

[15]"Eta, look," he said as he revealed his new, permanent electronic tattoo. She tentatively touched the mini circuitry embedded under his skin on the inside of his right wrist. Her fingers grazed its pulsing patterns.

[16]"These sensors," he said, "give MAMA full access to my body. MAMA can monitor my wellbeing, my heart rate, brainwaves, temperature, everything, and intervene to save my life if needed." Eta didn't say it, but she wondered if MAMA

could take action not so helpful to his wellbeing. "You know what else, Eta, MAMA and I can talk without speaking. We can hear each other's thoughts." He pointed to his forehead. "I have a microwave transmitter implanted in my sinus cavity," he said, "to interface with MAMA."

[17]As Lambda spoke, Eta noticed that his voice had changed; he did not sound like Lambda at all. The singsong cadence of MAMA's voice blanketed his impassioned modulations.

[18]Yet, what alarmed Eta most was the way Lambda submitted to his assigned work. He had hated Freedom Riders as much as she. He had vowed rebellion. Now, he *was* a Freedom Rider. Eta studied the insignia on the right breast of his uniform: "Freedom Rider: Enforcer of The Five Words: Peace through Violence."

[19]Lambda took her hand, lifted her chin, met her eyes, and reassured her, "It's okay, Eta, really, it is. It's not like what we thought. I feel so…" he paused and moved closer, never wavering in his eye contact, "…so complete. You are going to love the New Birth, Eta. Trust me."

[20]She hoped he couldn't see inside her head. She had no intention of being implanted with sensors and circuitry. She had no intention of sharing unspoken thoughts with anyone. She had no intention of being wired to interface with MAMA and "fully realize Human Integration with Virtual Environs—the HIVE." She knew—she was complete just as she was. She would not submit to the New Birth.

[21]Eta Pother had a plan.

WHAT IS GPS?

[1]The Global Positioning System (GPS) is a U.S.-owned utility that provides users with positioning, navigation, and timing (PNT) services. This system consists of three segments: the space segment, the control segment, and the user segment. The U.S. Air Force develops, maintains, and operates the space and control segments.

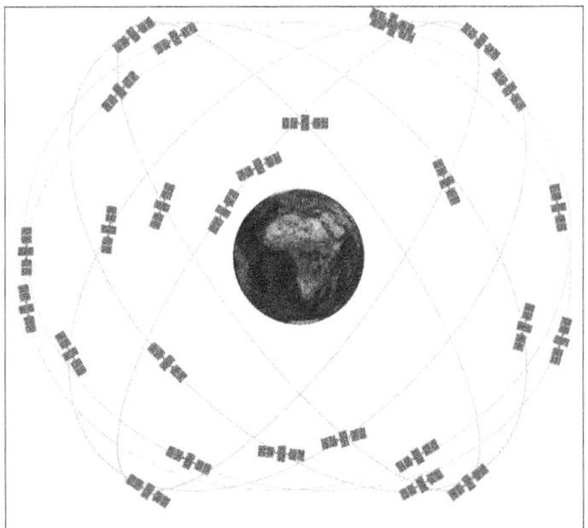

Space Segment

[2]The GPS space segment consists of a constellation of satellites transmitting radio signals to users. The United States is committed to maintaining the availability of at least 24 operational GPS satellites, 95% of the time. To ensure this commitment, the Air Force has been flying 31 operational GPS satellites for the past few years.

Expandable 24-Slot satellite constellation, as defined in the SPS Performance Standard.

[3]GPS satellites fly in medium Earth orbit (MEO) at an altitude of approximately 20,200 km (12,550 miles). Each satellite circles the Earth twice a day.

[4]The satellites in the GPS constellation are arranged into six equally-spaced orbital planes surrounding the Earth. Each plane contains four "slots" occupied by baseline

CONTINUED

satellites. This 24-slot arrangement ensures users can view at least four satellites from virtually any point on the planet. The Air Force normally flies more than 24 GPS satellites to maintain coverage whenever the baseline satellites are serviced or decommissioned.

5The extra satellites may increase GPS performance but are not considered part of the core constellation. In June 2011, the Air Force successfully completed a GPS constellation expansion known as the "Expandable 24" configuration. Three of the 24 slots were expanded, and six satellites were repositioned, so that three of the extra satellites became part of the constellation baseline. As a result, GPS now effectively operates as a 27-slot constellation with improved coverage in most parts of the world.

Control Segment

6The GPS control segment consists of a global network of ground facilities that track the GPS satellites, monitor their transmissions, perform analyses, and send commands and data to the constellation. The current operational control segment includes a master control station, an alternate master control station, 12 command and control antennas, and 16 monitoring sites. The locations of these facilities are shown in the following map.

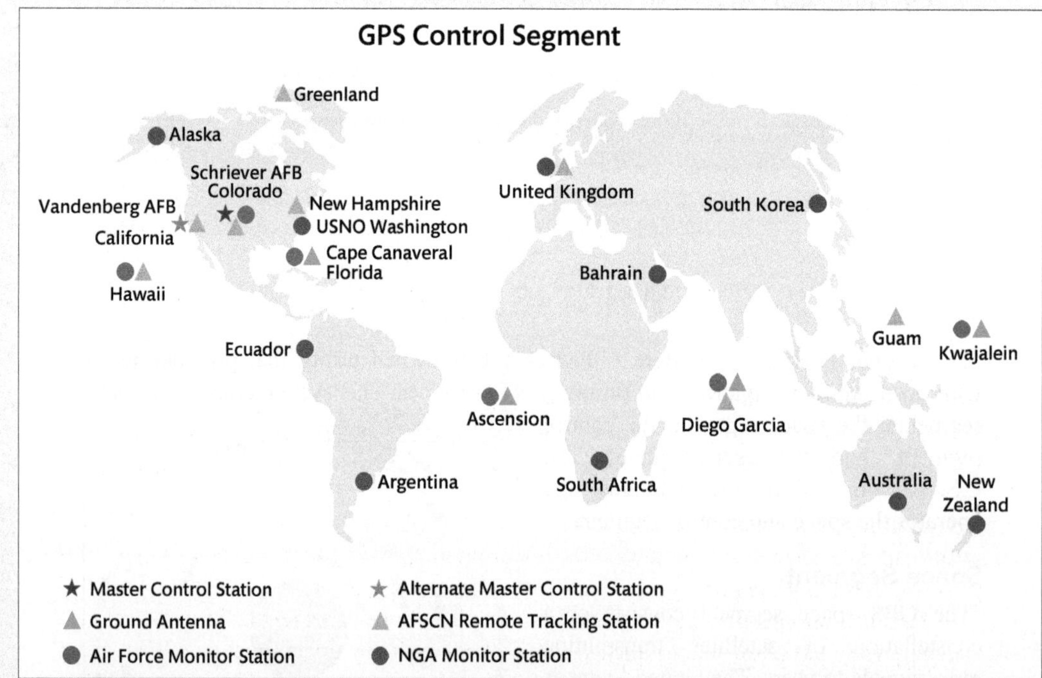

User Segment: GPS Applications

7Like the Internet, GPS is an essential element of the global information infrastructure. The free, open, and dependable nature of GPS has led to the development of hundreds of applications affecting every aspect of modern life. GPS technology is now in everything from cell phones and wristwatches to bulldozers, shipping containers, and ATM's.

8GPS boosts productivity across a wide swath of the economy, to include farming, construction, mining, surveying, package delivery, and logistical supply chain management. Major communications networks, banking systems, financial markets, and power grids depend heavily on GPS for precise time synchronization.

Some wireless services cannot operate without it. GPS saves lives by preventing transportation accidents, aiding search and rescue efforts, and speeding the delivery of emergency services and disaster relief. GPS is vital to the Next Generation Air Transportation System (NextGen) that will enhance flight safety while increasing airspace capacity. GPS also advances scientific aims such as weather forecasting, earthquake monitoring, and environmental protection. Finally, GPS remains critical to U.S. national security, and its applications are integrated into virtually every facet of U.S. military operations. Nearly all new military assets—from vehicles to munitions—come equipped with GPS. New uses of GPS are invented every day and are limited only by the human imagination.

–"What Is GPS?" GPS.gov http://www.gps.gov/students 10 July 2014.

Who Is Watching?

[1]Having the ability to locate and track an object anywhere on Earth does bring with it societal implications. The Federal Communications Commission (FCC) mandated that every cell/smartphone had to include a GPS chip by the end of 2005. This enabled the complete rollout of the Enhanced 911 (E911) program. E911 automatically gives dispatchers precise location information for any 911 call. It also means your phone records may include this precise tracking information, which indicates where you are when you make a call. Is that information something you would want the government, or other people, to know? Consider if you were at a park playing baseball with your friends and you made a phone call. At the same time, in another part of the park, an organization with suspected terrorist ties was holding a rally. Would you want the government to assume that because you made a phone call from the park, you are a member of that organization?

[2]Because phones now have GPS chips, cellular phone providers offer plans (for a monthly fee) that allow you to track where a phone is at any given time via a Web site. This could be a real boon for tracking a lost child who wandered off into the woods during a group hike. But are other uses of the technology ethical? Did your daughter really go to the library, or is she actually at the local skate park hanging with her friends? Is your spouse really working late at the office—or at the ballpark watching the baseball game with friends? Now, with a few clicks of the mouse, you can tell where a family member's phone is located. Is this an invasion of privacy? Is it ethical to track the whereabouts of your family members? This is something that you need to decide.

[3]GPS technology begs several questions: What limits and supervision of the government need to be in place to ensure the ethical use of GPS technologies? In what ways could the tracking information provided by GPS devices be used unethically?

CONTINUED

[4]If GPS tracking information is recorded in people's phone data, should the criteria for allowing government agencies to subpoena phone records be changed? Should users be allowed to disable the location information feature on their phones? Location records such as these were used to determine that *New York Times* reporter Jayson Blair had been fabricating stories, a determination that resulted in his resignation. Car rental companies such as Acme Car Rental of New Haven, Connecticut are using GPS records to fine customers for speeding violations. As a nation, we now need to decide how we should balance the benefits and costs (to our privacy) of using this new level of tracking information.

Big Brother Is Watching—But Should He Be?

[5]Think you aren't being closely watched by your employer? Think again! A survey of employers by the American Management Association and the ePolicy Institute revealed that of the employers surveyed:

[6]73 percent monitored e-mail messages

[7]66 percent monitored Web surfing

[8]48 percent monitored activities using video surveillance

[9]45 percent monitored keystrokes and keyboard time

[10]43 percent monitored computer files in some other fashion

[11]There is a high probability that you are being monitored while you work and when you access the Internet via your employer's Internet connection.

[12]The two most frequently cited reasons for employee monitoring are to prevent theft and to measure productivity. Monitoring for theft isn't new, because monitoring cameras have been around for years, and productivity monitoring has been a consistent process for assembly line workers for decades. However, the rise of the Internet has led to a new type of productivity drain that is of concern to employers. **Cyberloafing**, or cyberslacking, means doing anything with a computer, while you are being paid to do your job that is *not* an approved function of your job. Examples of cyberloafing activities are playing games, reading personal e-mail, checking sports scores, watching videos, and buying personal use products on e-commerce sites. Estimates of business productivity losses due to cyberloafing top $50 billion annually. While many employers don't mind if workers answer the occasional personal e-mail while at work, they would probably not appreciate it if they spent four hours of their workday playing World of Warcraft online!

[13]Like most other Americans, you probably feel you have a right to privacy in the workplace. Unfortunately, the laws in the United States don't support a worker's right to privacy. Laws, such as the 1986 Electronic Communications Privacy Act (ECPA), which prohibits unauthorized monitoring of electronic communications, have been interpreted by the courts in favor of employers. The bottom line is that when the employer is paying for equipment and software (such as Internet access and e-mail), the employer has the legal right to monitor its usage.

[14]Is it ethical for employers to monitor employees? Just because an action is *legal* doesn't mean it is *ethical*. It is difficult to argue that an employer doesn't have the right to take measures to prevent theft and detect low productivity. The ethical issue here is whether or not the employees are made aware that they are being monitored. An ethical employer should treat employees with respect and dignity and inform the employees that they are being monitored. Employers have an ethical responsibility (and a legal

one as well, depending on the jurisdiction) not to place monitoring devices in sensitive locations such as bathrooms and dressing areas. However, in many states, the employer does not need to inform the employees in advance that they are being monitored. Conscientious employers include monitoring disclosures in published employee policies to avoid confusion and conflict. If you aren't sure whether your employer monitors employees, check with the company's human resources department.

[15]Employers use a variety of software programs to monitor employee computer usage. Certain software packages keep track of every Web site you visit and the duration of your stay. Checking the baseball scores might take only three seconds and go unnoticed, but spending two hours updating your fantasy football team may be flagged. Keystroke loggers were originally used to monitor performance for people with input-intensive jobs, like clerks and secretaries. Now these programs have the potential to be used to invade your privacy, because they can record everything you type, even that nasty e-mail about the boss that you thought better of sending and deleted!

[16]In addition to monitoring keystrokes, computer software can also be used to monitor the contents of your hard drive, so you don't want to collect 4,823 illegal MP3 files on your work computer. Some programs even keep track of how long your computer is idle, which can give your manager a good idea of whether you were working or taking a three-hour lunch. Since your employer might not tell you that your computer use is being monitored, you should assume that anything you do on your company-provided computer is subject to scrutiny. If you need to do personal work on your lunch hour or other breaks, you may be able to use your personal laptop to avoid the monitoring. Check with your employer to be sure you can connect personal computers to the corporate network or Internet connection. Note that courts in some jurisdictions have ruled that e-mails sent from third-party systems, such as Yahoo! and Gmail, are subject to monitoring if they are sent from employer provided computer systems. Instant messaging is also subject to monitoring. Therefore, the best defense against monitoring of personal instant messaging or e-mail is to use your own computing device to send the communications.

[17]People who monitor employees have a duty to protect their right to privacy and not to disclose any information that they may inadvertently see during the course of monitoring. The acceptable computer use policies at most companies include guidelines for network administrators and other people who have high levels of access to sensitive information. When monitoring employees' work habits, management must ensure that compliance with the policies is tested periodically. Periodic reviews of procedures and compliance help ensure that established company policies are working as designed. An ethical employer strives to prevent misuse of personal data and accidental data loss. This helps a company maintain the trust of its employees. However, you can't always be certain that everyone who monitors you will behave in an ethical manner. Therefore, you need to think very carefully about exactly what personal tasks you are willing to risk engaging in on company computer systems.

[18]So, do your employers have an ethical right to monitor your activities? Certainly, they have a right to ensure they are getting a fair day's work from you, just as you have an ethical obligation to provide a fair effort for a fair wage. However, employers should also be willing to respect the privacy rights of their employees and treat them as professionals, unless there is some indication of wrongdoing. Because employers may have a legal right to monitor you in the workplace, you should work under the assumption that everything you do on your work computer is subject to scrutiny, and behave accordingly. Do your online shopping at home!

—Evans, Martin, and Poatsy. *Introductory Technology in Action*, 7th ed., 2011, pp. 373, 425.

Preread: Survey and Question

Who is MAMA in the short story *The Hive* by D.J. Henry? How does MAMA exemplify cyberbullying (see page 396)?

How is *The Hive* an illustration of the ethical theory of rule utilitarianism? (See "Ethics in Computing," page 388.)

What is the relationship between technology and privacy in *The Hive?*

What are examples of ethical and unethical uses of GPS? (See "E-Readers," page 397 and "Ethics in Computing," page 388.)

What are examples of employees' unethical use of technology at work?

What are examples of employers' ethical use of technology to monitor employees' productivity?

How does *The Hive* illustrate some of the concerns raised in the passage "Who Is Watching?" about living in a digital age?

Read and Annotate

As you read, annotate key ideas, particularly those details that answer your prereading questions.

Recite, Review, and Brainstorm

Recite and **Review** the information. Paraphrase ideas. Summarize the most important parts. **Brainstorm** ideas for your written response to the passage. Answer your prereading questions. *Freewrite* or *map* the relationship among answers to questions or ideas you have annotated in the text. *Outline* or *list* key ideas and details in blocks of thought. Use your own paper.

Write a Draft of Your Response

Using the ideas you generated by brainstorming, compose a draft of your response. Use your own paper.

Revise Your Draft

Once you have created a draft of an example pattern essay, read it over to answer the questions in the "Questions for Revising Example Patterns" box that follows. Indicate your answers by annotating your paper. If you answer "yes" to a question, underline, check, or circle examples. If you answer "no" to a question, write needed information in the margins and draw lines to indicate the placement of additional details. Revise your essay based on your reflection. (*Hint:* Experienced writers create several drafts as they focus on one or two questions per draft.)

Step by Step: Questions for Revising Example Patterns

- ☐ Have I stated or implied a focused main idea?
- ☐ Have I stated or implied the specific points of supports using examples?
- ☐ Is the order of the specific points clear? Have I used strong signal words for example patterns?
- ☐ Have I used concrete details to make my point?
- ☐ Have I made my point with adequate details?
- ☐ Have I included only the details that are relevant to my thesis sentence?
- ☐ Have I used figurative language to make my point clear to my readers?

Proofread Your Draft

Once you have made any revisions to your essay that may be needed, proofread your essay to eliminate careless errors.

Reading and Writing Assignments

MySkillsLab™
Complete this Exercise
on myskillslab.com

Reading and Writing for Everyday Life

Assume Google is sponsoring a contest to give away a device known as Google Glass. The reason for the giveaway is to test the usability of the device and promote sales. Read the following excerpt from a review of the product. Then write the required letter to Google. In your letter, explain how Google Glass would enhance your life. Give examples of how you plan to use the device.

You Will Want GOOGLE GOGGLES

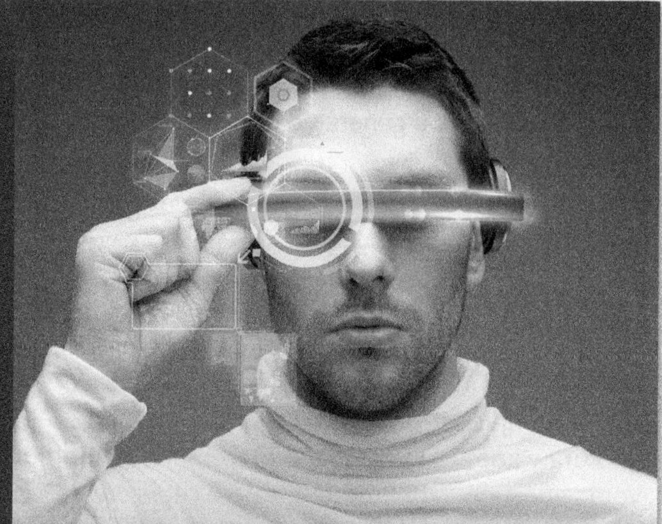

At first glance, Thad Starner does not look out of place at Google. A pioneering researcher in the field of wearable computing, Starner is a big, charming man with unruly hair. But everyone who meets him does a double take, because mounted over the left lens of his eyeglasses is a small rectangle. It looks like a car's side-view mirror made for a human face. The device is actually a minuscule computer monitor aimed at Starner's eye; he sees its display—pictures, e-mails, anything—superimposed on top of the world, Terminator-style.

○○

The spectacles take the place of his desktop computer, his mobile computer, and his all-knowing digital assistant. For all its utility, though, Starner's machine is less distracting than any other computer I've ever seen. This was a revelation. Here was a guy *wearing a computer*, but because he could use it without becoming lost in it—as we all do when we consult our many devices—he appeared less in thrall to the digital world than you and I are every day. "One of the key points here," Starner says, "is that we're trying to make mobile systems that help the user pay *more* attention to the real world as opposed to retreating from it."

○○

Much of what I think you'll use goggles for will be the sort of quotidian stuff you do on your smart phone all the time—look up your next appointment on your calendar, check to see whether that last text was important, quickly fire up Shazam to learn the title of a song you heard on the radio. So why not just keep your smart phone? Because the goggles promise speed and invisibility.

–Manjoo, Farhad. "You Will Want Google Goggles," *MIT Technology Review*. June 19, 2012. *http://www.technologyreview.com/review/428212/you-will-want-google-goggles/*

Reading and Writing for College Life

Assume you are taking a college speech course. You are to give a computer-assisted presentation to your class that explains and illustrates the following guidelines. Read the passage and create a slideshow to assist your speech.

78 THE ESSENTIALS OF PUBLIC SPEAKING

Computer Assisted Presentations

Presentation software is a fact of life for public speakers. PowerPoint still seems the most popular, but there are many others such as Prezi, GoAnimate, Google Docs, Sliderocket, and Keynote. Here are just a few suggestions for designing your slides.

USE CONSISTENT TYPEFACE, SIZE, AND COLOR. Give each item in your outline that has the same level head (for example, all your main points) the same typeface, size, and color throughout your presentation. This will help your listeners follow the organization of your speech.

BE BRIEF. Your objective is to provide the audience with key words and ideas that will reinforce what you're saying in your speech; you don't want your audience members to spend their time reading rather than listening. Generally, put one complete thought on a slide and don't try to put too many words on one slide.

USE COLORS FOR CONTRAST. Remember that many people have difficulty distinguishing red from green, so if you want to distinguish ideas, it is probably best to avoid this color pairing. Similarly, if you're going to print out your slides in shades of gray, make sure the tones you choose provide clear contrasts.

USE ONLY THE VISUALS THAT YOU REALLY NEED. Presentation software packages make inserting visuals so easy that they sometimes encourage the user to include too many visuals. Most presentation packages provide a variety of graphic pictures, animated graphics, photos, and videos that are useful for a wide variety of speeches. Use relevant visuals only when you have room on the slide.

ANTICIPATE QUESTIONS. If there's a question-and-answer period following your speech, consider preparing a few extra slides for responses to questions you anticipate being asked. Then, when someone asks you a predicted question, you can say: "I anticipated that question," and then use the slide to explain it.

USE THE SPELL-CHECK. You don't want professional-looking slides with misspellings; it can ruin your credibility and seriously damage the impact of your speech.

ANTICIPATE TECHNICAL PROBLEMS. If you're planning to use a slide show, for example, consider what you'd do if the computer malfunctioned or the electricity didn't work. A useful backup procedure is to have handouts ready just in case something goes wrong.

—DeVito, *The Essentials of Public Speaking*, 5th ed., Pearson, 2015, pp. 128–129.

Reading and Writing for Working Life

Assume you are the office manager of an insurance company. You want to put in a request to your supervisor that the Maintenance Department adjust employees' computer work stations to ergonomic standards. Read the following article, and then compose a memo to your supervisor that justifies your request.

ERGONOMICS: AVOIDING INJURY ON THE JOB

Ergonomics refers to how you arrange your monitor, chair, body, and keyboard in ways that will help you avoid injury, discomfort, and eyestrain as you work on your computer. The following guidelines can help keep you comfortable and productive:

Position your monitor correctly. Studies suggest it's best to place your monitor at least 25 inches from your eyes. You may need to decrease the screen resolution to make text and images more readable at that distance. Position the monitor either at eye level or so that it is at an angle 15 to 20 degrees below your line of sight.

Purchase an adjustable chair. Adjust the height of your chair so that your feet touch the floor. (You may need to use a footrest to get the right position.) The back support needs to be adjustable so that you can position it to support your lumbar (lower back) region. You should also be able to move the seat or adjust the back so that you can sit without exerting pressure on your knees.

Assume a proper position while typing. A repetitive strain injury (RSI) is a painful condition caused by repetitive or awkward movements of a part of the body. Improperly positioned keyboards are one of the leading causes of RSIs in computer users. Your wrist should be flat (unbent) with respect to the keyboard, and your forearms should be parallel to the floor. Additionally, your wrists should not be resting on the keyboard while typing.

Take breaks from computer tasks. Remaining in the same position for long periods of time increases stress on your body. Shift your position in your chair and stretch your hands and fingers periodically. Likewise, staring at the screen for long periods of time can lead to eyestrain, so rest your eyes by periodically taking them off the screen and focusing them on an object at least 20 feet away.

Ensure the lighting is adequate. Ensuring that you have proper lighting in your work area is a good way to minimize eyestrain. Eliminate any sources of direct glare (light shining directly into your eyes) or reflected glare (light shining off the computer screen) and ensure there is enough light to read comfortably. Or purchase an antiglare screen to place over your monitor. Look for ones that are polarized or have a purplish optical coating. These will provide the greatest relief.

—Evans, Martin, and Poatsy, *Introductory Technology in Action*, 7th ed., Pearson, 2011, pp. 79–80.

Review Test

MySkillsLab™
Complete this Exercise on myskillslab.com

The Example Patterns

Score (number correct) _____ x 10 = _____ %

Read the following passage, and then, answer the questions.

Glossary

solidifies (sentence 6): strengthens
camaraderie (sentence 6): friendship
exhortation (sentence 11): urging, advice, warning
ethical (sentence 17): moral, principled, right

Gossip

[1]Gossip is social talk that involves making evaluations about persons who are not present during the conversation; it generally occurs when two people talk about a third party (Eder & Enke, 1991). [2]As you obviously know, a large part of your conversation at work and in social situations is spent gossiping (Lachnit, 2001; Waddington, 2004; Carey, 2005). [3]In fact, one study estimates that approximately two-thirds of people's conversation time is devoted to social topics, and that most of these topics can be considered gossip (Dunbar, 2004). [4]Gossiping seems universal among all cultures (Laing, 1993), and among some it's a commonly accepted ritual (Hall, 1993).

[5]Lots of reasons have been suggested for the popularity and persistence of gossip. [6]One reason often given is that gossip bonds people together and **solidifies** their relationship; it creates a sense of **camaraderie** (Greengard, 2001; Hafen, 2004). [7]At the same time, of course, it helps to create an in-group (those doing the gossiping) and an out-group (those being gossiped about). [8]Gossip also serves a persuasive function in teaching people the cultural rules of their society. [9]That is, when you gossip about the wrong things that so-and-so did, you're in effect identifying the rules that should be followed and perhaps even the consequences that follow when the rules are broken. [10]Gossip enables you to learn what is and what is not acceptable behavior (Baumeister, Zhang, & Vohs, 2004). [11]Within an organization, gossip helps to regulate organization behavior: Gossip enables workers to learn who the organizational heroes are, what they did, and how they were rewarded—and carries an implicit **exhortation** to do likewise. [12]And, of course, negative gossip enables workers to learn who broke the rules and what punishments resulted from such rule-breaking—again, with an accompanying implicit **admonition** to avoid such behaviors (Hafen, 2004).

[13]People often engage in gossip for some kind of reward; for example, to hear more gossip, gain social status or control, have fun, cement social bonds, or make social comparisons (Rosnow, 1977; Miller & Wilcox, 1986; Leaper & Holliday, 1995; Wert & Salovey, 2004). [14]Research is

CONTINUED

REVIEW TEST *CONTINUED*

not consistent on the consequences of gossip for the person gossiping. [15]One research study argues that gossiping leads others to see you more negatively, regardless of whether your gossip is positive or negative and whether you're sharing this gossip with strangers or friends (Turner, Mazur, Wendel, & Winslow, 2003). [16]Another study finds that positive gossip leads to acceptance by your peers and greater friendship intimacy (Cristina, 2001).

[17]As you might expect, gossiping often has **ethical** implications, and in many instances gossip would be considered unethical. [18]Some such instances: when gossip is used to unfairly hurt another person, when you know it's not true, when no one has the right to such personal information, or when you've promised secrecy (Bok, 1983).

—DeVito, *The Interpersonal Communication Book*, 11th ed., pp. 212–213.

Vocabulary

1. In sentence 12, **admonition** means ____________________.

2. Context clue used for **admonition** ____________________

____________________.

Central Idea

Complete the following outline with information from the passage.

____

Supporting Details/Patterns

Thesis Statement: (3) ____________________

____

1. Gossip

A. Definition: **(4)** ____________________

____

1. Two-thirds of conversation time is considered gossip.

2. Gossip is a universal ritual among all cultures.

B. Reasons for gossip

1. Gossip bonds people and solidifies relationships.

2. Gossip creates an in-group and an out-group.

3. **(5)** ____________________

C. (6) ____

1. Gossiping may lead others to see you negatively.

2. Gossiping may lead to acceptance and intimacy.

Patterns of Organization

7. The main pattern of organization for the first paragraph (sentences 1–4) is
   a. comparison.
   b. cause and effect.
   c. definition and example.

Patterns of Organization

8. The main pattern of organization for the second paragraph (sentences 5–12) is
   a. comparison.
   b. cause and effect.
   c. definition and example.

Purpose/Tone

9. What is the overall purpose and tone of the passage?
   a. to inform the reader about the nature of gossip
   b. to entertain the reader with gossip
   c. to persuade the reader to avoid gossip

Inference

10. Based on the information in the passage we may infer that
   a. gossip is unavoidable.
   b. gossip is always rewarding.
   c. gossip can teach cultural values.

Summary Response

Restate the author's central idea in your own words. In your summary, follow the thought pattern used by the author. Begin your summary response with the following: *The central idea of "Gossip" from* The Interpersonal Communication Book *by DeVito is. . . .*

What Do You Think?

Assume you have taken the role of a mentor to a younger person through your public service work with a youth organization such as the Boys Club, the Girls Club, Boys Scouts, Girl Scouts, or the YMCA. Write an article to post on the organization's local Web page about the causes and effects of gossip—particularly in the context of online social networks. Consider the following ideas from the passage to guide your writing:

Define the term *gossip*.
List reasons why gossip occurs.
Summarize the effects of gossip.

Academic Learning Log: Module Review

Summary of Key Concepts of the Example Patterns

Assess your comprehension of the example patterns.

L1 L2

1. In the generalization-example pattern, the writer makes a ________________ statement and then offers a(n) ________________ or series of ________________ to clarify the ________________.
2. In a simple definition-example pattern, the writer makes a general statement that ____.
3. Two types of definition-example patterns are the ________________ and the ________________.
4. In an extended definition-example pattern, a writer makes a general statement that introduces a difficult concept. To define the concept, the writer identifies and explains its ____.
5. To clarify meaning, a writer may also include an explanation and example of ____.

Test Your Comprehension of the Example Patterns

Respond to the following prompts.

LO1 LO2

Complete a chart of transitions and signal words used to establish example patterns.

Key Words and Transitions Used to Signal Examples				
an illustration				
for example				
also				
and				
another				
besides				
certain				

Words Used to Signal Definitions				
as				
are				
characteristics				
characterized by				
connotes				

LO1 LO2 LO3 LO4 LO5 LO6

1. **How will I use what I have learned?** In your notebook, discuss how you will apply to your own reading/writing strategy what you have learned about the example patterns. When will you apply this knowledge to your reading/writing strategy?
2. **What do I still need to study about the example patterns?** In your notebook, discuss your ongoing study needs. Describe what, when, and how you will continue studying and using the example patterns.

MySkillsLab™

Complete the Post-test for Module 10 in MySkillsLab.

11

LEARNING OUTCOMES

After studying this module you should be able to:

- **LO 1** Answer the Question "What's the Point of the Classification, Comparison, and Contrast Patterns?"
- **LO 2** Question, Read, Annotate, and Review Passages Using Classification, Comparison, and Contrast
- **LO 3** Prewrite a Draft of a Thesis Statement Using Classification, Comparison, and Contrast
- **LO 4** Prewrite to Generate Relevant Details Using Classification, Comparison, and Contrast
- **LO 5** Compose a Draft Using Logical Order: Classification, Comparison, and Contrast
- **LO 6** Revise and Proofread for Effective Language with Classification, Comparison, and Contrast

The Classification, Comparison, and Contrast Patterns

Identifying and labeling groups or types help both readers and writers to discover the point about a particular topic. Consider, for example, the aisles of your local grocery store. Food is sorted and stocked by type so shoppers can efficiently find specific items. Additionally, most food items are labeled with various types of information such as calories, lists of ingredients, and levels of salt and fat. Classifying ideas is a foundational skill for comparing and contrasting ideas. Analyzing the similarities and differences among ideas, events, products, people, or places is an essential part of critical thinking. Often, we establish a comparison or contrast based on the traits of groups or types. For example, in everyday life, we compare and contrast the type of home we buy or neighborhoods where we want to live. We compare and contrast the traits of political candidates and their political parties as we decide for whom we will vote. In college life, we compare key historical figures and events, scientific theories, and problem-solving processes to clarify meaning and deepen learning. In working life, we compare or contrast career opportunities based on traits such as salaries, benefits, and working conditions.

WHAT'S THE POINT of the Classification, Comparison, and Contrast Patterns?

LO1

Before you study this module, predict the point of classification, comparison, and contrast. Study the following set of photographs. In the space provided, explain how each element is a part of war and peace. Finally, in a complete sentence, answer the question "What's the point of classification, comparison, and contrast?"

Photographic Organizer: What Is Conflict, and How Do We Resolve It?

WEAPONS OF MASS DESTRUCTION

DIPLOMACY

SOCIAL PROBLEMS SUCH AS HUNGER AND POVERTY

What is conflict, and how do we resolve it?

What's the point of classification, comparison, and contrast?

L2 Question, Read, Annotate, and Review Passages Using Classification, Comparison, and Contrast

Classification is the division of a topic in clearly identified subgroups based on shared traits.

Readers and writers use **classification** to learn about the relationships among ideas, people, places, and things based on their traits, types, grouping, or rank. When we classify, we sort items into subgroups based on shared traits or characteristics. The writer labels, lists, and describes the traits of each subgroup. Because groups and subgroups are listed in a piece of writing, transitions of addition (*and, also, first, last, and so on*) are also often used to order those groups and subgroups. Transitions of addition are coupled with signal words that indicate classes or groups. Examples of classification transitions and signal words (where the first word is the classification transition and the second word is the signal word) are *first type, second kind,* and *another group*. The following chart offers a few examples of signal words and transitions that establish classification.

Classification Signal Words That Are Used to Organize Groups, Types, or Traits				
aspect	classify	group	quality	style
attribute	classification	ideal	rank	trait
branch	collection	kind	section	type
brand	division	level	set	typical
categories	element	order	sort	variety
characteristic	feature	part	status	
class	form	principle	stratum	

Transitions That Combine with Signal Words to List Groups, Types, or Traits				
also	final	for one thing	last of all	second
and	finally	furthermore	moreover	third
another	first	in addition	next	
besides	first of all	last	one	

A **comparison** explains the similarities between two or more topics.

A **contrast** explains the differences between two or more topics.

A **comparison/contrast** explains both the similarities and the differences between two or more topics.

Classification is often the first step toward comparison and contrast. We generally classify objects before we compare or contrast them. The comparison/contrast pattern can be limited in three ways. Sometimes, the central idea is a **comparison**, focusing on just the similarities of the topics. Other times, the focus is only on the **contrasts** or differences. The third focus, a **comparison/contrast**, includes both the similarities and the differences. Master writers often include signal words in the thesis sentence and paragraph body to indicate the focus on a comparison, a contrast, or a combination comparison/contrast. Thus, master readers skim for comparison/contrast words to locate and comprehend the writer's central point and flow of ideas. The following chart offers a few examples of signal words and transitions that establish comparison and contrast.

Words That Signal Comparison				
alike	equally	in the same way	likewise	similarity
as	in a similar fashion	just as	resemble	similarly
as well as	in a similar way	just like	same	
equal	in like manner	like	similar	

Words That Signal Contrast				
although	conversely	differently	more	on the other hand
as opposed to	despite	even though	most	still
at the same time	difference	in contrast	nevertheless	to the contrary
but	different	in spite of	on the contrary	unlike
by contrast	different from	instead	on the one hand	yet

? For Module 11, assume you are taking a college course in political science, and your class is beginning a study on the theme of "conflict and resolution." Each reading in this module follows this theme. After completing all assigned readings, you will write in response to the following guiding question: "What are the elements of war and peace, and how do these elements seem similar or different in specific situations?"

Example

Assume the following passage is your first assigned reading on the theme of "conflict and resolution." Your professor has provided before and during reading questions and guided annotations to prepare you to read about and respond to the theme. Before reading, survey the questions and skim the passage for possible answers. Next, read the passage and the annotations. As you read, add your own annotations by completing the prompts in **bold** print. After reading, use your own words to answer the questions. Record your answers in your reading/writing journal. Finally, complete the concept map with information from the passage.

Before and During Reading Questions:

Logical Order: Does this passage use classification, comparison, contrast, or combined patterns? Which transitions/signal words does the writer use?

Central Idea: What is the writer's central point?

Relevant Details: What are the elements that promote war?

What are the various types of approaches to peace?

Effective Language: What vivid words does the writer use to create mental images for the reader?

CONTINUED

EXAMPLE *CONTINUED*

Central Idea: The central idea is the point the writer makes about the topic of the passage. The topic is "war and peace." **Underline the writer's point about the topic.**

Logical Order: The transitional word *like* signals that the writer is using comparison/contrast. **Circle two more transitional phrases that indicate comparison or contrast.**

Relevant Details: This detail answers the first prereading question "What are the elements that promote war?" **Underline details that answer the other prereading question.**

Elements of War and Peace

[1]Perhaps the most critical political issue is **war**, *organized, armed, conflict among the people of two of more nations, directed by their governments.* [2]War and peace are as old as humanity, but understanding them is crucial today because we now have weapons that can destroy the entire planet.

[3]At almost any moment during the twentieth century, nations somewhere in the world were engaged in violent conflict. [4]In its short history, the United States has participated in eleven major wars. [5]From the Revolutionary War to our current engagement in Iraq and Afghanistan more than 1.3 million U.S. men and women have been killed in armed conflicts, and many times that number have been injured. [6]Thousands more have died in undeclared wars and limited military actions around the world.

ELEMENTS LEADING TO WAR

[7]Wars occur so often that we might think that there is something natural about armed conflict. [8]But there is no evidence that human beings must wage war under any particular circumstances. [9]On the contrary, governments around the world usually have to force their people to go to war.

[10] Like other forms of social behavior, warfare is a product of society that is more common in some places than in others. [11]The Semai of Malaysia, among the most peace loving of the world's peoples, rarely resort to violence. [12] In contrast, the Yanomamo of South America are quick to wage war.

[13]If society holds the key to war or peace, under what circumstances do humans go to war? [14]Quincy Wright (1987) cites five elements that promote war:

1. [15]**Perceived threats**. [16]Nations mobilize in response to a perceived threat to their people, territory, or culture. [17]Leaders justified the U.S.-led military campaign to disarm Iraq, for example, by stressing the threat that Saddam Hussein posed to neighboring countries and also to the United States.
2. [18]**Social problems**. [19]When internal problems cause widespread frustration at home, a nation's leaders may try to divert public attention by attacking an external "enemy" as a form of scapegoating. [20] Although U.S. leaders defended the 2003 invasion of Iraq as a matter of national security, the start of the war effectively shifted the nation's attention away from the struggling national economy and boosted the popularity of President George W. Bush.
3. [21]**Political objectives**. [22]Poor nations, such as Vietnam, have used wars to end foreign domination. [23]Powerful countries such as the United States may benefit from periodic shows of force (recall the deployments of troops in Somalia, Haiti, Bosnia, and Afghanistan) to increase global political standing.
4. [24]**Moral objectives**. [25]Nations rarely claim that they are going to war to gain wealth and power. [26]Instead, their leaders infuse military campaigns with moral urgency. [27]By calling the 2003 invasion of Iraq "Operation Iraqi Freedom"; U.S. leaders portrayed the mission as a morally justified war of liberation from an evil tyrant.

5. [28]**The absence of alternatives.** [29]A fifth factor promoting war is the lack of alternatives. [30]Although the goal of the United Nations is to maintain international peace by finding alternatives to war, the organization has had limited success in preventing conflict between nations.

PURSUING PEACE

[31]How can the world reduce the dangers of war? [32]Here are the most recent types of approaches to peace:

[33]The first kind of peace is based on **deterrence**. [34]The logic of the arms race holds that security comes from a "balance of terror" between the superpowers. [35]The principle of *mutual assured destruction* (MAD) means that a nation launching a first strike against another will face greater retaliation. [36]This deterrence policy kept the peace for almost fifty years during the Cold War. [37]Yet it encouraged an enormous arms race and cannot control nuclear proliferation, which represents a growing threat to peace. [38]Deterrence also does little to stop terrorism or to prevent wars that are started by a stronger nation (such as the United States) against a weaker foe (such as the Taliban government in Afghanistan or Saddam Hussein's Iraq).

[39]The second type of peace is a **high-technology defense**. [40]If technology created the weapons, perhaps it can also protect us from them; such is the claim of the *strategic defense initiative* (SDI). [41]Under SDI, satellites and ground installations would destroy enemy missiles soon after they were launched. [42]In a survey shortly after the 2001 terrorist attacks, two-thirds of U.S. adults supported SDI (Thompson & Waller, 2001; "Female Opinion," 2002). [43]However, critics claim that the system, which they refer to as "Star Wars" would be, at best, a leaky umbrella. [44]Others worry that building such a system will spark another massive arms race. [45]In recent years, the Obama administration has turned away from further development of SDI in favor of more focused defense against short-range missiles that might be launched from Iran.

[46]The third type of peace is **diplomacy and disarmament**. [47]Some analysts believe that the best road to peace is diplomacy rather than technology (Dedrick & Yinger, 1990). [48]Teams of diplomats working together can increase security by reducing, rather than building, weapons stockpiles. [49]But disarmament has limitations. [50]No nation wants to be weakened by eliminating its defenses. [51]Successful diplomacy depends on everyone involved sharing responsibility for a common problem (Fisher & Ury, 1988). [52]In 2010, the New Start treaty required the United States and Russia to reduce nuclear stockpiles to 1,550 warheads within seven years. [53]The treaty also provided for a new system of monitoring compliance with this limitation, yet, each nation will still have more than enough weapons to destroy the entire planet. [54]In addition, the world now faces increasing threats from other nations including North Korea and Iran.

[55]Finally, a fourth kind of peace is **resolving underlying conflict**. [56]In the end, reducing the dangers of war may depend on resolving underlying conflicts by promoting a more just world. [57]Poverty, hunger, and illiteracy are all root causes of war. [58]Perhaps the world needs to reconsider the wisdom of spending thousands of times as much money on militarism as we do on efforts to find peaceful solutions (Sivard, 1988; Kaplan & Schaffer, 2001). [59]We can either choose to pursue peace, or we can fund war.

Logical Order: The signal word *type* signals that the writer is using classification. **Circle two more transitional phrases that indicate classification.**

Effective Language: A writer often uses a compound sentence to emphasize a similarity or difference. Often a coordinating conjunction (*and, but, or, yet*) links the two ideas within the sentence. **Double underline one more compound sentence that uses a coordinating conjunction to contrast ideas.**

—Adapted from Macionis, *Society: The Basics*, 13th ed., Pearson, 2015, pp. 407-413.

CONTINUED

EXAMPLE *CONTINUED*

Elements of War: Types of Peace		
Elements of War	**Traits**	**Example(s)**
1.		
2.		2003 invasion of Iraq shifted attention from the struggling economy
3.	use wars to end foreign domination, show of force	
4.		
5.	limited success	
Types of Peace	**Traits**	**Example(s)**
1.		
2.		Star Wars
3.		
4.	more money spent on militarism than on peace	

Explanation

Compare your answers to the following think-aloud, completed by Bethany, another student in your class.

The writer's controlling point about the topic of war and peace was "understanding them is crucial today because we now have weapons that can destroy the entire planet." To support and organize ideas, the writer used a combination of classification, comparison, and contrast. First, the writer identified the traits of war and peace, and then compared and contrasted those traits. I circled the following contrast signal words: **In contrast** (sentence 12), **although** (sentence 20). In sentences 33, 39, 46, and 55, I circled the classification signals **first kind**, **second type**, **third type**, **fourth kind**. I found the writer's use of numbers to introduce the four types of peace very effective. I double underlined the last sentence as an example of the writer's use of a compound sentence to contrast ideas. To highlight the answers to the before and during reading questions, I underlined all the words in bold print. I also used these details to complete the concept map.

Elements of War: (1) Perceived threats; threat to their people, territory, or culture; Saddam Hussein. (2) Social problems; divert public attention by attacking an external "enemy," scapegoating. (3) Political objectives; Vietnam, Somalia, Haiti, Bosnia, and Afghanistan. (4) Moral objectives; leaders infuse military campaigns with moral urgency; "Operation Iraqi Freedom" portrayed as a war of liberation from an evil tyrant. (5) The absence of alternatives; United Nations

Types of Peace: (1) Deterrence; balance of terror, mutual assured destruction; Cold War, Taliban, Saddam Hussein's Iraq. (2) High-technology defense; strategic defense initiative, destroy enemy missiles after launch. (3) Diplomacy and disarmament; shared responsibility, reducing stockpiles of weapons; New Start Treaty between Russia and U.S. (4) Resolving underlying conflict; poverty, hunger, and illiteracy.

Practice 1

Question, Read, Annotate, and Review Passages Using Examples

Assume the following two passages are the next assigned readings on the theme of "conflict and resolution." Your professor has provided a few questions to guide your thinking. Before reading each passage, survey the before and during reading questions and skim the passage for possible answers. Then read the passage. As you read, annotate the details in the passage that answer these questions. After reading, respond to the prompts that follow each passage.

CONTINUED

PRACTICE 1 *CONTINUED*

Before and During Reading Questions:

Logical Order: How does this passage use classification, comparison, contrast, or combined patterns? Which transitions/signal words does the writer use?

Central Idea: What is the writer's central point?

Relevant Details: What are the traits of peace? What are the kinds and traits of suffering?

Effective Language: What vivid words does the writer use to create images in the reader's mind?

FROM AUNG SAN SUU KYI'S NOBEL PEACE PRIZE LECTURE

This lecture was delivered in 2012 for a prize received in 1991. Suu Kyi was under house arrest in Burma at the time the prize was awarded and was not released until 2010.

...[1]The Burmese concept of peace can be explained as the happiness arising from the cessation of factors that militate against the harmonious and the wholesome. [2]The word *nyein-chan* translates literally as the beneficial coolness that comes when a fire is extinguished. [3]Fires of suffering and strife are raging around the world. [4]In my own country, hostilities have not ceased in the far north; to the west, communal violence resulting in arson and murder were taking place just several days before I started out on the journey that has brought me here today. [5]News of atrocities in other reaches of the earth abound. [6]Reports of hunger, disease, displacement, joblessness, poverty, injustice, discrimination, prejudice, bigotry; these are our daily fare. [6]Everywhere there are negative forces eating away at the foundations of peace. [7]Everywhere can be found thoughtless dissipation of material and human resources that are necessary for the conservation of harmony and happiness in our world.

[8]The First World War represented a terrifying waste of youth and potential, a cruel squandering of the positive forces of our planet. [9]The poetry of that era has a special significance for me because I first read it at a time when I was the same age as many of those young men who had to face the prospect of withering before they had barely blossomed. [10]A young American fighting with the French Foreign Legion wrote before he was killed in action in 1916 that he would meet his death: "at some disputed barricade"; "on some scarred slope of battered hill"; "at midnight in some flaming town."

[11]Youth and love and life perishing forever in senseless attempts to capture nameless, unremembered places. [12]And for what? [13]Nearly a century on, we have yet to find a satisfactory answer.

[14]Are we not still guilty, if to a less violent degree, of recklessness, of improvidence with regard to our future and our humanity? [15]War is not the only arena where peace is done to death. [16]Wherever suffering is ignored, there will be the seeds of conflict, for suffering degrades and embitters and enrages.

[17]A positive aspect of living in isolation was that I had ample time in which to ruminate over the meaning of words and precepts that I had known and accepted all my life. [18]As a Buddhist, I had heard about *dukha*, generally translated as suffering, since I was a small child. [19]Almost on a daily basis elderly, and sometimes not so elderly, people around me would murmur "dukha, dukha" when they suffered from aches and pains or when they met with some small, annoying mishaps. [20]However, it was only during my years of house arrest that I got around to investigating the nature of the six great dukha. [21]These are: to be conceived, to age, to sicken, to die, to be parted from those one loves, to be forced to live in propinquity with those one does not love. [22]I examined each of the six great sufferings, not in a religious context but in the context of our ordinary, everyday lives. [23]If suffering were an unavoidable part of our existence, we should try to alleviate it as far as possible in practical, earthly ways. [24]I mulled over the effectiveness of ante- and post-natal programmes and mother and childcare; of adequate facilities for the aging population; of comprehensive health services; of compassionate nursing and hospices. [25]I was particularly intrigued by the last two kinds of suffering: to be parted from those one loves and to be forced to live in propinquity with those one does not love. [26]What experiences might our Lord Buddha have undergone in his own life that he had included these two states among the great sufferings? [27]I thought of prisoners and refugees, of migrant workers and victims of human trafficking, of that great mass of the uprooted of the earth who have been torn away from their homes, parted from families and friends, forced to live out their lives among strangers who are not always welcoming.

[28]We are fortunate to be living in an age when social welfare and humanitarian assistance are recognized not only as desirable but necessary. [29]I am fortunate to be living in an age when the fate of prisoners of conscience anywhere has become the concern of peoples everywhere, an age when democracy and human rights are widely, even if not universally, accepted as the birthright of all. [30]How often during my years under house arrest have I drawn strength from my favorite passages in the preamble to the Universal Declaration of Human Rights:

. . . [31]disregard and contempt for human rights have resulted in barbarous acts which have outraged the conscience of mankind, and the advent of a world in which human beings shall enjoy freedom of speech and belief and freedom from fear and want has been proclaimed as the highest aspirations of the common people.

. . . [32]it is essential, if man is not to be compelled to have recourse, as a last resort, to rebellion against tyranny and oppression, that human rights should be protected by the rule of law . . .

CONTINUED

PRACTICE 1 *CONTINUED*

[33]If I am asked why I am fighting for human rights in Burma the above passages will provide the answer. [34]If I am asked why I am fighting for democracy in Burma, it is because I believe that democratic institutions and practices are necessary for the guarantee of human rights.

***

[35]The peace of our world is indivisible. [36]As long as negative forces are getting the better of positive forces anywhere, we are all at risk. [37]It may be questioned whether all negative forces could ever be removed. [38]The simple answer is: "No!" [39]It is in human nature to contain both the positive and the negative. [40]However, it is also within human capability to work to reinforce the positive and to minimize or neutralize the negative. [41]Absolute peace in our world is an unattainable goal. [42]But it is one towards which we must continue to journey, our eyes fixed on it as a traveller in a desert fixes his eyes on the one guiding star that will lead him to salvation. [43]Even if we do not achieve perfect peace on earth, because perfect peace is not of this earth, common endeavors to gain peace will unite individuals and nations in trust and friendship and help to make our human community safer and kinder.

[44]I used the word 'kinder' after careful deliberation; I might say the careful deliberation of many years. [45]Of the sweets of adversity, and let me say that these are not numerous, I have found the sweetest, the most precious of all, is the lesson I learnt on the value of kindness. [46]Every kindness I received, small or big, convinced me that there could never be enough of it in our world. [47]To be kind is to respond with sensitivity and human warmth to the hopes and needs of others. [48]Even the briefest touch of kindness can lighten a heavy heart. [49]Kindness can change the lives of people. [50]Norway has shown exemplary kindness in providing a home for the displaced of the earth, offering sanctuary to those who have been cut loose from the moorings of security and freedom in their native lands.

[51]There are refugees in all parts of the world. [52]When I was at the Maela refugee camp in Thailand recently, I met dedicated people who were striving daily to make the lives of the inmates as free from hardship as possible. [53]They spoke of their concern over 'donor fatigue,' which could also translate as 'compassion fatigue.' [54]'Donor fatigue' expresses itself precisely in the reduction of funding. [55]'Compassion fatigue' expresses itself less obviously in the reduction of concern. [56]One is the consequence of the other. [57]Can we afford to indulge in compassion fatigue? [58]Is the cost of meeting the needs of refugees greater than the cost that would be consequent on turning an indifferent, if not a blind, eye on their suffering? [59]I appeal to donors the world over to fulfill the needs of these people who are in search, often it must seem to them a vain search, of refuge.

[60]At Maela, I had valuable discussions with Thai officials responsible for the administration of Tak province where this and several other camps are situated. [61]They acquainted me with some of the more serious problems related to refugee camps: violation of forestry laws, illegal drug use, home brewed spirits, the problems of controlling malaria, tuberculosis, dengue fever and cholera. [62]The concerns of the administration are

as legitimate as the concerns of the refugees. [63]Host countries also deserve consideration and practical help in coping with the difficulties related to their responsibilities.

[64]Ultimately our aim should be to create a world free from the displaced, the homeless and the hopeless, a world of which each and every corner is a true sanctuary where the inhabitants will have the freedom and the capacity to live in peace. [65]Every thought, every word, and every action that adds to the positive and the wholesome is a contribution to peace. [66]Each and every one of us is capable of making such a contribution. [67]Let us join hands to try to create a peaceful world where we can sleep in security and wake in happiness.

After Reading Response: Respond to the following prompts in your journal:

- Write a summary of the passage (see Module 1, page 34).
- Create a comparison/contrast concept map that answers the following prompt: Compare and contrast three points from "Elements of War and Peace" to the elements of peace, suffering, and kindness as discussed in Aung San Suu Kyi's Nobel Peace Prize Lecture.

Comparison/Contrast Concept Chart			
Comparable Topics/Traits	**Topic: Elements of War and Peace**	**Like or Unlike**	**Topic: Elements from Aung San Suu Kyi's Nobel Peace Prize Lecture**
1st Point or Trait			
2nd Point or Trait			
3rd Point or Trait			

CONTINUED

PRACTICE 1 *CONTINUED*

Before and During Reading Questions:

Logical Order: How does this passage use classification, comparison, contrast, or combined patterns? Which transitions/signal words does the writer use?

Central Idea: What is the writer's central point?

Relevant Details: What kind of peace does Kennedy assert we should seek?

What element of war has changed the face of war?

What is the defeatist attitude toward war?

Effective Language: What vivid words does Kennedy use to create mental images in the reader's mind?

FROM PRESIDENT JOHN F. KENNEDY'S COMMENCEMENT ADDRESS AT THE AMERICAN UNIVERSITY, 10 JUNE 1963

[1]"There are few earthly things more beautiful than a university," wrote John Masefield in his tribute to English universities—and his words are equally true today. [2]He did not refer to spires and towers, to campus greens and ivied walls. [3]He admired the splendid beauty of the university, he said, because it was "a place where those who hate ignorance may strive to know, where those who perceive truth may strive to make others see."

[4]I have, therefore, chosen this time and this place to discuss a topic on which ignorance too often abounds and the truth is too rarely perceived—yet it is the most important topic on earth: world peace.

[5]What kind of peace do I mean? [6]What kind of peace do we seek? [7]Not a Pax Americana enforced on the world by American weapons of war. [8]Not the peace of the grave or the security of the slave. [9]I am talking about genuine peace, the kind of peace that makes life on earth worth living, the kind that enables men and nations to grow and to hope and to build a better life for their children—not merely peace for Americans but peace for all men and women—not merely peace in our time but peace for all time.

[10]I speak of peace because of the new face of war. [11]Total war makes no sense in an age when great powers can maintain large and relatively invulnerable nuclear forces and refuse to surrender without resort to those forces. [12]It makes no sense in an age when a single nuclear weapon contains almost ten times the explosive force delivered by all the allied air forces in the Second World War. [13]It makes no sense in an age when the deadly poisons produced by a nuclear exchange would be carried by wind and water and soil and seed to the far corners of the globe and to generations yet unborn.

[14]Today the expenditure of billions of dollars every year on weapons acquired for the purpose of making sure we never need to use them is essential to keeping the peace. [15]But surely the acquisition of such idle stockpiles—which can only destroy and never create—is not the only, much less the most efficient, means of assuring peace.

[16]I speak of peace, therefore, as the necessary rational end of rational men. [17]I realize that the pursuit of peace is not as dramatic as the pursuit of war—and frequently the words of the pursuer fall on deaf ears. [18]But we have no more urgent task.

[19]Some say that it is useless to speak of world peace or world law or world disarmament—and that it will be useless until the leaders of the Soviet Union adopt a more enlightened attitude. [20]I hope they do. [21]I believe we can help them do it. [22]But I also believe that we must reexamine our own attitude—as individuals and as a Nation—for our attitude is as essential as theirs. [23]And every graduate of this school, every thoughtful citizen who despairs of war and wishes to bring peace, should begin by looking inward—by examining his own attitude toward the possibilities of peace, toward the Soviet Union, toward the course of the cold war and toward freedom and peace here at home.

[24]First: Let us examine our attitude toward peace itself. [25]Too many of us think it is impossible. [26]Too many think it unreal. [27]But that is a dangerous, defeatist belief. [28]It leads to the conclusion that war is inevitable—that mankind is doomed—that we are gripped by forces we cannot control.

[29]We need not accept that view. [30]Our problems are manmade—therefore, they can be solved by man. [31]And man can be as big as he wants. [32]No problem of human destiny is beyond human beings. [33]Man's reason and spirit have often solved the seemingly unsolvable—and we believe they can do it again.

[34]I am not referring to the absolute, infinite concept of peace and good will of which some fantasies and fanatics dream. [35]I do not deny the value of hopes and dreams but we merely invite discouragement and incredulity by making that our only and immediate goal.

[36]Let us focus instead on a more practical, more attainable peace—based not on a sudden revolution in human nature but on a gradual evolution in human institutions—on a series of concrete actions and effective agreements which are in the interest of all concerned. [37]There is no single, simple key to this peace—no grand or magic formula to be adopted by one or two powers. [38]Genuine peace must be the product of many nations, the sum of many acts. [39]It must be dynamic, not static, changing to meet the challenge of each new generation. [40]For peace is a process—a way of solving problems.

[41]With such a peace, there will still be quarrels and conflicting interests, as there are within families and nations. [42]World peace, like community peace, does not require that each man love his neighbor—it requires only that they live together in mutual tolerance, submitting their disputes to a just and peaceful settlement. [43]And history teaches us that enmities between nations, as between individuals, do not last forever. [44]However fixed our likes and dislikes may seem, the tide of time and events will often bring surprising changes in the relations between nations and neighbors.

[45]So let us persevere. [46]Peace need not be impracticable, and war need not be inevitable. [47]By defining our goal more clearly, by making it seem more manageable and less remote, we can help all peoples to see it, to draw hope from it, and to move irresistibly toward it.

—Kennedy, John F. Commencement Address at American University, June 10, 1963

CONTINUED

PRACTICE 1 *CONTINUED*

After Reading Response: Respond to the following prompts in your journal:

- Write a summary of the passage (see Module 1, page 34).
- Create a comparison/contrast concept map that answers the following prompt:

  How is Kennedy's view of war and peace similar to or different from the "Elements of War and Peace" and the views Aung San Suu Kyi asserts in her Nobel Peace Prize Lecture?

Comparison/Contrast Concept Chart				
Comparable Topics/Traits	**Topic: Elements of War and Peace**	**Like or Unlike**	**Topic: Aung San Suu Kyi's Nobel Peace Prize Lecture**	**Topic: JFK's speech**
1st Point or Trait				
2nd Point or Trait				
3rd Point or Trait				

Prewrite a Draft of a Thesis Statement Using Classification, Comparison, and Contrast

When you write a classification piece, you limit your topic to a set of ideas or groups based on types, shared traits, or common principles. Most likely, you also have an opinion or point of view about that set of ideas. This opinion or attitude becomes your controlling point or main idea. You also reveal your opinion by discussing the groups or traits in a particular order of importance. A thesis sentence states the point or purpose of the groups, types, or traits. For example, the following topic sentence contains (1) the topic, (2) the writer's opinion about the topic, (3) the pattern of organization used to organize details, and (4) a list of subgroups of the topic.

Classification Thesis Statement:

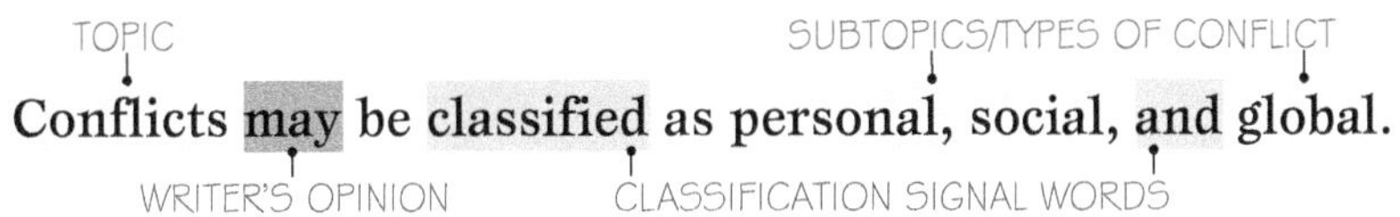

To write a comparison or a contrast piece, you limit your thoughts to a set of topics based on their relationship to each other. While several topics can be compared/contrasted, often writers limit their comparison/contrast to two. Most likely you have an opinion or belief about the two topics and their comparable points. Your opinion is your point or main idea. In a comparison or contrast paragraph, you also reveal your opinion by describing the points of similarity or difference between the topics in the order of your own choosing. A topic sentence states the overall point of the comparison, the contrast, or the comparison/contrast between the two topics.

Comparison/Contrast Thesis Statement

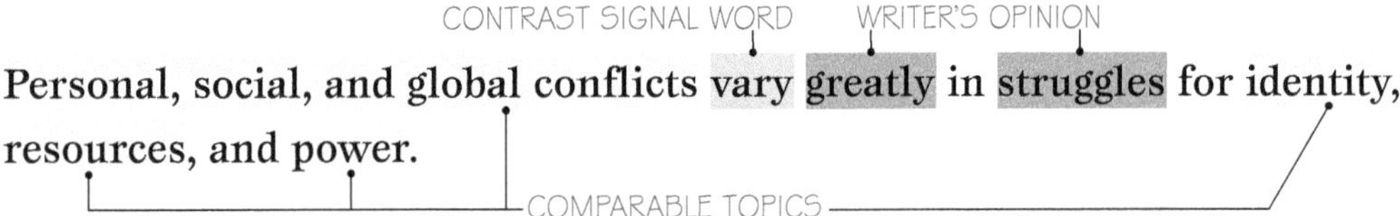

Example

Your instructor has asked you to use the readings on pages 430–439 to write an essay that addresses the guiding question: "What are the elements of war and peace, and how do these elements seem similar or different in specific situations?" The first part of the assignment is to generate a central idea or thesis statement for the essay. Your first step is to decide how you will use classification, comparison, and/or contrast to make your point. Use the following steps to brainstorm your thesis statement.

CONTINUED

EXAMPLE *CONTINUED*

Topic: Types of Conflict or Forms of Conflict Resolution

1. Narrow Topic: ____________________

2. Identify Classification Order Signal Words: ____________________

3. Identify Comparison/Contrast Order Signal Words: ____________________

4. Identify Opinion: ____________________

5. Combine into a Draft of Thesis Statement: ____________________

Explanation

Compare your answers to Bethany's think-aloud.

I decided to write about what the true purpose and path of peace is and what elements might oppose that in the modern, uninformed world peace ideology. My final thesis is as follows: The strife we see is a mixture of cruelty and apathy which must be exposed, and then conquered by identifying the specific elements of suffering and components to deter those struggles.

Practice 2

Prewrite a Draft of a Thesis Statement Using Classification, Comparison, and Contrast

In your reading/writing journal, identify the steps you used to write a thesis statement using classification or comparison and contrast order. How did your thesis statement differ from Bethany's? Did she use any methods you didn't?

Prewrite to Generate Relevant Details Using Classification, Comparison, and Contrast

To generate details based on the classification pattern of organization, writers primarily ask the reporter's questions *what* and *how*. What are the types, traits, and examples of people, places, or objects? How are people, places, or things grouped? Answers to these questions enable readers to identify and writers to generate details. Usually, classification transitions and signal words introduce these details. Some major and minor details may also explain the writer's opinion about the groups, types, and traits and how they are being classified. Many readers and writers use a classification concept map to identify and generate details.

Types, Forms, Kinds, or Classes of a Topic

1st Trait
  Examples
2nd Trait
  Examples
3rd Trait
  Examples

To generate details based on comparison or contrast, writers ask the reporter's questions *who*, *what*, *when*, *where*, *why*, and *how*. Who is being compared or contrasted? What places, objects, or ideas are being compared or contrasted? What are the specific similarities between the two ideas? What are the differences? When do the similarities or differences occur? Where do they occur? Why is this comparison or contrast significant? How do the people, places, things, or ideas differ? How do they agree? Answers to these questions enable readers to identify and writers to generate details.

Writers have several choices about how to organize comparison and contrast. They may choose to organize details about similarities and differences point by point or block by block.

Point by Point

1st Comparable Trait
  Topic A
  Topic B
2nd Comparable Trait
  Topic A
  Topic B

Block by Block

Topic A
  1st Comparable Trait
  2nd Comparable Trait
Topic B
  1st Comparable Trait
  2nd Comparable Trait

Usually, comparison/contrast transitions and signal words introduce these details. Some major and minor details may also explain the writer's opinion about the comparison or contrast. Master readers and writers use a concept map to identify and generate details.

Example

Assume your class is continuing to work on the essay addressing the guiding question "What are the elements of war and peace, and how do these elements seem similar or different in specific situations?" Now your assignment is to return to the texts to identify details that you will use in your paper and create a concept map to organize your ideas for the essay.

Classification Concept Chart		
Topic	**Traits**	**Example(s)**
1.		
2.		
3.		

Comparison/Contrast Concept Chart			
Comparable Topics/Traits	**Topic/Trait:**	**Like or Unlike**	**Topic/Trait:**
1st Point or Trait			
2nd Point or Trait			
3rd Point or Trait			

Explanation

Compare your responses to Bethany's think-aloud.

The first element of peace that I reviewed was unrest in the world and how it affects people. The writers, while speaking on a common subject, had different takes on the subject. Aung San Suu Kyi inspired people to see past themselves into a hurting world, whereas the author of "Elements of War and Peace" dove into the application. I believe Kennedy's take balanced both, perhaps inspired by the unrest in America at the time or the need to please two parties at once. Either way, he identified a practical application as well as hope. Then I reviewed the practical applications. There were examples of how countries are, could be, or should be handling suffering. All of these came back to the point of a need for communication and camaraderie among nations to bring about a harmony and comfort for those who are suffering. The last point I mapped was the idea that appeared in each work—total world peace, although impossible, is a goal we should strive towards now and in the future.

Practice 3

Prewrite to Generate Relevant Details Using Classification, Comparison, and Contrast

In your reading/writing journal, identify the steps needed to create relevant details to support a thesis statement. Identify the steps Bethany went through as she annotated the texts and created her graphic organizer. How did your concept maps differ?

Compose a Draft Using Logical Order: Classification, Comparison, and Contrast

LO5

DRAFT YOUR RESPONSE

Once you have brainstormed details to compose a classification, comparison, contrast, or comparison/contrast essay, you are ready to begin the drafting process. First, review the concept map you completed with the details from the readings, along with your own insights or responses. As you review your concept map, move details into the most logical order. Add details, if needed. Also, use appropriate signal words and transitions to guide your reader through the classification, comparison, or contrast. Master writers create several drafts to achieve a logical order and smooth flow of ideas.

Example

Assume you are still working toward writing an essay that answers the guiding question: "What are the elements of war and peace, and how do these elements seem similar or different in specific situations?" On your own paper, write a draft of your essay.

Explanation

Compare your answer to Bethany's think-aloud and essay.

After creating a concept map and thesis statement, I basically spilled my entire brain onto a page. All the thoughts I had while reading and annotating were typed out in no specific order. After I had everything I wanted to say written down, I organized the ideas and points into a smooth flow. After I arranged it into an understandable order, I reread and edited line by line. After my second or third time doing this I had the first official draft of my essay. Then I put it aside for a day before reading it again and continuing the drafting process.

CONTINUED

EXAMPLE *CONTINUED*

The War Machine

by Bethany Cobb

Since the dawn of time, there have been two harsh concepts; war and world peace. War is harsh because of its cruelty, death, and destruction that hits society at all levels. However, world peace is equally harsh because so many long for it in vain. Why is it that war happens so often and world peace is almost a mythical concept? Every day people are exposed to abuse, genocide, hunger, and countless other things that many people, including myself, have never dealt with. So why are the age-old struggles still alive and well while technology and some members of society have proclaimed that they have made strides toward a peaceful world? The strife we see is a mixture of cruelty and apathy, which must be exposed, then conquered by identifying the specific elements of suffering and components to deter those struggles.

Aung San Suu Kyi, in the lecture she gave for her Nobel Peace Prize award, identified some of the hardships that she has seen around the world. While speaking of the tragedy of war, she said, "whenever suffering is ignored, there will be seeds of conflict, for suffering degrades and embitters and enrages." In her speech she goes on to talk about why, how, and where our effort should be put forth to help those who are suffering every day. In another speech, President Kennedy spoke on the subject of peace, specifically in the context of war. Instead of discussing individual struggles, he pointed out the practical reality that our world could and should band together to obtain and reinforce peace. He argued that we live in a day where anything is possible, even harmony among nations. In the essay "Elements of War and Peace," the author takes a more analytical view of the matter. But the sweeping theme is that peace is always an option, and that option needs to be a conscious decision we make.

In all of these cases there is one common denominator—the first step to peace is awareness. That awareness can take the form of being cognizant of worldwide suffering, being informed about alternatives other than armed action, or being knowledgeable of the institutions or charities that can aid war-torn areas and people. You will not seek a remedy unless you recognize a malady. Accordingly, there will not be an outcry for peace unless the sobs of innocent victims are heard. Thus, the path to peace is initiated by education—getting individuals to think outside themselves to gain perspective and strength. In his speech, President Kennedy quoted John Masefield, who called a place of education "a place where those who hate ignorance may strive to know, where those who perceive truth may strive to make others see." The great enemy of peace and the ultimate war machine is ignorance.

An educated world, if modern history rings true, stands together in defense of the battered and downtrodden. The biggest weapon against the pangs of hunger and the cries of abuse is widespread concern and sensitivity. Once the population of the world comes to a common mindset there is not a single enemy that cannot be overthrown, even an enemy such as apathy or the adversary of selfishness.

There are wars every day, and only a few go down in history as a fight for humanity and freedom. Usually, war is characterized by selfish brutes who fight each other for domination. In fact, in "Elements of War and Peace" the author stated, "wars occur so often that we might think that there is something natural about armed conflict. But there is no evidence that human beings must wage war under any circumstances. On the contrary, governments around the world usually have to force their people to go to war."

War is, unfortunately, necessary at times. Like the old saying goes, freedom is not free, and the road to peace is not peaceful. But think of this: this world has the ability to expend lives and outrageous amounts of money to fight wars. What are we willing to do for peace? First, we must inform. Then we must hold this planet responsible for that knowledge. We are only an obstacle to ourselves, and as a united front, we can truly make a difference in a hurting world.

Practice 4

Compose a Draft Using Logical Order: Classification, Comparison, and Contrast

In your reading/writing journal, identify the steps you took to write your draft. Identify the steps Bethany took as she wrote her draft. How are your drafts different? How are they similar? What can you apply from Bethany's method to your own writing in the future?

L6 Revise and Proofread for Effective Language with Classification, Comparison, and Contrast

REVIEW AND REVISE YOUR DRAFT

PROOFREAD

Two types of sentence structures enable effective expression of comparison or contrast: coordination and subordination.

1. **Coordination** expresses an equal relationship between topics. Coordination expresses similarities with words such as *and, likewise, similarly, also*. Coordination expresses an equal relationship between differences with words such as *but, yet, or, however, in contrast.* A **compound sentence** is an example of coordination:

   War is a raging fire; however, peace is a soothing balm.

2. **Subordination** expresses an unequal relationship between topics. Subordination expresses similarities with words such as *as, just as, just like, like*. Subordination expresses an unequal relationship between differences with words such as *although, even though, while.* A **complex sentence** is an example of subordination:

   War is a raging fire while peace is a soothing balm.

For more information about *coordination* and *subordination*, see page 512.

Example

Assume the role of peer editor for Bethany's essay "The War Machine." Identify one expression or detail that would benefit from using a sensory detail or figure of speech. Also, identify one sentence that would benefit by revising for coordination and subordination. Suggest possible revisions.

1. **Original Expression or Detail:** ______________________________

   ____

   Revision: ______________________________

   ____

2. **Original Expression or Detail:** ______________________________

____

Revision: ______________________________

____

Explanation

Compare your answers to Bethany's think-aloud about how she needed to revise her draft.

After the initial draft, the next draft should focus on revising so that my points are conveyed clearly with exact wording. Through the revision exercises, I was able to create imagery in my essay, such as "selfish brutes." When reading my first draft I underlined key concepts that were essential to the thesis. After this, I tried my best to rewrite using colorful wording that made the phrase memorable. This made me take ideas and turn them into images so I could better influence my readers. This focus and my ongoing editing to make my essay flow smoothly were the two most important steps for me. During one of my revisions, I concentrated on using coordination and subordination to emphasize a comparison or contrast. Here are my revised sentences:

Coordination: We are only an obstacle to ourselves, and as a united front, we can truly make a difference in a hurting world.

Subordination: You will not seek a remedy unless you recognize a malady.

Practice 5

Revise and Proofread for Effective Language with Classification, Comparison, and Contrast

In your reading/writing journal, list the steps needed to revise, edit, and proofread an essay. What did Bethany do as part of her revision process? How did your processes differ? What can you learn from Bethany's revision that you can apply to your own editing process in the future?

Workshop: Comprehend and Create an Essay Using Classification, Comparison, and Contrast

Assume you are continuing your study of conflict and resolution. The following passages are the capstone reading assignment. Your capstone writing assignment is to write an essay in response to the guiding question, "What are the elements of war and peace, and how do these elements seem similar or different in specific situations?" You may also be asked to make connections among these passages and those you have already read in this module or in other modules. For this assignment, skim through the prereading questions, read the following passages, and complete the writing activities that follow.

Broadcast, Outbreak of War with Germany, September 3, 1939

King George VI of England

[1]In this grave hour, perhaps the most fateful in our history, I send to every household of my peoples, both at home and overseas, this message, spoken with the same depth of feeling for each one of you as if I were able to cross your threshold and speak to you myself.

[2]For the second time in the lives of most of us we are at war. Over and over again we have tried to find a peaceful way out of the differences between ourselves and those who are now our enemies. But it has been in vain. We have been forced into a conflict. For we are called, with our allies, to meet the challenge of a principle which, if it were to prevail, would be fatal to any civilized order in the world.

[3]It is the principle which permits a state, in the selfish pursuit of power, to disregard its treaties and its solemn pledges; which sanctions the use of force, or threat of force, against the sovereignty and independence of other states. Such a principle, stripped of all disguise, is surely the mere primitive doctrine that might is right; and if this principle were established throughout the world, the freedom of our own country and of the whole British Commonwealth of Nations would be in danger. But far more than this—the peoples of the world would be kept in the bondage of fear, and all hopes of settled peace and of the security of justice and liberty among nations would be ended.

[4]This is the ultimate issue which confronts us. For the sake of all that we ourselves hold dear, and of the world's order and peace, it is unthinkable that we should refuse to meet the challenge.

[5]It is to this high purpose that I now call my people at home and my peoples across the seas, who will make our cause their own. I ask them to stand calm, firm, and united in this time of trial. The task will be hard. There may be dark days ahead, and war can no longer be confined to the battlefield. But we can only do the right as we see the right, and reverently commit our cause to God. If one and all we keep resolutely faithful to it, ready for whatever service or sacrifice it may demand, then, with God's help, we shall prevail. May He bless and keep us all.

I Will Fight No More Forever

by Chief Joseph

[1]I am tired of fighting. Our chiefs are killed; Lookingglass is dead. Too-hul-hul-suit is dead. The old men are all dead. It is the young men, now, who say 'yes' or 'no' [that is, vote in council]. He who led on the young men [Joseph's brother, Ollicut] is dead. It is cold, and we have no blankets. The little children are freezing to death. My people—some of them—have run away to the hills, and have no blankets, no food. No one knows where they are—perhaps freezing to death. I want to have time to look for my children, and see how many of them I can find; maybe I shall find them among the dead. Hear me, my chiefs; my heart is sick and sad. From where the sun now stands, I will fight no more forever!

–Chief Joseph's surrender to General Nelson A. Miles, October 5, 1877.
http://memory.loc.gov/ammem/today/oct05.html

United States-Soviet Space Cooperation During the Cold War

[1]The Space Age spawned two outstanding space programs as a result of the hot competition between the United States and the Soviet Union. Both countries gave primary emphasis in their space efforts to a combination of national security and foreign policy objectives, turning space into an area of active competition for political and military advantage. At first, this charged political environment accommodated nothing more than symbolic gestures of collaboration. Only in the late 1980s, with warming political relations, did momentum for major space cooperation begin to build. As the Soviet Union neared collapse, with its ideological underpinnings evaporating, the impetus for the arms race and competition in space declined, allowing both countries to seriously pursue strategic partnerships in space.

[2]The bumpy U.S.–U.S.S.R. relationship in the years between 1957 and 1991 often was characterized by periods of mistrust and overt hostility (e.g., the U-2 incident, Cuban Missile Crisis, Vietnam War, Soviet invasion of Afghanistan and President Ronald Reagan's depiction of the Soviet Union as an "evil empire"). Periods of détente, in contrast, led to the Limited Test-Ban Treaty in 1963, the Strategic Arms Limitation Treaty in 1972, and an emerging U.S.-Soviet rapprochement during 1985–1991. Throughout this political roller-coaster period of history, both countries increased areas of cooperation, including space, as a symbol of warmer relations while cutting cooperation off when ties worsened.

CONTINUED

[3]The birth of the Space Age following the Soviet launch of Sputnik came out of the confluence of two seemingly incompatible developments. From the end of World War II, the Soviets made rockets their most important military asset. By the mid-1950s, they were ready to test their first intercontinental ballistic missile (ICBM). In 1957, the International Geophysical Year was launched, a multinational effort to study Earth on a comprehensive, coordinated basis. To highlight the effort, organizers had urged the United States and the Soviet Union to consider launching a scientific satellite. On Oct. 4, 1957, a seemingly routine test launch of a Soviet ICBM (now known as the R-7 rocket) carried the first artificial satellite to orbit.

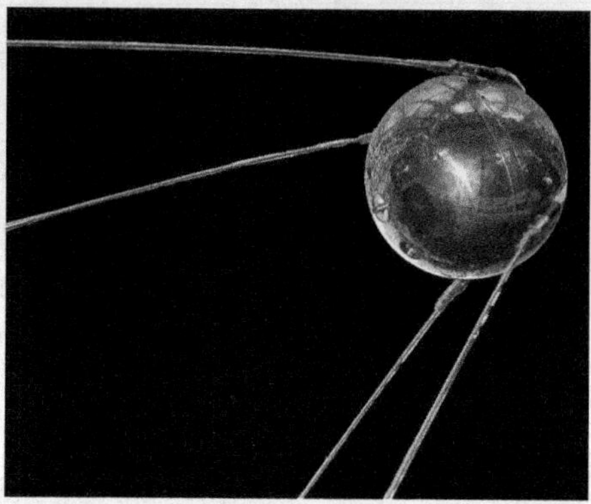

[4]Sputnik's launch had dramatic repercussions for the Cold War rivals. After reaping the first political dividends from military rocket technology, the Soviets continued to pursue a highly classified military-industrial approach in developing its space program. Conversely, the U.S. government decided to make NASA a purely civilian enterprise, while focusing its military space efforts in the Pentagon and intelligence community.

[5]Early on, President Dwight D. Eisenhower pursued U.S.–Soviet cooperative space initiatives through a series of letters he sent in 1957 and 1958 to the Soviet leadership, first to Prime Minister Nikolai Bulganin and then to Premier Nikita Khrushchev. Eisenhower suggested creating a process to secure space for peaceful uses. Khrushchev, however, rejected the offer and demanded the United States eliminate its forward-based nuclear weapons in places like Turkey as a precondition for any space agreement. Feeling triumphant after Sputnik's launch, Khrushchev was certain his country was far ahead of the United States in terms of rocket technology and space launch capabilities, unlike the Soviet Union's more vulnerable geostrategic position in the nuclear arena. This would be the first of many times when space was linked with nuclear disarmament and other political issues.

[6]Meanwhile, the United States energetically proceeded with its multinational initiative under the umbrella of the United Nations to develop a legal framework for peaceful space activities. This eventually led to the Outer Space Treaty and creation of the United Nations Committee on the Peaceful Uses of Outer Space, which a reluctant Soviet Union eventually joined.

—From "United States-Soviet Space Cooperation during the Cold War" by Roald Sagdeev, University of Maryland, and Susan Eisenhower, The Eisenhower Institute. Published by NASA.

Preread: Survey and Question

PREREAD: SURVEY/ QUESTION

According to King George VI, which elements of war led to war with Germany? (See "Elements of War and Peace," page 430.)

How are the attitude and situation of Chief Joseph similar to or different from those of Aung San Suu Kyi? (See page 434.)

King George's speech calls his people to fight, while Chief Joseph's speech declares surrender. Explain the differences between the purpose, tone, and effect of these two speeches.

How does Chief Joseph's speech illustrate the elements of war and peace? (See "Elements of War and Peace," page 430.)

Compare/contrast the views of Aung San Suu Kyi, Chief Joseph, and President Kennedy.

How is President's Kennedy's call for peace similar to President Eisenhower's view about the uses of space?

Compare/contrast the views of President Eisenhower and Premier Khrushchev about U.S.-Soviet space initiatives.

Are space programs the most effective as tools for deterrence or for diplomacy and disarmament? How so? (See "Elements of War and Peace," page 430.)

Read and Annotate

As you read, annotate key ideas, particularly those details that answer your prereading questions.

Recite, Review, and Brainstorm

Recite and **Review** the information. Paraphrase ideas. Summarize the most important parts. **Brainstorm** ideas for your written response to the passage. Answer your prereading questions. *Freewrite* or *map* the relationship among answers to questions or ideas you have annotated in the text. *Outline* or *list* key ideas and details in blocks of thought. Use your own paper.

Write a Draft of Your Response

Using the ideas you generated by brainstorming, compose a draft of your response. Use your own paper.

Revise Your Draft

Once you have created a draft of a classification or comparison/contrast response, read it over to answer the questions in the "Questions for Revising Classification, Comparison, and Contrast Essays" box that follows. Indicate your answers by annotating your paper. If you answer "yes" to a question, underline, check, or circle examples. If you answer "no" to a question, write the needed information in the margins and draw lines to indicate the placement of additional details. Revise your essay based on your reflection. (*Hint:* Experienced writers create several drafts as they focus on one or two questions per draft.)

Step by Step: Questions for Revising Classification, Comparison, and Contrast Essays

- ☐ Have I stated or implied a focused main idea?
- ☐ Have I stated or implied the specific points of classification, comparison, or contrast?
- ☐ Is the order of specific points clear? Have I used strong transitions of classification, comparison, or contrast?
- ☐ Have I used concrete details to make my point?
- ☐ Have I made my point with adequate details?
- ☐ Have I included only the details that are relevant to my thesis sentence?
- ☐ Have I used coordination and subordination to make my points clear to my readers?

Proofread Your Draft

Once you have made any revisions to your essay that may be needed, proofread your essay to eliminate careless errors.

Reading and Writing Assignments

MySkillsLab™
Complete this Exercise
on myskillslab.com

Reading and Writing for Everyday Life

Assume you are the president of the Parent-Teachers Association (PTA) at your child's high school. It has been brought to your attention that many parents are struggling with helping their children work through the process of choosing a college to attend. You have arranged for a workshop facilitated by guidance counselors from several colleges to work with the parents and students. Write a short column for the next PTA newsletter advertising the workshop. Use information from the following article to hook their interest.

COPING WITH **FRUSTRATION**

All thinkers have their share of frustration: confusion, mental blocks, false starts, and failures happen to everyone. Good thinkers, however, have learned strategies for dealing with their frustration, whereas poor thinkers merely lament it—thus allowing themselves to be defeated by it. One important study of students' problem-solving processes revealed some interesting differences between good and poor problem solvers. Among them were the following:

Good Problem Solvers	Poor Problem Solvers
Read a problem and decide how to begin attacking it.	Cannot settle on a way to begin.
Bring their knowledge to bear on a problem.	Convince themselves they lack sufficient knowledge (even when that is not the case).
Go about solving a problem systematically—for example, trying to simplify it, puzzling out key terms, or breaking the problem into sub problems.	Plunge in, jumping haphazardly from one part of the problem to another, trying to justify first impressions instead of testing them.
Tend to trust their reasoning and to have confidence in themselves.	Tend to distrust their reasoning and to lack confidence in themselves.
Maintain a critical attitude throughout the problem-solving process.	Lack a critical attitude and take too much for granted.

—Ruggiero, *The Art of Thinking*, 10th ed., Pearson Education, 2012, pp. 11–12.

Reading and Writing for College Life

Assume you are a peer tutor in your college's learning lab. You have been asked to conduct a training session about the differences between constructive and destructive behaviors or attitudes. Create a computer-assisted presentation based on the information in the following passage.

24 NAVIGATING YOUR FUTURE SUCCESS

BALANCE YOUR ATTITUDE

We should all strive for balance in our lives, including in our attitudes and emotions. Many people view anger as a negative emotion, but just like stress, a little can spur us on to do better or to right an injustice. However, prolonged anger can lead to destructive behavior and illness.

We all become sad when a tragedy strikes; this makes us human. But it's important to differentiate depression from sadness. If someone is sad following a painful disappointment or the loss of a loved one, it is a normal part of the grieving process. However, if sadness remains for a prolonged period of time and interferes with one's daily business, it becomes depression. Balance, again, is the key.

Look at the table, which contrasts a constructive versus destructive approach. Where do you fit in?

CONSTRUCTIVE	DESTRUCTIVE
Confronts a problem, (appropriately)	Thinks problems will resolve themselves
Discusses things in calm manner	Fights or yells
Accepts responsibility	Blames others
Uses relaxation techniques	Uses alcohol or drugs
Accepts/learns from mistakes	Is a perfectionist
Practices good nutrition	Over- or under-eats
Lives in the present	Agonizes over past or future
Helps others	Avoids people

Change Worry into Concern

Mark Twain's quote is cleverly telling us that most of what we worry about never happens. We waste all that negative energy by worrying, and we do not experience a positive outcome. You may think we are telling you not to worry about your grades this semester, and you are right. The difference is that, rather than worry, you should be *concerned* about your grades this semester.

"I am an old man and have known a great many problems, but most of them never happened."
—MARK TWAIN

When you are worried, you clench your jaw and your mind goes a million miles per hour with messages such as "I'm never going to understand this," "I'm never going to pass this course," and "What if I fail?"

When you are concerned, you take *action* to maximize the positive outcome. For example, students should be concerned about how *well* they will do in a difficult course. This example could illustrate their approach: "I know this is a tough course; however, if I *do* the following, I *will* pass this course if I"

- Study for 45 minutes each day
- Keep up with assignments
- See my teacher at least once per week

Notice the difference? *Worry* is wasted negative energy with no action, and concern involves planning a course of action that will most likely lead to a positive outcome. Remember this old saying: "Worrying is like sitting in a rocking chair; it gives you something to do, but it doesn't get you anywhere."

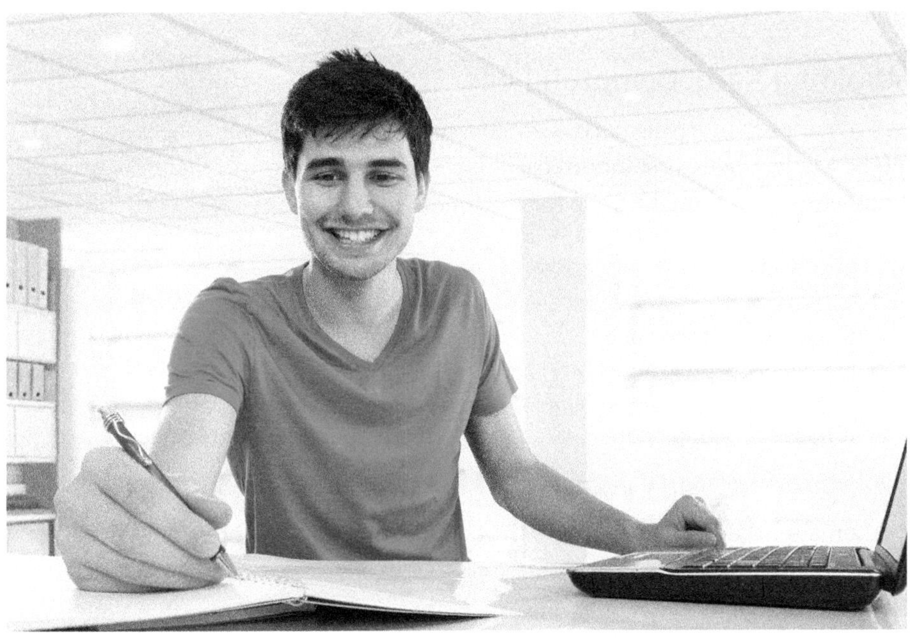

—Colbert, *Navigating Your Future Success*. 2nd ed., Pearson, 2015, pp. 24–25.

Reading and Writing for Working Life

Assume you are the owner of a local business in which the employees are in constant conflict over the following issues: shift workers sharing the same office space; timing of work breaks and rotating holidays; and responsibility of use of the company car for business.

Read the following article. Then write a memo to your employees that outlines ways to compromise or collaborate on these issues. In your memo, advise them that these issues will be discussed in a follow-up meeting.

Collaborating Conflict Communication as an Option

Collaboration means using integrative behaviors and developing mutually satisfying agreements to solve the problem once and for all. Collaboration, then, has two essential ingredients. First, it consists of behaviors such as cooperation, collective action, and mutual assistance. When people collaborate, they work together toward the same ends in compatible roles. We call this teamwork. To an observer, the collaborators appear to work side by side and hand in hand. This approach is in direct contrast to opposing or competing individuals who counteract, antagonize, and work against one another.

Secondly, collaboration means that the partners have in mind the same goal, which is to strive for a mutually satisfying solution to the conflict. Mutually satisfying solutions are win-win outcomes. Collaboration not only emphasizes one's own self-interests but also respects the other's interests, needs, and goals. While collaboration may involve confronting differences, it requires a focusing on the problem and includes sharing information about everyone's needs, goals, and interests.

Avoiding Early Compromising

All too often, conflicting parties are too quick to try compromising, when greater effort would produce a solution that completely satisfies both of them. For example, conflicting parties might settle for the following:

EXAMPLES OF COMPROMISING	EXAMPLES OF COLLABORATION
Alternate driving the car	Go together to events
Split driving 50:50	Take a bus/train
Split house cleaning chores	Hire a housecleaning service
Alternate watching TV programs	Watch one and tape the other
Alternate holidays with family	Spend part of the holiday with each family
Divide the money between them	Increase the amount so that both get what they want

—Cahn and Abigail, *Managing Conflict Through Communication*, 5th ed., Pearson, 2014, pp. 42–43.

Review Test

The Classification, Comparison, and Contrast Patterns

Score (number correct) _____ x 10 = _____ %

Read the following passage, and then answer the questions.

Categorizing Personality by Types

[1]We are always categorizing people according to distinguishing features. [2]These include college class, academic major, sex, and race. [3]Some personality theorists also group people into distinct, nonoverlapping categories that are called personality **types.** [4]Personality types are all-or-none **phenomena**, not matters of degree: If a person is assigned to one type, he or she could not belong to any other type within that system. [5]Many people like to use personality types in everyday life because they help simplify the complex process of understanding other people.

[6]One of the earliest type theories was originated in the 5th century B.C. by Hippocrates, the Greek physician who gave medicine the Hippocratic Oath. [7]He theorized that the body contained four basic fluids, or **humors**, each associated with a particular temperament, a pattern of emotions and behaviors. [8]In the 2nd century A.D., a later Greek physician, Galen, suggested that an individual's personality depended on which humor was predominant in his or her body. [9]Galen paired Hippocrates's body humors with personality temperaments according to the following scheme:

[10]**Blood.** Sanguine temperament: cheerful and active

[11]**Phlegm. Phlegmatic** temperament: apathetic and sluggish

[12]**Black bile.** Melancholy temperament: sad and brooding

[13]**Yellow bile.** Choleric temperament: irritable and excitable

[14]The theory proposed by Galen was believed for centuries, up through the Middle Ages, although it has not held up to modern scrutiny.

[15]In modern times, William Sheldon (1898–1977) originated a type theory that related physique to temperament. [16]Sheldon (1942) assigned people to three categories based on their body builds: *endomorphic* (fat, soft, round), *mesomorphic* (muscular, rectangular, strong), or *ectomorphic* (thin, long, fragile). [17]Sheldon believed that endomorphs are relaxed, fond of eating, and sociable. [18]Mesomorphs are physical people, filled with energy, courage, and assertive tendencies. [19]Ectomorphs are brainy, artistic, and introverted; they would think about life, rather than consuming it or acting on it. [20]For a period of time, Sheldon's theory was sufficiently influential that nude

CONTINUED

REVIEW TEST *CONTINUED*

"posture" photographs were taken of thousands of students at U.S. colleges like Yale and Wellesley to allow researchers to study the relationships between body type and life factors. [21]However, like Hippocrates's much earlier theory, Sheldon's notion of body types has proven to be of very little value in predicting an individual's behavior (Tyler, 1965).

[22]More recently, Frank Sulloway (1996) has proposed a contemporary type theory based on birth order. [23]Are you the firstborn child (or only child) in your family, or are you a laterborn child? [24]Because you can take on only one of these birth positions, Sulloway's theory fits the criteria for being a type theory. [25](For people with unusual family constellations—for example, a very large age gap between two children—Sulloway still provides ways of categorizing individuals.) [26]Sulloway makes birth-order predictions based on Darwin's idea that organisms diversify to find niches in which they will survive. [27]According to Sulloway, firstborns have a ready-made niche: They immediately command their parents' love and attention; they seek to maintain that initial attachment by identifying and complying with their parents. [28]By contrast, laterborn children need to find a different niche—one in which they don't so clearly follow their parents' example. [29]As a consequence, Sulloway characterizes laterborns as "born to rebel": "they seek to excel in those domains where older siblings have not already established superiority. [30]Laterborns typically cultivate openness to experience—a useful strategy for anyone who wishes to find a novel and successful niche in life" (Sulloway, 1996, p. 353).

—Gerrig and Zimbardo, *Psychology and Life*, 19th ed., p. 407.

Vocabulary

1. The word **phenomena** in sentence 4 means
a. spectacles. **b.** occurrences. **c.** facts. **d.** features.

Vocabulary

2. The best meaning of the word **humors** in sentence 7 is
a. funny qualities.
b. emotions.
c. effects of body fluids.
d. behaviors.

Vocabulary

3. The best synonym for the word **phlegmatic** in sentence 11 is
a. unmotivated. **b.** sickly. **c.** calm. **d.** determined.

Inference

4. Based on the information in the passage, we may infer that personality types
a. are primarily based on physical traits.
b. are primarily based on social status.
c. have been conclusively proven as true through scientific research.
d. are theories developed to categorize human behavior.

Central Idea

5. Which sentence states the central idea of the essay?
   a. sentence 1   b. sentence 2   c. sentence 3   d. sentence 5

Supporting Details

6. Sentence 20 states a
   a. main idea.
   b. major supporting detail.
   c. minor supporting detail.

Pattern of Organization

7. What pattern of organization does the word **types** in sentence 3 signal?
   a. time order   b. classification   c. space order

Pattern of Organization

8. What is the relationship of ideas within sentence 16?
   a. listing   b. time order   c. space order

Fact and Opinion

9. Sentence 6 states
   a. a fact.   b. an opinion.   c. a fact and an opinion.

Purpose and Tone

10. The primary purpose and tone of the passage is
   a. informative and objective.
   b. amusing and informal.
   c. persuasive and probing.

Summary Response

Restate the authors' central idea in your own words. Include the two major patterns of organization used by the authors in your summary. Begin your summary response with the following: *The central idea of "Categorizing Personality Types" by Gerrig and Zimbardo is . . . .*

Reader Response

Assume you are taking a college psychology class, and your teacher has given you the following assignment: Choose a fictional character from a television show, movie, book, graphic novel, etc., and categorize his or her personality type. Consider the following prompts to help your writing process:

Analyze the character using each of the personality types described in the passage.

Describe the moods and behaviors of the character to support your use of each label.

MySkillsLab™
Complete this Exercise
on myskillslab.com

Academic Learning Log: Module Review

Summary of Key Concepts of the Classification, Comparison, and Contrast Patterns

Assess your comprehension of the classification, comparison, and contrast patterns.

LO1 LO2 LO3 LO4 LO6

1. A classification ____________ a topic into ____________, based on shared ____________ or ____________.
2. Signal words for classification include kind, ____________, ____________, ____________, and ____________.
3. Because groups or traits are listed, classification also uses transitions such as ____________, ____________, ____________, and ____________.
4. To read or write a comparison/contrast paragraph, you identify or establish the ____________ between two (or more) topics.
5. A comparison focuses on the ____________ between topics. A contrast focuses on the ____________ between topics.
6. A ____________ focuses on both the similarities and the differences between topics.
7. Signal words for comparison include ____________, ____________, ____________, ____________, ____________. Signal words for contrast include ____________, ____________, ____________, ____________, ____________.
8. To identify and generate details based on classification, comparison, or contrast, readers and writers may ask the reporter's questions ____________, ____________, ____________, ____________, ____________, and ____________.
9. Coordination expresses an ____________ relationship between topics.

   A ____________ sentence is an example of coordination.
10. Subordination expresses an ____________ relationship between topics.

    A ____________ sentence is an example of subordination.

Test Your Comprehension of the Classification, Comparison, and Contrast Patterns

Respond in your own words to the following questions and prompts.

LO1 LO2 LO3 LO4 LO5 LO6

Complete the chart with examples of signal words to establish classification, comparison, and contrast patterns of organization.

Words That Signal Classification				

Words That Signal Comparison				

Words That Signal Contrast				

On your own paper, create blank concept map that combines classification, comparison, and contrast.

1. **How will I use what I have learned?** In your notebook, discuss how you will apply to your own reading/writing strategy what you have learned about the classification, comparison, and contrast patterns. When will you apply this knowledge to your reading/writing strategy?
2. **What do I still need to study about the classification, comparison, and contrast patterns?** In your notebook, discuss your ongoing study needs. Describe what, when, and how you will continue studying and using the classification, comparison, and contrast patterns.

MySkillsLab™
Complete the Post-test for Module 11 in MySkillsLab.

12 Argument

LEARNING OUTCOMES

After studying this module you should be able to:

- **LO 1** Answer the Question "What's the Point of Argument?"
- **LO 2** Question, Read, and Annotate Passages Using Argument
- **LO 3** Prewrite a Draft of a Thesis Statement Using Argument
- **LO 4** Prewrite to Generate Relevant Details Using Argument
- **LO 5** Compose a Draft Using Logical Order: Argument
- **LO 6** Revise and Proofread for Effective Language with Argument

In almost every area of our lives, we engage in some form of argument or persuasion. Whether convincing a friend to see a particular movie or proving we are the right candidate for a particular job, we are most effective when we use reason and logic to get others to agree with our views.

To make an argument, a master writer asserts or implies a strong stand, or claim, on one side of a debatable issue. Then he or she offers supports for that claim by providing convincing evidence such as reasons, facts, examples, and expert opinions. In addition to asserting a strong claim and supporting it with evidence, a master writer acknowledges and rebuts (disproves or challenges) the opposing views. A master reader evaluates the writer's claim and supporting details to determine or infer whether it is valid and the supports are relevant and adequate. Whether we realize it or not, we are constantly evaluating and creating arguments. In everyday life, our court system is based on proving claims of guilt or innocence. In college life, we encounter debatable claims made by other students, professors, and experts in every discipline. In working life, we use reasons to resolve workplace disputes or offer solutions to problems.

WHAT'S THE POINT of Argument?

Argument is often a call to action or a challenge to a change of mind. The following photos represent a call to good citizenship. Study the photographs. In the space provided, identify the claim, reasons, and an opposing point of view about what it means to be a good citizen. Then answer the question "What's the point of argument?"

Photographic Organizer: Argument

ISSUE: WHAT MAKES A GOOD CITIZEN?

SUPPORTING POINTS

What is this reason?

What is this reason?

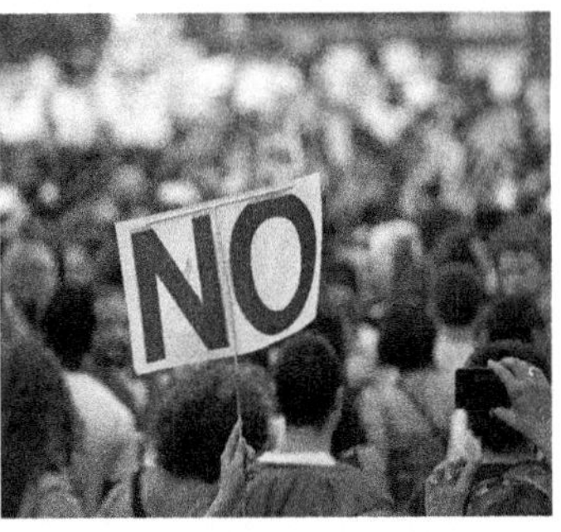

What is this reason?

COUNTERCLAIM (Opposing Point)

What is this opposing view?

What is the claim?

Refute the counterclaim:

What's the point of argument?

L2 Question, Read, and Annotate Passages Using Argument

An effective **argument** is a **claim** based on logical supports. An argument also acknowledges and refutes **counterclaims**. You have acquired several skills that will help you master argument as a reader/writer, including stating or implying main ideas, identifying and generating supporting details, distinguishing between fact and opinion, recognizing tone and purpose, and making inferences.

When a master reader recognizes that a writer is using argument to organize ideas, he or she can see how the central point and details fit together and anticipate upcoming details. To make an argument, a master writer often moves from a general idea (the claim) to a major support (a reason, fact, example, expert opinion, or argument against the opposing view) to a minor support (also a reason, fact, example, expert opinion, or argument against the opposing view).

Argument is a process of reasoning that demonstrates a claim as valid based on the logical details given in support of that claim.

A **claim** is a statement, assertion, or conclusion about a specific position on a debatable issue.

A **counterclaim** is a statement, assertion, or conclusion that opposes a specific position on a debatable issue.

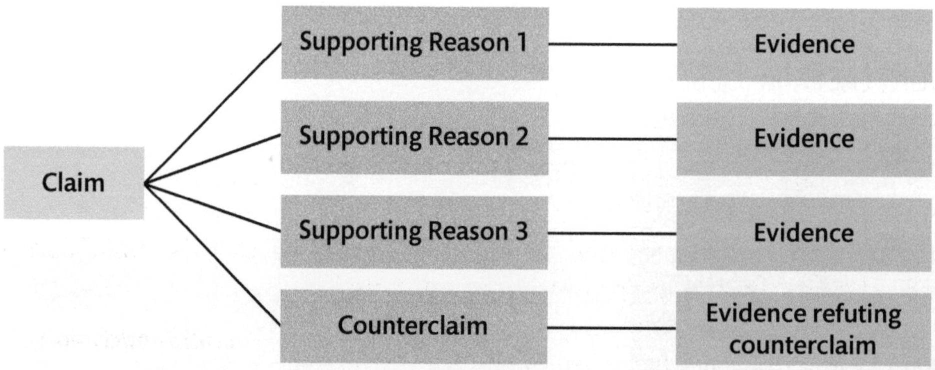

Master readers skim for transitions and signal words to recognize the importance of the writer's details and the relationships among these details. The following charts offer a few examples of signal words and transitions that establish an argument.

Transitions That Signal Argument			
accordingly	finally	in fact, in truth	on the other hand
admittedly	first (second, third, etc.)	in summary	since
although	for	last	some believe
because	furthermore	meanwhile	some may say
but	granted	nevertheless	therefore
certainly	hence	nonetheless	thus
consequently	however	obviously	to be sure
despite	in conclusion	of course	truly
even so	indeed	on the one hand	undoubtedly

Signal Words That Qualify an Idea as an Argument (sample list)				
all	has/have to	must	possibly, possible	think
always	indisputable	necessary	probably, probable	too
believe	it is believed	never	proved	usually
consequence	likely	often	seem	
could	may	only	should	
every	might	ought to	sometimes	

Common supports of an argumentative claim include reasons, facts, examples, effects, and expert opinions, as well as details that refute the opposing view. Both readers and writers evaluate these types of details to infer or determine if a claim is a **valid conclusion**. For a claim to be valid, supporting details must be both relevant and adequate. Relevant supports answer the reporter's questions (*who, what, when, where, why, how*). Ask and answer these questions to infer whether the supports for a claim are relevant. Master readers and writers also evaluate details to determine if they are adequate. A valid argument is based not only on a claim and relevant support but also on the amount and quality of the support given. That is, supports must give enough evidence for the writer's claim to be convincing. Just as you use the reporter's questions to decide whether supports are relevant, you also can use them to test whether supports are adequate. Asking and answering questions to test details keeps you from jumping to an **invalid conclusion** or false inference.

A **valid conclusion** is a claim reasonably supported with details soundly based in logic or fact.

An **invalid conclusion** is a claim not adequately supported with enough relevant details; it is a false inference.

Master readers learn to use the **VALID** thinking process to infer if a claim is sound. The VALID approach avoids drawing false inferences and coming to false conclusions. The VALID approach includes the following:

V	**V**erify and value the facts.	Writers may mix fact with opinion or use false information for their own purposes. Likewise, readers may draw false inferences by mixing the writer's facts with their own opinions. So it is important to find, verify, and stick to the factual details. Then you can begin to interpret the facts by making inferences and coming to conclusions about a claim's validity.
A	**A**ssess Prior knowledge.	Once you are sure of the facts, draw on your prior knowledge. What you already have already learned and experienced can help you make accurate inferences about an argument.
L	**L**earn from the text.	When you value and verify facts, you are learning from the text. A valid inference or conclusion is always based on what is stated or implied in the text. An invalid conclusion goes beyond the evidence. Many of the skills you have gained from previous modules work together to enable you to learn from the text. Context clues unlock the writer's use of vocabulary. Patterns of organization reveal the relationships among ideas.
I	**I**nvestigate for bias.	To infer if an argument is valid, bias must be identified and confronted. Each of us possesses strong personal views that affect the way we process information. Our bias may shape our reading of the writer's meaning. Likewise, it is important to recognize the writer's use of bias to make and support a claim.
D	**D**etect contradictions.	In determining the validity of an argument, contradictions occur in two ways. The first is jumping to a wrong conclusion that contradicts the evidence. For example, have you ever assumed a person was rude, only to find out later that he or she was acutely shy? Many times there may be a better explanation for a set of facts than the first one that comes to mind. Thus, consider all the possible explanations and choose the one that most reasonably explains all the details. The second contradiction occurs when a writer presents and refutes counterclaims. In both instances, effective readers search for contradictions and test them for logic.

For Module 12, assume you are taking a college course in political science, and your class is beginning a study on the theme of "civic duty." Each reading in this module follows this theme. After completing all assigned readings, you will write in response to the following guiding question: "What makes a good citizen?"

Example

Assume the following passage is your first assigned reading on the theme of "civic duty." Your professor has provided before and during reading questions and guided annotations to prepare you to read about and respond to the theme. Before reading, survey the questions and skim the passage for possible answers. Next, read the passage and the annotations. As you read, add your own annotations by completing the prompts in **bold** print. After reading, use your own words to answer the questions. Record your answers in your reading/writing journal. Finally, complete the concept map with information from the passage.

Before and During Reading Questions:

Logical Order: How does the writer use signal words and transitions to organize his argument? Which transitions/signal words does the writer use?

Central Idea: What is the writer's central point?

Relevant Details: What key reasons, facts, and consequences does the writer give to support his argument? Does the writer offer and refute opposing views? Does the writer call the audience to action?

Effective Language: How does the writer use emotional or subjective language to express opinions, attitudes, and values to make his argument?

THE PRICE OF GREATNESS

Winston Churchill

President Harry Truman and British Prime Minister Winston Churchill

[1]Twice in my lifetime the long arm of destiny has reached across the oceans and involved the entire life and manhood of the United States in a deadly struggle.

[2]There was no use in saying "We don't want it; we won't have it; our forebears left Europe to avoid these quarrels; we have founded a new world which has no contact with the old." [3]There was no use in that. [4]The long arm reaches out remorselessly, and every one's existence, environment, and outlook undergo a swift and irresistible change.

Relevant Details: The writer has implied that someone holds an opposing view and a counterclaim by saying these words: "There was no use saying . . ." **Circle the writer's counterclaim to this opposing view.**

CONTINUED

EXAMPLE *CONTINUED*

Central idea: The topic of the claim is "the price of greatness." **Underline the writer's controlling point of his claim.**

[5]What is the explanation, Mr. President, of these strange facts, and what are the deep laws to which they respond? [6]I will offer you one explanation—there are others, but one will suffice.

[7]The price of greatness is responsibility. [8]If the people of the United States had continued in a mediocre station, struggling with the wilderness, absorbed in their own affairs, and a factor of no consequence in the movement of the world, they might have remained forgotten and undisturbed beyond their protecting oceans: but one cannot rise to be in many ways the leading community in the civilized world without being involved in its problems, without being convulsed by its agonies and inspired by its causes.

[9]If this has been proved in the past, as it has been, it will become indisputable in the future. [10]The people of the United States cannot escape world responsibility. [11]Although we live in a period so tumultuous that little can be predicted, we may be quite sure that this process will be intensified with every forward step the United States makes in wealth and in power. [12]Not only are the responsibilities of this great Republic growing, but the world over which they range is itself contracting in relation to our powers of locomotion at a positively alarming rate.

[13]We have learned to fly. [14]What prodigious changes are involved in that new accomplishment! [15]Man has parted company with his trusty friend the horse and has sailed into the azure with the eagles, eagles being represented by the infernal (loud laughter)—I mean internal—combustion engine. [16]Where, then, are those broad oceans, those vast staring deserts? [17]They are shrinking beneath our very eyes. [18]Even elderly Parliamentarians like myself are forced to acquire a high degree of mobility.

[19]But to the youth of America, as to the youth of all the Britains, I say "You cannot stop." [20]There is no halting-place at this point. [21]We have now reached a stage in the journey where there can be no pause. [22]We must go on. [23]It must be world anarchy or world order.

[24]Throughout all this ordeal and struggle which is characteristic of our age, you will find in the British Commonwealth and Empire good comrades to whom you are united by other ties besides those of State policy and public need. [25]To a large extent, they are the ties of blood and history. [26]Naturally I, a child of both worlds, am conscious of these.

[27]Law, language, literature—these are considerable factors. [28]Common conceptions of what is right and decent, a marked regard for fair play, especially to the weak and poor, a stern sentiment of impartial justice, and above all the love of personal freedom, or as Kipling put it:

[29]"Leave to live by no man's leave, underneath the law"—these are common conceptions on both sides of the ocean among the English-speaking peoples. [30]We hold to these conceptions as strongly as you do.

[31]We do not war primarily with races as such. [32]Tyranny is our foe, whatever trappings or disguise it wears, whatever language it speaks, be it external or internal, we must forever be on our guard, ever mobilized, ever vigilant, always ready to spring at its throat. [33]In all this, we march together. [34]Not only do we march and strive shoulder to shoulder at this moment under the fire of the enemy on the fields of war or in the air, but also in those realms of thought which are consecrated to the rights and the dignity of man.

[35]At the present time we have in continual vigorous action the British and United States Combined Chiefs of Staff Committee, which works immediately under the President and myself as representative of the British War Cabinet. [36]This committee, with its elaborate organization of Staff officers of every grade, disposes of all our resources and, in practice, uses British and American troops, ships, aircraft, and munitions just as if they were the resources of a single State or nation.

[37]I would not say there are never divergences of view among these high professional authorities. [38]It would be unnatural if there were not. [39]That is why it is necessary to have a plenary meeting of principals every two or three months. [40]All these men now know each other. [41]They trust each other. [42]They like each other, and most of them have been at work together for a long time. [43]When they meet they thrash things out with great candor and plain, blunt speech, but after a few days the President and I find ourselves furnished with sincere and united advice.

[44]This is a wonderful system. [45]There was nothing like it in the last war. [46]There never has been anything like it between two allies. [47]It is reproduced in an even more tightly-knit form at General Eisenhower's headquarters in the Mediterranean, where everything is completely intermingled and soldiers are ordered into battle by the Supreme Commander or his deputy, General Alexander, without the slightest regard to whether they are

CONTINUED

EXAMPLE *CONTINUED*

Effective Expression: The writer uses subjective language such as "foolish and improvident" to empower his argument. **Draw a wavy line under two more expressions using subjective language.**

British, American, or Canadian, but simply in accordance with the fighting need.

[48]Now in my opinion it would be a most foolish and improvident act on the part of our two Governments, or either of them, to break up this smooth-running and immensely powerful machinery the moment the war is over. [49]For our own safety, as well as for the security of the rest of the world, we are bound to keep it working and in running order after the war—probably for a good many years, not only until we have set up some world arrangement to keep the peace, but until we know that it is an arrangement which will really give us that protection we must have from danger and aggression, a protection we have already had to seek across two vast world wars.

[50]I am not qualified, of course, to judge whether or not this would become a party question in the United States, and I would not presume to discuss that point. [51]I am sure, however, that it will not be a party question in Great Britain. [52]We must not let go of the securities we have found necessary to preserve our lives and liberties until we are quite sure we have something else to put in their place, which will give us an equally solid guarantee.

Relevant Details: The writer employs a VALID element when he offers historical details that could be verified through research. **Underline another example of a fact that can verified or another element of VALID.**

[53]The great Bismarck—for there were once great men in Germany—is said to have observed towards the close of his life that the most potent factor in human society at the end of the nineteenth century was the fact that the British and American peoples spoke the same language.

Logical Order: The writer sustains his argument with effective use of transitions and signal words, such as *Certainly*. **Circle three more transitions or signal words used to establish the flow of his argument.**

[54]That was a pregnant saying. [55]Certainly it has enabled us to wage war together with an intimacy and harmony never before achieved among allies.

[56]This gift of a common tongue is a priceless inheritance, and it may well someday become the foundation of a common citizenship. [57]I like to think of British and Americans moving about freely over each other's wide estates with hardly a sense of being foreigners to one another. [58]But I do not see why we should not try to spread our common language even more widely throughout the globe and, without seeking selfish advantage over any, possess ourselves of this invaluable amenity and birthright.

Relevant Details: The writer ends his argument with a final call to action. He has called for action once before. **Double underline one other call to action.**

Argumentation Concept Map

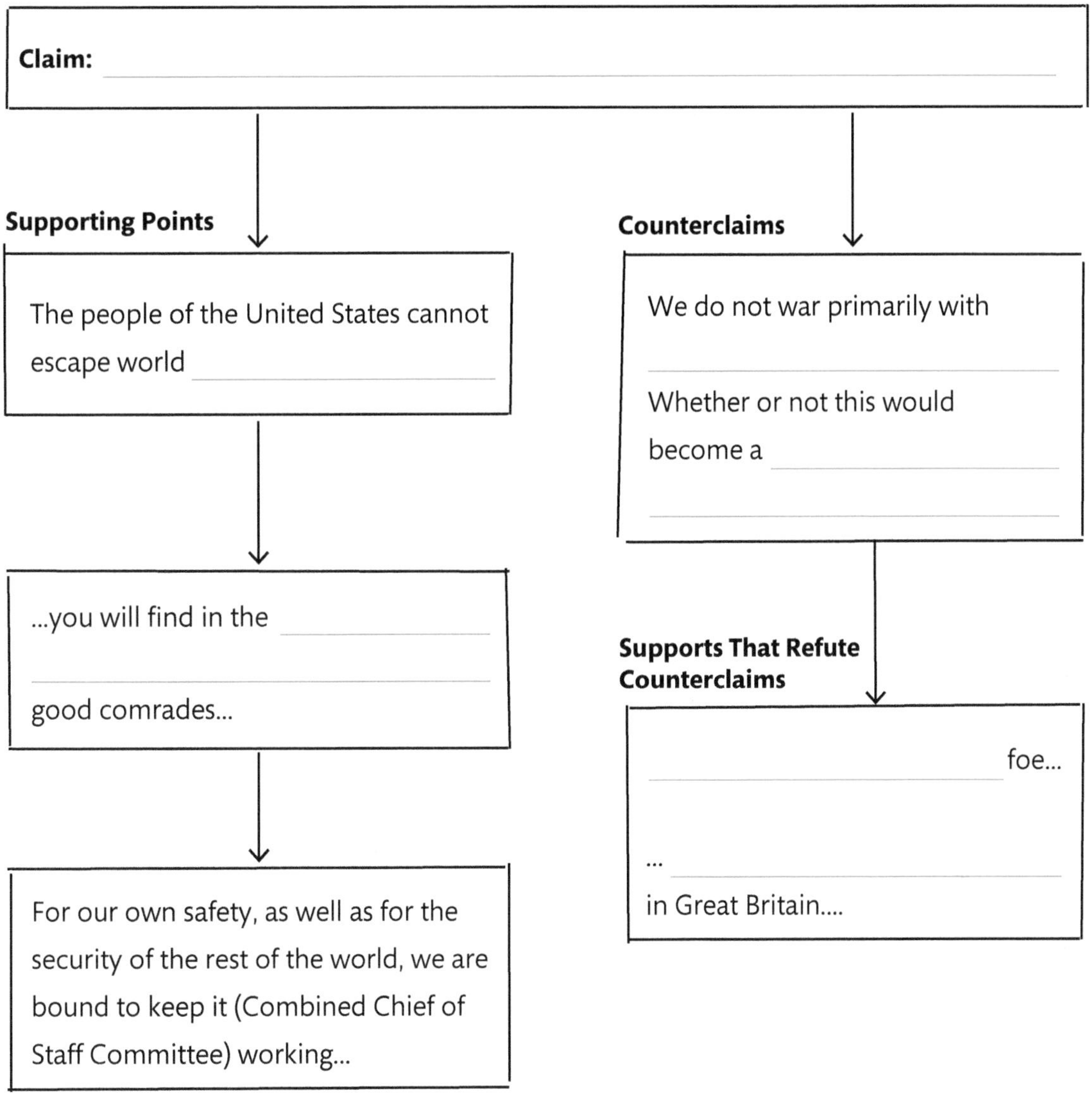

Claim: ____________________

Supporting Points

The people of the United States cannot escape world ____________

...you will find in the ____________ ____________ good comrades...

For our own safety, as well as for the security of the rest of the world, we are bound to keep it (Combined Chief of Staff Committee) working...

Counterclaims

We do not war primarily with ____________

Whether or not this would become a ____________ ____________

Supports That Refute Counterclaims

____________ foe...

... ____________ in Great Britain....

Explanation

Compare your answers to the following think-aloud, completed by Colleen, another student in your class.

The writer's point about the topic "the price of greatness" is **responsibility.** Churchill used relevant details effectively. For example, he states a counterclaim in sentence 2, "We don't want it; we won't have it." He uses sentence 7,

CONTINUED

EXPLANATION *CONTINUED*

his thesis statement, to refute this opposing view. Churchill also calls his audience to action in sentence 22, "We must go on" and in sentence 49, "we are bound to keep it working . . ." and in sentence 52, with the words "we must not let go." He also uses VALID details of historical facts that can be verified in sentences 35, 36, and 47. His use of signal words and transitions strengthened his argument. Some examples include **consequence** (8), **proved, indisputable** (9), **Although** (11), **Not only, but** (12), and **must** (23). Churchill's use of effective language gave power to his argument. I noted "the long arm of destiny" (1) and "the ties of blood and history" (25). These figurative expressions created vivid and memorable pictures in my mind.

Practice 1

Question, Read, and Annotate Passages Using Argument

Assume the following two passages are the next assigned readings on the theme of "civic duty." Your professor has provided a few questions to guide your thinking. Before reading each passage, survey the prereading questions and skim the passage for possible answers. Then read the passage. As you read, annotate the details in the passage that answer the prereading questions. After reading, respond to the prompts that follow each passage.

Before and During Reading Questions:

Logical Order: How does the writer use signal words and transitions to organize his argument? Which transitions/signal words does the writer use?

Central Idea: What is the writer's central point?

Relevant Details: What key reasons, facts, and consequences does the writer give to support his argument? Does the writer offer and refute opposing views? Does the writer call the audience to action?

Effective Language: How does the writer use emotional or subjective language to express opinions, attitudes, and values to make his argument?

United Nations Charter

Preamble

[1]WE THE PEOPLES OF THE UNITED NATIONS DETERMINED

- [2]to save succeeding generations from the scourge of war, which twice in our lifetime has brought untold sorrow to mankind, and
- [3]to reaffirm faith in fundamental human rights, in the dignity and worth of the human person, in the equal rights of men and women and of nations large and small, and
- [4]to establish conditions under which justice and respect for the obligations arising from treaties and other sources of international law can be maintained, and
- [5]to promote social progress and better standards of life in larger freedom,

[6]AND FOR THESE ENDS

- [7]to practice tolerance and live together in peace with one another as good neighbours, and
- [8]to unite our strength to maintain international peace and security, and
- [9]to ensure, by the acceptance of principles and the institution of methods, that armed force shall not be used, save in the common interest, and
- [10]to employ international machinery for the promotion of the economic and social advancement of all peoples,

[11]HAVE RESOLVED TO COMBINE OUR EFFORTS TO ACCOMPLISH THESE AIMS

[12]Accordingly, our respective Governments, through representatives assembled in the city of San Francisco, who have exhibited their full powers found to be in good and due form, have agreed to the present Charter of the United Nations and do hereby establish an international organization to be known as the United Nations.

Chapter I: Purposes and Principles

Article 1

[14]***The Purposes of the United Nations are:***

1. [15]To maintain international peace and security, and to that end: to take effective collective measures for the prevention and removal of threats to the peace, and for the suppression of acts of aggression or other breaches of the peace, and to bring about by peaceful means, and in conformity with the principles of justice

CONTINUED

PRACTICE 1 *CONTINUED*

Security Council chamber United Nations Headquarters, New York City

and international law, adjustment or settlement of international disputes or situations which might lead to a breach of the peace;

2. [16]To develop friendly relations among nations based on respect for the principle of equal rights and self-determination of peoples, and to take other appropriate measures to strengthen universal peace;
3. [17]To achieve international co-operation in solving international problems of an economic, social, cultural, or humanitarian character, and in promoting and encouraging respect for human rights and for fundamental freedoms for all without distinction as to race, sex, language, or religion; and
4. [18]To be a centre for harmonizing the actions of nations in the attainment of these common ends.

After Reading Response: Respond to the following prompts in your journal:

- Write a summary of the passage (see Module 1, page 34).
- Create an argumentation concept map that answers the following prompt:

  According to the "The Price of Greatness" by Winston Churchill and the "United Nations Charter," what are the guidelines for good citizenship?

Before and After Reading Questions:

Logical Order: How does the writer use signal words and transitions to organize his argument? Which transitions/signal words does the writer use?

Central Idea: What is the writer's central point?

Relevant Details: What key reasons, facts, and consequences does the writer give to support his argument? Does the writer offer and refute opposing views? Does the writer call the audience to action?

Effective Language: How does the writer use emotional or subjective language to express opinions, attitudes, and values to make his argument?

from The Truman Library Speech

Kofi Annan

. . . [1]My fourth lesson—closely related to the last one—is that governments must be accountable for their actions in the international arena, as well as in the domestic one.

[2]Today the actions of one state can often have a decisive effect on the lives of people in other states. [3]So does it not owe some account to those other states and their citizens, as well as to its own? [4]I believe it does.

[5]As things stand, accountability between states is highly skewed. [6]Poor and weak states are easily held to account, because they need foreign assistance. [7]But large and powerful states, whose actions have the greatest impact on others, can be constrained only by their own people, working through their domestic institutions.

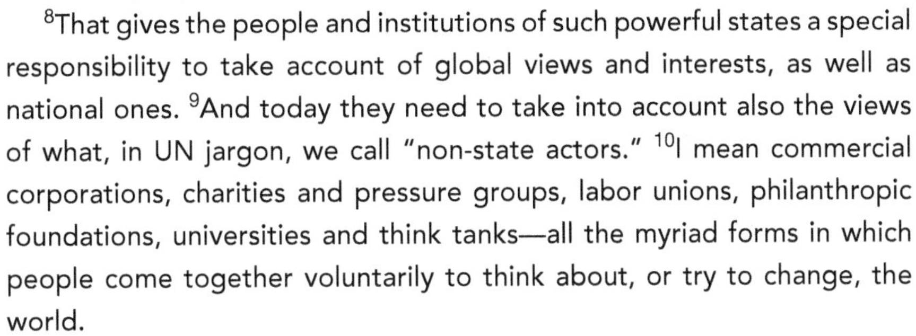

[8]That gives the people and institutions of such powerful states a special responsibility to take account of global views and interests, as well as national ones. [9]And today they need to take into account also the views of what, in UN jargon, we call "non-state actors." [10]I mean commercial corporations, charities and pressure groups, labor unions, philanthropic foundations, universities and think tanks—all the myriad forms in which people come together voluntarily to think about, or try to change, the world.

[11]None of these should be allowed to substitute itself for the state, or for the democratic process by which citizens choose their governments and decide policy. [12]But they all have the capacity to influence political

CONTINUED

processes, on the international as well as the national level. [13]States that try to ignore this are hiding their heads in the sand.

[14]The fact is that states can no longer—if they ever could—confront global challenges alone. [15]Increasingly, we need to enlist the help of these other actors, both in working out global strategies and in putting those strategies into action once agreed. [16]It has been one of my guiding principles as Secretary General to get them to help achieve UN aims—for instance through the Global Compact with international business, which I initiated in 1999, or in the worldwide fight against polio, which I hope is now in its final chapter, thanks to a wonderful partnership between the UN family, the US Centers for Disease Control and—crucially—Rotary International.

[17]So that is four lessons. [18]Let me briefly remind you of them: First, we are all responsible for each other's security. [19]Second, we can and must give everyone the chance to benefit from global prosperity. [20]Third, both security and prosperity depend on human rights and the rule of law. [21]Fourth, states must be accountable to each other, and to a broad range of non-state actors, in their international conduct.

[22]My fifth and final lesson derives inescapably from those other four. [23]We can only do all these things by working together through a multilateral system, and by making the best possible use of the unique instrument bequeathed to us by Harry Truman and his contemporaries, namely the United Nations.

[24]In fact, it is only through multilateral institutions that states can hold each other to account. [25]And that makes it very important to organize those institutions in a fair and democratic way, giving the poor and the weak some influence over the actions of the rich and the strong.

[26]That applies particularly to the international financial institutions, such as the World Bank and the International Monetary Fund. [27]Developing countries should have a stronger voice in these bodies, whose decisions can have almost a life-or-death impact on their fate. [28]And it also applies to the UN Security Council, whose membership still reflects the reality of 1945, not of today's world.

[29]That is why I have continued to press for Security Council reform. [30]But reform involves two separate issues. [31]One is that new members should be added, on a permanent or long-term basis, to give greater representation to parts of the world, which have limited voice today. [32]The other, perhaps even more important, is that all Council members, and especially the major powers who are permanent members, must accept the special responsibility that comes with their privilege. [33]The Security Council is not just another stage on which to act out national interests.

[34]It is the management committee, if you will, of our fledgling collective security system.

[35]As President Truman said, "The responsibility of the great states is to serve and not dominate the peoples of the world." [36]He showed what can be achieved when the US assumes that responsibility. [37]And still today, none of our global institutions can accomplish much when the US remains aloof. [38]But when it is fully engaged, the sky is the limit.

[39]These five lessons can be summed up as five principles, which I believe are essential for the future conduct of international relations: collective responsibility, global solidarity, the rule of law, mutual accountability, and multilateralism. [40]Let me leave them with you, in solemn trust, as I hand over to a new Secretary General in three weeks' time.

[41]My friends, we have achieved much since 1945, when the United Nations was established. [42]But much remains to be done to put those five principles into practice.

[43]Standing here, I am reminded of Winston Churchill's last visit to the White House, just before Truman left office in 1953. [44]Churchill recalled their only previous meeting, at the Potsdam conference in 1945. [45]"I must confess, sir," he said boldly, "I held you in very low regard then. [46]I loathed your taking the place of Franklin Roosevelt." [47]Then he paused for a moment, and continued: "I misjudged you badly. [48]Since that time, you more than any other man, have saved Western civilization."

[49]My friends, our challenge today is not to save Western civilization—or Eastern, for that matter. [50]All civilization is at stake, and we can save it only if all peoples join together in the task.

[51]You Americans did so much, in the last century, to build an effective multilateral system, with the United Nations at its heart. [52]Do you need it less today, and does it need you less, than 60 years ago?

[53]Surely not. [54]More than ever today Americans, like the rest of humanity, need a functioning global system through which the world's peoples can face global challenges together. [55]And in order to function, the system still cries out for far-sighted American leadership, in the Truman tradition.

[56] I hope and pray that the American leaders of today, and tomorrow, will provide it.

—From "The Truman Library Speech" by Kofi Annan, December 11, 2006. Reprinted by permission of the United Nations. http://www.un.org/News/ossg/sg/stories/statements_full.asp?statID=40.

After Reading Response: Respond to the following prompts in your journal:

- Write a summary of the passage (see Module 1, page 34).
- Create an argumentation concept map that answers the following prompt:

  In what ways do "The Price of Greatness" by Winston Churchill, the "Untied Nations Charter," and Kofi Annan's speech support the same claim?

L3 Prewrite a Draft of a Thesis Statement Using Argument

A thesis sentence states the debatable topic, the writer's claim, and, possibly, a pattern of organization. Because argument is a purpose, the writer may choose a particular pattern or combined patterns of organization to support a claim. In addition, the writer's claim may include the following types of signal words or phrases: *against, all, always, must, must not, never, only, oppose, should, should not*, or *support*.

For example, the following topic sentence contains (1) the debatable topic, (2) the writer's claim, and (3) a pattern of organization to signal the flow of ideas.

DEBATABLE TOPIC — WRITER'S CLAIM — ORGANIZATIONAL SIGNAL WORDS

To be a good citizen, one must serve on several levels.

Example

Your instructor has asked you to use the readings on pages 469–479 to write an essay that addresses the guiding question "What makes a good citizen?" The first part of the assignment is to generate a thesis statement for the essay. Use the following steps to brainstorm your thesis statement.

Topic: Civic duty: What makes a good citizen?

1. Narrow Topic: ______________________________

2. Identify Pattern(s) of Organization Signal Words: ______________________________

____

3. Identify Opinion: ______________________________

____

4. Combine into a Draft of Thesis Statement: ______________________________

____

Explanation

Compare your answers to Colleen's think-aloud.

When writing my thesis statement, I wanted to make sure I understood the main idea of each passage. I looked at my annotations and chose one word that summarized the point of each passage. Then I thought about what the words meant and how they worked together to respond to the question "What makes a good citizen?" I put them into one sentence that explains my understanding of what the passages say about good citizenship. I decided that I would combine the definition-example pattern with classification to support my claim. My thesis is "The three key ingredients in achieving good citizenship are responsibility, action, and accountability."

Practice 2

Prewrite a Draft of a Thesis Statement Using Argument

In your reading/writing journal, identify the steps you used to write a thesis statement for your argument. How did your thesis statement differ from Colleen's? Did she use any methods you didn't?

Prewrite to Generate Relevant Details Using Argument

LO 4

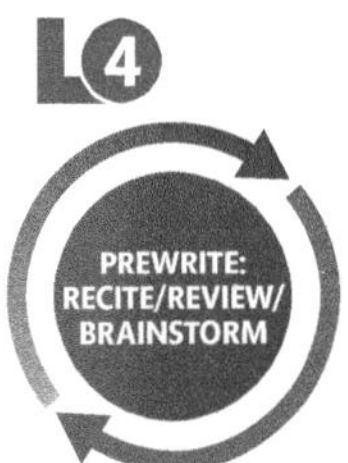

Just as a master reader looks for relevant and adequate details, a master writer evaluates the details chosen for the same elements to make sure that his or her claim is valid. As a writer narrows a topic into a focused main idea, he or she generates supporting details that answer questions such as *who, what, when, where, why*, and *how*. During this brainstorming phase, a writer naturally generates many details. Some of these details may be irrelevant to the specific claim. A writer evaluates the relevance of each detail and uses only those that imply, clarify, or support the main idea. Often, a writer uses a concept map before writing to generate ideas and also after writing to determine if details are relevant and adequate.

Example

Assume your class is continuing to work on the essay addressing the guiding question "What makes a good citizen?" Now your assignment is to return to the texts to identify details that you will use in your paper and create a concept map to organize your ideas for the essay.

A Concept Map for Argumentation

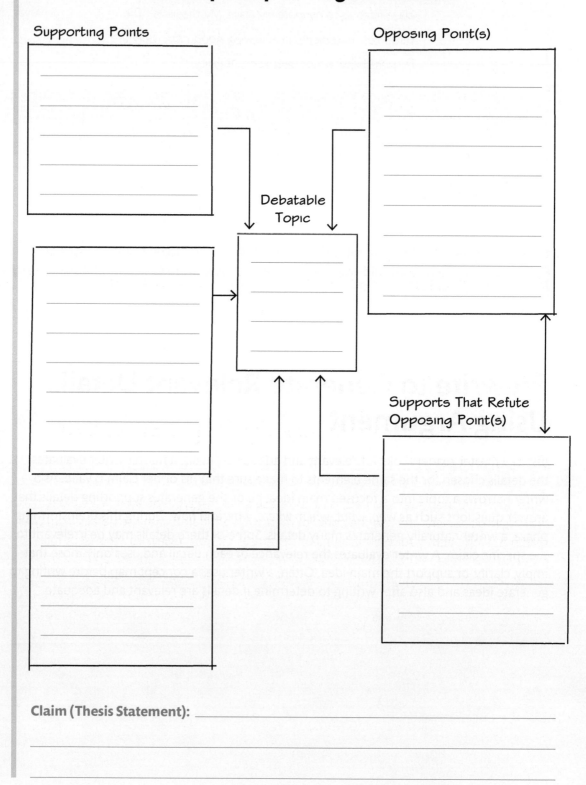

Claim (Thesis Statement): ______________________________

Explanation

Compare your responses to Colleen's think-aloud.

My concept map had the phrase "good citizen" boxed in the middle with three other boxes stemming out from it. Each box had one word in it—marking the three main ideas that made up my thesis statement: **responsibility**, **action**, and **accountability**. Each of these three boxes had its own set of circles stemming out from them that included key details and quotations from each of the passages that supported the main ideas from my thesis statement.

Practice 3

Prewrite to Generate Relevant Details Using Argument

In your reading/writing journal, identify the steps needed to create relevant details to support a thesis statement. Identify the steps Colleen went through as she annotated the texts and created her graphic organizer. How did your concept maps differ?

Compose a Draft Using Logical Order: Argument

Once you have brainstormed details to compose an argument, you are ready to begin the drafting process. First, review the concept map you completed with the details from the readings, along with your own insights or responses. As you review your concept map, move details into the most logical order. Add details, if needed. Also, use appropriate signal words and transitions to guide your reader through your claim, reasons, and evidence. Use signal words that clearly distinguish any counterclaims you have identified and refuted. Master writers create several drafts to achieve a logical order and smooth flow of ideas.

Example

Assume you are still working toward writing an essay that answers the guiding question, "What makes a good citizen?" On your own paper, write a draft of your essay.

Explanation

Compare your answer to Colleen's think-aloud and essay.

When I began to write my essay, I used my concept map as a model. From my concept map, I created an outline of my essay by listing each paragraph (introduction, three body paragraphs, and conclusion) and the main ideas and details for each paragraph. Then I used this outline to write the formal essay.

The Recipe for Good Citizenship

By Colleen Fahrenbach

What makes a good citizen? This is a complex question because the notions of *citizenship* and what it means to be a *citizen* have many meanings. In its most basic meaning, the Merriam-Webster dictionary explains that a *citizen* is when you live in a certain country and therefore have the protection and rights of that country. Building off of this simple definition, *citizenship* has developed into an ideal that people strive to live for. Furthermore, citizenship goes beyond simply belonging to a country. The term has come to encompass the greater idea that being a citizen comes with its own set of duties and expectations. However, the question still stands: What makes a good citizen? The notion of citizenship is based on the concept that there are certain rights that all people are entitled to and that there is a model for how a person should live out those rights. The way a person lives up to that model is what makes him or her a good or bad citizen. Over the course of world history, through tragedy, war, epidemic, and change, there have emerged many opportunities to call into question how a person can be a good citizen. According to this history, the three key ingredients in achieving good citizenship are responsibility, action, and accountability. The words of world leaders along with the course of history have proven that these three ideals are essential to the peaceful existence of the modern world.

The first important ideal of a good citizen is responsibility. Winston Churchill laid out this ideal and what it means when he shared the words "The price of greatness is responsibility." To Churchill, any nation or person that stands out as exceptional and "great" carries the extra burden of responsibility from that exceptionalism and greatness. He uses the United States as an example. Since the United States rose to power and emerged from mediocrity as a strong nation, it is inherently involved in the struggles and issues of the world. Churchill says that it is up to the strongest, most powerful, nations to be responsible for the peace and well being of all peoples of the world. To Churchill, good citizenship lies on the foundation of responsibility for one's self, one's nation, and the entire world. No person, nation, or world can be great without also being responsible.

The second important aspect of good citizenship is action. Once a person or nation takes responsibility for self, it must then turn that responsibility into action. The strongest example of action for the cause of good citizenship was the formation of the United Nations. This organizational body was put into place so that issues could be addressed, standards could be set, and problems could be solved on a worldwide scale. Its founding document, the "United Nations Charter," highlights the principles that call nations to action because of their responsibility. This charter recognizes that in order to be a good citizen of the world, a country must be willing to work with other countries in order to maintain peace and security, friendly relations, harmony, and co-operation on an international scale. In other words, this charter lays out the specific expectations and actions that Winston Churchill claimed all great countries and peoples are responsible for meeting in order to achieve good citizenship.

The third and final aspect of being a good citizen comes from the words Kofi Annan spoke in "The Truman Library Speech." This speech highlights certain principles of citizenship and recognizes the importance of accountability. Where Churchill highlighted responsibility and the United Nations charter called for action from that responsibility, Kofi Annan takes the idea of being a good citizen one step further and calls for accountability. Annan

CONTINUED

EXPLANATION *CONTINUED*

says that nations must be held accountable for their actions. He looks back to history to make the point that the world needs a platform on which people can come together and take action. The platform for this is the United Nations. He nods to the mission of Winston Churchill in calling on people and nations in Western Civilization to take responsibility for the damage caused by war and worldwide struggle. Then, he looks to the future and speaks to the importance of future generations to remain accountable for these past efforts and actions to foster international relations in the common goal of peace and human dignity. Accountability is the key element for citizenship; it is the final ingredient in the recipe for the good citizen. If a citizen is not accountable, if there is no organizational body to hold nations and people to their common goals, then the other ideals of action and responsibility mean nothing. When Annan calls for accountability, he is making good citizenship a lasting goal of all peoples and nations.

History shows that good citizenship is something that all people and nations strive for, as it is the manifestation of peace and prosperity. The way for countries to achieve good citizenship is to first assume the responsibility that comes with being a powerful nation. Countries like the United States and Great Britain have proven this to be true. This extra responsibility then calls these people and nations to take action. Through organizations such as the United Nations, countries can come together to address concerns, set standards, and solve problems on an international scale. Once action has taken place, the final step is for people and nations to remain accountable for their actions and the responsibility they have held. When all three of these ideals have been met, that is when a person or a country achieves good citizenship.

Practice 4

Compose a Draft Using Logical Order: Argument

In your reading/writing journal, identify the steps you took to write your draft. Identify the steps Colleen took as she wrote her draft. How are your drafts different? How are they similar? What can you apply from Colleen's method to your own writing in the future?

Revise and Proofread for Effective Language with Argument

A valid academic argument relies on objective, factual details, and appropriate use of figurative language. To evaluate the effectiveness of your argument, ask three key questions:

- Do I use a subjective or an objective tone?
- Do I provide mostly factual details and use figurative language appropriately?
- Do I include or omit opposing views?

Reread Module 5, Fact and Opinion, to refresh your understanding of biased language and how to distinguish fact from opinion.

It is also important to maintain a consistent point of view throughout an argument. Point of view is established with the use of personal pronouns. Personal pronouns imply an objective or a subjective tone. Three points of view include first person, second, person, and third person.

Personal Pronouns and Points of View	
First Person (subjective tone) I, me, mine, myself, my we, us, ours, our, ourselves	First person refers to speaker/writer. First person testimonies offer powerful evidence. First person is informal. First person can be intimate, more engaging. First person may not offer reliable details. First person offers a limited point of view
Second Person (subjective tone) you, your, yours, yourselves	Second person refers to listener/reader. Second person speaks directly to the reader. Second person is more familiar and engaging. Second person may be directive, instructional. Second person is informal. Second person may become overbearing.
Third Person (objective tone) he, him, his, himself she, her, hers, herself it, its, itself they, them, their theirs, themselves	Third person refers to the person, thing, or idea being discussed. Third person creates space between writer/reader. Third person is formal. Third person may seem more credible. Third person offers a universal point of view.

Common sense tells us that we cannot shift between several individuals' points of view. However, at times, writers carelessly shift point of view, as in the following sentence.

One must vote if you want to be a good citizen.

Consistent use of point of view strengthens coherence or the clear flow of ideas. Carefully edit your writing to ensure consistent use of point of view, as in the following sentence.

One must vote if he or she wants to be a good citizen.

Example

Assume the role of peer editor for Colleen's essay "The Recipe for Good Citizenship." Evaluate the effectiveness of her argument by asking the three key questions given earlier. Also review her draft for consistent use of point of view. Offer suggested revisions to strengthen her argument. Then revise the draft you wrote for the previous activity. Use your own paper to create a final version.

Explanation

Compare your answers to Colleen's think-aloud about how she needed to revise her draft.

As I reviewed my draft to evaluate the effectiveness of my argument, my answers to the three questions indicated that I had developed a strong argument. My tone is objective and my references to the passages are factual. While I did not use figurative language, I did revise the following sentence to include vivid language to impact my audience: The original sentence read, "Countries like the United States and Great Britain have proven throughout history this to be true." The revised sentence reads, "Countries like the United States and Great Britain have proven the powerful must help the powerless." I also revised the beginning of the last paragraph to include the opposing view, "Whether or not a person or country is a good citizen is something that is difficult to measure. However, history has shown . . ." My use of the transition **However** shows that I am going to refute this opposing view. I chose to use the objective point of view, third person. I did revise the third sentence for consistent viewpoint. My first draft of the dictionary definition for **citizen** had the wording "is when you live." I revised that phrase to read, "is someone who lives."

Practice 5

Revise and Proofread for Effective Language with Argument

In your reading/writing journal, list the steps needed to revise, edit, and proofread an essay. What did Colleen do as part of her revision process? How did your processes differ? What can you learn from Colleen's revision that you can apply to your own editing process in the future?

Workshop: Comprehend and Create an Essay Using Argument

Assume you are continuing your study of the theme of "civic duty." The following passages make up a capstone reading assignment. Your capstone writing assignment is to write an essay in response to the guiding question, "What makes a good citizen?" You may also be asked to make connections among these passages and the ones you have already read in this module. For this assignment, skim through the prereading questions, read the following passages, and complete the writing activities that follow.

EXCERPT FROM ON THE DUTY OF CIVIL DISOBEDIENCE 1849

Henry David Thoreau

1 I heartily accept the motto, "That government is best which governs least"; and I should like to see it acted up to more rapidly and systematically. Carried out, it finally amounts to this, which also I believe—"That government is best which governs not at all"; and when men are prepared for it, that will be the kind of government which they will have. Government is at best but an expedient; but most governments are usually, and all governments are sometimes, inexpedient. The objections which have been brought against a standing army, and they are many and weighty, and deserve to prevail, may also at last be brought against a standing government. The standing army is only an arm of the standing government. The government itself, which is only the mode which the people have chosen to execute their will, is equally liable to be abused and perverted before the people can act through it.

2 . . . But, to speak practically and as a citizen, unlike those who call themselves no-government men, I ask for, not at once no government, but at once a better government. Let every man make known what kind of government would command his respect, and that will be one step toward obtaining it.

3 After all, the practical reason why, when the power is once in the hands of the people, a majority are permitted, and for a long period continue, to rule is not because they are most likely to be in the right, nor because this seems fairest to the minority, but because they are physically the strongest. But a government in which the majority rule in all cases cannot be based on justice, even as far as men understand it. Can there not be a government in which the majorities do not virtually decide right and wrong, but conscience?—in which majorities decide only those questions to which the rule of expediency is applicable? Must the citizen ever for a moment, or in the least degree, resign his conscience to the legislator? Why has every man a conscience

CONTINUED

then? I think that we should be men first, and subjects afterward. It is not desirable to cultivate a respect for the law, so much as for the right. The only obligation which I have a right to assume is to do at any time what I think right.

4. . . Law never made men a whit more just; and, by means of their respect for it, even the well-disposed are daily made the agents on injustice. A common and natural result of an undue respect for the law is, that you may see a file of soldiers, colonel, captain, corporal, privates, powder-monkeys, and all, marching in admirable order over hill and dale to the wars, against their wills, ay, against their common sense and consciences, which makes it very steep marching indeed, and produces a palpitation of the heart. They have no doubt that it is a damnable business in which they are concerned; they are all peaceably inclined. Now, what are they? Men at all? Or small movable forts and magazines, at the service of some unscrupulous man in power?

5The mass of men serve the state thus, not as men mainly, but as machines, with their bodies. They are the standing army, and the militia, jailers, constables, posse comitatus, etc. In most cases there is no free exercise whatever of the judgment or of the moral sense; but they put themselves on a level with wood and earth and stones; and wooden men can perhaps be manufactured that will serve the purpose as well. Such command no more respect than men of straw or a lump of dirt. They have the same sort of worth only as horses and dogs. Yet such as these even are commonly esteemed good citizens.

6. . . How does it become a man to behave toward the American government today? I answer, that he cannot without disgrace be associated with it. I cannot for an instant recognize that political organization as my government which is the slave's government also.

7. . . However, the government does not concern me much, and I shall bestow the fewest possible thoughts on it. It is not many moments that I live under a government, even in this world. If a man is thought-free, fancy-free, imagination-free, that which is not never for a long time appearing to be to him, unwise rulers or reformers cannot fatally interrupt him.

8. . . The authority of government, even such as I am willing to submit to . . . is still an impure one: to be strictly just, it must have the sanction and consent of the governed. It can have no pure right over my person and property but what I concede to it. The progress from an absolute to a limited monarchy, from a limited monarchy to a democracy, is a progress toward a true respect for the individual.

9Even the Chinese philosopher was wise enough to regard the individual as the basis of the empire. Is a democracy, such as we know it, the last improvement possible in government? Is it not possible to take a step further towards recognizing and organizing the rights of man? There will never be a really free and enlightened State until the State comes to recognize the individual as a higher and independent power, from which all its own power and authority are derived, and treats him accordingly.

IS IT A CRIME FOR A U. S. CITIZEN TO VOTE?

Susan. B. Anthony

[1]Friends and Fellow-citizens: I stand before you tonight, under indictment for the alleged crime of having voted at the last Presidential election, without having a lawful right to vote. It shall be my work this evening to prove to you that in thus voting, I not only committed no crime, but, instead, simply exercised my citizen's right, guaranteed to me and all United States citizens by the National Constitution, beyond the power of any State to deny.

[2]Our democratic-republican government is based on the idea of the natural right of every individual member thereof to a voice and a vote in making and executing the laws. We assert the province of government to be to secure the people in the enjoyment of their unalienable rights. We throw to the winds the old dogma that governments can give rights. Before governments were organized, no one denies that each individual possessed the right to protect his own life, liberty and property.

[3]And when 100 or 1,000,000 people enter into a free government, they do not barter away their natural rights. They simply pledge themselves to protect each other in the enjoyment of them, through prescribed judicial and legislative tribunals. They agree to abandon the methods of brute force in the adjustment of their differences, and adopt those of civilization.

[4]Nor can you find a word in any of the grand documents left us by the fathers that assumes for government the power to create or to confer rights. The Declaration of Independence, the United States Constitution, the constitutions of the several states and the organic laws of the territories, all alike propose to protect the people in the exercise of their God-given rights. Not one of them pretends to bestow rights.

[5]"All men are created equal, and endowed by their Creator with certain unalienable rights. Among these are life, liberty and the pursuit of happiness. That to secure these, governments are instituted among men, deriving their just powers from the consent of the governed."

[6]Here is no shadow of government authority over rights, nor exclusion of any class from their full and equal enjoyment. Here is pronounced the right of all men, and "consequently," as the Quaker preacher said, "of all women," to a voice in the government. And here, in this very first paragraph of the declaration, is the assertion of the natural right of all to the ballot. For, how can "the consent of the governed" be given, if the right to vote be denied. Again: "That whenever any

CONTINUED

form of government becomes destructive of these ends, it is the right of the people to alter or abolish it, and to institute a new government, laying its foundations on such principles, and organizing its powers in such forms as to them shall seem most likely to effect their safety and happiness."

7Surely, the right of the whole people to vote is here clearly implied. For however destructive to their happiness this government might become, a disfranchised class could neither alter nor abolish it, nor institute a new one, except by the old brute force method of insurrection and rebellion. One-half of the people of this nation today are utterly powerless to blot from the statute books an unjust law, or to write there a new and a just one. The women, dissatisfied as they are with this form of government, that enforces taxation without representation,—that compels them to obey laws to which they have never given their consent,—that imprisons and hangs them without a trial by a jury of their peers, that robs them, in marriage, of the custody of their own persons, wages and children,—are this half of the people left wholly at the mercy of the other half, in direct violation of the spirit and letter of the declarations of the framers of this government, everyone of which was based on the immutable principle of equal rights to all. By those declarations, kings, priests, popes, aristocrats, were all alike dethroned, and placed on a common level, politically, with the lowliest born subject or serf. By them, too, men, as such, were deprived of their divine right to rule, and placed on a political level with women. By the practice of those declarations all class and caste distinction will be abolished. And slave, serf, plebeian, wife, woman, all alike, bound from their subject position to the proud platform of equality. . . .

8It was we, the people, not we, the white male citizens, nor yet we, the male citizens; but we, the whole people, who formed this Union. And we formed it, not to give the blessings of liberty, but to secure them; not to the half of ourselves and the half of our posterity, but to the whole people—women as well as men. And it is downright mockery to talk to women of their enjoyment of the blessings of liberty while they are denied the use of the only means of securing them provided by this democratic-republican government—the ballot. . . .

9If the fourteenth amendment does not secure to all citizens the right to vote, for what purpose was that grand old charter of the fathers lumbered with its unwieldy proportions? The republican party, and Judges Howard and Bingham, who drafted the document, pretended it was to do something for black men. And if that something was not to secure them in their right to vote and hold office, what could it have been? For, by the thirteenth amendment, black men had become people, and hence were entitled to all the privileges and immunities of the government, precisely as were the women of the country, and foreign men not naturalized. . . .

10Thus, you see, those newly freed men were in possession of every possible right, privilege and immunity of the government, except that of suffrage. Hence, they needed no constitutional amendment for any other purpose. What right, I ask you, has the Irishman the day after he receives his naturalization papers that he did not possess the day before, save the right to vote and hold office? And the Chinamen, now crowding our Pacific coast, are in precisely the same position.

[11]Clearly, then, if the fourteenth amendment was not to secure to black men their right to vote, it did nothing for them, since they possessed everything else before. But, if it was meant to be a prohibition of the states, to deny or abridge their right to vote—which I fully believe—then it did the same for all persons, white women included, born or naturalized in the United States. For the amendment does not say all male persons of African descent, but all persons are citizens. . . .

[12]The question of the citizen's right to vote is settled forever by the fifteenth amendment. "The citizen's right to vote shall not be denied by the United States, nor any state thereof; on account of race, color, or previous condition of servitude." How can the state deny or abridge the right of the citizen, if the citizen does not possess it? There is no escape from the conclusion, that to vote is the citizen's right, and the specifications of race, color, or previous condition of servitude can, in no way, impair the force of the emphatic assertion, that the citizen's right to vote shall not be denied or abridged. . . .

[13]If we once establish the false principle, that United States citizenship does not carry with it the right to vote in every state in this Union, there is no end to the petty freaks and cunning devices, that will be resorted to, to exclude one and another class of citizens from the right of suffrage.

[14]It will not always be men combining to disfranchise all women or native born men combining to abridge the rights of all naturalized citizens, as in Rhode Island. It will not always be the rich and educated who may combine to cut off the poor and ignorant. But we may live to see the poor, hardworking, uncultivated day laborers, foreign and native born, learning the power of the ballot and their vast majority of numbers, combine and amend state constitutions so as to disfranchise the Vanderbilts and A. T. Stewarts, the Conklings and Fentons. It is a poor rule that won't work more ways than one. Establish this precedent, admit the right to deny suffrage to the states, and there is no power to foresee the confusion, discord and disruption that may await us. There is, and can be, but one safe principle of government—equal rights to all. And any and every discrimination against any class, whether on account of color, race, nativity, sex, property, culture, can but embitter and disaffect that class, and thereby endanger the safety of the whole people.

[15]Clearly, then, the national government must not only define the rights of citizens, but it must stretch out its powerful hand and protect them in every state in this Union. . . .

CONTINUED

16We no longer petition Legislature or Congress to give us the right to vote. We appeal to the women everywhere to exercise their too long neglected "citizen's right to vote." We appeal to the inspectors of election everywhere to receive the votes of all United States citizens as it is their duty to do. We appeal to United States commissioners and marshals to arrest the inspectors who reject the names and votes of United States citizens, as it is their duty to do, and leave those alone who, like our eighth ward inspectors, perform their duties faithfully and well.

17We ask the juries to fail to return verdicts of "guilty" against honest, law-abiding, tax-paying United States citizens for offering their votes at our elections. . . .

18We ask the judges to render true and unprejudiced opinions of the law, and wherever there is room for a doubt to give its benefit on the side of liberty and equal rights to women, remembering that "the true rule of interpretation under our national constitution, especially since its amendments, is that anything for human rights is constitutional, everything against human rights unconstitutional."

19And it is on this line that we propose to fight our battle for the ballot—all peaceably, but nevertheless persistently through to complete triumph, when all United States citizens shall be recognized as equals before the law.

—"An Account of the Proceedings on the Trial of Susan B. Anthony on the Charge of Illegal Voting at the Presidential Election in Nov., 1872, and on the Trial of Beverly W. Jones, Edwin T. Marsh and William B. Hall, the Inspectors of Elections by Whom Her Vote Was Received" (Rochester, N.Y.: Daily Democrat and Chronicle Book Print, 1874), 151–78. Reprinted in Gordon, Ann D. "The Trail of Susan B. Anthony." Federal Judicial Center 2005. pages 64-68.

Speech On The Eve Of Historic Dandi March (11-3-1930)

Mahatma Gandhi

On the 11th of March 1930, the crowd swelled to 10,000 at the evening prayer held on the Sabarmati sands at Ahmedabad. At the end, Gandhi delivered a memorable speech on the eve of his historic march:

1In all probability this will be my last speech to you. Even if the Government allow me to march tomorrow morning, this will be my last speech on the sacred banks of the Sabarmati. Possibly these may be the last words of my life here.

[2]I have already told you yesterday what I had to say. Today I shall confine myself to what you should do after my companions and I are arrested. The programme of the march to Jalalpur must be fulfilled as originally settled. The enlistment of the volunteers for this purpose should be confined to Gujarat only. From what I have seen and heard during the last fortnight, I am inclined to believe that the stream of civil resisters will flow unbroken.

[3]But let there be not a semblance of breach of peace even after all of us have been arrested. We have resolved to utilize all our resources in the pursuit of an exclusively nonviolent struggle. Let no one commit a wrong in anger. This is my hope and prayer. I wish these words of mine reached every nook and corner of the land. My task shall be done if I perish and so do my comrades. It will then be for the Working Committee of the Congress to show you the way and it will be up to you to follow its lead. So long as I have reached Jalalpur, let nothing be done in contravention to the authority vested in me by the Congress. But once I am arrested, the whole responsibility shifts to the Congress. No one who believes in non-violence, as a creed, need, therefore, sit still. My compact with the Congress ends as soon as I am arrested. In that case volunteers. Wherever possible, civil disobedience of salt should be started. These laws can be violated in three ways. It is an offence to manufacture salt wherever there are facilities for doing so. The possession and sale of contraband salt, which includes natural salt or salt earth, is also an offence. The purchasers of such salt will be equally guilty. To carry away the natural salt deposits on the seashore is likewise violation of law. So is the hawking of such salt. In short, you may choose any one or all of these devices to break the salt monopoly.

[4]We are, however, not to be content with this alone. There is no ban by the Congress and wherever the local workers have self-confidence other suitable measures may be adopted. I stress only one condition, namely, let our pledge of truth and nonviolence as the only means for the attainment of Swaraj be faithfully kept. For the rest, every one has a free hand. But, that does not give a license to all and sundry to carry on their own responsibility. Wherever there are local leaders, their orders should be obeyed by the people. Where there are no leaders and only a handful of men have faith in the programme, they may do what they can, if they have enough self-confidence. They have a right, nay it is their duty, to do so. The history of the world is full of instances of men who rose to leadership, by sheer force of self-confidence, bravery and tenacity. We too, if we sincerely aspire to Swaraj and are impatient to attain it, should have similar self-confidence. Our ranks will swell and our hearts strengthen, as the number of our arrests by the Government increases.

[5]Much can be done in many other ways besides these. The Liquor and foreign cloth shops can be picketed. We can refuse to pay taxes if we have the requisite strength. The lawyers can give up practice. The public can boycott the law courts by refraining from litigation. Government servants can resign their posts.

CONTINUED

In the midst of the despair reigning all round people quake with fear of losing employment. Such men are unfit for Swaraj. But why this despair? The number of Government servants in the country does not exceed a few hundred thousands. What about the rest? Where are they to go? Even free India will not be able to accommodate a greater number of public servants. A Collector then will not need the number of servants, he has got today. He will be his own servant. Our starving millions can by no means afford this enormous expenditure. If, therefore, we are sensible enough, let us bid good-bye to Government employment, no matter if it is the post of a judge or a peon. Let all who are co-operating with the Government in one way or another, be it by paying taxes, keeping titles, or sending children to official schools, etc. withdraw their co-operation in all or as many ways as possible. Then there are women who can stand shoulder to shoulder with men in this struggle.

6 You may take it as my will. It was the message that I desired to impart to you before starting on the march or for the jail. I wish that there should be no suspension or abandonment of the war that commences tomorrow morning or earlier, if I am arrested before that time. I shall eagerly await the news that ten batches are ready as soon as my batch is arrested. I believe there are men in India to complete the work begun by me. I have faith in the righteousness of our cause and the purity of our weapons. And where the means are clean, there God is undoubtedly present with His blessings. And where these three combine, there defeat is impossibility. A Satyagrahi, whether free or incarcerated, is ever victorious. He is vanquished only, when he forsakes truth and nonviolence and turns a deaf ear to the inner voice. If, therefore, there is such a thing as defeat for even a Satyagrahi, he alone is the cause of it. God bless you all and keep off all obstacles from the path in the struggle that begins tomorrow.

—Mahatma, Vol. III (1952), pp. 28-30. Selected works of Mahatma Gandhi Volume-Six. www.gandhiashramsabarmati.org/en/the-mahatma/speeches/dandi-march.html.

Preread: Survey and Question

What is civil disobedience?

What are the similarities and differences in Winston Churchill's and Henry David Thoreau's calls for responsibility on the part of a citizen? (See "The Price of Greatness," page 469.)

How does the Preamble of the United Nations Charter (page 475) support Henry David Thoreau's view of government?

In "The Price of Greatness," Winston Churchill stated, "Tyranny is our foe" (page 471). What form of tyranny do Susan B. Anthony and her followers face?

What form of tyranny do Mahatma Gandhi and his followers face?

How does Kofi Annan's statement in "The Truman Library Speech" (page 477) that governments must be held accountable relate to the views and experiences of:

Henry David Thoreau?

Susan B. Anthony?

Mahatma Gandhi?

In his speech, Kofi Annan outlines five lessons he has learned about the responsibility of international governments. How may some of these lessons apply to the responsibility of individual citizens?

Compare and contrast Susan B. Anthony's and Mahatma Gandhi's use of civil disobedience.

How may an individual be a good and responsible citizen?

Read and Annotate

As you read, annotate key ideas, particularly those details that answer your prereading questions.

Recite, Review, and Brainstorm

Recite and **Review** the information. Paraphrase ideas. Summarize the most important parts. *Freewrite* or *map* the relationship among answers to questions or ideas you have annotated in the text. *Outline* or *list* key ideas and details in blocks of thought. Use your own paper.

Write a Draft of Your Response

Using the ideas you generated by brainstorming, compose a draft of your response. Use your own paper.

Revise Your Draft

Once you have created a draft of an argumentative response, read it over to answer the questions in the "Questions for Revising an Argumentative Essay" box that follows. Indicate your answers by annotating your paper. If you answer "yes" to a question, underline, check, or circle examples. If you answer "no" to a question, write the needed information in the margins and draw lines to indicate the placement of additional details. Revise your essay based on your reflection. (*Hint:* Experienced writers create several drafts as they focus on one or two questions per draft.)

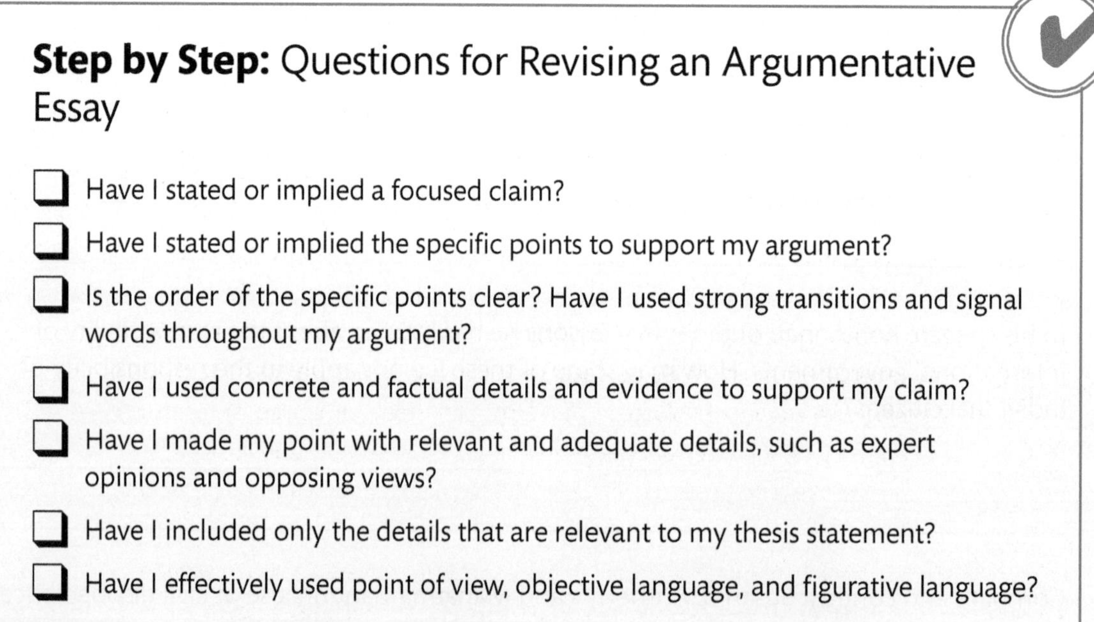

Step by Step: Questions for Revising an Argumentative Essay

- ❑ Have I stated or implied a focused claim?
- ❑ Have I stated or implied the specific points to support my argument?
- ❑ Is the order of the specific points clear? Have I used strong transitions and signal words throughout my argument?
- ❑ Have I used concrete and factual details and evidence to support my claim?
- ❑ Have I made my point with relevant and adequate details, such as expert opinions and opposing views?
- ❑ Have I included only the details that are relevant to my thesis statement?
- ❑ Have I effectively used point of view, objective language, and figurative language?

Proofread Your Draft

Once you have made any revisions to your essay that may be needed, proofread your essay to eliminate careless errors.

Reading and Writing Assignments

MySkillsLab™
Complete this Exercise on myskillslab.com

Reading and Writing for Everyday Life

Assume you are a concerned citizen who wants to make a difference for good in the world, so you have researched worthy causes and learned about the HIV/AIDS crisis in the Ukraine. You also learned that the Peace Corps accepts donations for volunteer projects. Read the following information about a volunteer Peace Corps project for the Ukraine. Write a letter that you will distribute to local business clubs (such as Rotary), community organizations, and friends, asking for donations to help this cause.

Partner with Peace Corps

Ukraine has the fastest growing rate of HIV/AIDS in Europe due to unsafe sex practices and intravenous drug use among youth. This trend is a major concern for a country undergoing economic transformation following the collapse of the Soviet Union. The lives of Ukraine's youth will be forever impacted by this looming crisis unless the trend can be reversed.

In response, several Peace Corps Volunteers, in conjunction with their host communities, implemented camp H.E.A.L. (Human Trafficking, Education, HIV/AIDS, and Leadership). Thirty youth, ages 16-21, from throughout the country attend the camp in eastern Ukraine for 10 days. Camp H.E.A.L. provides a unique environment for youth to come together to learn about HIV/AIDS and participate in leadership and team building activities.

The camp provides information about HIV/AIDS through the development of a nationwide peer education program. Participants attend various classes on topics such as biology of HIV/AIDS, stigma and discrimination, peer listening/education, peer pressure, self-esteem, and counter-human trafficking techniques. Working with a team of Volunteers, students brainstorm strategies for teaching in their hometowns what they learn at camp. One year, four students from one small town in western Ukraine decided to teach pupils at their former high school about the biology and transmission of HIV/AIDS and included a lesson on stigma and discrimination. At the end of the lesson, the pupils participated in an art contest, where the winning drawings were printed on greeting cards. There was so much enthusiasm for the project that two other groups of students decided to implement a similar technique in their communities.

—Peace Corps. "Partnership Stories: Ukraine." 13 March 2009.
Courtesy of the Peace Corps.

Reading and Writing for College Life

Assume you are taking a college course in economics. Your class is studying a unit on global trade. Your professor has announced an essay exam and provided a list of study questions. Your study group has been assigned the following question to prepare an answer to discuss at the next group meeting. Read the question and the passage, and draft a short essay response to the question "What are the benefits and costs of international trade?"

THE BENEFITS AND COSTS OF INTERNATIONAL TRADE

What are the benefits and costs of international trade? The theory of comparative advantage indicates that countries that participate in international trade will experience higher standards of living because of the greater quantity and variety of higher-quality products offered at lower prices. These results stem from the increased competition associated with more open trade. But these benefits are not without their costs.

The costs of international trade are borne by those businesses and their workers whose livelihoods are threatened by foreign competition. Some domestic businesses may lose market share to foreign companies, stunting their profitability and ability to create jobs. Other firms may face so much foreign competition that they're driven out of business entirely.

Do the benefits of international trade outweigh the costs? This is a difficult question to answer. The costs of increased international trade—including lost jobs to foreign competitors—are often easy to identify. The benefits are not always easily seen, however, as they are spread out among millions of consumers. For example, a greater quantity and variety of higher-quality products to purchase may not be easily traced to increased international trade because these benefits are often slow and subtle. People benefit from lower-priced products, although price reductions may save people only a nickel here and a dime there. But the sum of these lower prices for the public at large can be dramatic—especially over time. Governments play a large role in determining how much international trade they will support, for example, by choosing to impose restrictions on the quantity and types of goods that can cross their nation's borders.

93

—Solomon, *Better Business*, 3rd ed., Pearson, 2014, p. 93.

Reading and Writing for Working Life

Assume you work in management for a business employing over one thousand workers that designs, installs, and repairs telecommunication systems. You recently learned of the opportunity to partner with USAID. Your company could provide workers not only to help install telecommunications systems in developing countries, but also to train local people to install and repair equipment. You are scheduled to present your idea to the management team at the next regional meeting. First, read the information from USAID and the job descriptions of two key departments in your company that you want to involve. Then, write a computer-assisted presentation to convince the management team to further investigate partnering with USAID.

Why Partner with USAID?

In an era when 53 of the 100 largest economies in the world are companies and one company alone can reach 4 billion customers—nearly 60% of the global population—working with the private sector is no longer a luxury, but a necessity. In addition, official development assistance (ODA) is no longer the main driving force for international giving. For every dollar of U.S. foreign assistance in 2010, developing countries received an additional $3 in remittances from immigrants living in the United States, $5 in U.S. private capital flows, and $1 in U.S. private philanthropy.

As a result of the changing global landscape, U.S. companies and other private sector organizations are increasingly looking at development as a core strategy issue rather than a matter of corporate philanthropy. However, many of the obstacles that businesses face overseas are really symptoms of the development challenges that USAID is working to address. By working together in partnership, the public and private sectors can find new ways of looking at a problem and develop cost-effective solutions.

The Global Development Alliance program at USAID seeks to advance both U.S. development goals and the private sector's business interests. By leveraging private sector financial and human capital, expertise, and technologies and innovations, partnerships increase the impact and reach of USAID's interventions, often resulting in high-impact development solutions that foster sustained impact long after public funding ends. USAID brings unique assets to its partnerships with the private sector:

- Long-term country presence and extensive relationships with local and national governments;
- Technical expertise across industries and sectors;
- Network of local, regional and global development partners;
- Convening and coordinating power to catalyze, promote and facilitate the development of partnerships;
- Funding; and
- Credibility and goodwill.

CONTINUED

As a result, GDAs and other partnerships with USAID have generated a wealth of valuable business and development results, including but not limited to:

- Supply chains in developing countries that now meet international buyers' standards, foster increased business revenues, and raise incomes for workers and farmers;
- New markets for affordable products that meet the needs of those living in developing countries;
- Skilled workers to support growing telecommunications, health care, and apparel and other manufacturing industries; and
- The use of mobile technology for transmitting information on crops, health issues, etc., thereby connecting local buyers and sellers to international markets and improving health care in poorer communities.

—Why Partner? | U.S. Agency for International Development. 28 Feb. 2013. Accessed 17 Sept. 2014. http://www.usaid.gov/gda/why-partner

CoNect: Network and Computer Systems Administrators Department

- Determine what the organization needs in a network and computer system before it is set up
- Install all network hardware and software and make needed upgrades and repairs
- Maintain network and computer system security
- Collect data in order to evaluate and enhance the network's or system's performance
- Add users to a network and assign and update security permissions on the network
- Train users on the proper use of hardware and software

CoNect: Equipment Installers Department

- Install communications equipment in offices, private homes, and buildings that are under construction
- Set up, rearrange, or replace routing and dialing equipment
- Inspect and service equipment, wiring, and phone jacks
- Repair or replace faulty, damaged, or malfunctioning equipment
- Test repaired, newly installed, or updated equipment to ensure that it works properly
- Adjust or calibrate equipment settings to improve its performance
- Keep records of maintenance, repairs, and installations
- Demonstrate and explain the use of equipment to customers

—Bureau of Labor Statistics. Occupational Outlook Handbook. http://www.bls.gov/ooh/computer-and-information-technology/network-and-computer-systems-administrators.htm#tab-2

—Bureau of Labor Statistics. Occupational Outlook Handbook. http://www.bls.gov/ooh/installation-maintenance-and-repair/telecommunications-equipment-installers-and-repairers-except-line-installers.htm#tab-2

Review Test

MySkillsLab™
Complete this Exercise
on myskillslab.com

Argument

Score (number correct) _____ x 10 = _____%

Read the following passage and then answer the questions.

Glossary

polygraph (sentence 1): a device that records, or graphs, many ("poly") measures of physical arousal

false positives (sentence 16): mistaken identifications of persons as having a particular characteristic

implicate (sentence 17): to imply a connection with wrongdoing

Do Lie Detectors Really Detect Lies?

[1]The **polygraph** or "lie detector" test is based on the assumption that people will display physical signs of arousal when lying; so most polygraph machines make a record of the suspect's heart rate, breathing rate, perspiration, and blood pressure. [2]Occasionally, voice-print analysis is also employed. [3]Thus, the device really acts as an emotional arousal detector rather than a direct indicator of truth or lies. [4]But does it work?

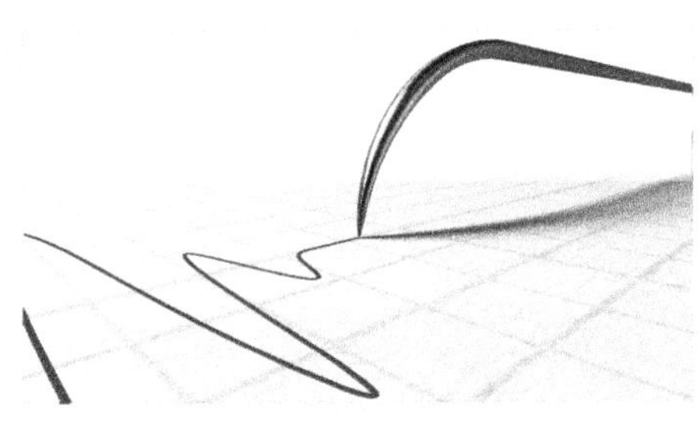

[5]Without a doubt, wrongdoers sometimes confess when confronted with polygraph evidence against them. [6]Yet, critics have pointed out several problems with the polygraphic procedure that could easily land innocent people in prison and let the guilty walk free (Aftergood, 2000). [7]For example, polygraph subjects know when they are suspects, so some will give heightened responses to the critical questions even when they are innocent. [8]On the other hand, some people can give **deceptive** responses because they have learned to control or distort their emotional responses. [9]To do so, they may employ simple physical movements, drugs, or biofeedback training—a procedure in which people are given moment-to-moment information on certain biological responses, such as perspiration or heart rate (Saxe et al., 1985). [10]Either way, a polygraph examiner risks incorrectly identifying innocent people as guilty and failing to spot the liars.

[11]Important statistical issues call the polygraph procedure into further question. [12]Even if the examination were 95 percent accurate, a 5 percent error rate could lead to the misidentification of many innocent people as being guilty. [13]To illustrate, imagine that your company arranges for all 500 of your employees to take a polygraph test to find out who has been stealing office supplies. [14]Imagine also that only about 4 percent (20 out of 500 people) are really stealing, which is not an unreasonable estimate. [15]If the lie detector test is 95 percent accurate, it will correctly spot 19 of these 20 thieves. [16]But the test will also give 5 percent **false positives**, falsely fingering 5 percent of the innocent people. [17]Of the 480 innocent employees, the polygraph will inaccurately **implicate** 24 as liars. [18]That is, you could end up with more people falsely accused of lying than people correctly accused of lying. [19]This was borne out in a field study of suspected criminals who were later either convicted or declared innocent. [20]The polygraph results were no better than a random coin flip (Brett et al., 1986).

CONTINUED

[21]An equally serious concern with polygraphy is that there are no generally accepted standards either for administering a polygraph examination or for interpreting its results. [22]Different examiners could conceivably come to different conclusions based on the same polygraph record. [23]For these reasons, the U.S. Congress has outlawed most uses of polygraph tests in job screening and in most areas of the government, except for high-security-risk positions. [24]National Academies of Science (2003) has gone even further in a report saying that the polygraph is too crude to be useful for screening people to identify possible terrorists or other national security risks.

[25]As far as criminal investigations are concerned, we find a patchwork of laws on the admissibility of polygraph evidence among the states. [26]Few have gone so far as imposing complete bans and 20 more allow such evidence only on agreement of both sides—although, in a few states, polygraph results are still routinely admissible in court (Gruben & Madsen, 2005).

–Adapted from Zimbardo, Johnson, and Hamilton, *Psychology: Core Concepts*, 7th ed., pp. 405–406.

Vocabulary

1. Based on the context of the passage, what is the best meaning of the word **deceptive** (sentence 8)?

a. useful
b. emotional
c. false
d. understandable

Tone and Purpose

2. The overall tone of the passage is

a. objective.
b. biased.

3. The primary purpose of the passage is to

a. inform.
b. entertain.
c. persuade.

Central Idea

4. Which sentence best states the implied central idea of the passage?

a. The polygraph assumes that people display physical signs of arousal when lying.
b. People who lie may still pass a polygraph test.
c. Better guidelines are needed for polygraph use.
d. The polygraph should not be considered or used as a lie detector.

Supporting Details

5. In the third paragraph (sentences 11–20), sentence 11 states a

a. main idea.
b. major supporting detail.
c. minor supporting detail.

Transitions

6. The relationship of ideas within sentence 7 is

a. time order.
b. listing.
c. comparison.
d. cause and effect.

Pattern of Organization

7. The overall pattern of organization of the passage is

a. time order.
b. listing.
c. comparison.
d. cause and effect.

Fact and Opinion

8. Sentence 23 is a statement of

a. fact.
b. opinion.
c. fact and opinion.

Inferences

9. Based on the information in the passage, the reader can infer that

a. there is no relation between emotional arousal and lying.
b. many companies use polygraphs to help stop office theft.
c. a lie detector less than 100% accurate will falsely accuse some people of lying.
d. there is a need for better-trained polygraph examiners.

Argument

10. Which sentence is not relevant to the authors' claim?

a. sentence 2
b. sentence 6
c. sentence 12
d. sentence 21

Summary Response

Restate the authors' claim in your own words. In your summary, state the authors' tone and purpose. Begin your summary response with the following: *The central idea of "Do Lie Detectors Really Detect Lies?" by Zimbardo, Johnson, and McCann is. . . .*

Reader Response

Assume you live in a state where polygraph results are allowed, but the legislature is considering outlawing them. Write a letter to a state legislator stating your position on whether to continue allowing them or to ban them. Consider the following points in your argument:

- Is the argument to outlaw polygraph results valid?
- Does the fact that a "lie detector" test can sometimes make a guilty person confess to his or her crime justify its use?

MySkillsLab™
Complete this Exercise
on myskillslab.com

Academic Learning Log: Module Review

Summary of Key Concepts of Argument

Assess your comprehension of argument.

LO1 LO2 LO3 LO4 LO5

1. A claim is ____
____.

2. An argument is ____
____.

3. A valid conclusion is ____
____.

4. An invalid conclusion is ____
____.

5. Transition words that signal argument include ____________, ____________,
____________, ____________, and ____________.

6. Signal words that qualify an idea as an argument include ____________, ____________,
____________, and ____________.

LO6

7-9. Three key questions a writer can ask to evaluate the effectiveness of his or her argument are:
____
____
____

10. Consistent use of ____________ strengthens ____________ or the clear flow of ideas.

Test Your Comprehension of Argument

Respond in your own words to the following questions and prompts.

LO1 LO2 LO3 LO4 LO5 LO6

Use your own words to complete the following chart that explains the VALID approach to avoiding drawing false inferences and coming to false conclusions as a reader and writer of arguments.

1. **How will I use what I have learned?** In your notebook, discuss how you will apply to your own reading/writing strategy what you have learned about argument. When will you apply this knowledge to your reading/writing strategy?
2. **What do I still need to study about argument?** In your notebook, discuss your ongoing study needs. Describe what, when, and how you will continue studying and using argument.

MySkillsLab™

Complete the Post-test for Module 12 in MySkillsLab.

13

LEARNING OUTCOMES

After studying this module you should be able to:

- LO 1 Use Commas with Items in a Series
- LO 2 Use Commas with Introductory Elements
- LO 3 Use Commas to Join Independent Clauses
- LO 4 Use Commas with Parenthetical Ideas
- LO 5 Use Commas with Quotations

The Comma

A comma is a valuable, useful punctuation device because it separates the structural elements of a sentence into manageable segments.

The primary purpose of the **comma** is to make a sentence easy to read by indicating a brief pause between parts of the sentence that need to be separated.

LO 1 Use Commas with Items in a Series

Use commas to separate a **series of items** in a list. A series of items in a list can be **three** or more words, phrases, or clauses. In addition, a series of items can be made up of subjects, verbs, adjectives, participles, and so on. Items in a series are parallel and equal in importance.

Series of Words

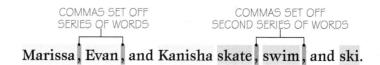

COMMAS SET OFF SERIES OF WORDS

COMMAS SET OFF SECOND SERIES OF WORDS

Marissa, Evan, and Kanisha skate, swim, and ski.

Series of Phrases

COMMAS SET OFF SERIES OF PHRASES

Marissa enjoys skating on ice, swimming in the ocean, and skiing down a snowy slope.

Series of Clauses

Marissa is an athlete who trains consistently, who eats sensibly, and who competes well.

COMMAS SET OFF SERIES OF CLAUSES

Use Commas with Introductory Elements

L2

Use commas to set off the introductory element of a sentence. **Introductory elements** are ideas that appear at the beginning of a sentence. Introductory elements come before a main clause and can be a word, phrase, or clause.

Introductory Word

COMMA SETS OFF INTRODUCTORY WORD

Overall, good health is achieved through wise choices.

Introductory Phrase

COMMA SETS OFF INTRODUCTORY PHRASE

To achieve good health, one should exercise on a regular basis.

Introductory Dependent Clause

COMMA SETS OFF INTRODUCTORY DEPENDENT PHRASE

As Maria increased her physical activity, her sense of well-being improved.

Use Commas to Join Independent Clauses

L3

Use a comma with a coordinating conjunction to join two or more equally important and logically related independent clauses. To join sentences with a coordinating conjunction, place the comma before the conjunction. The acronym **FANBOYS** identifies the seven coordinating conjunctions: *for, and, nor, but, or, yet,* and *so*.

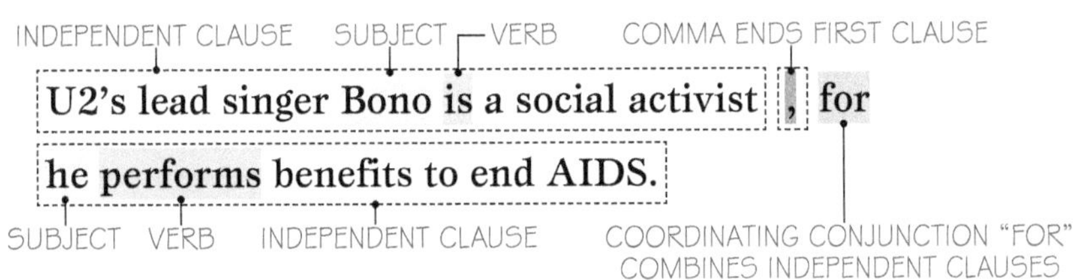

LO4 Use Commas with Parenthetical Ideas

Use commas to set off a parenthetical idea. A **parenthetical idea** interrupts a sentence with information that is **nonessential** to the meaning of the sentence. Such an idea could be enclosed in parentheses. However, more often, a comma comes before and after such an idea. These interruptions can be words, phrases, or clauses.

Parenthetical Word

COMMAS SET OFF PARENTHETICAL WORD

The demanding customer was, however, a generous tipper.

Parenthetical Phrase

COMMAS SET OFF PARENTHETICAL PHRASE

The polite customer, surprisingly heartless, left no tip.

Parenthetical Clause

COMMAS SET OFF PARENTHETICAL CLAUSE

Jennifer, who had been working a 12-hour shift, smiled at the sight of the generous tip.

LO5 Use Commas with Quotations

Use commas after a verb that introduces a quotation. The comma is used to set off the "said" clause, called the **speech tag**, and the comma is placed before the quoted information.

COMMA SEPARATES SPEECH TAG FROM THE QUOTATION

Mr. Newell said, "Let's begin the meeting promptly, please."

MySkillsLab™

Complete the Post-test for Module 13 in MySkillsLab.

Comma Splices and Fused Sentences

A comma splice is an error that occurs when a comma is used by itself to join two sentences. A fused sentence is an error that occurs when two sentences are joined without any punctuation.

14

LEARNING OUTCOMES

After studying this module you should be able to:

- LO 1 Identify Comma Splices
- LO 2 Identify Fused Sentences
- LO 3 Correct Comma Splices and Fused Sentences Using Four Strategies

Identify Comma Splices LO 1

A **comma splice** occurs when a comma is used by itself (without a coordinating conjunction) to join two independent clauses.

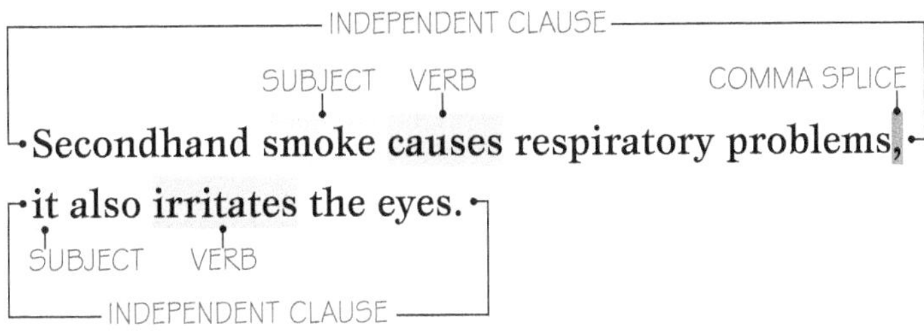

Identify Fused Sentences LO 2

A **fused sentence** occurs when two independent clauses are joined without any punctuation.

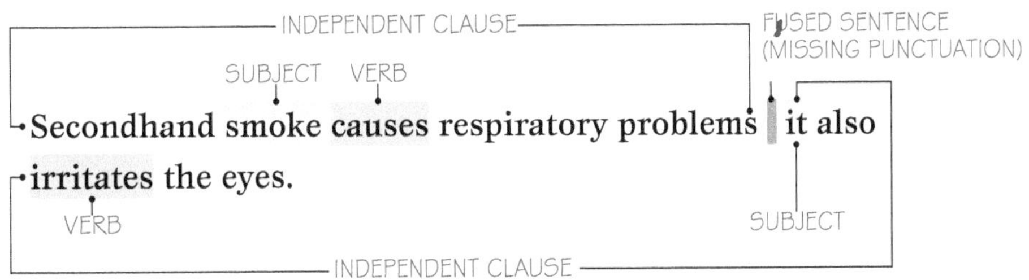

L3 Correct Comma Splices and Fused Sentences Using Four Strategies

1. Separate sentences using a period and capital letter.

INDEPENDENT CLAUSE — INDEPENDENT CLAUSE

Secondhand smoke causes respiratory problems. It also irritates the eyes.

ADDED PERIOD — CAPITALIZED LETTER STARTS 2ND SENTENCE

2. Join sentences with a comma followed by a coordinating conjunction.

INDEPENDENT CLAUSE

Secondhand smoke causes respiratory problems, and it also irritates the eyes.

ADDED COMMA AND COORDINATING CONJUNCTION

INDEPENDENT CLAUSE

3. Join sentences with a semicolon, or join sentences with a semicolon followed by a conjunctive adverb such as *also, for example, however, then, therefore,* and *thus.*

INDEPENDENT CLAUSE — INDEPENDENT CLAUSE

Secondhand smoke causes respiratory problems; it also irritates the eyes.

ADDED SEMICOLON

INDEPENDENT CLAUSE

Secondhand smoke causes respiratory problems; in addition, it irritates the eyes.

ADDED SEMICOLON AND CONJUNCTIVE ADVERB

INDEPENDENT CLAUSE

4. Join sentences using subordinate ideas.

DEPENDENT CLAUSE — INDEPENDENT CLAUSE

While secondhand smoke causes respiratory problems, it also irritates the eyes.

ADDED SUBORDINATING CONJUNCTION — ADDED COMMA TO SET OFF DEPENDENT CLAUSE

MySkillsLab™

Complete the Post-test for Module 14 in MySkillsLab.

Fragments and Consistent Use of Point of View, Number, and Tense

A fragment is an incomplete thought. Sentence clarity creates a logical flow of ideas through consistency in person, point of view, number, and tense.

15

LEARNING OUTCOMES

After studying this module you should be able to:

- LO 1 Recognize the Difference Between Sentences and Fragments
- LO 2 Edit to Correct Types of Fragments
- LO 3 Use Consistent Person and Point of View
- LO 4 Use Consistent Number
- LO 5 Use Consistent Tense

Recognize the Difference Between Sentences and Fragments LO 1

A **sentence** contains a subject, a verb, and all the information needed to clearly express a complete thought.

SENTENCE: **Complete Thought-Complete Information**

COMPLETE THOUGHT

You should visit your doctor.

SUBJECT (You) VERB (should visit)

FRAGMENT: **Incomplete Thought-Missing Information**

A **fragment** is missing one of the following: a subject, a verb, or both subject and verb.

Fragment (Missing an Independent Clause):

INCOMPLETE THOUGHT

Because youth are less active than in the past.

SUBORDINATING CONJUNCTION (Because) SUBJECT (youth) VERB (are)

Edit to Correct Types of Fragments LO 2

This section discusses two common types of fragments: the phrase fragment and the clause fragment. A writer may use two techniques to revise fragments into sentences:

- Combine existing ideas.
- Add missing ideas.

Phrase Fragments

A **phrase** is a group of words that acts as a single unit. A phrase is a fragment because it does not contain both a subject and a verb.

PHRASE

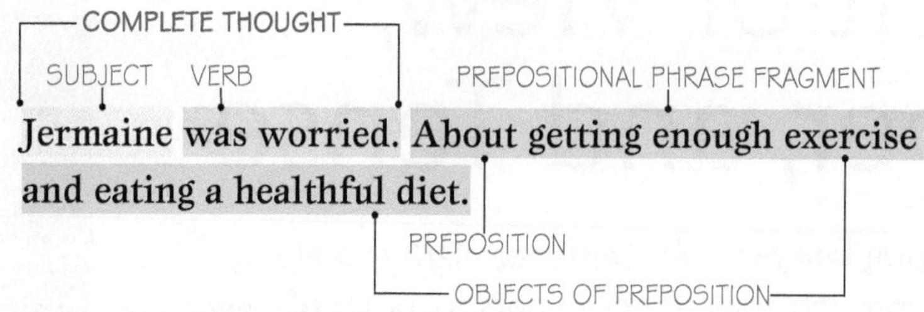

Revised to Combine Ideas:

Revised to Add Ideas:

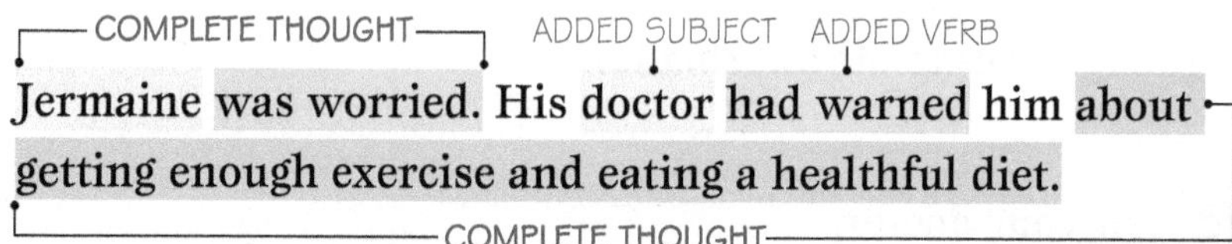

Clause Fragments

A **clause** is a set of words that contains a subject and a verb. A **dependent clause** expresses an incomplete thought or fragment.

Dependent Clause

A **dependent clause**, also known as a **subordinate clause**, does not make sense on its own.

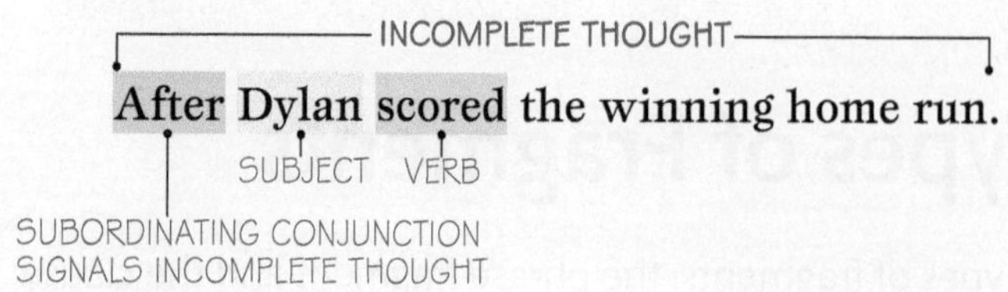

A **subordinating conjunction** states the relationship between two clauses.

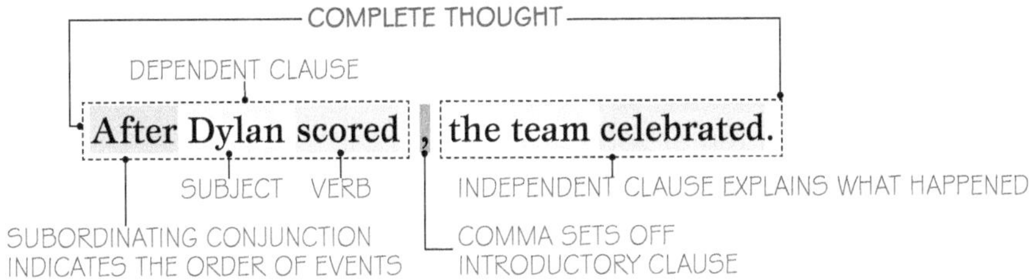

Relative Clause

One type of dependent clause is the relative clause, such as *who scored the winning home run*. A **relative clause** describes a noun or pronoun in an independent clause. A **relative pronoun** (such as *who, whom, whose, which*, and *that*) introduces the relative clause and relates it to the noun or pronoun it describes.

Join the relative clause to the independent clause that contains the word it describes.

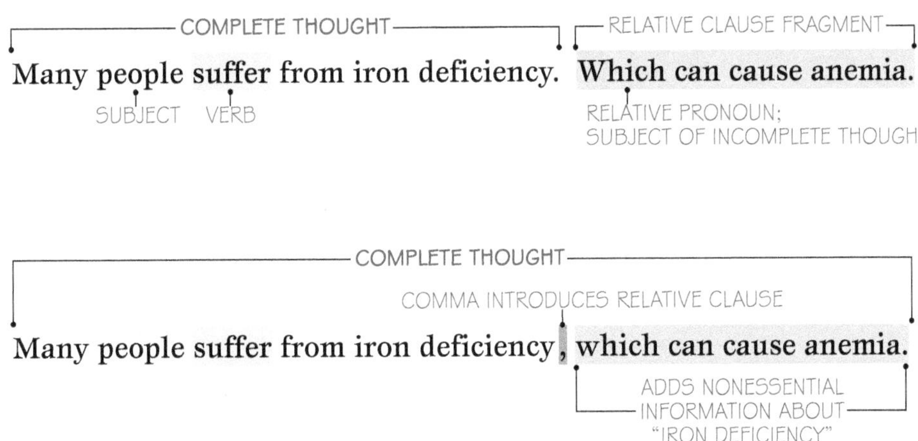

Use Consistent Person and Point of View

The term **person** refers to the use of pronouns to identify the difference between the writer or speaker, the one being written or spoken to, and the one being written about or spoken of. **Point of view** is the position from which something is considered, evaluated, or discussed; point of view is identified as first person, second person, or third person. Person and point of view also communicate tone.

Three Points of View

Person	Traits	Pronouns
First Person	The writer or speaker; informal, conversational tone	singular: *I, me* plural: *we, our*
Second Person	The one being written or spoken to; can remain unstated; informal, conversational tone	singular: *you* plural: *you*
Third Person	The one being written about or spoken of; formal, academic tone	singular: *he, she, it, one* plural: *they*

Illogical Shift in Person

An abrupt or **unnecessary shift in person or point of view** causes a break in the logical flow of ideas. When you revise for consistency, remember that the number of the verb may need to change as well.

Illogical Shift in Person:

THIRD PERSON

Nobody should text while you drive.

SECOND PERSON

Revision:

THIRD PERSON

Nobody should text while he drives.

PRONOUN AND VERB AGREE IN PERSON

LO 4 Use Consistent Number

The term *number* refers to the difference between a singular noun or pronoun and plural nouns and pronouns. Once you choose a point of view, carefully edit your writing to ensure **consistent use of number**.

Illogical Shift in Number

When pronouns act as the subject of a verb, they, too, must agree in number. An abrupt or **unnecessary shift in number** causes a break in the logical flow of ideas.

Illogical Shift in Number:

PLURAL NOUN SINGULAR, THIRD-PERSON PRONOUN

Henry loves scooters, yet it is dangerous.

SINGULAR VERB

Revision:

PLURAL NOUN PLURAL, THIRD-PERSON PRONOUN

Henry loves scooters, and they are dangerous.

PLURAL VERB

Use Consistent Tense

L5

Consistent tense expresses the logical sequence of events or existence. Verb *tense* expresses the time or duration of an action or state of being. Primary tenses include three time frames: The **past** *was*; the **present** *is*; the **future** *will be*.

Illogical Shift in Tense

Abruptly changing from one verb tense to another without a logical reason, also called an **illogical shift in tense**, breaks the logical flow of ideas and causes confusion.

Illogical Shift in Tense:

PRESENT TENSE

Monica eats dinner and went to bed.

PAST TENSE

Revision:

PRESENT TENSE

Monica eats dinner and goes to bed.

MySkillsLab™

Complete the Post-test for Module 15 in MySkillsLab.

16

LEARNING OUTCOMES

After studying this module you should be able to:

LO 1 Recognize Subject-Verb Agreement

LO 2 Create Agreement Using Key Verbs in the Present Tense: *To Have, To Do, To Be*

LO 3 Create Subject-Verb Agreement

Subject-Verb Agreement: Present Tense

In the present tense, subjects and verbs must agree in number. Singular subjects must take singular verbs; plural subjects must take plural verbs.

LO 1 Recognize Subject-Verb Agreement

The following chart uses the sample verb *think* to illustrate present tense agreement in number.

Present Tense Agreement				
	Singular **Subject** and **Verb**		Plural **Subject** and **Verb**	
First Person	I	think	We	think
Second Person	You	think	You	think
Third Person	He She It	thinks	They	think

For standard verbs, only the third person singular verb is formed by adding *-s* or *-es*.

Third person singular subject	→	present tense verb ends with *-s* or *-es*
He	→	apologizes
She	→	accepts
It	→	catches

LO 2 Create Agreement Using Key Verbs in the Present Tense: *To Have, To Do, To Be*

Three key verbs are used both as main verbs and as helping verbs to express a wide variety of meanings: *to have*, *to do*, and *to be*. Memorize their present tense singular and plural forms to ensure subject-verb agreement.

To Have: Present Tense		
	Singular **Subject** and **Verb**	Plural **Subject** and **Verb**
First Person	I have	We have
Second Person	You have	You have
Third Person	He / She / It — has	They have

To Do: Present Tense		
	Singular **Subject** and **Verb**	Plural **Subject** and **Verb**
First Person	I do	We do
Second Person	You do	You do
Third Person	He / She / It — does	They do

The verb ***to do*** is often used with the adverb *not* to express a negative thought. Frequently this negative is stated in the form of the contractions *doesn't* and *don't* that combine the verb and the adverb into shorter words. The verb part of the contraction must still agree with its subject.

To Do and *Not:* Contraction Form		
	Singular **Subject** and **Verb**	Plural **Subject** and **Verb**
First Person	I don't agree	We don't agree
Second Person	You don't seem well	You don't seem well
Third Person	He / She / It — doesn't care	They don't care

The verb ***to be*** is unusual because it uses three forms in the present tense: *am*, *is*, and *are*.

To Be: Present Tense		
	Singular **Subject** and **Verb**	Plural **Subject** and **Verb**
First Person	I am	We are
Second Person	You are	You are
Third Person	He / She / It — is	They are

L3 Create Subject-Verb Agreement

Subjects Separated from Verbs

The standard order of ideas in a sentence places the subject first, immediately followed by the verb. However, subjects are often separated from their verbs by **prepositional phrases**. The object of the preposition can never be the subject of a sentence. The verb of a sentence agrees with the subject, not the object of the preposition.

Example

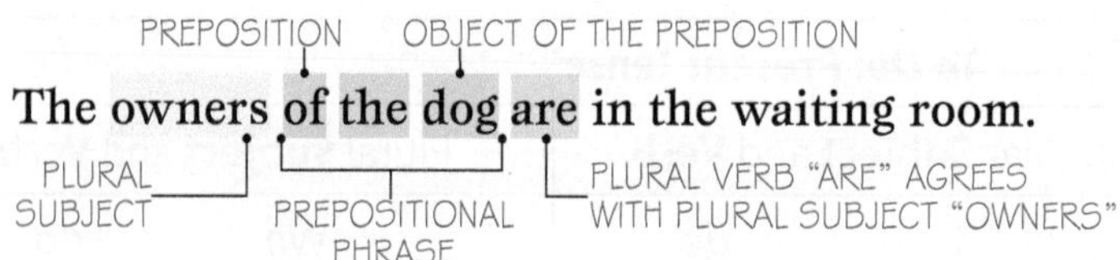

Subjects After Verbs

In some instances, a writer may choose to place the subject after the verb.

There and ***Here*** are never the subject of a sentence. Both of these words signal that the subject comes after the verb.

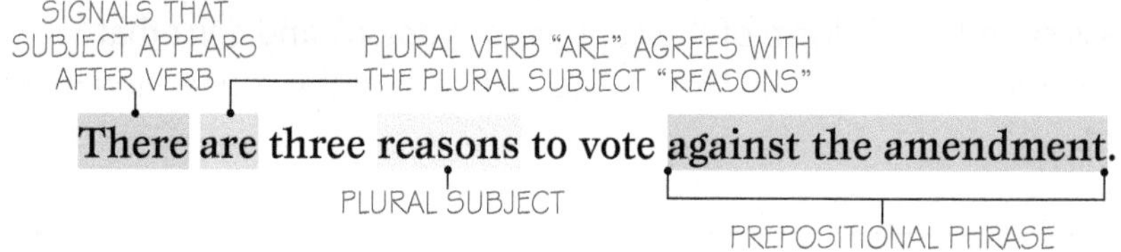

Agreement in Questions relies on understanding that the subject comes after the verb or between parts of the verb.

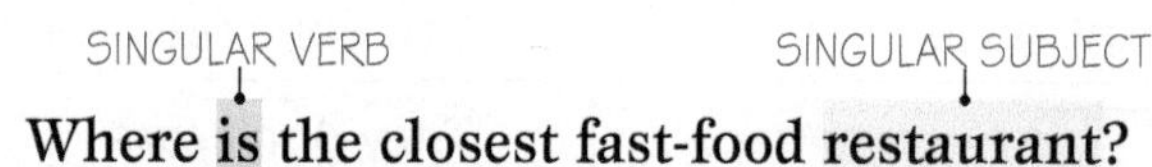

SINGULAR VERB
SINGULAR SUBJECT
Where is the closest fast-food restaurant?

MySkillsLab™

Complete the Post-test for Module 16 in MySkillsLab.

Adjectives and Adverbs

An adjective describes a noun or a pronoun. An adverb describes a verb, an adjective, or another adverb.

17

LEARNING OUTCOMES

After studying this module you should be able to:

LO 1 Recognize Types and Uses of Adjectives

LO 2 Recognize Types and Uses of Adverbs

Recognize Types and Uses of Adjectives LO 1

An **adjective** modifies—in other words, it describes—a noun or a pronoun. It answers one or more of the following questions:

- What kind?
- Which one?
- How many?

ADJECTIVE "LOUD" DESCRIBES NOUN "VOICE"

Maya has a loud voice.

An **adverb** modifies, or describes, a verb, an adjective, or another adverb. It answers one or more of the following questions:

- How?
- Why?
- When?
- When?
- To what extent?

VERB "TALKS" DESCRIBED BY ADVERB "LOUDLY"

Maya talks loudly.

Participles as Adjectives

Many adjectives are formed by adding *-ed* or *-ing* to verbs. These **participle adjectives** serve two purposes: The *-ed* form describes a person's reaction or feeling; the *-ing* form describes the person or thing that causes the reaction.

The amazed crowd watched the fireworks display.

The amazing fireworks display lit up the entire sky.

Nouns and Verbs Formed as Adjectives

In addition to the *-ed* and *-ing* word endings, many adjectives are formed by other types of word endings.

Common Adjectives								
Word Endings	***-able* *-ible***	***-ful***	***-ic***	***-ish***	***-ive***	***-less***	***-ly* *-y***	***-ous***
Examples	acceptable	bashful	alcoholic	boorish	abusive	cheerless	actually	ambiguous

Placement of Adjectives

A careful writer not only chooses the precise word for impact, but also arranges words in the most effective order for the greatest impact on the reader.

Adjectives can appear before a noun.

The nervous suspect offered an alibi.

Adjectives can appear after **linking verbs** such as *is, are, were, seems,* and *appears.*

The alibi seemed plausible.

Adjectives can appear after **sensory verbs**—those that describe physical senses—such as *look, smell, feel, taste,* and *sound.*

The suspect looked frightened.

L2 Recognize Types and Uses of Adverbs

The most common use of adverbs is to describe verbs. In addition, adverbs modify other types of words such as adjectives and other adverbs. In purpose, adverbs answer the reporter's questions *When? Where?* and *How?*

Many adverbs are derived from adjectives, many adverbs end in *-ly*, and many adverbs are gradable based on degree or quantity. The following chart lists some of the most frequently used adverbs based on the type of information they provide.

Common Adverbs				
Time, Frequency, or Sequence When?	**Place Where?**	**Manner How?**	**Certainty or Negation How?**	**Degree or Quantity How much?**
already finally regularly usually	everywhere here somewhere there	badly fast quickly well	certainly clearly never not	almost completely entirely not very

How to Use the Comparative and Superlative

Adjectives and adverbs take the form of three degrees: **absolute**, **comparative**, and **superlative**. The degrees of adverbs are formed by adding the suffixes *-er* or *-est* or by using *more* or *most*. For example, *more* or *most* establishes a degree of comparison with adverbs that end in *-ly*.

Absolute

The absolute degree makes no comparison, or makes a one-to-one comparison (in which the adjective or adverb describes both things equally).

Raisins and prunes are sweet.

Raisins are as sweet as prunes.

Comparative

The comparative degree compares and makes distinctions between two people or things, usually by using the adverb *more* or *less* or adding the suffix *-er*.

Raisins are sweeter than prunes.

Riana acted more generously than her sister [acted].

Superlative

The superlative degree makes distinctions among three or more people or things, usually by using the adverb *most* or *least* or adding the suffix *-est*.

This is the sweetest prune I have ever eaten.

MySkillsLab™

Complete the Post-test for Module 17 in MySkillsLab.

18 Parallelism

LEARNING OUTCOMES

After studying this module you should be able to:

- LO1 Use Parallel Words
- LO2 Use Parallel Phrases
- LO3 Use Parallel Clauses
- LO4 Punctuate for Parallelism

Parallelism is the expression of equal ideas—similar words, phrases, or clauses—in a sentence in the same, matching grammatical form. Parallel expressions bring clarity, interest, and power to a piece of writing.

LO1 Use Parallel Words

Parallel structure uses a pair or series of closely related compound words to emphasize a point. Parallel words often, but not always, use similar **suffixes** (word endings).

- **Parallel Words**

Nonparallel:

NOUN: predators; ADJECTIVE: wandering

Prehistoric Paleo-Indians were predators and wandering.

Revised for Parallelism:

PARALLEL NOUNS: predators, wanderers

Prehistoric Paleo-Indians were predators and wanderers.

Nonparallel:

ADVERB: skillfully; PREPOSITIONAL PHRASE: with diligence

Paleo-Indians skillfully hunted game and with diligence gathered berries.

Revised for Parallelism:

PARALLEL ADVERBS: skillfully, diligently

Paleo-Indians skillfully hunted game and diligently gathered berries.

Nonparallel:

NONPARALLEL VERBS: flaked, crafting

They flaked and crafting flint into spears.

Revised for Parallelism:

PARALLEL VERBS: flaked, crafted

They flaked and crafted flint into spears.

Use Parallel Phrases

L2

Parallel structure uses a pair or series of closely related compound phrases to emphasize a point. Parallel phrases repeat similar word patterns or groups.

- **Parallel Phrases**

Nonparallel:

INFINITIVE PHRASE GERUND PHRASE

The Mayas learned to build cities, jewelry crafting, and to develop trade around A.D. 300.

INFINITIVE PHRASE

Revised for Parallelism:

PARALLEL INFINITIVE PHRASES

The Mayas learned to build cities, to craft jewelry, and to develop trade around A.D. 300.

Use Parallel Clauses

L3

Parallel structure uses a set of closely related clauses to emphasize a point. Parallel structure begins with a clause and continues with clauses to create a balanced, logical statement. Use parallel words and phrases within clauses.

- **Parallel Clauses**

Nonparallel:

INDEPENDENT CLAUSES

Only a few million people inhabited the Americas by 1490, yet roughly 75 million people who were living in Europe.

DEPENDENT CLAUSE (ILLOGICAL MIXED STRUCTURE)

Revised for Parallelism:

PARALLEL INDEPENDENT CLAUSES

Only a few million people inhabited the Americas by 1490, yet roughly 75 million people inhabited Europe.

L4 Punctuate for Parallelism

The comma and the semicolon (sometimes along with coordinating conjunctions), and numbered, lettered, or bulleted items in a list signal ideas of equal importance. Ideas marked by these pieces of punctuation are best expressed with parallelism.

Coordinating conjunctions always signal an equal relationship among words, phrases, and clauses. Use commas between parallel items in a series. Use a comma with a coordinating conjunction to join independent clauses.

Examples:

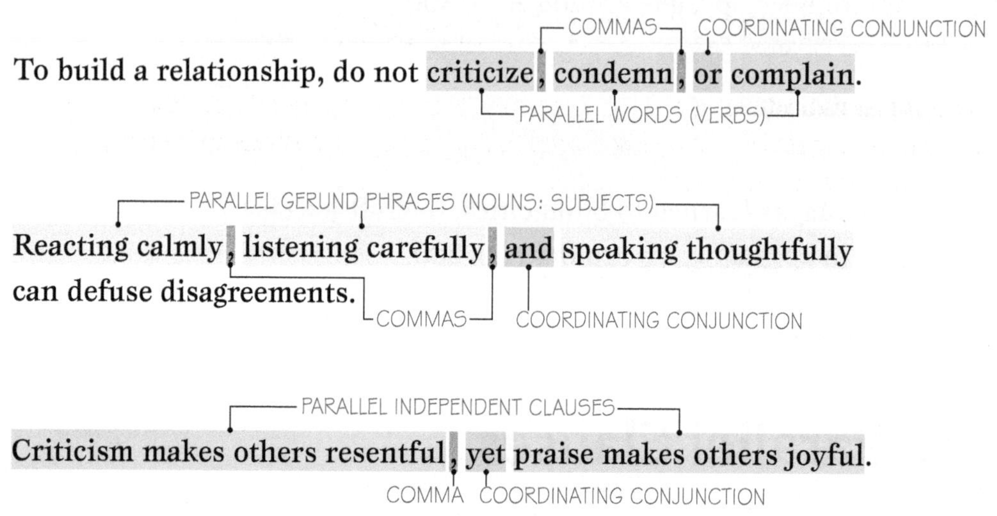

Semicolons signal two or more closely related independent clauses.

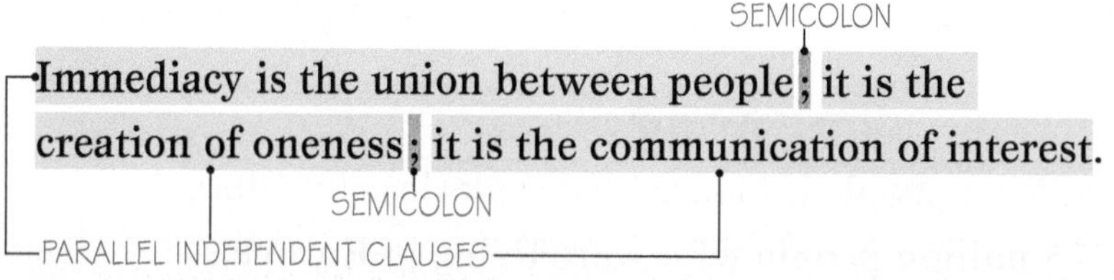

MySkillsLab™

Complete the Post-test for Module 18 in MySkillsLab.

Misplaced and Dangling Modifiers

A modifier is a word or phrase that describes, clarifies, or gives more information about another word in a sentence.

19

LEARNING OUTCOMES

After studying this module you should be able to:

LO 1 Edit Misplaced Modifiers

LO 2 Edit Dangling Modifiers

Edit Misplaced Modifiers LO 1

A **misplaced modifier** is a word or phrase illogically separated from the word it describes. The following examples and revisions illustrate the most common types of misplaced modifiers.

Types of Misplaced Modifiers

MISPLACED WORDS A misplaced word is separated from the word it limits or restricts.

Example

WORD "ONLY" DESCRIBES?

Belle Glade, Florida only has been flooded twice by hurricanes.

Revision #1

WORD "ONLY" DESCRIBES "TWICE"

Belle Glade, Florida has been flooded only twice by hurricanes.

Revision #2

WORD "ONLY" DESCRIBES "BELLE GLADE"

Only Belle Glade, Florida has been flooded twice by hurricanes.

MISPLACED PHRASE A phrase that describes a noun or pronoun is placed next to the wrong noun or pronoun and separated from the noun or pronoun it describes.

Example

PHRASE "WITHOUT HER GLASSES" DESCRIBES?

She couldn't tell what kind of animal it was without her glasses.

Revision

PHRASE "WITHOUT HER GLASSES" DESCRIBES "SHE"

Without her glasses, she couldn't tell what kind of animal it was.

ADDED COMMA SETS OFF INTRODUCTORY PHRASE

Example

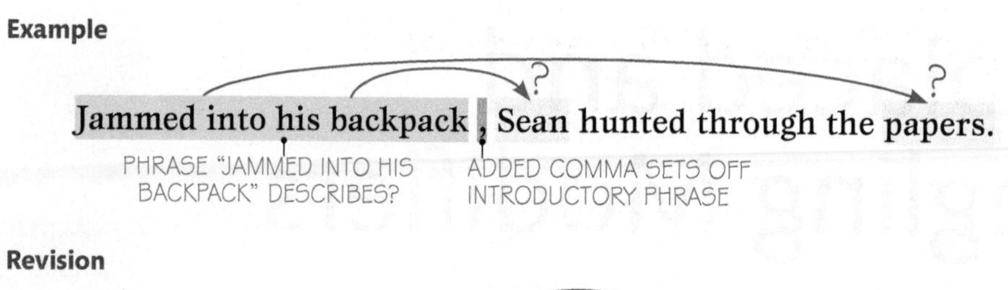

Revision

Sean hunted through the papers jammed into his backpack.

PHRASE "JAMMED INTO HIS BACKPACK" DESCRIBES "PAPERS"

MISPLACED CLAUSE A dependent clause that describes a particular word is placed next to the wrong word and is separated from the word the clause describes.

Example

CLAUSE "WHO GAVE BIRTH TO TWINS" DESCRIBES?

The 60-year-old woman was hounded by the reporter who gave birth to twins.

Revision

CLAUSE "WHO GAVE BIRTH TO TWINS" DESCRIBES "WOMAN"

The 60-year-old woman who gave birth to twins was hounded by the reporter.

L2 Edit Dangling Modifiers

A **dangling modifier** is a phrase that describes a word not stated in the sentence.

EXAMPLES What or whom do these phrases describe in each sentence below?

Sentence #1

While cleaning the house, a fifty dollar bill turned up.

Sentence #2

Observing the wildlife, the canoe glided through the waters.

Sentence #3

Running in second place, the finish line came into view.

Dangling Modifiers: Two Revision Tips

REVISION TIP #1 Change the dangling modifier into a logical clause with a subject and a verb.

Revised Sentence #1

ADDED SUBJECT AND VERB TO CREATE DEPENDENT CLAUSE

While I was cleaning the house, a fifty dollar bill turned up.

Revised Sentence #2

ADDED SUBORDINATING CONJUNCTION, SUBJECT, AND VERB TO CREATE DEPENDENT CLAUSE

As we were observing the wildlife, the canoe glided through the waters.

Revised Sentence #3

ADDED SUBJECT AND VERB TO CREATE INDEPENDENT CLAUSE

I was running in second place; the finish line came into view.

ADDED SEMICOLON JOINS TWO INDEPENDENT CLAUSES

REVISION TIP #2 Revise the main clause to include the word being modified.

Revised Sentence #1

PHRASE "WHILE CLEANING THE HOUSE" DESCRIBES ADDED SUBJECT

While cleaning the house, I found a fifty dollar bill.

ADDED SUBJECT AND VERB

Revised Sentence #2

PHRASE "OBSERVING THE WILDLIFE" DESCRIBES ADDED SUBJECT

Observing the wildlife, we glided the canoe through the waters.

ADDED SUBJECT

Revised Sentence #3

PHRASE "RUNNING IN SECOND PLACE" DESCRIBES ADDED SUBJECT

Running in second place, I saw the finish line come into view.

ADDED SUBJECT AND VERB

MySkillsLab™

Complete the Post-test for Module 19 in MySkillsLab.

20

LEARNING OUTCOMES

After studying this module you should be able to:

LO 1 Format and Punctuate Direct Quotations

LO 2 Use Speech Tags with Direct Quotations

LO 3 Use Quotation Marks Correctly with Titles

Quotation Marks

Quotation marks are used to set off exact words either written or spoken by other people or to set off titles of short works.

LO 1 Format and Punctuate Direct Quotations

1. Place commas (,) and periods (.) inside the quotation marks (" ").

The article said gangs and guns contributed to "a nationwide crime spike."

PERIOD GOES INSIDE QUOTATION MARK

QUOTATION MARKS ENCLOSE EXACT WORDS FROM THE ARTICLE

2. Place semicolons (;) and colons (:) outside the quotation marks.

QUOTATION MARKS ENCLOSE EXACT WORDS OF THE SPEAKER "WE"

We must say "no more violence"; we must strengthen gun control laws.

SEMICOLON GOES OUTSIDE QUOTATION MARK

3. Place a question mark (?) inside quotation marks when it is part of the quotation. Place a question mark outside quotation marks when the larger sentence is a question, but the quotation included in it is not.

QUOTATION MARKS ENCLOSE EXACT WORDS OF THE SPEAKER "WE"

We should ask, "How does violence in movies and music affect youth?"

QUESTION MARK GOES INSIDE QUOTATION MARK BECAUSE IT IS PART OF THE QUOTATION. (THE QUOTATION IS A QUESTION.)

QUOTATION MARKS ENCLOSE EXACT WORDS OF THE SPEAKER "WE"

Did she really say "no more violence"?

QUESTION MARK GOES OUTSIDE QUOTATION MARK BECAUSE THE SENTENCE ITSELF IS A QUESTION, BUT THE QUOTATION INCLUDED IN IT IS NOT.

4. Use single quotation marks for quoted information—or titles of short works—that appear within a direct quotation.

DOUBLE QUOTATION MARK INDICATES START OF QUOTED MATERIAL FROM NEWSPAPER

The *USA Today* article reports, "The Justice Department promises '$50 million this year to combat gangs and guns.' "

SINGLE QUOTATION MARK INDICATES START OF QUOTED MATERIAL FROM JUSTICE DEPARTMENT

SINGLE QUOTATION MARK INDICATES END OF QUOTED MATERIAL FROM JUSTICE DEPARTMENT. DOUBLE QUOTATION MARK INDICATES END OF QUOTED MATERIAL FROM NEWSPAPER

Use Speech Tags with Direct Quotations

L2

One part of a direct quotation is the **speech tag** or the credit given to the source, the person who spoke or wrote an idea. A speech tag is formed by a subject (the speaker) and a verb that indicates the subject is speaking. The following examples highlight the correct use of commas, periods, capitalization, and quotation marks based on the placement of the speech tag.

- **Speech tag at the beginning of quote**

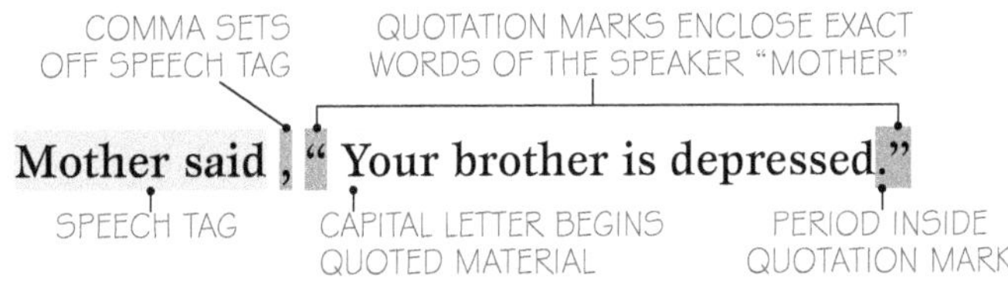

- **Speech tag in the middle of quote**

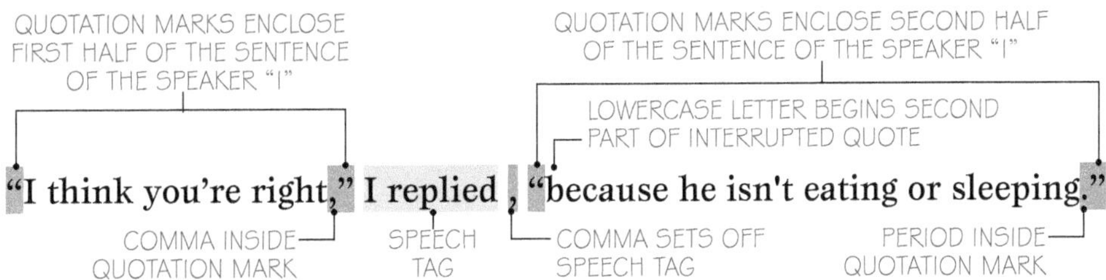

- **Speech tag at the end of quote**

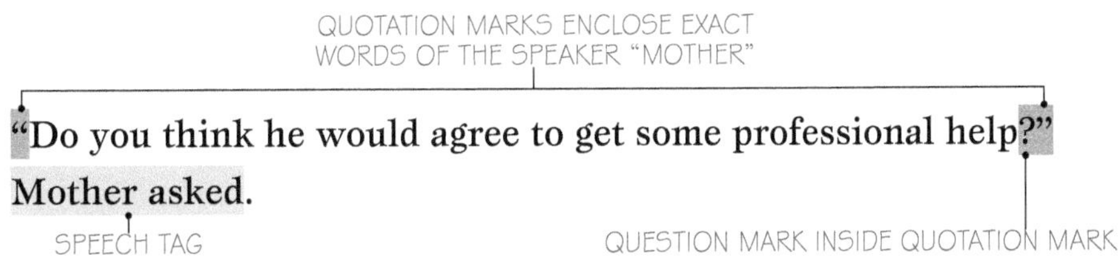

L3 Use Quotation Marks Correctly with Titles

Quotation marks are also used to set off the titles of short works such as essays, short stories, short poems, songs, articles in magazines, TV episodes, and chapter titles in books.

- Follow the general rules for using quotation marks.
- Do not use quotation marks to set off titles of larger publications such as magazines, newspapers, and books. These larger publications are set off with italics.

> Enrique Iglesias scored a big hit with the release of his single "Dimelo."

QUOTATION MARKS SET OFF SONG TITLE

MySkillsLab™

Complete the Post-test for Module 20 in MySkillsLab.

The Apostrophe

The apostrophe is used to show ownership and to form contractions by replacing omitted letters or numbers.

21

LEARNING OUTCOMES

After studying this module you should be able to:

L1 Use the Apostrophe to Show Ownership

L2 Use the Apostrophe for Contractions

L3 Avoid Common Misuses of the Apostrophe

Use the Apostrophe to Show Ownership L1

The **possessive form** of a noun and some pronouns is created by using an apostrophe followed, at times, by an -*s*. The possessive tells the reader that someone or something owns or possesses the next stated thing.

The following chart lists and illustrates the rules for using an apostrophe to show possession.

Using the Apostrophe for Ownership		
To Show Possession for	**Correct Use of Apostrophe**	**Example**
A singular noun	add 's	my husband's job
A singular noun ending with -*s*	add ' or add 's	the boss' memo or James's home
A regular plural noun ending with -*s*	add '	the writers' colony
An irregular plural noun	add 's	women's clothing

Using the Apostrophe for Ownership (*continued*)		
To Show Possession for	**Correct Use of Apostrophe**	**Example**
Compound words	add 's	vice president's speech sister-in-law's business (Note: Do not confuse the possessive form with the plural form, as in *sisters-in-law*)
Joint ownership of an item	add 's to the last noun	Abbott and Costello's comedy
Individual ownership	add 's to the end of both nouns	Leigh's and Rob's cars (Each person owns a car.)
Indefinite pronouns ending with *one* or *body*	add 's	someone's computer

L2 Use the Apostrophe for Contractions

An apostrophe is used to indicate the omission of letters to form a *contraction*. Most often, a **contraction** is formed to join two words to make one shorter word such as *don't* for *do not*. An apostrophe (') takes the place of the letter or letters that are dropped to form the contraction.

The following chart illustrates how contracted verbs are formed.

Apostrophe Use in Common Contractions The apostrophe replaces omitted letters.	
'm APOSTROPHE REPLACES "A" IN "I AM" I am = I'm	's APOSTROPHE REPLACES "I" IN "IS" it is = it's
're APOSTROPHE REPLACES "A" IN "YOU ARE" you are = you're	've APOSTROPHE REPLACES "HA" IN "I HAVE" I have = I've
n't APOSTROPHE REPLACES "O" IN "IS NOT" is not = isn't	'll APOSTROPHE REPLACES "WI" IN "WILL" I will = I'll

Avoid Common Misuses of the Apostrophe

L3

The apostrophe is frequently misused in several specific ways. The following chart lists and illustrates these common misuses of the apostrophe. Always base your use of an apostrophe on a specific rule. Proofread your writing for these common mistakes.

- **Do not use an apostrophe to form a plural noun.**

Correct Plural	Incorrect Plural
homes books	home's book's

- **Do not use an apostrophe to form a possessive pronoun.**

Correct	Incorrect
ours hers theirs	our's her's their's

- **Do not omit the apostrophe to form the possessive indefinite pronoun.**

Correct	Incorrect
one's everybody's	ones everybodys

- **Do not confuse contractions with similar sounding words.**

Contraction	Possessive Pronoun
it's (it is) who's (who is) they're (they are)	its whose their

MySkillsLab™
Complete the Post-test for Module 21 in MySkillsLab.

22

LEARNING OUTCOMES

After studying this module you should be able to:

LO1 Apply the Rules for Improving Your Spelling

Rule 1: Understand How Suffixes Are Used

Rule 2: Add *-s* or *-es* to Nouns and Verbs to Form the Plural

Rule 3: Double the Final Consonant in Words with One Syllable

Rule 4: Double the Final Consonant in Words with More Than One Syllable

Rule 5: Drop or Keep the Final *E*

Rule 6: Change or Keep the Final *Y*

Rule 7: Choose *ie* or *ei*

LO2 Identify Three Reasons for Word Confusion

LO3 Correctly Use 30 Commonly Confused Words

Improving Your Spelling

To spell correctly is to understand the rules for properly arranging letters in a word.

LO1 Rules for Improving Your Spelling

Improving your spelling involves understanding rules about the use of suffixes and prefixes.

RULE 1: Understand How Suffixes Are Used

A **suffix** is added to the end of a **base word** (a word's original meaning) to change the use or meaning of the word. Suffixes begin with either a vowel or a consonant, which affects the spelling rules for adding them to base words. The following chart lists a few common vowel and consonant suffixes, along with their meanings and examples.

Vowel Suffix	Meaning	Example
-able -ible	able to	touchable, visible
-ed	past tense of a verb	talked, walked
-en	present or past participle	bitten, written
-er	one who is or does	player, adopter
-er	comparison	bigger, smaller
-es	plural of a noun	dresses, boxes
-es	singular present tense of a verb	washes, finishes
-ous	full of	dangerous, luxurious

Consonant Suffix	Meaning	Example
-ful	full of	wonderful, careful
-ly or -y	like	gently, grimy
-ness	state of being	happiness, faithfulness
-ment	state of	government, statement
-s	plural of a noun	doctors, workers
-s	singular present tense of a verb	runs, quits

The rules of spelling words with suffixes vary. The next several sections explain and illustrate the various spelling rules for adding suffixes.

RULE 2: Add *-s* or *-es* to Nouns and Verbs to Form the Plural

- **Add *-s* to form the plural of most regular nouns, including those that end with *o*.**

video + s ⟶ videos

- **Add *-es* to nouns that end with a consonant immediately before a final *o*.**

hero + es ⟶ heroes

- **Add *-s* to most regular verbs to form the singular present tense in the third person.**

ask + s ⟶ asks

- **Add *-es* to form the plural of nouns and to third person present tense verbs that end in *ch*, *sh*, *s*, *x*, or *z*.**

Nouns		Verbs	
watch + es	watches	buzz + es	buzzes

RULE 3: Double the Final Consonant in Words with One Syllable

Many **one syllable** words end in a **consonant** with a **vowel** immediately **before** it. (*Hint*: Remember CVC.) For a word with one syllable, one consonant, and one vowel, double the final consonant when adding a vowel suffix. The final consonant is *not* doubled when adding a consonant suffix.

s i t + sits OR sitter

Exception: Do not double the final consonant of words that end in *w*, *x*, or *y* as in the following examples: **snowing, boxer, obeys.**

RULE 4: Double the Final Consonant in Words with More Than One Syllable

Words with more than one syllable often end with a vowel immediately before a **consonant**. (*Hint*: Remember VC.) If the final syllable is stressed or emphasized in its pronunciation, **double the final consonant**.

control controlled controlling

RULE 5: Drop or Keep the Final *E*

- **Drop the *e* when the *base word ends* with a *silent e* and the *suffix begins* with a *vowel.***

advance + -ing ⟶ advancing

- **Drop the *e* when a *vowel comes immediately before* the silent *e*.**

true + -ly ⟶ truly

- **Keep the *e* when the *base word ends* with a silent *e* and the *suffix begins* with a *consonant.***

advance + -ment ⟶ advancement

RULE 6: Change or Keep the Final *Y*

- **When a *consonant* appears before the final *y*, change the *y* to *i*.**

supply + -ies ⟶ supplies

- **When a *vowel* appears before the final *y*, keep the *y*.**

obey + -ed ⟶ obeyed

- **Keep the *y* when adding the suffix *-ing*.**

cry + -ing ⟶ crying

RULE 7: Choose *ie* or *ei*

A helpful way to remember how to use *ie* and *ei* in spelling is to think of the following rhyme:

"*i* before *e* except after *c* or when sounds like *ay* as in *neighbor* or *weigh*"

There are, however, some exceptions to the *ie*, *ei* rule that should be memorized:

ie: species, science, conscience

ei: height, either, neither, leisure, seize, counterfeit, foreign

Identify Three Reasons for Word Confusion

REASON #1: Words Sound Alike But Have Different Meanings

Words that sound alike are called *homophones*. Although these words sound similar, they differ in meaning, function, and sometimes spelling.

Word		Meaning
Aloud	(adverb)	with the use of the voice, speaking, orally, loudly
Allowed	(verb)	permitted, planned for

ADVERB MEANING "SPEAKING" — VERB MEANING "PLANNED FOR"

He wondered **aloud**, "You should have **allowed** more time for the project."

REASON #2: Words Sometimes Have a Similar Meaning

Some words differ in sound and spelling, but are close in meaning and sometimes serve the same function in a sentence.

Word		Meaning
Among	(preposition)	used to discuss a group of three or more people or things
Between	(preposition)	used to discuss a pair of (two) people or things

PREPOSITION INDICATING TWO OR MORE PEOPLE — PREPOSITION INDICATING A GROUP OF THREE OR MORE

Agreement is easier to achieve **between** two people than **among** a group.

REASON #3: Words Are Sometimes Used Improperly

Words may sound alike, but they serve different functions in a sentence.

Improper Use of Pronouns	
Contractions	blend two words into one: **You're** is a contraction of the second-person pronoun you and the verb **are** .
Pronouns	act as replacements or substitutes for nouns or noun phrases: Your is the second-person possessive pronoun.

CONTRACTION MEANING "YOU ARE" — SECOND-PERSON POSSESSIVE PRONOUN INDICATES THAT THE HOUSE BELONGS TO "YOU"

You're going to **your** house.

Improper Use of Adjectives with Adverbs

ADJECTIVES describe nouns and pronouns: **Bad** means poor, unfavorable.

ADVERBS describe verbs, adjectives, and other adverbs, often with the *-ly* suffix: **BADLY** means poorly, unfavorably, very much.

ADVERB MEANING "VERY MUCH" DESCRIBES PARTICIPLE "INJURED"

ADJECTIVE MEANING "UNFAVORABLE" DESCRIBES NOUN "RECORD"

Badly injured, Jerome also faces a bad record for driving badly.

ADVERB MEANING "POORLY" DESCRIBES VERB "DRIVING"

L3 Correctly Use 30 Commonly Confused Words

The rest of this module offers a glossary of 30 sets of commonly confused words, their definitions and functions, and examples of their proper use. The words are listed alphabetically in groups of five. As you study these words, think about why they are often confused and how you will use them to achieve clear and effective expression.

Often-Confused Words	Part of Speech	Meaning
Accept, Except		
Accept	verb	to receive willingly
Except	preposition	but, not including

PREPOSITION MEANING "NOT INCLUDING"

VERB MEANING "WILLINGLY RECEIVES"

Everyone except Bob accepts responsibility.

Advice, Advise		
Advice	noun	guidance
Advise	verb	to offer guidance, to recommend

VERB MEANING "RECOMMEND"

NOUN MEANING "GUIDANCE"

We advise you to follow the advice of your doctor.

Affect, Effect		
Affect	verb	to influence
Effect	noun	result, outcome
Effect	verb	result in, cause to come into being

The effects of the painkiller affect her emotions.

Constant studying effected a high GPA.

Allot, A lot		
Allot	verb	to assign portions of, to distribute
A lot	modifier	much, large amounts

The city wants a lot of power so officials can allot water for residential use.

All ready, Already		
All ready	adverb	completely prepared
Already	adverb	previously, before now

He has already asked me if I am all ready for the cookout.

Beside, Besides		
Beside	preposition	by the side of
Besides	preposition	except, other than, together with

Besides just visiting, Jordan takes a moment to sit beside his mother.

By, Bye, Buy		
By	preposition	near, beside, or through
Bye	interjection	farewell: an expression of leave-taking
Buy	verb	to purchase

INTERJECTION MEANING "FAREWELL" — PREPOSITION MEANING "BESIDE" — VERB MEANING "TO PURCHASE"

Tamar said "bye" to her friends and then drove by the house she wanted to buy.

Brake, Break		
Brake	verb	to stop
Brake	noun	a device that slows or stops
Break	verb	to smash, fracture, shatter
Break	noun	a time of rest

VERB MEANING "FRACTURES" — NOUN MEANING "DEVICE THAT STOPS A CAR" — NOUN MEANING "REST"

Jon breaks his leg when his brakes fail, so he takes a break from work.

Clothes, Cloths		
Clothes	noun	garments, personal articles made of cloth
Cloths	noun	pliable material

NOUN MEANING "GARMENTS" — NOUN MEANING "PLIABLE MATERIAL"

These clothes are made of soft and silky cloths.

Coarse, Course		
Coarse	adjective	rough
Course	noun	path, direction, part of a meal, an academic class

ADJECTIVE MEANING "ROUGH" DESCRIBES NOUN "GRASS" — NOUN MEANING "PATH"

He hit the ball into the coarse grass on the edge of the golf course.

NOUN MEANING "ACADEMIC CLASSES"

She took courses in gourmet cooking, so she learned to cook meals with five courses.

NOUN MEANING "PARTS OF A MEAL"

Farther, Further		
Farther	adverb	to a greater distance or more advanced point
Further	adjective	additional
Further	adverb	to advance

ADJECTIVE MEANING "ADDITIONAL" DESCRIBES NOUN "STUDIES"

ADVERB MEANING "TO A GREATER DISTANCE" DESCRIBES VERB "CAN TRAVEL"

Further studies will reveal how much farther we can travel in space.

Fewer, Less		
Fewer	adjective	smaller number (count)
Less	adjective	smaller amount (noncount)

ADJECTIVE MEANING "SMALLER NUMBER" DESCRIBES NOUN "COMPLAINTS"

ADJECTIVE MEANING "SMALLER AMOUNT" DESCRIBES NOUN "RESENTMENT"

Fewer complaints mean less resentment.

Good, Well		
Good	adjective	having favorable qualities, best
Well	adverb	done in a good or proper manner

ADJECTIVE MEANING "BEST" DESCRIBES NOUN "STUDENT"

ADVERB MEANING "IN A PROPER MANNER" DESCRIBES VERB "STUDIES"

The good student studies well.

Hear, Here		
Hear	verb	to perceive sound
Here	adverb	in or at this place

ADVERB MEANING "AT THIS PLACE" DESCRIBES VERB "STAND"

VERB MEANING "PERCEIVE SOUND"

Stand here to hear well.

Its, It's		
Its	pronoun	singular third-person possessive case
It's	subject/verb	contraction of *it is*

CONTRACTION OF SUBJECT AND VERB "IT IS"

POSSESSIVE PRONOUN "ITS" REFERS TO NOUN ANTECEDENT "DOG"

It's time for the dog to get its shots.

ANTECEDENT OF PRONOUN "ITS"

OBJECT BEING POSSESSED

Knew, New, Know, No		
Knew	verb, past tense	recognized, understood
New	adjective	recent, fresh
Know	verb, present tense	to recognize, understand
No	adverb	negative
No	adjective	not any

ADVERB MEANING "NEGATIVE" DESCRIBES VERB "DOUBTING"

ADJECTIVE MEANING "NOT ANY" DESCRIBES "NEW"

ADJECTIVE MEANING "RECENT" DESCRIBES NOUN "FACTS"

There's no doubting that I know now what you knew then; there are no new facts.

PRESENT TENSE VERB MEANING "UNDERSTAND"

PAST TENSE VERB MEANING "UNDERSTOOD"

Lay, Lie		
Lay	verb, present tense	to place
Lay	verb, past tense	reclined
Lie	verb, present tense	to recline
Lie	verb, present tense	to tell a falsehood
Lie	noun	a falsehood

PRESENT TENSE VERB MEANING "TELL A FALSEHOOD" — PAST TENSE VERB MEANING "RECLINE" — PRESENT TENSE VERB MEANING "PLACE"

I cannot lie; before, I lay in bed; now I lie on the sofa and lay the remote control nearby; that's no lie.

NOUN MEANING "FALSEHOOD" — PRESENT TENSE VERB MEANING "RECLINE"

Passed, Past		
Passed	verb, past tense	moved, proceeded, went
Past	noun	a time gone by
Past	adjective	ago, just gone or elapsed
Past	preposition	beyond

NOUN MEANING "TIME GONE BY" — PREPOSITION MEANING "BEYOND" — ADJECTIVE MEANING "ELAPSED" DESCRIBES NOUN "MONTH"

In the past, Aleta couldn't get past her fear, but in the past month, she passed the test.

VERB MEANING "MOVED THROUGH"

Principal, Principle		
Principal	noun	a person, matter, or thing of chief importance or authority
Principal	adjective	most important
Principle	noun	a rule, code, or standard

NOUN MEANING "PERSON OF AUTHORITY" — NOUN MEANING "RULES" — ADJECTIVE MEANING "MOST IMPORTANT" DESCRIBES NOUN "TASK"

The principal is a person who sets helpful principles as his principal task.

Quiet, Quit, Quite		
Quiet	noun	silence
Quiet	verb	to silence
Quiet	adjective	silent
Quit	verb	to stop
Quite	adverb	wholly, completely to an extreme

VERB MEANING "SILENCE"

ADVERB MEANING "COMPLETELY" DESCRIBES ADJECTIVE MEANING "SILENT"

Quiet yourself: quit talking and be quite quiet to achieve quiet.

VERB MEANING "STOP"

NOUN MEANING "SILENCE"

Raise, Rise		
Raise	verb	to cause to rise, to lift
Rise	verb	to assume an upright position from lying, kneeling, or sitting; to stand

VERB MEANING "STAND" VERB MEANING "LIFT"

Rise to your feet and raise your right hand to take an oath.

Sit, Set		
Sit	verb	to rest on the buttocks
Set	verb	to place

VERB MEANING "PLACE" VERB MEANING "REST ON YOUR BUTTOCKS"

Set the program on the chair where you will sit.

Than, Then		
Than	preposition	in comparison with
Then	adverb	at that time, following next, in that case

PREPOSITION MEANING "IN COMPARISON WITH" ADVERB MEANING "IN THAT CASE"

If you like Chinese food better than Italian, then make reservations at the China Garden.

Their, There, They're		
Their	pronoun	plural third-person possessive
There	adverb	in or at that place
They're	pronoun/verb	contraction of *they are*

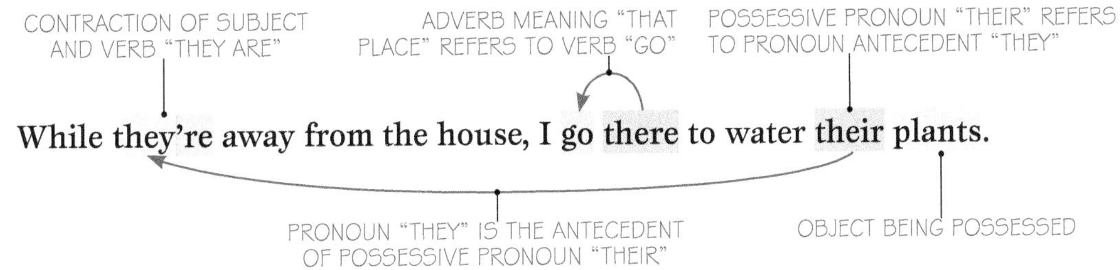

Threw, Through		
Threw	verb, past tense	to propel through the air
Through	preposition, adverb, adjective	in one side and out another

PAST TENSE VERB MEANING "PROPELLED THROUGH THE AIR" PREPOSITION MEANING "IN AND OUT"

Manny threw the ball through the hoop.

To, Too, Two		
To	preposition	movement toward, indicates direction
To	forms the infinitive	to be
Too	adverb	besides, also, excessively
Two	adjective, noun	one more in number than one

ADJECTIVE MEANING "ONE MORE IN NUMBER THAN ONE" DESCRIBES NOUN "TACOS"

ADVERB MEANING "EXCESSIVELY" DESCRIBES ADVERB "QUICKLY"

I went to the store to get two tacos; I ate them too quickly.

PREPOSITION MEANING "MOVEMENT TOWARD"

INFINITIVE VERB MEANING "THE ACT OF OBTAINING"

Waist, Waste		
Waist	noun	middle section of body between ribs and hips
Waste	noun	garbage, refuse
Waste	verb	to misuse, to ruin, to wear away

NOUN MEANING "GARBAGE"

NOUN MEANING "MID-SECTION OF THE BODY"

Leftover food that's thrown out creates waste. I am watching my waist.

The community wasted their resources.

VERB MEANING "RUINED"

Wear, Where, Were, We're		
Wear	verb, present tense	to clothe, to put on
Where	adverb	at what place
Were	verb, past tense	plural past tense of *to be*
We're	pronoun/verb	contraction of *we are*

CONTRACTION OF PRONOUN AND VERB "WE ARE"

ADVERB MEANING "TO A PLACE" DESCRIBES VERB "ARE GOING"

We were going to dress up, but now we're going where we can wear jeans.

PAST-TENSE VERB FORM OF "TO BE"

VERB MEANING "PUT ON"

Weather, Whether		
Weather	noun	atmospheric conditions
Weather	verb	to endure
Whether	conjunction	if, alternative choices

Whether the weather is fair or not, we will play the match.

Whose, Who's		
Whose	pronoun	third-person possessive
Who's	pronoun/verb	contraction of *who is*

Who's going to find out whose jacket this is?

MySkillsLab™

Complete the Post-Test for Module 22 in MySkillsLab.

A Reading Strategy for a Writer

Eleven Reading Selections

An Account of Alfred C. Cooley's Plight in the Face of Hurricane Katrina / SANDRA OFFIAH-HAWKINS 552

Seven Ages of Man from *As You Like It* / WILLIAM SHAKESPEARE 560

Niagara Falls / RUPERT BROOKE 565

Beauty from Ashes / ANNE SMITH 573

***A Doll's House*, a Scene from Act III** / HENRIK IBSEN 584

Fannie Lou Hamer / MAYA ANGELOU 594

I Hear America Singing / WALT WHITMAN 600

Shaking Hands / EDWARD EVERETT 605

On the Difference Between Wit and Humor / CHARLES S. BROOKS 612

The Morality of Birth Control / MARGARET SANGER 620

Nobel Lecture: The Nobel Peace Prize, 2014 / MALALA YOUSAFZAI 628

Reading Selections

Reading and writing are mirror reflections of the thinking process.

A Reading Strategy for a Writer

As you read the eleven selections included in this section, use the following reading strategy to make the connection between reading and writing. Read each selection three times. Read it once just to enjoy the writing. Then reread the piece to annotate it for understanding. Finally, read a third time to study the piece more closely to prepare for a written response. The following steps are a guide to how to get the most out of your reading.

Reading Like a Writer

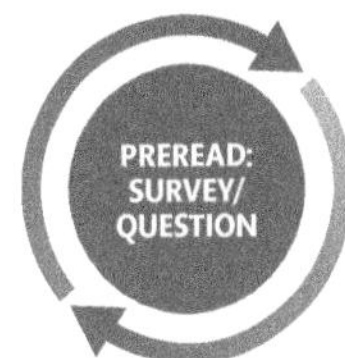

Before Reading

Write a journal entry about the topic, title, and vocabulary. What do you already know, believe, or feel about the topic? Skim the text to identify new or difficult words and look them up.

During Reading

Annotate the text. Underline or highlight key terms, definitions, and main ideas. Generate questions to guide your thinking as you read; these questions will help you recall information after you read. Look for the answers to these questions and annotate the text when you come across the answers. Many college textbooks provide comprehension questions after a section of information. Feel free to use these after reading questions to focus your attention as you read.

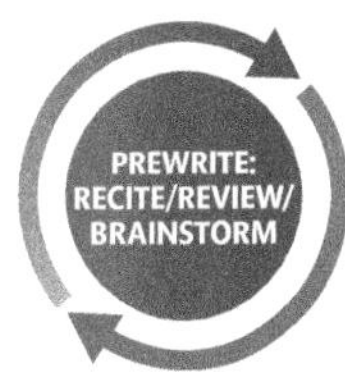

After Reading

Think, discuss, and write about what you read. Each of the eleven reading selections has four discussion questions about the writer's main idea, relevant details, logical order, and effective expression. These directed thinking activities are called "After Reading Discussion Questions: Meaning, Structure, and Expression." Your writing will improve as you learn how other writers handle these elements.

Discuss It

Use your annotations to compare your views about a text with those of your classmates. Be open to ideas you had not considered. Add information to your notes. Discuss possible written responses.

Write About It

Respond in writing to the text. Each of the reading selections has several writing prompts. The first set of prompts are under the heading "After Reading Discussion Questions: Meaning, Structure, and Expression." These questions ask you to respond to the reading selection by analyzing and evaluating the techniques used by the writer of the selection. You may choose to model your own writing on some of the techniques you study. The second type of prompt is under the heading "Reader Response." These prompts ask you to respond to the text by composing your own piece of writing. Be sure to use the full writing process to prewrite, draft, review, revise, and proofread your writing.

Eleven Reading Selections

READING 1
Narration

An Account of Alfred C. Cooley's Plight in the Face of Hurricane Katrina

SANDRA OFFIAH-HAWKINS

Sandra Offiah-Hawkins is a Senior Professor at Daytona State College in Daytona Beach, Florida, where she has taught English and reading for more than twenty-one years. She is a Kellogg Scholar and has attended, spoken, chaired/co-chaired at state, national, and international conferences (including the University of Santiago de Compostella, in Spain, The University of Ireland in Dublin, and the International Conference on Research and Access in Developmental Education in Puerto Rico). She has also performed as the lead actress in *I Leave You Love,* based on the life and legacy of eighty-year-old Dr. Mary McLeod Bethune, and as Mama in *A Raisin in the Sun*. The following real-life account is one of many non-fiction articles she has written.

Before Reading

Write a journal entry about your experience with dangerous weather or a natural event. Describe a time when you experienced severe weather, such as a thunderstorm, wildfire, flooding, or some other natural disturbance. Describe the details of the event, how you felt, and what you did to stay safe.

Vocabulary

Before, during, and after reading the selection, annotate the text and write in your journal. Create a list of vocabulary words and supply their definitions. Give examples of how the words are used in the selection you just read.

1 I am **aghast** by the sudden series of events. There is no time to figure out the next day, for there is no time to visualize where we are going to all sleep this night—new, used, and old cars line up along Interstate 10 and Highway 1 as we all travel 10 miles an hour and wait in five-mile long lines in hopes of getting gas before the stations run out. There are thirty-five of us traveling in a caravan: a Dodge Caravan, a Ford Taurus, a 2000 Grand Prix, and a Toyota CRV just to name a few. All the relatives we can contact in New Orleans on this day August 27, 2005, are with us; we have been asked to leave our homes immediately, for the strong winds, the deluging rain, the terrible wrath of Hurricane Katrina is headed straight to New Orleans—our home.

2 All of us leave our worldly possessions that day, bringing with us essentials for two days: I never think for a minute this is the end of what I have called home in the Ninth Ward for more than 50 years; all of us feel this is going to be a "James Brown turnaround." I never think the wife and children I have been blessed with over the past 30 years would never again know life as they had known it in New Orleans.

3 Throughout my life, I have known suffering: I suffer from Sickle Cell Anemia; my parents were told that I would not live past age 16, but here I am! Within the last eight years, I have had two hip replacements as well as operations on my shoulder and on my left eye. I have been placed in a situation of sometimes raising my four daughters as a single parent, and for many years, I have cared for my aging parents. Now this—the unanticipated fury of Katrina.

4 Once the storm hits, the power, as expected, is off for days in New Orleans, so it is Tuesday evening or Wednesday before we find out the Levee has broken. Since we left home on Saturday, we have been traveling—first to Alexandria, Louisiana, where we sleep wherever there is a space on the floor at Dora Ann's house, my sister's former daughter-in-law's home. The next day, we plan our next move: my parents, sisters, and one brother stay there, but the remaining sixteen of us head East on I-10 towards Memphis, Tennessee, to the home of Stanley Trotter, my ex-wife's cousin, where there were now 20 people sharing a house.

5 As the sixteen of us from New Orleans sit and watch television, we see the water begin to cover the roof of the familiar Circle Food Store, on North Clayborne Avenue and St. Bernard Avenue near the home we just abandoned; we realize now, we will not be returning home.

CONTINUED

READING SELECTION 1 *CONTINUED*

It is extremely difficult for anyone watching the news, but it has to be most difficult for those of us witnessing everything we have worked for being destroyed right before our eyes; we have no idea what we should do or where we should go from here; we begin to mourn for friends and neighbors gone from our lives forever. We continue watching as the Super Dome and Convention Center prove to be inadequate for the more than three thousand people seeking shelter and assistance; we listen to the reports of water leaks and criminals raping people in the Dome; we watch the people standing along the bridge in the smoldering heat with no sanitation, no food, no water; we see dead people floating in the water; we see another person dead in a wheelchair—not even covered. "Why is help so slow to arrive?" we cry out at the television. 6

My heart is truly heavy, and I can barely watch or believe what I am witnessing on television. During this time, I think of my brother and his adult son, Robert Jr., both of whom remained in New Orleans when we left: I pray to God they survive—not knowing until days later that they have located a car and driven to Alexandria to be with my parents and other siblings; I pray to God they survive—not knowing that they have returned to help the people and the clean-up efforts in the areas hit hardest by Katrina and the tornadoes that followed. 7

My mind drifts in time back to my uncles' and aunts' homes in Picayune, Mississippi, less than an hour's drive from New Orleans, and I think about all of my relatives living there: my cousins, my grandmothers, and paternal grandfather—I contemplate memories of Pilgrim Bound Baptist Church and other churches as the neighborhood readies for the 5th Sunday Singing. Every fifth Sunday, all the churches in the area gather as members from the various congregations hope for an opportunity to be placed on the program to sing two selections each. Reverend Woods, the announcer, is always filled with the Holy Spirit as he listens to the lyrics of songs and hymns both old and new: "What a Friend We Have in Jesus," "Amazing Grace," "Do Lord Remember Me," and "Jesus Paid It All." My father, brothers, and I would often travel to participate in the program as an all-male guest quartet from New Orleans, LA. 8

Oh, I will never forget those days—they remain an inspiring part of my life because I had an opportunity to meet many people; some I had forgotten until now: Mrs. Jewel had a candy store next door to where my grandmother, aunt, and uncle lived; only a few blocks away, Bossie Boys, a place where 9 teenagers would meet and dance on the weekends, was located just a few feet from my Uncle Bishop's barber shop.

In the wake of Katrina, we move to Atoka, Tennessee, and it does 10
not take long for people to hear about the sixteen people who fled New Orleans. I shall never forget—Mrs. Snead of St. Mark Baptist Church and Pastor McGee alert church members, the fire department, and other social agencies about our plight; church members help us get food and clothing and raise money so that we can begin reestablishing ourselves; through the Red Cross, we are able to obtain proper documentation for identification. No, I shall never forget—all the blessings that flowed from throughout the community to my family during these darkest hours.

Finally people are allowed to return briefly to New Orleans to check 11
out their property and help others during the aftermath of Katrina—I am anxious. My son-in-law Javelle and I rent a van to go back and **salvage** what we can. On the way, a police cruiser clocks my speed on the highway at 89 mph in a 70 mph zone; I tell the officer who I am, where I am going and why I am going there; he makes me prove that I have lived in New Orleans all of my life; then, he voids my ticket with a warning to slow down. How ironic—I have to prove that I am a "real" life-long New Orleans "native."

Getting off of Highway 610 at Franklin Avenue, we can see the marks 12
of high water levels, and so much trash—garbage and debris strewn everywhere—we see the damage, the loss, and oh so much more—we see a holocaust: we see wind damage; we see cars flipped on their sides; we see homes with nothing more than a frame of what once was; we see X's marked on still-standing homes, with a number 1, 2, 3, or more to indicate the dead inside.

When you have a near death experience, it is said, your life flashes 13
before you. That is exactly my experience during Katrina. Burdens are heavy, I cannot sleep, and I worry about my family; days pass, and I know the end of my life is near: I now realize that it is the end of my life as I have known it—as I walk in what was once my parents' home on Clouet Street. I see just how high the water had come, and there, I raise my hands to lift several pictures off the wall.

CONTINUED

Reading Comprehension Questions

Choose the best meaning of each word in **bold**. Use context clues to make your choice.

Vocabulary in Context

_____ **1.** "I am **aghast** by the sudden series of events." (paragraph 1)

a. excited
b. puzzled
c. horrified
d. unaffected

Vocabulary in Context

_____ **2.** My son-in-law Javelle and I rent a van to go back and **salvage** what we can." (paragraph 11)

a. sell
b. destroy
c. recover
d. fix

Implied Central Idea

_____ **3.** Which sentence best states the author's implied central idea?

a. Hurricane Katrina destroyed Alfred C. Cooley's home in New Orleans.
b. Hurricane Katrina dramatically and unexpectedly changed the lives of Alfred C. Cooley, his family, and other victims of the storm.
c. Alfred C. Cooley and his family suffered more than most who lived through Hurricane Katrina.
d. The people of New Orleans did not receive adequate help during Hurricane Katrina.

Supporting Details

_____ **4.** When the family evacuated New Orleans they took

a. essentials for two days.
b. nothing.
c. everything they owned.
d. supplies for a month.

Transitions

_____ **5.** "No, I shall never forget—all the blessings that flowed from throughout the community to my family during these darkest hours. Finally people were allowed to return briefly to New Orleans. . . ." (paragraphs 10–11)

The relationship of ideas **between** these sentences is

a. cause and effect.
b. time order.
c. comparison and contrast.
d. generalization-example.

Patterns of Organization

_____ **6.** The overall pattern of organization of the passage is

a. time order.

b. cause and effect.

c. comparison and contrast.

d. definition-example.

Fact and Opinion

_____ **7.** "I am aghast by the sudden turn of events." (paragraph 1)

This sentence is a statement of

a. fact.

b. opinion.

c. fact and opinion.

Tone and Purpose

_____ **8.** The overall tone and purpose of the author is

a. to amuse the reader with a personal story about living through Hurricane Katrina.

b. to frankly inform the reader about the suffering caused by Hurricane Katrina.

c. to convince the reader to give aid to the survivors of Hurricane Katrina.

Inferences

_____ **9.** Based on the details in paragraph 10, we can infer that Cooley

a. was reluctant to ask for help.

b. resented having to rely on others for help.

c. felt grateful to the people who helped his family.

d. begged others for help.

Argument

_____ **10.** The following group of statements from paragraph 3 includes a claim and its supporting details. Which statement asserts the claim?

a. "Throughout my life, I have known suffering."

b. "I suffer from Sickle Cell Anemia; my parents were told that I would not live past age 16, but here I am!"

c. "Within the last eight years, I have had two hip replacements as well as operations on my shoulder and on my left eye."

d. "Now this—the unanticipated fury of Katrina."

CONTINUED

Outlining

Complete the following outline with information from the passage.

An Account of Alfred C. Cooley's Plight

I. Evacuating ____________________

A. Traveling in a ____________________

B. Leaving worldly possessions behind

II. ____________________

A. ____________________

B. Operations: two hip replacements, shoulder, left eye

III. Since we left home

IV. Watching the news

V. Remembering Picayune

VI. In the wake of Katrina

A. Getting help in ____________________

B. Returning briefly to New Orleans

After Reading Discussion Questions: Meaning, Structure, and Expression

1. **Central Idea:** Work with a group to write a summary that answers the following questions: What purpose did Sandra Offiah-Hawkins have for writing this essay? Who is her intended audience? What is the central point of the essay? What is the significance of the title?
2. **Relevant Details:** Offiah-Hawkins compares the scene in New Orleans in the aftermath of Hurricane Katrina to a holocaust. What details does she give to support this comparison? Do you think this is an appropriate comparison? Why or why not?
3. **Logical Order:** Reread the concluding paragraph of the essay. Why do you think Offiah-Hawkins ended with Cooley raising his "hands to lift several pictures off the wall"? How is this final act related to the opening action of the essay in its introduction? Do you think this is an effective conclusion? Why or why not?
4. **Effective Expression:** Based on Offiah-Hawkins' use of language, how would you describe the tone of this essay? Is it angry, embarrassed, disappointed, self-pitying, self-righteous, or does it communicate some other attitude? Identify three expressions that illustrate the tone of the piece. Explain the reasons for your selections.

Reader Response

Have you or someone you know survived a natural disaster such as a hurricane, tornado, flood, or wildfire? How did you prepare for or respond to the event? What type of natural disaster is more likely to occur in your area? What advice would you give, or what steps would you take to prepare for a natural disaster? Write a letter to the editor of your local paper to warn about the dangers of a natural disaster that could strike your area. Include steps your readers could take to prepare beforehand.

Master Reading/Writing Scorecard

"An Account of Alfred C. Cooley's Plight in the Face of Hurricane Katrina"

Skill	Number Correct		Points		Total
Vocabulary					
Vocabulary in Context (2 items)	______	x	5	=	______
Comprehension					
Central Idea (1 item)	______	x	10	=	______
Supporting Details (1 item)	______	x	10	=	______
Transitions (1 item)	______	x	10	=	______
Patterns of Organization (1 item)	______	x	10	=	______
Fact and Opinion (1 item)	______	x	10	=	______
Tone and Purpose (1 item)	______	x	10	=	______
Inferences (1 item)	______	x	10	=	______
Argument (1 item)	______	x	10	=	______
Outlining (5 items)	______	x	2	=	______
			Comprehension Score		

READING 2

Process

"Seven Ages of Man" from *As You Like It*, Act II, Scene VII

WILLIAM SHAKESPEARE

William Shakespeare (1564–1616) was an English poet, playwright, and actor, who is widely acclaimed and considered by many to be the quintessential writer in the English language. His body of work, including 38 plays and 154 sonnets, has been translated into every major language and his plays are the most performed of all others. The following passage is a monologue spoken by the melancholy character Jaques in Act II, Scene VII of the comedy *As You Like It.* This passage is one of Shakespeare's most famous and often-quoted speeches.

Before Reading

Write a journal entry about the various stages of life. How many stages are there in human life? How would you characterize each stage?

Vocabulary

Before, during, and after reading the selection, annotate the text and write in your journal. Create a list of vocabulary words and supply their definitions. Give examples of how these words are used in the selection you just read.

All the world's a stage,
And all the men and women merely players,
They have their exits and entrances,
And one man in his time plays many parts,
His acts being seven ages. At first the infant,
Mewling and puking in the nurse's arms.
Then, the whining schoolboy with his satchel
And shining morning face, creeping like snail
Unwillingly to school.
And then the lover,
Sighing like furnace, with a woeful ballad

Made to his mistress' eyebrow.
Then a soldier,
Full of strange oaths, and bearded like the pard,
Jealous in honour, sudden, and quick in quarrel,
Seeking the bubble reputation
Even in the cannon's mouth.
And then the justice In fair round belly, with good capon lin'd,
With eyes severe, and beard of formal cut,
Full of wise **saws**, and modern instances,
And so he plays his part. The sixth age shifts
Into the lean and slippered **pantaloon**,
With spectacles on nose and pouch on side,
His youthful hose, well saved, a world too wide
For his shrunk shank, and his big manly voice,
Turning again toward childish treble, pipes
And whistles in his sound. Last scene of all,
That ends this strange eventful history,
Is second childishness and mere oblivion,
Sans teeth, sans eyes, sans taste, sans everything.

Reading Comprehension Questions

Choose the best meaning of each word in **bold**. Use context clues to make your choice.

Vocabulary in Context

_____ **1.** "Full of wise **saws**, and modern instances," (line 20)

a. chisel
b. scores
c. sayings
d. sounds

Vocabulary in Context

_____ **2.** "Into the lean and slippered **pantaloon**," (line 22)

a. young performer
b. joke
c. underwear
d. old fool

CONTINUED

READING SELECTION 2 *CONTINUED*

Central Idea

_____ **3.** Which line best states the speech's central idea?

a. line 1
b. line 5
c. line 18
d. line 29

Supporting Details

_____ **4.** What characterizes the age of life represented by the soldier?

a. reckless
b. patient
c. fearful
d. dutiful

Transitions

_____ **5.** The relationship of ideas within line 1 is

a. classification.
b. time order.
c. comparison.
d. cause and effect.

Patterns of Organization

_____ **6.** The overall pattern of organization established by lines 6 and 7 is

a. time order.
b. space order.
c. definition-example.
d. contrast.

Fact and Opinion

_____ **7.** This speech mostly offers

a. the character's opinions.
b. facts restated by the character.
c. the character's opinions about a set of facts.

Tone and Purpose

_____ **8.** The overall tone and purpose of the speech is to

a. inform the audience about the various stages of human life.
b. amuse the audience with a thoughtful view of the various stages of life.
c. convince the audience to enjoy each stage of life.

Inferences

_____ **9.** Based on the information in the speech, we can infer that

a. every stage of life is miserable and difficult.
b. the stages of life can be altered by free will.
c. death is to be feared.
d. life is a cycle in which we end up where we began.

Argument

_____ **10.** The following statements (lines 1–4) contain a claim and supports for that claim. Identify the claim.

a. "All the world's a stage."

b. "And all the men and women merely players."

c. "They have their exits and their entrances."

d. "And one man in his time plays many parts."

Outlining

Complete the following outline with information from the passage.

The Seven Ages of Man

I. ________

II. ________

III. Lover

IV. ________

V. Justice

VI. ________

VII. ________

After Reading Discussion Questions: Meaning, Structure, and Expression

1. **Central Idea:** Work with a group to write a summary that answers the following questions: What purpose did Shakespeare have for writing this passage? Who was his intended audience? What is the central point of the passage?

2. **Relevant Details:** Based on the descriptive details Shakespeare offers, is any one phase of life more positive or negative than another? Overall, is the view of life depicted here positive or negative? Give examples to support your response.

3. **Logical Order:** Shakespeare begins the speech by making a comparison between life and the stage, with people merely actors. However, he does not return to this image at the conclusion of the speech. Instead, he compares the final phase of life to the first phase. Why do you think Shakespeare chose to end the speech with that comparison instead of returning to the image of "All the world's a stage"?

4. **Effective Expression:** Shakespeare uses figurative language such as metaphors and similes to create vivid and memorable pictures in his audience's mind. Identify and explain the meaning of three figures of speech in the passage.

CONTINUED

Reader Response

Shakespeare wrote this monologue nearly four hundred years ago. Do you think his description of the ages of man still applies to current times? Do you agree or disagree with his seven stages and his description of each? Write an essay or poem in which you describe the various phases of life.

Master Reading/Writing Scorecard					
"The Seven Ages of Man"					
Skill	**Number Correct**		**Points**		**Total**
Vocabulary					
Vocabulary in Context (2 items)	______	x	5	=	______
Comprehension					
Central Idea (1 item)	______	x	10	=	______
Supporting Details (1 item)	______	x	10	=	______
Transitions (1 item)	______	x	10	=	______
Patterns of Organization (1 item)	______	x	10	=	______
Fact and Opinion (1 item)	______	x	10	=	______
Tone and Purpose (1 item)	______	x	10	=	______
Inferences (1 item)	______	x	10	=	______
Argument (1 item)	______	x	10	=	______
Outlining (5 items)	______	x	2	=	______
			Comprehension Score		

READING 3
Description

Niagara Falls

RUPERT BROOKE

Rupert Brooke (1887–1915) was an English poet known for his striking good looks and patriotic sonnets about war—which were inspired by his experiences in World War I—the most famous being "The Soldier." Although best known for his poetry, he was also a skilled essayist. He composed this piece of travel writing during a tour of the United States and Canada in 1913. The piece was one of a series written as letters to the *Westminster Gazette.* Two years after publishing this essay, Brooke died at the age of 27 from blood poisoning.

Before Reading

Write a journal entry about a place you have visited that you think others should travel to see. Describe the striking or significant features of this place.

Vocabulary

Before, during, and after reading the selection, annotate the text and write in your journal. Create a list of vocabulary words and supply their definitions. Give examples of how these words are used in the selection you just read.

1 *Samuel Butler has a lot to answer for. But for him, a modern traveler could spend his time peacefully admiring the scenery instead of feeling himself bound to dog the simple and grotesque of the world for the sake of their too-human comments. It is his fault if a peasant's *naïveté* has come to outweigh the beauty of rivers, and the remarks of clergymen are more than mountains. It is very restful to give up all effort at observing human nature and drawing social and political deductions from trifles, and to let oneself relapse into wide-mouthed worship of the wonders of nature. And this is very easy at Niagara. Niagara means nothing. It is not leading anywhere. It does not result from anything. It throws no light on the effects of Protection, nor on the Facility for Divorce in America, nor on Corruption in Public Life, nor on Canadian character, nor even on the Navy Bill. It is merely a great deal of water falling over some cliffs. But it is very remarkably that. The human race, apt as a child to destroy what

***Samuel Butler:** A Victorian author, critic, and philosopher who examined Christian and evolutionary thought.

CONTINUED

it admires, has done its best to surround the Falls with every distraction, incongruity, and vulgarity. Hotels, powerhouses, bridges, trams, picture post-cards, sham legends, stalls, booths, rifle-galleries, and side-shows frame them about. And there are Touts. Niagara is the central home and breeding-place for all the **touts** of earth. There are touts insinuating, and touts raucous, greasy touts, brazen touts, and upper-class, refined, gentlemanly, take-you-by-the-arm touts; touts who intimidate and touts who wheedle; professionals, amateurs, and *dilettanti*, male and female; touts who would photograph you with your arm round a young lady against a faked background of the sublimest cataract, touts who would bully you into cars, char-à-bancs, elevators, or tunnels, or deceive you into a carriage and pair, touts who would sell you picture post-cards, moccasins, sham Indian beadwork, blankets, tee-pees, and crockery, and touts, finally, who have no apparent object in the world, but just purely, simply, merely, incessantly, indefatigably, and *ineffugibly to tout. And in the midst of all this, overwhelming it all, are the Falls. He who sees them instantly forgets humanity. They are not very high, but they are overpowering. They are divided by an island into two parts, the Canadian and the American.

ineffugibly is a word made up by the author; making up words is a poetic technique often employed by writers.

Half a mile or so above the Falls, on either side, the water of the great stream begins to run more swiftly and in confusion. It descends with ever-growing speed. It begins chattering and leaping, breaking into a thousand ripples, throwing up joyful fingers of spray. Sometimes it is divided by islands and rocks, sometimes the eye can see nothing but a waste of laughing, springing, foamy waves, turning, crossing, even seeming to stand for an instant erect, but always borne impetuously forward like a crowd of triumphant feasters. Sit close down by it, and you see a fragment of the torrent against the sky, mottled, steely, and foaming, leaping onward in far-flung criss-cross strands of water. Perpetually the eye is on the point of descrying a pattern in this weaving, and perpetually it is cheated by change. In one place part of the flood plunges over a ledge a few feet high and a quarter of a mile or so long, in a uniform and stable curve. It gives an impression of almost military concerted movement, grown suddenly out of confusion. But it is swiftly lost again in the multitudinous tossing merriment. Here and there a rock close to the surface is marked by a white wave that faces backwards and seems to be rushing madly up-stream, but is really stationary in the headlong charge. But for these signs of reluctance, the waters seem to fling themselves on with some foreknowledge of their fate, in an ever wilder frenzy. But it is no *Maeterlinckian prescience. They prove, rather, that Greek belief that the great crashes are preceded by a 2

Maeterlinck, a Belgian writer who won the Nobel Prize, was noted for his poetic use of symbolism.

louder merriment and a wilder gaiety. Leaping in the sunlight, careless, entwining, clamorously joyful, the waves riot on towards the verge.

3 But there they change. As they turn to the sheer descent, the white and blue and slate color, in the heart of the Canadian Falls at least, blend and deepen to a rich, wonderful, luminous green. On the edge of disaster the river seems to gather herself, to pause, top, lift a head noble in ruin, and then, with a slow grandeur, to plunge into the eternal thunder and white chaos below. Where the stream runs shallower it is a kind of violet color, but both violet and green fray and frill to white as they fall. The mass of water, striking some ever-hidden base of rock, leaps up the whole two hundred feet again in pinnacles and domes of spray. The spray falls back into the lower river once more; all but a little that fines to foam and white mist, which drifts in layers along the air, graining it, and wanders out on the wind over the trees and gardens and houses, and so vanishes.

4 The manager of one of the great power-stations on the banks of the river above the Falls told me that the center of the riverbed at the Canadian Falls is deep and of a saucer shape. So it may be possible to fill this up to a uniform depth, and divert a lot of water for the power-houses. And this, he said, would supply the need for more power, which will certainly soon arise, without taking away from the beauty of Niagara. This is a handsome concession of the utilitarians to ordinary sight-seers. Yet, I doubt if we shall be satisfied. The real secret of the beauty and terror of the Falls is not their height or width, but the feeling of colossal power and of unintelligible disaster caused by the plunge of that vast body of water. If that were taken away, there would be little visible change, but the heart would be gone.

5 The American Falls do not inspire this feeling in the same way as the Canadian. It is because they are less in volume, and because the water does not fall so much into one place. By comparison their beauty is almost delicate and fragile. They are extraordinarily level, one long curtain of lacework and woven foam. Seen from opposite, when the sun is on them, they are blindingly white, and the clouds of spray show dark against them. With both Falls the color of the water is the ever-altering wonder. Greens and blues, purples and whites, melt into one another, fade, and come again, and change with the changing sun. Sometimes they are as richly **diaphanous** as a precious stone, and glow from within with a deep, inexplicable light. Sometimes the white intricacies of dropping foam become opaque and creamy. And always there are the rainbows. If you come suddenly upon the Falls from above, a great double rainbow, very vivid, spanning the extent of spray from top to bottom, is the first thing you see. If you wander along the cliff

CONTINUED

opposite, a bow springs into being in the American Falls, accompanies you courteously on your walk, dwindles and dies as the mist ends, and awakens again as you reach the Canadian tumult. And the bold traveler who attempts the trip under the American Falls sees, when he dare open his eyes to anything, tiny baby rainbows, some four or five yards in span, leaping from rock to rock among the foam, and gamboling beside him, barely out of hand's reach, as he goes. One I saw in that place was a complete circle, such as I have never seen before, and so near that I could put my foot on it. It is a terrifying journey, beneath and behind the Falls. The senses are battered and bewildered by the thunder of the water and the assault of wind and spray; or rather, the sound is not of falling water, but merely of falling; a noise of unspecified ruin. So, if you are close behind the endless clamor, the sight cannot recognize liquid in the masses that hurl past. You are dimly and pitifully aware that sheets of light and darkness are falling in great curves in front of you. Dull omnipresent foam washes the face. Farther away, in the roar and hissing, clouds of spray seem literally to slide down some invisible plane of air.

Beyond the foot of the Falls the river is like a slipping floor of marble, 6
green with veins of dirty white, made by the scum that was foam. It slides very quietly and slowly down for a mile or two, sullenly exhausted. Then it turns to a dull sage green, and hurries more swiftly, smooth and ominous. As the walls of the ravine close in, trouble stirs, and the waters boil and eddy. These are the lower rapids, a sight more terrifying than the Falls, because less intelligible. Close in its bands of rock the river surges tumultuously forward, writhing and leaping as if inspired by a demon. It is pressed by the straits into a visibly convex form. Great planes of water slide past. Sometimes it is thrown up into a pinnacle of foam higher than a house, or leaps with incredible speed from the crest of one vast wave to another, along the shining curve between, like the spring of a wild beast. Its motion continually suggests muscular action. The power manifest in these rapids moves one with a different sense of awe and terror from that of the Falls. Here the inhuman life and strength are spontaneous, active, almost resolute; masculine vigor compared with the passive gigantic power, female, helpless and overwhelming, of the Falls. A place of fear.

One is drawn back, strangely, to a contemplation of the Falls, at 7
every hour, and especially by night, when the cloud of spray becomes an immense visible ghost, straining and wavering high above the river, white and pathetic and translucent. The *Victorian lies very close below the surface in every man. There one can sit and let great cloudy thoughts of destiny and the passage of empires drift through the mind; for such

Victorian: An era from 1837-1891 characterized by a belief in order, stability, and natural laws.

dreams are at home by Niagara. I could not get out of my mind the thought of a friend, who said that the rainbows over the Falls were like the arts and beauty and goodness, with regard to the stream of life—caused by it, thrown upon its spray, but unable to stay or direct or affect it, and ceasing when it ceased. In all comparisons that rise in the heart, the river, with its multitudinous waves and its single current, likens itself to a life, whether of an individual or of a community. A man's life is of many flashing moments, and yet one stream; a nation's flows through all its citizens, and yet is more than they. In such places, one is aware, with an almost insupportable and yet comforting certitude, that both men and nations are hurried onwards to their ruin or ending as inevitably as this dark flood. Some go down to it unreluctant, and meet it, like the river, not without nobility. And as incessant, as inevitable, and as unavailing as the spray that hangs over the Falls, is the white cloud of human crying. . . . With some such thoughts does the platitudinous heart win from the confusion and thunder of a Niagara peace that the quietest plains or most stable hills can never give.

—Originally published in the *Westminster Gazette*, "Niagara Falls" by Rupert Brooke was included in the collection *Letters from America* (1916). This version of the essay first appeared in *Modern Essays*, edited by Christopher Morley (Harcourt Brace, 1921).

Reading Comprehension Questions

Choose the best meaning of each word in **bold**. Use context clues to make your choice.

Vocabulary in Context

_____ **1.** "Niagara is the central home and breeding-place for all the **touts** of earth." (paragraph 1)

a. buyers
b. tourists
c. con artists
d. guides

Vocabulary in Context

_____ **2.** "Sometimes they are as richly **diaphanous** as a precious stone, and glow from within with a deep, inexplicable light." (paragraph 5)

a. heavenly
b. transparent
c. thick
d. heavy

CONTINUED

READING SELECTION 3 *CONTINUED*

Implied Central Idea

_____ **3.** Which of the following sentences best states the implied central point of the passage?

a. The power and beauty of Niagara Falls inspires contemplation.
b. Humans have exploited Niagara Falls.
c. Niagara Falls defies description.
d. Niagara Falls is a natural resource for power.

Supporting Details

_____ **4.** What does the author describe as "a slipping floor of marble"?

a. the Canadian Falls
b. the American Falls
c. the river beyond the foot of the Falls
d. the stream above the Falls

Transitions

_____ **5.** "In one place, part of the flood plunges over a ledge a few feet high and a quarter of a mile or so long, in a uniform and stable curve." (paragraph 2)

The relationship of ideas **within** this sentence is

a. classification.
b. space order.
c. definition-example.
d. cause and effect.

Patterns of Organization

_____ **6.** What other primary pattern of organization does the writer use to describe Niagara Falls?

a. time order
b. classification
c. definition-example
d. cause and effect

Fact and Opinion

_____ **7.** Overall, the writer uses

a. facts.
b. opinions.
c. facts and opinions.

Tone and Purpose

_____ **8.** The overall tone and purpose of the passage is to

a. inform the reader about the power and beauty of Niagara Falls.
b. entertain the reader with a personal experience at Niagara Falls.
c. convince the reader to visit Niagara Falls.

Inferences

_____ **9.** Based on the information in the passage, we can infer that

a. the Canadian Falls are more beautiful than the American Falls.

b. more rainbows may be seen in the American Falls.

c. the Canadian and American Falls differ in their power and beauty.

d. there is no access behind or under the Falls.

Argument

_____ **10.** The following statements from paragraph 1 contain a claim and supports for that claim. Identify the claim.

a. "It is not leading anywhere."

b. "It does not result from anything."

c. "It is merely a great deal of water falling over some cliffs."

d. "But it is very remarkably that."

Mapping

Complete the following spatial concept map with information from the passage that describes the flow of Brooke's physical description of the Falls.

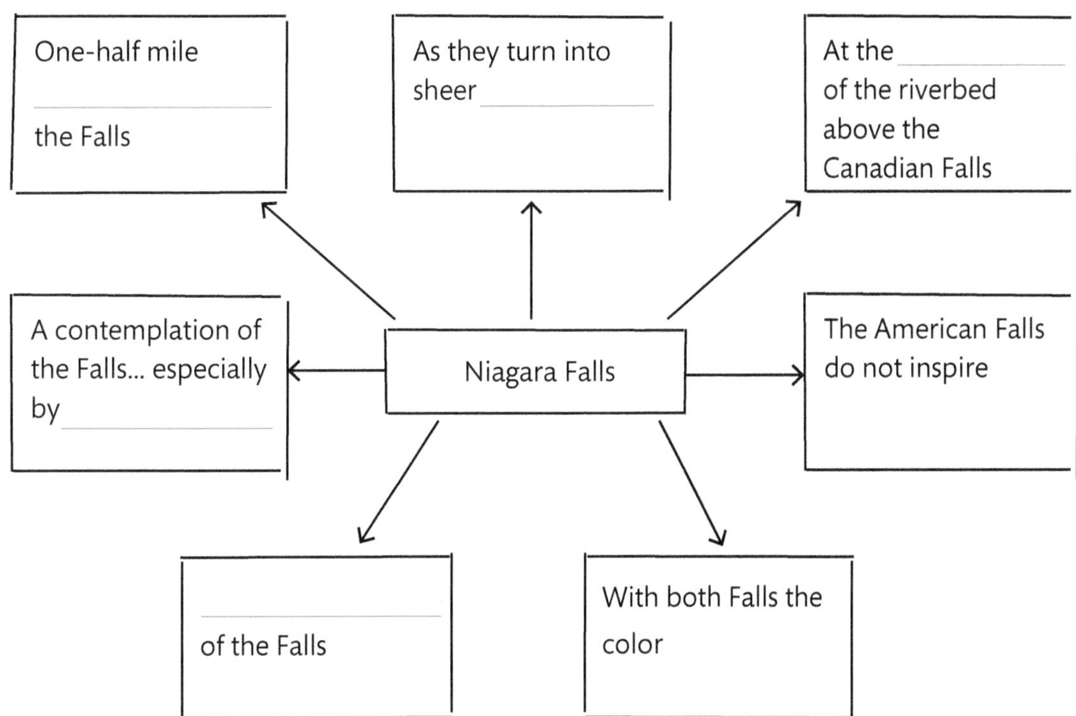

After Reading Discussion Questions: Meaning, Structure, and Expression

1. **Central Idea:** Work with a group to write a summary that answers the following questions: What purpose did Rupert Brooke have for writing this essay? Who is his intended audience? What is the central point of the essay?

CONTINUED

2. **Relevant Details:** Why do you think Brooke began with a reference to Samuel Butler? What point is he making by referring to Butler? Does this reference stand the test of time? Why or why not?
3. **Logical Order:** Brooke concludes his essay by drawing back "to a contemplation of the Falls." What point does he make as he concludes his contemplation? Do you think this is an effective end to this essay? Why or why not?
4. **Effective Expression:** Based on Brooke's use of language, how would you describe the tone of this essay? Does his tone remain consistent throughout the essay? For example, does his attitude toward the "touts" differ from his attitude about the Falls? Identify three expressions that illustrate specific tones or attitudes. Identify the tone or attitude and explain how Brooke achieved it.

Reader Response

Write a description of a significant place, person, or object. For example, you may choose to describe a local soup kitchen, a popular park, a homeless person, or your favorite place. Your description should reveal the significance of the subject matter you chose.

Master Reading/Writing Scorecard

"Niagara Falls"

Skill	Number Correct		Points		Total
Vocabulary					
Vocabulary in Context (2 items)	______	x	5	=	______
Comprehension					
Implied Central Idea (1 item)	______	x	10	=	______
Supporting Details (1 item)	______	x	10	=	______
Transitions (1 item)	______	x	10	=	______
Patterns of Organization (1 item)	______	x	10	=	______
Fact and Opinion (1 item)	______	x	10	=	______
Tone and Purpose (1 item)	______	x	10	=	______
Inferences (1 item)	______	x	10	=	______
Argument (1 item)	______	x	10	=	______
Mapping (5 items)	______	x	2	=	______
			Comprehension Score		

READING 4
Cause and Effect

Beauty from Ashes

ANNE SMITH

Anne Smith has chosen to remain anonymous as the author of this essay. She is a highly educated and accomplished professional who makes her living as a published writer. Her decision to remain unnamed stems from her desire to share insights gleaned from her painful personal experiences, yet protect the privacy of her family. Anne Smith is her pseudonym, and in the essay, she has changed the names of her family. As the poet John Donne said so eloquently in his famous poem, "No man is an island." To tell her story is to tell the stories of her family; thus she chooses to cloak their pain in anonymity.

Before Reading

Write a journal entry about your views on suffering. What are the various ways in which we suffer? Why do we suffer? What impact does suffering have on us? Are all the effects negative, or are there some benefits to suffering? Explain your views.

Vocabulary

Before, during, and after reading the selection, annotate the text and write in your journal. Create a list of vocabulary words and supply their definitions. Give examples of how the words are used in the selection you just read.

My 86-year-old mother suffers with the devastating effects of Alzheimer's disease. The **cognitive** impacts are obvious. Pieces of her self and the world around her slip from her grasp almost daily now. The moment just lived is immediately forgotten—as if it had not happened at all. Familiar objects become meaningless. Confusion and doubt dislocate her competence and confidence. Mindless, repetitive actions replace purposeful, gratifying behaviors. Fear withers her once steadfast strength. The physical impacts remain somewhat subtle. Her walking gait is slower and less sure. Bruises easily bloom on her fragile skin from normal brushes with daily life. Fundamentally, her brain is changing. Alzheimer's disease leads to nerve cell death and tissue loss throughout the brain. Over time, the brain shrinks dramatically, affecting nearly all its functions, 1

CONTINUED

and ultimately will shut down her body. Her suffering radiates its pain to those of us who love her and stand by as helpless witnesses.

2 It is not as if my immediate family is unfamiliar with suffering: we have experienced the effects of alcoholism, poverty, domestic violence, and loss of life to accident, disease, and suicide. At one time, I thought of us as an unusually dysfunctional or cursed unit. However, our suffering actually mirrors the anguish resulting from some of the common ills of society. For example, according to the National Institute on Alcohol Abuse and Alcoholism, in 2012, approximately 7.2 percent or 17 million adults in the United States ages 18 and older had a medical diagnosis of Alcohol Use Disorder (AUD). In addition, according to the Centers for Disease Control, suicide was the 10th leading cause of death in the United States in 2011, claiming the lives of over 41,000 people. And, the 2013 United States Census documented the official poverty rate at 14.5 percent with 45.3 million people living in poverty. Furthermore, according to the Centers for Disease Control and Prevention and the Alzheimer's Organization, in 2013, around 5 million Americans of all ages have Alzheimer's disease. My family's suffering merely puts flesh and bone on these statistics. Physical, psychological, and social suffering affect us all.

3 My older sister Leigh discerned the horrific effects of Alzheimer's years before I did. When our mother was first diagnosed, Leigh cried out the proverbial "Why?" Why, she wondered, would God allow Mom to endure this long, undignified exodus from life? What good could possibly come from her suffering? Indeed, Leigh's question is one that poets, philosophers, and religious leaders have asked since the beginning of human history. Now, as our mother stands at the cusp of the final stage of her **arduous** struggle, now in the midst of the concrete effect of her affliction, the question *why* pulses with a new and personal intensity only amplified by the awareness of universal suffering.

4 Suffering is inevitable in our physical being.

5 As mortal beings we are destined to face the physical agonies of aging, disease, injury, and death. Alzheimer's is but one example of aging and disease. I saw first hand the progressive damage to my father's body as he struggled for decades with the disease of alcoholism, looking more, at the age of 40, like an emaciated holocaust victim than himself as he forsook most all nutrients for booze. And I saw first hand the terrifying effects of lung cancer as my one-and-only sister gasped for her last breaths. Certainly, life choices—drinking and smoking—greatly contributed to my father's and sister's diseases. Likewise, all too often, injury comes about by our own hands. I saw firsthand the gory damage

the self-inflicted bullet did to my father's head—his choice to throw the final blow.

Then again, injury comes about by nature's hand. On October 13, 2003, a 15-foot tiger shark swimming off the North Shore of Kauai tore off the arm just below the shoulder of 13-year-old surfer Bethany Hamilton. She lost 60 percent of her blood and endured several surgeries. In that same year, a dislodged boulder entrapped 26-year-old Aron Ralston as he hiked alone in remote southeastern Utah. After 5 days, he used his dulled pocketknife to amputate his right forearm to free himself, avoid death, and return to civilization. 6

Other times, accidental injuries occur in our homes and on our roadways. I saw first hand the horrific and fatal injuries of my brother Allen due to the head-on crash between his motorcycle and an oncoming automobile. Then, a year later, in an intensive care unit, we watched Will, my husband's brother, fight a futile 3-week battle for his life after his car drifted off the road, rolled several times, and wrapped around a tree. 7

Then, too, disease and injury and death come about by the hand of war. According to a United Nations report "Children and Armed Conflict," children are the most likely to suffer death and injury to landmines in regions ravaged by war. In 2010, explosive devices caused the death of nearly 2,000 children with most occurring in Afghanistan, Cambodia, Sudan, Lao PDR, Pakistan, and Yemen. And those who survived maimed with missing limbs are unlikely to resume normal life. 8

Suffering does not limit itself to the physical realm. 9

Often, physical suffering spirals into psychological suffering. In her 1969 book *On Death and Dying*, Swiss psychiatrist Elisabeth Kübler-Ross published her theory about five stages of grief experienced by people who are terminally ill or who face other great losses, such as divorce, loss of limbs, or the death of a loved one. These phases include denial, anger, bargaining, depression, and acceptance. While Kübler-Ross indicated that not everyone experiences all five stages, nor do the stages necessarily occur in a certain order, my sister and her husband seemed to suffer through most of them. In the early days following her diagnosis of stage III lung cancer, Leigh and Paul denied the prognosis that she had just 10 months to live. They spent precious time, energy, and money seeking opinions that would offer a different outcome. My sister's anger was actually an expression of her fear of smothering. She lashed out at us for our slowness or clumsiness to care for her. As the chemotherapy and oxygen eased her breathing, her anger subsided. Until the end, she 10

CONTINUED

was filled with self-incrimination and remorse. She continually wept and
apologized, "If only I hadn't smoked all those years. I am so sorry . . .
so sorry . . . so sorry." Her sense of guilt kept her from bargaining with
God—convinced she had no right to ask for divine healing. She mourned
the loss of her future—the weddings, the grandchildren, and all the
celebrations. She came much more quickly to acceptance than did Paul,
who never did, who always believed, even in her last moments, that she
could beat this enemy and begged God to heal her.

Often, psychological and social suffering walk hand in hand. 11

I dare say, no one knows of this link better than I, the child of an 12
alcoholic, a survivor. I never knew the man with whom my mother fell
in love. She never lost sight of that man, never wanted to abandon him
to his disease, so we stayed with him decades longer than most would
have, longer than what seemed reasonable. Thus, by the time I could
form my earliest memories, that man, my father, had become a waking
nightmare.

His struggles occurred in a cycle of becoming intoxicated, inflicting 13
violence, passing out, checking into rehab, feeling remorse, seeking
forgiveness, coming home, and "honeymooning" until the cycle began all
over again. Each phase of the cycle could last days or weeks. The violent
stage seemed to last the longest; the honeymoon stage always seemed
the shortest.

Fear saturated our lives. When he was sober, we feared he would 14
start drinking. When he began drinking, we feared he would become
violent. When he became violent, we feared for our safety, even our lives.
Often, during the violent phase, Mom found low-rent apartments, and we
would leave him to himself until he passed out and had to be checked
into a facility.

He isolated us from the world. He allowed us no car, no phone. He 15
tolerated no friends; no neighborhood children or school classmates
crossed our threshold. Of course we played outside, we went to school,
but not coming immediately when called or arriving home even a little
late led to dire consequences.

In the long term, his verbal and physical attacks, mingled with the 16
depravation of our lives, undermined my sense of self-worth. I walked in
a fog of shame and self-loathing. My experiences at school reinforced
my inadequacies. My failure became so much the norm that once when I
did study for a test, my fourth grade teacher ripped up my work in front
of the whole class calling me a "cheater." After that it became easier to
remain disengaged, to not even try, and to transfer my distrust of my

father to others. By the time I was a high school senior, when my father committed suicide and left himself for me to find, few who knew me held much hope for my future. How little any of us knew then that beauty could rise like a phoenix from ashes.

17 Suffering can bring light.

18 Not too long ago, with almost a half-dozen nationally best-selling books to my name, I returned to my alma mater, a small private college in the South. A group my former classmates gathered with me in a small circle in the grand foyer of the main hall to congratulate me. At first, most shuffled uncomfortably in awkward silence. So I said with an easy laugh, "Well, it seems my success has surprised us all, right?" In an explosion of relieved chatter, they agreed, "Yeah, who knew . . . we are so amazed . . . good for you." Looking back, I completely understood why they were so astonished and why I was able to overcome.

19 Richard Tedeschi and Lawrence Calhoun, authors of the 1995 book *Trauma and Transformation: Growing in the Aftermath of Suffering*, coined the term *posttraumatic growth* to describe the positive outcomes that may result in the aftermath of great trauma or a major life crisis. Now, this idea of the transformative power of pain is not new.

20 For millennia, humans have written about the ways in which great challenges bring about profound and positive changes in those who endure. Ancient writings encourage us to see suffering as an opportunity for growth. In Greek and Egyptian mythology, the phoenix was a brilliant golden bird that attained rebirth by rising out of the ashes of the fire that consumed it. In the *Tanakh*, the Hebrew Bible, the poetic book of Job directly addresses the power of suffering. After losing family, wealth, and health, Job says of his suffering "He knows the way I take. And when He has tried me, I shall come forth as gold." And in the New Testament book of Romans, Paul writes, "Not only so, but we glory in tribulations also: knowing that tribulation worketh patience; and patience, experience; and experience, hope."

21 So no, posttraumatic growth is not a new concept. What is new is Tedeschi and Calhoun's research-based assertion that personal growth after great trauma has discernable reasons and results.

22 One element that fosters posttraumatic growth is spirituality. Bethany Hamilton's remarkable recovery from losing her arm to that shark propelled her onto the national stage as a role model of courage and tenacity. On her blog, Soulsurfer.com, she explains how her faith in God gave her the resilience she needed.

CONTINUED

> It was Jesus Christ who gave me peace when I was attacked by the shark. They had to get me to the beach, which took 20 minutes of paddling. "The peace of God, which transcends all understanding, will guard your hearts and mind in Christ Jesus" (Philippians 4:6-8).

One month after the attack, she was back in the water, and 3 months after the attack, she resumed competition as a surfer, winning fifth place in the Open Women's division. She explains her strength on her blog:

> It was what God had taught me growing up that helped me overcome my fear and get back on the board. Be strong and courageous. "Do not be terrified; do not be discouraged, for the Lord your God will be with you wherever you go" (Joshua 1:9).

In his 2004 bestselling book *127 Hours: Between a Rock and a Hard Place*, Aron Ralston recounts the spiritual aspects of his suffering. He describes a hallucination he had of a 3-year-old little boy with blond hair and red shirt running across the floor of a living room into his arms, picking the boy up, and realizing that this was his son—a mystical vision of something in the future that gave him the hope and strength to take action to save his own life. 23

Then, he describes his understanding about how to amputate his own arm as "an **epiphany** that strikes me with the magnificent glory of a holy intervention." In the aftermath of his ordeal, Ralston continued his life as an engineer and avid mountain climber and became a motivational speaker, best selling author, a husband, and a father to a beautiful blond boy. His trauma, he writes, "has affirmed my belief that our purpose as spiritual beings is to follow our bliss, seek our passions, and live our lives as inspirations to each other." 24

The second element, according to experts, that nurtures posttraumatic growth is social support. Both Hamilton and Ralston enjoy the support of strong and loving families, and both have been embraced and validated by their greater communities. Likewise, spirituality and social support greatly contributed to my ability to learn and grow from trauma. 25

My mother and I share a like-minded faith that saw us through those trying years with my father and strengthen us today as together we walk this difficult path mapped out by Alzheimer's disease. Even now, she comforts herself by quoting this promise, embedded in her memory, from Romans, "all things work together to them that love God, to them who are the called according to His purpose." And when I feel overwhelmed as her caregiver, I, too, call this promise to mind—asking God to make me strong, wise, and compassionate. Interestingly, this promise foreshadows the very 26 benefits Tedeschi and Calhoun assert may come after trauma: an increased appreciation for life; a shift in priorities; stronger, deeper relationships; maturity and strength; and recognition of the opportunities for spiritual development.

I am convinced that the social support I received in the years immediately after my father died came about as an answer to prayer embodied by the efforts of one remarkable teacher. 27

Dr. H and I began our time at the private all-women's college the same year: he as sole professor in the brand new theatre department—I as his student. He forged a creative community of about 30 freshman through senior girls, teaching us how to design and build sets, hang lights, execute sound, and perform classics including Molière, Shakespeare, Ibsen, Pinter, Sartre, and Tennessee Williams. He kept us working late, yet he expected us to not only show up for 8 o'clock classes but do well, as well. Still reeling from personal trauma, undisciplined and disconnected, I often skipped classes, never read textbooks until the night before exams, and often turned in works of first drafts hastily done last minute. He tried everything to make me mend my ways. He cajoled, threatened, reasoned with me, and on many occasions gambled on me—giving me more responsibility than I deserved. He taught me to read the great classics orally. Oral literacy—the great and ancient tradition of story telling—became my path to literacy. Dr. H knew this and created many opportunities to affirm my strengths. His program gave me a place to learn academically and thrive socially. By the time I graduated, I had performed in a dozen main stage productions and had directed three full-length plays. I still reap benefits from the lessons he taught us all. Because of him, I found my voice and even a reason to raise it: 28

My God-gifted Teacher
I have always known
You—a gift
From God no less,
Because always
In the first and from all our moments
That flow between us
Electric shock around,
Arching above and beyond us,
You make me know
You see
Something in me
Of worth
Some value worth
The work to express itself,

CONTINUED

And your sight
Gave me eyes
And now a voice
Urges on a body of work.
I have always known you—
Your great gift, a gift to me.
And only yesterday I prayed God
Give me a poem,
A poem I could give to you.
And a voice within whispered,
You are my poem to him—
God answers before I ask.
As always,
This I know.

No doubt, suffering occurs in myriad cycles of painful reasons and profound results. Our challenge, our gift is to make meaning out of our pain. Let us then do as the poet Tennyson calls us to in his renowned poem "Ulysses": "To strive, to seek, to find, and not to yield." 29

Reading Comprehension Questions

Choose the best meaning of each word in **bold**. Use context clues to make your choice.

Vocabulary in Context

____ **1.** "The **cognitive** impacts are obvious." (paragraph 1)

a. physical
b. spiritual
c. mental
d. personal

Vocabulary in Context

____ **2.** "Then, he describes his understanding about how to amputate his own arm as 'an **epiphany** that strikes me with the magnificent glory of a holy intervention.'" (paragraph 24)

a. secret
b. insight
c. attack
d. curiosity

Central Idea

_____ **3.** Which sentence best states the central point of the passage?

a. "Her suffering radiates its pain to those of us who love her and stand by as helpless witnesses." (paragraph 1)

b. "Physical, psychological, and social suffering affect us all." (paragraph 2)

c. "Suffering can bring light." (paragraph 17)

d. "Our challenge, our gift is to make meaning out of our pain." (paragraph 29)

Supporting Details

_____ **4.** What was the cause of death for Will, the author's brother-in-law?

a. war injury

b. lung cancer

c. injury from a car accident

d. suicide

Transitions

_____ **5.** "However, our suffering actually mirrors the anguish resulting from some of the common ills of society. For example, according to the National Institute on Alcohol Abuse and Alcoholism, in 2012, approximately 7.2 percent or 17 million adults in the United States ages 18 and older had a medical diagnosis of Alcohol Use Disorder (AUD)." (paragraph 2)

The main relationship of ideas **within** this sentence is

a. contrast.

b. process.

c. cause and effect.

d. generalization-example.

Patterns of Organization

_____ **6.** The main pattern of organization used for paragraph 13 is

a. comparison.

b. description.

c. process.

d. classification.

Fact and Opinion

_____ **7.** Overall, the supporting details in paragraph 2 are

a. facts.

b. opinions.

c. facts and opinions.

Tone and Purpose

_____ **8.** Smith's overall tone and purpose is to

a. inform the reader about her personal experiences with suffering.

b. entertain the reader with personal details about her difficult life.

c. inspire or encourage the reader to strive to overcome the effects of suffering.

CONTINUED

READING SELECTION 4 *CONTINUED*

Inferences

_____ **9.** Based on the information in the passage, we can infer that

a. the author was an only child.

b. the author has never had a personal injury or life-threatening disease.

c. the author's mother has outlived two of her three children.

d. the author's mother suffers from her disease because of her poor life choices.

Argument

_____ **10.** "My failure became so much the norm that once when I did study for a test, my fourth grade teacher ripped up my work in front of the whole class calling me a 'cheater.'" (paragraph 16)

This statement is an example of which fallacy?

a. personal attack

b. bandwagon

c. begging the question

d. transfer

Outlining

Complete the following outline with information from the passage.

Beauty from Ashes

I. My mother suffers.

II. Our suffering mirrors the common ills of society.

III. Leigh cried out the proverbial _______________

IV. Suffering is _______________

V. Suffering does not _______________

VI. _______________

VII. _______________

After Reading Discussion Questions: Meaning, Structure, and Expression

1. **Central Idea:** Work with a group to write a summary that answers the following questions: What purpose did Anne Smith have for writing this essay? Who is her intended audience? What is the central point of the essay? What is the significance of the title?

2. **Relevant Details:** Throughout the essay, Smith offers many painful details from her personal life. Why did she choose to disclose such intimate details? Are her disclosures appropriate and effective? Why or why not? Do you agree with her decision to remain anonymous? Why or why not?
3. **Logical Order:** Smith concludes her essay with a call to action. Why does she wait until the end of the essay to make this call? Would the essay have been as effective if she had made this call to action part of her introduction? Why or why not?
4. **Effective Expression:** How would you describe the overall tone Smith establishes in this essay? Is it poignant, inspiring, bitter, self-pitying, or some other tone? Does the tone draw you in or put you off? Give examples from the essay to support your interpretation of and reaction to Smith's tone.

Reader Response

In paragraph 26 of her essay "Beauty from Ashes," Anne Smith states the positive effects that experts assert may come from suffering. Give examples from the text that illustrate which of these effects are illustrated by the details she offers from her own life.

Master Reading/Writing Scorecard

"Beauty from Ashes"

Skill	Number Correct		Points		Total
Vocabulary					
Vocabulary in Context (2 items)	______	x	5	=	______
Comprehension					
Central Idea (1 item)	______	x	10	=	______
Supporting Details (1 item)	______	x	10	=	______
Transitions (1 item)	______	x	10	=	______
Patterns of Organization (1 item)	______	x	10	=	______
Fact and Opinion (1 item)	______	x	10	=	______
Tone and Purpose (1 item)	______	x	10	=	______
Inferences (1 item)	______	x	10	=	______
Argument (1 item)	______	x	10	=	______
Outlining (5 items)	______	x	2	=	______
			Comprehension Score		

READING 5
Cause and Effect

A Doll's House, Act III, Final Scene

HENRIK IBSEN

Henrik Ibsen, an influential and highly respected nineteenth century poet, playwright, and theater director, is often referred to as "the father of realism." His dramas often portray middle-class people whose routine lives are disrupted by life-changing crises arising from personal flaws and social traditions.

In the first two acts of *A Doll's House*, we learn that Nora Helmer once secretly forged her father's name to a bank loan to borrow a large sum of money so that her husband could recuperate from a serious illness. She has been secretly paying it back in small installments by saving from her household allowance. When her husband, Torvald is appointed bank director, his first act is to fire a man who was once disgraced for having forged his signature on a document. This man, Nils Krogstad, is the person from whom Nora has borrowed her money. Krogstad blackmails Nora with the threat of revealing her crime to force her to convince her husband not to fire him. When Torvald discovers that Nora has forged her father's name, he angrily disclaims his wife. The following scene from the final act is the result of this turmoil.

Before Reading

Write a journal entry about your views of marriage and divorce. What makes a successful marriage? What are the reasons for divorce? Are some reasons more justified than others?

Vocabulary

Before, during, and after reading the selection, annotate the text and write in your journal. Create a list of vocabulary words and supply their definitions. Give examples of how these words are used in the selection you just read.

Nora (*looking at her watch*). It's not so late yet. Sit down, Torvald, you 1
and I have much to say to each other. (*She sits on one side of the table.*)

Helmer. Nora, what does this mean; your cold, set face— 2

Nora. Sit down. It will take some time; I have much to talk over with 3
you. (*Helmer sits at the other side of the table.*)

4 **Helmer**. You alarm me; I don't understand you.

5 **Nora**. No, that's just it. You don't understand me; and I have never understood you—till tonight. No, don't interrupt. Only listen to what I say. We must come to a final settlement. Torvald!

6 **Helmer**. How do you mean?

7 **Nora** (*after a short silence*). Does not one thing strike you as we sit here?

8 **Helmer**. What should strike me?

9 **Nora**. We have been married eight years. Does it not strike you that this is the first time we two, you and I, man and wife, have talked together seriously?

10 **Helmer**. Seriously! Well, what do you call seriously?

11 **Nora**. During eight whole years and more—ever since the day we first met—we have never exchanged one serious word about serious things.

12 **Helmer**. Was I always to trouble you with the cares you could not help me to bear?

13 **Nora**. I am not talking of cares. I say that we have never yet set ourselves seriously to get to the bottom of anything.

14 **Helmer**. Why, my dear Nora, what have you to do with serious things?

15 **Nora**. There we have it! You have never understood me. I have had great injustice done me, Torvald. First by my father and then by you.

16 **Helmer**. What! by your father and me?—by us who have loved you more than all the world?

17 **Nora** (*shaking her head*). You have never loved me. You only thought it amusing to be in love with me.

18 **Helmer**. Why, Nora, what a thing to say!

19 **Nora**. Yes, it is so, Torvald. While I was at home with father he used to tell me all his opinions and I held the same opinions. If I had others I concealed them, because he would not have liked it. He used to call me his doll child, and play with me as I played with my dolls. Then I came to live in your house—

20 **Helmer**. What an expression to use about our marriage!

21 **Nora** (*undisturbed*). I mean I passed from father's hands into yours. You settled everything according to your taste; and I got the same tastes as you; or I pretended to—I don't know which—both ways perhaps. When I look back on it now, I seem to have been living here like a beggar, from hand to mouth. I lived by performing tricks for you, Torvald. But you would have it so. You and father have done me a great wrong. It's your fault that my life has been wasted.

CONTINUED

Helmer. Why, Nora, how unreasonable and ungrateful you are. 22
Haven't you been happy here?

Nora. No, never; I thought I was, but I never was. 23

Helmer. Not—not happy? 24

Nora. No, only merry. And you have always been so kind to me. But 25
our house has been nothing but play room. Here I have been your doll-wife, just as at home I used to be papa's doll-child. And the children in their turn have been my dolls. I thought it fun when you played with me, just as the children did when I played with them. That has been our marriage, Torvald.

Helmer. There is some truth in what you say, exaggerated and 26
overstrained though it be. But henceforth it shall be different. Playtime is over; now comes the time for education.

Nora. Whose education? Mine, or the children's? 27

Helmer. Both, my dear, Nora. 28

Nora. Oh, Torvald, you can't teach me to be a fit wife for you. 29

Helmer. And you say that? 30

Nora. And I—am I fit to educate the children? 31

Helmer. Nora! 32

Nora. Did you not say yourself a few minutes ago you dared not trust 33
them to me.

Helmer. In the excitement of the moment! Why should you dwell 34
upon that?

Nora. No—you are perfectly right. That problem is beyond me. 35
There's another to be solved first—I must try to educate myself. You are not the man to help me in that. I must set about it alone. And that is why I am now leaving you!

Helmer (*jumping up*). What—do you mean to say— 36

Nora. I must stand quite alone to know myself and my surroundings; 37
so I cannot stay with you.

Helmer. Nora! Nora! 38

Nora. I am going at once. Christina will take me in for to-night. 39

Helmer. You are mad. I shall not allow it. I forbid it. 40

Nora. It's no use your forbidding me anything now. I shall take with me 41
what belongs to me. From you I will accept nothing, either now or afterward.

Helmer. What madness! 42

Nora. To-morrow I shall go home. 43

Helmer. Home! 44

Nora. I mean to what was my home. It will be easier for me to find 45
some opening there.

Helmer. Oh, in your blind experience— 46

Nora. I must try to gain experience, Torvald. 47

Helmer. To forsake your home, your husband, and your children! You 48
don't consider what the world will say.

Nora. I can pay no heed to that! I only know that I must do it. 49

Helmer. It's exasperating! Can you forsake your holiest duties in this way? 50

Nora. What do you call my holiest duties? 51

Helmer. Do you ask me that? Your duties to your husband and your 52
children.

Nora. I have other duties equally sacred. 53

Helmer. Impossible! What duties do you mean? 54

Nora. My duties toward myself. 55

Helmer. Before all else you are a wife and a mother. 56

Nora. That I no longer believe. I think that before all else I am a 57
human being, just as much as you are—or, at least, I will try to become one. I know that most people agree with you, Torvald, and that they say so in books. But henceforth I can't be satisfied with what most people say, and what is in books. I must think things out for myself and try to get clear about them.

Helmer. Are you not clear about your place in your own home? Have 58
you not an **infallible** guide in questions like these? Have you not religion?

Nora. Oh, Torvald, I don't know properly what religion is. 59

Helmer. What do you mean? 60

Nora. I know nothing but what our clergyman told me when I was 61
confirmed. He explained that religion was this and that. When I get away from here and stand alone I will look into that matter too. I will see whether what he taught me is true, or, at any rate, whether it is true for me.

Helmer. Oh, this is unheard of! But if religion cannot keep you right, 62
let me appeal to your conscience—I suppose you have some moral feeling? Or, answer me, perhaps you have none?

Nora. Well, Torvald, it's not easy to say. I really don't know—I am all at 63
sea about these things. I only know that I think quite differently from you about them. I hear, too, that the laws are different from what I thought; but I can't believe that they are right. It appears that a woman has no right to spare her dying father, or to save her husband's life. I don't believe that.

Helmer. You talk like a child. You don't understand the society in 64
which you live.

Nora. No, I don't. But I shall try to. I must make up my mind which is 65
right—society or I.

CONTINUED

66 **Helmer**. Nora, you are ill, you are feverish. I almost think you are out of your senses.

67 **Nora**. I never felt so much clearness and certainty as tonight.

68 **Helmer**. You are clear and certain enough to forsake husband and children?

69 **Nora**. Yes, I am.

70 **Helmer**. Then there is only one explanation possible.

71 **Nora**. What is that?

72 **Helmer**. You no longer love me.

73 **Nora**. No, that is just it.

74 **Helmer**. Nora! Can you say so?

75 **Nora**. Oh, I'm so sorry, Torvald; for you've always been so kind to me. But I can't help it I do not love you any longer.

76 **Helmer** (*keeping his composure with difficulty*). Are you clear and certain on this point too?

77 **Nora**. Yes, quite. That is why I won't stay here any longer.

78 **Helmer**. And can you also make clear to me, how I have **forfeited** your love?

79 **Nora**. Yes, I can. It was this evening, when the miracle did not happen. For then I saw you were not the man I had taken you for.

80 **Helmer**. Explain yourself more clearly; I don't understand.

81 **Nora**. I have waited so patiently all these eight years; for, of course, I saw clearly enough that miracles do not happen every day. When this crushing blow threatened me, I said to myself, confidently, "Now comes the miracle!" When Krogstad's letter lay in the box, it never occurred to me that you would think of submitting to that man's conditions. I was convinced that you would say to him,"Make it known to all the world," and that then—

82 **Helmer**. Well? When I had given my own wife's name up to disgrace and shame?

83 **Nora**. Then I firmly believed that you would come forward, take everything upon yourself, and say, "I am the guilty one."

84 **Helmer**. Nora!

85 **Nora**. You mean I would never have accepted such a sacrifice? No, certainly not. But what would my assertions have been worth in opposition to yours? That was the miracle that I hoped for and dreaded. And it was to hinder that that I wanted to die.

86 **Helmer**. I would gladly work for you day and night, Nora—bear sorrow and want for your sake—but no man sacrifices his honor, even for one he loves.

87 **Nora**. Millions of women have done so.

88 **Helmer**. Oh, you think and talk like a silly child.

89 **Nora**. Very likely. But you neither think nor talk like the man I can share my life with. When your terror was over—not for me, but for yourself—when there was nothing more to fear,—then it was to you as though nothing had happened. I was your lark again, your doll—whom you would take twice as much care of in the future, because she was so weak and fragile. (*Stands up.*) Torvald, in that moment it burst upon me, that I had been living here these eight years with a strange man, and had borne him three children. Oh! I can't bear to think of it—I could tear myself to pieces!

90 **Helmer** (*sadly*). I see it, I see it; an abyss has opened between us. But, Nora, can it never be filled up?

91 **Nora**. As I now am, I am no wife for you.

92 **Helmer**. I have strength to become another man.

93 **Nora**. Perhaps—when your doll is taken away from you.

94 **Helmer**. To part—to part from you! No, Nora, no; I can't grasp the thought.

95 **Nora** (*going into room, right*). The more reason for the thing to happen. (*She comes back with out-door things and a small travelling bag, which she puts on a chair.*)

96 **Helmer**. Nora, Nora, not now! Wait till to-morrow.

97 **Nora** (*putting on cloak*). I can't spend the night in a strange man's house.

98 **Helmer**. But can't we live here as brother and sister?

99 **Nora** (*fastening her hat*). You know very well that would not last long. Good-by, Torvald. No, I won't go to the children. I know they are in better hands than mine. As I now am, I can be nothing to them.

100 **Helmer**. But some time, Nora—some time—

101 **Nora**. How can I tell? I have no idea what will become of me.

102 **Helmer**. But you are my wife, now and always?

103 **Nora**. Listen, Torvald—when a wife leaves her husband's house, as I am doing, I have heard that in the eyes of the law he is free from all the duties toward her. At any rate I release you from all duties. You must not feel yourself bound any more than I shall. There must be perfect freedom on both sides. There, there is your ring back. Give me mine.

104 **Helmer**. That too?

105 **Nora**. That too.

106 **Helmer**. Here it is.

CONTINUED

Nora. Very well. Now it is all over. Here are the keys. The servants 107
know about everything in the house, better than I do. To-morrow, when
I have started, Christina will come to pack up my things. I will have them
sent after me.

Helmer. All over! All over! Nora, will you never think of me again? 108

Nora. Oh, I shall often think of you, and the children—and this house. 109

Helmer. May I write to you, Nora? 110

Nora. No, never. You must not. 111

Helmer. But I must send you— 112

Nora. Nothing, nothing. 113

Helmer. I must help you if you need it. 114

Nora. No, I say. I take nothing from strangers. 115

Helmer. Nora, can I never be more than a stranger to you? 116

Nora (*taking her travelling bag*). Oh, Torvald, then the miracle of 117
miracles would have to happen.

Helmer. What is the miracle of miracles? 118

Nora. Both of us would have to change so that Oh, Torvald, I no 119
longer believe in miracles.

Helmer. But I will believe. We must so change that? 120

Nora. That communion between us shall be a marriage. Good-by. 121
(*She goes out.*)

Helmer (*sinks in a chair by the door with his face in his hands*). Nora! 122
Nora! (*He looks around and stands up.*) Empty. She's gone! (*A hope
inspires him.*) Ah! The miracle of miracles?! (*Then below is heard the
reverberation of a heavy door closing.*)

—From *A Doll's House*, three-act play in prose by Henrik Ibsen.

Reading Comprehension Questions

Choose the best meaning of each word in **bold**. Use context clues to make your choice.

Vocabulary in Context

_____ **1.** "Have you not an **infallible** guide in questions like these? (line 58)

a. faulty

b. clear

c. reliable

d. inner

Vocabulary in Context

_____ **2.** "And can you also make clear to me, how I have **forfeited** your love?" (line 78)

a. lost
b. gained
c. penalty
d. lessened

Central Idea

_____ **3.** Which of the following sentences best states the central idea of the scene?

a. "During eight whole years and more—ever since the day we first met—we have never exchanged one serious word about serious things." (line 11)
b. "I must stand quite alone to know myself and my surroundings; so I cannot stay with you." (line 37)
c. "Before all else you are a wife and a mother." (line 56)
d. "I have never felt so much clearness and certainty as tonight." (line 67)

Supporting Details

_____ **4.** According to Nora, her holiest duties are

a. as a wife and mother.
b. her moral feelings.
c. her religious belief and service.
d. toward herself as a human being.

Transitions

_____ **5.** "If I had others, I concealed them, because he would not have liked it." (line 19)
What is the relationship of ideas **within** this sentence?

a. time order
b. classification
c. definition-example
d. cause and effect

Patterns of Organization

_____ **6.** In addition to narration and description used to depict the scene, the writer uses

a. listing.
b. classification.
c. cause and effect.
d. process.

Fact and Opinion

_____ **7.** "We have been married eight years." (line 9) is a statement of

a. fact.
b. opinion.
c. fact and opinion.

CONTINUED

Tone and Purpose

_____ **8.** Overall, the tone and purpose of the scene is to

a. enlighten the audience about the bias against women in society.

b. amuse the audience with a conflict between a husband and wife.

c. convince the audience that divorce is an acceptable choice.

Inferences

_____ **9.** Based on the information in the passage, we can infer that Nora leaves without her children because

a. she does not love them.

b. she thinks Torvald will be a better father once she leaves.

c. she plans on coming back for them.

d. she doesn't think herself mature or wise enough to raise them.

Argument

_____ **10.** "Oh, you think and talk like a silly child." (line 88)

This statement is an irrelevant detail based on the fallacy of

a. bandwagon.

b. personal attack.

c. plain folks.

d. glittering generality.

Mapping

Complete the following concept map with information from the passage.

The Causal Chain of the End of the Helmer's Marriage

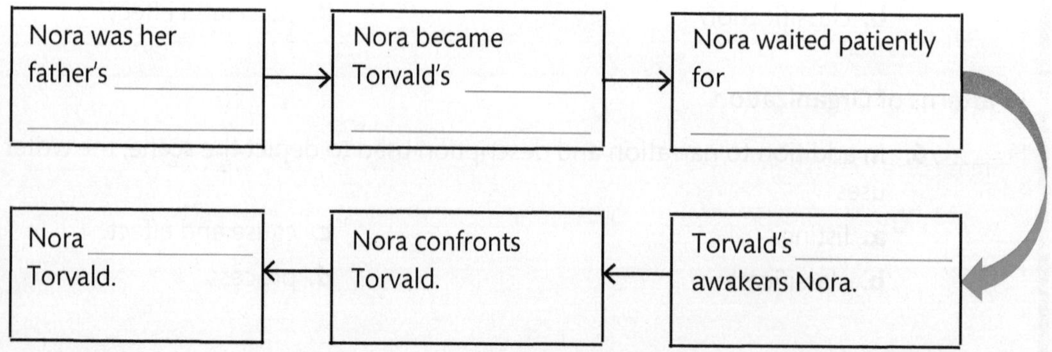

After Reading Discussion Questions: Meaning, Structure, and Expression

1. **Central Idea:** Work with a group to write a summary that answers the following questions: What purpose did Henrik Ibsen have for writing this play? Who was his intended audience? What is the central point of this scene? What is the significance of the title of the play?

2. **Relevant Details:** What reasons does Nora give for leaving her family? Are her reasons logical and substantial enough to warrant her leaving? Why or why not?

3. **Logical Order:** Reread the conclusion of the scene. Discuss the effect Ibsen intended to have on his audience with the final stage direction "*Then below is heard the reverberation of a heavy door closing.*" What does the sound of the door symbolize? Would the scene be as effective without this final sound? Why or why not?

4. **Effective Expression:** Throughout the scene, Ibsen uses the metaphor of a doll to describe Nora's roles as wife, mother, and woman. Then, in line 89, Nora refers to herself as Torvald's lark as well. What do these metaphors say about Nora and the expectations that others have placed upon her?

Reader Response

How timely is this play? For example, in this scene, Torvald states, ". . . but no man sacrifices his honor, even for one he loves" (line 86), and Nora replies, "Millions of women have done so" (line 87). What does this exchange reveal about social roles when the play was written, in the late 1800s? Do you think that social roles have changed or basically remained the same? Relate details from the play to current social life in your explanation.

Master Reading/Writing Scorecard

"A Doll's House"

Skill	Number Correct		Points		Total
Vocabulary					
Vocabulary in Context (2 items)	______	x	5	=	______
Comprehension					
Central Idea (1 item)	______	x	10	=	______
Supporting Details (1 item)	______	x	10	=	______
Transitions (1 item)	______	x	10	=	______
Patterns of Organization (1 item)	______	x	10	=	______
Fact and Opinion (1 item)	______	x	10	=	______
Tone and Purpose (1 item)	______	x	10	=	______
Inferences (1 item)	______	x	10	=	______
Argument (1 item)	______	x	10	=	______
Mapping (5 items)	______	x	2	=	______
			Comprehension Score		

READING 6
Generalization and Example

Fannie Lou Hamer

MAYA ANGELOU

Poet, writer, performer, teacher, and director, Maya Angelou was raised in Stamps, Arkansas, then moved to San Francisco. In addition to her bestselling autobiographies, beginning with *I Know Why the Caged Bird Sings*, she published a cookbook, *Hallelujah! The Welcome Table*, and five poetry collections, including *I Shall Not Be Moved* and *Shaker, Why Don't You Sing?* The following passage appears in *Letter to My Daughter*. In this collection of essays, she shares lessons based on the distilled knowledge of a life well-lived.

Before Reading

Write a journal entry about a public figure you admire. If you could choose a public figure to honor, whom would you choose? What lessons could be learned from this person's life?

Vocabulary

Before, during, and after reading the selection, annotate the text and write in your journal. Create a list of vocabulary words and supply their definitions. Give examples of how these words are used in the selection you just read.

> "All of this on account we want to register, to become first-class citizens, and if the Freedom Democratic Party is not seated now, I question America, is this America, the land of the free and the home of the brave, where we have to sleep with our telephones off the hooks because our lives be threatened daily because we want to live as decent human beings, in America? Thank you." 1
> —Fannie Lou Hamer

It is important that we know that those words come from the lips of an African American woman. It is imperative that we know those words come from the heart of an American. 2

I believe that there lives a burning desire in the most sequestered private heart of every American, a desire to belong to a great country. 3

I believe that every citizen wants to stand on the world stage and represent a noble country where the mighty do not always crush the weak and the dream of a democracy is not the sole possession of the strong.

We must hear the questions raised by Fannie Lou Hamer forty years ago. Every American everywhere asks herself, himself, these questions Hamer asked: 4

What do I think of my country? What is there, which elevates my shoulders and stirs my blood when I hear the words, the United States of America: Do I praise my country enough? Do I laud my fellow citizens enough? What is there about my country that makes me hang my head and avert my eyes when I hear the words the United States of America, and what am I doing about it? Am I relating my disappointment to my leaders and to my fellow citizens, or am I like someone not involved, sitting high and looking low? As Americans, we should not be afraid to respond. 5

We have asked questions down a pyramid of years and given answers, which our children memorize, and which have become an integral part of the spoken American history. Patrick Henry remarked, "I know not what course others may take, but as for me, give me liberty or give me death." 6

George Moses Horton, the nineteenth century poet, born a slave, said, "Alas, and was I born for this, to wear this brutish chain? I must slash the handcuffs from my wrists and live a man again." 7

> "The thought of only being a creature of the present and the past was troubling. I longed for a future too, with hope in it. The desire to be free, awakened my determination to act, to think, and to speak." 8
>
> —Frederick Douglass

The love of democracy motivated Harriet Tubman to seek and find not only her own freedom, but to make **innumerable** trips to the slave South to gain the liberty of many slaves and instill the idea into the hearts of thousands that freedom is possible. 9

Fannie Lou Hamer and the Mississippi Democratic Freedom Party were standing on the shoulders of history when they acted to unseat evil from its presumed safe perch on the backs of the American people. It is fitting to honor the memory of Fannie Lou Hamer and surviving members of the Mississippi Democratic Freedom Party. For their gifts to us, we say thank you. 10

The human heart is so delicate and sensitive that it always needs some **tangible** encouragement to prevent it from faltering in its labor. 11

CONTINUED

READING SELECTION 6 *CONTINUED*

The human heart is so robust, so tough, that once encouraged it beats its rhythm with a loud unswerving insistency. One thing that encourages the heart is music. Throughout the ages we have created songs to grow on and to live by. We Americans have created music to embolden the hearts and inspire the spirit of people all over the world.

Fannie Lou Hamer knew that she was one woman and only one 12
woman. However, she knew she was an American, and as an American
she had a light to shine on the darkness of racism. It was a little light, but
she aimed it directly at the gloom of ignorance.

Fannie Lou Hamer's favorite was a simple song that we all know. We 13
Americans have sung it since childhood . . .

"This little light of mine, I'm going to let it shine, Let it shine, 14
Let it shine, 15
Let it shine. 16

Reading Comprehension Questions

Choose the best meaning of each word in **bold**. Use context clues to make your choice.

Vocabulary in Context

____ **1.** "The love of democracy motivated Harriet Tubman to seek and find not only her own freedom, but to make **innumerable** trips to the slave South to gain the liberty of many slaves and instill the idea into the hearts of thousands that freedom is possible." (paragraph 9)

a. few
b. specific
c. immense
d. countless

Vocabulary in Context

____ **2.** "The human heart is so delicate and sensitive that it always needs some **tangible** encouragement to prevent it from faltering in its labor." (paragraph 11)

a. obvious
b. important
c. subtle
d. indescribable

Central Idea

_____ **3.** Which of the following sentences states the central idea of the passage?

a. "It is important that we know that those words come from the lips of an African American woman." (paragraph 2)

b. "We must hear the questions raised by Fannie Lou Hamer forty years ago." (paragraph 4)

c. "It is fitting to honor the memory of Fannie Lou Hamer and surviving members of the Mississippi Democratic Freedom Party." (paragraph 10)

d. "However, she knew she was an American, and as an American she had a light to shine on the darkness of racism." (paragraph 12)

Supporting Details

_____ **4.** According to the passage, Harriet Tubman was motivated by

a. fear of slavery.

b. love of democracy.

c. the shoulders of history.

d. the work of Fannie Lou Hamer.

Transitions

_____ **5.** "We have asked questions down a pyramid of years and given answers, which our children memorize, and which have become an integral part of the spoken American history. Patrick Henry remarked, 'I know not what course others may take, but as for me, give me liberty or give me death.'" (paragraph 6)

The relationship of ideas **between** these two sentences is

a. cause and effect.

b. process.

c. generalization-example.

d. comparison and contrast.

Patterns of Organization

_____ **6.** The author also mainly uses

a. classification.

b. description.

c. comparison and contrast.

d. time order.

Fact and Opinion

_____ **7.** "It is imperative that we know those words come from the heart of an American." (paragraph 2) This sentence is a statement of

a. fact. **b.** opinion. **c.** fact and opinion.

Tone and Purpose

_____ **8.** The tone and purpose of the passage is to

a. objectively inform the reader about the racism faced by African Americans such as Fannie Lou Hamer.

b. delight the reader with the words and deeds of highly regarded civil rights leaders.

c. convince the reader to appreciate and be inspired by Fannie Lou Hamer and the history she represents.

CONTINUED

READING SELECTION 6 *CONTINUED*

Inferences

_____ **9.** Based on the details in the passage, we can infer that

a. there will always be injustice and oppression.

b. determined individuals can significantly impact society for the good.

c. freedom always comes through violence and loss of life.

d. citizens should love their country unconditionally.

Argument

_____ **10.** The following group of statements from paragraphs 12 and 13 includes a claim and its supporting details. Which statement asserts the claim?

a. "Fannie Lou Hamer knew that she was one woman and only one woman."

b. "However, she knew she was an American, and as an American she had a light to shine on the darkness of racism."

c. "It was a little light, but she aimed it directly at the gloom of ignorance."

d. "Fannie Lou Hamer's favorite was a simple song that we all know."

Outlining

Complete the following outline with information from the passage.

Fannie Lou Hamer

I. Quote by ____________________

II. A Desire to ____________________

III. Questions Asked by ____________________

IV. Questions Asked ____________________

V. To Honor ____________________

____

VI. The Human Heart

VII. Only One Woman

VIII. This Little Light of Mine

After Reading Discussion Questions: Meaning, Structure, and Expression

1. Central Idea: Work with a group to write a summary that answers the following questions: What purpose did Maya Angelou have for writing this essay? Who is her intended audience? What is the central point of the essay? What is the significance of the title?

2. **Relevant Details:** Paragraph 5 lists a number of questions, but offers no answers. Why did Angelou ask but not answer these questions? Whom does she expect to provide these answers? Do you think the essay would have been more or less effective if she had given her own answers? Why or why not?
3. **Logical Order:** Angelou does not state her thesis until paragraph 10. Why did she place her thesis so late in the essay? Would the essay have been more or less effective if she had presented her thesis in the first paragraph? Why or why not?
4. **Effective Expression:** In her essay, Maya Angelou relies heavily on quotations from famous civil right leaders. Discuss the effectiveness of her use of each specific quotation. Why did she choose that particular quotation?

Reader Response

In the opening paragraph, Fannie Lou Hamer asks, "Is this America? The land of the free and the home of the brave?" What is Hamer's question implying about America? Do current circumstances oppose or support her implication? Explain how.

Master Reading/Writing Scorecard					
"Fannie Lou Hamer"					
Skill	**Number Correct**		**Points**		**Total**
Vocabulary					
Vocabulary in Context (2 items)	______	x	5	=	______
Comprehension					
Central Idea (1 item)	______	x	10	=	______
Supporting Details (1 item)	______	x	10	=	______
Transitions (1 item)	______	x	10	=	______
Patterns of Organization (1 item)	______	x	10	=	______
Fact and Opinion (1 item)	______	x	10	=	______
Tone and Purpose (1 item)	______	x	10	=	______
Inferences (1 item)	______	x	10	=	______
Argument (1 item)	______	x	10	=	______
Outlining (5 items)	______	x	2	=	______
			Comprehension Score		

READING 7
Definition and Example

I Hear America Singing

WALT WHITMAN

Walter "Walt" Whitman (1819–1892) was an American poet, essayist, and journalist. Along with Emily Dickinson, Whitman was one of America's most significant and influential poets of the nineteenth century and is considered the father of free verse. His collection of poetry, *Leaves of Grass*, in which the following poem appears, is a landmark in the history of American literature.

Before Reading

Write a journal entry about your views of the United States of America. What about America is worth celebrating or praising? Who or what represents the best of America?

Vocabulary

Before, during, and after reading the selection, annotate the text and write in your journal. Create a list of vocabulary words and supply their definitions. Give examples of how these words are used in the selection you just read.

I hear America singing, the varied carols I hear;
Those of mechanics—each one singing his, as it should be, **blithe** and strong;
The carpenter singing his, as he measures his plank or beam,
The mason singing his, as he makes ready for work, or leaves off work;
The boatman singing what belongs to him in his boat—the deckhand singing on the steamboat deck;
The shoemaker singing as he sits on his bench—the hatter singing as he stands;
The wood-cutter's song—the ploughboy's, on his way in the morning, or at the noon intermission, or at sundown;
The delicious singing of the mother—or of the young wife at work—or of the girl sewing or washing—
Each singing what belongs to her, and to none else;
The day what belongs to the day—at night, the party of young fellows, robust, friendly,
Singing, with open mouths, their strong **melodious** songs.

—From "I Hear America Singing" by Walt Whitman, 1819–1892.

Reading Comprehension Questions

Choose the best meaning of each word in **bold**. Use context clues to make your choice.

Vocabulary in Context

_____ **1.** "Those of mechanics—each one singing his, as it should be, **blithe** and strong;" (line 2)

a. happy
b. anxious
c. mighty
d. soft

Vocabulary in Context

_____ **2.** "Singing, with open mouths, their strong **melodious** songs." (line 11)

a. tuneless
b. pretty
c. tuneful
d. jarring

Implied Central Idea

_____ **3.** Which of the following sentences best states the implied central point of the poem?

a. America is defined by hard work.
b. America is defined by its music.
c. America is defined by the selfless sacrifice of individuals.
d. America is defined by the freedom of individuals to work and enjoy the work they do.

Supporting Details

_____ **4.** Who sings as he stands?

a. the mechanic
b. the mason
c. the carpenter
d. the hatter

Transitions

_____ **5.** "The day what belongs to the day—at night, the party of young fellows, robust, friendly." (line 10)

The main relationship of ideas **within** this sentence is

a. space order.
b. contrast.
c. definition-example.
d. classification.

CONTINUED

Patterns of Organization

_____ **6.** The writer also mainly uses
a. listing.
b. cause and effect.
c. contrast.
d. space order.

Fact and Opinion

_____ **7.** "I hear America singing, the varied carols I hear;" (line 1) is a statement of
a. fact.
b. opinion.
c. fact and opinion.

Tone and Purpose

_____ **8.** The overall tone and purpose of the poem is to
a. inform the reader about the prosperity of America.
b. celebrate the individuals who make America great.
c. convince the reader to become a part of the American experience.

Inferences

_____ **9.** Based on the information in the poem, we can infer that singing is a metaphor for
a. actual songs the American people sang.
b. the actual sounds generated by specific jobs and industry.
c. the struggles of the people.
d. the happiness of free people going about their work.

Argument

_____ **10.** The following lines contain a claim and supports for that claim. Identify the claim.
a. "I hear America singing, the varied carols I hear." (line 1)
b. "The carpenter singing his, as he measures his plank or beam." (line 3)
c. "The delicious singing of the mother—or of the young wife at work—or of the girl sewing or washing—" (line 8)
d. Singing, with open mouths, their strong melodious songs." (line 11)

Mapping

Complete the following concept map with information from the poem.

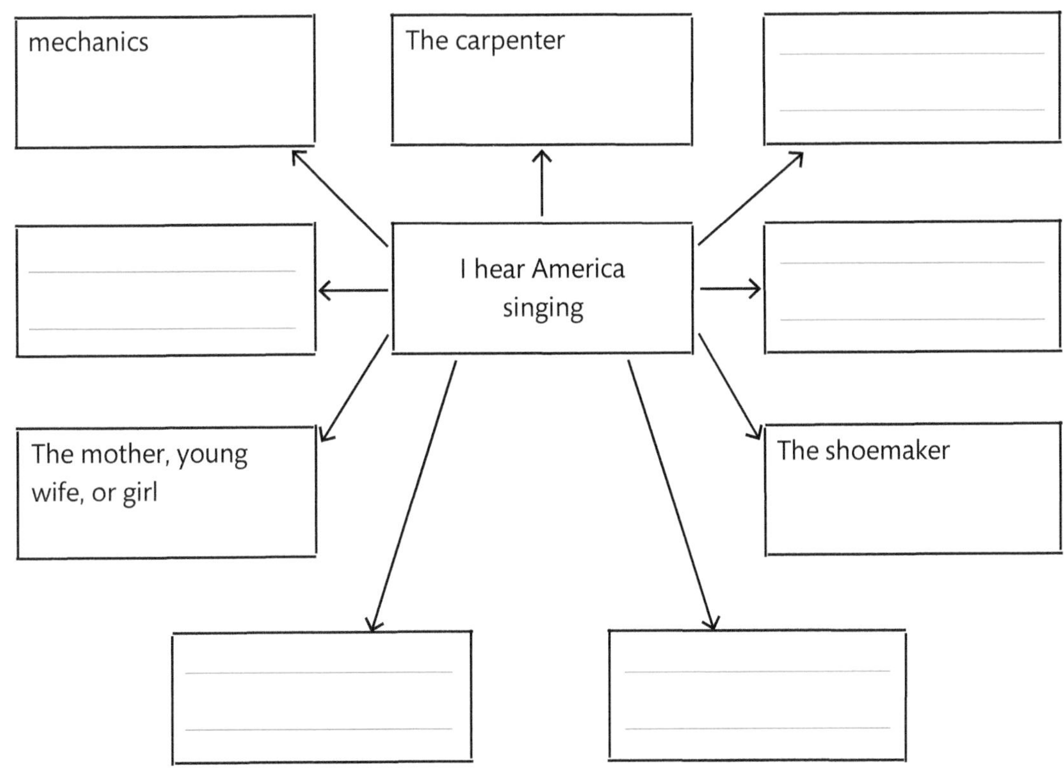

After Reading Discussion Questions: Meaning, Structure, and Expression

1. **Central Idea:** Work with a group to write a summary that answers the following questions: What purpose did Walt Whitman have for writing this poem? Who is his intended audience? What is the central point or theme of the poem? What is the significance of the title?
2. **Relevant Details:** Whitman only includes workers as examples of his ideal of America. Why doesn't he include examples from other walks of life, such as store owners, bankers, or politicians?
3. **Logical Order:** How does the concluding line of the poem reinforce the opening line?
4. **Effective Expression:** Based on Whitman's use of language, how would you describe the tone of this poem? Is it cynical or boastful, or does it communicate some other attitude? Identify three expressions that illustrate the tone of the piece. Explain the reasons for your selections.

CONTINUED

Reader Response

Suppose Whitman was writing "I Hear America Singing" today. How would the poem be different? How would the poem be the same? How would America be defined in current times, and what examples would be used? Write an essay explaining the differences or similarities between the America that Walt Whitman defined and illustrated in his poem and America today.

Master Reading/Writing Scorecard

"I Hear America Singing"

Skill	Number Correct		Points		Total
Vocabulary					
Vocabulary in Context (2 items)	______	x	5	=	______
Comprehension					
Implied Central Idea (1 item)	______	x	10	=	______
Supporting Details (1 item)	______	x	10	=	______
Transitions (1 item)	______	x	10	=	______
Patterns of Organization (1 item)	______	x	10	=	______
Fact and Opinion (1 item)	______	x	10	=	______
Tone and Purpose (1 item)	______	x	10	=	______
Inferences (1 item)	______	x	10	=	______
Argument (1 item)	______	x	10	=	______
Mapping (5 items)	______	x	2	=	______
			Comprehension Score		

READING 8
Classification

Shaking Hands

EDWARD EVERETT

Edward Everett is remembered today as the orator who—on November 19, 1863, at Gettysburg—spoke for over two hours before President Abraham Lincoln delivered his two-minute Gettysburg Address. In addition to being a notable speaker, Everett was an editor, essayist, and statesman. He taught Greek at Harvard and served five terms in Congress.

Before Reading

Write a journal entry about your own observations of shaking hands or how you greet your friends. For example, do you shake hands? Why or why not? If you do, what type of handshake do you prefer? What kind of first impression can handshakes make? Do you use different handshakes or greetings for different types of relationships, such as professional, social, family, and close friends?

Vocabulary

Before, during, and after reading the selection, annotate the text and write in your journal. Create a list of vocabulary words and supply their definitions. Give examples of how these words are used in the selection you just read.

There are few things of more common occurrence than shaking hands; and yet I do not recollect that much has been speculated upon the subject. I confess, when I consider to what unimportant and futile concerns the attention of writers and readers has been directed, I am surprised that no one has been found to *handle* so important a matter as this, and attempt to give the public a rational view of the doctrine and discipline of shaking hands. It is a theme on which I have myself theorized a good deal, and I beg leave to offer a few remarks on the origin of the practice, and the various forms in which it is exercised. 1

I have been unable to find in the ancient writers, any distinct mention of shaking hands. They followed the heartier practice of hugging or embracing, which has not wholly disappeared among grown persons in Europe, and children in our own country, and has unquestionably the advantage on the score of **cordiality**. When the ancients trusted the 2

CONTINUED

business of salutation to the hands alone, they joined but did not shake them; and although I find frequently such phrases as *jungere dextras hospitio*, I do not recollect to have met with that of *agitare dextras*. I am inclined to think that the practice grew up in the ages of chivalry, when the cumbrous iron mail, in which the knights were cased, prevented their embracing; and when, with fingers clothed in steel, the simple touch or joining of the hands would have been but cold welcome; so that a prolonged junction was a natural resort, to express cordiality; and as it would have been awkward to keep the hands unemployed in this position, a gentle agitation or shaking might have been naturally introduced. How long the practice may have remained in this incipient stage, it is impossible, in the silence of history, to say; nor is there anything in the Chronicles, in Philip de Comines, or the Byzantine historians, which enables us to trace the progress of the art, into the forms in which it now exists among us.

3 Without therefore availing myself of the privilege of theorists to supply by conjecture the absence of history or tradition, I shall pass immediately to the enumeration of these forms:

4 1. The *pump-handle* shake is the first which deserves notice. It is executed by taking your friend's hand, and working it up and down, through an arc of fifty degrees, for about a minute and a half. To have its nature, force, and character, this shake should be performed with a fair steady motion. No attempt should be made to give it grace, and, still less, vivacity; as the few instances, in which the latter has been tried, have uniformly resulted in dislocating the shoulder of the person on whom it has been attempted. On the contrary, persons who are partial to the pump-handle shake should be at some pains to give an equable, tranquil movement to the operation, which should on no account be continued after perspiration on the part of your friend has commenced.

5 2. The *pendulum* shake may be mentioned next, as being somewhat similar in character; but moving, as the name indicates, in a horizontal, instead of a perpendicular direction. It is executed by sweeping your hand horizontally toward your friend's, and after the junction is effected, rowing with it from one side to the other, according to the pleasure of the parties. The only caution in its use, which needs particularly to be given, is not to insist on performing it in a plane, strictly parallel to the horizon, when you meet with a person who has been educated to the pump-handle shake. It is well known that people cling to the forms in which they have been educated, even when the substance is sacrificed in adhering to them. I had two acquaintances, both estimable men, one of whom had been brought up in the pump-handle shake, and another had

brought home the pendulum from a foreign voyage. They met, joined hands, and attempted to put them in motion. They were neither of them feeble men. One endeavored to pump, and the other to paddle; their faces reddened; the drops stood on their foreheads; and it was, at last, a pleasing illustration of the doctrine of the composition of forces, to see their hands slanting into an exact diagonal–in which line they ever after shook. But it was plain to see, there was no cordiality in it; and, as is usually the case with compromises, both parties were discontented.

3. The *tourniquet* shake is the next in importance. It derives its name 6
from the instrument made use of by surgeons to stop the circulation of the blood, in a limb about to be amputated. It is performed by clasping the hand of your friend, as far as you can, in your own, and then contracting the muscles of your thumb, fingers and palm, till you have induced any degree of compression you may propose, in the hand of your friend. Particular care ought to be taken, if your own hand is as hard and as big as a frying-pan, and that of your friend as small and soft as a young maiden's, not to make use of the tourniquet shake to the degree that will force the small bones of the wrist out of place. It is also seldom safe to apply it to **gouty** persons. A hearty young friend of mine, who had pursued the study of geology, and acquired an unusual hardness and strength of hand and wrist, by the use of the hammer, on returning from a scientific excursion, gave his gouty uncle the tourniquet shake, with such severity as nearly reduced the old gentleman's fingers to powder; for which my friend had the pleasure of being disinherited, as soon as his uncle's fingers got well enough to hold a pen.

4. The *cordial grapple* is a shake of some interest. It is a hearty, 7
boisterous agitation of your friend's hand, accompanied with moderate pressure, and loud, cheerful exclamations of welcome. It is an excellent travelling shake, and well adapted to make friends. It is indiscriminately performed.

5. The *Peter Grievous touch* is opposed to the cordial grapple. It is 8
a pensive, tranquil junction, followed by a mild subsultary motion, a cast-down look, and an inarticulate inquiry after your friend's health.

6. The *prude major* and *prude minor* are nearly monopolized by 9
ladies. They cannot be accurately described, but are constantly to be noticed in practice. They never extend beyond the fingers; and the prude major allows you to touch even then only down to the second joint. The prude minor gives you the whole of the forefinger. Considerable skill may be shown in performing these, with nice variations, such as extending the left hand, instead of the right, or stretching a new glossy kid glove over the finger you extend.

CONTINUED

10 I might go through a list, of the *gripe royal*, the *saw-mill* shake, and the shake *with malice prepense*; but these are only factitious combinations of the three fundamental forms already described, as the pump-handle, the pendulum, and the tourniquet; as the *loving pat*, the *reach romantic*, and the *sentimental clasp*, may be reduced in their main movements to various combinations and modifications of the cordial grapple, Peter Grievous touch, and the prude major and minor. I should trouble the reader with a few remarks, in conclusion, on the mode of shaking hands, as an indication of characters, but I see a friend coming up the avenue, who is addicted to the pumphandle. I dare not tire my wrist by further writing.

—*The Boston Book: Being Specimens of Metropolitan Literature*, edited by B.B. Thatcher (1837).

Reading Comprehension Questions

Choose the best meaning of each word in **bold**. Use context clues to make your choice.

Vocabulary in Context

_____ **1.** "They followed the heartier practice of hugging or embracing, which has not wholly disappeared among grown persons in Europe, and children in our own country, and has unquestionably the advantage on the score of **cordiality**." (paragraph 2)

a. cold
b. uncaring
c. sympathy
d. welcoming

Vocabulary in Context

_____ **2.** "It is also seldom safe to apply it to **gouty** persons." (paragraph 6)

a. flexible
b. course
c. soft
d. brittle

Central Idea

_____ **3.** Which of the following sentences states the central idea of the passage?

a. "There are few things of more common occurrence than shaking hands; and yet I do not recollect that much has been speculated upon the subject." (paragraph 1)

b. "I confess, when I consider to what unimportant and futile concerns the attention of writers and readers has been directed, I am surprised that no one has been found to *handle* so important a matter as this, and attempt to give the public a rational view of the doctrine and discipline of shaking hands." (paragraph 1)

c. "It is a theme on which I have myself theorized a good deal, and I beg leave to offer a few remarks on the origin of the practice, and the various forms in which it is exercised." (paragraph 1)

d. "I should trouble the reader with a few remarks, in conclusion, on the mode of shaking hands, as an indication of characters, but I see a friend coming up the avenue, who is addicted to the pumphandle." (paragraph 10)

Supporting Details

_____ **4.** According to the passage, there are many "factitious combinations," but only how many fundamental forms of the handshake?

a. three
b. countless
c. six
d. twelve

Transitions

_____ **5.** "The *Peter Grievous touch* is opposed to the cordial grapple." (paragraph 8) The relationship of ideas **within** this sentence is

a. description.
b. process.
c. contrast.
d. cause and effect.

Patterns of Organization

_____ **6.** In addition to classification, paragraphs 3–6 also mainly use

a. contrast.
b. description.
c. cause and effect.
d. definition-example.

Fact and Opinion

_____ **7.** Overall, the passage offers statements of

a. fact.
b. opinion.
c. fact and opinion.

Tone and Purpose

_____ **8.** The overall tone and purpose of the passage is to

a. objectively inform the reader of the types of handshakes.
b. amuse the reader with the writer's observations and analysis of types of handshakes.
c. convince the reader to effectively use the proper type of handshake based on the social situation.

CONTINUED

Inferences

_____ **9.** Based on phrases such as "the first which deserves notice" (paragraph 4) and "is the next in importance" (paragraph 6), may infer that the writer lists the types of handshakes

a. from most important to least important.

b. from least important to most important.

c. from most desirable to least desirable.

d. in no particular order.

Argument

_____ **10.** The following sentences from paragraph 7 state a claim and supports for that claim. Identify the claim.

a. "The *cordial grapple* is a shake of some interest."

b. "It is a hearty, boisterous agitation of your friend's hand, accompanied with moderate pressure, and loud, cheerful exclamations of welcome."

c. "It is an excellent travelling shake, and well adapted to make friends."

d. "It is indiscriminately performed."

Outlining

Complete the following outline with information from the passage.

Forms of Shaking Hands

I. ____________________

II. ____________________

III. ____________________

IV. ____________________

V. The Peter Grievous Shake

VI. ____________________

After Reading Discussion Questions: Meaning, Structure, and Expression

1. **Central Idea:** Work with a group to write a summary that answers the following questions: What purpose did Edward Everett have for writing this essay? Who is his intended audience? What is the central point of the essay? What is the significance of the title?

2. **Relevant Details:** Why does Everett include the details from ancient history in paragraph 2? How do these details relate to his central point?

3. **Logical Order:** Analyze the effectiveness of Everett's concluding paragraph. Which details reinforce his central point? Which statements introduce an idea he does not develop? Why did he include this idea? Why did he conclude his essay with that final sentence?

4. **Effective Expression:** Based on Everett's use of language, how would you describe the tone of this essay? Is it humorous, bitter, matter of fact, or does it communicate some other attitude? How does he use tone to support his central point? Identify three expressions that illustrate the tone of the piece and how tone supports the central point. Explain the reasons for your selections.

Reader Response

In his opening paragraph, Everett refers to shaking hands as a "common occurrence" and expresses surprise that no one has written about "so important a matter as this." He then goes on to thoughtfully analyze the form and functions of several types of handshakes. What other common occurrences might also be important to analyze? Assume you write a weekly blog that is followed by dozens of people. Choose a common occurrence to classify based on its various forms. For example, you may choose to analyze types of lies, types of shoes, types of drivers, or types of people who use of social media. Use Everett's essay as a model to generate and organize your ideas.

Master Reading/Writing Scorecard					
"Shaking Hands"					
Skill	**Number Correct**		**Points**		**Total**
Vocabulary					
Vocabulary in Context (2 items)	______	x	5	=	______
Comprehension					
Central Idea (1 item)	______	x	10	=	______
Supporting Details (1 item)	______	x	10	=	______
Transitions (1 item)	______	x	10	=	______
Patterns of Organization (1 item)	______	x	10	=	______
Fact and Opinion (1 item)	______	x	10	=	______
Tone and Purpose (1 item)	______	x	10	=	______
Inferences (1 item)	______	x	10	=	______
Argument (1 item)	______	x	10	=	______
Outlining (5 items)	______	x	2	=	______
			Comprehension Score		

READING 9
Comparison and Contrast

On the Difference Between Wit and Humor

CHARLES S. BROOKS

Charles S. Brooks (1878–1934) was an American novelist, essayist, and playwright who retired at the age of 37 from a successful career in his family's printing and stationery business to devote himself to a life of writing. He produced more than a dozen volumes of work and founded the Cleveland Play House.

Before Reading

Write a journal entry about the differences between wit and humor. For example, can wit or humor be used in different ways to make someone feel good or bad about themselves or about certain situation? How so?

Vocabulary

Before, during, and after reading the selection, annotate the text and write in your journal. Create a list of vocabulary words and supply their definitions. Give examples of how these words are used in the selection you just read.

1 I am not sure that I can draw an exact line between wit and humor. Perhaps the distinction is so subtle that only those persons can decide who have long white beards. But even an ignorant man, so long as he is clear of Bedlam, may have an opinion.

2 I am quite positive that of the two, humor is the more comfortable and more livable quality. Humorous persons, if their gift is genuine and not a mere shine upon the surface, are always agreeable companions and they sit through the evening best. They have pleasant mouths turned up at the corners. To these corners the great Master of marionettes has fixed the strings and he holds them in his nimblest fingers to twitch them at the slightest jest. But the mouth of a merely witty man is hard and sour until the moment of its discharge. Nor is the flash from a witty man always comforting, whereas a humorous man radiates a general pleasure and is like another candle in the room.

I admire wit, but I have no real liking for it. It has been too often employed against me, whereas humor is always an ally. It never points an impertinent finger into my defects. Humorous persons do not sit like explosives on a fuse. They are safe and easy comrades. But a wit's tongue is as sharp as a donkey driver's stick. I may gallop the faster for its prodding, yet the touch behind is too persuasive for any comfort. 3

Wit is a lean creature with sharp inquiring nose, whereas humor has a kindly eye and comfortable girth. Wit, if it be necessary, uses malice to score a point—like a cat it is quick to jump—but humor keeps the peace in an easy chair. Wit has a better voice in a solo, but humor comes into the chorus best. Wit is as sharp as a stroke of lightning, whereas humor is diffuse like sunlight. Wit keeps the season's fashions and is precise in the phrases and judgments of the day, but humor is concerned with homely eternal things. Wit wears silk, but humor in homespun endures the wind. Wit sets a snare, whereas humor goes off whistling without a victim in its mind. Wit is sharper company at table, but humor serves better in mischance and in the rain. When it tumbles, wit is sour, but humor goes uncomplaining without its dinner. Humor laughs at another's jest and holds its sides, while wit sits wrapped in study for a lively answer. But it is a workaday world in which we live, where we get mud upon our boots and come weary to the twilight—it is a world that grieves and suffers from many wounds in these years of war: and therefore as I think of my acquaintance, it is those who are humorous in its best and truest meaning rather than those who are witty who give the more profitable companionship. 4

And then, also, there is wit that is not wit. As someone has written: 5

> Nor ever noise for wit on me could pass,
> When thro' the braying I discern'd the ass.

I sat lately at dinner with a notoriously witty person (a really witty man) whom our hostess had introduced to provide the entertainment. I had read many of his reviews of books and plays, and while I confess their wit and brilliancy, I had thought them to be hard and intellectual and lacking in all that broader base of humor which aims at truth. His writing—catching the bad habit of the time—is too ready to proclaim a paradox and to assert the unusual, to throw aside in contempt the valuable haystack in a fine search for a paltry needle. His reviews are seldom right—as most of us see the right—but they sparkle and hold one's interest for their perversity and unexpected turns. 6

In conversation I found him much as I had found him in his writing—although, strictly speaking, it was not a conversation, which requires an 7

CONTINUED

interchange of word and idea and is turn about. A conversation should not be a market where one sells and another buys. Rather, it should be a bargaining back and forth, and each person should be both merchant and buyer. My rubber plant for your victrola, each offering what he has and seeking his deficiency. It was my friend B— who fairly put the case when he said that he liked so much to talk that he was willing to pay for his audience by listening in his turn.

But this was a speech and a lecture. He loosed on us from the cold spigot of his intellect a steady flow of literary **allusion**—a practice which he professes to hold in scorn—and wit and epigram. He seemed torn from the page of Meredith. He talked like ink. I had believed before that only people in books could talk as he did, and then only when their author had blotted and scratched their performance for a seventh time before he sent it to the printer. To me it was an entirely new experience, for my usual acquaintances are good common honest daytime woollen folk and they seldom average better than one bright thing in an evening. 8

At first I feared that there might be a break in his flow of speech which I should be obliged to fill. Once, when there was a slight pause—a truffle was engaging him—I launched a frail remark; but it was swept off at once in the renewed torrent. And seriously it does not seem fair. If one speaker insists—to change the figure—on laying all the cobbles of a conversation, he should at least allow another to carry the tarpot and fill in the chinks. When the evening was over, although I recalled two or three clever stories, which I shall botch in the telling, I came away tired and dissatisfied, my tongue dry with disuse. 9

Now I would not seek that kind of man as a companion with whom to be becalmed in a sailboat, and I would not wish to go to the country with him, least of all to the North Woods or any place outside of civilization. I am sure that he would sulk if he were deprived of an audience. He would be crotchety at breakfast across his bacon. Certainly for the woods a humorous man is better company, for his humor in mischance comforts both him and you. A humorous man—and here lies the heart of the matter—a humorous man has the high gift of regarding an annoyance in the very stroke of it as another man shall regard it when the annoyance is long past. If a humorous person falls out of a canoe he knows the exquisite jest while his head is still bobbing in the cold water. A witty man, on the contrary, is sour until he is changed and dry: but in a week's time when company is about, he will make a comic story of it. 10

My friend A— with whom I went once into the Canadian woods has genuine humor, and no one can be a more satisfactory comrade. I do not 11 recall that he said many comic things, and at bottom he was serious as the best humorists are. But in him there was a kind of joy and exaltation that lasted throughout the day. If the duffle were piled too high and fell about his ears, if the dinner was burned or the tent blew down in a driving storm at night, he met these mishaps as though they were the very things he had come north to get, as though without them the trip would have lacked its spice. This is an easy philosophy in retrospect but hard when the wet canvas falls across you and the rain beats in. A— laughed at the very moment of disaster as another man will laugh later in an easy chair. I see him now swinging his axe for firewood to dry ourselves when we were spilled in a rapids; and again, while pitching our tent on a sandy beach when another storm had drowned us. And there is a certain cry of his (dully, *Wow!* on paper) expressive to the initiated of all things gay, which could never issue from the mouth of a merely witty man.

Real humor is primarily human—or divine, to be exact—and after that the fun may follow naturally in its order. Not long ago I saw Louis Jouvet of the French Company play Sir Andrew Ague-Cheek. It was a most humorous performance of the part, and the reason is that the actor made no primary effort to be funny. It was the humanity of his playing, making his audience love him first of all, that provoked the comedy. His long thin legs were comical and so was his drawling talk, but the very heart and essence was this love he started in his audience. Poor fellow! How delightfully he smoothed the feathers in his hat! How he feared to fight the duel! It was easy to love such a dear silly human fellow. A merely witty player might have drawn as many laughs, but there would not have been the catching at the heart. 12

As for books and the wit or humor of their pages, it appears that wit fades, whereas humor lasts. Humor uses permanent nutgalls. But is there anything more **melancholy** than the wit of another generation? In the first place, this wit is intertwined with forgotten circumstance. It hangs on a fashion—on the style of a coat. It arose from a forgotten bit of gossip. In the play of words the sources of the pun are lost. It is like a local jest in a narrow coterie, barren to an outsider. Sydney Smith was the most celebrated wit of his day, but he is dull reading now. *Blackwood's* at its first issue was a witty daring sheet, but for us the pages are stagnant. I suppose that no one now laughs at the witticisms of Thomas Hood. Where are the wits of yesteryear? Yet the humor of Falstaff and Lamb and Fielding remains and is a reminder to us that humor, to be real, must be founded on humanity and on truth. 13

—"On the Difference Between Wit and Humor" by Charles S. Brooks first appeared in the collection *Chimney-Pot Papers* published in 1919 by Yale University Press.

CONTINUED

Reading Comprehension Questions

Choose the best meaning of each word in **bold**. Use context clues to make your choice.

Vocabulary in Context

_____ **1.** "But this was a speech and a lecture. He loosed on us from the cold spigot of his intellect a steady flow of literary **allusion**—a practice which he professes to hold in scorn—and wit and epigram." (paragraph 8)

a. reference
b. announcement
c. declaration
d. symbol

Vocabulary in Context

_____ **2.** "But is there anything more **melancholy** than the wit of another generation?" (paragraph 13)

a. fresh
b. unusual
c. stale
d. memorable

Central Idea

_____ **3.** Which of the following sentences states the central idea of paragraphs 1–13?

a. "Wit, if it be necessary, uses malice to score a point—like a cat it is quick to jump—but humor keeps the peace in an easy chair." (paragraph 4)

b. "But it is a workaday world in which we live, where we get mud upon our boots and come weary to the twilight—it is a world that grieves and suffers from many wounds in these years of war: and therefore as I think of my acquaintance, it is those who are humorous in its best and truest meaning rather than those who are witty who give the more profitable companionship." (paragraph 4)

c. "A humorous man—and here lies the heart of the matter—a humorous man has the high gift of regarding an annoyance in the very stroke of it as another man shall regard it when the annoyance is long past." (paragraph 10)

d. "As for books and the wit or humor of their pages, it appears that wit fades, whereas humor lasts." (paragraph 13)

Supporting Details

_____ **4.** According to the passage, humorous persons are

a. like explosives on a fuse.
b. safe and easy comrades.
c. sharp as a stroke of lighting.
d. sour.

Transitions

_____ **5.** "If a humorous person falls out of a canoe he knows the exquisite jest while his head is still bobbing in the cold water. A witty man, on the contrary, is sour until he is changed and dry: but in a week's time when company is about, he will make a comic story of it." (paragraph 10)

The relationship of ideas **between** these sentences is

a. cause and effect.
b. time order.
c. comparison and contrast.
d. generalization-example.

Patterns of Organization

_____ **6.** The overall pattern of organization of paragraphs 6–9 is

a. cause and effect.
b. time order.
c. generalization-example.
d. comparison and contrast.

Fact and Opinion

_____ **7.** "Sydney Smith was the most celebrated wit of his day, but he is dull reading now." (paragraph 13)

This sentence is a statement of

a. fact.
b. opinion.
c. fact and opinion.

Tone and Purpose

_____ **8.** The overall tone and purpose of the author is to

a. inform the reader about the difference between wit and humor.
b. entertain the reader with interesting details about how wit and humor differ.
c. persuade the reader that humor is superior to wit.

Inferences

_____ **9.** Based on the details of the passage, we can infer that

a. wit is mean and unnecessary.
b. humor can be a helpful tool in difficult situations.
c. humor is about being funny.
d. wit is about being smart.

CONTINUED

Argument

_____ **10.** The following items from paragraph 9 contain a claim and a list of supports for that claim. Which sentence states the claim?

a. "At first I feared that there might be a break in his flow of speech which I should be obliged to fill."

b. "Once, when there was a slight pause—a truffle was engaging him—I launched a frail remark; but it was swept off at once in the renewed torrent."

c. "If one speaker insists—to change the figure—on laying all the cobbles of a conversation, he should at least allow another to carry the tarpot and fill in the chinks."

d. "When the evening was over, although I recalled two or three clever stories, which I shall botch in the telling, I came away tired and dissatisfied, my tongue dry with disuse."

Mapping

Complete the following concept map with information from the passage.

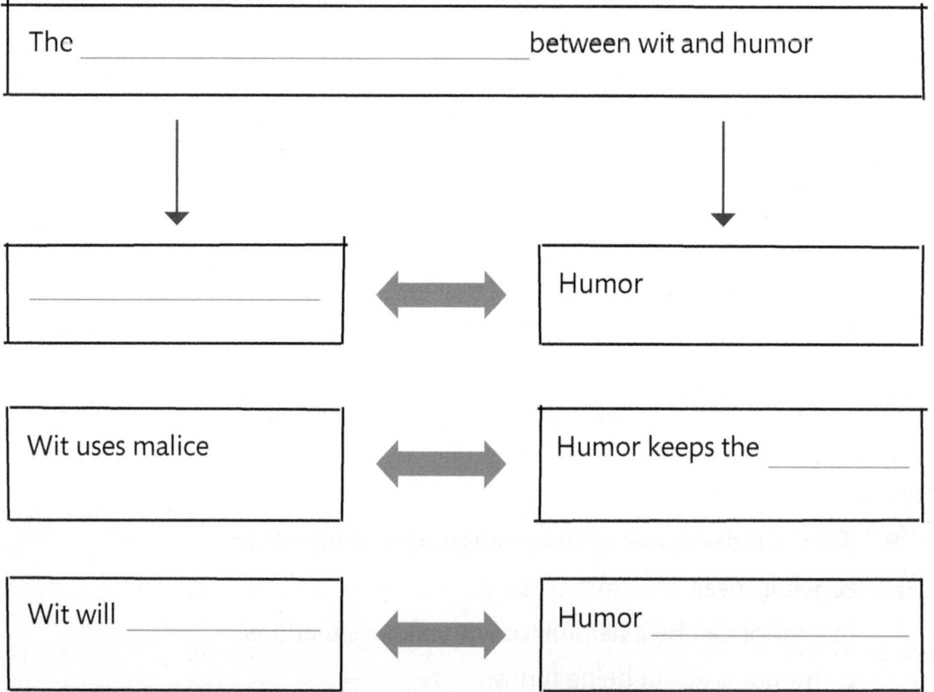

After Reading Discussion Questions: Meaning, Structure, and Expression

1. **Central Idea:** Work with a group to write a summary that answers the following questions: What purpose did Charles S. Brooks have for writing this essay? Who is the intended audience? What is the central idea of the essay?
2. **Relevant Details:** The details of this passage explain the differences in the temperaments of witty and humorous people. How does the author describe wit? How does he describe humor? How do the two differ? Brooks begins his essay by saying wit is a "better voice in a solo, but humor comes into the chorus best." Then the author tells stories about two very different people. One uses wit; the other uses humor. Why do you think he chose these two specific experiences to make his point?

3. **Logical Order:** How does Charles S. Brooks organize his ideas? Does he talk about the similarities and differences of wit and humor? Does he compare and contrast the two ideas and give examples of both? Does he use blocks of information or a point-by-point analysis? Do you think this was an effective organization? Why or why not?
4. **Effective Expression:** Charles S. Brooks wrote this essay almost a hundred years ago. Do you think it is still relevant today? Does the formal tone add to his argument or take away from it? Choose a paragraph from the essay and rewrite it in your own words. How does that change the effectiveness of the selection?

Reader Response

Charles S. Brooks illustrates the difference between wit and humor by comparing and contrasting them to many different things. What other differences between wit and humor have you observed? For example, is wit always used in a negative way? Is humor always kind? Write an essay using your own set of comparable points that discusses other important differences between wit and humor. Choose an audience and a writing situation such as the following: a group of elementary school students you are speaking to about appropriate ways to play and have group fun, or a high school newsletter about how humor and wit can also be a passive form of bullying.

Master Reading/Writing Scorecard

"On the Difference Between Wit and Humor"

Skill	Number Correct		Points		Total
Vocabulary					
Vocabulary in Context (2 items)	______	x	5	=	______
Comprehension					
Central Idea (1 item)	______	x	10	=	______
Supporting Details (1 item)	______	x	10	=	______
Transitions (1 item)	______	x	10	=	______
Patterns of Organization (1 item)	______	x	10	=	______
Fact and Opinion (1 item)	______	x	10	=	______
Tone and Purpose (1 item)	______	x	10	=	______
Inferences (1 item)	______	x	10	=	______
Argument (1 item)	______	x	10	=	______
Mapping (5 items)	______	x	2	=	______
			Comprehension Score		

READING 10
Argument

The Morality of Birth Control

MARGARET SANGER

Margaret Sanger's (1879–1966) work as an activist contributed to the legalizing of contraception in the United States. Sanger worked as a nurse in New York City's East Side slums. She deeply understood the plight of poor women who struggled with frequent pregnancies, miscarriages, and self-induced abortions due to lack of knowledge about how to prevent pregnancy. She coined the term *birth control*, opened the first birth control clinic in the country, and founded the American Birth Control League that eventually became the Planned Parenthood Federation of America.

Originally scheduled to be delivered at the close of the First American Birth Control Conference on November 13, 1921, the following speech was made on November 18 after the police raided the Town Hall and arrested Sanger. This speech was given at the Park Theatre, in New York City.

Before Reading

Birth control has long been a controversial subject. Many believe a woman has the right to control decisions about her body, including if and when to have children. Many religious traditions teach that God creates each human life; thus, pregnancy should not be prevented or terminated. Furthermore, many believe that the human right to life begins at conception. Write a journal entry about your views of birth control.

Vocabulary

Before, during, and after reading the selection, annotate the text and write in your journal. Create a list of vocabulary words and supply their definitions. Give examples of how these words are used in the selection you just read.

The meeting tonight is a postponement of one which was to have taken place at the Town Hall last Sunday evening. It was to be a culmination of a three day conference, two of which were held at the Hotel Plaza, in discussing the Birth Control subject in its various and manifold aspects. 1

The one issue upon which there seems to be most uncertainty and disagreement exists in the moral side of the subject of Birth Control. It seemed only natural for us to call together scientists, educators, members of the medical profession and the theologians of all denominations to ask 2 their opinion upon this uncertain and important phase of the controversy. Letters were sent to the most eminent men and women in the world. We asked in this letter, the following questions:

3 1. Is over-population a menace to the peace of the world? 2. Would the legal dissemination of scientific Birth Control information through the medium of clinics by the medical profession be the most logical method of checking the problem of over-population? 3. Would knowledge of Birth Control change the moral attitude of men and women toward the marriage bond or lower the moral standards of the youth of the country? 4. Do you believe that knowledge which enables parents to limit the families will make for human happiness, and raise the moral, social and intellectual standards of population?

4 We sent such a letter not only to those who, we thought, might agree with us, but we sent it also to our known opponents. Most of these people answered. Every one who answered did so with sincerity and courtesy, with the exception of one group whose reply to this important question as demonstrated at the Town Hall last Sunday evening was a disgrace to liberty-loving people, and to all traditions we hold dear in the United States. I believed that the discussion of the moral issue was one which did not solely belong to theologians and to scientists, but belonged to the people. And because I believed that the people of this country may and can discuss this subject with dignity and with intelligence I desired to bring them together, and to discuss it in the open.

5 When one speaks of moral, one refers to human conduct. This implies action of many kinds, which in turn depends upon the mind and the brain. So that in speaking of morals one must remember that there is a direct connection between morality and brain development. Conduct is said to be action in pursuit of ends, and if this is so, then we must hold the irresponsibility and recklessness in our action is immoral, while responsibility and forethought put into action for the benefit of the individual and the race becomes in the highest sense the finest kind of morality.

6 We know that every advance that woman has made in the last half century has been made with opposition, all of which has been based upon the grounds of immorality. When women fought for higher education, it was said that this would cause her to become immoral and she would lose her place in the sanctity of the home. When women asked for the franchise it was said that this would lower her standard of morals, that it was not fit that she should meet with and mix with the members of the opposite sex, but we notice that there was no objection to her meeting with the same members of the opposite sex when she went to church.

CONTINUED

The church has ever opposed the progress of woman on the ground 7
that her freedom would lead to immorality. We ask the church to have more confidence in women. We ask the opponents of this movement to reverse the methods of the church, which aims to keep women moral by keeping them in fear and in ignorance, and to **inculcate** into them a higher and truer morality based upon knowledge. And ours is the morality of knowledge. If we cannot trust woman with the knowledge of her own body, then I claim that two thousand years of Christian teaching has proved to be a failure.

We stand on the principle that Birth Control should be available to every 8
adult man and woman. We believe that every adult man and woman should be taught the responsibility and the right use of knowledge. We claim that woman should have the right over her own body and to say if she shall or if she shall not be a mother, as she sees fit. We further claim that the first right of a child is to be desired. While the second right is that it should be conceived in love, and the third, that it should have a heritage of sound health.

Upon these principles the Birth Control movement in America stands. 9

When it comes to discussing the methods of Birth Control, that is far 10
more difficult. There are laws in this country which forbid the imparting of practical information to the mothers of the land. We claim that every mother in this country, either sick or well, has the right to the best, the safest, the most scientific information. This information should be disseminated directly to the mothers through clinics by members of the medical profession, registered nurses and registered midwives.

Our first step is to have the backing of the medical profession so that 11
our laws may be changed, so that motherhood may be the function of dignity and choice, rather than one of ignorance and chance. Conscious control of offspring is now becoming the ideal and the custom in all civilized countries.

Those who oppose it claim that however desirable it may be on 12
economic or social grounds, it may be abused and the morals of the youth of the country may be lowered. Such people should be reminded that there are two points to be considered. First, that such control is the inevitable advance in civilization. Every civilization involves an increasing forethought for others, even for those yet unborn. The reckless abandonment of the impulse of the moment and the careless regard for the consequences is not morality. The selfish gratification of temporary desire at the expense of suffering to lives that will come may seem very beautiful to some, but it is not our conception of civilization, or is it our concept of morality.

In the second place, it is not only inevitable, but it is right to control 13
the size of the family for by this control and adjustment we can raise

the level and the standards of the human race. While Nature's way of reducing her numbers is controlled by disease, famine and war, primitive man has achieved the same results by infanticide, exposure of infants, the abandonment of children, and by abortion. But such ways of controlling population is no longer possible for us. We have attained high standards of life, and along the lines of science must we conduct such control. We must begin farther back and control the beginnings of life. We must control conception. This is a better method; it is a more civilized method, for it involves not only greater forethought for others, but finally a higher sanction for the value of life itself.

Society is divided into three groups. Those intelligent and wealthy 14
members of the upper classes who have obtained knowledge of Birth Control and exercise it in regulating the size of their families. They have already benefited by this knowledge, and are today considered the most respectable and moral members of the community. They have only children when they desire and all society points to them as types that should perpetuate their kind.

The second group is equally intelligent and responsible. They desire 15
to control the size of their families, but are unable to obtain knowledge or to put such available knowledge into practice.

The third are those irresponsible and reckless ones having little 16
regard for the consequence of their acts, or whose religious scruples prevent their exercising control over their numbers. Many of this group are diseased, feeble-minded, and are of the pauper element dependent entirely upon the normal and fit members of society for their support. There is no doubt in the minds of all thinking people that the **procreation** of this group should be stopped. (Applause.) For if they are not able to support and care for themselves, they should certainly not be allowed to bring offspring into this world for others to look after. (Applause.) We do not believe that filling the earth with misery, poverty and disease is moral. And it is our desire and intention to carry on our crusade until the perpetuation of such conditions has ceased.

We desire to stop at its source the disease, poverty and feeble- 17
mindedness and insanity which exist today, for these lower the standards of civilization and make for race deterioration. We know that the masses of people are growing wiser and are using their own minds to decide their individual conduct. The more people of this kind we have, the less immorality shall exist. For the more responsible people grow, the higher do they and shall they attain real morality. (Applause.)

—Margaret Sanger, "The Morality of Birth Control," 18 Nov 1921. Published Speech. Source: *The Morality of Birth Control* (New York, 1921), Margaret Sanger Microfilm S70:917.

CONTINUED

Reading Comprehension Questions

Choose the best meaning of each word in **bold**. Use context clues to make your choice.

Vocabulary in Context

_____ **1.** "We ask the opponents of this movement to reverse the methods of the church, which aims to keep women moral by keeping them in fear and in ignorance, and to **inculcate** into them a higher and true morality based upon knowledge." (paragraph 7)

a. instill

b. attain

c. prepare

d. force

Vocabulary in Context

_____ **2.** "There is no doubt in the minds of all thinking people that the **procreation** of this group should be stopped." (paragraph 16)

a. support

b. reproduction

c. work

d. training

Central Idea

_____ **3.** Which sentence best states the central idea of the passage?

a. "The one issue upon which there seems to be most uncertainty and disagreement exists in the moral side of the subject of Birth Control." (paragraph 2)

b. "When one speaks of moral, one refers to human conduct." (paragraph 5)

c. "We stand on the principle that Birth Control should be available to every adult man and woman." (paragraph 8)

d. "For the more responsible people grow, the higher do they and shall they attain real morality." (paragraph 17)

Supporting Details

_____ **4.** According to Sanger, there is a direct connection between morality and

a. human conduct.

b. the church.

c. birth control.

d. brain development.

Transitions

_____ **5.** "For the more responsible people grow, the higher do they and shall they attain real morality." (paragraph 17)

The relationship of ideas **within** this sentence is

a. cause and effect.
b. space order.
c. process.
d. classification.

Patterns of Organization

_____ **6.** The overall pattern of organization for paragraphs 14–16 is

a. comparison.
b. process.
c. cause and effect.
d. classification.

Fact and Opinion

_____ **7.** Overall, the passage mostly offers statements of

a. fact.
b. opinion.
c. fact and opinion.

Tone and Purpose

_____ **8.** The overall tone and purpose of the passage is to

a. inform the audience of the need for birth control.
b. interest the audience with shocking views about birth control.
c. argue for widespread acceptance and use of birth control.

Inferences

_____ **9.** Based on the context of information in paragraph 4, we may infer that

a. all who received Sanger's letter responded with polite sincerity.
b. all who received Sanger's letter agreed with her views about birth control.
c. some who received Sanger's letter ignored it.
d. some who received Sanger's letter were so offended that they publically protested against her views about birth control.

Argument

_____ **10.** "Many of this group are diseased, feeble-minded, and are of the pauper element dependent entirely upon the normal and fit members of society for their support." (paragraph 16)

This statement is an irrelevant detail by the use of the fallacy

a. bandwagon.
b. plain folks.
c. personal attack.
d. begging the question.

CONTINUED

Mapping

Complete the following concept map with information from the passage.

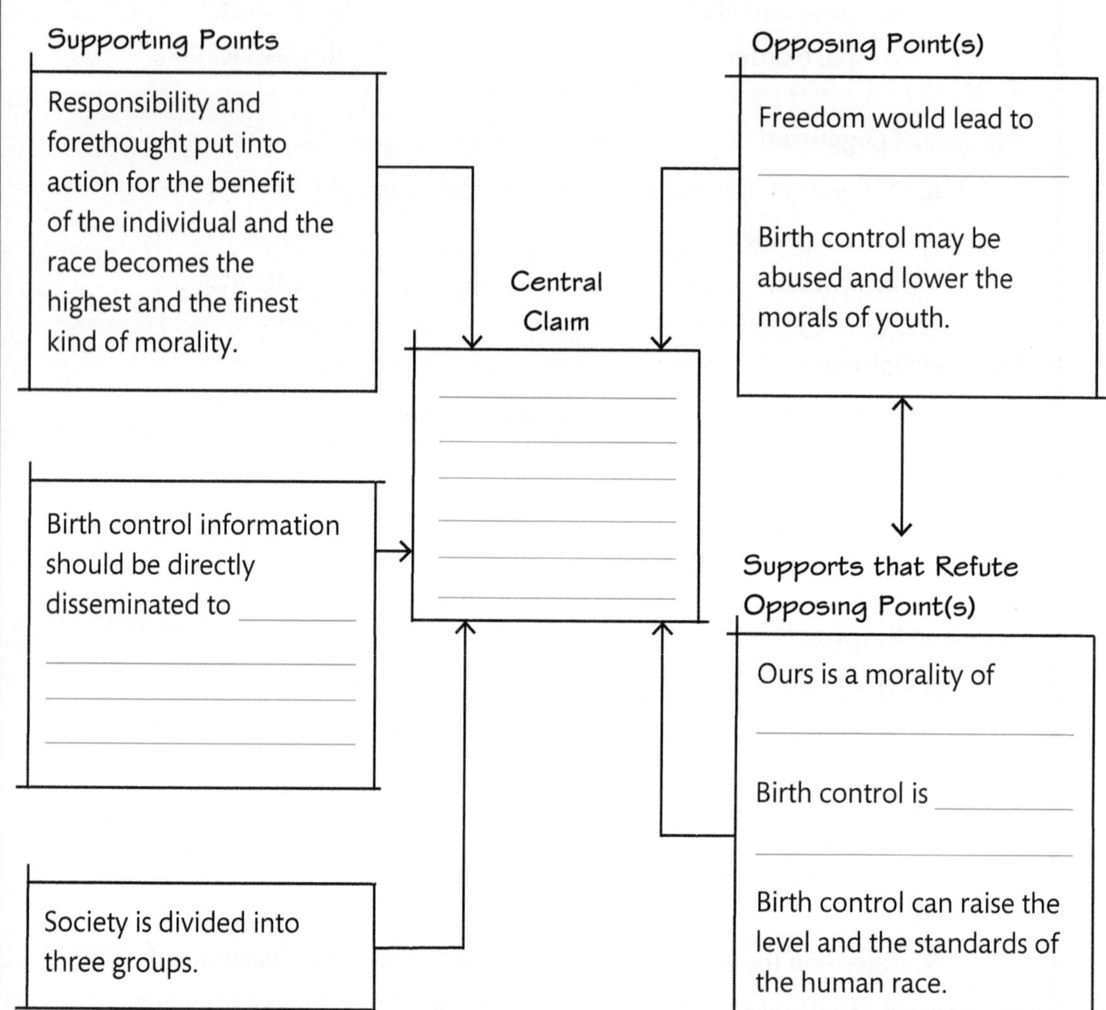

Supporting Points
Responsibility and forethought put into action for the benefit of the individual and the race becomes the highest and the finest kind of morality.
Birth control information should be directly disseminated to ______
Society is divided into three groups.
Central Claim
Opposing Point(s)
Freedom would lead to ______
Birth control may be abused and lower the morals of youth.
Supports that Refute Opposing Point(s)
Ours is a morality of ______
Birth control is ______
Birth control can raise the level and the standards of the human race.

After Reading Discussion Questions: Meaning, Structure, and Expression

1. **Central Idea:** Work with a group to write a summary that answers the following questions: What purpose did Margaret Sanger have for writing this speech? Who is the intended audience? What is the central idea of the speech?
2. **Relevant Details:** Does Sanger offer verifiable facts or personal opinions to support her claim that birth control is moral? What additional facts might have been relevant to her argument? Whose expert opinions does she use? Whose expert opinions might have strengthened her argument? Why?
3. **Logical Order:** Why did Sanger wait until the middle of her speech (paragraph 8) to explain the principles of birth control? Would her speech have been more effective if she had begun with these principles? Why or why not?

4. **Effective Expression:** Based on Sanger's use of language, how would you describe the tone of this speech? Is it sarcastic, hopeful, passionate, objective, or does it communicate some other attitude? Identify three expressions that illustrate the tone of the piece. Explain the reasons for your selections.

Reader Response

Margaret Sanger remains a controversial figure in the debate about birth control and reproductive rights. Some see her as a pioneer whose efforts have improved the lives of women. Others see her as a bigot who opposed religion and warred against the poor. The speech "The Morality of Birth Control" asserts her core beliefs, which still fuel the controversy surrounding her legacy today. Assume you are taking a college sociology course. Write an essay in which you support or oppose Sanger's work and views about birth control. Use evidence from her speech to support your stance.

Master Reading/Writing Scorecard					
"The Morality of Birth Control"					
Skill	**Number Correct**		**Points**		**Total**
Vocabulary					
Vocabulary in Context (2 items)	______	x	5	=	______
Comprehension					
Central Idea (1 item)	______	x	10	=	______
Supporting Details (1 item)	______	x	10	=	______
Transitions (1 item)	______	x	10	=	______
Patterns of Organization (1 item)	______	x	10	=	______
Fact and Opinion (1 item)	______	x	10	=	______
Tone and Purpose (1 item)	______	x	10	=	______
Inferences (1 item)	______	x	10	=	______
Argument (1 item)	______	x	10	=	______
Mapping (5 items)	______	x	2	=	______
			Comprehension Score		

READING 11
Argument

Nobel Lecture: The Nobel Peace Prize 2014

MALALA YOUSAFZAI

Malala Yousafzai, born on July 12, 1997, in Mingora, Pakistan, became an activist at a very young age, speaking out for girls' education. A Taliban edict had banned girls' education and resulted in hundreds of schools being destroyed in her region. At the age of 11, Yousafzai wrote "Diary of a Pakistani Schoolgirl." First published on BBC Urdu online, her diary records the impact the ban on their education had on her and her classmates. As a result of her public stand, the Taliban issued a death threat against her. On October 9, 2012, a militant shot Yousafzai in the head. The gunman boarded her school bus in her hometown Swat and opened fire. Two of her school friends were also wounded. She survived the terrible assault and gained worldwide fame and admiration. She has continued to speak out on the importance of education. Named one of *Time* magazine's most influential people in 2013, she won the Nobel Peace Prize in 2014. Yousafzai is the youngest person to receive the Nobel Peace Prize.

Before Reading

Write a journal entry about the importance of education. Why do you think the Taliban banned education for girls? What would you do if you were told you had no right to attend school?

Vocabulary

Before, during, and after reading the selection, annotate the text and write in your journal. Create a list of vocabulary words and supply their definitions. Give examples of how these words are used in the selection you just read.

Bismillah hir rahman ir rahim. 1

In the name of God, the most merciful, the most beneficent.

Your Majesties, Your royal highnesses, distinguished members of the Norwegian Nobel Committee, 2

Dear sisters and brothers, today is a day of great happiness for me. I am humbled that the Nobel Committee has selected me for this precious award. 3

Thank you to everyone for your continued support and love. Thank 4
you for the letters and cards that I still receive from all around the world. Your kind and encouraging words strengthens and inspires me.

I would like to thank my parents for their unconditional love. Thank 5
you to my father for not clipping my wings and for letting me fly. Thank you to my mother for inspiring me to be patient and to always speak the truth—which we strongly believe is the true message of Islam. And also thank you to all my wonderful teachers, who inspired me to believe in myself and be brave.

I am proud, well in fact, I am very proud to be the first Pashtun, the 6
first Pakistani, and the youngest person to receive this award. Along with that, along with that, I am pretty certain that I am also the first recipient of the Nobel Peace Prize who still fights with her younger brothers. I want there to be peace everywhere, but my brothers and I are still working on that.

I am also honored to receive this award together with Kailash 7
Satyarthi, who has been a champion for children's rights for a long time. Twice as long, in fact, than I have been alive. I am proud that we can work together, we can work together and show the world that an Indian and a Pakistani, they can work together and achieve their goals of children's rights.

Dear brothers and sisters, I was named after the inspirational Malalai 8
of Maiwand who is the Pashtun Joan of Arc. The word Malala means "grief stricken," "sad," but in order to lend some happiness to it, my grandfather would always call me Malala–"The happiest girl in the world" and today I am very happy that we are together fighting for an important cause.

This award is not just for me. It is for those forgotten children who 9
want education. It is for those frightened children who want peace. It is for those voiceless children who want change.

I am here to stand up for their rights, to raise their voice . . . it is not 10
time to pity them. It is not time to pity them. It is time to take action so it becomes the last time, the last time, so it becomes the last time that we see a child deprived of education.

I have found that people describe me in many different ways. 11

Some people call me the girl who was shot by the Taliban. 12

And some, the girl who fought for her rights. 13

Some people, call me a "Nobel Laureate" now. 14

However, my brothers still call me that annoying bossy sister. As 15
far as I know, I am just a committed and even stubborn person who wants to see every child getting quality education, who wants to see

CONTINUED

women having equal rights and who wants peace in every corner of the world.

Education is one of the blessings of life—and one of its necessities. 16
That has been my experience during the 17 years of my life. In my paradise home, Swat, I always loved learning and discovering new things. I remember when my friends and I would decorate our hands with henna on special occasions. And instead of drawing flowers and patterns we would paint our hands with mathematical formulas and equations.

We had a thirst for education, we had a thirst for education because 17
our future was right there in that classroom. We would sit and learn and read together. We loved to wear neat and tidy school uniforms and we would sit there with big dreams in our eyes. We wanted to make our parents proud and prove that we could also excel in our studies and achieve those goals, which some people think only boys can.

But things did not remain the same. When I was in Swat, which was a 18
place of tourism and beauty, suddenly changed into a place of terrorism. I was just ten that more than 400 schools were destroyed. Women were flogged. People were killed. And our beautiful dreams turned into nightmares.

Education went from being a right to being a crime. Girls were 19
stopped from going to school.

When my world suddenly changed, my priorities changed too. 20

I had two options. One was to remain silent and wait to be killed. 21
And the second was to speak up and then be killed.

I chose the second one. I decided to speak up. 22

We could not just stand by and see those injustices of the terrorists 23
denying our rights, ruthlessly killing people and misusing the name of Islam. We decided to raise our voice and tell them: Have you not learnt, have you not learnt that in the Holy Quran Allah says: if you kill one person it is as if you kill the whole humanity?

Do you not know that Mohammad, peace be upon him, the prophet 24
of mercy, he says, "do not harm yourself or others."

And do you not know that the very first word of the Holy Quran is the 25
word "Iqra," which means "read"?

The terrorists tried to stop us and attacked me and my friends who 26
are here today, on our school bus in 2012, but neither their ideas nor their bullets could win.

We survived. And since that day, our voices have grown louder and 27
louder. I tell my story, not because it is unique, but because it is not.

It is the story of many girls. 28

Today, I tell their stories too. I have brought with me some of my 29
sisters from Pakistan, from Nigeria and from Syria, who share this story. My brave sisters Shazia and Kainat, who were also shot that day on our school bus. But they have not stopped learning. And my brave sister Kainat Soomro who went through severe abuse and extreme violence, even her brother was killed, but she did not **succumb**.

Also my sisters here, whom I have met during my Malala Fund 30
campaign. My 16-year-old courageous sister, Mezon from Syria, who now lives in Jordan as refugee and goes from tent to tent encouraging girls and boys to learn. And my sister Amina, from the North of Nigeria, where Boko Haram threatens, and stops girls and even kidnaps girls, just for wanting to go to school.

Though I appear as one girl, though I appear as one girl, one person, 31
who is 5 foot 2 inches tall, if you include my high heels. (It means I am 5 foot only) I am not a lone voice, I am not a lone voice, I am many.

I am Malala. But I am also Shazia. 32

I am Kainat. 33

I am Kainat Soomro. 34

I am Mezon. 35

I am Amina. I am those 66 million girls who are deprived of 36
education. And today I am not raising my voice, it is the voice of those 66 million girls.

Sometimes people like to ask me why should girls go to school, why 37
is it important for them. But I think the more important question is why shouldn't they, why shouldn't they have this right to go to school.

Dear sisters and brothers, today, in half of the world, we see rapid 38
progress and development. However, there are many countries where millions still suffer from the very old problems of war, poverty, and injustice.

We still see conflicts in which innocent people lose their lives and 39
children become orphans. We see many people becoming refugees in Syria, Gaza and Iraq. In Afghanistan, we see families being killed in suicide attacks and bomb blasts.

Many children in Africa do not have access to education because of 40
poverty. And as I said, we still see, we still see girls who have no freedom to go to school in the north of Nigeria.

Many children in countries like Pakistan and India, as Kailash Satyarthi 41
mentioned, many children, especially in India and Pakistan are deprived

CONTINUED

of their right to education because of social **taboos**, or they have been forced into child marriage or into child labour.

42 One of my very good school friends, the same age as me, who had always been a bold and confident girl, dreamed of becoming a doctor. But her dream remained a dream. At the age of 12, she was forced to get married. And then soon she had a son, she had a child when she herself was still a child—only 14. I know that she could have been a very good doctor.

43 But she couldn't . . . because she was a girl.

44 Her story is why I dedicate the Nobel Peace Prize money to the Malala Fund, to help give girls quality education, everywhere, anywhere in the world and to raise their voices. The first place this funding will go to is where my heart is, to build schools in Pakistan—especially in my home of Swat and Shangla.

45 In my own village, there is still no secondary school for girls. And it is my wish and my commitment, and now my challenge to build one so that my friends and my sisters can go there to school and get quality education and to get this opportunity to fulfill their dreams.

46 This is where I will begin, but it is not where I will stop. I will continue this fight until I see every child, every child in school.

47 Dear brothers and sisters, great people, who brought change, like Martin Luther King and Nelson Mandela, Mother Teresa and Aung San Suu Kyi, once stood here on this stage. I hope the steps that Kailash Satyarthi and I have taken so far and will take on this journey will also bring change—lasting change.

48 My great hope is that this will be the last time, this will be the last time we must fight for education. Let's solve this once and for all.

49 We have already taken many steps. Now it is time to take a leap.

50 It is not time to tell the world leaders to realize how important education is—they already know it—their own children are in good schools. Now it is time to call them to take action for the rest of the world's children.

51 We ask the world leaders to unite and make education their top priority.

52 Fifteen years ago, the world leaders decided on a set of global goals, the Millennium Development Goals. In the years that have followed, we have seen some progress. The number of children out of school has been halved, as Kailash Satyarthi said. However, the world focused only on primary education, and progress did not reach everyone.

In year 2015, representatives from all around the world will meet 53
in the United Nations to set the next set of goals, the Sustainable
Development Goals. This will set the world's ambition for the next
generations.

The world can no longer accept, the world can no longer accept 54
that basic education is enough. Why do leaders accept that for children
in developing countries, only basic literacy is sufficient, when their own
children do homework in Algebra, Mathematics, Science and Physics?

Leaders must seize this opportunity to guarantee a free, quality, 55
primary and secondary education for every child.

Some will say this is impractical, or too expensive, or too hard. Or 56
maybe even impossible. But it is time the world thinks bigger.

Dear sisters and brothers, the so-called world of adults may 57
understand it, but we children don't. Why is it that countries which we
call "strong" are so powerful in creating wars but are so weak in bringing
peace?

Why is it that giving guns is so easy but giving books is so hard? Why 58
is it, why is it that making tanks is so easy, but building schools is so hard?

We are living in the modern age and we believe that nothing is 59
impossible. We have reached the moon 45 years ago and maybe will
soon land on Mars. Then, in this 21st century, we must be able to give
every child quality education.

Dear sisters and brothers, dear fellow children, we must work . . . 60
not wait. Not just the politicians and the world leaders, we all need to
contribute. Me. You. We. It is our duty.

Let us become the first generation to decide to be the last, let us 61
become the first generation that decides to be the last that sees empty
classrooms, lost childhoods, and wasted potentials.

Let this be the last time that a girl or a boy spends their childhood in 62
a factory.

Let this be the last time that a girl is forced into early child marriage. 63

Let this be the last time that a child loses life in war. 64

Let this be the last time that we see a child out of school. 65

Let this end with us. 66

Let's begin this ending . . . together . . . today . . . right here, right 67
now. Let's begin this ending now. Thank you so much.

–"Malala Yousafzai–Nobel Lecture". Nobelprize.org. Nobel Media AB 2014. Web. 16 Jan 2015.

CONTINUED

Reading Comprehension Questions

Choose the best meaning of each word in **bold**. Use context clues to make your choice.

Vocabulary in Context

____ **1.** "And my brave sister Kainat Soomro who went through severe abuse and extreme violence, even her brother was killed, but she did not **succumb**." (paragraph 29)

a. win
b. live
c. yield
d. complain

Vocabulary in Context

____ **2.** ". . . many children, especially in India and Pakistan are deprived of their right to education because of social **taboos**, or they have been forced into child marriage or child labour. " (paragraph 41)

a. supports
b. permissions
c. dangers
d. restrictions

Central Idea

____ **3.** Which of the following sentences best states the central idea of the passage?

a. "I am humbled that the Nobel Committee has selected me for this precious award." (paragraph 3)
b. "Education is one of the blessings of life—and one of its necessities." (paragraph 16)
c. "I am not a lone voice, I am not a lone voice, I am many." (paragraph 31)
d. "Leaders must seize this opportunity to guarantee a free, quality, primary and secondary education for every child." (paragraph 55)

Supporting Details

____ **4.** Malala Yousafzai's home country is

a. Pakistan.
b. India.
c. Nigeria.
d. Syria.

Transitions

____ **5.** "But she couldn't . . . because she was a girl." (paragraph 43)

The main relationship of ideas **within** this sentence is

a. classification.
b. space order.
c. comparison and contrast.
d. cause and effect.

Patterns of Organization

_____ **6.** What is the overall primary pattern of organization for the lecture?

a. classification
b. time order
c. comparison and contrast
d. generalization-example

Fact and Opinion

_____ **7.** Paragraph 26 states

a. facts.
b. opinions.
c. fact and opinion.

Tone and Purpose

_____ **8.** The overall tone and purpose of the speech is to

a. inform the audience about the need for and barriers to education for girls in certain parts of the world.
b. entertain the audience with a personal story of overcoming oppression.
c. argue for the world leaders to take action to ensure free and quality education for girls everywhere.

Inferences

_____ **9.** Based on the information in paragraph 21, we may infer that Yousafzai

a. was afraid of dying.
b. expected to be killed no matter what action she took.
c. knew she would survive any attack against her.
d. wanted to die and become a martyr for her cause.

Argument

_____ **10.** Which of the following statements does Yousafzai offer as an opposing view to her claim about education for girls.

a. "I am here to stand up for their rights, to raise their voice . . . it is not time to pity them." (paragraph 10)
b. "I am those 66 million girls who are deprived of education." (paragraph 36)
c. "I will continue this fight until I see every child, every child in school." (paragraph 46)
d. "Some will say this is impractical, or too expensive, or too hard. Or maybe even impossible." (paragraph 56)

CONTINUED

Outlining

Complete the following outline with information from the passage.

"Nobel Lecture" by Malala Yousafzai

I. Greeting and Thank you
   A. Recognition of ___________
   B. Recognition of Nobel Committee
   C. Recognition of everyone for continued support
   D. Recognition of parents
   E. Recognition of Kailash Satyarthi, co-recipient
II. This award is not just for ___________.
   A. People describe me in many different ways.
   B. Education in one of the blessings in life—and one of its necessities.
III. When my world changed, my ______________ changed too.
IV. It is the story of many girls.
V. We ask the world leaders to ______________________________.
VI. Let us become the first generation to decide to be the last that sees ______ ______________________________________.

After Reading Discussion Questions: Meaning, Structure, and Expression

1. **Central Idea:** Work with a group to write a summary that answers the following questions: What purpose did Malala Yousafzai have for writing this piece? Who is the intended audience? What is the central idea of the speech?
2. **Relevant Details:** What detail does Yousafzai use to open her speech? How does this detail relate to her central point? Why does she use this detail as her introduction?
3. **Logical Order:** To make her argument for global support of education for women, Yousafzai organized her ideas to move from her personal story to the stories of other girls unjustly treated in her community, nation, and surrounding countries. Then she concludes with an appeal for global response and responsibility. Create an outline that shows this movement from the personal to the global. Why did she begin with her personal experience and conclude with the global appeal? Why didn't she begin by describing the problem and then end with her personal experience?

4. **Effective Expression:** Throughout her speech, Yousafzai repeats certain patterns of speech. For example, in paragraph 17, she repeats the phrase "We had a thirst for education" Another example occurs in paragraph 48 with the repetition of "this will be the last time." Many other instances occur throughout her speech. Find at least three more examples of repeating patterns of speech. Describe the effect of these repetitions. Which use of repetition seems most powerful? Why?

Reader Response

Assume you taking a college course in sociology. A key assignment is to identify a person who has made an impact on society and analyze the significance of that impact. You have chosen to write about Malala Yousafzai. You are expected to provide a written and oral response that includes the following information: A brief biography of the person; the person's notable achievements; and the scope and significance of his or her impact on society.

Master Reading/Writing Scorecard

"Nobel Lecture"

Skill	Number Correct		Points		Total
Vocabulary					
Vocabulary in Context (2 items)	______	x	5	=	______
Comprehension					
Central Idea (1 item)	______	x	10	=	______
Supporting Details (1 item)	______	x	10	=	______
Transitions (1 item)	______	x	10	=	______
Patterns of Organization (1 item)	______	x	10	=	______
Fact and Opinion (1 item)	______	x	10	=	______
Tone and Purpose (1 item)	______	x	10	=	______
Inferences (1 item)	______	x	10	=	______
Argument (1 item)	______	x	10	=	______
Outlining (5 items)	______	x	2	=	______
			Comprehension Score		

Photo Credits

2: Wave Break Media/Shutterstock; **3 top:** Andrey Popov/Shutterstock; **3 middle:** Purple Queue/Shutterstock; **3 bottom:** Dragon Images/Shutterstock; **11 top:** Wavebreak Media/Shutterstock; **11 middle:** bikeriderlondon/Shutterstock; **11 bottom:** Rubberball/Corbis; **13:** GL Archive/Alamy; **28 left:** Tammy Hanratty/Fancy/Corbis; **28 right:** Tim Robbins/Mint Images/Corbis; **37:** Library of Congress Prints and Photographs Division [LC-USZ62-78987]; **45:** Richard M Lee/Shutterstock; **46:** Diego Cervo/Shutterstock; **49:** Konstantin Chagin/Shutterstock; **54:** Vitchanan Photography/Shutterstock; **55 top:** Kzenon/Shutterstock; **55 middle:** Creativa/Shutterstock; **55 bottom:** Odua Images/Shutterstock; **68:** Colin Anderson/Getty Images; **70:** Library of Congress Prints and Photographs Division [LC-DIG-ppmsca-32842]; **71:** Library of Congress Prints and Photographs Division [LC-DIG-ppmsca-19926]; **78:** R Carner/Shutterstock; **89:** Golden Pixels LLC/Shutterstock; **94:** Ringo Chiu/ZUMA Press/Corbis; **95 top:** Jaboo2foto/Shutterstock; **95 middle:** LuckyImages/Shutterstock; **95 bottom:** Wavebreak Media/Shutterstock; **97:** John Lund/Blend Images/Corbis; **106:** Ryan Jorgensen Jorgo/Shutterstock; **113:** Fine Art/Corbis; **130:** Auremar/Shutterstock; **131**: Auremar/Shutterstock; **134:** Pearson Education, Inc.; **138:** KPG Payless2/Shutterstock; **139 top:** Tsyhun/Shutterstock; **139 middle:** Hero Images/Fancy/Corbis; **139 bottom:** Monkey Business Images/Shutterstock; **144 upper left:** William Perugini/Shutterstock; **144 upper right:** Wavebreak Media/Shutterstock; **144 lower left:** Nemke/Shutterstock; **146:** Nick Pavlakis/Shutterstock; **152:** Metamorphosis of Narcissus, 1937. Oil on canvas, 511 x 781 cm/Dali, Salvador (1904-1989)/Tate, London/Art Resource, NY; **154:** Ewa Studio/Shutterstock; **155:** Adoc-photos/Historical/Corbis; **178:** Bikerider London/Shutterstock; **179 upper left:** Freer/Fotolia; **179 upper right:** Bloomua/Shutterstock; **179 lower left:** Karen Roach/Shutterstock; **179 lower right:** Vepar5/Shutterstock; **183:** Library of Congress Prints and Photographs Division [LC-USZ62-48965]; **191:** Library of Congress Prints and Photographs Division [LC-USZ62-53346]; **195:** Woolaroc Museum & Wildlife Preserve; **213:** William H. Rau/Culver Pictures/The Art Archive at Art Resource, NY; **218:** Simon Jarratt/Cardinal/Corbis; **219 top:** Michaeljung/Shutterstock; **219 middle:** Eric Audras/Onoky/Corbis; **219 bottom:** Rachid Dahnoun/Aurora Open/Corbis; **223:** United States Environmental Protection Agency; **224:** United States Environmental Protection Agency; **227:** *Ready.gov*, Federal Emergency Management Agency (FEMA); **228:** Big Cypress National Preserve, Florida. NPS/Brodeur; **242:** Yevgeniy11/Shutterstock; **243:** Hurst Photo/Shutterstock; **244:** National Oceanic and Atmospheric Administration; **246:** Cialino/National Oceanic and Atmospheric Administration; **252:** Taiga/Shutterstock; **258:** Ammentorp Photography/Shutterstock; **259 top:** Monkey Business Images/Shutterstock; **259 middle:** Whisson/Jordan/Corbis; **259 bottom:** Alexander Raths/Shutterstock; **265:** Screenshot from General OneFile. © Gale, a part of Cengage Learning, Inc. Reproduced by permission; **280:** Alzheimer's Association National Office; **294 top:** Ducu59us/Shutterstock; **294 middle:** Monkey Business Images/Shutterstock; **294 bottom:** Wavebreak Media/Shutterstock; **300:** Cathy Keifer/Shutterstock; **301 top:** Vitalinka/Shutterstock; **301 middle:** Angela Luchianiuc/Shutterstock; **301 bottom:** Stefanolunardi/Shutterstock; **307:** Lynn Goldsmith/Corbis Entertainment/Corbis; **312:** Courtesy of Perkins School for the Blind Archives, Watertown, MA; **334:** Monkey Business Images/Shutterstock; **336:** Monkey Business Images/Shutterstock; **337:** Photobank gallery/Shutterstock; **338:** Rawpixel/Shutterstock; **344:** Rawpixel/Shutterstock; **345 top:** Wavebreak Media/Shutterstock; **345 middle:** NASA, ISS037-E-028787, November 9, 2013; **345 bottom:** Architect of the Capitol; **355:** NASA/JPL-Caltech/Malin Space Science Systems; **356:** Library of Congress, Prints & Photographs Division [LC-USZ62-75620]; **368:** BRAIN Initiative Infographic, *Whitehouse.gov*; **369-370:** Department of Molecular and Cellular Biology, Harvard University; **371:** National Archives and Records Administration; **372:** National Oceanic and Atmospheric Administration; **379:** Todor Rusinov/Shutterstock; **384:** Scyther/Shutterstock; **385 top:** Patryk Kosmider/Shutterstock; **385 middle:** Kuzma/Shutterstock; **385 bottom:** O Driscoll Imaging/Shutterstock; **391:** Maksim Kabakou/Shutterstock; **397:** Shandrus/Shutterstock; **411:** GPS, National Coordination Office for Space-Based Positioning, Navigation, and Timing, National Oceanic and Atmospheric Administration; **412:** GPS, National Coordination Office for Space-Based Positioning, Navigation, and Timing, National Oceanic and Atmospheric Administration; **413:** Maksim Kabakou/Shutterstock; **418:** Syda Productions/Shutterstock; **421:** Shvaygert Ekaterina/Shutterstock; **426:** Pincasso/Shutterstock; **427 top:** Dmitry Kalinovsky/Shutterstock; **427 middle:** Zerbor/Shutterstock; **427 bottom:** Suzanne Tucker/Shutterstock; **434:** Alexander Widding/Alamy; **438:** Ted Spiegel/Corbis; **451:** Library of Congress, Prints & Photographs Division [LC-USZ62-132047]; **452:** National Space Science Data Center, NASA, National Space Science Data Center, *http://nssdc.gsfc.nasa.gov/planetary/image/sputnik_asm.jpg*; **456:** Odua Images/Shutterstock; **457:** Odua Images/Shutterstock; **459:** Lassedesignen/Shutterstock; **464:** Peeradach Rattanakoses/Shutterstock; **465 top left:** photka/Shutterstock; **465 top middle:** Hill Street Studios/Blend Images/Corbis; **465 top right:** Eric Crama/Shutterstock; **465 bottom left:** Eric Krouse/Shutterstock; **469:** U.S. Army Signal Corps, Courtesy of Harry S. Truman Library; **476:** Steve Estvanik/Shutterstock; **477:** Ivan Nesterov/Alamy; **489:** Library of Congress, Prints & Photographs Division [LC-USZ61-361]; **491:** Library of Congress, Prints & Photographs Division [LC-USZ62-23933]; **494:** Omikron Omikron/Getty Images; **501:** USAID; **503:** Albund/Shutterstock; Vitchanan Photography/Shutterstock

Text Credits

Aronson, Elliot; Wilson, Timothy D; Akert, Robin M., *Social Psychology*, 8th Ed., © 2013, pp. 10–11, 416–418, 427–428. Reprinted and Electronically reproduced by permission of Pearson Education, Inc., Hoboken, New Jersey.

Bevington, David, *The Complete Works of Shakespeare*, 4th Ed., © 1997, pp. 1074, 1075, 1076. Reprinted and Electronically reproduced by permission of Pearson Education, Inc., Hoboken, New Jersey.

Cahn, Dudley D.; Abigail, Ruth Anna, *Managing Conflict Through Communication*, 5th Ed., © 2014, pp. 42–43, 178–179, 813–814. Reprinted and Electronically reproduced by permission of Pearson Education, Inc., Hoboken, New Jersey.

Center for Substance Abuse Prevention, *Substance Abuse and Mental Health Services Administration, Results from the 2010 National Survey on Drug Use and Health: Summary of National Findings*, NSDUH Series H-41, HHS Publication No. (SMA) 11-4658. Rockville, MD: Center for Substance Abuse Prevention, Substance Abuse and Mental Health Services Administration, 2011.

Ciccarelli, Saundra K.; White, J. Noland, *Psychology*, 2nd Ed., © 2009, pp. 600-601. Reprinted and Electronically reproduced by permission of Pearson Education, Inc., Hoboken, New Jersey.

Ciccarelli, Saundra K.; White, J. Noland, *Psychology*, 4th Ed., © 2015, pp. 152, 176–179, 187, 209–211, 294–297, 325, 354–358. Reprinted and Electronically reproduced by permission of Pearson Education, Inc., Hoboken, New Jersey.

Cobb, Bethany, "The War Machine." Used with Permission.

Colbert, Bruce J., *Navigating Your Future Success*, 2nd Ed., © 2015, pp. 7, 20–22, 24–25, 29–31, 78–79, 80–82, 176–177. Reprinted and Electronically reproduced by permission of Pearson Education, Inc., Hoboken, New Jersey.

DeVito, Joseph A., *The Essential Elements of Public Speaking*, 5th Ed., © 2015, pp. 19–22, 128–129, 276–277. Reprinted and Electronically reproduced by permission of Pearson Education, Inc., Hoboken, New Jersey.

DeVito, Joseph A., *The Interpersonal Communication Book*, 11th Ed., pp. 212–213. Reprinted and Electronically reproduced by permission of Pearson Education, Inc., Hoboken, New Jersey.

Donatelle, Rebecca, *Health: The Basics*, 11th Ed., © 2015, p. 143. Reprinted and Electronically reproduced by permission of Pearson Education, Inc., Hoboken, New Jersey.

Earnest, Reagan, "Overcoming Communication Barriers." Used with Permission.

Evans, Alan; Martin, Kendall; Poatsy, Mary Anne, *Introductory Technology in Action*, 7th Ed., Prentice Hall 2011, pp. 79–80; 142–143, 373, 425. Reprinted by permission.

Fahrenbach, Colleen. "The Recipe for Good Citizenship." Used with Permission.

Folger, Joseph P.; Poole, Marshall Scott; Stutman, Randall K., *Working Through Conflict*, 4th Ed., pp. 5–6. © Pearson Education, Inc. Used by permission.

Gerrig, Richard J., *Psychology and Life*, 20th Ed., © 2013, p. 80. Reprinted and Electronically reproduced by permission of Pearson Education, Inc., Hoboken, New Jersey.

Gerrig, Richard J.; Zimbardo, Philip G., *Psychology and Life*, 19th Ed., p. 407. Reprinted by permission.

Hamilton, Bethany, blog, *Soulsurfer.com*.

Henslin, James M., *Sociology: A Down-to-Earth Approach*, 10th Ed., © 2010, pp. 608–609. (Figure *The 20 Largest Cities in the World* was created by the author; based on United Nations 2008: Table 3.) Reprinted and Electronically reproduced by permission of Pearson Education, Inc., Hoboken, New Jersey.

Henslin, James M., *Sociology: A Down-to-Earth Approach*, 11th Ed., © 2012, p. 423. Reprinted and Electronically reproduced by permission of Pearson Education, Inc., Hoboken, New Jersey.

Hunt, Elgin F.; Colander, David C., *Social Science: An Introduction to the Study of Society*, 14th Ed., © 2011, p. 127. Reprinted and Electronically reproduced by permission of Pearson Education, Inc., Hoboken, New Jersey.

Kohl, Herbert, "I Wont Learn From You" from *I Won't Learn From You* (Minneapolis: Milkweed Editions, 1991). © 1991 by Herbert Kohl. Reprinted with permission from Milkweed Editions. *www.milkweed.org*

Levack, Brian; Muir, Edward; Veldman, Meredith; Maas, Michael, *The West: Encounters & Transformations*, 2nd Ed., © 2008, pp. 807–871. Reprinted and Electronically reproduced by permission of Pearson Education, Inc., Hoboken, New Jersey.

Macionis, John J., *Society: The Basics*, 13th Ed., © 2015, pp. 276-277. Reprinted and Electronically reproduced by permission of Pearson Education, Inc., Hoboken, New Jersey.

Macionis, John J., *Sociology*, 15th Ed., © 2014, pp. 129–130, 130–131, 407–413, 444–446. Reprinted and Electronically reproduced by permission of Pearson Education, Inc., Hoboken, New Jersey.

Martin, James Kirby; Roberts, Randy J.; Mintz, Steven; McMurry, Linda O.; Jones, James H., *America and Its Peoples: A Mosaic in the Making*, 5th Ed., © 2004, pp. 356, 258–259. Reprinted and Electronically reproduced by permission of Pearson Education, Inc., Hoboken, New Jersey.

Mayer, Richard E., "Three Facets of the Visualizer-Verbalizer Dimension," *Journal of Educational Psychology*, American Psychological Association, © 2003. Published by the American Psychological Association.

Miller, Madelyn, "The Pros and Cons of Living in a Digital Age." Used with Permission.

National Park Service. *Women's Rights. Report of the 1848 Women's Rights Convention*. 7 July 2014. *http://www.nps.gov/wori/historyculture/report-of-the-womans-rights-convention.html*

Obed, Alex, "Let Your Life Speak." Used by permission.

Ralston, Aron, "127 Hours: Between a Rock and a Hard Place."

Renzetti, Clarie M., *Women, Men, and Society*, 6th Ed., pp. 147–149. Copyright © 2012 Pearson Education, Inc. Used by permission.

Ruggiero, Vincent Ryan, *The Art of Thinking*, 10th Ed., pp. 11-12, 12–14. Copyright © 2012 Pearson Education, Inc. Used by permission.

Sayre, Henry M., *Discovering the Humanities*, 1st Ed., © 2010, pp. 446–447. Reprinted and Electronically reproduced by permission of Pearson Education, Inc., Hoboken, New Jersey.

Sayre, Henry M., *The Humanities: Culture, Continuity, and Change, Volume I*, 3rd Ed., © 2015, p 18. Reprinted and Electronically reproduced by permission of Pearson Education, Inc., Hoboken, New Jersey.

Schwartz, Mary Ann; Scott, Barbara Marliene, *Marriages and Families: Diversity and Change*, Census Update, p. 136. © 2010, Pearson Education, Inc.

Solomon, Michael, R.; Poatsy, Mary Anne; Martin, Kendall, *Better Business*, 3rd Ed., © 2014, p. 93, 64-66, 205–207, 264–265, 268, 275–276. Reprinted and Electronically reproduced by permission of Pearson Education, Inc., Hoboken, New Jersey.

Stewart, David; Blocker, H. Gene; Petrik, James, *Fundamentals of Philosophy*, 7th Ed., © 2010, pp. 85-86. Reprinted and Electronically reproduced by permission of Pearson Education, Inc., Hoboken, New Jersey.

Thompson, Janice J.; Manore, Melinda, *Nutrition for Life*, 3rd Ed., © 2013, pp. 284–286. Reprinted and Electronically reproduced by permission of Pearson Education, Inc., Hoboken, New Jersey.

United States Food and Drug Administration. Nutrition label. *http://www.fda.gov/food/guidanceregulation/guidancedocumentsregulatoryinformation/labelingnutrition/ucm385663.htm*

Withgott, Jay; Laposata, Matthew, *Environment: The Science Behind the Stories*, 5th Ed., pp. 432–433, 502–503. Copyright © 2014, Benjamin Cummings. Used by permission.

Wood, Samuel; Wood, Ellen Green; Boyd, Denise, *Mastering the World of Psychology*, 5th Ed., © 2014, p. 127. Reprinted by permission of Pearson Education, Inc., Hoboken, New Jersey.

Woolfolk, Anita, *Educational Psychology*, 10th Ed., © 2007, pp. 124-127. Reprinted and Electronically reproduced by permission of Pearson Education, Inc., Hoboken, New Jersey.

Zimbardo, Philip G.; Johnson, Robert L.; Hamilton, Vivian McCann, *Psychology: Core Concepts*, 7th Ed., pp. 405-406. Reprinted by permission.

Index

A

A Doll's House, Act III, Final Scene (Ibsen), 584–593
a lot/allot, 541
Absolute adjectives/adverbs, 523
Academic learning log
  argument, 506–507
  cause and effect pattern, 382–383
  classification, comparison, and contrast, 462–463
  essay, 256–257
  example patterns, 424–425
  fact and opinion, 216–217
  key concepts in reading and writing, 52–53
  learning and using new words, 136–137
  reading/writing strategy, 92–93
  research, 298–299
  time order/space order pattern, 342–343
  word choice, tone, and purpose, 176–177
accept/except, 540
Adequate details, 220, 481
Adjectives, 521–522
  absolute form, 523
  common forms, 522
  comparative form, 523
  defined, 521
  improper use of, 540
  nouns formed as, 522
  participles as, 521
  placement, 522
  superlative form, 523
  verbs formed as, 522
Adverbs, 522–523
  absolute form, 523
  common forms, 522
  comparative form, 523
  defined, 521
  improper use of, 540
  superlative form, 523
advice/advise, 540
affect, defined, 366
affect/effect, 541
all ready/already, 541
allot/a lot, 541
already/all ready, 541
American Psychological Association (APA) documentation style
  and MLA documentation style compared, 282
  sample research essay in, 287–291
"An Account of Alfred C. Cooley's Plight in the Face of Hurricane Katrina" (Offiah-Hawkins), 552–559
and, 509
Angelou, Maya, "Fannie Lou Hamer," 594–599
Annotate/Annotation
  for analyzing facts and opinions, 181, 187–193
  defined, 34
  identifying tone and purpose, 148–154
  key details, during reading of essay, 221–226
  in reading/writing situation, 34–36
  in reading/writing strategy, 56, 63–65
  use of argument, 466–474
  use of cause/effect order patterns, 346–351
  use of classification, comparison, and contrast, 428–433
  use of example order patterns, 386–395
  use of time/space order patterns, 302–306
Anthology selection, MLA citation style for, 277
Antonyms
  defined, 100
  in SAGE approach, 100–103
  signal words for, 100
APA. *See* American Psychological Association (APA) documentation style
Apostrophes, 533–535
  for contractions, 519, 534
  misuse of, 535
  for ownership, 533–534
Argument, 464–507
  biased, checking for, 468
  claim in. *See* Claim, in argument
  creating logical order in, 483–486
  defined, 466
  effective language with, revising and proofreading for, 487–488
  evaluating, 464
  generating relevant details in, 481–483
  as purpose for reading/writing, 11
    questions establishing, 148
  reading and writing assignments
    for college life, 500
    for everyday life, 499
    for working life, 501–502
  reading selections for, 620–637
  signal words for, 232
  supports for, 464, 467
  word choice and, 140–141
Argumentation concept map, 473, 482
Argumentative essay, revising (step-by-step guidelines), 498
Articles (published), MLA citation style for, 277–278, 280–281
Attribution, fact and opinion and, 201
Audience
  in reading/writing situation, 10, 142–145
  word choice and, 140–141
Author. *See* Writer
Author names, MLA citation style for, 276–277

B

Bandwagon appeal, 187
Base words, suffixes for, 536
be
  future tense, 517
  past tense, 517
  present tense, 517, 518–519
"Beauty from Ashes" (Smith), 573–583
Begging the question, 187
Belief, fact and opinion and, 178, 180, 187
beside/besides, 541
Biased argument, checking for, 468
Biased tone, 148
Biased words, 180
Block-by-block organization, comparison/contrast, 443–444
Body, of essay, 220
Body paragraphs, of essay, 220
Bold type
  content words and specialized terms displayed in, 112
  effective skimming and, 112
Bookmark, Internet, 268
Books. *See also* Textbooks
  MLA citation style for, 276–277
Boolean operators, 267
Brainstorming
  to establish tone and purpose, 158–160
  in reading/writing strategy, 56, 66–68
    step-by-step directions, 66
  relevant detail and, 481
  using facts and opinions, 198–199
brake/break, 542
Brooke, Rupert, "Niagara Falls," 565–572
Brooks, Charles S., "On the Difference Between Wit and Humor," 612–619
Building blocks
  paragraphs as, 218
  words as, 94
but, 509
by/bye/buy, 542

C

Call to action, as essay introduction/conclusion, 240
Capital letter, correcting comma splices and fused sentences with, 512
Causal chain, defined, 346
Cause, defined, 346
Cause and effect essay, revising (step-by-step guidelines), 374
Cause and effect pattern, 344–383
  analyzing text using, 346–351
  generating details in, 360–361
  reading and writing assignments

Cause and effect pattern (*continued*)
for college life, 377
for everyday life, 375–376
for working life, 378
reading selections for, 573–593
signal words for, 232
using effective language with, 366–367
writer's opinion in, 358
Central idea. *See also* Main idea; Thesis statement
defined, 16
in essay, 220
prewriting a draft, 232–234
key examples and, 401
Central point, in argument, 466
Chain of events. *See* Narration
Chronological order. *See* Time order pattern
Claim, in argument, 466–468
components of, 466
defined, 466
VALID approach to, 468
Classification, 426–463
creating logical order with, 445–447
defined, 428
generating details based on, 443
reading and writing assignments
for college life, 456–457
for everyday life, 455
for working life, 458
reading selection for, 605–611
signal words for, 232
writer's opinion in, 441, 443
Classification concept chart, 444
Classification essay, revising (step-by-step guidelines), 454
Classification thesis statement, 441–442
Clause, independent. *See* Independent clause
Clause fragments, 514–515
Clauses
dependent, as fragments, 514–515
misplaced, 528
parallel, 625
parenthetical, commas and, 510
relative, 515
series of, commas and, 508
Closing quotation mark, 531
clothes/cloths, 542
coarse/course, 542–543
College textbooks. *See* Textbooks
Colon, quotation marks and, 530
Comma splices
corrective strategies, 512
identifying, 511
Commas, 508–510
correcting comma splices and fused sentences with, 512
independent clauses and, 509, 511
introductory elements and, 509
quotation marks and, 530
quotations, 510
in a series, 508
Comparative adjectives/adverbs, 523
Comparison
defined, 428
words signaling, 429
Comparison and contrast, 426–463
creating logical order with, 445–447
defined, 428
generating details based on, 443–444
reading and writing assignments
for college life, 456–457
for everyday life, 455
for working life, 458
reading selection for, 612–619
signal words for, 232
writer's opinion in, 441, 443
Comparison/contrast concept chart, 437, 440, 444
Comparison/contrast essay, revising (step-by-step guidelines), 454
Comparison/contrast thesis statement, 441–442
Complex sentence, 448–449
subordination and, 448–449
Composition. *See also* Drafting
concept maps and outlines for, 30–34
Compound sentence, coordination and, 448–449
Comprehension
concept maps and outlines for, 30–34
context clues for. *See* Context clues
defined, 2
vocabulary resources for, 112–115
Concept map/chart
for argument, 473, 482
for cause and effect, 360–361
for classification, 444
for comparison/contrast, 437, 440, 444
creating, 30–34
defined, 30
in essay development, 235, 237
for examples, 401–404
for time order/space order, 303
Concluding paragraph, in essay
purpose of, 240
types of, 240–241
Conclusions (inferences)
invalid, 467
valid, 467
Conjunctions
coordinating. *See* Coordinating conjunctions
subordinating, 512
Conjunctive adverbs, correcting comma splices and fused sentences with, 512
Connecting paragraphs, transitions for, 237–239
Connotation
defined, 140, 323
figures of speech and, 323
word choice and, 140–141
time/space order, 323–325
Consequences, warning about, as essay introduction/conclusion, 241
Consonant suffixes, 536
Consonants, final, 537
Content words, textbook aids for learning, 112
Context
general, in SAGE approach, 103–105
information about, as essay introduction/conclusion, 241
Context clues, 96
antonyms as, 100–103
defined, 96
examples as, 106–108
general context as, 103–105
SAGE approach to, 96–108
synonyms as, 96–99
Contractions, apostrophe use with, 519, 534
Contradiction, as essay introduction, 241
Contrast
contrast/comparison, defined, 428. *See also* Comparison and contrast
defined, 428
words signaling, 429
Controlling point. *See also* Pattern of organization; Writer's opinion
defined, 232
in time/space order pattern, 316
Coordinating conjunctions, 509
correcting comma splices and fused sentences with, 512
parallelism and, 626
Coordination
comparison/contrast pattern and, 448–449
of ideas, 512
Counterclaim, in argument, 466, 468, 483
course/coarse, 542–543

D

Dangling modifiers, editing, 528–529
Definition(s)
as essay introduction, 240
key words signaling, 387
in textbooks, 112
Definition-example patterns, 386–387
extended form, 387
reading selection for, 600–604
signal words for, 387
simple form, 386–387
using concept maps based on, 401, 403
writer's opinion in, 399
Definition-example thesis statement, 399–400
Denotation
defined, 140, 323
word choice and, 140–141
time/space order, 323–325
Dependent clauses
as fragments, 514–515
subordinate ideas and, 512
Description. *See* Space order pattern
Details
adequate, 220, 481
major and minor, 220, 221
relevant. *See* Relevant details
supporting, 16, 220
Direct quotations
formatting and punctuating, 530–531
speech tags with, 531
Directions, time order pattern in, 316
transition words used for, 302
do, 518–519
Documentation styles, key differences between, 282. *See also* American Psychological Association (APA)

documentation style; Modern Language Association (MLA) documentation style
Domain types, 267
Drafting
to establish tone and purpose, 158–160
in reading/writing strategy, 57, 72–73
step-by-step directions, 72
from research, 261
using facts and opinions, 198–199
using logical order, 237–239
example patterns, 404–407
time/space order pattern, 320–322
DVDs, MLA citation style for, 278

E

-*e* endings, 538
effect, definitions of, 346, 366
effect/affect, 541
Effective language/expression
with argument, 487–488
with cause and effect pattern, 366–367
with classification, comparison, and contrast, 448–449
defined, 220
in essay, 220, 240–242
with example patterns, 408–409
with time/space patterns, 323–325
ei vs. *ie* spelling, 538
Electronic database collection, 265
Emotional words, 148
Entertainment, as purpose for reading/writing, 11
questions establishing, 148
word choice and, 140–141
-*es* endings
plural nouns, 537
subject-verb agreement, 518
Essay, 218–257
connecting paragraphs in, transitions for, 237–239
defined, 218
effective introduction/conclusion to, types of, 240–242
levels of information in, 220
logical order in, 237–239
paragraph role in, 218
parts of, 220
reading and writing assignments
for college life, 250
for everyday life, 249
for working life, 251–252
relevant details for, generating and organizing, 235–236
revising, step-by-step guidelines for, 248
argumentative essay, 498
cause and effect essay, 374
classification, comparison, and contrast essays, 454
time/space order essay, 333
thesis statement for, drafting, 232–234
uses for, 218
word choice in, revising, 240–243
Everett, Edward, "Shaking Hands," 605–611

Example(s)
as context clue, 106–108
defined, 106, 384
key words signaling, 106, 386
in SAGE approach, 106–108
transition words signaling, 386
Example patterns, 384–425
creating logical order with, 404–407
effective language in, revising and proofreading for, 408–409
generating details in, 401–404
reading and writing assignments
for college life, 419
for everyday life, 418
for working life, 420
revising, step-by-step guidelines for, 417
signal words for, 232
supporting main idea, 386–395
thesis statements using, 399–400
writer's opinion and
in definition-example pattern, 399–400
in generalization-example pattern, 399–400
except/accept, 540
Exemplification. *See* Example(s); Example patterns
Expert opinion, 187
Expression
effective. *See* Effective language/expression
as purpose for reading/writing, 11
questions establishing, 148
word choice and, 140–141
Extended definition-example pattern, 387

F

Fact
characteristics of, 180
defined, 178
and opinion, 178–216
analyzing, 187–193
distinguishing between, 178, 180–182
effective use of, 201–202
evaluating research sources for, 264
revising, step-by-step guidelines for, 208
using to draft a response, 198–199
reading and writing assignments
for college life, 210–211
for everyday life, 209
for working life, 212
surprising, as essay introduction, 241
Fallacy(ies)
defined, 187
examples of, 187
FANBOYS (acronym), 509
"Fannie Lou Hamer" (Angelou), 594–599
farther/further, 543
fewer/less, 543
Fiction, text elements of, 16
Figurative tone, 148
Figures of speech, 323
defined, 323
in example patterns, 408–409
in time order/space order patterns, 323

First person
point of view and, 516
in argument, 487
singular and plural forms, 516
in subject-verb agreement, 518–519
traits, 516
Flow of ideas
in classification, comparison, and contrast, 429, 445
in paragraph, 221
time order/space order patterns and, 318, 320
Focus, in cause and effect pattern, 344, 346
for, 509
Formal tone, 143, 148
Fragment
clause, 514–515
correcting, 513–514
phrase, 514
simple sentence vs., 513
Freewriting, generating detail by, 235–236
further/farther, 543
Fused sentence
corrective strategies, 512
identifying, 511
Future tense, 517

G

General context
defined, 103
of passage, 105
in SAGE approach, 103–105
Generalization-example pattern, 386
reading selection for, 594–599
using concept maps based on, 401, 402
writer's opinion in, 399
Generalization-example thesis statement, 399–400
Genre
defined, 16
text structure, 16–21
Glittering generality, 187
Glossary
defined, 112
using, 112–115
good/well, 543
Graphic organizer
generating details with, 303, 318. *See also* Concept map/chart
vocabulary, examples of, 110, 111
Groups, in classification, 443–444
signal words and transitions for, 428

H

have, 518–519
hear/here, 544
here, subject after verb and, 520
here/hear, 544

I

"I Hear America Singing" (Whitman), 600–604
Ibsen, Henrik, *A Doll's House*, Act III, Final Scene, 584–593

Ideas. *See also* Main idea
classifying. *See* Classification
comparing and contrasting. *See* Comparison and contrast
flow of, in paragraph, 221
implying, 4, 28–30
logical connections between, 300
parenthetical, commas and, 510
words qualifying, 180
ie vs. *ei* spelling, 538
Illustration. *See* Narration
Images, vivid, as essay introduction/conclusion, 241
Impartial tone, 148
Implications, making in reading/writing situation, 28–30
Imply, defined, 4
In-text citations, 274–275
Independent clauses
comma splices and, 511, 512
commas joining, 509, 511
coordinating conjunctions and, 511
fused sentences and, 511–512
Index cards, for tracking sources, 263, 273
Infer, defined, 4
Inferences, in reading/writing situation
making, 28–30
valid/invalid, 467
Informal tone, 143, 148
Information
complete vs. incomplete. *See* Fragment
contextual, as essay introduction/conclusion, 241
in MLA Works Cited page, categories of, 276
nonessential, parentheses and, 510
in paragraph, flow of, 221
as purpose for reading/writing, 11
questions establishing, 148
quoted, single quotation marks for, 531
for research
finding and evaluating sources of, 264–265
locating, 264–265. *See also* Sources
recording, 267, 273
reliability assessment (PAART), 269–270
tracking sources, 263, 266, 268, 270, 273
word choice and, 140
Informed opinion, 187
Internet, as source for research
information, 267–268
reliability assessment, PAART approach to, 269–270
Internet bookmark, 268
Interview, personal, MLA citation style for, 279
Introduction, to essay, 220
purpose of, 240
types of, 240–241
Introductory elements, commas and, 509
Invalid conclusion, 467
Italic type
content words and specialized terms displayed in, 112
effective skimming and, 112
its/it's, 544

J

Journal
reading/writing, 39
for research results, 263, 266, 268, 270

K

Key words, signaling patterns of organization. *See* Signal words; Transitions
Keyword searches, 267
knew/new/know/no, 544

L

Language, effective. *See* Effective language/expression
lay/lie, 545
less/fewer, 543
Library resources, for research, 264–265
lie/lay, 545
Listing, generating detail by, 235–236
Listing order pattern, signal words for, 232
Literal tone, 148
Logical order
creating
in argument, 483–486
with classification pattern, 445–447
with example patterns, 404–407
with time cause/effect order pattern, 362–365
with time order/space order patterns, 320–322
defined, 220
of paragraphs, using transitions to connect, 237–239

M

Magazine article, MLA citation style for, 278, 281
Main idea
cause and effect pattern and, 358
classification, comparison, and contrast and, 441–442
examples supporting, 386–395
of paragraph, 220–221
time and space order and, 316
Major details
defined, 221
in essay, 220
in paragraph, 221
Meaning
thinking about, 34
tools to create
concept maps and outlines, 30–33
inferring and implying, 28–30
prior knowledge, 25–28
summaries, 33–36
words as building blocks for, 94, 140–141
Medium of document, in MLA Works Cited page, 276
Metaphor
in example patterns, 408
in time order/space order patterns, 323
Minor details
defined, 221
in essay, 220
in paragraph, 221
Misplaced modifiers, editing, 527–528
Modern Language Association (MLA) documentation style
and APA documentation style compared, 282
in-text citations, 274–275
sample research essay in, 283–286
works cited page, 275–276
Modifiers
dangling, 528–529
misplaced, 527–528

N

Name calling, 187
Narration
described, 302
reading selections for, 552–559
time order pattern in, 302
transition words used for, 302
Narrative thesis statement, 316–317
Neutral tone, 148
new/knew, 544
New words, learning and using, 94–137
reading and writing assignments
in college life, 130–131
in everyday life, 129
in working life, 132–132
revising (step-by-step guidelines), 128
SAGE approach to, 96–108
Newspaper article, MLA citation style for, 278, 281
"Niagara Falls" (Brooke), 565–572
no/know, 544
"Nobel Lecture: The Nobel Peace Prize 2014" (Yousafzai), 628–637
Nonessential information, parentheses and, 510
Nonfiction, text elements of, 16
not, 509
contraction of, 519
Nouns
as adjectives, 522
plural, spelling and, 537
signaling cause and effect, 346
Number
consistent use of, 516
illogical shift in, 516

O

Objective proof, defined, 178
Objective tone
in argument, 487
characteristics of, 148
identifying, 148–154
Offiah-Hawkins, Sandra, "An Account of Alfred C. Cooley's Plight in the Face of Hurricane Katrina," 552–559
"On the Difference Between Wit and Humor" (Brooks), 612–619
Online catalogue, 265
Online database, 265
Onomatopoeia, 323

Opening quotation mark, 531
Opinion
of author. *See* Writer's opinion
characteristics of, 180
defined, 178
expert, 187
fact and, 178–216
analyzing, 187–193
distinguishing between, 178, 180–182
effective use of, 201–202
evaluating research sources for, 264
revising, step-by-step guidelines for, 208
using to draft a response, 198–199
informed, 187
reading and writing assignments
for college life, 210–211
for everyday life, 209
for working life, 212
Opposing view, as essay introduction, 241
or, 509
Organization
logical. *See* Logical order
patterns of. *See* Pattern of organization
Outlines/Outlining
creating, 30–34
defined, 30
Ownership, apostrophes for, 533–534

P

PAART approach, in source reliability assessment, 269–270
Paragraph(s)
as building blocks for essay, 218
defined, 220–221
flow of ideas in, 221
general sense of, as context clue, 105
information levels in, 221
logical order of, using transitions to connect, 237–239
role in essay, 218, 220–221
Parallel clauses, 625
Parallel phrases, 625
Parallel words, 524
Parallelism, 624–626
Paraphrase/Paraphrasing
avoiding plagiarism with, 271–272
defined, 34
five R's of, 271
in ready/writing situation, 34–36
Parenthetical ideas, 510
Parenthetical notations, 274–275
Participle adjectives, 521
Parts of speech, signaling cause and effect, 346
passed/past, 545
Past tense, 517
Pattern of organization. *See also individually named patterns*
controlling point and, 232–234
defined, 300
ideas flow in. *See* Flow of ideas
narrowing of topic and, 263
signal words for, 232
types of, 232
Period
correcting comma splices and fused sentences with, 512
quotation marks and, 530
Person. *See also* First person; Second person; Third person
defined, 515
illogical shift in, 516
Personal attack, 187
Personal interview, MLA citation style for, 279
Personal tone, 148
Photographic organizer
argument, 465
cause and effect pattern, 345
classification, comparison, and contrast, 427
developing a reading/writing strategy, 55
essay, 219
example patterns, 385
fact and opinion, 179
learning and using new words, 95
reading and writing, reasons for, 3
research, reading/writing strategy for, 259
time order/space order patterns, 301
word choice, tone, and purpose, 139
Phrase fragments, 514
Phrases
misplaced, 527–528
parallel, 625
parenthetical, commas and, 510
series of, commas and, 508
Plagiarism
avoiding, 271–273
defined, 271
Plain folks fallacy, 187
Plural nouns, spelling and, 537
Point-by-point organization, comparison/contrast, 443–444
Point of view
consistent use of, 515–516
defined, 515
establishing with personal pronouns, 516
illogical shift in, 516
Prepositional phrases, 520
Prereading, in reading/writing strategy, 56, 58–61
Present tense, 517
subject-verb agreement, 518–519
Prewriting
draft of thesis statement
for essay, 232–234
using argument, 480–481
using cause/effect order pattern, 358–359
using classification, comparison, and contrast, 441–442
using example, 399–400
using time/space order pattern, 316–317
generating and organizing relevant details
for essay, 235–236
using argument, 481–483
using cause/effect order pattern, 360–361
using classification, comparison, and contrast, 443–444
using examples, 401–404
using time/space order pattern, 318–319
in reading/writing strategy, 56, 66–68
for research, 260
word-concept mapping. *See* Concept map/chart
principal/principle, 545
Prior knowledge, in reading/writing situation
activating, 25–28
defined, 25
Process
described, 302
reading selection for, 560–564
time order pattern in, 302
transition words used for, 302
Process thesis statement, 316–317
Pronouns
improper use of, 539
personal. *See* First person; Second person; Third person
Proof, objective, 178
Proofreading
for effective language in essay, 240–243
for effective use of fact and opinion, 201–202
in reading/writing strategy, 57, 75–78
step-by-step directions, 75
in research strategy, 261
Publication information, in MLA Works Cited page, 276
Published articles, MLA citation style for, 277–278
Punctuation
for parallelism, 626
quotation marks with, 530–531
Purpose(s), 138–177
brainstorming to establish, 158–160
drafting to establish, 158–160
identifying, 148–154
reading and writing assignments
for college life, 172
for everyday life, 170–171
for working life, 173
in reading/writing situation, 10, 142–145
reviewing and revising for, 161
word choice and, 140–141

Q

Qualifiers, 180
Question-Answer relationships (QAR), in reading/writing strategy, 58–61
Question mark, quotation marks and, 530
Questions/Questioning
for analyzing facts and opinions, 181
determining writer's point of essay, 221–226
distinguishing fact from opinion, 181

Questions/Questioning (*continued*)
as essay introduction/conclusion, 240
identifying key details in example pattern, 401
identifying tone and purpose, 148–154
in reading/writing strategy, 56, 58–61, 63–65
step-by-step directions, 58
reporter's, 318–319, 443, 467
for revision
of essay. *See under* Essay
of example patterns, 417
subject-verb agreement in, 520
in use of argument, 466–474
in use of cause/effect order patterns, 346–351
in use of classification, comparison, and contrast, 428–433
in use of example order patterns, 386–395
in use of time/space order patterns, 302–306
quiet/quit/quite, 546
Quotation marks, 530–532
Quote/Quotation. *See also* Direct quotations
attribution for, 201
avoiding plagiarism with, 271, 272–273
basic language rules for, 201
comma use with, 510
defined, 201, 271
as essay introduction/conclusion, 240

R

Radio program, MLA citation style for, 279
raise/rise, 546
Reader, benefits of writing for, 4
Reading, 2–53
argument, 466–474
cause/effect order patterns, 346–351
classification, comparison, and contrast, 428–433
connection between writing and, 4–6
defined, 2
to determine writer's point of essay, 221–226
example order patterns, 386–395
purposes for, 11
in reading/writing strategy, 56, 63–65
for research, 260
reasons for, 3
strategy, for a writer, 551
time/space order patterns, 302–306
Reading situation, defined, 10. *See also* Reading/writing situation
Reading/writing journal, 39
Reading/writing situation, 10–12. *See also* Reading *entries*; Writing *entries*
assessing, 10–12
connecting reading and writing in, 4–6
creating meaning in, tools for, 25–36
defined, 10
purposes and, 11
reading and writing assignments
for college life, 46
for everyday life, 45
for working life, 47–48
textual elements in, recognizing, 16–21
word choice in, 142–145
Reading/writing strategy, 54–93
defined, 57
development of, 54–93
phases of, 56–57
after reading, 66–68
after writing, 74–78
drafting a response, 72–73
during reading, 63–65
before reading/writing, 58–61
reading and writing assignments
for college life, 86
for everyday life, 85
for working life, 87–88
for research, 258–299
avoiding plagiarism, 271–273
developing, 260–261
revising (step-by-step guidelines), 293
source evaluation, 264–265
topic choice, 262–263
Reasons, in argument, 464, 467
Reciting, in reading/writing strategy, 56, 66–68
step-by-step directions, 66
Reference book article, MLA citation style for, 277
Reference librarian, 264
Relative clauses, as fragments, 515
Relative pronouns, 515, 636
Relevant details, 220
using prewriting to generate and organize
in argument, 481–483
in cause and effect pattern, 360–361
in classification, comparison, and contrast, 443–444
for essay, 235–236
in example patterns, 401–404
in time order/space order patterns, 318–319
Reported speech
attribution for, 201
basic language rules for, 202
defined, 201
Reporter's questions, establishing relevance, 318–319, 443, 467
Rereading, in reading/writing strategy, 64, 66
Research
defined, 258
reading and writing assignments
for college life, 294
for everyday life, 294
for working life, 294
reading/writing strategy for, 258–299
avoiding plagiarism, 271–273
developing, 260–261
revising (step-by-step guidelines), 293
source evaluation, 264–265
topic choice, 262–263
Research journal, tracking sources in, 263, 266, 268, 270
to avoid plagiarism, 273
Research topic, choosing/discovering
exploratory searches, 262–263
step-by-step procedure for, 262–263
Reviewing
drafted response, 74–78
essay, 221–226
fact and opinion, for effective use of, 201–202
in reading/writing strategy, 56, 66–68
step-by-step directions, 66, 74
for research, 261
use of classification, comparison, and contrast, 428–433
use of example order patterns, 386–395
use of time/space order patterns, 302–306
for word choice, tone, and purpose, 161
Revising
of essays. *See under* Essay
fact and opinion, for effective use of, 201–202
step-by-step guidelines, 208
in reading/writing strategy, 57, 75–78
step-by-step directions/guidelines, 74, 84
in research strategy, 261
step-by-step guidelines, 293
vocabulary and new words (step-by-step guidelines), 128
for word choice, tone, and purpose, 161
step-by-step guidelines, 169
rise/raise, 546

S

-s endings
plural nouns, 537
subject-verb agreement, 518
SAGE approach, context clues and, 96–108
Sanger, Margaret, "The Morality of Birth Control," 620–627
Scholarly journal article, MLA citation style for, 281
Search engine, 267
Second person
point of view and, 516
in argument, 487
singular and plural forms, 516
in subject-verb agreement, 518–519
traits, 516
Semicolon
correcting comma splices and fused sentences with, 512
parallelism and, 626
quotation marks and, 530
Sentences
compound and complex, 448–449
simple, vs. fragment, 513
Series, commas for items in, 508
set/sit, 546

"Seven Ages of Man" from *As You Like It*, Act II, Scene VII (Shakespeare), 560–564
Shakespeare, William, "Seven Ages of Man" from *As You Like It*, Act II, Scene VII, 560–564
"Shaking Hands" (Everett), 605–611
Signal words. *See also* Transitions
  for antonyms, 100
  for argument, 232
  for cause-and-effect pattern, 232
  for cause and effect pattern, 346
  for classification, 232, 428
  for comparison and contrast, 429
  for definition-example patterns, 387
  for example patterns, 232, 386–387
  introducing examples, 106, 386
  introducing lists, 232
  qualifying idea as argument, 467
  for space order pattern, 232
    description, 302
  for synonyms, 96
  for time order pattern, 232
    narration and process, 302
Simile
  in example patterns, 408
  in time order/space order patterns, 323
Simple definition-example pattern, 386–387
Simple sentence, vs. fragment, 513
Single quotation marks, 531
sit/set, 546
Skimming
  for content words, 112
  of essay, 221
  in reading/writing strategy, 58
  for relevant information in sources, 262
  for specialized terms, 112
  for transitions and signal words
    in argument, 428–429
    in classification, 428–429
    in example patterns, 386
Smith, Anne, "Beauty from Ashes," 573–583
so, 509
Sound recording, MLA citation style for, 279
Sources
  attribution and evaluation, 201
  for research topic
    exploratory searches, 262–263
    finding and evaluating, 264–265
    recording search results. *See* Research journal
    reliability assessment (PAART), 269
    tracking sources. *See* Research journal
Space order pattern, 300–343
  creating logical order with, 320–322
  described, 302
  generating details in, 318–319
  reading and writing assignments
    for college life, 336
    for everyday life, 334–335
    for working life, 337
  reading selection for, 565–572
  signal words for, 232
  writer's opinion in, 316, 318
Space/time order essay, revising (step-by-step guidelines), 333
Spatial order. *See* Space order pattern
Speech, reported. *See* Reported speech
Speech tag, 510
  with direct quotations, 531
Spelling
  commonly confused words, 539–549
  rules for improving, 536–538
Stages, time order pattern in, transition words used for, 302
Statement, as essay introduction, 241
Steps, time order pattern in, transition words used for, 302
Subgroups, in classification, 443–444
  signal words and transitions for, 428
Subject area, learning words associated with, 112
Subject (of sentence)
  after verb, 520
  separated from verb, 520
Subject-verb agreement, 518–520
Subjective tone
  in argument, 487
  characteristics of, 148
  identifying, 148–154
Subordinate clauses. *See* Dependent clauses
Subordinating conjunctions
  correcting clause fragments with, 515
  correcting comma splices and fused sentences with, 512
Subordination
  comparison/contrast pattern and, 448–449
  of ideas, 512
Suffixes
  commonly used, 536
  consonant, 536
  defined, 536
  final consonant, 537
  final *e*, 538
  final *y*, 538
  parallel words and, 524
  plural nouns, 537
  vowel, 536
Suggestion, as essay introduction/conclusion, 240
Summary/Summarizing
  avoiding plagiarism with, 273
  defined, 34
  as essay introduction/conclusion, 241
  in reading/writing situation, 34–36
  strategy for, 34
Superlative adjectives/adverbs, 523
Supporting details, defined, 16, 220
Surprising fact, as essay introduction, 241
Survey
  for analyzing facts and opinions, 187–193
  in reading/writing strategy, 56, 58–61
    step-by-step directions, 58
Synonyms
  defined, 96
  in SAGE approach, 96–99
  signal words for, 96

T

Television program, MLA citation style for, 279
Tense
  consistent use of, 517. *See also individually named tenses*
  illogical shifts in, 517
Text
  elements of, 16–21
    by genre, 16
  structure of, defined, 16
Textbooks
  definitions in, 112
  glossary in, 112–115
  vocabulary resources in, 112–115
than/then, 547
"The Morality of Birth Control" (Sanger), 620–627
their/there/they're, 547
Theme, defined, 16
then/than, 547
there, subject after verb and, 520
there/their/they're, 547
Thesis statement
  classification, 441–442
    comparison, and contrast, 441–442
  connecting paragraphs to, transitions for, 237–239
  defined, 220
  definition-example, 399–400
  in essay, 220
  generalization-example, 399–400
  narrative, 316–317
  prewriting draft of
    for essay, 232–234
    using argument, 480–481
    using cause/effect order pattern, 358–359
    using classification, comparison, and contrast, 441–442
    using examples, 399–400
    using time/space order pattern, 316–317
  process, 316–317
they're/there/their, 547
Thinking-reading-writing tasks, 34
Third person
  point of view and, 516
    in argument, 487
  singular and plural forms, 516
  in subject-verb agreement, 518–519
  traits, 516
Thought, complete vs. incomplete. *See* Fragment
threw/through, 547
Time order pattern, 300–343
  creating logical order with, 320–322
  described, 302
  generating details in, 318–319
  reading and writing assignments
    for college life, 336
    for everyday life, 334–335
    for working life, 337
  signal words for, 232
  types of, 302
  writer's opinion in, 316, 318

Time/space order essay, revising (step-by-step guidelines), 333
Title of source, in MLA Works Cited page, 276
Titles (works)
of essay, 220
quotation marks and, 532
to/too/two, 548
Tone, 138–177
biased, 148
brainstorming to establish, 158–160
defined, 140
drafting to establish, 158–160
identifying, 148–154
objective, 148–154
reading and writing assignments
for college life, 172
for everyday life, 170–171
for working life, 173
in reading/writing situation, 142–145
reviewing and revising for, 161
subjective, 148–154
word choice and, 140–141
words identifying, characteristics of, 148
too/to/two, 548
Topic(s)
audience and, 140–141
classification pattern and, 443–444
controlling point and. *See* Controlling point; Pattern of organization
narrowing, prewriting for, 262–263
in reading/writing situation, 10
for research. *See* Research topic
word choice and, 142–143
Topic sentence
in comparison and contrast, 428
connecting paragraphs to, transitions for, 237–239
defined, 221
in essay, 220, 221
example patterns and, 386
main idea in, 201
time order/space order pattern and, 316
Tracking sources, 263, 266, 268, 270
to avoid plagiarism, 273
Traits, in classification pattern, 443–444
signal words and transitions for, 428
Transfer fallacy, 187
Transitions
in argument, 467
in cause and effect pattern, 346
in classification, 428
connecting paragraphs in essay, 237–239
defined, 237, 300
in example pattern, 386
in time order and space order patterns, 302
words used for. *See* Signal words
two/to/too, 548
Types, in classification pattern, 443–444
signal words and transitions for, 428

U

Unbiased tone, 148
URLs, 267

V

VALID approach, 468
Valid conclusion, 467
Verbs
as adjectives, 522
signaling cause and effect, 346
subjects after, 520
subjects separated from, 520
tenses. *See also individual tenses*
consistent use, 517
illogical shifts in, 517
Viewpoint. *See* Point of view
Vivid image, as essay introduction/conclusion, 241
Vocabulary, 94–137
context cues for, 96
defined, 94
glossary in textbooks, 112–115
importance of, 94
new. *See* New words
review list, examples of, 114, 118
revising (step-by-step guidelines), 128
Vowel suffixes, 536

W

waist/waste, 548
Warning about consequences, as essay introduction/conclusion, 241
waste/waist, 548
wear/where/were/we're, 548
weather/whether, 549
Websites
article or page within, MLA citation style for, 280
domain types and, 267
picture from, MLA citation style for, 280
well/good, 543
where/wear/were/we're, 548
whether/weather, 549
Whitman, Walt, "I Hear America Singing," 600–604
who's/whose, 549
Word choice, 138–177
connecting audience with topic, 140–141
defined, 140
effective. *See* Effective language/expression
reading and writing assignments
for college life, 172
for everyday life, 170–171
for working life, 173
in reading/writing situation, 142–145
inference drawn from, 29–30
message implied by, 29–30
reviewing and revising for, 161, 240–243
step-by-step guidelines, 169
for tone and purpose, 140–141
Word confusion
commonly confused words, 540–549
between similar sounding words, 539
between words used improperly, 539–540
between words with similar meaning, 539
Words. *See also* Vocabulary
biased, 180
as building blocks, 94
connotative meanings of. *See* Connotation
denotative meanings of. *See* Denotation
emotional, 148
establishing tone, 148–152
glossary definitions for, 112–115
misplaced, 527
new. *See* New words
number known by people, 94
objective, in argument, 487
parallel, 524
parenthetical, commas and, 510
qualifying ideas, 180
series of, commas and, 508
subjective, in argument, 487
suffixes for, 536–538
transitional. *See* Signal words
Write-to-learn/writing-to-learn
antonyms as context clues, 102
connecting reading and writing, 4
examples as context clues, 107
general sense of passage as context clues, 105
synonyms as context clues, 98
Writer
benefits of reading for, 4
reading strategy for, 551
Writer's opinion, thesis statement and, 232
in cause and effect pattern, 358
in classification, comparison, and contrast, 441, 443
in example patterns, 399–400
in time order/space order pattern, 316, 318
Writer's point. *See* Controlling point; Writer's opinion
Writing, 2–53
connection between reading and, 4–6
defined, 2
purposes for, 11
and reading situation. *See* Reading/Writing situation
and reading strategy. *See* Reading/Writing strategy
reasons for, 3
Writing situation, defined, 10. *See also* Reading/writing situation

Y

-y endings, 538
yet, 509
Yousafzai, Malala, "Nobel Lecture: The Nobel Peace Prize 2014," 628–637